Archaic and Classical Greece

Archaic and Classical Greece

A selection of ancient sources in translation

MICHAEL H. CRAWFORD
Professor of Ancient History,
University College London

DAVID WHITEHEAD
Professor of Classics,
The Queen's University, Belfast

CAMBRIDGE
UNIVERSITY PRESS

PUBLISHED BY THE PRESS SYNDICATE OF THE UNIVERSITY OF CAMBRIDGE
The Pitt Building, Trumpington Street, Cambridge, United Kingdom

CAMBRIDGE UNIVERSITY PRESS
The Edinburgh Building, Cambridge CB2 2RU, UK   http://www.cup.cam.ac.uk
40 West 20th Street, New York, NY 10011–4211, USA   http://www.cup.org
10 Stamford Road, Oakleigh, Melbourne 3166, Australia
Ruiz de Alarcón 13, 28014 Madrid, Spain

© Cambridge University Press 1983

First published 1983
Reprinted in 1984, 1986, 1988, 1989, 1991, 1992, 1994, 1998, 2000

Printed in the United Kingdom at the University Press, Cambridge

Library of Congress catalogue card number: 82–4355

British Library Cataloguing in Publication data
Crawford, Michael
Archaic and classical Greece
1. Greece—History
I. Title.   II. Whitehead, David
938   DF213

ISBN 0 521 22775 5 hardback
ISBN 0 521 29638 2 paperback

PP

Contents

List of figures vii
List of maps viii
Preface ix
Conventions and abbreviations xi
Glossary xiv
Weights, measures, money xvii
Introduction I Greek society 1
II The sources 4

PART I   THE ARCHAIC PERIOD

1 The development of the *polis* and its values (**1–13**) 27
2 Exploration and colonisation (**14–20**) 52
3 Tyranny (**21–35**) 66
4 The institutions of the *polis* (**36–43**) 87
5 Sparta (**44–62**) 95
6 Athens (**63–73**) 128
7 Kleisthenes and the *dēmos* (**74–80**) 152
8 Diversity and unity (**81–89**) 168
9 The Persian Empire (**90–100**) 183
10 Persia and the Greeks (**101–118**) 205

PART II   THE FIFTH CENTURY

11 The development of Athenian democracy (**119–128**) 235
12 The Athenian Empire (**129–140**) 246
13 Athenian political life (**141–149**) 262
14 The culture of Athens (**150–157**) 277
15 Economic and social developments in Athens (**158–163**) 287
16 Athens and Sparta in the Pentekontaëtia (**164–175**) 301
17 The prelude to the Peloponnesian War (**176–181**) 322

Contents

PART III   THE PELOPONNESIAN WAR

18 Spartan strategy in the Archidamian War (**182–193**)   337
19 Athenian strategy in the Archidamian War (**194–201**)   362
20 The uneasy peace, 421–416 (**202–206**)   379
21 Athenian politics during the war (**207–216**)   385
22 Athens and Sicily (**217–227**)   406
23 The Spartan offensive (**228–234**)   437
24 The defeat of Athens (**235–243**)   447
25 Post-war Athens, 404–399 (**244–248**)   456

PART IV   THE FOURTH CENTURY

26 Spartan imperialism (**249–255**)   475
27 The resurgence of Athens (**256–263**)   488
28 Sparta, Athens and Thebes (**264–275**)   497
29 The *polis* and its economy (**276–287**)   521
30 War and revolution (**288–302**)   538
31 Athenian politics and society (**303–315**)   558
32 Thessaly and Persia (**316–320**)   580
33 The rise of Makedonia (**321–332**)   587
34 Philippos and Greece (**333–350**)   600

Chronological table   618
Table of rulers   621
Index of ancient sources   623
Index of Greek words   626
Index of names   628
Index of subjects   633

Figures

1 Cult relief   2
2 Characteristic archaic scripts   20
3 Attic inscription   22
4 Offering at the Menelaion   29
5 Population trends in Attika   30
6 Plan of Megara Hyblaia   60
7 *Chōra* of Metapontion   61
8 The *agora* and *akropolis* of Miletus   92
9 The Alkmaionidai   133
10 The growth of Delphi   156
11 Ostraka   164
12 Greek works of art in Asia Minor   184
13 The Philaïdai   216
14 The growth of Athens   280
15 The Long Walls   305

Maps

1 The Aegean and Ionia xviii
2 The Peloponnesos and Attika xx
3 Central Greece and Attika xxi
4 Attika xxii
5 Italy and Sicily xxiii

Acknowledgement is due to the following for their permission to reproduce the drawings and figures listed below:
Fig. 2a, Oxford University Press; Fig. 2b, British School at Athens; Fig. 2c, Oxford University Press (originally published in R. P. Austin, *Stoichedon Style in Greek Inscriptions*); Fig. 5, Prof. A. M. Snodgrass; Fig. 6, Ecole des Hautes Etudes en Sciences sociales (plan adapted from that published in paper by Georges Vallet in *Problèmes de la terre en Grèce ancienne* (Mouton, The Hague)); Fig. 8, Walter de Gruyter & Co. (plan after A. von Gerkan, *Griechische Städteanlagen* (1924)); Figs. 11 and 14c and d, Agora Excavations, American School of Classical Studies, Athens; Fig. 12, Svenska Institutet i Athen; Figs. 14a and b, 15, Thames and Hudson.

Preface

Considerable in extent, but still inadequate, the sources which form the basis of our knowledge of ancient Greek history have in many cases survived either by pure chance or for literary reasons unconnected with their historical significance. Within the necessarily restricted confines of a single volume, we have tried both to represent the diversity of the Greek historical tradition and to present what we hope is a balanced picture of ancient Greek society. What we offer is a selection from the selection already created by time and chance, but it is at least a deliberate one. There is of course much that cannot be documented from written sources, and we have tried to draw attention to archaeological and other evidence, just as we have tried to explain difficulties and uncertainties in the written sources. The book has been born from and improved by our own teaching experiences. It is also in its final form the result of prolonged discussion of the parts for which each of us provided a first draft. Traces of our different interests and approaches no doubt remain. We shall be grateful for the comments of our colleagues and above all for those of the students for whom the book is intended to provide, through the medium of their own language, an approach to one of the most absorbing human societies of all time. That the book exists at all is due to a very large extent to the interest and encouragement of the Cambridge University Press. We warmly thank those concerned.

M. H. C.
D. W.

Conventions and abbreviations

Dates. Unless otherwise stated all dates are B.C.

Proper names. In general, for both persons and places we use transliterated Greek forms in preference to the once traditional Latinised versions: thus (for example) Perikles[1] not Pericles, Boiotia not Boeotia. Note however:

(a) We adopt the Latinised forms for *authors,* whether quoted, cited or merely mentioned: thus 'Thucydides' is the great Athenian historian (pp.10–11). 'Thoukydides' his (?) grandfather the politician (**145–146**).

(b) In a few cases, usually place names, we retain familiar *anglicised* forms where it seemed pedantic to do otherwise: thus Athens (not Athenai), Sparta, Thebes, Corinth, Delphi, Sicily, Italy, Syracuse, Sardinia, Corsica, Rhodes, Troy, Egypt, Cyprus; note also Alexander (not Alexandros) the Great.

Brackets occurring within the passages from the sources are of two kinds: square brackets [thus] indicate parts of the document itself, usually an inscription, which are lost or illegible and have been 'restored' by modern scholars; round brackets (thus) enclose matter which we supply for explanation, expansion or connection.

References to sources. These should be self-explanatory: all authors are given their full names in the index of passages, together with any abbreviation of them and/or their works employed in short references (e.g. Hdt. for Herodotus); an asterisk attached to a reference indicates abridgement. Inscriptions we cite where possible by reference not to the standard collection *Inscriptiones Graecae (IG)* but to more modern and accessible editions, chiefly:

Meiggs and Lewis	R. Meiggs and D. M. Lewis, *A Selection of Greek Historical Inscriptions to the end of the fifth century* B.C. (Oxford, 1969)
Tod	M. N. Tod, *A Selection of Greek Historical Inscriptions* (Oxford, vol. I (1933), vol. II (1948)). (The numbering of inscriptions in the two volumes is continuous.)

For *translations* of inscriptions note the following abbreviation:

Fornara	C. W. Fornara, *Archaic Times to the End of the Peloponnesian War* (Translated Documents of Greece and Rome 1) (Johns Hopkins University Press, Baltimore and London, 1977; second ed., Cambridge, 1982).

---

[1] All syllables in Greek are pronounced; and we indicate long vowels as ā, ē, ō in transliterated words other than proper names.

Abbreviations

References to modern works. Books and articles cited only once or twice are given a full reference each time. Note the following abbreviations for periodical journals:

CQ	*Classical Quarterly*
CR	*Classical Review*
GRBS	*Greek, Roman and Byzantine Studies*
JHS	*Journal of Hellenic Studies*
PCPhS	*Proceedings of the Cambridge Philological Society*
REG	*Revue des Études Grecques*

Note also that the following books are referred to by short title:

Adkins, *Moral Values*	A. W. H. Adkins, *Moral Values and Political Behaviour in Ancient Greece* (London, 1972)
Andrewes, *Society*	A. Andrewes, *Greek Society* (Harmondsworth, 1971)
Andrewes, *Tyrants*	A. Andrewes, *The Greek Tyrants* (London, 1956)
Austin and Vidal-Naquet, *Economy*	M. M. Austin and P. Vidal-Naquet, *Economic and Social History of Ancient Greece: an introduction* (London, 1977)
Boardman, *Greeks Overseas*	J. Boardman, *The Greeks Overseas* (London, 1980)
Burford, *Craftsmen*	A. Burford, *Craftsmen in Greek and Roman Society* (London, 1972)
Burn, *Persia*	A. R. Burn, *Persia and the Greeks: the defence of the West, c.546–478 B.C.* (London, 1962)
Bury and Meiggs, *Greece*	J. B. Bury and R. Meiggs, *A History of Greece to the Death of Alexander the Great* (fourth edition, London, 1975)
Cartledge, *Sparta*	P. A. Cartledge, *Sparta and Lakonia: a regional history 1300–362 B.C.* (London, 1979)
Connor, *Politicians*	W. R. Connor, *The New Politicians of Fifth-Century Athens* (Princeton, 1971)
Davies, *Democracy*	J. K. Davies, *Democracy and Classical Greece* (Hassocks, Sussex, 1978)
Davies, *Families*	J. K. Davies, *Athenian Propertied Families 600–300 B.C.* (Oxford, 1971)
Ehrenberg, *Greek State*	V. L. Ehrenberg, *The Greek State* (second edition, London, reprinted with corrections, 1974)
Ellis, *Philip II*	J. R. Ellis, *Philip II and Macedonian Imperialism* (London, 1976)
Finley, *Early Greece*	M. I. Finley, *Early Greece: the Bronze and Archaic Ages* (second edition, London, 1981)
Finley, *Economy*	M. I. Finley, *The Ancient Economy* (London, 1973)
Finley, *Odysseus*	M. I. Finley, *The World of Odysseus* (second edition, London, 1977)
Finley, *Sicily*	M. I. Finley, *Ancient Sicily* (revised edition, London, 1979)
Finley, *Use and Abuse*	M. I. Finley, *The Use and Abuse of History* (London, 1975)
Forrest, *Emergence*	W. G. G. Forrest, *The Emergence of Greek Democracy: the character of Greek politics 800–400 B.C.* (London, 1966)
Forrest, *Sparta*	W. G. G. Forrest, *A History of Sparta 950–192 B.C.* (second edition, London, 1980)

von Fritz and Kapp, *Aristotle* — K. von Fritz and E. Kapp, *Aristotle's Constitution of Athens and related texts* (New York, 1950)

Gomme, *Commentary* i–v — A. W. Gomme, A. Andrewes and K. J. Dover, *A Historical Commentary on Thucydides* (Oxford, five volumes, 1945–81)

Graham, *Colony* — A. J. Graham, *Colony and Mother City in Ancient Greece* (Manchester, 1964)

Hammond and Griffith, *Macedonia* — N. G. L. Hammond and G. T. Griffith, *A History of Macedonia*, vol II, 500–336 B.C. (Oxford, 1979)

Hignett, *Constitution* — C. Hignett, *A History of the Athenian Constitution to the end of the fifth century B.C.* (Oxford, 1952)

Hignett, *Xerxes* — C. Hignett, *Xerxes' Invasion of Greece* (Oxford, 1963)

Isager and Hansen, *Aspects* — S. Isager and M. H. Hansen, *Aspects of Athenian Society in the fourth century B.C.* (Odense, 1975)

Jeffery, *Archaic Greece* — L. H. Jeffery, *Archaic Greece: the city-states c.700–500 B.C.* (London, 1976)

Jones, *Democracy* — A. H. M. Jones, *Athenian Democracy* (Oxford, 1957)

Jones, *Sparta* — A. H. M. Jones, *Sparta* (Oxford, 1967)

Lacey, *Family* — W. K. Lacey, *The Family in Classical Greece* (London, 1968)

Lewis, *Sparta* — D. M. Lewis, *Sparta and Persia. Lectures . . . in memory of Donald W. Bradeen* (Cincinnati Classical Studies new series, vol. I; Leiden, 1977)

Meiggs, *Empire* — R. Meiggs, *The Athenian Empire* (Oxford, 1972)

Momigliano, *Alien Wisdom* — A. D. Momigliano, *Alien Wisdom: the limits of Hellenization* (Cambridge, 1975)

Moore, *Aristotle* — J. M. Moore, *Aristotle and Xenophon on Democracy and Oligarchy* (London, 1975)

Murray, *Early Greece* — O. Murray, *Early Greece* (Hassocks, Sussex, 1980)

Parke, *Festivals* — H. W. Parke, *Festivals of the Athenians* (London, 1977)

Pritchett, *War* I and II — W. K. Pritchett, *The Greek State at War* (Los Angeles etc., two volumes, 1974)

Rhodes, *Boule* — P. J. Rhodes, *The Athenian Boule* (Oxford, 1972)

de Ste Croix, *Origins* — G. E. M. de Ste Croix, *The Origins of the Peloponnesian War* (London, 1972)

Snodgrass, *Archaic Greece* — A. Snodgrass, *Archaic Greece—the age of experiment* (London, 1980)

Westlake, *Essays* — H. D. Westlake, *Essays on the Greek Historians and Greek History* (Manchester, 1969)

Whitehead, *Ideology* — D. Whitehead, *The Ideology of the Athenian Metic* (*PCPhS* Supplementary Volume IV, 1977)

Glossary

We give here a brief definition of some basic Greek words and terms *which will not normally hereafter be translated*. (Plural forms appear in parentheses.)
See also Weights, measures, money (p. xvii).

AGORA. The market-square, and generally civic centre, of a city or town; somewhat like a Roman *forum*. See **9**, etc.

APOIKIA (–IAI). Traditionally translated 'colony' but in fact a wholly independent settlement founded by one *polis* (*q.v.*) and constituting another. The settlers involved are the *apoikoi*. See further pp. 52–3, and *emporion*, below.

ARCHŌN (–ONTES). Literally a 'ruler': sometimes therefore a governor imposed by a superior power upon an inferior (as **338**); more commonly and neutrally a city's chief executive official. In Athens the (eponymous) *archōn*, together with the *basileus*, the *polemarchos* (*q.v.*) and the six *thesmothetai* constituted each year the nine *archontes*. See also *stratēgos*.

ASTU. The urban nucleus of a *polis* (*q.v.*).

BARBAROS (–ROI). Anyone other than a Greek: see **1**.

BOULĒ. In Athens (and elsewhere: see **38**), the council or standing committee of the citizen assembly (**77**). Its members (500 in Athens) are the *bouleutai*, meeting in the *bouleutērion*.

CHŌRA. The territory of a *polis* (*q.v.*).

DĒMOS. A collective term for 'the people' of a place; sometimes, in a restricted (and derogatory) sense, the common people; sometimes, in a technical sense (especially in inscriptions), the people constituted as a citizen assembly (*ekklēsia*). Note also *dēmos* (*-oi*) as a local subdivision, natural or artificially created, of a *polis* (**76, 92,** etc.); this we always give in English (deme, demes).

DIKASTĒRION (–RIA). A jury-court in classical Athens (**67, 123**), manned by large panels (e.g. 201, 501) of the annual pool of 6,000 *dikastai*.

EKKLĒSIA. The assembly of adult male citizens, in Athens and elsewhere.

EMPORION (–RIA). In contradistinction to an *apoikia* (*q.v.*), a purely commercial settlement or trading-post without the characterising institutions of a *polis* (*q.v.*).

GEROUSIA. The council of 28 elders or *gerontes* in Sparta; see **51**.

HĒGEMONIA. Literally 'leadership', a concept prominent in Greek inter-state relations: a *hēgemōn* (whether state or individual) controls subordinate allies without abolishing their separate identities. Thus, for example, the Athenian empire (see Ch. 12), so-called, is in this respect quite unlike the Roman (or British).

METOIKOS (–KOI). In Athens and elsewhere (**83, 160**), an immigrant of free status; not a citizen, but not a slave either (though sometimes an *ex*-slave).

NAUKLĒROS. A merchant who carries his wares aboard a ship which he himself owns or captains, as opposed to a merchant who must pay a *nauklēros* to carry them for him.

NOMOS (–MOI). Either a law or a conventional practice; the context will usually, though not always, make clear which. Frequently a component part of such concepts as *eunomia* (**12B, 45, 47**) and *isonomia* (**34, 73, 89, 102**, etc.).

OIKOS (–KOI). A household or family in its broadest sense, personal and material: theoretically a self-sufficient economic unit; in practice (see **7**) part of a larger community.

PHYLĒ (–LAI). A tribe, i.e. an ethnic subdivision either of the Greek race *in toto* (see **3**) or else those Greeks resident in a particular place (Snodgrass, *Archaic Greece*, 25–8, is probably wrong to connect the two); the citizens of archaic Athens, for example, belonged to one of four (Ionian) *phylai*. By or during the classical period most states changed over to subdivision by territorial area, not kinship groupings (for Athens see **76**), but the old kinship terminology, including 'tribe', was often retained.

POLEMARCHOS. In Athens, the *archōn* (*q.v.*) with particular responsibility for *polemos*, war, until superseded in that respect by the *stratēgoi* (*q.v.*), which left the polemarch as above all a judicial officer, especially in matters involving non-citizens.

POLIS (–LEIS). An independent 'city-state', comprising an urban centre (*astu*) and surrounding land (*chōra*). (A state lacking the urban centre, and the institutions that went with it, was an *ethnos*; see p. 168.) Its constitutional form is the *politeia*, and its citizen members collectively the *politai* (plural of *politēs*). See further pp. 1–4

PROXENOS (–NOI). A citizen of one state who served as the representative there of the citizens of another, at their request; see **43** (and *xenia*, below).

PRYTANEIA. One-tenth of the Athenian administrative year, during which the 50 representatives of a tribe, the *prytaneis*, convened and presided over the *boulē* and *ekklēsia* (above); see **65C, 134**, etc. Note also *prytaneion*, in Athens and elsewhere the equivalent of a town hall (**63, 172B**, etc.).

PSĒPHISMA (–MATA). A decree voted through the Athenian *ekklēsia* (above) or equivalent body elsewhere.

STASIS. Inter-factional strife or civil disturbance, sometimes running to civil war.

STĒLĒ (–LAI). A block or slab of stone, usually marble, cut with a view to its bearing an inscription; see further p.21.

STRATĒGOS (–GOI). A general, usually a member of a board of generals. In fifth-century Athens the ten *stratēgoi* superseded the *archontes* (*q.v.*) as the chief civil as well as military executive.

TRIĒRĒS. From the late sixth century onwards the usual type of Greek warship, with a crew of *c*.200 (most of them rowers). But note that we adopt the accepted English form (trireme, triremes).

XENIA. Hospitality, or what a host should offer his guest (*xenos*): in archaic Greece the individual exchange of gifts (see **5**), joined in the classical period by such institutionalised aspects as the *proxenos* (above) and official civic hospitality for ambassadors (e.g. **172**B). However, not all strangers were in practice welcome as guests, and *xenos* (*–noi*) often had the sense of our 'foreigner'.

Weights, measures, money

Like all peoples, the Greek *poleis* had their own measures, weights and coinage, all following the same basic pattern, though with some variations. Measures of length were calculated in terms of parts of the human body, obviously varying as a result; the *stadion*, stade, the distance normally covered by a single draught of a plough, contained 600 feet and was thus *of the order of* 200 metres.

Measures of capacity were calculated in terms of the *kotyle*, cup, of about ¼ of a litre; four made up a *choinix*, which was therefore about a litre; 48 *choinikes* made up a *medimnos*.

The basic Greek weight was a drachma, the silver equivalent of six iron spits, obols; silver and other precious metals by weight were produced in the form of coinage from about 600 in Ionia, from rather later in the rest of Greece. A coin worth $\frac{1}{6}$ of a drachma was naturally called an obol. This system was grafted onto one derived ultimately from Babylonia and covering the higher values; a talent was always worth 60 *minai*, minas, but since the weight of the drachma varied, so did the number to the mina – 100 at Athens, 70 on Aigina.

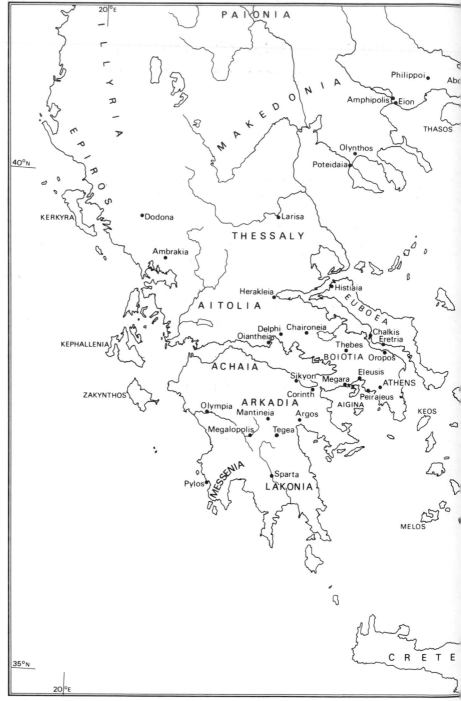

1 The Aegean and Ionia (adapted from W. W. Tarn, *Hellenistic Civilization* (3rd ed. London, 1952), 8–9)

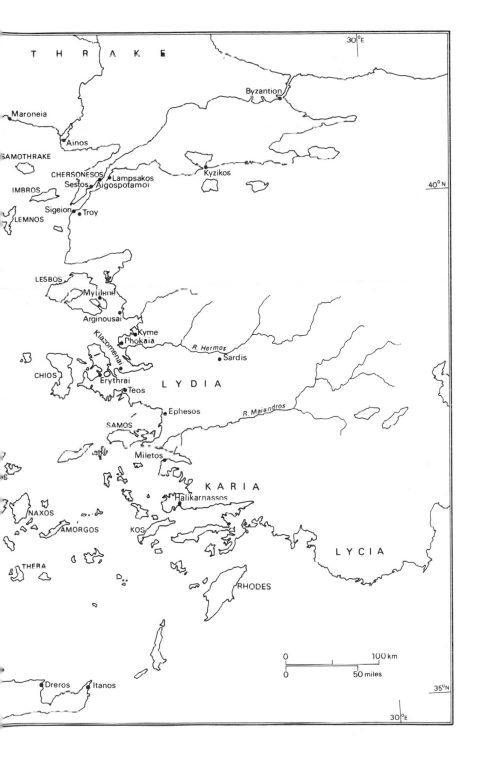

THRAKE

Byzantion

Maroneia

Ainos

SAMOTHRAKE

CHERSONESOS
Sestos
IMBROS
Lampsakos
Aigospotamoi

Kyzikos

40°N

Sigeion
Troy

LEMNOS

LESBOS
Mytilene

Arginousai

Klazomenai
Kyme
Phokaia
R. Hermos
Sardis

CHIOS
Erythrai
Teos

LYDIA

Ephesos
R. Maiandros

SAMOS

Miletos

KARIA
Halikarnassos

NAXOS

KOS

LYCIA

AMORGOS

THERA

RHODES

| 0 | | 100 km |
| 0 | | 50 miles |

Dreros
Itanos

35°N

30°E

30°E

2 The Peloponnesos and Attika

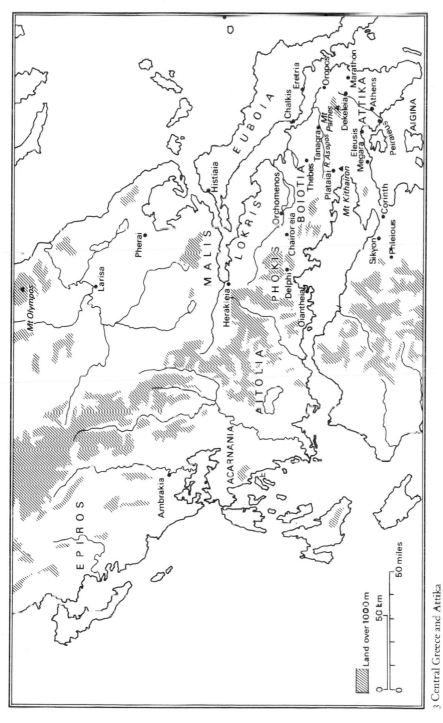

3 Central Greece and Attika

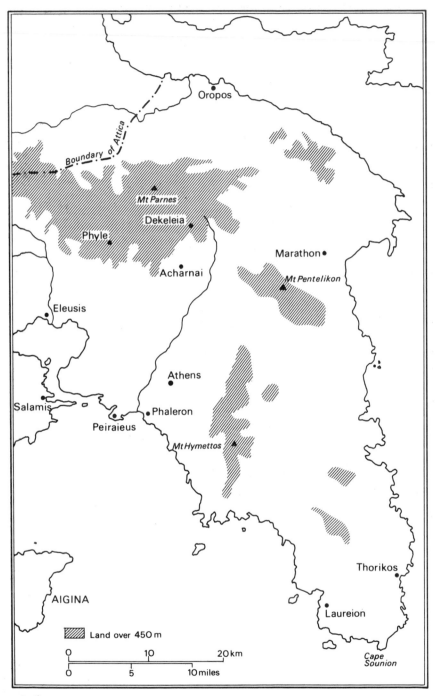

Oropos

Boundary of Attica

▲ *Mt Parnes*

Dekeleia ◆

Phyle ●

●Acharnai

Marathon ●

Mt Pentelikon ▲

Eleusis ●

Athens ●

Salamis ●

●Phaleron

Peiraieus

Mt Hymettos ▲

AIGINA

 Land over 450 m

| 0 | 10 | 20 km |
| 0 | 5 | 10 miles |

Thorikos ●

● Laureion

Cape Sounion

4 Attika

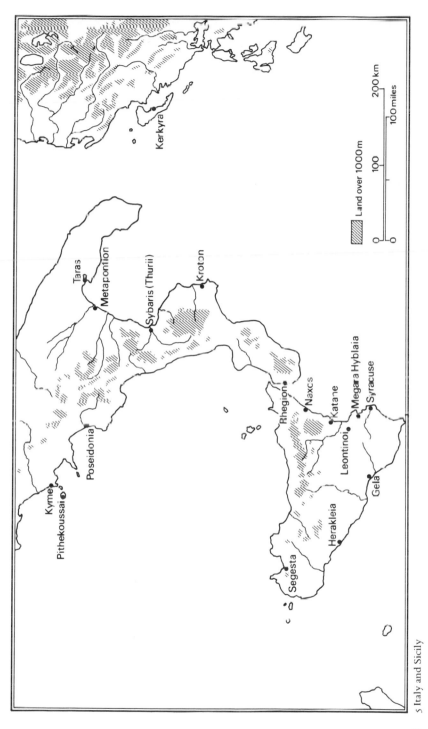

Land over 1000m

200 km

100 miles

100

Kerkyra

Taras
Metapontion
Sybaris (Thurii)
Kroton

Poseidonia

Kyme
Pithekoussai

Rhegion
Naxos
Katane
Megara Hyblaia
Syracuse
Leontinoi
Gela

Segesta
Herakleia

5 Italy and Sicily

Introduction

I Greek society

The study of the history of ancient Greece is both exciting and infuriating – exciting because of the inherent interest of the way in which Greek society organised itself, and because the members of that society still seem able through their writings to communicate as individuals with us who are the inheritors of much which they created; infuriating because in the course of transmission over two and half millennia much information has disappeared, and because the information which remains often shatters on inspection the first impression of similarity between the Greeks and ourselves.

We hope that the texts and other sources presented here will provide a coherent and comprehensible picture of ancient Greece; certain things, however, need some comment.

The characteristic institution of the Greek world was the *polis*, a small, independent community, consisting of an urban nucleus, or *astu*, and territory, or *hōra*. Although a few Greeks chose to spend much or all of their lives away from the place of their birth, for most Greeks existence outside their *polis* was unthinkable. An exile was prepared to go to almost any lengths to secure his return and if a *polis* was destroyed by one great power and restored by another, as sometimes happened, the survivors of the destruction returned to re-people their home. If a colony *apoikia* was destroyed, its men were likely to return to the *polis* which had sent them out. A *polis*, indeed, *was* its citizens *politai*; thus in two significant incidents at the turn of the fifth and fourth centuries, Nikias can tell the Athenian army in danger of being stranded in Sicily (see Ch. 22) that they could constitute themselves into a *polis*; and the Greek mercenaries, who actually found themselves stranded in Central Asia by the death of the Persian pretender for whom they had fought (see **252**), behaved like a *polis* on the move as they fought their way back to Greece.

Second, the religious basis of the Greek *polis*: with the possible (but by no means certain) exception of some philosophers, being a member of a *polis* was for a Greek inseparable from worshipping the gods of that *polis*. At the same time, Greek values depended on the context of the *polis*. It is

I

Athena   Dēmos   worshipper

1 Cult relief (S. Reinach, *Repertoire de reliefs grecs et romains* II (Paris, 1912), 332

not surprising that one important facet of the emergence of the *polis* was the achievement of ascendancy of the gods of the *polis* over the gods of the countryside, and the insertion of many important rural cults into the political framework of the community. The characteristic manifestations of Greek religion, cult statue, temple and altar, are already taken for granted by Homer. Furthermore, the practices of Greek religion were quite unlike those of the Judaeo-Christian tradition; a priest was not given any special training and his presence was not necessary for the performance of sacrifice, yet no *polis* was without its priests and the fact that the priests were the priests of the *polis* is crucial. A whole dimension of Greek life, which came forcibly to the front of the stage in 415 (see **214**), is missing if one does not place the religion of a *polis* at the centre of one's understanding of it. Again, the Greeks did not distinguish as we do between myth and history; their stories, *mythoi*, about their gods merged imperceptibly into their stories about what we call their early history; and throughout their history, their myths served to represent and explain their cosmology, their value system and their society. The tragedies of Aeschylus, Sophocles, Euripides and others (see p.7) were primarily acts of worship, which characterised and investigated the relationship of men as moral beings to the gods and to other men.

The aim of the *polis* was normally self-sufficiency; and the geological and climatic uniformity of much of the Mediterranean world meant that large-scale transfer of commodities, with one general and one particular exception, was not necessary. The general exception is provided by the different metals; some parts of the Greek world had none and none had all that were necessary. It was indeed the search for metals that led to the rediscovery of the outside world after the Dark Ages (see **14**). The particular exception is provided by Athens, which by the middle of the fifth century contained a population larger than could be fed from the resources of Attika; dependence on imported corn was the consequence.

But for most of the Greek world trade was a marginal activity. It was, moreover, marginal not only in quantitative terms; at Athens and as far as we can tell elsewhere trade was largely in the hands of outsiders, not *politai.* The values of the *polis* were predominantly those of farmers and soldiers.

The organisation of production was also vastly different from our own: insofar as production was not in the hands of men who owned and lived without additional labour off their own land or their own business, labour was not characteristically provided by men who worked for a wage; of course, this practice existed, but the characteristic form of additional labour, certainly in Athens from the late sixth century, was slave labour, the labour of men (and women) whose *persons* were owned and controlled by another (see **162**). This is not to say that slaves formed numerically the largest group of labourers in the Greek world as a whole – apart from the existence of labourers for a wage, there were also people in bondage for debt and freed slaves bound to perform services for their former masters; and since some areas of the Greek world never achieved the clear distinction between *polites,* free non-*polites* and slave which emerged at Athens, labour provided by means of various forms of customary dependance continued to exist, not to mention the labour of a once free population, now enslaved, exploited by Sparta (see **44**). And when the Greeks moved to settle areas outside Greece, they often reduced the native population to a form of dependence between free and slave (see **19**).

The parenthetical addition of 'women' in the previous paragraph draws attention to another point in which the Greek world was radically different from our own. Neither progressive Athens nor conservative Sparta, nor any other *polis*, conferred even the smallest political role on women; this fact was invariable, though their social role and their function in relation to the transmission of property varied widely. When the Athenian comic poet Aristophanes (see p.8) in two of his plays explored the possibility of rule by women, it was just a fantasy, parallel in its genre to the occasional speculations by philosophers on the possibility of a world without slaves.[1]

---

[1] See J. P. Gould, 'Law, custom and myth: aspects of the social position of women in classical Athens', *JHS* 100 (1980), 38–59.

The unit which lay between a man and a society was of course the family, understood always in a much more extended sense than the nuclear family normal in the modern western world. It was the family which presented a man for registration as a *politēs* and which guaranteed whatever qualifications of descent or ownership of land were necessary. Within this uniformity, however, there was enormous diversity, illustrated by the fact that at Sparta women became substantial owners of property, while at Athens a woman who became an heiress was forced to marry her nearest male agnate, both divorcing their existing spouses if they had them, in order to return property to the family.

It is indeed precisely the diversity of ancient Greece that we wish to emphasise. Particularly in the fifth and fourth centuries the period called classical from the supposed perfection of the art which it produced, it is all too easy to talk of Athens and think one is talking of Greece. Politically fragmented, socially at various stages of development, economically diverse, archaic and classical Greece was a mosaic of *poleis*, not a nation.

The Greeks indeed defined themselves only in relation to barbarians who were not Greeks, and then with some difficulty: the criteria were largely linguistic, hardly cultural and not at all racial. Even the rule that one Greek should not enslave another was far from universally observed. The *polis* was at the centre of a man's life, consisting above all of the men who composed its citizen body and only secondarily involving a geographical location – the Athenians, the Spartans, and not Athens, Sparta; to see this it is only necessary to read together Thucydides' account of the disaster which befell the Amprakiots in 426 (III. 109–113) and his account of the Athenian disaster in Sicily (VIII. 1). It is as a presentation and interpretation of the Greek *polis* that we should like this book to be seen.[2]

II The sources

While it is certainly possible to acquire a more or less adequate knowledge of the major events and main characteristics of a period of history from books and articles written about it by modern scholars, the serious student must be prepared to come to grips at first hand with the original texts and documents which those scholars have themselves consulted. This primary source-material falls under two obvious head-

---

2 For a selection of important recent work on the 'deep structure of ancient Greek thinking about the social nature of man' (J. P. Gould), with which we are not primarily concerned see R. L. Gordon (ed.), *Myth, religion and society. Structuralist essays by M. Detienne, L. Gernet, J. P. Vernant and P. Vidal-Naquet* (Cambridge, 1981).

ings: (a) written (sometimes called literary) sources and (b) archaeological finds, including inscriptions and coins.

(a) WRITTEN SOURCES

This rubric covers a large and disparate body of material, united only by
the means of its transmission to us – the fact that it has been handed
down to the age of printing only by repeated copying and recopying in a
manuscript tradition[3] – and by the fact that *where it exists* (and often it
does not, for particular topics or even whole periods or areas of enquiry)
it is usually the type of evidence from which the historian tends to
expect, and sometimes gets, the most. Indeed the most obvious way of
pinpointing the beginning of the History of a people or society, as
opposed to its Prehistory, is to link that demarcation with the appearance
of literacy there, and hence with the production sooner or later of what
comes to serve as the historian's written source-material; written either at
or near the time of the events in question or else (more usually) with
reference back to them; written either with an eye to posterity or else
(more usually) for consumption and effect at the time. On this criterion,
at any rate, Greek History may be deemed to begin in the eighth century,
for it was then that Greeks started to write their own language in an
alphabetic script (see **4**).

Homer

At first this new and useful facility of reading and writing, in accordance
with its Phoinikian origins, perhaps served mainly commercial ends, but
before long it had its impact too upon less ephemeral products of the
Greek experience – specifically upon two massive epic poems or songs,
the *Iliad* and the *Odyssey*. The Greeks themselves ascribed them to the
authorship of one man, HOMER (Homeros), but if any single individual(s)
did play a decisive role in bringing them to completion, that fact is less
important for the historian than the clarification, during the modern era
of scholarly work, of their essential nature and origins. They were not in
fact 'written' – by Homer or anyone else – in the same sense that Vergil
wrote the *Aeneid* or Milton *Paradise Lost*; they evolved, as the culmination of several centuries of oral, pre-literate poetic composition and
performance, in a highly stylised and formulaic manner, by many
generations of creative bards who passed on the subject-matter (and their
own skills in transmitting and extending it) from one to another.[4] The
whole process was a dynamic one, creative rather than merely repetitive,

3 See on this L. D. Reynolds and N. G. Wilson, *Scribes and Scholars: a guide to the
transmission of Greek and Latin literature* (second edition, Oxford, 1974).
4 See in detail G. S. Kirk, *The Songs of Homer* (Cambridge, 1962).

until a crucial conjunction of events occurred in the eighth century: (*a*) the two songs attained to such monumental size and scope as to be hardly capable of further extension, or even satisfactory preservation, by oral techniques, and (*b*) the art of writing made its (re)appearance in the Greek world. On the debit side this meant the end of the creative phase of epic composition – for it is an anthropological commonplace that the advent of literacy has a destructive impact on such oral poetry; but it meant also that the two enormous songs could indeed at last be 'written', i.e. written down, before the techniques and circumstances that had given rise to them had utterly died away.

The *Iliad* and *Odyssey* thus constitute the earliest written source-material for the historian of Greece; however, their character and origins, as just described, present him at the outset with an interpretative dilemma. They purport to depict the world of Mycenean Greece (*c.*1400–*c.*1150), and do indeed make mention of artefacts and institutions which belong to that early period. Some scholars have therefore been content without further ado to see them as a reflection of, and thus a source for, the Mycenean period – the fourteenth, thirteenth and twelfth centuries.[5] In 1954, however, M. I. Finley (in *The World of Odysseus*) put forward the view that Homeric society was essentially that of the *tenth* century, the so-called Dark Age which followed the collapse of the Mycenean palace-civilisation; and his thesis received striking and unforeseen support from the decipherment, between 1950 and 1955, of the Mycenean Linear B script, which gave scholars contemporary documentation from Mycenean Greece itself and revealed it to be a society significantly different from that depicted in the Homeric poems.[6] Since the controversies of the 1950s detailed work on the poems, hand in hand with archaeology, has come to appreciate them as an anachronistic amalgam of the institutions and artefacts of all the centuries during which they were growing to their maturity. But one may still ask whether in basic essentials they are rooted in one period or another; and although some scholars emphasise the obstacles to such a belief (see especially A. M. Snodgrass, 'An historical Homeric society?', *JHS* 94 (1974), 114–25), more generally Finley's positive answer to the question, once heretical, is now very much the orthodoxy; indeed many today would advocate a date even later than his and think of the ninth rather than the tenth century. If this is correct (as the authors of this book believe), the *Iliad* and perhaps especially the *Odyssey* become sources of prime importance for the evolution of archaic Greek society out of the

5 E.g. A. J. B. Wace and F. H. Stubbings (eds.), *A Companion to Homer* (London, 1962).
6 See J. Chadwick, *The Decipherment of Linear B* (second edition, Cambridge, 1967).

preceding Dark Age; and we have utilised Homeric evidence accordingly (see **2, 5, 6, 9, 14, 17**).[7]

Other evidence from poetry

Given the nature of its composition, the epic represented an inevitably impersonal, collective poetic effort rather than a single voice; but the rest of archaic Greek poetry, or what survives of it, is very much a matter of distinctive personalities and individual viewpoints.[8]

First, certainly in time (*c.*700) and arguably in importance also, comes HESIOD (Hesiodos), who lived at Askra in Boiotia, though he tells us that his father had migrated there from Kyme in Asia Minor. Poems of various sorts, all written in the epic vocabulary and metre, were ascribed to him in antiquity, but his main interest for the historian lies in his authorship of the *Works and Days*, an idiosyncratic miscellany of moral advice and practical wisdom, and our first direct insight into the problematical social conditions of the early archaic period (see **10**); he is also the source of much of our knowledge of early Greek agriculture (see Austin and Vidal-Naquet, *Economy* nos. 10 and 31). Indeed many of the poets of this epoch, writing in an unprecedentedly subjective mode, give us evidence direct or indirect of the social and (increasingly) political tensions and changes of their time – in Sparta (TYRTAEUS: **45, 49**), in Athens (SOLON: **66–68**), in Megara (THEOGNIS: **21, 36**) and across the Aegean in Mytilene (ALCAEUS: **24**). Others, however, preferred to see and to emphasise order rather than conflict, continuity rather than change: thus the Sicilian IBYCUS (**33**) and – prolonging the archaic ethos into the middle of the fifth century – the Boiotian PINDAR (Pindaros) (**12**) still sang of the epic heroes, in songs to honour men who still aspired to emulate their virtues and achievements.[9]

But otherwise Greek poetry was never to be so personal again – not at any rate until the Hellenistic period, which lies outside the scope of this book. Instead the classical period, and particularly the fifth century, saw in Athens the flowering of genres of poetic expression and performance in which the concerns of the individual gave way to the concerns of the whole community: political genres in the purest Greek sense of the term, poetry of and for the *polis*. At the centre of the life of any *polis* was its

---

7 The second edition of *The World of Odysseus* (London, 1977) takes account of developments in the argument since 1954; see especially Appendix 1, 'The world of Odysseus revisited'. For studies of 'Homeric' values which acknowledge a debt to Finley and follow his general approach see especially A. W. H. Adkins, *Merit and Responsibility: a study in Greek values* (Oxford, 1960), chs.2–3, and *Moral Values*, ch.2; and see **5–6**.

8 See in general M. L. West in K. J. Dover (ed.), *Ancient Greek Literature* (Oxford, 1980), ch.3.

9 On Pindar see C. M. Bowra, *Pindar* (Oxford, 1964).

7

Introduction

calendar of religious festivals; and it was at the festivals in Athens, in the late sixth and early fifth centuries, that dramatic poetry first took on recognisable shape. In celebration of the god or goddess, sets of stage plays, both tragedies and comedies, came to be submitted in annual competition. The products of this might well have been purely ephemeral – for each play was performed only the once; yet what actually evolved, during the course of the fifth century, was a succession of enduring poetic and dramatic masterpieces.[10] After such sixth-century pioneers as Thespis (whence our word 'thespian'), the first of the three great names in Attic tragedy is Aeschylus (525/4–456); and his two successors-in-chief are both represented in this book: SOPHOCLES (**158**) and EURIPIDES (**160**). Only rarely were their subjects overtly contemporary ones – Aeschylus' *Persians* of 472 being the obvious surviving example; in so far as it is temporally located at all, the world which tragedy inhabits is akin to the Homeric one, and can only be described as the world of myth;[11] yet even so the nature of the genre was such as to reflect indirectly many of the contemporary political and moral issues prominent at the time of writing. The use of this sort of evidence by historians has sometimes been heavy-handed, but it would be folly to ignore it.[12] As to comedy, its supreme exponent was ARISTOPHANES, whose eleven surviving plays give us invaluable insights into the social and political fabric of Athens between 425 and 388 (see **147, 156, 160, 163, 180, 201, 211, 261**). The genre was a uniquely uninhibited and eclectic one, but within a plot, usually, of escapist fantasy a preoccupation with contemporary issues and personalities is plain to see; and every historian of the period must attempt to evaluate the evidence, biased and distorted as it often is, that these plays provide.[13]

Fifth-century prose

Meanwhile, however, various genres of prose literature had been developed also; and these, necessarily, will usually provide the historian with his most direct sources of literary evidence. Prose-writing had evolved in the *poleis* of sixth-century Ionia, as part of an intellectual revolution which had been taking place there: a range of enquiries into

10 See in general K. J. Dover in *Ancient Greek Literature* (n.8, above), ch.4.
11 See B. M. W. Knox, *Word and Action: essays on the ancient theater* (Baltimore, 1979), ch.1, 'Myth and Attic Tragedy'.
12 For some guidance in this see K. J. Dover, *Greek Popular Morality* (Oxford, 1974), 14–18.
13 For recent discussions of the problems here see Meiggs, *Empire*, 391–5; de Ste Croix, *Origins*, 232–4 (with the criticisms of G. A. H. Chapman, *Acta Classica* 21 (1978), 59–70) and 355–76; Dover, *Greek Popular Morality*, 18–33. On the genre in general see K. J. Dover, *Aristophanic Comedy* (London, 1972) and *Ancient Greek Literature* (1980), ch.5.

8

the observable phenomena of the world had begun to be undertaken, all of them written in prose rather than verse, as almost a declaration in itself of the supremacy of rational thought and investigation over the unexaminable nexus of religion, magic and superstition.[14] This progressive climate had given rise to what the Greeks called *historia* – asking questions.

With the benefit of hindsight we can separate *historia* into various strands. In its earliest and most austere form we should describe it as philosophy, a combination of natural science and metaphysics, with the city of Miletos producing the three great figures – Thales (see **92**), Anaximandros and Anaximenes. But in the fifth century its scope increasingly extended into ethical and political philosophy (the questions raised by the life of human beings as individuals and members of society), in the hands of men whom for convenience we collectively call the Sophists (*sophistai*).[15] Not more than a tiny fraction of their writings survives; for an example here see **243** (DEMOCRITUS); but their influence can be traced in broad terms upon a surprisingly large proportion of the literature, both prose and poetry, of the second half of the fifth century. Just as important, by now, as the substance of an argument or enquiry was its *form*, and hence its power to convince, right or wrong; and a fair, if not very distinguished, example of these newly-formulated rules of rhetorical presentation would be the Athenian 'OLD OLIGARCH' (see **135, 140, 143** (with Intro.), **160**).

For our purposes, though, it is more germane to note that there had been developing meanwhile another aspect of *historia* which during the course of the fifth century becomes our principal source of written evidence: genuine historical research and exposition, as we ourselves would understand it. Again Ionia was the place of origin, for there in the late sixth century the new spirit of rational investigation had been interacting with the epic tradition of story-telling and song. Precise beginnings are obscure, but it is clear enough that beside the epic poets and reciters had appeared a crop of writers for whom enquiry into the doings of men, as opposed to gods or heroes, was the chief concern; again their medium was prose, not verse, and these *logographoi* (as they were called), such as another Milesian, Hecataeus (see **102**), were instrumental in furthering an intellectual curiosity and a tradition of disinterested research designed to satisfy it which continued throughout the fifth century and on into the fourth (see below). Their names and their (almost entirely lost) works, opening up fields of study which today we should term geography, ethnography, mythography, etc., need not

14 See on this G. E. R. Lloyd, *Magic, Reason and Experience: studies in the origins and development of Greek science* (Cambridge, 1979).
15 See in general W. K. C. Guthrie, *The Sophists* (Cambridge, 1971).

be recited here; more important is to introduce the two fifth-century historians of major stature who dominate any source-book of this kind, as will be obvious from the Index, and whose achievements in their different fields remained unequalled ever after – HERODOTUS of Halikarnassos, and the Athenian THUCYDIDES.

Herodotus, [16] the earlier of the two (born in the 480s), put a lifetime of travel and tireless curiosity to the service of a great historical work of unprecedented size and scope, best described in the words of his own preface: 'this is an exposition of the *historia* of Herodotus of Halikarnassos, its object to ensure that the passage of time does not erase the past from men's minds and that the great and astonishing achievements of both Greeks and *barbaroi* [see I] do not go unsung, and to find out in particular why the two peoples made war upon each other'. The work culminated, therefore, in a full-dress narrative of the two unsuccessful Persian invasions of Greece (in 490 and 480: see Ch. 10) – but not before Herodotus had incorporated into it, with apparently effortless ease, a whole mass of historical, ethnographical and anecdotal material relating to Greece and the Near East (including Egypt) during the sixth and early fifth centuries. This was the product to some extent, it would seem, of his reading in the works of the *logographoi*, but for the most part the fruits of his own travels and enquiries, his own first-hand *historia*. A consummate story-teller (albeit in prose) in the epic manner, Herodotus could nonetheless evaluate his material with a rational scepticism inherited from the Ionian natural scientists and philosophers, and speak in an ironic tone of stories which seemed to him implausible (the *locus classicus* is VII. 152); so his ancient title of Father of History is not unjustified. In so far as his standards of accuracy and level of insight fall below our modern expectations, they do so in any case very largely by (unfair) comparison with his indubitably more sophisticated successor Thucydides (born *c*.460–455), the historian of the great Peloponnesian War of 431–404. [17] With Thucydides too his aims and objectives in writing are best

16 Work on H. published up to 1966 is reviewed by G. T. Griffith in *Fifty Years (and Twelve) of Classical Scholarship* (Oxford, 1968), 184–8 and 227–9; since then the most important study is C. W. Fornara, *Herodotus: an interpretative essay* (Oxford, 1971). See also A. D. Momigliano, *Studies in Historiography* (London, 1969), ch.8, 'The place of Herodotus in the history of historiography'; G. E. M. de Ste Croix, *Greece and Rome* 24 (1977), 130–48.

17 There are brief bibliographical surveys by Griffith, *Fifty Years (and Twelve)*, 188–92 and 229–32, and (more fully and idiosyncratically) by K. J. Dover, *Thucydides* (*Greece and Rome*, New Surveys in the Classics no. 7, 1973). See also de Ste Croix, *Origins*, 5–34, and M. I. Finley's introduction to recent editions (since 1972) of the *Penguin Classics* translation by Rex Warner. An indispensable aid to our understanding of Thuc. and our use of his work is A. W. Gomme, A. Andrewes and K. J. Dover, *A Historical Commentary on Thucydides* (5 vols, Oxford, 1945–1981); see especially Gomme's long introduction to Vol. 1 (pp. 1–87).

conveyed in his own prefatory words: 'Thucydides, an Athenian, has written of how the Peloponnesians and the Athenians went to war with each other – beginning right at the war's outset, in the expectation that it would be a major one, and more noteworthy than any of the wars of the past; this he concluded from the fact that both sides, as they went into it, were at their peak and fully prepared, and he saw too that the rest of the Greek world was either already committed to one side or the other or else planning to be; for this was certainly the greatest upheaval to affect the Greeks and, in part, the *barbaroi* as well – in short, the majority of the human race' (compare v.26). Thucydides thus carried historical method a crucial stage further than had Herodotus, in that besides looking into the events of the recent past, to establish the war's underlying origins, he was setting himself the task of chronicling and analysing a conflict yet to unfold year by year, before his eyes. A highly intelligent and intellectually rigorous man (who makes an appearance in his own narrative as one of Athens' generals: see IV.102–108), he was fully aware, and concerned to make his readers fully aware also, of the extraordinary difficulties of such a project (see especially 1.20–22), and it cannot be said that he succeeded in overcoming them all; his work is nonetheless a record, and an achievement, of the very highest order, always our principal source for the war itself and an important authority too on earlier periods and topics.

Oratory

The many direct speeches which Thucydides included in his History, while in a formal sense a continuation of the Herodotean (and ultimately the epic) tradition, in fact pose problems at a genuinely historical level, as he clearly intended them to be a record, in some (notoriously indefinable) sense, of what was really said at the time.[18] Some scholars insist that in Thucydides we do have preserved virtually the *ipsissima verba* of leading figures of the Peloponnesian War period; others prefer on a number of grounds to emphasise the element of Thucydides' own composition and analysis in most of the speeches; and the authors of this book admit to a strong inclination in the latter direction. But we do in any event possess a means of reading, and thus of exploiting as evidence, actual speeches delivered by known individuals in the fifth and fourth centuries. Here again, as with tragedy and comedy, one is essentially speaking of

---

18 See in general P. A. Stadter (ed.), *The Speeches in Thucydides* (Chapel Hill, N.C., 1973). Thuc.'s own statement, in 1.22.1, of what the speeches are has defeated its explanatory object by being so ambiguous (see for instance Gomme, *Commentary* 1, 140–1; de Ste Croix, *Origins*, 7–11). We translate: 'the speeches, while keeping as closely as possible to the overall gist of what the various speakers actually said on each occasion, represent essentially what in my opinion it was necessary for them to say'.

democratic Athens: in the Athenian citizen assembly or before enormous juries speeches were made and the techniques of rhetorical persuasion brought to a high pitch. To use the material which this political and forensic oratory offers is not easy, as the speaker's aim was simply to win over his audience, not necessarily to tell them (or us) the truth; where two surviving speeches refer to the same events (Aeschines III and Demosthenes XVIII – see below) their disagreement *on facts* is radical; the genre as a whole thus calls for treatment and use on the same lines as comic (or tragic) drama, which is to say that individual and ostensibly factual statements will be often less significant, certainly less reliable, than the tacit assumptions shared between speaker and audience which underpin the argument as a whole.[19]

In terms of what survives, the evidence of oratory is a feature of the late fifth and above all the fourth century: in this book the authors represented are LYSIAS (**144, 244, 246**) and ANDOCIDES (**307**), both active in the last years of the fifth century and on into the fourth; ISOCRATES, born in 436 and still alive and at work 98 years later in 338 (**80, 247, 260, 276, 303, 314, 319**); and the two great rivals of the 340s and 330s, AESCHINES (**248, 305, 310, 313**, etc.) and DEMOSTHENES (**163, 278, 279, 281, 305**, etc.). With the exception of Isocrates, who preferred to write and circulate tracts in speech form, all these men were actively involved in the political life of their period; even Lysias, who as a Syracusan by birth was ineligible to address the Athenian citizen assembly in person, could write speeches for others to do so (**246**), besides seeking legal redress for wrongs suffered by himself and his family (**244**); and for Aeschines and Demosthenes the assembly and the courts served equally well as the arena for their great power-struggle over the Makedonian issue (see Ch. 34).

Fourth-century historians and researchers

As matters stand, then, the fifth century *for us* is the era of great historical writing, the fourth century that of great oratory; this is mainly a simple accident of source survival or loss. Fifth-century oratory, both political and forensic, did exist but little is preserved. As to history, though, the situation is more complex: plenty of it was written, whether actually in or referring retrospectively back to the fourth century, but subsequently lost, save for snippets preserved in quotation or paraphrase; even if it had survived in abundance, however, one doubts whether very much of it would be as centrally important to us for its period as the accounts of Herodotus and Thucydides are for their earlier times. Thucydides in

---

19 For critical principles see Dover, *Greek Popular Morality*, 5–14 and 23–45; see also, more generally, his *Ancient Greek Literature*, ch.8.

particular had preached, and practised, standards of such severe perfection that no successor was found equal to them, much as several seem deliberately to have invited the comparison – by beginning their own Greek History (*Hellēnika*) at precisely the point, in the year 411, where Thucydides' narrative had prematurely broken off. THEOPOMPOS of Chios (born *c.*378) did so, for instance; though he, a product of the rhetorical academy established and run in Athens by Isocrates, is better known as the author of a later and wider-ranging work, the *Philippika*, in which his strong personal likes and especially dislikes appear to have been given free rein (see **322**).[20] Another continuator of Thucydides has so far defied all attempts to identify him by name. To the general statement that we owe our Greek literary sources to a manuscript tradition of repeated recopying (p.5) must be added the important rider that during the last 200 years the discovery of literary texts on *papyrus* (the paper of the ancient world), written from the last third of the fourth century onwards, with Alexander the Great's conquest of Egypt, and preserved in the dry sands there, has been steadily increasing the sum of Greek literature which can once again be read; much of what is turned up is very fragmentary, and of interest only to the specialist papyrologist, but occasionally the find is substantial and spectacular; and both adjectives are appropriate to the anonymous 'HELLENICA OXYRHYNCIA', the first and most substantial extract of which was found on papyrus at Oxyrhynchos (Behnesa) in 1906. What we have covers the period 396–5 (see **254, 258**), and its high quality makes one wish there were more.[21] Instead, however, the successor of Thucydides who has to matter most to us is the Athenian XENOPHON, for his is the *Hellēnika* which provides the only continuous and contemporary account of Greek history between 411 and 362. Xenophon (*c.*428–*c.*354) was an active man of many parts, and a writer of great versatility, as a glance at the Index of this book will show; amongst his smaller works excerpted here are his *Constitution of the Spartans, Recollections of Sokrates (Memorabilia)*, which reflects the emergence of the new genre of biography, and the undervalued *Ways and Means (Poroi)*, which puts forward suggestions for curing the economic and social ills of Athens in the mid fourth century (see **161, 277, 286**); but he was perhaps jack of too many trades to be master of any one of them, and certainly as an historian his failings are

---

20 See K. von Fritz, 'The historian Theopompus', *American Historical Review* 46 (1941), 765–87; W. R. Connor, *Theopompus and Fifth-Century Athens* (Washington, D.C., 1968); I. A. F. Bruce, 'Theopompus and classical Greek historiography', *History and Theory* 9 (1970), 86–109. (Note that a *Hellēnika* and a *Philippika* were also amongst the output of his contemporary ANAXIMENES of Lampsakos (**323**).)

21 See in brief Griffith in *Fifty Years (and Twelve)*, 192–4; I. A. F. Bruce, *An Historical Commentary on the Hellenica Oxyrhyncia* (Cambridge, 1967); for the fragments most recently identified, L. Koenen, *Studia Papyrologica* 15 (1976), 55ff.

many and obvious.[22] A valuable supplement and corrective to Xenophon would have been available to us in the World History, from earliest times down to his own day, by another pupil of Isocrates, Ephorus of Kyme (born c.405),[23] but sadly it survives only through its extensive use by the derivative DIODORUS (see below).

Yet if the fourth century is a disappointment to us after the fifth in terms of historical *insight*, a real grasp of events and their causes and effects, its compensation lies in an improvement (or so it would seem) in historical *method*, in the sense at least of serious documentary research within limited fields. During the course of the fifth century Ionian *historia* had developed in two rather different directions: thanks to the great stature of Herodotus we see the more clearly its tendency towards anecdotal history, which in other hands led to little more than mere curiosity and gossip-mongering, but at the same time there was another strand of the logographic tradition, less flamboyant but more serious-minded, which had set itself the task of sober historical research. Hecataeus the Milesian has already been mentioned, and he it was, so far as we can tell, who pioneered (amongst other genres) what may be termed regional history or ethnography. A fair idea of the scope and character of this sort of material and approach is provided by the early books of Herodotus, who, as explained earlier, took the perceptive step of using it in the service of a grander historical design. Others, however, preferred to keep the various elements of the logographic tradition separate and to refine some of them still further: thus *regional* history led on to *local* history, with a writer such as Ephorus (above) cutting his teeth on a history of his native *polis* before attempting more grandiose projects. In this field, as in several others, Hellanicus of Lesbos was the great name of the second half of the fifth century, most particularly because it was he who researched and wrote the first *Atthis*, a local history and chronography of Athens and Attika (disparagingly mentioned by Thucydides, 1.97.2); and in the fourth and third centuries a whole succession of these Atthidographers — Athenians themselves, by then — transmitted this specialised body of material from one to another and zealously unearthed documentary and archival sources to refine and improve it.[24] Frustratingly little of the work of the six principal

22 See in brief Griffith in *Fifty Years (and Twelve)*, 196–8; W. P. Henry, *Greek Historical Writing* (Chicago, 1967); J. K. Anderson, *Xenophon* (London, 1974). C. H. Grayson (in B. M. Levick (ed.) *The Ancient Historian and his Materials: essays . . . C. E. Stevens* (Farnborough, Hants., 1975), 31–43) overplays his hand in arguing that X. did not *intend* his work to be treated as history; nonetheless, any modern equivalent of it might best be described as memoirs (thus for instance G. L. Cawkwell's introduction to recent editions (since 1978) of the *Penguin Classics* translation by Rex Warner).

23 See G. L. Barber, *The Historian Ephorus* (Cambridge, 1935).

24 See in brief Griffith in *Fifty Years (and Twelve)*, 195–6. The classic study is Felix Jacoby, *Atthis: the local chronicles of ancient Athens* (Oxford, 1949).

Atthidographers has survived to us; those represented in this book are ANDROTION (**79**; see also **338**) and PHILOCHORUS (**79, 313, 347**).

A genre such as the *Atthis* was obviously one of parochial horizons, by definition; but equally obviously those horizons could be transcended if the local research was undertaken as an element of some comprehensive programme of research into political philosophy. Of the two towering figures of philosophy in fourth-century Athens, the first, PLATO (427–347), was temperamentally disinclined to undertake any such project, so the evidence which we extract from his philosophical dialogues – despite, in many cases, their real Athenian setting – is hardly ever of this direct kind (see **17, 141, 247, 248, 283, 303**). But his most distinguished pupil ARISTOTLE (Aristoteles) (384–322) was a different sort of thinker, an empiricist who liked to draw out general truths and patterns from a systematic and logical study of specific data; so *his* political and moral generalisations (see **7, 22, 23, 40**, etc.) are much more often grounded directly or indirectly in hard facts and real historical developments; and the same can be said of his own pupil, and successor, THEOPHRASTUS (see **315**). Indeed to put it in modern terms Aristotle created and ran a research institute, the Lykeion, in fourth-century Athens, with pupils and collaborators from all over the Greek world engaged in projects in all the many areas of his own interest. And in the field of historically-oriented political thought the product of their labours was a collection of no fewer than 158 constitutional histories (*politeiai*) of all the major Greek and in some instances non-Greek cities of any significance – this to supply the master with working material for his general synthetic theories of political and social evolution. Sadly this great thesaurus is almost entirely lost, save for quotation and paraphrase in other writers;[25] however, by a fortunate accident the *Constitution of the Athenians* (*Athenaion Politeia*) came to light in 1890 on papyrus rolls acquired by the British Museum, and we have naturally drawn heavily upon the evidence of this, the only surviving *Atthis* (see especially Chs.6 and 11). There is still no general agreement amongst scholars as to whether the *Ath. Pol.* is from the hand of Aristotle himself or (as the authors of this book are inclined to think) one of his associates;[26] but on either view the information in it must always be assessed on its own merits, and questioned where necessary.

Later writers

As well as the literary source-material surviving from the archaic and classical periods themselves (and contemporary in that sense), we look

25 For a preserved fragment of the *Constitution of Massalia* (Marseilles) see **19**.
26 For the arguments involved see for example von Fritz and Kapp, *Aristotle*, 3–7, and Hignett, *Constitution*, 27–30 (with J. J. Keaney, 'Hignett's *HAC* and the authorship of the *Athenaion Politeia*', *Liverpool Classical Monthly* 5,3 (March 1980), 51–6).

also to a miscellany of later writers, from the second century B.C. to the second A.D., who provide information retrospectively about earlier epochs. During the late fourth and the third centuries, in the wake of the conquests of Alexander the Great, Greek culture spread over an area immeasurably larger than the old 'Greek world' as Herodotus or Thucydides or even Aristotle would have conceived it; and the literature produced in this period, in centres old (such as Athens) and new (such as Alexandria), was different in character and outlook from anything that had gone before, reflecting this new, expanding and cosmopolitan society. And then, in the second and first centuries, the Hellenistic Greek kingdoms succumbed one by one to the power of Rome. The changes in taste and mentality which accompanied and resulted from these successive transformations of the political map form a complex subject which cannot be dealt with here,[27] but one aspect of them is plain enough – an upsurge of interest, on the part both of the conquering Romans and the conquered Greeks, in precisely those periods of Greek history and culture which are the subject of this book. This often led to the inclusion of incidental information concerning Greek history in works devoted to other subjects: thus for example POLYBIUS, the second-century historian of the rise of Rome, adds to our knowledge of the fourth century also (**312, 348**), while the philosopher and polymath POSIDONIUS (born *c.*135) and the Roman annalist LIVY both augment our meagre data on the archaic colonisation movement (**15, 19**); and there is also much Greek history to be extracted from the *Roman Antiquities* and other works of DIONYSIUS of Halikarnassos, the Augustan literary critic and antiquarian, whose interest in classical Athenian oratory gives us our only surviving source of information on an abortive constitutional change in late fifth-century Athens (**246**). Closer to the historical mainstream, the genre of World History, largely ignored since its creation by Ephorus (p.14), took on a new and obvious attraction with the dominance of Rome. In the second half of the first century DIODORUS of Agyrion (in Sicily; hence Diodorus Siculus) compiled such a history, in 40 volumes, from earliest times down to his own day. Most of it is now lost; for our purposes the most important surviving section is books 11–20, which cover the years 480 to 302. Through most of this period (books 11–16) Diodorus followed, to a degree which today would be unacceptable plagiarism, the work of his predecessor Ephorus; the value of Diodorus is that of his sources, for in his own right he was hopelessly second-rate; we are obliged to use him simply because for so many periods and on so many topics there is no alternative; on matters of chronology, in particular, he

---

27 See in brief J. Griffin in K. J. Dover (ed.), *Ancient Greek Literature* (1980), ch.9.

is notoriously confused and confusing.[28] A more distinguished example of the genre, possibly, was that written by the Asiatic Greek STRABO (born 64/3), but it has not survived; fortunately, though, we do have his 17-book *Geography* which preserves a great deal of valuable geographical and antiquarian material, especially in books 8–10 on Greece (see **1, 3, 15, 20**, etc.).

And this antiquarian nostalgia for the history and culture of the Greek, and above all the Athenian, past intensified in the late first and on throughout the second centuries A.D. with the Renaissance-like movement known as the Second Sophistic. Again, we cannot pursue its many manifestations here,[29] but simply be thankful for another crop of writers whose backward-looking perspective, however uncritical or distorted it often is, preserves further historical detail from oblivion: witness for instance PAUSANIAS (c.A.D.150), not only a geographer but an active traveller and sightseer in the Herodotean mould, whose *Periēgēsis* (*Description of Greece*) contains a wealth of topographical and antiquarian matter – its reliability confirmed, for the most part, by still-surviving remains – as well as historical material which is not always so trustworthy (see **11, 57, 84**, etc.); or ATHENAEUS of Naukratis (in Egypt), whose rambling and anecdotal *Deipnosophistai* (*Dons at Dinner*) reflects wide reading in sources which were subsequently lost (see **19, 73, 331**). However, much the most interesting and useful of these retrospective writers is the Greek PLUTARCH (Ploutarchos) of Chaironeia (c.A.D.46 – after 120), whose *Parallel Lives* pair together prominent Greeks and Romans; and extracts from fifteen of his Greek biographies are presented here. Not that Plutarch was a biographer of the modern type, concerned with historical accuracy and chronological precision no less than the historian in other genres; rather he was a moral essayist, who in these works (and he wrote many others besides, known collectively as the *Moralia*) chose the biographical format as a framework for analysing the characters of the well-known individuals concerned; and the realisation of this by modern scholars has brought about a more favourable estimate of his work than was once the norm, and more sensitive guidance on how best to use it.[30] Besides, Plutarch enjoyed access to a great many

28 See Gomme, *Commentary* I, 51–4; Meiggs, *Empire*, 447–64.
29 See G. W. Bowersock, *Greek Sophists in the Roman Empire* (Oxford, 1969), E. L. Bowie, 'Greeks and their past in the Second Sophistic', in M. I. Finley (ed.), *Studies in Ancient Society* (London, 1974), 166–209; E. L. Bowie in K. J. Dover (ed.), *Ancient Greek Literature* (1980), ch. 10; J. J. Winkler and Gordon Williams (eds.), *Later Greek Literature* (Cambridge, 1982).
30 A pioneer was Gomme, *Commentary* I, 54–84; amongst recent studies see D. A. Russell, *Plutarch* (London, 1973), and A. E. Wardman, *Plutarch's Lives* (London, 1974). For the genre as a whole, A. D. Momigliano, *The Development of Greek Biography* (Cambridge, Mass., 1971).

writers who are now lost; he read widely in them, and cites and quotes from them liberally; so on several levels his *Lives* make a major contribution to any study of archaic and classical Greece.

Having briefly assessed the surviving literary source-material, we must now clearly state and appreciate its limitations. And the prime point to be understood is what a paltry fraction we have of what once existed: seven plays of Sophocles, for example, out of more than 120; only one, as mentioned, of the 158 Aristotelian *politeiai*; and surely no more than 5 per cent, perhaps far less, of historical writing.[31] No doubt it is a cliché to liken one's task in studying a period of history to that of assembling a jigsaw puzzle; but as regards the ancient Greek world what must be borne in mind is that the great majority of the pieces are and always will be missing. All we have is a glimpse of a shape here, a suggestion of colour there, and we must recognise and resist the temptation of making these scraps of the total picture fit together too neatly, and of believing that even when properly located they can answer all the questions that we care to ask. To take only the two most obvious biases: it will have been plain from the preceding discussion that there is a massive preponderance of source-material from, or at any rate about, Athens, which leaves us not only with wholly inadequate specific information about other places but also in danger of formulating generalisations on the basis of that single and in many ways untypical *polis*; and also – less obvious but every bit as important – these written sources naturally tell us far more about the concerns, collective and individual, of the educated, literate adult males who produced them than about other sectors of society. In general terms, then, the historian of archaic and classical Greece will regard the evidence as paramount, a set of precious clues to be examined and re-examined until they have yielded up all the enlightenment they can; but having done this he will endeavour to go further, seeing beyond the fragmentary record to the basic characteristics of the society which produced it (some of them adumbrated above, pp. 1–4), and seeking to bridge the gaps in explicit documentation by the disciplined exercise of inference, extrapolation and conjecture.

(b) ARCHAEOLOGICAL EVIDENCE, INSCRIPTIONS AND COINS

If the Greek historian's only resort was the written source material just described, he could hope to reach a satisfactory understanding of some few topics and periods, and an acceptable working familiarity with rather

31 See L. Pearson, 'Lost Greek historians judged by their fragments', *Greece and Rome* 12 (1943), 43–56.

more; but in other cases he would make little or no progress at all. We are fortunate, then, in that other types of evidence are available, and that even if they do not always link up with the literary sources as neatly as we would like, they may shed light instead upon matters about which we should otherwise be extremely ill-formed.

Perhaps the most striking difference to our knowledge of ancient Greece is made by the evidence of archaeology, whether through the study of burials in eighth-century Attika (p.28) or through our knowledge of the building programme of Periklean Athens or of the Royal cemetery of Makedonia (p. 587). For the Greeks both commissioned sacred and secular buildings, which were intended to serve as public symbols for a community, and left behind traces of their private life; some of the public buildings of ancient Greece have survived more or less complete and archaeological investigation has both excavated the ruins of others and told us much also about aspects of Greek society which hardly figure in the literary sources. The harvest is obviously richest for the earliest periods, but much can be learnt even for later periods – looking at the *akropolis* of Athens, it is hard not to feel admiration for the *dēmos*, which chose the architects and sculptors for most of its buildings.[32]

As already explained, our conventional written sources have come down to us, over two and a half millennia and more, as a result of conscious decisions to preserve and transmit them; however, we also have other written evidence that has survived in its original form simply because of the durability of its medium: this is *epigraphical* evidence, or that of inscriptions. Epigraphical evidence is constantly on the increase – much more so than literary source material – as a result both of archaeological excavation and of chance discovery. Once the inscriptions have come to light they become the concern of specialist epigraphists, who will prepare a text of the stones (or bronzes) for publication, usually accompanied by a commentary on their contents, and thus add them to the general body of the historian's data. The techniques which epigraphists employ in studying and publishing inscriptions, and their criteria for restoring (if, as is so often the case, they are incomplete), classifying and dating them are clearly and expertly explained by Woodhead;[33] it will suffice here to give a general indication of the scope of epigraphical evidence, so far as it is presented in this book, together with some remarks about aspects of Greek society that it highlights simply by existing at all.

32 See in general A. M. Snodgrass, in M. H. Crawford (ed.), *Sources for Ancient History* (1982).
33 A. G. Woodhead, *The Study of Greek Inscriptions* (1981); and F. G. B. Millar, in M. H. Crawford (ed.), *Sources for Ancient History* (1982).

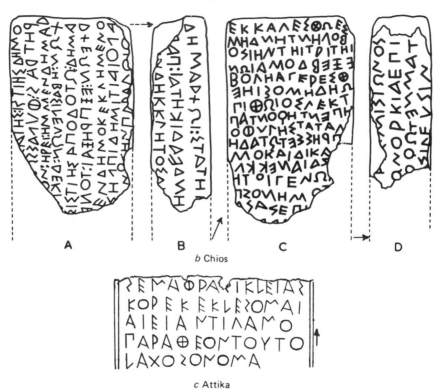

a Megara Hyblaia

b Chios

c Attika

2 Characteristic archaic scripts (L. H. Jeffery, *Local Scripts of Archaic Greece* (Oxford, 1961))

Obviously enough, the origins of Greek epigraphy, as of the other manifestations of literacy in the Greek world, lie in the eighth century: while Hesiod was penning his *Works and Days*, an anonymous contemporary in the Greek settlement on Pithekoussai (**15**) was, in a more modest literary endeavour, inscribing poor verse on his drinking cup ('Nestor's Cup': Meiggs and Lewis no. 1). And it must be emphasised that in terms of simple quantity this sort of purely private epigraphy – including what today we would call graffiti – represents for all periods the bulk of the evidence: dedications (see **12A, 42B**), curses, and above all, in their tens of thousands, epitaphs (**41, 43**); and the social historian, in particular, will make full use of this testimony, bringing us as it does close to the life and death of ordinary men and women. But on the whole it is the various categories of public inscriptions that chiefly concern us –

the documentary evidence of laws, decrees, treaties, inventories and all manner of other transactions which whole communities, each employing their characteristic local script (see Figs 2–4) and dialect, acquired the habit of having inscribed by masons upon stone blocks (*stēlai*) as a matter of public record. Early examples included here are **16B** (actually a fourth-century document copied from an archaic original), **37, 38, 39** and **42A**; and the practice became a firmly established one in the classical period and beyond (see **127, 134,** etc.).

The reasons for this were manifold, some of them fairly obvious, others less so. On a simple material level, public documents and records which were not ephemeral in character and application (and those which were, of course, are now wholly lost to us)[34] called for preservation *somehow or other*, and in the absence of all our modern methods of data storage and retrieval it might be said that the Greeks had little real alternative but to use the stone, usually marble, that lay around them in such abundance. Nor should one discount fashion as a factor, as the epigraphical habit and an appreciation of its uses spread from one city to another. But the basic question still remains, why would a visitor to Athens in the late fifth century have found its *akropolis* and *agora* full to overflowing with stone *stēlai*? For whose benefit was this parading of transactions and proceedings? Once put in these terms the question answers itself, and indeed reveals an important correlation: the extent to which any Greek community, in this period, publicised its business on inscriptions set up in public places may be seen as directly related to (a) the extent to which it was, or became, democratically governed, and (b) its general level of literacy. Crude as it is in many ways, the Sparta/Athens dichotomy (for which see **182–183**) inevitably arises here, as a pointer to the two extremities of the scale. In Sparta, as will be seen, the uniquely conservative nature of society and government, ever more anachronistic in a changing world, went hand in hand with a restriction of literacy, *de facto*, to a small ruling élite; and Spartan public inscriptions are virtually non-existent.[35] Athens, by contrast, was the pioneer, as we shall see, of open and particularly democratic government; and this fact was both a concomitant of and a stimulus to a relatively high level of literacy amongst Athenians,[36] with the consequence that between the

---

34 As regards Athens, for example, we hear of *leukōmata* (whitened tablets), which evidently served as notice-boards for transitory business (Lysias IX. 6; Demosthenes XXIV. 23).

35 For a rare example see **188**. On the only surviving epigraphical instance, recently discovered, of a fifth-century Spartan treaty see P. A. Cartledge, 'Literacy in the Spartan oligarchy', *JHS* 98 (1978), 25–37 at 35.

36 See **121**, with some reservations on this point. One must remember that Greek inscriptions were probably not easy to read (Fig. 3) and that their proliferation at Athens in part did no more than symbolise the existence of an open system of government.

3 Attic inscription: Record of accounts of 410/09 B.C. (IG I². 304A) (B. D. Meritt, *Athenian Financial Documents* (Ann Arbor, 1932), pl. 6)

middle of the fifth century and the end of our period the volume of public inscriptions from Athens outweighs by a colossal margin the epigraphical evidence from any other single city (see Fig. 3). And between these two extremes come all the other communities – most of them, unfortunately, nearer in this respect to the Spartan end of the spectrum than to the Athenian. It is obviously a matter for regret that other cities did not, to anything approaching the Athenian extent, put their public business on record in this way, and thus enable us to supplement the usually meagre literary sources. We must simply count ourselves fortunate that one community did do so, and that we may still today handle, read and use the contemporary records of the Athenian *ekklēsia* (citizen assembly) and of its decisions in domestic and foreign policy.

We have just seen that when the Greek *poleis* became literate in and after the eighth century they used a script which differed from one area to another; their separateness appears also from the fact that when coinage appeared in the Greek world in the middle of the sixth century, each *polis* coined for itself.

The adoption of a weight of metal as a monetary unit probably goes back in most *poleis* at least to the eighth century; when coinage was invented it was in economic terms a relatively trivial step, probably taken in Lydia around 600, perhaps in order to simplify the payment of mercenaries. The institution was then taken up by one Greek *polis* after another, partly as a way of symbolising its independence, partly as a vehicle for public fiscal activity. The history of Greek coinage thereafter reveals much that is relevant to the history of the Greek world: thus, before 400 it is only at Athens, where a market economy developed relatively early, that there is an adequate supply of small denominations.[37]

37 See in general M. H. Crawford, in M. H. Crawford (ed.), *Sources for Ancient History* (1982).

Part I

The Archaic Period

1 The development of the polis and its values

The archaic period – conventionally the eighth, seventh and sixth centuries – is a uniquely interesting and important era of Greek history. It is also uniquely difficult to study in detail, especially through the medium of a source-book of this kind, chiefly because (as already explained, p. 5) the developments which characterise it were already under way before the appearance of any record, literary or epigraphical, to document them. Already by the eighth century, for example, the Greeks probably perceived themselves as an entity, racial and cultural, distinct from all others (see 1–2), and although the part played by the formation of a shared system of values can often be adequately illustrated (5, 6, 12, 13), it remains extraordinarily hard to make sense of the period and its trends, and marshal the meagre and diverse data in the service of some sort of explanation of what was happening. One theme predominates: the evolution of what was to become, and remain, the characteristic form and expression of Greek society – the *polis*. (See above, pp. 1–4. There is an excellent discussion of this (problematical) historical development by Austin and Vidal-Naquet, *Economy*, 49–53.)

At the beginning of the first millennium, Greek communities formed the population of mainland Greece, the Aegean islands, some areas of western Asia Minor and parts of Cyprus (the last two as a result of recent settlement). In the core of this area – Greece, the Aegean and coastal Asia Minor – they lived in small, poor, static communities, with little contact with the rest of the Mediterranean. Five centuries later, the communities of this core of the Greek world were – by ancient standards – wealthy, organised and creative; and similar communities were spread throughout the Mediterranean and the Black Sea. Archaeological evidence makes it possible to trace the development of contact with the Mediterranean (see 14, in Ch. 2), but it is not clear how far this contact can account for the development of self-awareness and communal institutions which is also observable. In many cases the Greeks of the tenth century and later were returning to places already visited by way of trade, or even settled, during the Mycenean period (before 1200), when such contact had had no effect on the economy or society of the Mycenean kingdoms. It seems that after these kingdoms succumbed to attack in c. 1200 the society and economy which replaced them were already potentially open ones, dominated only in general terms by hereditary aristocracies. The aristocracies were themselves disunited and far from sure how to react to the changes that were taking place; their members certainly attempted to exploit these changes but were unable to monopolise the resulting increase in wealth.

At all events by *c*.800 certain important features of the archaic (and indeed classical) Greek world were already in existence, notably its division into distinct cultural and political entities. Within the general pottery-style known as Geometric, the pottery of each area (Argolis, Corinthia, etc.) is quite distinct. Also, each area presumably already spoke a distinct dialect. Certainly when the art of writing reappeared in the Greek world in the eighth century (4) each area used a different and distinctive script.

The eighth century was indeed crucial in a number of ways. In cases where it had not already done so, monarchy now disappeared from the core of the Greek world (with the exception of Sparta: see 50), while an oral epic tradition purporting to recall the deeds of the Mycenean kings now crystallised, as already explained, into the *Iliad* and *Odyssey* – which themselves during the seventh century spawned a number of imitations known, collectively, as the Epic Cycle. (See also Snodgrass, *Archaic Greece*, 68–72, for vase paintings.) Offerings at Mycenean graves identified as the tombs of heroes begin, in the overwhelming majority of instances, in *c*.750; and shrines such as the Agamemnoneion at Mykenai itself or the Menelaion at Sparta provide important evidence for the emergence of a sense of community and a sense of history, whether or not one sees them as brought into being by the influence of the epic tradition (see J. N. Coldstream, 'Hero-cults in the age of Homer', *JHS* 96 (1976), 8–17). For the emergence of this sense of community it is symptomatic, too, that both the *Iliad* and Hesiod portray institutions for the administration of justice (see 9–10); and it is likely that some institutions which are first documented only much later than the eighth century had already begun to evolve (see in general Ch.4).

In Attika and Argolis, and probably elsewhere also, the population began to grow dramatically (for Attika see Fig. 5). Eretria, on the island of Euboia, was laid out as an urban centre between 800 and 750; Athens became a single urban centre instead of a collection of villages in the same period (8), Corinth perhaps a little later; and both Athens and Corinth acquired temples *c*.700. Numerous communities seem in fact to have begun the process of development into fully-fledged *poleis* by building a temple: see Snodgrass, *Archaic Greece*, 58–64.

Nor are eighth-century developments confined to the internal affairs of the *poleis*: the archaeological evidence for the use of the great

4 Offering at the Menelaion (*Kadmos* (1976), 145)

pan-Hellenic religious centres, for instance, also effectively dates their emergence as such to the eighth century (see **11**).

For excellent photographs and ground plans of the sites of many *poleis* see R. V. Schoder, *Ancient Greece from the Air* (London, 1974).

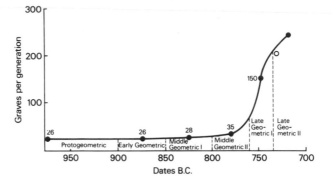

5 Population trends in Attika, expressed in terms of burials per generation with extrapolated figures for the subdivisions of Late Geometric (A. M. Snodgrass, *Archaeology and the Rise of the Greek State* (Cambridge, 1977))

1. Greeks and barbarians

One need only read the famous preface to the *History* of Herodotus, recording as it does 'the great and astonishing achievements of both Greeks and non-Greeks' (p.10, above), to realise that the Greeks had, or developed, an unusually high level of awareness of themselves as a unique and distinct people. A Greek (or as he would always have called himself, a Hellene, living in Hellas) was Greek; all others were *barbaroi*. One might compare the equally all-embracing distinction between Jews and Gentiles – but with caution: the (untranslatable) term *barbaros* pointed to a division founded less upon religion than upon language and culture (see for instance H. D. F. Kitto, *The Greeks* (Harmondsworth, 1967), 7–11). In the passages which follow, two Greek writers discuss the division with particular reference to the terminology employed in the Homeric poems.

(A) Something else which, to me, is a good sign that the men of long ago were weak is this: evidently before the Trojan War no enterprise was undertaken by Hellas as a whole. It seems to me in fact that at that time the whole country did not yet have its name. Before the time of Hellen the son of Deukalion the name did not exist at all; for the most part the various peoples such as the Pelasgians lent their names to their districts. But after Hellen and his sons had come to power in Phthiotis[1] and had been invited as allies into the other *poleis*,[2] this connection led to the various states changing their name to that of Hellenes. It was a long time, though, before this name superseded all the others. The best witness to this is Homer: although he was born long after the Trojan War he never calls the whole Greek army Hellenes; this term he reserves for the followers of Achilles from Phthiotis – who were indeed the original Hellenes[3] – and speaks otherwise in his poems of Danaans, Argives and

Achaians. He does not even use the word *barbaroi*. This is because the Hellenes had not yet, it seems to me, been separated off under a single distinctive name. At all events, these various Hellenic peoples – so called later, by the one name, when they were living in *poleis* and beginning to understand each other's languages – did nothing in concert before the Trojan War, for they were weak and had no contact with one another; and for that expedition they came together only because by then they were making more use of the sea.

Thucydides I.3

(B) When the poet[4] says 'Then Masthles led the Karians, of barbarian speech (*barbarophōnoi*)',[5] we have no cause to ask how it is that, although he knew so many barbarian peoples, it is only the Karians that he calls 'of barbarian speech' – and nowhere at all mentions *barbaroi*. So Thucydides is wrong[6] in maintaining that Homer does not use the word *barbaroi* because the Hellenes had not yet been separated off under a single distinctive name. The poet himself refutes the idea that there were no Hellenes yet, when he says 'My husband, whose fame is wide through Hellas and mid Argos', or elsewhere 'If you wish to journey through Hellas and mid Argos';[7] and how could he properly have described people as *barbarophōnoi* unless the name for them was *barbaroi?* So Thucydides is assuredly mistaken; and so is Apollodorus the grammarian,[8] who says that the Hellenes employed the general term in a peculiar and abusive way against the Karians – the Ionians doing so particularly, out of hatred for the Karians as enemies with whom they were constantly at war . . . I would think that the word *barbaros* was at first spoken onomatopoeically, with reference to people whose pronunciation of words was difficult, harsh and rough – just as one speaks of stammering, lisping or faltering;[9] for we are naturally inclined to denote sounds by words that sound like them, because they are homogeneous . . . So, with everyone whose pronunciation was thick being called *barbaroi* in this way, the pronunciation of all alien peoples – other than the Hellenes, I mean – seemed to be of this sort. Thus they called these people *barbaroi*, in this idiomatic sense. Initially this was an insult, implying that their pronunciation was thick and harsh; but later we misused the word as a term of general ethnology, signifying a difference between Greeks and all others. In fact, however, through much familiarity and involvement with the *barbaroi*, it became clear that the way they speak arises not from any thickness of accent or unsuitability of the organs of speech but from the peculiarities of their various languages.

Strabo XIV.2.28*

1 Achaia Phthiotis, a region of north central Greece (unimportant in later times).

2 The word is strictly anachronistic for this period – as the passage goes on to illustrate.

3 See *Iliad* II. 681–685.

4 I.e. Homer, who for the Greeks was 'the poet' *par excellence*.

5 *Iliad* II. 867, where the name is actually Nastes.

6 In I.3 (A, above).

7 *Odyssey* I.344, XV.80 (and elsewhere).

8 An eminent Athenian scholar of the second century.

9 The Greek words, coined by onomatopoeia, are *battarizein, traulizein* and *psellizein.*

2. The Phoinikians

One of the first non-Greek peoples whom the Greeks perceived as having a particular, characteristic identity were the Phoinikians. This was because from at least the tenth century onwards they were the Mediterranean explorers and traders *par excellence* – at a time when seafaring by Greeks was an almost exclusively parochial affair. Based on the coast of (modern) Syria and Lebanon, the Phoinikians 'sailed from one end of the known world to the other, carrying slaves, metal, jewellery and fine cloth' (Finley, *Odysseus*, 70). This was no organised, centralised 'mercantile empire', which is a misleading creation of modern scholarship (thus, rightly, C. R. Whittaker, 'The western Phoenicians: colonisation and assimilation', *PCPhS* n.s.20 (1974), 58–79; see further, p.52), but Phoinikian trading *links* certainly stretched as far west as Spain, and by their great foundation at Carthage (traditional date 814; more probably mid-eighth century) they were to come into close contact, and conflict, with the Greeks of Sicily and southern Italy (see **35, 118, 294, 295, 296**). It was also to the Phoinikians that the Greeks owed what we today call the Greek alphabet (see **4**). But despite all this – or perhaps because of it – their image in Greek eyes was an unfavourable one. As early as the Homeric poems they are portrayed as unscrupulous folk, given over to profit at the expense of honour and propriety: as well as passage A, below, which is part of a yarn spun by the disguised Odysseus, see for instance *Odyssey* XV.415–84, where the abduction story is of the same type as the one retailed by Herodotus here (passage B). (It is represented as something out of character when Phoinikians pass up an opportunity for profit, as in *Odyssey* XIII.271–286!)

See further: D. Harden, *The Phoenicians* (revised edition, London, 1963); S. Moscati, *The World of the Phoenicians* (London, 1968).

(A) 'I stayed (in Egypt) for seven years and made a lot of money out of the Egyptians, generous men all of them. But in the course of the eighth year a Phoinikian turned up, a cunning rogue, and a confirmed trouble-maker to his fellow men. He took me aside for a talk and won me over to the idea of a voyage to Phoinikia, where he had a house and property, and there I stayed with him for a whole year. Then, when the months and days had been brought to completion and the seasons of a second year started back on their course, he put me on board a sea-going ship bound for Libya. This was a trick: ostensibly I was to help him in shipping the cargo, but his scheme was to get a good price by selling me into slavery.'

Homer, *Odyssey* XIV.285–297

(B) For the origin of the quarrel[1] Persian historians maintain that the Phoinikians were to blame. These people, they say, came from the so-called Red Sea[2] to this sea of ours,[3] where they settled in the territory in which they still live now. Very soon they were making long sea voyages, taking Egyptian and Assyrian goods as cargo; and among their ports of call was Argos, which was at that time the most important place in all the country now called Hellas. In Argos the Phoinikians were showing off their cargo. On the fifth or sixth day after their arrival, by which time they had almost completely sold out, some women came down to the sea. Among them was the daughter of king Inachos, whose name – Greek sources confirm this – was Io. As these women were standing by the stern of the ship, buying what they wanted from the goods on sale, the Phoinikians egged each other on and made a rush at them. The majority of the women escaped, of course; but Io, amongst others, was caught. The men boarded the ship and sailed off for Egypt. (2) So this was how Io came to Egypt, according to the Persians, though the Greek version is different; and the incident triggered off a whole series of outrages. Subsequently, they say, certain Greeks – probably Cretans, though their names have gone unrecorded – called at the Phoinikian city of Tyros and abducted the king's daughter Europa; a case of tit for tat.

Herodotus I.1–2.1

1 Between the Greeks and the *barbaroi*, culminating in the fifth-century Persian Wars – the unifying theme of Herodotus' *History* (see p.10).
2 Part for whole: we would say the Indian Ocean. Compare I.180.1, II.158.1–4, etc.
3 The Mediterranean, not the Aegean.

3. The tribes of Greece

The simple distinction between Greeks and *barbaroi* was open to refinement on both sides of the divide: the open mind of a Herodotus could appreciate the differences between the various non-Greek peoples, while conversely the Greeks were well aware (Hdt.VIII.73, Thuc.I.2, etc.) that they were a people formed, historically, out of a number of tribes which had migrated down into the Balkans at different times and which perpetuated different dialects of their common language. The correlation between dialects and migrating groups may not in fact be a simple one. What is, however, clear is that the last of these migrations, that of the Dorians, was culturally and historically the most far-reaching, both at the time and also in its later effects and manifestations: for while many of the tribal and other kinship distinctions fell away with the development of new focuses of solidarity and identity, a polarity persisted, and solidified, between Dorians and non-Dorians (which meant especially, though not exclusively, Ionians). Attempts to interpret and explain the whole of Greek history in tribal terms inevitably exaggerate the issue, but it is true, and important, to say that at virtually any time (see for instance **217**) the division might come to the fore. By Strabo's day, though, the subject was purely one for scholarly discourse.

N.B. Doubts about the historicity of the Dorian 'invasion', first raised long ago by the great German historian K. J. Beloch, have recently been renewed by J. Chadwick ('Who were the Dorians?', *La Parola del Passato* 31 (1976), 103–17) and J. T. Hooker (*Mycenean Greece* (London, 1977)), who by somewhat different routes both arrive at a similar conclusion: that the Dorians had been in Greece all along, in subjection to the Myceneans. But this theory has provoked strong and (in our view) convincing rejoinders: see for instance P. A. L. Greenhalgh, *Acta Classica* 21 (1978), 1–38, esp. 27–37, and (on Sparta, for which see further Ch. 5) Cartledge, *Sparta*, 75–101. For the literary tradition see now N. G. L. Hammond, *Cambridge Ancient History*, vol. II part 2 (1975), 678–99; on the evolution of the Greek language, J. Chadwick, *ibid.* 805–19; L. R. Palmer, *The Greek Language* (London, 1980), chs. 1–3.

There are many tribes in Greece, but the most important correspond in number to the dialects of Greek which we recognise – namely four. We may say, though, that one of them, the Ionic, is the same as the ancient Attic; for the people of Attika used then to be called Ionians, and their descendants were the Ionians who colonised Asia[1] and who use the speech now called Ionic. We may also say that the Doric dialect is the same as the Aiolic; for with the exception of the Athenians and the Megarians and also the Dorians round about (Mount) Parnassos,[2] all the peoples north of the Isthmos (of Corinth) are called Aiolians to this very day. As for the Dorians, it is fair to say that because they are few in number, live in the most rugged part of the country and keep themselves to themselves, they have altered their speech and their other habits so as to lose much of their former homogeneity (with the Aiolians). Just the same happened with the Athenians: through inhabiting a rugged country with a thin soil they remained free of the ravages of invaders. Thucydides maintains that they were thought of as indigenous, in that they always occupied the same land, from which nobody tried to expel them and of which nobody wanted to dispossess them.[3] No doubt this was precisely the reason why, although few in number, they remained distinct in their speech and habits.

Strabo VIII.1.2

1 I.e. the coast of Asia Minor and its offshore islands.
2 Mention of Parnassos would normally call Delphi to mind, but presumably
  Str. means the region further north west, actually called Doris (see for instance
  Thuc.1.107.2).
3 Thuc.1.2.5–6 (= **158A**).

4. The alphabet

Mycenean Greece, as the Linear B tablets show (p.6), was a literate society, if
only to the extent that a handful of scribes made official inventories for storage in
palace vaults (see J. Chadwick, *The Decipherment of Linear B* (second edition,
Cambridge, 1967), 101–33). But as Mycenean civilisation dissolved into the Dark
Age, literacy was amongst a number of its accomplishments swept away and
forgotten, save for such vestigial memories as the 'sinister signs' (*sēmata lugra*) in
the Homeric version of the story of Bellerophon (*Iliad* VI.168). So the Greeks
believed that they were becoming literate for the first time when, apparently in
the early eighth century, they took over and modified to suit their own
language's requirements a medium much more valuable, potentially, than the
Minoan syllabary: the fully alphabetic script of the Phoinikians. With the version
of Herodotus, given here, compare Diodorus III.67.1 and V.74.1, Josephus,
Contra Apionem 1.10 and Tacitus, *Annals* XI.14.

See further: in brief, A. G. Woodhead, *The Study of Greek Inscriptions*
(Cambridge, 1981), 12–23; in detail, L. H. Jeffery, *The Local Scripts of Archaic
Greece* (Oxford, 1961).

The Gephyraioi, (a family) to which the murderers of Hipparchos
belonged,[1] originated in Eretria,[2] according to their own account;
however, I have investigated the matter personally and I find that they
were Phoinikians, descended from those Phoinikians who came with
Kadmos to the land now called Boiotia,[3] where they were allotted the
district around Tanagra to settle in. Later, after the Kadmeians had been
expelled by the Argives, these Gephyraioi too were ejected, by the
Boiotians, and turned to Athens. The Athenians received them as their
own *politai*, on specified terms which excluded them merely from a few
minor privileges. (58) And these Phoinikians who came with Kadmos,
the Gephyraioi amongst them, settled in Greece and taught the Greeks
many things above all, the alphabet, which as far as I can see the Greeks
did not previously possess. At first they used the characters in the same
way as did all the Phoinikians, but as time went on, changes in their
language brought changes in the shape of the letters also. At this time
most of the Greeks who lived in the lands round about were Ionians. It
was they who were taught the letters by the Phoinikians and took them
over, adopting them with a few changes in shape; and as was only right –

given that the Phoinikians had introduced them into Greece – they called them Phoinikian letters.[4]

Herodotus V.57–58.2

1 See **72**.
2 One of the principal cities on the island of Euboia (see **81**).
3 Kadmos: brother of Europa (see **2B**). Boiotia: see Map 3.
4 So called in an inscription (*c*.470) from Teos, on the coast of Asia Minor: Meiggs and Lewis no.30, lines 35–41. See also **39**, the *poinikastēs*.

5. Heroic values

As well as evolving values and behaviour patterns to suit its collective needs (see **36**), the *polis* inevitably inherited and perpetuated attitudes from the earlier, *oikos*-based stages of society also. These 'heroic' values are thus important for our full understanding of the values of the *polis*, and where we find them is in the Homeric poems; see Adkins, *Moral Values*, ch.2. At their heart is the concept of *aretē*, excellence, a term which embraced all the qualities of mind and body that an aristocrat should possess; and if he did possess and display them, *timē*, honour and respect, was his due from others. See *Iliad* I.503–510, IX.496–498, XV.641–644, XX.407–412, etc. Although the word *aretē* does not occur in passage A, below, it clearly underlies what Sarpedon says to Glaukos – both of them, we may note, fighters not on the Greek but on the Trojan side. In B, two warriors, a Greek and a Trojan, meet on the battlefield and discover that their families have an ancestral link of guest-friendship (*xenia*) – which persuades them to stop trying to kill each other. See in general Finley, *Odysseus*, 64 and (esp.) 99–103; Murray, *Early Greece*, 50–2. Such reciprocal exchange of gifts is of course aristocratic in essence, and thus especially characteristic of the aristocratic stage of Greek society; but there were aristocrats in the classical period too, who had their *xenoi* (e.g. the Athenian statesman Perikles and the Spartan king Archidamos: see Thuc.II.13.1), even if by then the less exclusive ideas of *proxenia* (see **43**) – protection by a member of one *polis* of all the members of another *polis* – and *philoxenia* (**158**) – benevolence to foreigners in general – might be more useful to the community as a whole.

(A) Thus his spirit spurred on godlike Sarpedon to rush at the wall and break through the battlements. At once he spoke to Glaukos, son of Hippolochos. 'So why is it, Glaukos, that we two have been given so much *timē* in Lykia, with pride of place, meat on our plates and plenty to drink, and everyone looking at us as if we were gods? And what of the great estate (*temenos*) we were allotted by the banks of the Xanthos, with its fine orchards and wheatfields? All this means that now we must take our stand in the forefront of the Lykians and face up to the heat of battle, so that when the well-armoured Lykians see us there they will say, "Yes indeed, these kings of ours who rule Lykia are not inglorious: they eat fat sheep and drink the best sweet wine, but they are strong and brave, fighting at the head of the Lykians.'" . . . So said Sarpedon, and Glaukos did not turn away or disobey him, but the two of them advanced straight ahead, leading all the Lykians.

Homer, *Iliad* XII. 307–330*

(B) That was the story he told[1] – and Diomedes, he of the loud battle-cry, was delighted: sticking his spear in the fruitful earth, he spoke warmly to the prince. 'It is clear that you are my guest-friend, thanks to links established by our forefathers long ago. For once noble Oineus[2] entertained great Bellerophon in his palace for twenty days, and they exchanged fine tokens of their friendship. Oineus gave a belt of bright purple-red, and Bellerophon a gold cup with two handles; I left it in my own house before coming here. Tydeus[3] I cannot remember, as I was still a baby when he left to join the Achaian force which perished at Thebes.[4] Anyway, now I am your friend and host in the heart of Argos, and you are mine in Lykia, should I ever come to that country. Let us avoid each other's spears, even in the general throng: there are plenty of the Trojans and their famous allies to be my victims, should the gods give me speed to catch them, and for you there are lots of Achaians to try to overcome. And let us exchange our armour, so that all may see we are proud to continue the friendship of our forefathers.' So they spoke, the two of them, and dismounted to clasp hands with one another and pledge their faith. But then Zeus the son of Kronos stole away Glaukos' wits: he gave Tydeus' son Diomedes gold armour and was given bronze in return – a hundred oxen's worth in exchange for nine!

Homer, *Iliad* VI.212–236

1 Glaukos has just recounted (lines 145–211) the story of Bellerophon, his grandfather.
2 Grandfather of Diomedes, and king of Kalydon.
3 Father of Diomedes, and one of the 'Seven against Thebes' (see n.4).
4 The expedition of the 'Seven against Thebes' – the subject of the play of that name by the great Athenian tragedian Aeschylus (525/4–456/5).

6. Homeric society: kings, nobles and commoners

The society depicted in the Homeric poems is in principle a strictly hierarchical one, with hierarchies of authority, allegiance, privilege and general worth. Detail and nuance are irrecoverable, but the main lines of the relationship between the three principal elements of the hierarchy – the supreme King, the lesser kings (or nobles) and everyone else – emerge from this famous scene set in the Greek camp at Troy, as do the tensions which were already present. King Agamemnon's plan

37

is to test the morale of his men by inviting them, disingenuously, to sail for home; and the army takes him at his word.

On the episode see Finley, *Odysseus*, 111–12; and compare the debate at Ithaka in *Odyssey* II (where the hierarchies are less rigid).

When he[1] came to one of the kings or noblemen, he went up and endeavoured to restrain him by speaking politely. 'Sir, it would be improper for me to intimidate you, as I would a villain, but please stay where you are, and keep your men in check. You do not yet know what Agamemnon's plan is: what is happening now is a test, and he will soon force the army back to heel. Did we not hear, all of us, what he said in council? I hope he will not be angry with the men and punish them. These kings are men of such great pride, divinely favoured as they are; omniscient Zeus loves them, so we must honour them.' But when, on the other hand, he spotted one of the common soldiers holding forth, he struck him with his sceptre and issued a rebuke. 'You sir, sit still! A coward and a weakling like you, counting for nothing in war or council, must wait for orders from his betters. There is no way that all of us here can be king, and too many people giving the orders is a bad thing anyway. Let there be a single lord and king – the one given to us by Zeus, son of crafty Kronos . . .' So they all took their seats and order was established – with one exception: Thersites, who could never keep quiet, carried on talking. He was a man never at a loss for insults, pointless and disruptive jibes designed to vex the kings as much as they amused everyone else. The ugliest man of all those who had come to Troy, he was bandy-legged and lame in one foot; his shoulders were so rounded that they practically met across his chest; and above them was a pointed head boasting a sparse covering of hairs. He had many enemies, notably Achilles and Odysseus, for they were the men he made a habit of insulting; but on this occasion the target of his shrill complaints and criticisms was the noble Agamemnon – with whom the men were by now extremely angry. Shouting to Agamemnon in a loud and jeering voice, 'Son of Atreus,' he said, 'what are you grumbling about this time? What is it you want? Your huts are full of bronze, as well as large numbers of the best women: we always offer you first choice from the captives taken when we sack a town. Can it be that you are short of gold, the ransom that some rich Trojan may bring along from Troy to exchange for his son, captured and brought in by one of the Greeks – myself, perhaps? Or are you pining with love for a new woman, to sleep with and keep on one side for your own personal use? You are our leader, you know, and it is not right that the ways into which you lead us are such wicked ones! And as for you, my friends, you pitiful specimens of Greek womanhood – I cannot call you *men* any longer – let us indeed sail our ships home and leave the fellow here at Troy enjoying his prerogatives to the full; he will soon realise what he is reduced to without our support . . .'

That was the gist of Thersites' taunts against king Agamemnon; and in a flash he found the noble Odysseus standing by him, with a black look and a fierce rebuke. 'Shut up, Thersites, you babbler! You may be adept at public speaking, but you should not try to antagonise the kings – you of all men, whom I would call the most worthless of all those who came to Troy with the sons of Atreus.[2] How dare you bandy the kings' names back and forth in insults, trying to engineer a voyage home . . . Now you listen carefully to me, for I mean what I say: if ever I catch you being stupid like this again, may my head no longer sit on my shoulders and may I no more be called the father of Telemachos if I do not take you and strip off your clothes – cloak, tunic, and whatever you wear to hide your naked shame – and throw you out of the assembly with a good thrashing, to run away and cry down by the ships.' So saying, he struck him on the back and shoulders with his sceptre. Thersites doubled up in pain, and a large tear fell from his eye; a bloody weal, raised by the golden sceptre, stood out on his back. He sat down in pain and alarm, looking helplessly round about, and brushed away the tear. The rest of the men, angry as they were, enjoyed the joke enormously and exchanged approving looks with one another. 'Well, my friend,' said one to his neighbour, 'I must say, Odysseus has done so very many good things, what with the clever plans he thinks up and his leadership in the war, but this service to us, now, must be his greatest ever – getting that loud-mouthed ranter to hold his peace! We can be sure that *he* won't be man enough to come back here a second time and vex the kings with his insults.'

Homer, Iliad II.188–277*

1 Odysseus, whom the gods have delegated to intervene and prevent the departure.
2 I.e. Agamemnon and his younger brother Menelaos (husband of the abducted Helen).

7. The formation of the 'polis'

Near the beginning of his great work *Politics* – which literally means 'things relating to the *polis*' – the fourth-century philosopher Aristotle has a discussion of how a *polis* comes into being. (His argument is characteristically concise; for an expansion and further comments, see E. Barker, *The Politics of Aristotle* (Oxford, 1946), 2–8.) It is a discussion, as will be seen, in the abstract, and yet – typically of Aristotle – it is sufficiently grounded in common sense for us to regard it as a basically valid representation of the actual historical evolution in question; and as a *conceptualisation* of the process its influence is still felt today through such works as *La cité antique* (1864) of N. D. Fustel de Coulanges (on which see M. I. Finley, 'The Ancient City: from Fustel de Coulanges to Max Weber and beyond', *Comparative Studies in Society and History* 19 (1977), 305–27). See further **8**, and in general Lacey, *Family*, 51–83.

It will be found that in this subject, as in all others, the best mode of investigation is to begin at the beginning and to consider things as they grow. First of all it is inevitable that those who cannot live without each other will form a union. Male and female do so, for instance, to reproduce the species – not from conscious choice, this, but from a natural instinct, common to all animals and plants, to leave behind something akin to themselves. Another example is the natural conjunction of ruler and ruled, for their mutual preservation: it is natural that the ability to exercise intelligence and foresight will belong to the ruling and dominant element, while the partner with the capacity for physical labour will be a subject, and naturally a slave; hence master and slave have the same interest. So there is a natural difference between the female and the slave. Nature, you see, is not mean in what she makes, as are the smiths who produce the Delphian knife;[1] everything in nature has one function only, and any tool is best turned out if it is designed to serve a single purpose, not a multiplicity. Among the *barbaroi*, though, female and slave do fill the same position. The reason for this is that the *barbaroi* possess no naturally ruling element: for them, the marital union is that of a female slave with a male slave. That is why the poets say 'Right it is that Greeks rule *barbaroi*'[2] – the implication being that *barbaros* and slave are by nature one and the same.

So from these two partnerships[3] the primary outcome is the *oikia*;[4] and Hesiod was right when he wrote 'First *oikos*, wife, and ox for the plough'[5] – the ox, you see, is the poor man's slave. Anyway, the natural unit established to meet all man's daily needs is thus the *oikos*, (comprising) those whom Charondas[6] calls 'fellows at the meal-tub', and the Cretan Epimenides[7] 'fellows at the manger'. Then, when a number of *oikiai* are first united for the satisfaction of something more than day-to-day needs, the result is the village (*kōmē*). It would seem most natural to think of the village as an *apoikia* of an *oikia*, made up of people whom some call fellow-nurselings, that is sons and sons' sons. Thus it was that at first the *poleis* used to have kings, and the *ethnē* still do:[8] it was kings who ruled the parts from which they were made up. An *oikia* is always ruled, monarchically, by its eldest member, and so too were the colony-villages, because of the kinship between the two. This is what

Homer is talking about in his line 'Each lays down right and wrong for sons and for wives';[9] for they[10] were living in scattered groups, as people did in early times. This is why everyone says that the gods too have a king (Zeus): it is because they themselves still have one, or else once did, and since they visualise the gods in human form they suppose them to lead human lives.

Finally the ultimate partnership, made up of numbers of villages and having already attained the height, one might say, of self-sufficiency – this is the *polis*. It has come into being in order, simply, that life can go on; but it now exists so as to make that life a good life. Consequently each *polis* is a natural thing, if that is what its constituent associations are, for it is what they are leading up to; and for a process to reach its consummation is only natural. What each thing is when fully developed, this we call its nature – be it a man, a horse, or an *oikia*. Besides, the reason why anything exists, its destiny, is its chief good; and self-sufficiency is the best destiny of all.

So from all this it is evident that the *polis* exists by natural processes, and that it is natural for a man to live in a *polis*.[11] Anyone who has no *polis*, not by accident but by reason of his own nature, must be subhuman – or else superhuman! He is like the man reviled by Homer as 'Without clan, law or hearth'.[12] Any such man must be a lover of war; he is just like an isolated piece in a game of draughts.

Aristotle, Politics (I) 1252 a 24–1253 a 7

1 This was evidently a multi-purpose implement.

2 Euripides, *Iphigeneia in Aulis* 1400.

3 I.e. male/female and master/slave.

4 This means the same as *oikos* (i.e. household); the two nouns are used interchangeably in this passage.

5 Hesiod, *Works and Days* 405; see **10**.

6 A lawgiver (*nomothetēs*) of Katane in Sicily: **40A**, **174**.

7 A mystic and miracle-worker said to have visited Athens in the late seventh (or in other versions sixth) century.

8 This is sometimes seen as pointing a contrast between the Greeks, with their characteristic *poleis*, and the *barbaroi*, who could be described only in terms of their tribes, nations or nation-states; but there were *ethnē* with monarchies within the Greek world too, notably the Makedonian *ethnos*, which in the lifetime of Aristotle came to control the Greek world (Chs.33–4).

9 *Odyssey* IX.114–115.

10 The one-eyed giant Kyklopes (see **17A**).

11 This is the famous phrase, misleading in its usual translation, 'man is a political animal'.

12 *Iliad* IX.63.

8. 'Synoikismos'

The processes discussed by Aristotle as an abstract matter in **7** could be subsumed, when considered as actual historical developments, under one general heading: *synoikismos*, an act of 'settling together'. In Aristotle's terms this would be, most significantly, where a number of villages (*kōmai*) merge into a single *polis*; in fact it might mean any one or more of a variety of things, at different stages of a state's formation and evolution. Common to the majority of cases, as the word itself suggests, would be some actual movement of population – small communities physically combining into larger ones – but this was not the invariable rule, and what was really the essence of *synoikismos* was a centralisation (and thereby an upgrading) of institutions, political and religious. This is pre-eminently so in the case discussed here by Thucydides, that of Attika: separate population-centres continue to exist but only as components, politically speaking, of the one all-embracing *polis* and urban nucleus, Athens. Where possible the Greeks always liked to attribute such processes and developments to one time and preferably one man; the inclination of most modern scholars, however, would be to see the role ascribed here to Theseus (for which compare Plut. *Thes.* 24) as purely symbolic of a much more lengthy and piecemeal stage of development.

On *synoikismos* in general, see further (though in brief) Ehrenberg, *Greek State*, 24 and 27. On topographical and other problems in this passage, Gomme, *Commentary* II, 48–61. For the cult of Theseus see **18**.

From very early times, in fact, this[1] had been more the case with the Athenians than with others. For in the time of Kekrops[2] and the first kings down to Theseus the people of Attika always lived in (their own) *poleis*, each one with its own administrative buildings and officials; unless there was some common danger they would not come together in council with the king, but each individual *polis* would govern itself in accordance with its own decisions. And on occasion some of these communities actually went to war with Athens – Eumolpos and the men of Eleusis, for instance, against (king) Erechtheus.[3] But then Theseus came to the throne. An intelligent man as well as a powerful one, it was he who organised the *chōra* on a proper basis, chiefly by doing away with the multiplicity of *poleis* and their separate councils and governments; on his scheme there was only one *polis*, the present one, and one seat of decision-making and administration. Thus the *synoikismos* was total:[4] everyone was free, just as before, to look after his own affairs, but there was now only one place – Athens – which Theseus allowed them to treat as a *polis*; so that with everyone joining in the union it was a great city indeed that Theseus bequeathed to posterity. And he inaugurated a celebration of this unification, a festival in honour of the goddess, which the Athenians still keep, at public expense, to this very day.

In earlier times the *polis* consisted simply of what is now the Akropolis and the area below it, especially to the south. Proof of this lies in two facts: the location of the temples of other deities too[6] is on the Akropolis itself, and those not on the Akropolis are to be found more in this part of the *polis* than anywhere else – the temples of Olympian Zeus, Pythian Apollo, Ge (Earth) and Dionysos-in-the-Marshes, in whose honour the Athenians celebrate the more ancient Dionysia, during the month of Anthesterion; so also, to this day, do the Ionians who came from Athens.[8] Other ancient temples are also hereabouts. Also there is the spring which today we call the Nine Fountains – for so the tyrants[9] constructed it to be – but which long ago, when the waters simply flowed out of the ground, went by the name of Fair Stream: because it lay close at hand the people then used to draw on it for all their needs, and from this ancient usage comes the present-day practice of using its water in the ceremonies before a marriage and for other cult purposes. Furthermore because long ago it was a place of habitation the Athenians still refer today to their Akropolis as 'the *polis*'.[10]

Thucydides II.15

1 I.e. living, most of them, in the countryside (Thuc. II.14). Strictly speaking, one should of course say that until the political completion of the *synoikismos* the people of Marathon, Brauron, Eleusis, etc. were not 'Athenians' at all, at least in the later sense of that designation.
2 The mythical first king of Athens.
3 Eleusis was traditionally the last (in the eighth or even seventh century) of the townships of Attika to succumb to the primacy of Athens.
4 See introduction: not (in this case) physical movement but amalgamation of institutions.
5 I.e. Athena, a deity associated with Athens as such.
6 I.e. besides that of Athena.
7 And the month gave this festival its more common name: Anthesteria. On all these cults see Parke, *Festivals*.
8 See **3**.
9 See **69–72**.
10 There are numerous examples of this in the language of Athenian official documents, including ones quoted by Thucydides himself (V.18.10, 23.5 and 47.11); also (e.g.) Meiggs and Lewis no.90, lines 23–4.

9. Justice

In *Iliad* XVIII the god Hephaistos is forging wonderful new armour for Achilles, and on the hero's great shield he depicts scenes in two cities, one at peace and one at war. The central event in the former is one which we may take, as we are invited to, as a typical feature of the early *polis*: the orderly resolution of disputes by pronouncement of the aristocratic elders of the community. Naturally the practice is presented here in idealised form; for the other side of the coin see **10**.

See in general Murray, *Early Greece*, 60–3 (simplifying the problem of the *polis* in Homer).

Then he fashioned two fine *poleis*, full of people. In the first of them weddings and revels were in progress: the young brides were being led out from their chambers and up through the *astu*, to the light of blazing torches; the wedding-hymn rose up loud and clear, while to the din of flutes and lyres the youths whirled about in a hectic dance. The womenfolk stood and watched in wonder, each lingering to enjoy the proceedings from her own doorstep. Their husbands, however, had all gone off in a body to the *agora*, where a dispute had arisen between two individuals over a man's death and the blood-money payable as recompense for it. One party[1] was declaring for all to hear his intention to make payment in full, while the other[2] was adamant that he would not take a penny; and both of them were insisting that the issue be settled by arbitration. Both sides had plenty of supporters there to cheer them on, and heralds were doing their best to maintain orderly behaviour in the crowd. As for the elders, they sat in a circle on the sacred seats hewn from stone; the clear-voiced heralds handed them their sceptres, and each came forward with it when his turn came to say what was just. And in the midst of everything lay two talents of gold – a prize for whichever of them pronounced the fairest verdict.

Homer, Iliad XVIII.490–508

1 The one responsible, evidently, for the man's death – the defendant.
2 Presumably a relative of the deceased.

10. Injustice

The Boiotian poet and pessimist Hesiod (see p.7) will have been familiar with the Homeric description of the Shield of Achilles (**9**); his own view of the dispensation of justice, however, is a strikingly different one. In the scene on the Shield the implication is clear that the ordinary man can hope to get a fair deal from his aristocratic judges, even if one party will necessarily be the loser. But as Hesiod sees it the dice are loaded: the financial reward which Homer's elders can aspire to *after* a (fair) verdict now comes *before* it, in the shape of bribes; and common folk can only keep faith in a higher Justice, that of the gods, which will ultimately redress the balance (compare **99**).

See further: G. Nussbaum, 'Labour and status in the *Works and Days*', *CQ* n.s.10 (1960), 213–20; P. Walcot, 'Hesiod and the law', *Symbolae Osloenses* 38 (1963), 5–21; M. Gagarin, '*Dikē* in the *Works and Days*', *CPh* 68 (1973), 81–94. In general, M. L. West, *Hesiod: Works and Days* (Oxford, 1978).

But you, Perses,[1] should listen to Right, and not let insolence thrive. Insolence is an evil thing for poor folk, and even their betters cannot bear it with ease but are weighed down by it once they have fallen into blind delusions. No, pass it by, and pursue the course of justice by another, better path. Right is more potent than insolence – ultimately; this is what poor fools learn from what they suffer. When judgments are crooked, Horkos[2] is fast upon the scene, and there is uproar when the goddess Justice is dragged back and forth to suit men who gobble up bribes before pronouncing their crooked and unfair verdicts: cloaked in mist she fastens, lamenting, on to *poleis* and the haunts of men and punishes those who have thrown her out in order to persist in their wickedness. When judgments are fair – alike for strangers as for the local folk – and the judges undiverted from what is right, then a *polis* blooms and the people in it prosper. For such a place Zeus, all-seeing, does not ordain the misery of war, so the young men grow up in the land in peace. Men of justice know nothing of famine or ruin, as they feast upon the produce of their fields: the earth offers them a life of plenty, with acorns[3] from the trees of the mountain-tops and honey from the foothills, and the sheep are weighed down by their great woolly fleeces. As for the women, they bring forth sons to match their fathers. So their blessings are perpetual: the fertile land yields up its crops – and they never set foot on a ship. But when men care only for insolence, evil and wickedness, the son of Kronos, all-seeing Zeus, has the right punishment in store! Often a whole *polis* has suffered because of the evil of one man who is a sinful and wicked schemer: the son of Kronos sends down from heaven a great and universal calamity, famine and plague at the same time, so that the people waste away; no children are born to the women, and *oikoi* die out; such is the decision of Olympian Zeus. Or again, at other times, the son of Kronos destroys a great army of theirs, or their walls, or sinks their ships on the high seas.

So you, the kings, you too must reflect upon this punishment, because the immortals are here in the midst of mankind, observing those who do not hold the gods in awe but grind each other down with crooked judgments. Thrice ten thousand of them are here on the bountiful earth, keeping everlasting watch for Zeus over mortal men; cloaked in mist they roam, assuredly, through all lands, as custodians of the retribution that follows abominable acts. Then too there is Zeus's virgin daughter, noble Justice, whom the gods of Olympos hold in honour. I tell you, whenever any man treats her with devious scorn and does her harm, she is quick to take her seat at the side of her father Zeus, the son of Kronos, and cry out against unjust men and their devices, so that the people may atone for the sinful delusions of kings who with sinister intent turn aside from the just way by their devious pronouncements. Keep these things in mind, kings, bribe-gobblers, and rectify your verdicts: forget crooked decisions once and for all. A man who works evil against another works it really against himself, and bad advice is worst for the one who devised it. The eye of Zeus sees all things and observes all things, so this too he watches, if such be his wish, and it does not escape his notice what sort of justice this really is that a *polis* keeps within its walls. If the more unjust man gets better justice, the right thing for a man is to be bad – in which case I wish neither myself nor a son of mine to act justly in our dealings with men!⁵ I trust, though, that Zeus, wise in council, will never bring such a thing to pass.

Hesiod, *Works and Days* 213–273

1 Hesiod's brother, to whom the poem and its stock of advice and admonition are addressed. See M. Gagarin, 'Hesiod's dispute with Perses', *Transactions of the American Philological Association* 104 (1974), 103–11; West, *op. cit.* 30–40.
2 The personification of an oath, as the god who pursues and punishes perjurers.
3 Possibly nuts in general: see West, *op. cit.* 214–15.
4 This was a blessing indeed, as far as Hesiod was concerned: see above all lines 618–694.
5 This 'paradox-wish' (West, *op. cit.* 225) is even more paradoxical in the Greek of this sentence, but for clarity in an English idiom its three components are best presented, as here, in reverse order.

11. The Olympic Games

The history of the original Olympic, or Olympian, Games stretches unbroken for over a thousand years, from their first celebration in (traditionally) 776 to their suppression in A.D. 393 by the Christian emperor of Rome, Theodosius I: see M. I. Finley and H. W. Pleket, *The Olympic Games: the first thousand years* (London, 1976). But the contests held quadriennially in Zeus's sacred grove at Olympia in the north-west Peloponnesos have their roots in even earlier Greek history, and indeed in the Greek character itself. When Homer's aristocratic warriors were not on the battlefield they were often channelling their aggression and mutual rivalry into games and contests – not so much a recreation, in the modern sense, as a celebratory and reinforcing affirmation of the prowess and worth of the heroes, living and dead: witness above all the Funeral Games for Patroklos in *Iliad* XXIII. In post-Homeric times the element of individual competition was joined, though not superseded, by a communal religious function: the Olympic (and other) festivals were at the same time institutions which served as focuses of unity in the world of the *poleis* and occasions when the aristocratic values of the Homeric world were reaffirmed. The Olympic festival, as this passage from Pausanias indicates, grew in stature and in complexity throughout its history, but the precise details of its early stages were obscure to later investigators (see Fornara no.3) and remain so today; Pausanias' discussion, beginning in the realm of mythology, is a characteristic attempt to fill a vacuum.

As to the Olympic contest,[1] the antiquarian scholars of Elis[2] say that Kronos was the first king in heaven and that a temple for him was built at Olympia by the men of that time, who were called the Golden Race. And when Zeus was born, they say, Rhea[3] entrusted the care of her son to the Daktyls of (Mount) Ida, who are the same as those called Kouretes; Herakles,[4] Paionaios, Epimedes, Iasios and Idas, who all came from the Cretan Ida. Herakles was the eldest of them, and he organised, as a game, a running-race between his brothers, crowning the victor with a branch of wild olive; they had so much of this wild olive there that they made beds of it to sleep on while the leaves were still green . . . Herakles of Ida, then, has the reputation of being the first to hold the contest – on the occasion I mentioned – and to call it Olympic; and since he and his brothers were five in number he established the custom of holding it every fifth year.[5] Of course, some maintain that Zeus wrestled there with Kronos himself, to see which of them should rule, while others say that it was precisely to celebrate his victory over Kronos that Zeus held the contest. And the record of victors includes, amongst others, the name of Apollo, who defeated his opponent Hermes in the foot-race and also overcame Ares at boxing. This is the reason, they say, for the playing of the Pythian flute during the jumping stage of the pentathlon: the music of the flute is sacred to Apollo, and Apollo won Olympic victories. (8) . . . After the reign of Oxylos[6] – who also held the contest – it was discontinued until the time of Iphitos. However, when Iphitos reinstated the contest, as I have already stated,[7] men could not remember what had happened in the early days; so as the memory of it began to come back, little by little, they would make addition of whatever aspects of the competition they had been able to recollect. There is clear proof of this in the foot-race: it was first offered for competition at the time from which the continuous tradition of Olympiads begins,[8] and it was won by an Eleian, Koroibos. There is no statue of Koroibos, admittedly, at Olympia (itself), but his tomb is situated on the borders of Elis.[9] Subsequently, at the fourteenth Olympiad (724), the two-lap race was added, and the crown of wild olive offered for it was won by Hypenos, a man from Pisa;[10] and at the one after that, Akanthos of Sparta won the long-distance race. For the eighteenth Olympiad (708) they remembered to restore the pentathlon and the wrestling competition; Lampis won the former and Eurybatos the latter – Spartans again, both of them. At the twenty-third Olympiad (688) prizes for boxing were given again, and the victor was Onomastos from Smyrna, which was already at that time part of Ionia.[11] At the twenty-fifth (680) they gave recognition to the race for full-grown horses, and the winner proclaimed in the chariot-race was a Theban, Pagondas. At the eighth Olympiad after that (648) they admitted the men's *pankration*[12] and the horse-race. The horse-race was won by

Krauxidas of ~~Krannon~~, while Lygdamis, a Syracusan, defeated all comers in the ~~pankration~~. There is a monument to this man Lygdamis near the stone quarries at Syracuse.[13] I do not myself know whether he really was a match in size for Herakles of Thebes, but the Syracusans do say so.

Pausanias v.7.6–8.8★

1 The Greek word, here and throughout, is *agōn*: see further, **12**.
2 The state which, from 572 onwards, had control of Olympia and its festival, having usurped it from its original and (geographically speaking) natural custodians the Pisatans: see in brief Bury and Meiggs, *Greece*, 101–2. (Note, however, the possibility that the state of Pisa may be a fiction invented in the course of fourth-century political controversies: Bury and Meiggs, *Greece*, 524 n.14; Andrewes, *Tyrants,* 62–3.)
3 Wife (and sister) of Kronos, and mother of Zeus.
4 Not to be confused, Pausanias evidently believed, with Herakles of Thebes (who is mentioned later in the passage), the most widely worshipped of all the Greeks' quasi-divine heroes; in fact, however, the two figures are probably incompatible aspects of the same jungle of myth and cult. Other accounts are happy enough to credit the orthodox Herakles-figure with having instituted the Games.
5 The Greeks computed intervals inclusively; in English we would say every *fourth* year.
6 See Strabo VIII.3.33.
7 In VI.4.5–6.
8 I.e. 776.
9 And presumably it recorded his victory.
10 See n.2 above.
11 See **3** and **92**.
12 A fearsome event combining the techniques of boxing and (virtually) all-in wrestling.
13 The stone quarries: see **225**.

12. Victory at the Games

The Olympic Games are a prime illustration of that potent instinct of competitiveness – the concept of the *agōn,* or struggle – which was evidently central to the Greek character from the very earliest period (see intro. to **11**). But the word *agōn* also came to have a more formal sense, denoting one of the most typical institutions of Greek life: a public festival, generally in honour of a particular god or goddess, at which competitors vied with each other for prizes. In some of them, such as the Athenian Dionysia, the main element was a cultural one; more usually, though, the chief competitive events retained their Homeric character as contests of physical skill and prowess – in short, as Games. The four-yearly ones at Olympia (**11**) were the most prestigious and 'international' of all, but there were three others of scarcely lesser rank: the Pythian Games at Delphi, in honour of Apollo, also every fourth year; and two festivals at two-yearly intervals – the Nemean, for Zeus, and the Isthmian, for Poseidon. Victory at such a gathering was naturally the occasion for pride and celebration, whether a private dedication to the deity under whose auspices the success had been achieved (A) or a full-blown victory ode commissioned from a poet such as the Boiotian Pindar (B).

(A) Aristis dedicated me to Lord Zeus, son of Kronos, after four victories in the *pankration*[1] at Nemea – (Aristis) son of Pheidon of Kleonai.
Semi-metrical inscription from Nemea, *c*.560 (Meiggs and Lewis no.9)

(B) Thrice victorious at Olympia is the *oikos* I am praising,[2] amenable to fellow-townsmen and thoughtful for strangers besides. I shall come to know happy Corinth, Poseidon's portal on the Isthmos, glorious in her young men. For there dwells Lawfulness (*Eunomia*), secure foundation-stone of cities, with her brood-sisters Justice and Peace. They are stewards of men's wealth, these golden daughters of the wise counsellor Right (*Themis*), and their wish is to ward off rash-speaking Insolence, mother of surfeit.

I have a fine tale to tell, and courage prompts my tongue to speak it straight out. There is no fighting, or hiding, what nature has inbred.[3] To you, sons of Aletes,[4] the flower-laden Seasons many times brought the brightness that comes with victory, when you scaled the heights of excellence in the sacred contests; many times, too, the clever contrivances of men's hearts were put there by them, long ago – and the deed belongs to its inventor, no one else. Where did the graces of Dionysos with the ox-driven dithyrambs appear from? Who added the bridle and bit to a horse's harness, or the king of birds[6] to crown the gods' temples, front and rear? Here the sweetly murmuring Muse flourishes, and Ares also, amidst the deadly spears of young men.

Father Zeus, lord of Olympia and ruler far and wide, be ever generous to our words. Keep this people free from harm, and do not let the fortunes of Xenophon blow off course: accept from him the crowns and due measure of praise which he brings from Pisa's plains,[7] winner in the foot-race and in the pentathlon besides, a feat never before achieved by mortal man. Two wreaths of wild celery garlanded him on his appearance at the Isthmian Games, and Nemea showed him no hostility either. As for his father Thessalos, the glory of his running is stored up by Alpheus' streams;[8] at Delphi he has the honour of the foot-race and the two-lap race in the space of a single day. In that same month, one fleeting day at rocky Athens crowned his hair for three fine wins, and he was a Hellotian victor seven times over.[9] Of the triumphs won at Poseidon's games between the two seas by Terpsias and Eritimos with their father

49

Ptoiodoros[10] it would take too long to sing; and your successes[11] at Delphi and in the Lion's pastures?[12] – there are many of us who struggle to mark their number and their splendour. Am I to know, and tell, how many pebbles there are in the ocean?

Pindar, *Olympian* XIII.1–46b

1 See **11** n.12.
2 That of Xenophon of Corinth, winner (in 464) in both the foot-race and the pentathlon; Pindar claims this as an unprecedented 'double'. The third victory referred to is that of his father Thessalos (lines 35–36).
3 This is a sentiment calculated to appeal to Pindar's aristocratic patrons and clients.
4 The Corinthians; Aletes was the legendary Heraklid king of Corinth.
5 The dithyramb was a choral song to the god Dionysos, said (Hdt.1.23) to have originated in Corinth. 'Ox-driven' may refer, obscurely, to the prize offered in dithyrambic competitions.
6 The eagle.
7 See **11** n.2.
8 I.e. Olympia.
9 The festival of Athena Hellotis was a Corinthian one.
10 Obviously these are other relatives of Xenophon's, but their exact relationship to him is problematical.
11 This either refers to the three men just mentioned or, more likely, to the family as a whole.
12 I.e. Nemea. The allusion is to Herakles killing the Nemean Lion as one of his Twelve Labours.

13. 'Banausia'

In the classical period our sources regularly describe, and despise, certain occupations and tasks as 'banausic', and those who fulfil them (whether from choice or necessity) as *banausoi*. Aristotle, for example, declared that 'the best *polis*' should not have *banausoi* amongst its *politai* (*Politics* 1278 a 8), by which he meant that banausic occupations should be fulfilled by immigrants (see **160**) and, above all, slaves (**162**); and we know of *poleis* where these divisions did coincide in a way which he would presumably have approved. Yet Aristotle was also enough of a realist to assert (*Politics* 1291 a 1–4) that a *polis* was uninhabitable without the crafts (*technai*), basic and luxury, which the banausic sector pursued. So is all this simply the prejudice of a leisured upper class (Plato, Xenophon, Aristotle and others)? Certainly the élitist origins and bias of our surviving evidence, in this respect as in others, is undeniable, but so is the fact that there were strong feelings at *all* levels of society about which life-styles were acceptable – given a choice in the matter – and which were not. 'In the Greek scale of values, the crucial test was not so much the nature of the work (within limits, of course) as the condition or status under which it was carried on' (M. I. Finley, *Historia* 8

(1959), 148). For some passages illustrating anti-banausic prejudice see Whitehead, *Ideology*, 117–19; here, however, we give a more detached opinion, from Herodotus, on the question of how the attitude first arose. In view of the fact that Aristotle, amongst others, was poised on the brink of a grand equation between slaves, *barbaroi* and *banausoi* (see **7**) it is a pleasing irony that Herodotus believed the concept to be non-Greek in origin.

There are seven classes of Egyptians: the priests, the warriors, the cowherds, the swineherds, the tradesmen, the interpreters and the steersmen. Such is the classification, and the names derive from their crafts (*technai*). The warriors are those known as Kalasirians and Hermotybians. The whole of Egypt is of course divided into districts, and the districts where the warriors live are as follows. (165) In the case of the Hermotybians: Bousiris, Sais, Chemmis, Papremis, the island known as Prosopitis, and half of Natho. At their most numerous there were 160,000 of them; they are trained for war, and none of them has the slightest knowledge of *banausia*. (166) As to the Kalasirians, their districts are Thebes, Boubastis, Aphthis, Tanis, Mendes, Sebennys, Athribis, Pharbaithis, Thmouis, Onouphis, Anytis and Myekphoris; Myekphoris is an island opposite the city of Boubastis. At their most numerous there were 250,000 of them; they too have an exclusively military training, passed from father to son, and are forbidden to follow any craft (*technē*). (167) Now whether this too is something which the Greeks learned from the Egyptians[1] I cannot determine for certain, seeing that Thrakians and Skythians and Persians and Lydians and indeed almost all the *barbaroi* consider those who learn a *technē*, and their descendants, inferior in status to the rest of the *politai*. Only men exempted from making things with their hands, and the full-time warriors above all, are thought to possess any nobility. But certainly all the Greeks have learned this attitude, particularly the Spartans;[2] it is the Corinthians who despise craftsmen least.

Herodotus II.164–167

1 Throughout Book II Hdt. has been giving examples of Greek borrowings (in his opinion) from Egypt, e.g. the names of their twelve principal gods (II.4.2).
2 See **53**.

2 Exploration and colonisation

Perhaps the most remarkable, and certainly – because of the different sorts of evidence available – the best-documented, aspect of the archaic period is the process whereby Greeks settled throughout the length and breadth of the Mediterranean Sea, from Spain to Syria and from the Crimea to North Africa. The very earliest settlements were unlike the vast majority of later ones and were trading-posts (*emporia*, at Al Mina in Syria, at Pithekoussai (on Ischia in the Bay of Naples), perhaps at Sinope and Trapezous on the Black Sea, at Naukratis in Egypt. Al Mina was settled by Greeks before 800, Pithekoussai about 775, some Black Sea sites (and some in the Troad and on the Sea of Marmara) perhaps soon afterwards, Naukratis in the late seventh century. This last *emporion* was itself unlike the other *emporia*, as far as we know, since it was a venture in which a number of Greek *poleis* shared and was established under the control of the kingdom of Egypt. (It is also worth noting in passing that large numbers of Greeks settled in Egypt as soldiers of Pharaoh (see **94**).)

Greek *apoikiai* proper, on the other hand, were self-supporting, self-governing agricultural communities. The literary sources always assume that they were organised ventures of established communities (see **16**), but it is an open (and important) question how far the need to send out an *apoikia* was not itself sometimes a factor in the process of self-definition of a *polis*.

Shortage of land as a result of the growth of population in the eighth century (p.28) presumably lies behind the need to found settlements overseas, and our sources for the colonisation of Kyrene (see **16**) record that the *apoikoi* were compelled to go; one should note, however, that the sources describe the compulsion as being religious in character, and it is in general clear that religious sanction for the foundation of an *apoikia* was always sought, usually from the oracle at Delphi. The contrast between the vast majority of Greek *apoikiai* and the vast majority of Phoinikian and Carthaginian colonies is striking, though some of the latter were agricultural and some of the former were trading-posts (C. R. Whittaker, 'The western Phoenicians. Colonisation and assimilation', *PCPhS* n.s.20 (1974), 58–79, emphasises the agricultural character of some Phoinikian settlements).

The relationship of a Greek *apoikia* with the native population and the hinterland was indeed crucial, and it is striking that the classic case of friendly coexistence is provided by Massalia, whose wealth derived as much from trade as from agriculture (see **19**). Some *apoikiai* clearly succeeded in subjugating the native population and using it as agricultural labour (see **19** for the case of Herakleia, perhaps typical of many); in some cases the native population acquired under Greek influence a differentiated social structure, with a partially Hellenised élite, urban centres and monumental temples.

Those hungry for land were not the only source of potential conflict which the mother city (*mētropolis*) removed by founding an *apoikia*; every *apoikia* had a founder (*oikistēs*), presumably an aristocrat, and other ambitious or dissatisfied aristocrats could and probably did accompany him. At least in the case of Kyme (**15A**), where a group of rich tombs belongs to the first generation of the *apoikia*, it is clear that an élite was there from the start and not a later development.

Aristocratic government was not the only institution which the *apoikoi* took with them; the dialect and script of the *mētropolis* was that of the *apoikia*; distinctive cults and characteristic names of officials were likewise transferred (the institutions of Megara can indeed be reconstructed from the evidence provided collectively by her *apoikiai*); at Pithekoussai (see above) the excavators found, probably from the earliest levels, a weight which is on the same standard as that later characteristic of the *poleis* of Euboia, which had therefore established a standard weight by the early eighth century. The colonial movement thus provides important evidence for the level of development of the core of the Greek world at the time. And the relationship now created between a *mētropolis* and its *apoikia* remained an important factor in the whole of the rest of the history of the two communities.

It is also desirable to ask what are likely to have been the consequences of the colonising movement; one effect must have been to spread a somewhat larger number of Greeks over a much greater expanse of land and to generate thereby a bigger agricultural surplus; whence presumably an economic capacity reaching beyond the bare necessities of life and an increasing trade in luxuries (we think it fantasy to suppose in the archaic period any significant trade in agricultural staples between *apoikiai* and *mētropoleis*). It is interesting that Thucydides saw an increase in wealth as a feature of the archaic period (see **81**, also **21**) and significant that the middle of the seventh century saw the emergence in almost all *poleis* of a large group of people able to afford body-armour and hence of heavy infantry (see **22**); it is also significant that in temple building the architectural great leap forward occurs at the end of the seventh century.

It is necessary at the end to bear in mind that many Greek *poleis* played no effective part in the colonising movement; Sparta adopted the alternative approach of conquering neighbouring Messenia (see **45**); Athens retained her growing population in Attika, whence perhaps both the upheavals of the end of the archaic period (see Chs.6–7) and the spectacular achievements of the fifth century (for Athenian dependence on imported grain see **281**).

See in general, Graham, *Colony*, esp. chs.2–4; Boardman, *Greeks Overseas*.

14. The search for metals

Greece possessed few deposits of bronze or iron and it was the search for these metals which, already before 800, took Greeks back to coastal areas of the Near East visited by Greeks in the Bronze Age. The leadership of the earliest ventures, as later of *apoikiai*, presumably lay in the hands of members of the aristocracy, who went to sea in the first instance to engage in piratical raiding (see Murray, *Early Greece*, 52–4), but who were ready to turn their hand to trading in metals when necessary or desirable – they doubtless needed to see to the arming of their followers and were anxious to share in any new source of wealth. But since there were presumably similar aristocracies with similar needs almost everywhere in Greece, their existence cannot explain the particular phenomenon of Euboian trade in the eighth century. Given the Euboian presence at Al Mina from 800 to 700 (when Euboian pottery is replaced by Corinthian) and in the west, it looks as though one area is witnessing the emergence of specialised traders. During the eighth century, in any case, the import of bronze and iron into Greece became commonplace, and body-armour reappeared towards the end of the century (see **22**); at the same time Greek exploration of the Mediterranean was preparing the way for Greek settlement.

For the essentially timeless vignette presented here see Finley, *Odysseus*, 66–8. For aristocratic interest in sources of wealth overseas at the end of the sixth century see **100**, for the seventh-century trader Kolaios of Samos see **16**.

And the goddess Athena with the gleaming eyes answered him: 'Of course I shall tell you truthfully what you wish to know; I am proud to be called Mentes, son of wise Anchialos, and I rule over the sea-faring Taphians.[1] And at the moment I am here with my ship and my men on my way across the wine-dark sea to foreign lands, to Temese in search of copper; I carry shining iron. My ship is moored away from the *polis*, in the harbour of Reithron, below wooded Neion. As for us, we are *xenoi*, as our fathers were before us.'

Homer, Odyssey I.178–188

---

1 Athena had chosen this disguise in order to converse with Telemachos, son of Odysseus. The place names outside Ithaka are unidentifiable and probably fictional.

15. The earliest settlements in the west

Knowledge of the Mediterranean, usually gained in the course of trade, was obviously a necessary preliminary to settlement proper. In the case of the *emporion* on Pithekoussai, the subsequent foundation of an agricultural community of Kyme on the mainland opposite is explicitly attested.

(A) (The Neapolitans) came from Kyme; the Kymians came from Chalkis in Euboia. They exercised great influence along the shore of that sea by which they live, having first landed on the islands of Aenaria and Pithekoussai and then dared to transfer their settlement to the mainland.[1]

Livy VIII.22.5–6

(B) And Ephorus says that these were the first Greek cities to be founded in Sicily, in the tenth generation after the Trojan War. For earlier men feared the pirates from Etruria and the savagery of the natives in the area, so that they did not even sail there by way of trade. But Theokles the Athenian was carried to Sicily by the wind and observed both the weakness of the natives and the richness of the land; when he returned, he failed to persuade any Athenians, but took many of the Chalkidians of Euboia and some of the Ionians (of Asia Minor) and even some of the Dorians, of whom the majority were Megarians, and so sailed. And the Chalkidians founded Naxos and the Dorians Megara, which was earlier called Hybla.[2] And the cities no longer exist, but the name of Hybla persists, because of the quality of Hyblaian honey.

Strabo VI.2.2

1 Livy slightly misrepresents the true situation, dramatically revealed by the excavations on the island of Pithekoussai (Roman Aenaria, now Ischia): the settlers lived there and worked iron ore brought from Ilva (Elba). It is now clear that the settlement on Ischia was a trading post: see D. Ridgway, in C. F. C. and S. Hawkes (eds.), *Greeks, Celts and Romans* (London, 1972), 5–38.
2 For a discussion of chronological and other problems see Gomme, *Commentary* IV, 198–210.

16. The colonisation of Kyrene and the role of Delphi

Despite the increasing amount of archaeological evidence, Kyrene remains the best known of all colonial ventures, thanks to the narrative of Herodotus and a fourth-century inscription from Kyrene, which claims to reproduce a version of the original decision of the community of Thera. Herodotus and the inscription seem to provide independent and mutually confirmatory accounts (though unfortunately the inscription is damaged at one crucial point), and it is likely that Herodotus draws on an authentic tradition and (despite suggestions of forgery) that the inscription reproduces at least the sense of an archaic document.

The Kyrene inscription also provides important evidence for the enduring relationship between an *apoikia* and its mother city; this relationship meant, amongst other things, that if an *apoikia* itself founded an *apoikia*, the *oikistēs*, founder, was drawn from the original mother city; the interference of Athens in the dealings of Corinth with her colonies of Kerkyra and Poteidaia was a factor in the outbreak of the Peloponnesian War (see **176–177**); and a hoard of bronze coins of Leontinoi from Greece is perhaps the pathetic relic of a citizen of Leontinoi on his way back to Chalkis (Leontinoi having been founded from Chalkidian Naxos, for which see **15**) after the destruction of his city in 423.

See further: commentary of Fornara (no.18) and Meiggs and Lewis, with bibliography.

(A) Up to this point the Lakedaimonians and the Therans tell the same story, but as for what follows only the Therans claim that this is how it happened. Grinnos son of Aisanios, a descendant of the Theras of whom I have spoken and the king of the island of Thera, went to Delphi with an offering of a hundred victims from the *polis*; a number of the *politai* went with him, including Battos son of Polymnestos, belonging to the family of the Euphemidai, of the race of the Minyans.[1] And while Grinnos the king of the Therans was asking about quite other things, the priestess commanded him to found a *polis* in Libya. So he replied, 'Lord Apollo, I am now too old and inactive to set off; you should command one of these younger men to do this.' And as he spoke, he pointed to Battos. That was all that occurred, and afterwards they went away and forgot about the oracle, not knowing where on earth Libya was and not daring to send an *apoikia* to an uncertain destination. (151) For the next seven years it did not rain on Thera and in their course every tree on the island except one died of drought. And when the Therans asked (the oracle at Delphi what to do), the priestess brought up the *apoikia* in Libya. There was still no end to their troubles, so they sent some of their people to Crete to find out if any of the Cretans or the foreigners resident there had ever been to Libya. And as they wandered around Crete, they came to the *polis* of Itanos and there met a fisherman called Korobios, who claimed that he had once been carried to Libya by the wind and had landed on the island of Platea off the coast. By offering him a reward they persuaded him to come back to Thera and a reconnoitring expedition set sail from Thera, only a few men in the first instance. Guided by Korobios, they reached the island of Platea and left Korobios there with supplies for a number of months and themselves sailed for Thera, with all possible speed, to report on the island. (152) They were away for longer than had been agreed and all Korobios' supplies ran out; but a Samian ship, sailing to Egypt under the command of a certain Kolaios, was carried (by the wind) to the same island of Platea; the Samians, when they had had the whole story from Korobios, left him enough food for a year . . . (There follows the account of the Samian visit to Tartessos and the comparison of their profits with those of Sostratos of Aigina)[2] . . . (152.5). As a result of this affair, the close friendship between the Kyrenaians and Therans and the Samians first came into existence. (153) The Therans who had left Korobios on the island in due course reached Thera and announced that an island off the coast of Libya had been settled by them. The Therans agreed to send a contingent of men out, with brother drawing lots with brother and each one of the seven villages participating, and that their leader and king should be Battos. And in this way they despatched two fifty-oared ships to Platea . . . (There follows a different account, drawn from sources in Kyrene, of how Battos found himself heading for Libya with two fifty-oared ships; he consulted the oracle at Delphi over his stammer and his initial neglect of the command to found an *apoikia* in Libya brought trouble to himself and to Thera) . (156.2). They reached Libya, but could not think what to do, and so sailed back to Thera. But the Therans attacked them as they put in and did not let them land, but ordered them to sail back again. Thus constrained, they sailed back again and settled the island off the coast of Libya, whose name is Platea, as I have already said. And it is said to be equal in size to the present *polis* of the Kyrenaians. (157) They lived there for two years, but nothing went well for them, so they left one man there and all the others sailed to Delphi; when they reached the oracle, they asked what they should do, saying that they had settled in Libya and that despite living there they were no better off. And the priestess replied to their question: 'If you who have not been there know sheep-rearing Libya better than I who have, your knowledge is truly wonderful.' On hearing this, Battos and his followers sailed back again; for Apollo was not prepared to regard his command as executed until they reached Libya itself. Having reached the island, they picked up the man they had left and settled a site in Libya itself opposite the island called Aziris; it is surrounded on both sides by beautiful valleys and a river flows past one side. (158) They lived there for six years; and in the seventh year the Libyans convinced them that they would take them to a better site, so they decided to leave. And the Libyans took them thence and moved them west, and so that the Greeks should not see the best of the sites as they moved, they worked out the time of day and took them through it by night. And this place is called Irasa. And taking the Greeks to a spring said to be sacred to Apollo, they remarked 'Men of Hellas, here you must settle; for here there is a hole in the sky.'[3] (159) And under Battos, the founder of Kyrene, who ruled for forty years, and his son Arkesilaos, who ruled for sixteen years, the Kyrenaians in the settlement remained the same in number as had originally been sent out to the colony; but under the third king, Battos surnamed the Fortunate, the priestess (at

Delphi) encouraged all the Greeks to sail in order to settle Libya jointly
with the Kyrenaians; for these were summoning others to come and
share in the parcelling out of the land. And the oracle was 'Whoever
comes too late to attractive Libya, when the land is being parcelled out, I
say that he shall later regret it.' A large population thus developed at
Kyrene and the Libyans who lived in the neighbourhood found themselves deprived of a great deal of land; so they and their king, whose
name was Adikran, on the grounds that they were being deprived of
their land and were being treated insolently by the Kyrenaians, sent to
Egypt and put themselves under the protection of Apries, king of Egypt.
And he collected a large army of Egyptians and sent it against Kyrene.
But the Kyrenaians marched out to the place called Irasa and the well
called Thestes and joined battle with the Egyptians and were victorious.
It was no doubt because the Egyptians had no previous experience of war
with the Greeks and belittled them that they suffered a defeat so severe
that only a few got back to Egypt. As a result the Egyptians blamed
Apries for the defeat and rebelled against him . . . (Herodotus goes on to
narrate the later vicissitudes of the monarchy at Kyrene.)

Herodotus IV. 150–159*

(B) God.4 Good fortune. Damis son of Bathykles proposed: concerning
the matters which the Therans raise, (whose spokesman is) Kleidamas
son of Euthykles, in order that the *polis* may prosper and the *dēmos* of the
Kyrenaians enjoy good fortune the Therans shall be given *politeia*
according to the ancestral customs which our forefathers established,
both those who founded Kyrene from Thera and those who remained at
Thera, just as Apollo granted Battos and the Therans who founded
Kyrene to enjoy good fortune if they abided by the sworn agreement
which our ancestors concluded with them when they sent out the *apoikia*
according to the command of Apollo Archagetas. With good fortune. It
has been resolved by the *dēmos* that the Therans shall continue to enjoy
equal *politeia* in Kyrene according to the same conditions (as before). All
the Therans who are domiciled in Kyrene shall swear the same oath
which the others once swore and shall be assigned to a *phylē* and
p(hr)atria and nine *hetaireiai*. This decree shall be inscribed on a marble
stēlē and the *stēlē* shall be placed in the ancestral shrine of Pythian Apollo;
and the sworn agreement also shall be inscribed on the *stēlē* which was
concluded by the settlers when they sailed to Libya with Battos, from
Thera to Kyrene. As to the expenditure necessary for the *stēlē* or for the
inscribing, let the superintendents of the accounts provide it from the
revenues of Apollo. The sworn agreement of the settlers. It has been
resolved by the *ekklēsia*. Since Apollo spontaneously told Battos and the
Therans to settle Kyrene, it seems good to the Therans to send Battos to

Libya as *archagetass* and king and for the Therans to sail as his companions. On equal and fair terms are they to sail according to their *oikos* and one son is to be conscripted [about 21 letters missing] the adults and of the [other] Therans those who are free [about 6 letters missing] are to sail.[7] And if the *apoikoi* establish the settlement, kinsmen who sail later to Libya shall share in *politeia* and offices and shall be given lots from the land which has no owner. But if they do not establish the settlement and the Therans are unable to give it assistance and they are oppressed by hardship for five years, they shall depart without fear from the land to Thera, to their own property, and they shall be *politai*. And if any man does not wish to go when the *polis* sends him he shall be liable to the death penalty and his property shall belong to the *dēmos*. And the man harbouring him or concealing him, whether he be a father (aiding his) son or a brother his brother, is to suffer the same penalty as the man who does not wish to sail. On these conditions a sworn agreement was made by those who stayed there and by those who sailed to found the settlement and they invoked curses against those who transgress it or do not abide by it, whether they were those who settled in Libya or those who remained there. They made waxen images and burnt them, calling down (the following) curse, everyone having gathered together, men, women, boys, girls, 'The person who does not abide by this sworn agreement, but transgresses it, shall melt away and dissolve like the images, himself, his descendants and his property; but those who abide by the sworn agreement, those sailing to Libya and those staying in Thera, shall have every good thing, both themselves and their descendants.'[8]

Meiggs and Lewis, no. 5

1 According to Herodotus, one of the early races inhabiting Greek lands.
2 For the activities of Kolaios and Sostratos see Boardman, *Greeks Overseas*, 114 and 206.
3 The remark may be understood, if one does not mind rationalising it, to refer to the abundant rainfall of Kyrene.
4 The precise way in which the invocation should be expanded is not clear.
5 The cult title of Apollo in this context and the designation of Battos are the same, 'ruler who leads'.
6 *Phratria* and *hetaireia* are both groups within the *polis*, the former by implication a kin group.
7 Traces on the stone perhaps suggest 'and those who are chosen are to be those who are the adults and of the other Therans only those who are free are to sail'; the implication is of a differentiation of the population of Thera into members of a recognised *oikos*, others who are not members but are still free, and slaves.
8 Yet another account of the foundation of Kyrene is provided by a local historian, Menecles of Barka, writing in the second century (Fornara no. 17).

17. The foundation of an 'apoikia'

Throughout their history, the Greeks believed that it was men who made a *polis*; the men of Attika always referred to themselves as 'the Athenians', in contrast to the way in which we talk of 'Britain', 'France', etc., being involved in some action; the concept appears in the poetry of Alcaeus in the sixth century, and also underlies the evacuation of Athens in 480 (see **112**) and the behaviour of the Athenian fleet on Samos in 411 (see **227B**); but the Greeks also always had a clear and consistent notion of what was involved in the foundation of a *polis*, a city *and* its *chōra*, a notion unchanged in its essentials from Homer to Plato (see p.1).

(A) The Phaiekians had previously lived in the broad lands of Hypereie, near the Kyklopes, aggressive types who ravaged their lands and were stronger than they. So the godlike Nausithoos took them away from

6 Plan of Megara Hyblaia (M. I. Finley (ed.), *Problèmes de la terre en Grèce ancienne* (The Hague, 1973), 85)

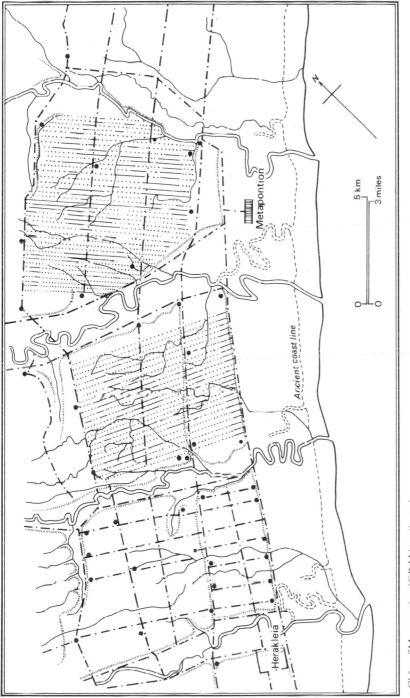

Metapontion

Ancient coast line

Herakleia

5 km

3 miles

7 *Chōra* of Metapontion (*CRAI* (1976), 112)

61

there and settled them in Scherie, far from the bustle of men. And he built a wall around the *polis* and constructed houses and erected temples of the gods and divided up the land.[1]

Homer, *Odyssey* VI.4–10

(B) As for the next stage, the first thing to do is to designate a site for the *polis*[2] as far as possible in the centre of its *chōra* and to pick a site which possesses the other characteristics which are favourable to the foundation of a *polis*; there is no difficulty in knowing or stating what these are. The next thing to do is to divide the whole into twelve parts, but first it is necessary to designate a sacred area for Hestia, Zeus and Athena,[3] to call it the *akropolis* (citadel) and to build a wall round it; then it is possible to lay out the twelve parts, both in the *polis* itself and in the *chōra* as a whole. And the twelve parts must be equal, with the parts made up of good land being small and those of worse land being larger. And one must create 5,040 lots and in every case divide each lot into two and make each lot up of two parts, so that every lot consists of land which is close (to the centre) and of land which is at a distance; and a plot near the *polis* goes with a plot near the frontier and a second plot near the *polis* goes with a second plot near the frontier and so on. And, bearing in mind what has just been said about poverty and richness of soil, it is necessary to exercise care over the two separate plots, making the whole of a lot equal by varying the size of what is distributed. And it is necessary to divide the men up into twelve parts and to assign as far as possible the entire extent of non-landed property into twelve equal parts, on the basis of a complete declaration. And after this one must designate twelve lots for the Twelve Gods[4] and name and consecrate the lot which falls to each god and name a *phylē* after each god.[5] And then one must divide up the twelve parts of the *polis* in the same way in which the *chōra* as a whole has been assigned; and everyone must be given two houses, one near the centre and one near the edge. And thus the foundation is complete.[6]

Plato, *Laws* 745B–E

1 Compare Hdt. 1.166 for the importance of temples in new foundations; the excavations of Megara Hybla(ia) have shown that the *apoikoi* set aside land for temples which were not built for some time (see **15B** and Fig. 6); aerial photography and excavation at Metapontion have revealed traces of settlement in the *chōra* in the sixth century and of a division of the *chōra* according to a rectilinear plan at a later date (Fig. 7).

2 Note the ambiguity between *polis* = 'city' and *polis* = urban centre.

3 Hestia is the goddess of the hearth, Zeus the king of the gods, Athena the goddess of Athens (whence Plato derived many of the institutions which he recommended in the *Laws*).

4 Zeus, Hera, Poseidon, Demeter, Apollo, Artemis, Hephaistos, Athena, Ares, Aphrodite, Hermes and Hestia: see Hdt. II.4.2.

5 See **75–76**.

6 Apart from the obtrusion of a Platonic obsession with symmetry ($5,040 = 1 \times 2 \times 3 \times 4 \times 5 \times 6 \times 7$), the process described here is a standard one; we doubt (against Austin and Vidal-Naquet, *Economy*, 375, who follow Vernant) whether 'the antithesis between the city and the country-side is growing deeper' in the fourth century and this passage is a protest against it.

18. The cult of the founder ('oikistēs')

Just as each *phylē* within a *polis* had a divine or mythical patron, to whom cult was offered, so every *polis* worshipped a founder; the best-documented case is that of the mythical Theseus, regarded as responsible for the *synoikismos* of Athens (see **8**); but the practice is unlikely to have been very different for the founders of *apoikiai*. In addition to the example quoted, one may compare the case of Miltiades on the Thrakian Chersonesos (Hdt. VI.38) and the *mnēma*, memorial, of Glaukos son of Leptines, a friend of the poet Archilochus and someone known to have been involved in the Parian colonisation of Thasos in the seventh century (Meiggs and Lewis no.3).

(A) And after the Persian Wars, when Phaidon was *archōn* (in Athens, in 476/5), the priestess (at Delphi) commanded the Athenians in the course of a consultation to collect the bones of Theseus and give them honourable burial at Athens and keep them there. But there was considerable difficulty involved in finding the tomb and taking the bones because of the hostility to outsiders and savage nature of the Dolopians who lived there (on Skyros). But Kimon took the island, as has been narrated in his *Life*,[1] and, being eager to find the bones, dug at a place which came to his notice by the action of providence; for, as is said, an eagle was pecking at a place where there was something of a mound and tearing it open with its talons. And there emerged the tomb of a man of giant stature, with a bronze spear and a sword beside him. So Kimon brought these relics back on his ship and the Athenians were delighted and received them with a dazzling procession and with sacrifices as if Theseus himself were returning to the town. And he lies in the centre of the *polis* beside what is now the gymnasium and the place is a place of refuge for slaves and all members of the lower orders and those who fear the strong, since Theseus himself was as it were a champion and helper of such men and gladly listened to the requests of members of the lower orders. And the chief sacrifice which they offer to him is on the eighth of Pyanepsion, the day on which he returned from Crete with the young people (whom he had rescued from the Minotaur), but they honour him also on the eighth day of every month . . .

Plutarch, *Theseus* 36

(B) The Teians acted in much the same way as the Phokaians;[2] for when Harpagos overcame their fortifications by building a ramp, they all went on board their ships and sailed off to Thrake and there founded the *polis* Abdera, where Timesios of Klazomenai had earlier tried to settle but whence he had been driven out by the Thrakians; he now receives cult as a hero from the Teians in Abdera.

Herodotus 1.168

1 Compare *Kimon* 8.
2 See **92**.

19. Relations with natives

One of the most crucial problems which faced any *apoikia* was its relationship with the native population (note Hdt. 1.146 and IV.186 for intermarriage with native women); the well-documented cases of Massalia (on which see Momigliano, *Alien Wisdom*, 51–7) and Herakleia probably represent something fairly close to the two extremes on the range of possibilities; uneasy co-existence with intermittent hostilities was perhaps normal (see also **16** and **46**).

(A) Posidonius, the Stoic philosopher, says in the eleventh book of the *Histories*: 'Many people, who are unable to manage themselves because of the weakness of their intellect, surrender themselves voluntarily into the service of more intelligent men, in order that they may secure from them provision for their daily needs and may themselves give in return, through their own labours, whatever they are capable of in the way of service. And in this way the Mariandynoi subjected themselves to the Herakleots, promising to serve them for ever, so long as they provided for their needs; and they stipulated in addition that there should be no sale of them outside Herakleot territory, but only in their own territory.'

Posidonius fr. 60 Edelstein and Kidd (= Athenaeus VI.263C–D[1])

(B) And Aristotle records a similar story in the *Massalioton Politeia*; he says: 'The Phokaians, the trading people from Ionia, founded Massalia. Euxenos of Phokaia was a *xenos* of Nannos the king;[2] that was his name. Now this Nannos was celebrating the nuptials of his daughter when Euxenos happened to be present, so he invited him to the feast. And the nuptials were conducted thus: the procedure was for the daughter to come in after the dinner and give a cup of wine to whomsoever she wished of the suitors who were present; and to whomsoever she gave it, he was the bridegroom. Now the daughter came in and either at random or for some reason gave the cup to Euxenos; and the daughter was called Petta. And when this happened and the father asked him to take her on the grounds that the gift was ordained by providence, Euxenos took her as his wife and lived with her, changing her name to Aristoxene; and there is a family in Massalia to this day descended from her and called Protiadai; for the son of Euxenos and Aristoxene was Protis.'

Aristotle fr. 549 Rose (= Athenaeus XIII.576A–B)

1 Compare Strabo XII.3.2–4; Paus. V.26.7.
2 Of the Celts in the hinterland.

20. Corinth and Syracuse

The prosperity of a community which had shed its excess population may be illustrated by the case of Tenea in the territory of Corinth.

It is said that most of the *apoikoi* who accompanied Archias when he set off to found the *apoikia* at Syracuse came from the village of Tenea[1] and that afterwards this village prospered more than the others and that finally it followed its own political line, abandoned Corinth, joined the Romans and survived when the *polis* was destroyed (in 146). And there is record of an oracle given to someone from one of the peoples in Asia who asked if it would be to his advantage to move to Corinth: 'Blest is Corinth, but would that I were from Tenea.'

Strabo VIII.6.22

1 For Corinth as a group of villages in the period of her colonial ventures from the 730s onwards (including the foundation of Syracuse) see C. Roebuck, 'Some aspects of urbanisation in Corinth', *Hesperia* 41 (1972), 96.

3 Tyranny

'Tyranny' in the Greek context simply means unconstitutional rule by an individual. Few Greek *poleis*, apart from Sparta, avoided a period of such rule during the archaic age (even if the date was different in different *poleis*), and so the temptation to see archaic Greek tyranny as a general phenomenon and to seek general explanations is a strong one. But few of those which have been advanced, from the alleged rise of a mercantile class to the appearance of the hoplite phalanx (for which see **22**), stand up to examination.

The source problems are grave: Herodotus preserves much information (even if it contains already a large 'fairy-tale' element), but within a chronological framework rejected by most Greek scholars of the fourth century and later (see p.618). *Their* information, however, must also be treated with caution; Aristotle distinguishes not, as we do today, between tyranny down to the Persian Wars and tyranny of the late fifth century or later, but between the tyrants of his own day and all earlier tyrants; Dionysios of Syracuse (tyrant from 406 to 367) was for Aristotle one of the *archaioi tyrannoi* (tyrants of old), and it is clear on some points and likely on others that what is reported of archaic tyrants in our sense of the term is heavily influenced by the career of Dionysios.

A few general points may, however, be made. We have seen that the Greek world after 800 was in a state of flux, with its growing and often hungry population and with the development of the colonial movement; aristocratic control was no longer unquestioned and a distinct class from which heavy infantry was drawn *did* appear as a new factor after 700. It is also clear that aristocratic rule in the archaic age involved bitter competition between individual aristocrats and that sole rule was for such men a desirable and not a shameful objective. Tyranny may indeed be seen as a natural outcome of aristocratic government and therefore as a possibility in the Greek world at all times; it was only temporarily suppressed in most areas in the fifth century by powerful communal institutions (it is important in this context to note the early emergence of communal institutions at Sparta, see Ch. 5) and by the existence for a time of democratic Athens and oligarchic Sparta as focuses for universal polarisation.

66

It is in any case important to remember that tyranny was not democratic in intention; *any* means might be used to seize power and the hoplite class was only one potential source of support (see **22**); as at Sparta, it could facilitate the appearance of a quite different form of government. But power once seized had to be retained if possible and the retention of power is quite different from its seizure; a populist streak at this stage in an archaic tyranny comes as no surprise and the reverence of the lower orders for the aristocracy as a whole was necessarily weakened when it was seen to be subject to the will of one man (the case of Athens is here illuminating, see Ch.6). It is also worth remarking that tyranny in the archaic period was an institution grafted on to and not replacing the institutions of the *polis.*

A few other features may be mentioned: the strong links often existing between tyrants in different *poleis,* recalling the attitude to *xenia* of the Homeric world (see **5**), the imperialist attitudes of some tyrants, their role as patrons of the arts. As a general account, Andrewes, *Tyrants,* remains standard; note, however, the arguments of Snodgrass, *Archaic Greece,* 111–16; see also M. E. White, 'Greek tyranny', *Phoenix* 9 (1955), 1–18.

21 The complaint of Theognis of Megara

This picture of a society in which aristocratic contempt for *parvenus* and envy of their wealth (however derived) were both to be found relates to Megara in the middle of the sixth century, in the aftermath of the ill-attested tyranny of Theagenes (see also **64**); but it is probably true of other *poleis* and earlier periods. For the moral vocabulary used compare **5** and **6**; see also P. A. L. Greenhalgh, 'Aristocracy and its advocates in archaic Greece', *Greece and Rome* 19 (1972), 204–7.

We always, Kyrnos,[1] make sure that we get rams and donkeys and horses of good stock and one always tries to breed from good females; but a good man does not hesitate to marry the bad daughter of a bad man,[2] provided she brings him a rich dowry; nor does a woman disdain to be the wife of a bad man, so long as he is rich, and she prefers wealth to quality. For everyone prizes wealth, and a good man marries into a bad family and *vice versa.* Wealth has ruined breeding. So do not be surprised, son of Polypaos, that the good breeding of your fellow-citizens *(astoi)* is disappearing; for the good is mingled with the bad.

Kyrnos, this *polis* is in travail, and I fear lest it may bring forth a sole ruler who will rein in our evil insolence. For our fellow-citizens *(astoi)* are still well-behaved, but our leaders have turned their hands to much evil.

Good men, Kyrnos, have never yet ruined a *polis*, but when bad men turn to insolence and corrupt the *dēmos* and treat wrong as right for the sake of their own enrichment and advancement, do not expect a *polis* to be quiet for long, even if it is now completely calm. This will change, once evil men have chosen to enhance their own wealth amid public suffering.[3] For this leads to *stasis* and internecine killing and despotism – may this *polis* never turn to this.

Theognis 183–192 and 39–52

1 Kyrnos, son of Polypaos, is the lover of Theognis.
2 Compare the views expressed by Odysseus in **6**.
3 *Dēmosion kakon*, compare **43**.

22. The 'polis' and its army

Aristotle here analyses the effect of changes in the composition of the armed strength of the *polis*; the link made with changes in the government of the *polis* presumably owes much to observation of the association between the importance of the fleet at Athens and the radical democracy. Differing views on the 'hoplite revolution' are expressed by A. M. Snodgrass, 'The hoplite reform and history', *JHS* 85 (1965), 110–22; P. Cartledge, 'Hoplites and heroes', *JHS* 97 (1977), 11–27 (with special reference to Sparta); J. Salmon, 'Political Hoplites?', ibid. 84–101; Snodgrass, *Archaic Greece*, 101–7. For the nature of hoplite fighting and for its implications for the *polis* see Murray, *Early Greece*, ch.8. An interesting consequence of the emergence of the hoplite phalanx must have been a greatly increased demand for metal and, probably, new means of supplying it, as opposed to earlier 'trading' by aristocrats seeking to arm their followers (see **14**).

And the first form of government which emerged in Greece after kingship was that of the warrior group, originally a government of cavalrymen; for the crucial aspect of warfare was cavalry fighting, since the hoplite is useless without being in formation and there was no knowledge of such things or hoplite drill originally, so that the strength of an army lay in the cavalry. But as *poleis* grew in size and the numbers in them capable of bearing arms increased, a larger number of people shared in the government. So what we now call *politeiai*[1] men at an earlier stage called democracies. But early forms of government can readily be regarded as oligarchic or even monarchic; for because of their small numbers those of middling status had little power, so that the lower orders, being few in number and disorganised, more readily accepted the rule of others.

Aristotle, *Politics* (IV)1297b16–28

1 Here Aristotle means what we would call moderate oligarchies.

23. The legality of tyranny

It was not at the time and is not now easy to draw dividing lines on the spectrum which runs from tyrants via elective tyrants (*aisymnētai*) to Solon (see Ch.6); associated with this fact is the fact that even among those without ambitions for sole rule the word *tyrannos* (which is of non-Greek origin) did not necessarily have evil connotations. The orthodox view of a tyrant as necessarily a bad thing is a later development (see **25**).

These then (Spartan and barbarian) are two forms of monarchy, but there is another which existed among the ancient Greeks, whom they call *aisymnetai*. And this is to put it simply an elective tyranny, differing from the barbarian form of monarchy not by reason of being outside the law, but only by reason of not being hereditary. Some *aisymnetai* ruled for life, others for a specific period or purpose, as when the Mytilenaians chose Pittakos to deal with the exiles under Antimenides and Alcaeus. The poet Alcaeus shows in one of his drinking songs that they *chose* Pittakos as tyrant, for he reproaches them because 'they made Pittakos, the destroyer of his country, tyrant of the meek and ill-fated *polis*, together offering their praises'. Such cases then are and were tyrannical because of the possession of irresponsible power, but kingly because of their being elective and ruling over willing subjects.

Aristotle, *Politics* (III) 1285 a 29–b 4[1]

1 Compare 1274b.

24. Alcaeus and Pittakos

The hostile picture of the tyrant no doubt derives in part from the aristocracies whom the tyrants rendered powerless, in the case of Mytilene on Lesbos the friends of Alcaeus the poet, who here vents his helpless bitterness. On the tyranny on Lesbos see in general D. L. Page, *Sappho and Alcaeus* (Oxford, 1955), 147–243; Andrewes, *Tyrants*, 92–9.

Let him, since he has married into the house of the Atreidai,[1] devour the *polis* as he did with Myrsilos,[2] until Ares[3] wishes to turn us (again) to our armour. May we utterly forget this anger; let us abate our soul-consuming strife and civil war, which a god in heaven has unleashed, bringing the *dēmos* to ruin, but giving longed-for glory to Pittakos.

Alcaeus in D. L. Page, p.235, D12 lines 6–13

1 Pittakos married a woman of the Penthilidai, a family in Mytilene whose position was similar to that of the Bakchiadai (see **27**) in Corinth and who claimed descent from Orestes son of Agamemnon, son of Atreus, kings of Mykenai in Homer.

2 An earlier associate in power.
3 God of war.

25. The classical view of tyranny

Partly because tyrants did sometimes behave tyrannically and partly because of the triumph of democracy at Athens (see Plut. *Per.* 3–7 and **180** for the propaganda against Perikles as a tyrant), tyranny came in the fifth century to have a bad name; that did not, however, prevent its recrudescence elsewhere and Athenian fear of tyranny in the fourth century is perhaps less odd than it seems at first sight. The context of the *psēphisma* which forms the second passage below is the aftermath of the final defeat of Athens by Philippos of Makedon at Chaironeia in 338 (see **349**), when the consequences of the defeat in Sicily in 413 (see **225**) were no doubt very much in men's minds; the fear of the council of the Areiopagos, stripped of its powers in 462 (see **123**), is remarkable. For another classical view of tyranny see **89**.

(A) (The Spartans offer the Athenians their advice on the Persian peace proposals in 480/79, mediated by Alexandros I of Makedon.) 'Do not let Alexandros the Makedonian convince you, with his attractive account of the proposals of Mardonios;[1] for this is the way he has to behave; for as a tyrant himself he naturally does the work of a tyrant. But you must not behave in this way, if you have your senses about you, for you should know that *barbaroi* are neither trustworthy nor honourable.'

Herodotus VIII. 142.4–5

(B) In the archonship of Phrynichos, in the ninth prytany, (that) of Leontis, for which Chairestratos son of Ameinias of (the deme) Acharnai was secretary; of the *proedroi*[2] Menestratos of (the deme) Aixone put the matter to the vote; Eukrates son of Aristotim[3] 3 proposed: to the good fortune of the *dēmos* of the Athenians; the *nomothetai*[3] have agreed: if anyone moves against the *dēmos* with a view to establishing a tyranny or helps to establish a tyranny or overthrows the *dēmos* of the Athenians or the democracy of the Athenians, whoever kills anyone who does any of these things is to be immune from punishment; and if the *dēmos* or the democracy at Athens is overthrown, it is forbidden for any of the *bouleutai* who are members of the *boulē* of the Areiopagos to go up onto the Areiopagos or to sit down in council or to consider any matter; and if, when the *dēmos* or the democracy at Athens has been overthrown, any of the *bouleutai* of the Areiopagos goes up onto the Areiopagos or sits down in council or considers any matter, he is to be deprived of all rights, both he and his descendants after him, and his property is to belong to the *dēmos* and a tithe is to be given to Athena. And the secretary of the *boulē* is to inscribe this *nomos* on two stone *stēlai* and place one at the entrance to the Areiopagos where one goes into the *bouleutērion*[4] and the other in the *ekklēsia*; and the *tamias*[5] of the *dēmos* is to give 20 drachmas for the inscription of the *stēlai* from the money which the *dēmos* expends in connection with *psēphismata*.

SEG XII.87

1 The Persian commander, see Ch.10.
2 Chairmen appointed by lot for each session of the *boulē* or *ekklēsia*.
3 See **307**.
4 Council-building. Although the *boulē* of 500 (see **77**) was the Council *par excellence* of democratic Athens the Areiopagos (see **123**) was a council, and *boulē* and cognate words were used in connection with it.
5 Financial official.

26. The tyranny of Sikyon and the aristocracies of Greece

The search for a husband for Agariste, daughter of the tyrant Kleisthenes of Sikyon, provided an occasion both for a dazzling display of a type familiar to readers of Homer and for an ostentatious reinforcement of Homeric values (see **5**). The story in its present form clearly derives from Athenian and indeed Alkmaionid sources; the favourable view taken of links between Athenian aristocrats and tyrants is striking; see in general Andrewes, *Tyrants*, 61.

Later on, in the next generation, Kleisthenes the tyrant of Sikyon raised the family (of the Alkmaionidai at Athens) to even greater heights, with the result that it became a subject of conversation among the Greeks to a greater extent than before. Kleisthenes, who was the son of Aristonymos and grandson of Myron and great-grandson of Andreas, had a daughter who was called Agariste; he wanted to find the best of all the Greeks and to give her to him as his wife. So on the occasion of the Olympic Games,[1] in which he himself won the four-horse chariot race, Kleisthenes proclaimed that whoever of the Greeks thought himself worthy to be the son-in-law of Kleisthenes should come not later than the sixtieth day to Sikyon, since Kleisthenes proposed within a year from that day to celebrate the marriage of his daughter. So all the Greeks who had any claim to fame either on their own account or because of their lineage came along as suitors. Kleisthenes prepared a race-track and a wrestling-ring and got down to business. (127) From Italy there came Smindyrides son of Hippokrates of Sybaris, who was the one man above all others with a reputation for luxurious living – Sybaris was at the height of its fortunes at the time; also from Italy there came Damasos son of Amyris of Siris – Amyris who was nicknamed 'the Wise'. From the shores of the Ionian Sea there came Amphimnestos son of Epistrophos of Epidamnos;

there was also Males from Aitolia, brother of that Titormos who was the strongest man in Greece and who had fled from human company to the borders of Aitolia. From the Peloponnesos there came Leokedes son of Pheidon, the tyrant of Argos who established a set of measures for the Peloponnesos and who was responsible for the greatest act of insolence of any Greek – he displaced the Eleian supervisors of the (Olympic) Games and himself organised the contest;[2] there was also Amiantos son of Lykourgos of Trapezous in Arkadia and Laphanes son of Euphorion of the *polis* of Paios in Azania – Euphorion who once entertained the Dioskouroi in his house, so runs the tale they tell in Arkadia, and thereafter kept open house for all strangers; there was also Onomastos son of Agaios of Elis. There came from Athens Megakles, son of that Alkmaion who had visited Kroisos, and also Hippokleides son of Teisandros, the richest and most handsome of all the Athenians. Lysanias came from Euboia, which was in a flourishing state at that period, but he was the only one. From Thessalia there came Diaktorides of Krannon of the (family of the) Skopadai, and Alkon from the (tribe of the) Molossoi. (128) These then were the suitors; and when they all arrived on the appointed day, Kleisthenes first of all enquired of them what their lineage was and who their family were; then, keeping them with him for the whole of the year, he investigated their bravery and spirit and education and bearing, consorting with each one individually and with the group as a whole. And he accompanied the younger ones among them to the gymnasium and – most important of all – investigated their conduct at dinner; and all the time that he kept them he carried out his investigations and at the same time entertained them magnificently. Now the suitors who pleased him most were the two from Athens, and of them Hippokleides son of Teisandros had a slight edge both because of his bravery and because he was connected through his family with the Kypselidai of Corinth.[3] (129) Finally, the crucial day came on which the marriage was to be announced and Kleisthenes was to say whom he chose out of all the suitors; so he sacrificed a hundred oxen and feasted them all along with all the Sikyonians. When they rose from dinner, the suitors held a competition among themselves in musicianship and table-talk. The drinking went on and Hippokleides was winning easily; but now he ordered the flautist to play him a tune and when the man obeyed he danced to it. No doubt he danced to his own satisfaction, but when Kleisthenes saw him he took it rather ill. Hippokleides now paused for a bit, but then ordered a table to be brought and, when it came, first danced Lakonian and then Attic dances on it and finally put his head on the table and danced with his legs in the air. Kleisthenes, during the first and second dances, had been repelled by the thought that Hippokleides with his dancing and his lack of self-respect might be his son-in-law; but he had restrained himself, wishing to avoid an outburst against him; but when he saw him dancing with his legs in the air he could hold himself back no longer and said, 'Son of Teisandros, you have danced away your marriage.' And Hippokleides simply replied, 'Hippokleides does not care', (130) which has become a saying. Kleisthenes now called for silence and spoke as follows to them all: 'You who are suitors of my daughter, I think highly of you all and if I could I should satisfy you all, not choosing one of you nor rejecting the rest; but since I am dealing with the marriage of only one daughter I cannot please you all; so to those of you who are rejected in their suit I am giving a talent of silver as a gift to each one,[4] to reward you for wishing to marry into my family and for your absence from home; my daughter Agariste I betroth to Megakles son of Alkmaion according to the customs of the Athenians.' And when Megakles announced that he accepted the betrothal the whole thing was formalised by Kleisthenes. (131) This then was what happened in the competition of the suitors and this was how the Alkmaionidai became a byword in Greece.

Herodotus VI. 126–131

1 See 11.
2 The presence of a son of Pheidon at a gathering in 570 poses chronological problems, see p.618. We see no objection to placing Pheidon around 600, rather than in 700 or earlier, where the Greek antiquarian tradition placed him.
3 For the family tree see Fig. 13 on p.216.
4 Compare 5B.

27. Kypselos and Periandros

The tyranny at Corinth is almost an archetype for tyranny in the core of the Greek world, with its romantic aura, its relationships with other tyrannies, its imperialism and its patronage of the arts; see in general Andrewes, *Tyrants*, ch.4 (discussing other sources), and, for the chronological problem, p.618.

The government at Corinth was an oligarchy and the family known as the Bakchiadai ruled the *polis*, giving and taking in marriage only among themselves. Amphion, who was one of them, had a daughter who was lame and who was called Labda. None of the Bakchiadai wished to marry her, so Eetion son of Echekrates married her, a man from the village of Petra, of the families of the Lapithai and Kaineidai. Now he had no children either by her or by any other woman so he went to Delphi to enquire about an heir; and as he went in the priestess addressed him at once in these terms: 'Eetion, no one honours you although you deserve much honour; Labda is pregnant and she will bear a millstone; and it will fall upon the rulers and it will bring justice to Corinth.' Although the oracle was given to Eetion it was somehow reported to the Bakchiadai; they had not been clear about an earlier prophecy delivered to Corinth, but bearing on the same matter as that of Eetion and in these terms: 'An eagle on the rocks is pregnant and it will bear a mighty, ravening lion; and it will loose the knees of many. Give heed now to these matters, Corinthians who live by lovely Peirene and rocky Corinth.' This oracle, then, delivered earlier had not been clear to the Bakchiadai, but then when they heard the one delivered to Eetion they understood the earlier one since it fitted with that of Eetion. They kept quiet about their discovery, intending to kill the child which was to be born to Eetion. And as soon as the woman gave birth they sent ten of their number to the village in which Eetion lived to kill the child . . . It was ordained, however, that suffering should come to Corinth from the child of Eetion (and the plot failed. The baby was hidden by his mother in a chest, *kypselē,* whence his name Kypselos.)[1] In due course Kypselos grew up and consulted the oracle and received at Delphi an ambiguous prophecy; but he believed it and successfully set out to seize Corinth; this was the prophecy: 'Fortunate is this man who steps into my house, Kypselos son of Eetion, king of famous Corinth, he and his sons, but not the sons of his sons.' This was the prophecy, and Kypselos became tyrant and this is how he behaved. He exiled many Corinthians and deprived many of their property and many more of their lives. He ruled for thirty years and ended his life at the height of his power and his son Periandros succeeded him in the tyranny. At the beginning he was a much milder ruler than his father, but then he got in touch with Thrasyboulos the tyrant of Miletos and became even more savage than Kypselos. For he sent a messenger to Thrasyboulos to ask what was the best way to ensure safe control of affairs and to manage the *polis.* Now Thrasyboulos took the man who had come from Periandros outside the town and going into a field of growing corn he went through the crop, asking him and questioning him about his mission from Corinth and at the same time cutting off any of the ears of wheat which stood out from the rest and throwing it away, until in this way he had destroyed the best and richest of the crop. And when he had gone through the field he sent the man away without a further word. When he got back to Corinth, Periandros was eager to find out what the advice was, but the man said that Thrasyboulos had given him no advice and that he was surprised that he had been sent to see such a man, since he was quite mad and destroyed his own property; and he went on to tell what he had seen in the company of Thrasyboulos. Periandros understood his behaviour and realised that Thrasyboulos had recommended him to kill anyone who stood out among the townspeople; he now revealed all the evil side of his nature to his fellow

74

politai. Anything Kypselos had left undone in the way of murder or banishment, Periandros finished off.

Herodotus v.92β–η.1★

1 This part of the story at least is clearly an aetiological invention to explain the name Kypselos.

28. Periandros and Kerkyra

The tyranny of Periandros is also remarkable for an attempt to form the *apoikiai* of Corinth into an overseas empire, ruled by members of the tyrannical house (compare the activities of Peisistratos, Ch.6, also **106**). In the end, the attempt was unsuccessful; but it involves an approach which recalls the in many other ways untypical tyrannies in Sicily (see **35**). It is instructive also to compare the later relationship between Corinth and Kerkyra (see **176**).

The Corinthians, too, gladly helped towards the despatch of the (Spartan) expedition to Samos; for they too had suffered an insult at the hands of the Samians a generation before the expedition took place, about the same time as the seizure of the mixing bowl (on its way from Sparta to Kroisos). For Periandros son of Kypselos had sent three hundred boys from the leading families of Kerkyra to Alyattes in Sardis to be castrated; but when the Corinthians who were taking them thither put in to Samos, the Samians discovered the reason why they were being taken to Sardis; so they told the boys to take refuge in the temple of Artemis and then refused to countenance the suppliants being dragged from the temple. The Corinthians then tried to deprive the boys of sustenance, but the Samians instituted a festival, which they still celebrate in the same way: as long as the boys remained as suppliants, when night came on they held dances of girls and boys and when they held the dances they established a rule that cakes of sesame and honey should be carried, so that the boys from Kerkyra could snatch them and so get food; and this went on until the Corinthians guarding the boys went home and left them; and the Samians took the boys back to Kerkyra.[1] (49) Now if there had been friendly relations between Corinth and Kerkyra after the death of Periandros, the Corinthians would never have been led by this incident to take part in the expedition to Samos because of this incident. But as it is, ever since they settled the island, the Corinthians and the Kerkyrans have been at loggerheads with each other; so as a result the Corinthians bore a grudge against the Samians. Periandros had selected the boys from the leading families of Kerkyra and sent them to Sardis to be castrated in order to get his revenge; for the Kerkyrans had started things first by perpetrating a terrible crime against him. (50) Periandros had murdered his own wife Melissa and another

75

disaster like the first then befell him: he had two sons by Melissa, one seventeen and one eighteen. Their maternal grandfather Prokles, who was tyrant of Epidauros, invited them to stay and entertained them well, as one would expect since they were his daughter's children. But when he was sending them back, he said as he bade them farewell, 'Do you know, my children, who killed your mother?' The elder of the two paid no attention to this speech, but the younger, who was called Lykophron, was so deeply hurt by what he had heard that when he got back to Corinth he refused to speak to his father, regarding him as his mother's murderer, and did not even answer when addressed and gave no reason when asked. Finally Periandros became angry with him and drove him out of the house. (51) When he had done this, he enquired of the elder what their grandfather had said to them. And he reported how he had entertained them well, but since he had paid no attention he did not remember the speech which Prokles had delivered as he bade them farewell. But Periandros insisted that in no way was it possible that he had not made some remark to them and kept on begging him to tell. And finally he remembered and told. And Periandros, taking the matter to heart and not wishing to be in any way soft, sent to the people with whom his son had gone to live when he had been driven out and forbade them to have him in their house. And when Lykophron was driven out and went to another house, he was driven out of that also, since Periandros threatened them for receiving him and ordered them to exclude him; and when he was driven out, he went to another house belonging to friends and they took him in as being a son of Periandros, despite their fears. (52) Finally Periandros made an announcement that anyone who took him into their house or even spoke to him should be made to pay a certain sum which should be given to Apollo. As a result of this announcement no one was prepared to speak to him or to take him into their house and, what is more, even Lykophron did not think that he ought to try what was forbidden, but steeled himself and slept in the *stoai*.[2] On the fourth day Periandros saw him in a wretched state, unwashed and unfed, and took pity on him; he abandoned his anger and went up to him and said, 'My son, which is preferable, your present state or the inheritance of the tyranny and the good things which I now enjoy, if you serve your father's interests? You have chosen a beggar's life, though you are my son and can be king[3] of wealthy Corinth, because you resist and are angry with the person whom you should least treat in this way. If any disaster has occurred recently in which you have reason to suspect my hand at work, it is after all a disaster which has affected me and I suffer from it the more since I was responsible for it. You should realise that it is much better to be envied than to be pitied and know what it is to be angry with one's parents and one's superiors; so go home.'

Periandros spoke to him thus, but he only replied to his father that he should now pay the sum to the god since he had spoken to him. Periandros realised that the evil state of mind of his son was quite irremediable and despatched him from his sight by ship to Kerkyra, which he controlled. Having got rid of him, he marched against his father-in-law Prokles, as being largely responsible for his present troubles, and captured Epidauros and Prokles himself and kept him prisoner. (53) Finally Periandros grew old and realised that he was no longer able to oversee and organise affairs and sent to Kerkyra and summoned Lykophron back to take over the tyranny. For he saw no hope in his elder son; indeed he seemed very stupid to him. But Lykophron did not even deign to reply to the messenger. So Periandros, making much of the young man, sent to him again, this time his sister, his own daughter, thinking that he would be most likely to obey her. So she came and said, 'My brother, do you want the tyranny to fall into other hands and the line of your father to be blotted out rather than to come home and hold the power yourself? Come home and stop punishing yourself. Pride is a dangerous thing; do not meet evil with evil. Most men regard mercy as better than justice. Many men before you have lost the power of their fathers by espousing their mother's causes. A tyranny is hard to keep, many others want it; our father is now an old man and past his prime. Do not hand over the good things which are yours to others.' Instructed by her father, she spoke as persuasively as possible to him, but he replied that he would not in any circumstances return to Corinth as long as he knew that his father was alive. When she reported this back, Periandros sent for the third time and offered himself to go to Kerkyra, but bade him to come to Corinth and take over the tyranny. And when his son agreed to these terms, Periandros prepared to go to Kerkyra and his son to Corinth. But the Kerkyrans heard of the whole arrangement and killed the son to prevent Periandros coming to their land. And it was for this that Periandros wanted his revenge on the Kerkyrans.

Herodotus III.48–53

1 It may be suspected that much of the story derives from an attempt to explain the conduct of the festival.
2 Covered colonnades surrounding public squares.
3 Herodotus here uses the 'respectable' term *basileus*.

29. Patronage of the arts

The later tyrants, at Samos (see **31–34**), Athens (see Ch.6) and in the west (see **35**), were conspicuous patrons of the arts, those at Athens initiating a major building programme and those in the west commissioning many of the victory odes of Pindar (see **12**). The archaeological evidence for the earlier tyrants is a great deal less explicit than for the later, but the picture of Corinth drawn by the literary sources is plausible, at the very least.

(A) (The story tells of) Arion of Methymna (on Lesbos) who was carried on a dolphin to Tainaron.[1] He was a poet second to none of his period and the first person we know of to compose what is known as a dithyrambos;[2] he named it and recited it at Corinth. (24) They say that this Arion, who spent the bulk of his time at the court of Periandros, desired to sail to Italy and Sicily and, having made a great deal of money, to sail back to Corinth. So he set out from Taras and, trusting no sailors more than Corinthian ones, he hired a ship from some men of Corinth; but they plotted during the voyage to throw Arion overboard and seize his money. He realised what they were up to and fell at their feet, offering them his money, but begging for his life. (Arion was forced to jump overboard, but was carried to Tainaron by a dolphin and returned to Corinth to confound the crew.) This is the story which the Corinthians and the Lesbians tell and there is a small bronze dedication of Arion at Tainaron, a man sitting on a dolphin.[3]

Herodotus I.23–24*

(B) Boutades, a potter from Sikyon, was the first to make likenesses in clay by the use of that material; the discovery took place at Corinth and was provoked by his daughter; she was in love with a young man and when he went abroad she drew in outline on the wall the silhouette cast from his face by a lantern; her father made a relief by filling the outline with clay and produced it hardened by fire along with the rest of his pots; they say that the relief was preserved in the Nymphaion until Mummius destroyed Corinth (in 146). (152) (Pliny goes on to report an alternative tradition about the discovery.) Boutades also discovered the addition of red colouring to clay or the use of red clay and he first placed masks on the outer tiles of roofs . . .

Pliny, *Natural History* XXXV.151–152*

1 In Lakonia.
2 See **12** n.5.
3 Is this invented to lend verisimilitude to the story or is it the origin of it?

30. Tyranny at Sikyon

We have already come across Kleisthenes of Sikyon finding a husband for his daughter Agariste (see **26**); Herodotus also records a curious set of his measures taken with respect to the internal organisation of Sikyon, where tyranny had existed since the seventh century (see Andrewes, *Tyrants*, 57–8; the papyrus fragment of (?) Ephorus is Fornara no. 10; it is an interesting piece of fiction). The first two measures of Kleisthenes are intelligible as reported, if a trifle naive; we suspect à propos of the third measure that the new names of the Dorian tribes of Sikyon were, in some way which we do not understand, more neutral than they now seem, and we doubt whether they are an indication of 'racial prejudice' against the Dorians.

For Kleisthenes, having gone to war against the Argives, stopped the rhapsodists competing at Sikyon in the recitation of the Homeric epics, since the Argives and Argos are highly praised in them. He also wished to expel from the land Adrastos son of Talaos, who had and has a shrine in the *agora* at Sikyon, as being an Argive. So he went to Delphi and asked whether he should expel Adrastos; but the priestess replied and said that Adrastos was king of the Sikyonians while he (Kleisthenes) was a stone-thrower.[1] So when the god did not grant his wish, he went back home and thought of a way to ensure that Adrastos left of his own accord. And when he thought that he had found one, he sent to Thebes in Boiotia and said that he wished to introduce Melanippos son of Astakos (by building him a shrine); and the Thebans gave him permission. So Kleisthenes introduced Melanippos and designated a *temenos* (sacred enclosure) for him actually in the *prytaneion* and settled him there in the greatest possible security. Now Kleisthenes introduced Melanippos, it must be explained, as being the greatest possible enemy of Adrastos, since he killed both his brother Mekistes and his son-in-law Tydeus. And when he had designated the *temenos* for him, he took away the sacrifices and festivals which had been the due of Adrastos and gave them to Melanippos. The Sikyonians had been accustomed to pay very great honour to Adrastos; for their country had once belonged to Polybos, who was the maternal grandfather of Adrastos and, dying without a son, bequeathed his kingdom to Adrastos. Now the Sikyonians paid Adrastos various honours and indeed, what is more, they celebrated his life story in choral performances, thus honouring Adrastos instead of Dionysos.[3] But Kleisthenes transferred the choral performances to Dionysos, the other sacrifices to Melanippos. (68) This then was what Kleisthenes did to Adrastos, but he also changed the names of the Dorian *phylai* (of Sikyon), so that the names should not be the same for the Sikyonians and the Argives. As a result he had a good laugh at the expense of the Sikyonians; for he derived the names from the pig and the ass and the piglet and then added the terminations, but he behaved differently with his own *phylē* to which he assigned a name derived from his own position; his fellows were called Archelaoi (rulers of the people), the others Hyatai, Oneatai and Choireatai (pig-men, ass-men and

79

piglet-men). These then were the names for the *phylai* which the Sikyonians used under Kleisthenes and after his death for another sixty years; but then they discussed the matter among themselves and changed to Hylleis, Pamphyloi and Dymanatai;⁴ and they added to them a fourth *phyle* called Aigialeis, taking the name from Aigialeus son of Adrastos.

Herodotus v.67–68

1 The precise significance of the insult is obscure.
2 See **41**.
3 The god normally honoured in such performances.
4 The three traditional Dorian tribes.

31. Tyranny at Samos

The last of the great archaic tyrannies, apart from that at Athens and those of the west, is the one at Samos, set up in the mid 530s, which clearly captured the imagination of Herodotus, perhaps not least because of the proximity of Samos to his place of birth, Halikarnassos. See in general Andrewes, *Tyrants*, 117–23.

While Kambyses¹ was at war with Egypt, the Lakedaimonians also mounted an expedition against Samos and Polykrates son of Aiakes, who had seized power and now held the island. In the beginning he had divided control of the *polis* with his two brothers Pantagnotos and Syloson, but later he killed the former and drove out Syloson, who was the younger of the two, and held the whole of Samos. While in that position he entered into friendly relations with Amasis king of Egypt, sending gifts and receiving them from him in turn.² And now the affairs of Polykrates soon prospered and became the talk of Ionia and the rest of Greece; for wherever he decided to fight, everything went well for him. He had a hundred fifty-oared ships and a thousand archers; and he ravaged and plundered everyone without distinction; for he said that he would give more pleasure to a friend by giving him back what he had taken than by not taking anything in the first place. He captured many of the islands and many of the towns of the mainland also; and he even captured the Lesbians who had come to the help of the Milesians with all their forces after defeating them in a sea-battle; the captives were forced to dig, in chains, the whole of the moat which surrounds the wall of Samos. (There follows the story of the ring which Polykrates attempted unsuccessfully to get rid of in order to preserve his good fortune.) (44) So the Lakedaimonians mounted an expedition against this Polykrates, a man for whom everything went well; the Samians who afterwards settled Kydonia in Crete had called them in. For Polykrates, without the Samians knowing, had sent to Kambyses son of Kyros while he was collecting his army for the campaign against Egypt,[3] asking him to send to him in Samos and request a contingent. When Kambyses heard this he gladly sent to Samos, requesting from Polykrates that he send a naval contingent with him against Egypt. So he selected those whom he most suspected of plotting rebellion and sent them off in forty triremes and instructed Kambyses not to send them back again. (45) Some report that the Samians who were sent off never reached Egypt, but when they got to Karpathos on their voyage discussed the matter among themselves and decided to sail no further; others report that they did reach Egypt and were put under guard, but escaped. They sailed back to Samos and Polykrates met them with his ships and a battle ensued; the returning exiles were victorious, but when they landed and fought again they were defeated; so they sailed off to Sparta. There are some who report that those returning from Egypt defeated Polykrates, but I do not think they can be right. For if they had been able to defeat Polykrates by themselves, they would not have needed to call in the Lakedaimonians; and it is not reasonable to suppose that someone who had large numbers of mercenary supporters and native archers available should be defeated by a small group of returning exiles. Anyway, Polykrates gathered the children and wives of those of the *politai* who were under his control into the ship-sheds and kept them there, proposing to burn them to death along with the sheds, if any of the *politai* betrayed him to the exiles. (46) And when those of the Samians who had been driven out by Polykrates reached Sparta, they came before the *archontes* and made a long speech, as one would expect in the case of men with a desperate plea. But when they came before them the first time, the *archontes* replied that they had forgotten the first part of their speech and not understood the rest. So when they later came before them for the second time, they brought a bag with them and simply remarked that the bag needed barley in it. The *archontes* replied to them that they had wasted their effort by mentioning the bag; but they agreed to help them.[5] (47) So the Lakedaimonians made their preparations and set off against Samos; the Samians report that they were repaying the kindness which they had done when they had earlier come themselves by ship to help them against the Messenians; but the Lakedaimonians report that they did not set off wishing to help the Samians in answer to their request, but wishing to take revenge for the seizure of the mixing-bowl[6] which they were conveying to Kroisos and of the breast-plate which Amasis king of Egypt had sent to them as a gift. For the Samians had seized the breast-plate the year before the mixing bowl . . .[7]

Herodotus III. 39 and 44–47

1 The King of Persia.

2 Compare **5B**.
3 See **93**.
4 Presumably the *ephoroi*, see **52**.
5 Herodotus allows himself a joke at the expense of the notorious Spartan penchant for brevity; compare **87** and P. Cartledge, 'Literacy in the Spartan oligarchy', *JHS* 98 (1978), 25–37.
6 See **28**.
7 For piracy in the archaic period see **82**. For early fleets in general and that of Polykrates in particular see **81**.

32. Tyrants and public works

As we have seen, the tyrants were remembered as builders, by Herodotus in the case of Samos with admiration; the building programme of the tyranny at Athens was an important centralising factor, though it is doubtful whether the archaic tyrants had the motives which Aristotle attributes to them and whether their subjects saw their building activity as Aristotle did; at least in one case Polykrates used foreign captives (see **31**) and it is likely that the analysis of Aristotle is here heavily influenced by the career of Dionysios of Syracuse.

(A) I have spent rather a long time on the Samians, since they are responsible for three of the greatest things achieved by any of the Greeks: the first is a tunnel dug right underneath a mountain 900 feet high; the length of the tunnel is seven stades and its height and breadth are both eight feet; and for its whole length it carries a channel twenty cubits deep and three feet wide, along which water conveyed in pipes reaches the *polis*, brought from a freely flowing spring. The craftsman responsible for the tunnel was Eupalinos son of Naustrophos of Megara. This is one of the three things; the second is a breakwater in the sea around the harbour, going out to a depth of twenty fathoms and over two stades long. And the third thing is the biggest of all known temples; the first craftsman in charge of it was Rhoikos son of Phileus of Samos.[1] These are the reasons why I have spent rather a long time on the Samians.

Herodotus III.60[2]

(B) And it is a mark of tyrants to impoverish their subjects, so that *they* pay for a bodyguard, and being occupied with their daily affairs will not have the leisure to plot. An example of the approach is provided by the pyramids in Egypt and the votive offerings of the Kypselidai and the building of the Olympion[3] by the Peisistratidai and the works of Polykrates among those on Samos – all these enterprises had the same effect, the occupation and impoverishment of the subject.[4]

Aristotle, *Politics* (V) 1313 b19–25

1 The temple designed by Rhoikos had been burnt down about 540 and its replacement commissioned by Polykrates was still incomplete in the time of Herodotus. The other works cannot be dated. (Remains of all three works are still visible today.)

2 Compare 1.51; IV.88 for Samian crafts and craftsmen.

3 Temple of Zeus, eventually completed by Hadrian.

4 Compare 135B.

33. Flattery of a tyrant

The court of Polykrates attracted the poet Ibycus, who sang of the heroes of the Trojan War and ended his poem with a graceful assimilation of Polykrates to them.

But now it is not my desire to sing of Paris the deceiver of his *xenos* or of slim-ankled Kassandra or of the other children of Priamos or of the inglorious day on which high-gated Troy was taken, nor yet of the proud *aretē*[1] of the heroes whom the hollow ships with their nailed sides brought as destroyers to Troy, noble heroes; their leader was the lord Agamemnon, of the house of the Pleisthenidai, the king, the leader of men, the son of Atreus,[2] a noble father . . . They shall always have beauty hereafter and you, Polykrates, shall now have undying renown, just as I have renown for my song.

Ibycus 263 Page, lines 10–22 and 46–48

1 Worth, in a military and a moral sense, see 5A.

2 See 24 n.1.

34. The vicissitudes of a tyranny

For someone who had once acquired a tyranny it was hard to let it go, as appeared in the case of Samos – and, later, in the case of the Athenians and their subjects (Ch.12).

Maiandrios son of Maiandrios held sway in Samos, having taken over the tyranny from Polykrates in his absence; he was someone who wished to behave as justly as possible, but failed. When he heard of the death of Polykrates, this is what he did: first he established an altar of Zeus Eleutherios[1] and marked out a sacred enclosure (*temenos*) round it, which is still there, outside the built-up area; then, when he had done this, he summoned an *ekklēsia* of all the citizens (*astoi*) and spoke as follows: 'As you yourselves know, the throne of Polykrates and his entire sway have been handed over to me and it now falls to me to rule over you; but as far

83

as possible I shall not do anything which I disapprove of in another; for I did not approve of the way in which Polykrates lorded it over men who were like himself nor do I approve of anyone else who behaves in this way. Polykrates has now met his end, so I hereby surrender the tyranny and proclaim the advent of equal rights (*isonomia*).[2] I ask, however, for certain rights for myself, the right to take six talents from the possessions of Polykrates for myself, and in addition I claim the priesthood of Zeus Eleutherios for myself and for my descendants;[3] for I have established the shrine myself and I give you your freedom.' This is what he proclaimed to the Samians, but one of them got up and said: 'You are not in any case fit to rule over us, since you are base-born and a scoundrel; what you ought to do is render an account of the moneys which you have handled.' (143) The spokesman was a man respected among the citizens (*astoi*), who was called Telesarchos. Maiandrios realised that if he let go the tyranny someone else would be set up as tyrant instead of him and so decided not to let it go; rather, when he had got back onto the *akropolis*, he sent in turn for everyone involved on the pretext that he was going to render an account of the moneys, but seized them and imprisoned them. After they had been seized, Maiandrios fell ill. His brother, who was called Lykaretos, expected him to die and in order that he might the more easily seize power on Samos put all the prisoners to death. So, it seems, the Samians did not wish to be free. (And in due course the Persians imposed Syloson, brother of Polykrates, on Samos.)

Herodotus III.142–143

1 That is, as god of freedom.
2 Compare **73**.
3 Compare **35** with n.2.

35. Tyranny in the west

The Greek cities of Italy and Sicily also experienced tyrannies in the archaic period. Particularly in the case of the latter, the phenomenon was associated with violent upheavals and destructions of cities; yet even here, where tyrannies also persisted later than they did in the core of the Greek world, tyranny is something which is grafted onto the *polis* as a parallel institution. It is striking that the coinages of *poleis* ruled by tyrants continue to bear simply the appropriate ethnic (e.g. 'of the Syracusans') as a legend. See in general Andrewes, *Tyrants*, 128–36; Finley, *Sicily*, ch.4; for the involvement of Carthage (important also later in the case of Dionysios) **118**; for Sicily and Athens **172A**.

(The Greeks have sent to Sicily to ask for help against the Persian invasion of 480.) The ancestor of this Gelon, one of the original settlers at Gela, came from the island of Telos which lies off Triopion;[1] he did not get left behind when Gela was settled by Lindians from Rhodes under Antiphemos. In the course of time his descendants became priests of the underworld deities and kept the position once Telines, one of the ancestors of Gelon, had got it. This is how he did it: some men of Gela, worsted in civil strife, took refuge in Maktorion which lies in the hills above Gela. These men Telines brought back to Gela, not by exercising any mortal force but by possessing the sacred objects of the underworld deities. Whence he had got them or how he came to possess them, that I cannot say; but he was trusted because of them and so brought the exiles back, on condition that his descendants should be priests of the deities[2] . . . (154) Now when Kleandros son of Pantares, who had been tyrant of Gela for seven years, came to the end of his life – murdered by Sabyllos, a man of Gela – his brother Hippokrates took over the reins of power. And Gelon, the descendant of Telines the priest, was one of Hippokrates' bodyguards along with Ainesidemos son of Pataikos and many others. After a while he was appointed commander of the entire cavalry force because of his outstanding qualities; for Hippokrates was involved in attacks on the Kallipolitans and the Naxians and the Zanklaians[3] and the Leontines and the Syracusans and many of the native communities and in all these wars Gelon was clearly the most outstanding figure. Of all the *poleis* I have mentioned none escaped enslavement by Hippokrates except for Syracuse; and they were saved by the Corinthians and the Kerkyrans after they had been defeated in battle[4] on the river Heloros, and they were only saved by coming to terms and agreeing to surrender Kamarina to Hippokrates; for originally Kamarina had belonged to the Syracusans. (155) Finally it fell to Hippokrates to be killed before the *polis* of Hybla after ruling for the same number of years as his brother Kleandros, in the course of a campaign against the Sikels;[5] Gelon pretended to protect his sons Eukleides and Kleandros, since the *politai* were no longer willing to be their subjects, but once he had defeated the Gelans in battle he in fact ruled them himself and deposed the sons of Hippokrates. After this plot, Gelon gained control of Syracuse also; the so-called *gamoroi*[6] among the Syracusans had been driven out by the *demos* and by their own slaves[7] called Kyllyrioi, but they were restored by Gelon from the *polis* of Kasmenai (whither they had fled); the *demos* of Syracuse handed over the *polis* and itself to Gelon when he approached. (156) Once he had control of Syracuse, he was less interested in his rule over Gela, but handed it over to his brother Hieron, while he lorded it over Syracuse, which was everything to him. And it immediately began to grow and to flourish; for he brought all the Kamarinaians to Syracuse and made them *politai* and pulled Kamarina to the ground; he also did to over half the inhabitants of Gela what he had done to the Kamarinaians. He then dealt similarly with Megara in Sicily, which had been besieged by him and come to terms; he transferred the upper classes to Syracuse and made them *politai*, although they had started the war against him and expected to be executed as a result; he also brought to Syracuse and sold into slavery to be exported from Sicily the *dēmos* of Megara, which was in no way responsible for the war and did not expect to suffer any harm. And Gelon did exactly the same, operating the same criterion, to Euboia in Sicily. He did this to both *poleis* since he regarded the *dēmos* as something very unpleasant to associate with. This was the way in which Gelon became a very powerful tyrant.

Herodotus VII.153–156*

1 Telos lies near Rhodes.
2 Compare **34** with n.3.
3 See Hdt. VI.22–24 for the story.
4 Note Corinth and Kerkyra here acting in concert, in contrast to the situation in **28**.
5 The native population.
6 The landowning aristocracy.
7 Probably native serfs, see **19**.

4 The institutions of the polis

Colonisation and tyranny are not the only phenomena common to many archaic *poleis*; between the eighth and the sixth centuries these acquired communal institutions which were defined and recorded, a process where the evidence of inscriptions supplements the literary evidence. Whatever form of constitution a *polis* developed, whether aristocracy, oligarchy or democracy, the rules for its government and for the administration of justice were laid down and known; they could be discussed, justified, attacked or changed and the rule of custom which persisted, whether it functioned well or ill and whether it commanded admiration or its opposite (see **9** and **10**), had gone for ever.

36. Co-operative values

Although Homer always remained *the* great educational poet for the Greeks, the competitive values which he idealised (though not to the exclusion of justice, see **5** and **9**) were clearly not always at a premium in the classical *polis*. There must have been some development of co-operative values, even though on the one hand a belief in justice, community and rationality (G. E. R. Lloyd, *Magic, Reason and Experience* (Cambridge, 1979), esp. 264–7) were probably always elements in the mental make-up of the Greeks, and on the other hand the *polis* continued to provide an arena for competition. Striking early expression of a belief in justice is to be found in a poem of Theognis (see Adkins, *Moral Values*, 42–3, who, however, exaggerates the contrast with Homer).

Be willing to lead a pious life with few possessions rather than be rich as a result of their unjust acquisition. In a word, all virtue is to be found in justice and everyone who is just, Kyrnos,[1] is an excellent man.

Theognis 145–148

1 See **21** n.1.

37. Legislation at Dreros in Crete (650–600)

This is the earliest of a series of cases where a contemporary epigraphic document survives to reveal the process whereby an archaic community created and defined the institutions according to which it proposed to live. We do not know whether the reference to a *polis* at the beginning is to an assembly or to a body of officials, or who the *dāmioi* (the local spelling of *dēmioi*) or 'twenty of the *polis*' are; but the mere fact of the existence of the measures is important, and the document also reveals already an administration comprising different functions. See further the discussion of Meiggs and Lewis.

May God be kind. The following points were agreed by the *polis*: when a man has been *kosmos*,[1] the same man shall not be *kosmos* for ten years; if he be *kosmos*, whatever judgment he give, he shall owe double (the penalty which he hands down) and he shall be without rights for as long as he lives and whatever he do as *kosmos* shall be void. The *kosmos* and the *dāmioi* and the twenty of the *polis* shall swear.

Meiggs and Lewis no.2

1 The chief *polis* official characteristic of Crete.

38. Legislation at Chios (575–550)

Despite the fragmentary nature of this inscription from Chios (it *may*, although found there, actually be an inscription of Erythrai on the mainland opposite), it reveals a *dēmos* which approves *rhētrai* (ordinances), officials who include a *dēmarchos* and a college of *basileis* (literally, kings), and a procedure for the administration of justice involving *dēmos*, *dēmarchos*, and *boulē*.

Side A.]of Hestia,[1] observing the *rhētrai* of the *dēmos*[
           ](rhētra) which will declare; if a man who is *dēmarchos* or *basileus*[
           ]of Hestia let the man who is *dēmarchos* grant to exact[
           ]in the presence of the *dēmos* having been summoned . . .[2]
           ]double penalty[

Side B.]if the case subject to appeal[
           ]but if he is wronged, before the *dēmarchos*, staters[

Side C.]let him appeal to the *boulē* of the *dēmos*.[3] On the third day after the Hebdomaia[4] let the *boulē* of the *dēmos*, with power to inflict penalties, assemble, chosen fifty from a *phylē*. Let it deal with the other affairs of the *dēmos* and all the cases subject to appeal in the month[

Side D. (Artemision)[
           ]let him make oaths[
           ]to the *basileis*[

Meiggs and Lewis no.8

1 See **17** n.3.
2 We cannot translate the word *aloiai* which occurs here.
3 The phrase has been taken to imply the existence of two *boulai* and this alleged

fact cited in the debate about whether a Solonian council of 400 existed in Athens beside the Areiopagos (see **67**); but we see no grounds for believing in two *boulai* at Chios – the use of the phrase *consilium publicum* at Rome does not imply that there was another similar body beside the Senate.

4 A festival on the seventh day of the month; the *boulē* thus meets (given the Greek system of inclusive reckoning) on the ninth day.

5 The name of a month.

39. The need for records

This inscription on bronze, from Crete at the end of the archaic period, shows a curious blend of the primitive and the advanced. (The identity of the *polis* does not emerge with certainty from the text and the inscription has no secure provenance; but script and dialect suffice to attribute it to Crete and to about 500.) The *polis* concerned makes a contract with a scribe; he is known as the *poinikastēs* because of the Phoenician origin of the Greek alphabet (see 4), and is clearly an innovation, but the post is to be hereditary; a variety of officials appears, but payment by the *polis* is still in kind. (Despite much that has been written since the original publication, text and translation are both in places conjectural.)

Side A

Gods. The Dataleis resolved[1] and we the *polis* pledged to Spensithios, five men from each of the *phylai*, subsistence[2] and immunity from all taxes to him and to his descendants, so that he be for the *polis* its scribe and recorder in public affairs both sacred and secular. No one else is to be scribe and recorder for the *polis* in public affairs, neither sacred nor secular, except Spensithios himself and his descendants, unless Spensithios himself should induce and bid the *polis*, or else the majority of his sons, as many as be adult. (The *polis*) is to give annually as payment to the scribe fifty jugs of must and [about 9 letters missing] of twenty drachmas weight or ? more; and the must is to be given from whichever ?plot he wishes to take it . . . (Fragmentary regulations dealing with the infringement of this last clause follow.)

Side B

The scribe is to have equal share, and the scribe too may be present at and participate in sacred and secular affairs in all cases wherever the *kosmos*[3] may be; and to whatsoever deity has not a priest to conduct its own (sacrifices) the scribe is to make the public sacrifices and to have the precinct dues, and there is to be no ?scizure, and no security is to be taken from the scribe; [?????] but otherwise, it shall be invalid. As lawful dues to the mess (*andreion*)[4] he shall give ten axes weight of dressed meat, if ?the others also make offerings; (he shall give) the yearly offering also, and shall ?collect the ?portion, but nothing else is to be compulsory if he does not wish to give it. The sacred matters (?of the *andreion*) are to be (reserved) for the ?senior member (despite the privileges of the scribe).

L. H. Jeffery and A. Morpurgo Davies, *Kadmos* (1970), p.118

1 Perhaps a body within the *polis* of uncertain identity and function, rather than the *polis* itself.
2 Probably grain only, in the light of what is specified later.
3 See **37** n.1.
4 Compare **54** for the common messes at Sparta.

40. The tradition of the lawgiver

The acquisition by a *polis* of its various institutions was normally no doubt a piecemeal process; but the Greeks themselves tended to attribute everything or almost everything to a single lawgiver (*nomothetēs*), conspicuously so in the case of Sparta (Ch.5); only in the case of Athens is the tradition good enough to distinguish the contributions of different people and periods. Some of the impetus towards the tendency no doubt derives from the nature of the act of colonisation (see Ch.2); note also the role of Demonax of Mantineia as a mediator in the internal strife at Kyrene in the sixth century (Hdt. IV.161–162).

(A) There is nothing special in what Charondas[1] laid down (for the city of Katane) except for the trials for false witness, for he first introduced the procedure of denunciation; but in the detailed provisions of his laws he is more exact even than the lawgivers of today.[2]

Aristotle, *Politics* (II) 1274b 5–8

(B) Zaleukos was by origin a Lokrian from Italy, of noble birth and widely admired for his upbringing, a follower of Pythagoras the philosopher.[3] He gained a large following in his native country and was chosen as lawgiver;[4] he laid down a new set of laws from scratch, beginning first with those concerning the gods. For right at the beginning of his whole set of laws he laid down that it was necessary for the inhabitants of the *polis* above all to accept and believe that the gods existed, and for them to contemplate in their minds the heaven and its arrangement and order, and to see that all this was not the result of chance or of human action; and it was necessary for them to revere the gods as the source of everything that was noble and good in the life of men and to keep their souls pure from every evil, since the gods take no delight in the sacrifices and gifts of wicked men, but only in the upright and noble observances of good men. Having thus at the beginning summoned his fellow *politai* to be pious and upright, he added the injunction that no *politēs* was to contract an irreconcilable enmity with anyone, but that they were to contract any enmity on the assumption that they would in due course be reconciled and become friends again; and anyone who behaved otherwise should be regarded by his fellow *politai* as wild and savage in spirit. And he bade the officials not to be wilful or overbearing, nor to judge cases with reference to enmities or friendships. And in the details of his set of laws he included many of his own ideas, which were admirably intelligent.⁵

Diodorus XII.20

1 See **7** n.6 and **174**.
2 Aristotle here shows himself critical of a presumably adulatory and largely fictitious tradition; Diodorus XII.11.3–19.3 records the laws of Charondas at length, but attributes him to Thourioi (see **174**) and the mid-fifth century.
3 An exile from Samos, who taught in Kroton and whose teachings had political implications.
4 Compare **23** for the *aisymnetēs*, and the resolution of conflict.
5 Diodorus goes on to discuss at length the attempt of Zaleukos to control private morality and dismisses in a sentence his provisions for contracts and similar matters.

41. The 'polis' and its buildings

Tyrants were great builders (see **32** and **70** Intro.), but even without their intervention all Greek *poleis* came to acquire the buildings, in addition to temples, which were necessary for the conduct of their political and social life: meeting places for *ekklēsia, boulē* and *prytaneis*, and gymnasia (see Fig. 8). This inscription from Sigeion (of 575–550) is remarkable both for the early mention of a *prytaneion* (compare **42**) and also for the religious function of the gifts of Phanodikos; for the *prytaneion* of Athens see **172**B and, in general, S. G. Miller, *The Prytaneion* (Berkeley, 1978). For accounts of what the physical appearance of a *polis* ought to be see Catullus 63.60; Strabo XI.3.1; Paus. X.4.1.

I am (the gravestone) of Phanodikos son of Hermokrates of Prokonnesos; and he gave a mixing-bowl and a stand and a strainer for the *prytaneion* to the Sykecis.¹
I also am (the gravestone) of Phanodikos son of Hermokrates of Prokonnesos; I gave a mixing-bowl and a stand and a strainer for the *prytaneion* as a memorial (of myself) to the Sigeueis; and if I suffer any damage, look after me, men of Sigeon; and Aisopos and his brothers made me.

SIG no.2²

1 Note the erratic spelling throughout the inscription.
2 The two versions were engraved, probably simultaneously, the first in the Ionic script and dialect of Phanodikos' home town, the second in the script and

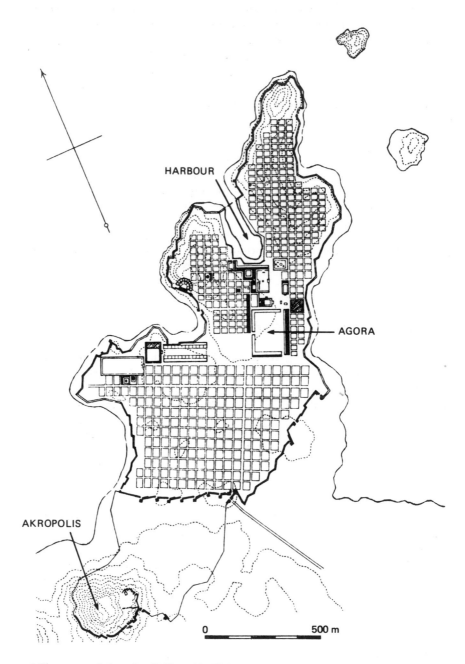

HARBOUR

AGORA

AKROPOLIS

0   500 m

8 The *agora* and *akropolis* of Miletus (G. Kleiner, *Die Ruinen von Milet* (Berlin, 1968), 26)

dialect of the Athenians who controlled Sigeion (on the Hellespont) probably from 550; the second version uses the first person indiscriminately of the gravestone and of Phanodikos.

42. The 'polis' and its finances

We have seen that the establishment of a metallic weight standard probably comes early in the development of the *polis* (p.53) and that the establishment of a set of measures is attributed to Pheidon of Argos (see **26**); once a metallic weight standard existed, a *polis* doubtless used it as a monetary unit for accounting purposes, notably in the assessment of fines (see **28**) and in the calculation of income and expenditure; the sixth-century Manes inscription below shows a remarkably complex set of taxes in existence in archaic Kyzikos. At the same time, individuals will also have come to use the local monetary unit for private accounting purposes, as in B below, from Samos, of 580–570. Coinage, on the other hand, is a relatively late invention, appearing about 600 in Asia and the islands of the east Aegean (see Hdt. 1.94.1 for the development of a bi-metallic coinage of gold and silver in Lydia) and about 550 in Greece and the islands of the west Aegean; when it did appear, coinage will have been simply the expression of a familiar monetary unit and initially of little significance either fiscally or economically (see further p.22). See in general C. M. Kraay, *Archaic and Classical Greek Coins* (London, 1976), ch. 2.

(A)]the *polis* gave this *stēlē* to Manes son of Medikes.
In the term of office of Maiandrios
The *polis* granted the children of Aisepos and Medikes and their descendants immunity and hospitality in the *prytaneion*,[1] except for the tax on the *nayssos* and on the use of the public balance and on the sale of a horse and the 25 per cent tax and the tax on the sale of a man; but they are to be immune from all others;[2] and the *dēmos* made a sworn agreement[3] on these terms. And the *polis* gave this *stele* to Manes son of Medikes.

SIG 4[4]

(B) [?]niskos son of Xenodokos, Demis son of Pythokles, native Perinthians, dedicated a tithe to Hera, making a golden gorgon, a silver siren, a silver dish, a bronze lamp, all worth 212 Samian staters with the inscription.

SEG XII.391

1 See **41**.
2 The tax on the *nayssos* (if this is the right reading) and the 25 per cent tax are both obscure; the taxes from which the children of Aisepos and Medikes *are* immune are probably direct levies on property.
3 Compare **16B**.
4 The inscription bears the last line of the sixth-century version and the whole of the first-century copy; the reasons for the re-inscription are unknown.

43. International relationships: Lokris and Kerkyra

The archaic period also saw the Greek *poleis* begin to work out ways of organising their relationships with each other; the process involved the recognition of the sanctity of the four great shrines and of the truce for their festivals (see **11, 12)**, the establishment of rules of war and the emergence of the *proxenos,* a citizen of one *polis* who served as the representative there of the citizens of another *polis.* The post was honorific and often hereditary, having its roots in *xenia* (see **5B**) and often retaining an aristocratic aura. See M. B. Wallace, 'Early Greek *proxenoi*', *Phoenix* 24 (1970), 189–208; also Austin and Vidal-Naquet no.41.

This is the monument of Menekrates son of Tlasiaos of Oiantheia[1] by origin, and the *dēmos*[2] made it for him, for he was a *proxenos* who was a friend of the *dēmos*; but he died at sea and public suffering[3] [came upon everyone]. And Praximenes coming from his native land placed this monument of his brother for him in association with the *dēmos*.

Meiggs and Lewis no.4

1 In Lokris, see **83**.
2 Of Kerkyra, where the inscription was found.
3 *Dēmosion kakon,* compare **21**.

5 Sparta

To Sparta one must devote its own chapter; inevitably so, for Sparta was, or became, unique. As successive waves of Greek-speaking peoples migrated down into the Balkans towards the end of the second millenium, most of them simply displaced the previous inhabitants of whatever area they chose to settle in. Hence, in large measure, the eastward flowing 'colonisation' of the Aegean islands and the coast of Asia Minor between *c.*1050 and *c.*950 (not to be confused with the later and more organised colonising movement documented in Ch.2). But the Dorians, who by *c.*1000 were pressing on down to the southern Peloponnesos and occupying the Eurotas valley, took a different course – to subjugate the population which they found there and to subordinate it totally to their own requirements. Such a policy was not, in point of fact, unparalleled outside Sparta and Lakonia, as we have already seen (**19**, Austin and Vidal-Naquet, *Economy*, 65, 86–9), but there is every reason to believe that the problems which the Spartans (or more properly Lakedaimonians) thereby created for themselves became in the end uniquely severe – particularly when they took the step of annexing neighbouring Messenia also, in much the same fashion (**45**); and certainly without parallel was their own course of action once the full extent of those problems had become apparent. Already odd in various ways (possessing, for instance, a dual monarchy: **50**), Sparta changed during the seventh and sixth centuries in aspects and at levels so fundamental as to be revolutionary. Indeed the Spartans themselves, and the Greeks in general, believed in such a revolution as a tangible event, which in the normal Greek way (compare **8, 40**) they attached to the name of one man, Lykourgos (**47**); but he, if he ever existed, is simply one feature of the 'mirage' which ever since antiquity itself has obscured and distorted the truth about how, when and why it was that the Spartans came to have not merely an extraordinary constitution (**48–52**), but also and more importantly an extraordinary educational system, social and economic structure, way of life and cast of mind (**53–56**; see in general the excellent study by Finley, *Use and Abuse*, ch.10). The net effect, thanks again to the 'mirage', has always been to encourage exaggeration, particularly as regards the supposedly immediate and deleterious effects on culture and art (Cartledge, *Sparta*, 154–7, is sensible on this), but certainly those who looked at Sparta in the fifth and fourth centuries, from Herodotus (**13**) to Aristotle (**267**), saw a people whose entire life-style was shaped and dominated by a single categorical imperative: to maintain their position as masters of Lakonia and Messenia (see de Ste Croix, *Origins*, 89–94).

44. The Spartan occupation of Lakonia

Greek tradition and modern archaeology are not substantially at variance about the early history of Lakonia, even if only the former caters to an appetite for detail. Mycenean Sparta disappeared, along with the rest of Mycenean civilisation, around 1200, and the Eurotas valley lay open, as did Greece as a whole, to occupation by fresh invaders. By *c.*1000 they had arrived, in the shape of a Greek tribe called the Dorians (see **3**), who overran and took possession of the Peloponnesos in general and Lakedaimon in particular. And it was they, clearly, who originated the idea – to legitimise these conquests – that they were a people *returning* to their rightful heritage, as the Herakleidai, descendants of the hero Herakles (compare Hdt. IX.26).

See further: Forrest, *Sparta*, chs.2 and 3; Cartledge, *Sparta*, chs.6 and 7.

According to Ephorus[1] the Herakleidai, Eurysthenes and Prokles,[2] took possession of Lakonia, divided it into six parts and turned the *chōra* into *poleis*. One of these divisions, Amyklai, they picked out as a gift for the man (Philonomos) who had betrayed Lakonia to them and who had persuaded its ruler of that time to come to an agreement and emigrate, with the Achaians, to Ionia. Sparta they designated as their own, and the royal seat. To the other places they sent kings, with the authority to take in any strangers (*xenoi*) who wished to live with them – this because the population was so small. Because of its good harbour they made use of Las as a naval station, while Aigys became a base for operations against their enemies, since its territory bordered upon those of the neighbouring peoples. Pharis[3] served as the treasury, since it afforded security against external attack. And although all the *perioikoi*[4] were subjects of the Spartiatai,[5] they enjoyed legal equality nonetheless, sharing in *politeia* and public offices. However, Agis the son of Eurysthenes deprived them of this equality of status and had them pay tribute to Sparta. Most submitted – but the Heleians, who occupied Helos and were called helots, rose in revolt. A war ensued in which they were forcibly taken prisoner and pronounced to be slaves; and it was laid down that whoever owned one of them could neither set him free nor sell him beyond the frontiers. This then was known as the War against the Helots. And one might almost call Agis and his associates the inventors of the whole helot system, which persisted right down to the Roman conquest:[6] the Spartans maintained these men in a sort of public slavery, assigning them places to live and particular duties.[7]

Strabo VIII.5.4

1 See p.14. His *World History* took the return of the Herakleidai as its starting-point.
2 Said to be the fathers of Agis (mentioned later in the passage) and Eurypon, the eponyms of the two branches of the Spartan royal family (see **50**).
3 Or possibly Pheraia; the text of these few lines is very poor.
4 The *perioikoi* (literally 'dwellers-round-about') were the free inhabitants of the towns, other than Sparta itself and Amyklai, of Lakonia and (after its conquest: **45**) Messenia; 24 such communities are named by Pausanias as existing by his day (III.21.6–7). Their status, which evolved from diverse origins, emerged ultimately as a compromise between independence and subordination: on the one hand *perioikoi* were, as individuals, free men and members of communities which our sources consistently call *poleis*; on the other, the perioikic communities were actually part, together with 'the Spartans' in a narrow sense (see next note), of the *polis* (and army) of 'the Lakedaimonians'. See further Forrest, *Sparta*, 30–1; Jones, *Sparta*, 8; R. T. Ridley, 'The economic activities of the Perioikoi', *Mnemosyne* 27 (1974), 281–92; Cartledge, *Sparta*, 178–93 and *passim*.
5 This term designated 'the Spartans' in the strictest sense, i.e. the full citizens of Sparta itself. Another name for them (see for instance **50B**) was the Equals (*Homoioi*).
6 In the second century.
7 On the helots compare Myron of Priene *apud* Athenaeus 657C D (Fornara no. 13); Thuc. IV.80.1–4; Plut. *Lyk.* 28. And see further Forrest, *Sparta*, 31 and *passim*; Jones, *Sparta*, 9–11; de Ste Croix, *Origins*, 89–94; Cartledge, *Sparta*, 160–77 and *passim* (including, at 347–56, a dossier of ancient sources in translation).

45. The Messenian Wars

To the west of Sparta and the Eurotas valley, across the formidable Taygetos range of mountains, lay Messenia. Here too the 'Heraklid' Dorians had taken possession; but in the second half of the eighth century (c.730–c.710) the Spartans' wish to infiltrate and interfere culminated in a full-dress war of conquest and annexation. Clearly enough Sparta wanted to possess, or exploit, more land, and chose a very much more uncompromising way of doing so than that of encouraging potential landowners to join in the foundation of overseas *apoikiai* (Ch.2): Messenia as well as Lakonia now became a territory peopled by *perioikoi* and, above all, Helots (see **44**). The profit to Sparta was self-evident. But it was counterbalanced, arguably outweighed, by the ever-present burden and threat, thereafter, of a massive subject population. In the seventh century, as Strabo relates, there was a second Messenian War – or revolt – and more lay ahead (see

169); and the constant *likelihood* of revolt was to mould much of Spartan history, policy and psychology until well into the fourth century.

With Strabo's account, given here, compare Diod. xv.66.2–4. And see further Forrest, *Sparta*, ch.4; Cartledge, *Sparta*, ch.8.

Often the Spartans went to war because of the Messenians' revolts. Tyrtaeus says in his poems that the first conquest of Messenia took place in the time of his father's father,[1] and the second on the occasion when the Messenians chose as their allies the men of Argos and Elis and Pisa[2] [and Arkadia],[3] and rose in revolt; the Arkadians supplied as their general Aristokrates, the king of Orchomenos, and the Pisatans Pantaleon the son of Omphalion. It was in this war, Tyrtaeus maintains, that he himself acted as general for the Spartans, for in his elegiac poem called *Eunomia*[4] he says that he came from Sparta: 'For the son of Kronos himself, Zeus, spouse of fair-crowned Hera, has given this *polis* to the Herakleidai, with whom we left windy Erineos[5] and came to the broad island of Pelops.'[6] So either these elegies are not authentic or else we must give no credence to Philochorus[7] when he asserts that Tyrtaeus was an Athenian, from (the deme) Aphidna: the story goes – and it is also in Callisthenes and several other writers – that Tyrtaeus came from Athens at the request of the Spartans, whom an oracle had instructed to apply to the Athenians for a leader.[8] Anyway, the second war did occur in Tyrtaeus' time.

Strabo VIII.4.10

1 Tyrtaeus flourished *c*.650.
2 See **11** with n.2.
3 These words do not appear in the transmitted text, but the context demands them.
4 Lawfulness. We have already met the word in a context (**12B**) which makes clear its aristocratic overtones, and perhaps 'law and order' captures its flavour even more exactly – certainly to the extent that it became a central catchword in the authoritarian, disciplinary ethos of the Spartan revolution: see A. Andrewes, 'Eunomia', *CQ* 32 (1938), 89–102; and **47**.
5 One of the cities of Doris in north-central Greece, the eponymous homeland of the Dorians (compare **3** with n.2).
6 I.e. the Peloponnesos. This is Tyrtaeus fragment 2 in West's collection; for others see **49** and Fornara no.12.
7 See p.15.
8 The story is scarcely credible; better to accept what the poet (and general) himself claims.

46. Taras

The foundation (*c*.706) of Taras, in the 'instep' of southern Italy, is the only certain exception to the generalisation that Sparta played no part in the colonising movement of the archaic period (Ch. 2). The story of the Partheniai, in its various versions – compare with Strabo's account, given here, Aristotle *Politics* (v) 1306 b 22–31, Diodorus VIII.21 and Athenaeus 271C–D – may well have undergone elaboration in the course of attempts to explain the word itself, but to see the origins of the episode in some sort of social and economic unrest following the (first) Messenian War is plausible enough. For the problems of interpretation beyond that, see Forrest, *Sparta*, 61–2; Jones, *Sparta*, 11–12; Cartledge, *Sparta*, 123–4.

In speaking of the foundation (of Taras), Antiochus[1] says that after the Messenian War[2] those Spartans who had not taken part in the campaign were adjudged to be slaves and were named helots;[3] and those children who were born while the campaign was in progress they called Partheniai,[4] and decided to deny them citizen rights. But the Partheniai, who were numerous, would not tolerate this and formed a plot against the government. When this came to light, some men were sent in to pretend to be sympathetic to the plotters and to report back, if possible, what they had in mind. One of these men was Phalanthos, who was thought to be their ringleader but who in fact was not altogether satisfied with those who had been named in connection with the conspiracy. Anyway, it was agreed to make the attempt in the Amyklaion,[5] during the celebration of the games at the Hyakinthia (festival) and at the moment when Phalanthos put on his leather cap; not to wear anything on the hair was the mark of a citizen. However, Phalanthos and the others secretly reported back these plans, and when the contest was under way a herald came up and told Phalanthos not to put on his cap; so the conspirators realised that their plot had been betrayed. Some of them began to run away, others to plead for mercy. The authorities put them under guard, telling them not to worry, and sent Phalanthos to (the temple) of the god[6] to ask about an *apoikia*. And this was the response: 'I give you Satyrion and the rich land of Taras to live in, and to become a bane to the Iapygians.' So the Partheniai went off there, with Phalanthos . . .

(3) Ephorus, on the other hand, tells of the foundation as follows. The Spartans were at war with the Messenians, who had killed their king Teleklos when he went to Messene to sacrifice, and they had sworn an oath not to return home again until either they had destroyed Messene or they were themselves all killed; and when the expedition set out, the youngest and oldest of the *politai* were left behind to guard the *polis*. Later, however, in the tenth year of the war, the women of Sparta met together and chose representatives to go and complain to their husbands that they were fighting the Messenians on unequal terms: their argument was that the Messenians were staying at home and producing children while the Spartans had left their wives as widows, to go and campaign in

an enemy land, and so were in danger of seeing the fatherland run short of men. Now the Spartans were keeping to their oath, but at the same time they took to heart what the women had said, so what they did was to send back from the army the most robust men they could find – who were of course also the youngest men: it was recognised that they had not participated in the oaths, since when they went out with the men of military age they themselves had still been boys. So these men were ordered, all of them, to have sexual intercourse with all the virgin girls – the belief being that this was the best way to produce the most children; and when this was done, the children were named Partheniai. Subsequently, after nineteen years of war, Messene was taken . . . and its territory divided out; but when the Spartans returned home they would not give the Partheniai the same status as others, on the grounds that they had been born out of wedlock. So the Partheniai joined forces with the helots in a plot against the Spartans, and agreed to raise a Lakonian cap in the *agora* to signify when the attack should begin. Some of the helots told the authorities of this, but it was felt that a counter-attack would be difficult against men who were so numerous and besides, all of the same mind, regarding one another almost as brothers. So those who were about to raise the signal were simply ordered to leave the *agora*. Realising of course that their undertaking had been betrayed, the conspirators held back; and the Spartans then used the influence of their fathers to persuade them to go away and found an *apoikia*. If they could get hold of a satisfactory site, they were to stay there; if not, they could return and receive a fifth part of Messenia in the distribution.[7] So the Partheniai were sent out and . . . founded Taras.

Strabo VI. 3.2–3*

1 Antiochus of Syracuse, a fifth-century writer on the history of Sicily.
2 I.e. the first war, or conquest (**45**).
3 See **44**.
4 Sons of 'virgins' (i.e. unmarried mothers).
5 The temple of Apollo at Amyklai.
6 Delphic Apollo.
7 'Surely a claim to Messenian land had lain behind the original quarrel' (Forrest, *Sparta*, 61).

47. Lykourgos

The Spartans of the classical period, and those who fell under their spell, did not generally care to believe that the basis of Sparta's extraordinary constitutional machinery, social structure and educational system had come together piecemeal; they saw a coherence in it, and a need to preserve it from change and decay, both of which called forth the view that it had been deliberately established at one specific time in the past. As to when that time was, the pundits were at variance – in addition to the two passages here see the testimony collected as Fornara no.2. There was substantial agreement, however, that the measures could be attributed to, or at the very least discussed in connection with, one man, Lykourgos, around whom there gathered sufficient biographical detail for Plutarch to write his biography (see B).

See further: Andrewes, *Tyrants*, 76–7; Jones, *Sparta*, 5–7; Cartledge, *Sparta*, 103; and **88**.

(A) So this[1] was the state of affairs in Athens at the time when Kroisos was making his enquiries.[2] As for the Spartans, he discovered that in their war against Tegea they had survived a number of serious setbacks to emerge, by now, victorious. During the reign of Leon and Agasikles in Sparta, the Spartans had been successful against all their enemies, with the sole exception of the resistance put up by the men of Tegea.[3]

At an earlier time still,[4] the Spartans had had a system of laws which was practically the worst in all Greece, both domestically speaking and in terms of their dealings with foreign states – which were in fact non-existent;[5] but then they made changes with a view to law and order (*eunomia*), and this is how this came about. Lykourgos, one of the Spartans of noble birth, went to Delphi to consult the oracle, and immediately upon his entering the shrine the priestess of Apollo spoke to him as follows: 'Lykourgos, dear to Zeus and to all (the other gods) who have their homes on Olympos, you have come to my rich temple. Shall I pronounce you god, or man? I cannot tell – but I would wish and hope a god, Lykourgos.' Of course there are those who assert that in addition to this the priestess also revealed to him the constitution which the Spartans have maintained to this day, but they themselves, the Spartans, deny this: their story is that Lykourgos brought over the institutions from Crete[6] after he had become regent for the young king Leobotes, his nephew.[7] They point to the fact that as soon as he became regent he changed all the laws, and also saw to it that, thus changed, they should not be broken. And it was Lykourgos too, later, who created the military institutions – the *enōmotiai* and the *triakades*,[8] and the *messes*[9] – and established the *ephoroi*[10] and the *gerontes*[11] besides. (66) So these were the changes which brought about *eunomia*, and when Lykourgos died they built a temple to honour him – which they still do, greatly. And thus, thanks to their fine *chora* and abundant manpower they very quickly shot up and flourished.

Herodotus 1.65–66.1

(B) No general statement can be made about Lykourgos the lawgiver (*nomothetēs*) which is not controversial: the accounts of his origins, his travels, his death, and – above all – his measures to deal with the *nomoi* and the *politeia* are all different; and there is least agreement of all about the time when the man lived. For some, including the philosopher Aristotle, say that his heyday coincided with that of Iphitos, and that the two of them actually collaborated in establishing the Olympic truce.[12] Aristotle cites as proof of this the discus at Olympia upon which the inscribed name of Lykourgos is preserved. On the other hand, those who calculate dates from the Spartan king-lists, such as Eratosthenes and Apollodorus,[13] reveal that Lykourgos antedates the first Olympiad by many years. As for Timaeus,[14] he has voiced the suspicion that there may have been *two* Lykourgoi at Sparta, at different times, and that to one of them – the more famous – the achievements of both have been ascribed. The earlier of the two, in his opinion, lived not far from the time of Homer; and there are some who conjecture that he actually met Homer, face to face. Then again, according to Xenophon[15] Lykourgos lived in the time of the Herakleidai,[16] but this view looks suspiciously simplistic: even the most recent of the Spartan kings were of course 'Herakleidai' by descent, but Xenophon apparently wishes to indicate by this name the original Herakleidai, Herakles' immediate descendants. At all events, although the enquiry strays into such complexities I shall try to give my own version by following those writers whose accounts of the man spend the least time in contesting alternative views, or which cite the weightiest authorities.

Plutarch, Lykourgos 1.1–3

1 See **69**.
2 In *c*.550 Kroisos, king of Lydia (see **90, 91**), sought links of alliance with the most powerful of the Greek cities – which meant, so he was told, Athens and Sparta.
3 *c*.580–*c*.550: see **58**.
4 See n.7, below.
5 It is odd, indeed mistaken, that Hdt. should think xenophobia a feature only of *pre*-Lykourgan Sparta: see **56**.
6 See further **88**.
7 His reign can be assigned notional dates of *c*.870–*c*.840. (Note, however, that Hdt. himself would have thought more in terms of *c*.1000.)
8 See Forrest, *Sparta*, 45–6.
9 See **54**.
10 See **52**.
11 See **51**.
12 'The Eleians regulated the details of the Olympiad and formally proclaimed by heralds the commencement of the Olympic truce (*ekecheiria*) during which all violation of Eleian territory by an armed force was a sin against Zeus' (Pritchett, *War* I, 121). See in general **11**.

13 Scholars and polymaths of the third (E.) and second (A.) centuries, whose
    writings included works on chronology.
14 A Sicilian historian, *c.*356–260.
15 Xen. *Lak. Pol.* x.8.
16 See **44**.

48. The mixed constitution

A second identifiable element, besides the Lykourgos-figure, in the 'mirage'
which distorts our view of the Spartan revolution is the fact that the constitution
which emerged from it came later to be seen as the embodiment of a principle
valid on a universal basis – that of a *mixed* constitution, combining in stable
equilibrium the characteristics of monarchy, aristocracy and democracy. (See in
brief Cartledge, *Sparta*, 131–3.) We cannot trace in detail the origin and
development of the idea, and ideal, of a mixed constitution as such (though note
the hint in Thuc. VIII.97.2: see **227B**); but on its way to becoming a commonplace
of Hellenistic philosophy it seems to have gained ground in oligarchically-
inspired Athenian political thought of the fourth century, in such works as
Plato's *Laws* and Aristotle's *Politics.* For Aristotle's views on Sparta, in addition
to the passage given here see *Pol.*(II) 1269 a 29–1271 b 19 and (VII) 1333 b 12–35.

Some people maintain that the best *politeia* must be a mixture of all the
politeiai, and they therefore praise that of the Spartans. This is because –
on one view – it is a combination of oligarchy,[1] monarchy and
democracy: those who see it this way call the kings the monarchic
component[2] and the office of the *gerontes* the oligarchic,[3] while the office
of the *ephoroi* provides the element of democracy,[4] since the *ephoroi* are
drawn from the *dēmos* as a whole. Others, however, declare the ephorate
a tyrannical feature and see democracy in the system of messes[5] and the
other aspects of daily life.

Aristotle, Politics (II) 1265 b 33–42

1 Or aristocracy.
2 See **50**.
3 See **51**.
4 See **52**.
5 See **54**.

49. The Rhētra

According to Plutarch, 'Lykourgos did not lay down written laws; in fact one of
the so-called *rhētrai* forbids it' (*Lyk.* 13.1). The 'Lykourgan' system was thus seen
as resting upon these *rhētrai*, unwritten compacts or covenants between the
lawgiver and his people which apparently derived their ultimate authority (and

perhaps phraseology also) from oracles (*ibid*.13.6). Paradoxically, however, Plutarch did find preserved in one of his sources – probably Aristotle – what gives every impression of having been the most crucial *rhētra* of all, concerned as it is with the basic constitutional relationship between the kings, the *gerousia* and the citizen assembly, and (ostensibly in a rider or amendment) with modifications therein. A secure interpretation of this enigmatic document, together with the accompanying fragment of Tyrtaeus, would resolve many of the most fundamental and mystifying obscurities which surround the Spartan revolution, but there is scant agreement amongst modern scholars about its date, historical context, and the exact meaning and significance of its constitutional provisions. All things considered, we believe in a date somewhere between *c*.700 and *c*.650; further precision than that is guesswork. We also see the Rhētra as embodying what Andrewes (*Tyrants*, ch.6) has aptly called 'the Spartan alternative to tyranny', i.e. the establishment of a form and procedure of democratic decision-making which, however archaic and reactionary it was to appear in the context of later constitutional developments elsewhere, was ahead of its own time. But beyond that, difficulties such as the relationship between the Rhētra itself and the rider (and the absence from the document of the *ephoroi*: **52**) remain baffling.

See further: H. T. Wade-Gery, *Essays in Greek History* (Oxford, 1958), 37–85; A. H. M. Jones, 'The Lycurgan Rhetra', in *Ancient Society and Institutions: Studies . . . Ehrenberg* (Oxford, 1966), 165–75; Forrest, *Sparta*, 40–60; Cartledge, *Sparta*, 131–5.

So eager was Lykourgos to establish this office[1] that he brought an oracle from Delphi about it, which they call a *rhētra*. This is what it contains: 'When a temple of Zeus Syllanios and Athena Syllania has been built,[2] the people divided into *phylai* and *ōbai*, and thirty men – including the *archagetai*[4] – appointed as a *gerousia*, from time to time *apellai*[5] shall be held between Babyka and Knakion; thus questions shall be introduced and withdrawals made.[6] But the people (*dāmos*) shall have the supreme power to decide.'[7] In these provisions, the clause about division into *phylai* and *ōbai* refers to the separation and distribution of the populace into, respectively, tribes and local communities; *archagetai* is the name for the kings; and *apellai* signifies meetings of the citizen assembly, so called because it was the oracle of Pythian Apollo which was originally responsible for the *politeia*. The Babyka is now known as Cheimarros and the Knakion as Oinous – though according to Aristotle the Knakion is a river but the Babyka a bridge.[8] Between these they used to hold the assemblies, for there were no colonnades or any other buildings: Lykourgos considered such things to be not conducive to good counsel – indeed actually detrimental to it, reducing to nonsense and frivolity the deliberations of those who were met together in assembly but instead were gazing around absentmindedly at statues and paintings or theatrical stage-settings or excessively embellished roofs of council-chambers. When the populace had been brought together, the *gerousia* and the kings would bring forward a motion, which the *dēmos* had the authority to accept or reject. No one else was permitted to propose a motion. Subsequently, however, when the masses were twisting and distorting the motions by removing or adding clauses, Polydoros and Theopompos the kings[9] wrote in this addition to the Rhētra: 'But if the people choose a distorted (motion), the old men and the *archagetai* shall be setters-aside' – that is to say, shall not ratify the decision but order a complete withdrawal and dissolution of the assembly, on the grounds that it is improperly perverting and altering the motion. And in fact they persuaded the *polis* that it was the god (Apollo) who was prescribing this, as Tyrtaeus tells us in the following lines: 'When Phoibos (Apollo) had spoken, they brought home from Delphi the oracles and prophetic words of the god. "The kings, divinely honoured, shall be supreme in council, they who care for the fair *polis* of Sparta, with the august *gerontes*; and next the men of the *dēmos*, duly obeying straightforward *rhetrai*."'[10]

Plutarch, *Lykourgos* 6

1 The *gerousia*: see below, and **51.**
2 The meaning of these epithets of Zeus and Athena, and therefore their significance here, is unknown.
3 The explanation of these terms which Plut. gives later in the passage is a mere tautology. Consult Forrest, *Sparta*, 42–6.
4 The kings (as explained later).
5 Feasts (possibly monthly) in honour of Apollo, which were evidently to serve as occasions for the assembly to meet. Plutarch's explanation (later) is dubious. See de Ste Croix, *Origins*, 346–7.
6 'Withdrawals', i.e. 'after discussion the *gerousia* shall stand aside to reconsider the question in the light of the discussion and subsequently, if it sees fit, submit a proposal to a reconvened assembly for ratification' (Forrest, *Sparta*, 48).
7 The Greek of this clause is badly garbled; we reconstruct it from Plutarch's gloss (below).
8 Presumably it was more usual to regard both as rivers. In any event their location cannot now be determined.
9 Their reigns coincided in the first quarter of the seventh century.
10 Tyrtaeus frag.4 West. Diodorus' version (VII.12.6) has a different introductory couplet and four further lines in the oracle itself.

50. The kings

In most of Greece the archaic period saw the disappearance of the monarchies that we see in Homer (6) in favour of aristocratic rule: instead of recognising allegiance to an Agamemnon-figure, the nobles, formerly his advisors, now shared out his power amongst themselves; and the king himself either vanished altogether or, as at Athens (see **63**), was reduced and transformed into a priest and archōn. Monarchy survived, however, at colonial Kyrene (**16**) and also, more importantly, at Sparta – partly, no doubt, because of the role it was allotted in the 'Lykourgan' constitution, and partly because it must have derived strength and durability from one unique feature: it was a *dual* monarchy, with kings drawn in pairs from the Agiad and Eurypontid royal families. (For how this may have come about see Forrest, *Sparta*, 28–9; Cartledge, *Sparta*, 103–6.) The following passages indicate that in the fifth and fourth centuries the Spartan kings, though certainly what we would call constitutional monarchs, had survived with some substantial powers still intact.

See further: Jones, *Sparta*, 13–16.

(A) The Spartans have given their kings the following privileges: two priesthoods, of Zeus Lakedaimon and Heavenly Zeus, and the right to declare war against any territory they wish; any Spartan who opposes this is put under a curse. On a campaign it is the kings who go out first and return last, guarded by a hundred picked men, and during these expeditions they are allowed as many cattle and sheep as they like; also they receive the skins and backs of any beast offered in sacrifice. (57) So much for matters of war. In peacetime their prerogatives are these: at any sacrifice celebrated at public expense it is the kings who sit down to dinner first and are served first, each of them receiving twice as much of everything as the other diners; also they initiate the libations[1] and receive the skins of the sacrificial victims. On the first and the seventh days of every lunar month each king is given at the public cost a full-grown sacrificial beast to offer at the temple of Apollo, together with a *medimnos*[2] of barley and a Lakonian measure of wine. At all the games they have the choice front seats.[3] It is their right to choose whom they like from the citizens for appointment as *proxenoi*, and in addition they each select two Pythioi; these are the official sacred delegates to Delphi, and they dine with the kings at public expense.[4] If the kings do not go to dinner (in the mess), two *choinikes* of barley and a *kotylē* of wine[5] are sent to each of them at home; if they do attend, they are given double servings of everything, and this same honour is paid to them by private individuals who invite them home to dine. All oracles are in the safe keeping of the kings – in collaboration with the Pythioi – and they have sole authority in certain law-suits: concerning young heiresses – if their fathers have not betrothed them to anyone, the kings decide who shall marry them; concerning the public roads; and concerning adoption, where the procedure requires the kings to be present. They sit in council with the *gerontes*, who are 28 in number; and if they, the kings, do not attend, those of the *gerontes* who are their closest relatives take over their prerogatives and cast two votes, in addition to the one for themselves.[6]

Herodotus VI.56–57

(B) I shall also give an account of the power and status which Lykourgos prescribed for a king on campaign. First of all, while they are on military service the king and his staff are maintained at the expense of the *polis*. The senior officers (*polemarchoi*) share his quarters, in order that they may be constantly available should the need arise for collective discussions. So, too, do three of the Equals;[8] it is their business to see to all the supplies, so that (the leaders) are not distracted from concentrating on the campaign itself. However, I shall go back to the beginning and speak of how the king sets out with an army. First of all he offers a sacrifice at home to Zeus the Leader and the (gods) associated with him. If the omens are favourable, the fire-bearer takes fire from the altar and leads the way to the frontiers of the *chōra*. There the king offers a second sacrifice, to Zeus and Athena; and only when both deities have accepted it does he cross the frontiers of the *chōra*. The fire from these ceremonies leads the way, never quenched, and all sorts of sacrificial beasts follow behind. Always when he offers a sacrifice the king begins the task during the morning twilight, in the hope of making an early bid for the god's goodwill; and in attendance at the sacrifice are *polemarchoi*, company-commanders (*lochagoi*),[9] divisional-commanders (*pentēkontēres*),[9] commanders of foreign troops (*xenagoi*), commanders of the baggage-train, and also any general from the (allied) *poleis* who wishes to be there. Also present are two of the *ephoroi*, who do not interfere in the proceedings – except at the king's request – but observe everyone and see to it that they act with appropriate decorum.[10] When the ceremonies are over the king calls everyone together and announces the orders of the day. One really would think, to see all this, that the Lakedaimonians are the only true craftsmen in matters of warfare, while everyone else makes up soldiering as they go along![11]

(xv) I should like also to give an account of the compact established by Lykourgos between king and *polis*: for this is of course the only government which continues exactly as it was initially set up; other *politeiai*, it will be found, have undergone and are still undergoing changes. He laid down that the king, by virtue of his descent from a god,[12] should offer all the public sacrifices on behalf of the *polis*, and that he should lead the army to wherever the *polis* might despatch it. He also gave him the privilege of receiving portions from the sacrificial beasts, and allotted him choice land in many of the perioikic *poleis*, enough to ensure him a moderate supply of everything but not riches in excess. In order that the kings, as well as everybody else, should mess out of doors he assigned them a public mess-tent; and he gave them the further honour of double helpings at dinner – not to enable them to eat enough for two, but so that they might have the means, thereby, to honour anyone of their choice. He also granted each king the right to select two messmates, who are known as Pythioi, and to take a piglet from every litter of pigs. This was in order that a king, should he ever need to take counsel with the gods, might never be without sacrificial victims. As regards water, there is a lake near the house which supplies it in abundance; and how useful *that* is, in all sorts of ways, will best be recognised by those without it! And everybody rises from their seats for a king – everybody except the *ephoroi*, who remain seated on their thrones of office. Kings and *ephoroi*, moreover, exchange oaths with one another each month, the *ephoroi* on behalf of the *polis* and each king on his own behalf: the kings' oath binds them to rule in accordance with the established *nomoi* of the *polis*; while the *polis* undertakes, in return for their abiding by this oath, to maintain the monarchy undisturbed.

These then are the domestic honours given to a king during his lifetime, and they are scarcely much greater than those of private individuals. This is because it was not thought desirable either for the kings to start behaving with the arrogance of tyrants or for the *politai* to grow envious of their power.

Xenophon, *Lakedaimonion Politeia* XIII.1–5; XV.1–8

(c) Of course it is easy to perceive that there are many kinds (of monarchy) and that there is no single mode of ruling common to them all. Take the monarchy in the Spartan *politeia*, which is seen as the prime example of a monarchy regulated by law (*kata nomon*). There the king is not sovereign in everything, though when he leaves the *chōra* to wage a war he is the leader in matters relating to it; and religious affairs too have been allotted to the kings. So this monarchy is a sort of plenipotentiary generalship (*stratēgia*) held for life.[13] Except in an emergency, you see, the king has no power of life and death, of the sort summarily exercised during their military campaigns by the kings of old.

Aristotle, *Politics* (III) 1285 a 1–10

1 Offerings of drink, usually wine, poured out to the gods.
2 See p.xvii.
3 Reservation of front seats (*proedria*) was a common mark of esteem and reward in the ancient world.
4 See further below, B; and P. A. Cartledge, 'Literacy in the Spartan oligarchy', *JHS* 98 (1978), 25–37 at p.30.
5 See p. xvii. (Two *choinikes* is a quantity, appropriately for the kings, twice that of one man's normal daily needs.)
6 That the kings cast two votes is polemically denied by Thucydides (1.20.3). See Gomme, *Commentary* I, 137–8.
7 Xen. is right to use the singular, since from the late sixth century only one of the kings was permitted to be away, at any given time, on campaign: see 75.
8 See 44 with n.5.

9 These equivalents are purely notional, and the internal organisation of the
   Spartan army notoriously problematical (see for instance Gomme, *Commentary* IV, 110–17).
10 The *ephoroi*: see further, below, and **52**.
11 Compare Plut. *Pelop.* 23.3, and **270**.
12 I.e. Zeus, who fathered Herakles.
13 The formulation is reiterated in (III) 1285 b 26 28. In 1285 b 33–37 Spartan
    kingship is set at the opposite extreme from absolute monarchy (*pambasileia*).

51. The 'gerousia'

The *gerousia*, as we have already seen (**47–50**), was Sparta's council of elders. Like
so much else its creation was ascribed to Lykourgos – thus, for instance, by
Herodotus (**47A**) and, in the passage given here, by Plutarch – but if this is
anything more than unthinking accretion it is a misunderstanding of the *Rhētra*
(**49**): the kings of Sparta must always have had some such body of venerable
aristocrats to advise them, and the most that 'Lykourgos' can have done is to
have given it formal definition, in size, as a council of 28 *gerontes* sitting in
deliberation with the two kings.

  See further: Forrest, *Sparta*, 46–51; Jones, *Sparta*, 17–19; A. Andrewes, 'The
government of classical Sparta', in *Ancient Society and Institutions: Studies . . .
Ehrenberg* (Oxford, 1966), 1–20; de Ste Croix, *Origins*, 124–38 and 349–54; Lewis,
Sparta, 36–42.

Among the many innovations made by Lykourgos the first, and the
greatest, was his establishment of the *gerousia*. This, as Plato says, when
mixed with the 'feverish' rule of the kings and possessing voting equality
with them in matters of the greatest importance, created a government
secure and sensible.[1] Previously the *politeia* had been wayward, inclining
at some times in the direction of the kings, towards tyranny, and at
others in the direction of the masses, towards democracy. Now,
however, it had the office of the *gerontes* set at its centre, creating
equilibrium just as a ship's ballast does, and thus securing the safest and
most orderly arrangement: when a stand needed to be made against
democracy the 28 *gerontes* invariably sided with the kings, yet they also
added strength to the *dēmos* in preventing the establishment of a tyranny.
As regards the figure of 28, Aristotle asserts that this was fixed because in
setting up the *gerousia* Lykourgos had had 28 associates – originally 30,
but two men had lost their nerve and deserted the enterprise. Sphaerus,
on the other hand,[2] maintains that from the outset those involved in the
scheme numbered 28. Possibly the figure's significance lies in its being
the product of seven multiplied by four; it is also equal to the sum of its
own parts, and thus the next perfect number after six.[3] My own opinion,
though, is that Lykourgos prescribed precisely this number of *gerontes* so

as to produce an overall figure of thirty, when the two kings were added to the 28.

(26) It was Lykourgos himself, as has been mentioned, who appointed the first *gerontes*, from those who had been his associates and advisors; for the future, however, he laid down a procedure whereby vacancies resulting from a member's death were filled by electing the most outstanding candidate from men over sixty years of age. And of all the contests[4] in which men engage, this one, surely, was the greatest – and the most contentious! . . . This is how the choice was made. When the people had been brought together in assembly, selected men were shut up in a nearby room, from which they could neither see nor be seen, but merely hear the cries of those assembled; for it was by their normal practice of shouting[5] that they decided between the contenders. These appeared not all together in a body but one by one, introduced in an order determined by lot and passing in silence through the assembly; and thus the incarcerated judges, who had writing-tablets with them, indicated the volume of the cry for each man – not knowing his identity but simply that he had been brought in first or second or third or whatever. And the man for whom the shouting was loudest and longest was declared elected . . .

Plutarch, Lykourgos 5.6–8; 26.1–3★

1 Plato, *Laws* 691E.
2 Sphaerus of Borysthenes, third-century philosopher, and advisor to the reforming Spartan king Kleomenes III.
3 Compare Plato's pride (in *Laws* 737E–738A) in the arithmetical possibilities of the number 5,040; see also **17B** with n.6.
4 *Agōnes*: compare **12**.
5 Compare **183B**.

52. The 'ephoroi'

The constitutional procedures laid down by the Rhētra (**49**) make mention of kings, *gerousia* and assembly – but not of *ephoroi*. This did not, though, prevent the creation of that office from being credited to Lykourgos (by Herodotus, for instance (see **47A**), and implied by Xenophon in passage B, below). Others, including Aristotle (*Politics* (v) 1313 a 25–8) and Plutarch (passage A, below), preferred king Theopompos, *c*.720–675, which for them made it a post-Lykourgan development. In plain truth, the state of our knowledge of Spartan history before the mid-sixth century does not allow us to say with certainty whether 'creation' of the ephorate (as opposed to adaptation or upgrading of a pre-existing office) is even the proper issue for discussion, or to interpret with certainty the hints in later procedure (**50B**) that the post was somehow anti-monarchist in origin. All that is clear is that by the fifth and fourth centuries the ephoroi, a board of (by that time) five men chosen annually, enjoyed such extensive administrative, executive and judicial powers as to make them, within the constraints of the 'mixed' constitution (48), the mainspring of the Spartan governmental system.

See further: de Ste Croix, *Origins*, 148–9; P. A. Rahe, 'The selection of ephors at Sparta', *Historia* 29 (1980), 385–401.

(A) This was how Lykourgos achieved the mixture in his political system.[1] The oligarchical element in it, however, was still unmixed and strong; and his successors, seeing it, as Plato says, 'swelling and fuming, set the power of the *ephoroi* as a kind of bridle on it'.[2] It was about 130 years after Lykourgos, during the reign of king Theopompos, that the first *ephoroi*, Elatos and his colleagues,[3] were appointed. The story goes[4] that when Theopompos was being criticised by his wife on the grounds that he would be handing on to his sons a lesser monarchy than the one he had inherited, he replied, 'No, a greater one – in that it will be a longer one.' And in point of fact, by avoiding excess the monarchy managed also not to arouse jealousy and the danger that accompanies it, so as a result the Spartan kings did not share the treatment inflicted by their peoples on the kings of Messenia and Argos, who were inflexible in their refusal to yield any of their power to the *dēmos*.

Plutarch, *Lykourgos* 7.1–2

(B) Now we all know that Sparta is the place above all others where men obey the officials and the *nomoi*.[5] I personally believe, however, that Lykourgos did not so much as attempt to establish this sort of disciplined behaviour until he had persuaded the most powerful men in the *polis* to share his views. My proof of this? In other *poleis* the more influential men do not wish even to give the appearance of being afraid of those in office, which they consider to be an attitude of servility. Yet in Sparta it is the leading men who are most deferential to the officials, and whose greatest pride is to abase themselves – to *run*, not walk, whenever they are called upon. They do this in the belief that if they themselves lead the way in eager obedience the rest will follow; and this is exactly what has happened. It is likely also that these same men helped to set up the power of the ephorate, once they had realised what a great blessing obedience is – in a *polis*, in an army, and in an *oikos*: their view was that the more power this office could be given, the more it would frighten the *politai* into obedience. Accordingly the *ephoroi* are competent to fine anyone they like, and empowered to exact payment on the spot; they also have the authority to suspend (other) officials from duty, and even to imprison them and lodge a capital charge against them. So great, in fact, is their power that they do not allow (other) elected officials to rule as they like throughout their whole year's term, as would happen in other *poleis*, but instead they act like tyrants – or presidents of the games – and punish an offence the minute they see it being committed.[6]

Xenophon, Lakedaimonion Politeia VIII.1-4

1 I.e. by the Rhētra.
2 Plato, *Laws* 692A.
3 One member of each board, the eponymous *ephoros*, lent his name to each year, for dating and other purposes; compare the eponymous *archōn* in Athens.
4 The source is Aristotle, *Politics* (v) 1313 a 28–33.
5 See further, on this theme, **55**.
6 In Athens, for example, an official's conduct in office was not normally scrutinised until his term was over (at the *euthynai*: see **65**B).

53. Land and property

The Spartiatai, full citizens of Sparta, were all Equals (*Homoioi*). One obvious and crucial expression of this equality was its political embodiment, *via* the Rhētra (**49**), in a sovereign assembly. Another was, or might be, regulations and norms concerning the ownership of property – which, for a state as conservative as Sparta was forcing herself to be, meant property in land above all else. In the latter part of the archaic period (and then throughout Greek history as a whole), the redistribution of land became a standard revolutionary cry in many *poleis*, so it is not unduly sceptical to suspect that the land-allotments and property-regulations of 'Lykourgos' owe much of their substance to idealised retrojections by later historians and political theorists; see for instance Jones, *Sparta*, 40–3. Yet it is clear that equality, in Forrest's sense of 'not falling below a certain minimum' (*Sparta*, 51), was no less true of the Spartan system of land tenure than in the political context, and in many ways more important: *above* the 'certain minimum' there was ample scope, regulations or not, for some Spartiatai to be very much more Equal than others (see **265**), but each and every one of them was a landowner whose possession of an inalienable plot (*klēros*) expressed and guaranteed his position as a component part of this unique *polis*.

The second of Lykourgos' schemes for the *polis*,[1] and a most innovative one, was his redistribution of the land. This was necessary because there was terrible inequality: many men had no property at all and were a burden on the *polis* in their helplessness, while wealth was entirely concentrated in the hands of a small minority. He therefore resolved to banish insolence and envy and crime and luxury, at the same time as those two much more old-established and serious diseases which afflict a *politeia* – wealth and poverty. This he sought to do by persuading them to pool all their land together and divide it out afresh: they were to live with each other, one and all, as equals, with plots of the same size ensuring them life's necessities, and with their wish to be pre-eminent expressing itself in the pursuit of excellence[2] – the ethos being that between one man and another there is no difference or inequality other than that determined by reproach for shameful actions and praise for good ones. That was the theory, and what it meant in practice was a distribution of land: 30,000 *perioikoi*[3] were given plots in Lakonia, while the territory belonging to the *astu* itself, Sparta, was divided into 9,000 plots, that being the number of Spartiatai. In some versions, however, Lykourgos distributed (only) 6,000, with 3,000 being added later by Polydoros;[4] and sometimes it is asserted that Lykourgos distributed (only) half of the 9,000, and Polydoros half. Each individual's plot was large enough to give a yield of 70 *medimnoi* of barley for a man and twelve for his wife,[5] with a proportionate amount of the liquid crops.[6] A plot of this size, in his view, would be adequate for men who would need sustenance sufficient for their vigour and health but nothing more than that. And the story goes that when, some time later, on returning from foreign parts he was passing through the *chōra* just after harvest-time and saw the identical piles of grain in their parallel lines, he smiled and remarked to those with him that the whole of Lakonia was looking like a family estate freshly shared out amongst many brothers.

(9) He also set about dividing up their moveable property, in such a way as to abolish the inequality and disparity once and for all; but when he saw that they were not at all happy about having it taken from them directly, he adopted another course and overcame their greed by political measures. First of all he declared all gold and silver coinage invalid and prescribed the use of iron currency only. Furthermore, to a great and weighty bulk of this he assigned a trifling face value, so that a quantity worth ten minas required a large household storeroom to keep it in and a pair of oxen and a cart to move it about![7] With this established as the currency, Lakedaimon saw the last of many sorts of crime. Who, for instance, would think of stealing money, or accepting it as a bribe? Who would be likely to commit fraud, or robbery with violence?[8] The stuff could not be concealed, there was nothing to be envied in possessing it, and there was not even any profit in cutting it up, given the use – so we are told – of vinegar to quench the red-hot iron, which took away its temper and left it brittle, unworkable and useless for anything else.

After this he also banished, as undesirable aliens, the unnecessary and superfluous crafts (*technai*).[9] And even without someone driving them out, most of them would doubtless have departed along with the regular coinage, once there was no medium for the sale of their products: this was because nobody could carry the iron currency into the rest of

Greece, where in any case it was considered worthless and ludicrous. So the result was that the Spartans were not able to buy any foreign goods or bric-à-brac; no merchantmen brought in cargo to their harbours; and unwilling even to set foot in Lakonia were the teachers of rhetorical argument, the vagabond prophets, the pimps, and the ornamental gold- and silver-smiths – simply because there was no coined money there. What happened instead was that luxury, thus deserted, little by little, by that which gives it life and sustenance, died out by itself; their wealth gave the rich no advantage, for affluence had no means of expressing itself openly but was stored away at home in idleness. And so it came about that Lakonian craftsmanship in such articles of everyday necessity as couches and chairs and tables was of the very highest, and the Lakonian drinking-cup, as Critias says,[10] was held in particularly high repute for military campaigns; its colour concealed the unpleasant appearance of the water that soldiers are obliged to drink, while its inward-curving rim kept the foul sediment back inside and allowed only the purer part to fill the drinker's mouth. For this too they had the lawgiver to thank: freed from useless tasks, the skilled craftsmen were able to show off the beauty of their workmanship in articles which everybody needed.

Plutarch, Lykourgos 8–9

1 I.e. after the Rhētra.
2 *Aretē*: see 5A, 33 n.1.
3 See 44 n.4.
4 King *c*.700–665; see 49.
5 I.e. annually. The high proportion for the man, the *klēros*-holder himself, is because of the contributions required of him to his mess (see 54); but beyond that, Plutarch's figures create more problems than they solve (see Cartledge, *Sparta*, 169–71).
6 I.e. wine and oil.
7 Ten minas of (e.g.) Attic silver currency, by contrast, weighed less than 10 lb.
8 The answer to these rhetorical questions is, of course, anyone (inside or outside Sparta) with access to other currencies – see 265. Note, however, that this moralising explanation of Sparta's decision not to coin silver had a sound basis in economics: unlike, for instance, Attika (see 161), Lakonia and Messenia had no silver deposits of their own – but iron ore in abundance.
9 Compare 13. 'Lakonian' craftsmanship was therefore largely, though not entirely, the craftsmanship of the *perioikoi*: see P. A. Cartledge, 'Did Spartan citizens ever practise a manual *tekhnē*?', *Liverpool Classical Monthly* 1 (1976), 115–19 (summarised in his *Sparta*, 183–5). For pictures of Lakonian artefacts see L. F. Fitzhardinge, *The Spartans* (London, 1980), chs.3–8.
10 A fifth-century Athenian writer and revolutionary: see 244.

54. The messes

As a complete training and inculcation in the habits of toughness, discipline and service – military service above all – to the community, from the cradle to (almost) the grave, every Spartiate (with the curious exception of heirs-apparent to the throne: Plut. *Ages.* 1) passed through the *agōgē*, a uniquely rigorous and elaborate system of state education described at length by Xenophon (*Lak. Pol.* I–IV) and Plutarch (*Lyk.* 14–25); see in general Forrest, *Sparta*, 51–5, and Jones, *Sparta*, 34–9. Some of its features, such as the various initiation rites, find parallels in other *poleis* and indeed other societies altogether: 'what was unique about Sparta was the way all these elements were combined into a coherent structure, and the pivotal organising mechanism . . . as a pattern of life for the young and as an attempt to fix the individual Spartan's behaviour and ideology for a lifetime' (Finley, *Use and Abuse*, 175–6). Individuals, in fact, were subordinated to the community, which as a principle was nothing extraordinary in the world of the *poleis*: compare **149**, an utterly different *ethos* yet fundamentally the same result. However, the extent to which for a Spartiate community also came before *family* was a very much rarer and less characteristic Greek attitude (see in general Lacey, *Family*, esp. 196–208). Family life in Sparta was not absolutely non-existent, but there were potent alternatives – and none more so than the institution of the *sussition* (mess) to which every adult Spartiate belonged and contributed.

With Xenophon's account, given here, compare Plut. *Lyk.* 10–12.

So Lykourgos found the Spartiates boarding at home, just like the rest of the Greeks, and he realised that this was a perfect prescription for a life of indolence, so he brought the messes out into the open, thinking that this would be the best way to combat disobedience. And he stipulated an amount of food for them sufficient to allow them to eat, but not too much – though there can be many unexpected extras from the spoils of the hunt, as well as occasions when the wealthy members contribute bread made from wheat instead (of barley); and the result is that until they retire to their own quarters the table is neither bare of food nor extravagantly laid out with it. What is more, he put a stop to the obligatory drinking-bouts which are the undoing of body and mind alike: each man was to drink whenever he felt thirsty, which in his view created the circumstances in which wine does the least harm and gives the most pleasure. So with this as the procedure in the messes, how could anyone ruin either himself or his *oikos* by gluttony or drunkenness? Of course in other *poleis* it is generally the case that men of the same age are grouped together – the worst possible recipe for decent behaviour – but at Sparta Lykourgos intermixed the age-groups so as to have the younger men educated, for the most part, by the experience of their elders. And in point of fact since it is the Spartan custom for the topic of conversation at the mess-table to be that of great deeds done in the *polis*, the result is little or no insolence, little or no drunkenness, and little or no indecency in behaviour and talk.

Xenophon, Lakedaimonion Politeia v.2–6

1 This confirms the impression given in other passages (50A, 53) that barley, not wheat, was the staple cereal consumed, by humans as well as animals, in Sparta (see Cartledge, *Sparta*, 171). The same could be said of Athens (Isager and Hansen, *Aspects*, 18), and was doubtless true in general, but the unpalatability of Spartiate mess fare was notorious: see for instance Plut. *Lyk.* 12.6–7 on the 'black broth' (*melas zōmos*).

55. The Spartans and the law

Obedience to the laws (*nomoi*) was a requirement in all *poleis* (for Athens see **149** and passages there cited), but we have already seen (e.g. **52B**) that in Sparta it had an importance even more central than for most – and we have also seen the reason for this: as masters of Lakonia and Messenia the Spartiatai had turned themselves into virtually full-time soldiers, and what was required of them thereafter was the soldier's unquestioning obedience. Here the deposed Spartan king Demaratos, accompanying the Persian invasion of Greece in 480, is made by Herodotus to explain this to Xerxes, the Great King of Persia, who finds it incredible that the Spartans will dare to stand up to him.

'I knew, my lord, right from the start that if I spoke the truth you would not be pleased by what I am telling you; nonetheless you insisted on the absolute truth, so I told you how things are with the Spartiates. And yet you of all people know what hatred I feel for them now, for taking away my honours and ancestral privileges and sending me away in exile from my *polis*.[1] Your father (Dareios), by contrast, took me in and granted me the means to set up my own *oikos*, and for any sensible man it cannot be reasonable[2] to reject kindness when it is shown to him; surely his main response will be loving gratitude. Personally I do not claim to be able to fight ten men, or even two. Given the choice, I would not take on even *one* opponent singlehanded! However, if it were essential, if there were some great struggle (*agōn*) to urge me on, then it would give me the greatest pleasure to fight one of these men of yours who maintain that they are a match, each of them, for three Greeks. And so it is with the Lakedaimonians: in single combat they are as good as any, but when they fight together they are the best soldiers in the world. And the reason for this? Well, they are free men, certainly, but their freedom is not absolute: they have a master set over them, Law (*nomos*), whom they fear much more than your subjects fear you. At any rate, whatever this master orders, they do; and what he orders is always the same thing – never flee

from the battlefield, no matter how large the opposing forces, but stay in
the line, to conquer or to die.[3]

That is what you insisted upon hearing, my lord. If you believe that
what I say is nonsense, I am quite content to keep quiet in future. I hope,
however, that events turn out as you wish.'

Herodotus VII.104

1 Demaratos was the Eurypontid king of Sparta between *c.*515 and 491. This
   meant that his reign largely overlapped with that of the Agiad Kleomenes (**61**,
   etc.). Relations between the two of them were bad from at least 506 (see **75**),
   and it was Kleomenes who engineered the deposition of Demaratos in 491 on a
   charge of illegitimacy; D. then fled to Persia.
2 Some manuscripts repeat the word *oikos*, but the variant reading *eikos*
   (reasonable) is what the sense requires.
3 The character of a hoplite's armour (see P. A. Cartledge, *JHS* 97 (1977), 12–17)
   made it imperative that *the whole phalanx stood firm, not just courageous
   individuals*.

56. Xenophobia

Spartan *eunomia* presupposed above all else a changeless stability in which no
reason could arise for the excellence of the laws and the wisdom of the lawgiver
to be called into question or contrasted adversely with practices and attitudes
elsewhere. Of course no *polis* could actually survive in complete and utter
isolation, hermetically sealed off from all contact with, even knowledge of, the
outside world, but at Sparta the *desirability* of such isolation was always
self-evident, and a constant counterpoise to the requirements and ambitions of a
state which wished also, paradoxically, to dominate the rest of the Peloponnesos
(see **57–62**); so an ethos arose in which visits by others to Sparta and by Spartans
to other places were equally, if possible, to be avoided. On the specific institution
of the *xenēlasiai* (expulsions of aliens) compare Hdt. III.148; Thuc. I.144.2 and
II.39.1; Aristoph. *Birds* 1012–1014; Plato, *Protagoras* 342c; also Xen. *Lak. Pol.*
XIV.4 (see **265B**).

This was the reason[1] why (Lykourgos) did not grant them the freedom
to leave home, if they wanted to, and wander around picking up alien
habits and imitating the lives of uneducated peoples who lived under
different political systems. On the contrary he actually drove away the
multitudes who had streamed into the *polis* for no useful purpose. This
he did not, as Thucydides asserts, out of apprehension that they might
wish to copy his *politeia* and learn something advantageous about the
pursuit of excellence (*aretē*), but in order to prevent their becoming
teachers of any sort of evil. For the inevitable fact is that alien people
bring in with them alien principles; and from novelty in principles

follows novelty in decisions, something which is bound to give rise to many experiences and policies destructive to the harmony, as it were, of the established *politeia*. So he thought it more necessary to protect the *polis* from being filled with bad habits than to keep out infectious diseases.

Plutarch, *Lykourgos* 27.3–4

1 To preserve good behaviour.
2 *Aretē*: see 5A, **33** n.1. (In Thuc. II.39.1, the passage to which Plut. is referring, the subject is actually *military* secrecy.)

57. The battle of Hysiai

Once dominant in Lakonia and Messenia, the Spartans had the southern half of the Peloponnesos to themselves. To the north, however, lay other states – in chief, Argos and the cities of Arkadia – which might pose a threat, with or without provocation. The history of archaic Argos, which had its own Lykourgos-like figure in the shadowy king Pheidon (see **26**), is obscure and controversial in itself, but the indications are that in the first half of the seventh century it was Argos, not Sparta, which was in a position to attempt to overpower her neighbours (see for instance Andrewes, *Tyrants*, 31–42); and one of the foundations upon which this picture rests is a tantalising reference by Pausanias to an Argive victory over the Spartans at Hysiai in 669/8. Since Hysiai is in *Argive* territory it is usual to infer that Argos was defending itself – successfully – against Spartan aggression. But did the battle really happen? Since Pausanias is our only (surviving) authority for it, the question is a fair one (see T. Kelly, 'Did the Argives defeat the Spartans at Hysiai?', *American Journal of Philology* 91 (1970), 31–42; also, broader in scope, 'The traditional enmity between Sparta and Argos: the birth and development of a myth', *American Historical Review* 75 (1970), 971–1003; and now his *History of Argos to 500* B.C. (Minneapolis, 1976)); but the case for scepticism is ultimately unconvincing.

On returning to the road which leads (from Argos) to Tegea one sees, on the right of what is called the Wheel,[1] Kenchreai. Why this name has been given to the place is not recorded, unless in this case also it was so called because of Kenchreas the son of Peirene.[2] Here are common graves of the Argives who conquered the Lakedaimonians in battle at Hysiai. This conflict (*agōn*) took place, I discovered, when Peisistratos was *archōn* at Athens,[3] in the fourth year of the twenty-seventh Olympiad (669/8), when Eurybotos, an Athenian, won the foot-race. Dropping to a lower level one finds the ruins of Hysiai, once a *polis* in Argive territory. Here it was, we are told, that the misfortune fell upon the Lakedaimonians.

Pausanias II.24.7

1 Presumably a round hill.
2 In II.2.3 Paus. gives a mythological derivation of the name of the more famous Kenchreai (Corinth's Aegean harbour) from Kenchreas son of Poseidon, patron god of Corinth, and the nymph Peirene.
3 An ancestor, in all probability, of Peisistratos the tyrant (**68–72**).

58. Sparta and Tegea

By the end of the seventh century Sparta will have recovered from the shocks of the Messenian revolt (**45**) – which may well have accelerated, if it did not altogether occasion, the adoption of *eunomia* – and the defeat at Hysiai (**57**); and for the next fifty years or so her territorial ambitions, reawakened after the period of reform and retrenchment, focussed themselves upon her northern neighbour, Arkadian Tegea. Herodotus alludes briefly (in I 65.1: see **47A**) to a series of Spartan setbacks in this connection during the reigns of Leon and Agasikles, i.e. between *c*.580 and *c*.560; and the Battle of the Fetters, described in the passage given here, was presumably the most serious of them. The implication of the episode, it should be noted, is that the Spartans planned at this stage to treat Tegea in much the same way as they had treated Messenia – as a wholly subordinate territory of helots and *perioikoi*. But the failure of this approach, this time, seems to have caused a radical change of policy: under the next pair of kings, Anaxandridas and Ariston (who coincided between *c*.560 and *c*.550), we see a new approach, perhaps to be associated with the name of Chilon, eponymous *ephoros* in *c*.556. Integral to it, as even Herodotus' jejune narrative makes clear, was the element of propaganda, with the bones of Orestes. But the real crux of 'this sea-change in Lakonian affairs' (Cartledge, *Sparta*, 138) lay in the fact that it marked a shift in Spartan policy from absorption to hegemony: when the Spartans did gain the upper hand over Tegea, what they did with it was to make it, in effect, the founder-member of (what modern scholars call) the Peloponnesian League – a network of treaty-alliances, under Spartan leadership, which was to be one of the dominant forces in Greek warfare and politics for two centuries thereafter.

See further: Forrest, *Sparta*, 73–6; Jones, *Sparta*, 44–5; de Ste Croix, *Origins*, 96–124, esp. 96–7; Cartledge, *Sparta*, 137–9. Fornara no.27 is a Spartan treaty with Tegea (mentioned in a fragment of Aristotle preserved by Plutarch), apparently from the time of the *rapprochement* in the 550s, in which Tegea undertook not to harbour or enfranchise Messenians.

And then, of course,¹ the Spartans were no longer content to live a quiet life: it seemed self-evident to them that they were superior to the men of Arkadia, so they consulted the oracle at Delphi with a view to conquering that entire territory. This was the response which the priestess gave them: 'You ask me for Arkadia? You ask a great deal – and I shall not give it to you. In Arkadia there are many men, acorn-eaters, and they will keep you out. But I shall not grudge you everything: I shall give you

Tegea to dance in with stamping feet, and its fine plain to measure out with the line.' When the Spartans heard this reply they ignored the rest of Arkadia and set off on a campaign against Tegea, carrying with them fetters, for all the world as if the men of Tegea were about to become their slaves – such was their faith in a deceptive oracle: it was they themselves who lost the battle, and those who were taken prisoner were made to 'measure out with the line' the Tegean plain by the labour of cultivating it, wearing the very fetters that they themselves had brought! And these fetters in which they were bound were in fact still preserved in Tegea during my own lifetime; they were hanging up round the temple of Athena Alea.

(67) So in this earlier war against Tegea the Spartans had been constantly and continuously getting the worst of it; but by the time of Kroisos,[2] and the reigns at Sparta of kings Anaxandridas and Ariston, the Spartans gained the upper hand in the war. This is how they did it. After a long series of Tegeate victories the Spartans sent sacred delegates to Delphi and asked which of the gods they should pray to in order to win the war against Tegea; and the priestess' response was that they would be successful once they had brought home the bones of Orestes the son of Agamemnon. They were unable, however, to find Orestes' tomb, and sent again to the oracle to ask where his remains were to be found. And this is the reply which the priestess gave to the Spartan representatives: 'In Arkadia there is Tegea, in its level plain. There, under mighty constraint, two winds breathe; blow falls upon blow, and woe upon woe. That is where the life-giving earth keeps the son of Agamemnon. Bring him away and you will be master of Tegea.'[3] That is what the Spartans were told – but it brought them no nearer to the end of their search; so they kept on looking, high and low, until a Spartiate called Lichas found the answer. He was one of the so-called *Agathoergoi*,[4] who are the five oldest men who leave the cavalry every year and who must then spend the whole of the year after their discharge on whatever errands and missions the Spartan state may give them.

(68) Lichas was one of these when he made his discovery in Tegea – by a combination of luck and sagacity. Since by this time the two states were on better terms with each other, Lichas was able to go to Tegea, where he visited a forge and watched iron being hammered out. This in his eyes was a miraculous process, and when the smith saw how amazed he was[5] he stopped work and said, 'Surprised, are you, my Lakonian friend? Well, your surprise at coming upon such a marvel as this, the working of iron, would be nothing to your astonishment if you had seen what I saw. I was wanting to make a well, you see, here in the yard, and as I was digging I came upon a coffin – seven cubits long! It seemed incredible that men were ever bigger than they are today, so I opened it;

and there I saw the corpse, just as long as the coffin![6] I measured it, and filled in the hole again.' That was the story; and after pondering upon what he had been told Lichas came to the conclusion that this was what the oracle meant – this was Orestes. The two 'winds', as he saw it, were the smith's two pairs of bellows; 'blow falls upon blow' signified the hammer and the anvil; and 'woe upon woe' stood for the hammered-out iron – the point being, or so he conjectured, that the discovery of iron was a bad thing for mankind. With this interpretation Lichas returned to Sparta and told the Lakedaimonians everything that had happened. They, however, brought up some fabricated charge against him and threw him out; so he went back to Tegea, told the smith his story and endeavoured to lease the yard from him. At first the smith refused, but eventually Lichas persuaded him and took up residence there – whereupon he excavated the tomb, collected the bones and went off home with them to Sparta. And ever since that time the Spartans, who had already subdued most of the Peloponnesos,[7] were far stronger than the men of Tegea in any war which either initiated.

Herodotus I.66–68

1 I.e. (in Hdt.'s view) after the reforms of Lykourgos had had their beneficial effects: see **47A**, from which this passage follows directly on.
2 See **47A** with n.2.
3 'Sparta was now ceasing to regard herself as a purely Dorian power and was claiming to be heir to the "Achaean" hegemony of Agememnon , ... whose son Orestes was said to have succeeded his uncle Menelaus as Sparta's king' (de Ste Croix, *Origins*, 96–7).
4 'Those who render good service'.
5 How and Wells observe in their *Commentary on Herodotus* (vol.I (Oxford, 1912), 91) that surprise at the working of iron is much too primitive a feature in this sixth-century story; but Spartan unfamiliarity with craftsmanship of *any* sort (**13, 53**) must be the real point here.
6 About ten feet. The bones themselves were possibly those of large prehistoric animals: see G. L. Huxley, 'Bones for Orestes', *GRBS* 20 (1979), 145–8.
7 Something of an exaggeration until the defeat of Argos: see **59**.

59. Sparta and Argos

Whether or not Sparta and Argos fought each other at Hysiai in 669/8 (see **57**), it could fairly be said that they were bound to clash sooner or later. While the Spartans had been taking hold in Lakonia and Messenia, the easternmost parts of the Peloponnesos had been left for their fellow-Dorians of Argos to dominate – principally (from the Spartan viewpoint) a thin strip of territory extending from Argos itself, in the north, down through Hysiai, Thyrea and Kynouria to Cape Malea and the offshore island of Kythera (on which note Hdt. VII.235). The indications are – for instance Paus. III.7.5 – that there was inconclusive fighting in the first half of the sixth century; but the issue came to a head in *c*.545 with the episode described here, the Battle of the Champions. See Forrest, *Sparta*, 79; Jones, *Sparta*, 46; Cartledge, *Sparta*, 140–2.

At this time[1] the Spartans themselves happened to be engaged in a quarrel of their own, with the Argives, over the territory known as Thyrea. The Spartans had cut it off and were occupying it, despite its being part of the Argolid: indeed Argos possessed everything as far as (Cape) Malea and the west,[2] both the mainland territory and also Kythera and the other islands. The Argives came out to oppose this seizure of their land, and reached an agreement with the Spartans to the effect that 300 men from each side should fight it out, with the territory going to the winners; the remainder of the two armies were to go home rather than stay to watch the contest, which might lead to assistance being given by either side to its champions if they were seen to be losing. With this arrangement made the two sides went away, leaving behind their picked men; and the fight began.[3] It proved to be an evenly-balanced one, such that at the end of it only three of the 600 men were left – two Argives, Alkenor and Chromios, and the Spartan Orthryades; and they owed their survival, these three, only to the onset of darkness. Naturally enough the two Argives felt that they had won, and ran back to Argos with the news. Orthryades the Spartan, however, stripped the Argive dead of their arms and armour, carried the spoils to his own camp, and remained there alone at his post. On the following day, when they had heard the news, the two sides came together again. For a while, of course, they both claimed the victory: the Argives pointed out that more of their men had survived, while the Spartans reasoned that the two Argives had run away, leaving Orthryades behind to strip the enemy corpses. And the dispute led in the end to their fighting a battle, in which after heavy losses on both sides the Spartans were victorious. It was from this time that the Argives, who had previously been bound by custom to wear their hair long, adopted their present practice of having it cropped close to the head. They also enacted a law forbidding, on pain of a curse, any man of Argos to grow his hair and any woman to wear 'gold until Thyrea had been recovered. As for the Spartans, the law[4] which *they* established was just the opposite – to wear their hair long, which they had not previously done.[5] And Orthryades, the sole survivor of the three hundred? He, the story goes, was ashamed to return to Sparta after the death of his comrades, and killed himself there at Thyrea.[6]

Herodotus I.82

1 When Kroisos of Lydia appealed for help (**47A**, **91**).
2 To us it would be more natural to say the south.

3 On this curiously formalistic, even ritualistic, aspect of Greek warfare see J. A. O. Larsen, *CPh* 44 (1949), 258–9; Pritchett, *War* II, 173, 249, 252. As Cartledge observes (*Sparta*, 140), the episode 'remained indelibly stamped on the consciousness . . . of the Argives, who actually proposed a return match on the same terms in 420 (Thuc. v.41.2)' – when this territory was *still* sought by both states.

4 Or possibly 'custom'; *nomos* is often ambiguous.

5 According to Aristotle, *Rhetoric* 1367 a 28–33, the wearing of long hair was particularly associated with the Spartans, and a reflection of their uninvolvement in banausic occupations (**13**).

6 Compare the case of the sole survivor of an even more famous Spartan Three Hundred, from Thermopylai: Hdt. VII.229–232 and IX.71.

60. Sparta and the tyrants

During the second half of the sixth century the issue which appears chiefly to have preoccupied the Spartans – or with which, at any rate, their name came chiefly to be associated – was not a domestic one, nor even something confined to the evolving Peloponnesian League, but a matter with much wider Greek and Aegean ramifications: the tyrants (above, Ch.3). Certain episodes and relationships are well enough attested – with Polykrates of Samos (Hdt. III.39–56) and the Peisistratids in Athens (see **74**), for example; and late sources glibly supply other names, plausible and implausible (e.g. [Plut.] *Moralia* 859C–D). Does all this then amount to a Spartan 'crusade against tyranny and in favour of constitutional government' (Andrewes, *Tyrants*, 127)? Any general validity in the thesis must derive in the main from the passage of Thucydides translated here.

See further: Forrest, *Sparta*, 79–84; Jones, *Sparta*, 45–7.

In the Greek *poleis* which had tyrants, the tyrant's sole concern was for his own affairs, that is to say his personal safety and the aggrandisement of his private *oikos*. This meant that the *poleis* were governed, as far as was possible, with a single end in view – security; and as a result nothing worth mentioning was achieved, beyond the sort of issues, purely local in their significance, which gave the tyrants in Sicily a position of such power.[1] For a long time the situation everywhere in Greece was such that nothing of note was being accomplished by joint effort, and the *poleis* individually were somewhat timid in what they did. (18) But eventually, a few years before the battle at Marathon where the Persians fought the Athenians,[2] the Spartans expelled the tyrants both from Athens and – with the exception of the ones in Sicily – from the rest of Greece as well, where on the whole they had established themselves earlier than in Athens.[3] From the time when the present Dorian inhabitants settled there, Sparta suffered throughout most of her recorded history from *stasis*, despite the great antiquity of her *eunomia* – and the fact that she has

123

never been ruled by tyrants: for a little over 400 years, reckoning to the end of this present war,4 the Spartans have had the same *politeia*, which has given them the capacity both to be strong themselves and to determine affairs in the other *poleis*.

Thucydides I.17–18.1

1 See **35, 118**.

2 In 490: see **108**. In the context of Thuc.'s rapid survey of several centuries, 'a few years' can be interpreted with some freedom.

3 For the Athenian episode see **74**. Note, however, that subsequent developments there (**75**) were so little to the Spartans' taste that only a few years later they were seeking to restore the man they had ejected (Hdt. v.91)!

4 I.e. the Peloponnesian War (431–404; see Chs.18–25). The possibility that Thuc.'s phrase (also in I.8.1 and 13.3) refers to, and counts back from, the end of the first *phase* of the War (in 421) is sometimes important for questions of dating, but scarcely here.

61. The accession of Kleomenes I

Before the second half of the sixth century no Spartan king seems to stand out, for us, as a definable personality pursuing an identifiable policy or policies. That they then begin – some, at any rate – to do so is attributable to the fact, above all else, that *c*.550 marks the beginning of the information collected and related by Herodotus; and it is perfectly obvious that the eighth-, seventh- and sixth-century kings included some important and influential figures – especially so in a period before the other elements in the 'Lykourgan' constitution had fully bitten into their freedom of action. As the evidence stands, though, one has to say that the availability of Herodotus' testimony coincides, happily, with the reign of one of the most striking, energetic and ambitious of all Sparta's kings, in *any* period: Kleomenes I (*c*.520–490). On his controversial accession see Forrest, *Sparta*, 82–3; Jones, *Sparta*, 48–9.

At Sparta the king was no longer Anaxandridas the son of Leon;[1] he had died, and on the throne now was his son Kleomenes. It was his birth, not any manly qualities of his own, which had given Kleomenes the succession, and this is how it came about. Anaxandridas had married his sister's daughter, and was devoted to her, but they had no children; and it was on this score that he was called to appear before the *ephoroi*. 'If you insist on neglecting your own interests,' they said to him, 'you leave us no choice but to see to it ourselves that the house of Eurysthenes[2] does not die out. You have one wife at the moment, but she is not bearing you children – so send her away and marry another. Do this and the Spartans will be pleased with you.' Anaxandridas, however, said in reply that he would do neither of these things: it was bad advice, their urging him to send away his present wife – who had done him no wrong – and marry another, and he would not do it. (40) At this the *ephoroi* and the *gerousia* held further discussions and then approached Anaxandridas with another proposal. 'We see how attached you are to your present wife; so make no objection to what we tell you to do, or else the Spartans may think of some other way of dealing with you! We do not ask you to divorce the wife you have now. On the contrary, do continue to give her everything that you give her now – but marry another wife as well, to bear you children.' Anaxandridas agreed to what they had said, and afterwards had two wives and lived in two separate households – a most un-Spartan thing to do. (41) And after a short time had passed the second wife gave birth to a son, this Kleomenes, thus providing the Spartans with an heir to the throne. But at the same time the strangest thing happened to the first wife: she, who had previously been childless, somehow or other became pregnant! There was no doubt about it; and when the news reached the relatives and friends of the second wife they began to make a nuisance of themselves by suggesting that the woman's claim was false and that she intended to pass off another's child as her own. After these angry accusations the *ephoroi* grew suspicious, as the time went by, and they adopted the safeguard of sitting round the woman's bed as she was giving birth. This they did, and saw her produce Dorieus. Very soon afterwards came another son, Leonidas, and then another soon after that, Kleombrotos – though some say that Kleombrotos and Leonidas were twins.[3] As for the second wife, who was the daughter of Prinetadas the son of Demarmenos, she had no more children after Kleomenes.

(42) Now Kleomenes, so it is said, was not of sound mind but on the verge of madness. Dorieus, on the other hand, was quite outstanding in his age-group, and took it for granted that his manly qualities would secure him the throne; so it came as a nasty shock to him when, on the death of Anaxandridas, the Spartans followed their usual practice and put the eldest son, Kleomenes, on the throne.

Herodotus v.39–42.2

1 *c*.560–*c*.520.

2 See **44**.

3 Presumably they were born in private! Leonidas succeeded his half-brother Kleomenes in 490.

62. Sparta, Athens and Plataiai

The reign of Kleomenes is documented in some detail, if unsystematically, by Herodotus. Out of several episodes we give here an early one, recorded in a digression from Herodotus' main Persian War narrative. In addition to illustrating Kleomenes' willingness to interfere – by appearing *not* to interfere – in affairs north of the Isthmos of Corinth, its interest lies in the origin of the special relationship between Athens and the small Boiotian *polis* of Plataiai which was to last for more than a century and a half (see **108, 184–186, 289**).

See in general on the reign of Kleomenes: Forrest, *Sparta*, 85–94; Jones, *Sparta*, 48–55; Jeffery, *Archaic Greece*, 123–7; Cartledge, *Sparta*, 143–54 and *passim*; Murray, *Early Greece*, 249–53. For Kleomenes and Athens, **74** and **75**.

When the Athenian forces had been drawn up in the precinct of the temple of Herakles,[1] the Plataians sent out their entire army to join and help them. This was because the Plataians had put themselves in the Athenians' hands, and before this occasion the Athenians had frequently been of service to the Plataians in their difficulties. It had come about like this:[2] when Plataiai was under attack from the Thebans, and getting the worst of it, the Plataians offered their allegiance to Kleomenes the son of Anaxandridas and the Spartans – simply because they were the first people on the spot.[3] But the Spartans refused the offer. 'We live too far away,' they said, 'and it would be cold comfort to you to have the sort of support we could give: you would be reduced to slavery many times over before any of us got to hear of it! Our advice to you is to submit yourselves to the Athenians, who are your neighbours, and no mean champions of anyone looking for revenge.' The Spartans gave this advice not so much out of goodwill towards the Plataians as because it was their wish to see the Athenians at loggerheads with the Boiotians. The Plataians took it nonetheless; and while the Athenians were making sacrifices to the Twelve Gods,[4] the Plataians came to them as suppliants and sat down by the altar; this meant that they had put themselves in the Athenians' hands. When the Thebans got to hear of this they mounted an expedition against Plataiai, and the Athenians sent an army to defend it. Battle was about to commence when some Corinthians, who happened to be on hand, intervened to stop it: they effected a reconciliation between the two sides, at their request, and fixed the frontier between the two territories. A condition of this was that the Thebans should not interfere with any Boiotians who chose not to be reckoned as part and parcel of Boiotia. After giving this decision the Corinthians left. So too did the Athenians – but on their way they were attacked by the Boiotians. It was the Athenians, though, who successfully defended themselves in the battle, and won it; and having done so they crossed the frontier which the Corinthians had fixed for Plataiai and made the (river) Asopos itself the frontier where Theban territory met that of Plataiai and Hysiai.[5] This then was how and why the Plataians put themselves in the hands of the Athenians; and so it was that they came to support the Athenians at Marathon.[6]

Herodotus VI.108

1 To fight the Persians at Marathon in 490: see **108**.
2 Hdt. gives no date for this, nor even a hint of one; but Thuc. III.68.5 says that
  the capture and destruction of Plataiai by the Spartans in 427 took place in the
  ninety-third year after this alliance with Athens, which would put the alliance
  in 519. (Suggested textual emendations which produce 509, or even 499, are
  unnecessary and improper: see Gomme, *Commentary* II, 358; Forrest, *Sparta*,
  85.)
3 We do not know what Kleomenes was doing or where exactly he was. Jones's
  suggestion of the Megarid (*Sparta*, 49; stated as a fact by Cartledge, *Sparta*,
  144) seems hardly near enough.
4 See **17** n.4.
5 Hysiai: a small Boiotian *polis* to the east of Plataiai (not to be confused with the
  one in Argive territory – see **57**).
6 See n.1.

6 Athens

Athens no less than Sparta lays claim to separate treatment and documentation, at any rate from about the last third of the seventh century. But here the reason is different, and altogether simpler: the richness (comparatively speaking) of the surviving source-material from, or relating to, Athens shows us in greater detail than for any other single *polis* the operation of the factors and developments already outlined (in Chs. 2–4) in general terms. And it must be clearly understood that this is a reflection not so much of any real and actual importance of Athens in the archaic period as of the consuming interest of a later age, of men such as Herodotus, Thucydides and Aristotle, in the origins and early history of a city which *by then*, in its achievements both external and internal, had become something very much out of the ordinary. Little enough of this could have been predicted in the eighth and the seventh centuries, and perhaps not even in the first half of the sixth, when in most respects Athens was seemingly following the trends rather than setting them. We need the benefit of hindsight to appreciate (and dimly enough, even so) just how crucial the sixth century was in bringing Athens and Attika to a point of development – political, social and economic – which, with the stimulus of the Kleisthenic revolution (Ch. 7), led on directly to their fifth-century greatness. The abolition of debt-bondage (**66–67**), for example, can be seen as a major step in the development of Athens as a 'modern' *polis*, to use the terminology of Austin and Vidal-Naquet (*Economy*, 80–1 and 94) – that is to say, one in which the status of different groups in the population was clearly differentiated. And at a more tangible level both Solon and the Peisistratid tyrants took steps to increase the wealth of Attika – both in the traditional and basic area, agriculture (e.g. Plut. *Sol.* 24.1, and **70**), and also in the non-landed sectors which were later to assume such importance (Chs. 15 and 29). In the field of Attic pottery production, for instance, the period saw great advances in both quantity and quality: in the seventh century, the black-figure wares of Corinth were supreme throughout the Greek world, but from *c*.600 this position was steadily eroded by similar products made in Athens; and from *c*.530 the technically more versatile red-figure, an Athenian invention, went on to dominate the next two centuries. (See R. M. Cook, *Greek Painted Pottery* (second edition, London, 1972).)

63. The early constitutional development of Athens

The opening of the Aristotelian *Athenaion Politeia* (*Constitution of the Athenians;* see p.15) is lost, and the first two preserved chapters – or rather a chapter and a fragment – concern the conspiracy of Kylon and its aftermath (see **64** and **66**). In chapter 3, however, the writer reverts to earlier times and gives a brief general survey of Athenian constitutional developments in the archaic period down to the latter part of the seventh century. The *synoikismos* (8), we are to conclude, has taken place, and the main area of change and development is seen as involving the evolution of the collegiate office of the *archontes*.

For the many problems presented by this chapter, see further: Hignett, *Constitution*, 38–85; von Fritz and Kapp, *Aristotle*, 150–2; Moore, *Aristotle*, 210–12.

The ancient *politeia*, before Drakon,[1] was ordered as follows. The officials were appointed on grounds of birth and wealth, and they held office at first for life and later for a term of ten years. The most important of the offices, as well as the earliest, were those of the king (*basileus*) and the *polemarchos* and the *archōn*. The earliest of these was that of the king – which was in fact traditional. Then came a second office, that of the *polemarchos*, introduced because of the military inadequacy of some of the kings;[3] this is why they sent for Ion when a crisis arose.[4] And last was the office of the *archōn*. According to most accounts it was established during the reign of Medon, though some say that of Akastos[5] – citing as proof the fact that the nine *archontes*[6] swear to fulfil their oaths 'as under Akastos', which seems to show that it was in his reign that the descendants of Kodros gave up their monarchy in return for the powers given to the *archōn*. Whichever of the two accounts is true, it makes little difference chronologically. That the office of *archōn* was last (of the three) is clear from the fact that, unlike the king and the *polemarchos*, the *archōn* does not administer any of the traditional duties but only those which were added later. This is why the office became a major one only recently, once it had been enlarged in stature by the additions. As for the *thesmothetai*, they were not (first) elected until many years later, by which time the offices were already annual. Their function was to record the statutes (*thesmia*) and preserve them for the settlement of disputes. It is because of this[7] that this is the only one of the archonships which was never held for longer than a year.

Such then was the chronological sequence of the archonships. And not all of the nine *archontes* lived together. The king occupied what is now called the Boukoleion, near the *prytaneion*: this is shown by the fact that even now the union and marriage of the king's wife with (the god) Dionysos takes place there.[8] The *archōn* had the *prytaneion* (itself), and the *polemarchos* the Epilykeion; this had once been known as the *polemarcheion* but was renamed the Epilykeion after being rebuilt and fitted out by Epilykos after his term as *polemarchos*. As to the *thesmothetai*, they had the *thesmotheteion*. In Solon's time, however,[9] the whole nine came together in the *thesmotheteion*. At that time they were fully competent to judge lawsuits themselves, rather than merely holding the preliminary hearings as they do now.

So much for the position of the officials. As regards the Council of the Areiopagos, it had the task of watching over the *nomoi*, and it enjoyed many important regulatory powers over the *polis* and its affairs by virtue of possessing supreme authority in the punishment and fining of all offenders. The *archontes* were appointed on grounds of birth and wealth, and it was (ex-)*archontes* who made up the Areiopagos. That is why it is the only one of the offices held for life which has survived to the present day.

?Aristotle, *Athenaion Politeia* 3

1 See **65**.
2 This seems to be a rather awkward way of saying that the elective office of king derived directly from the position of the hereditary monarch; note **50** Intro. As Plato put it (*Menexenos* 238D), 'kings are always with us – whether hereditary or elected'.
3 The word means 'war-*archōn*', which may be enough to cast some doubt on the writer's insistence in this passage that the order was king/*polemarchos*/*archōn*; see Hignett, *Constitution*, 42. On the *polemarchos* see further **108**.
4 See Hdt. VIII.44.2.
5 Son of Medon, and grandson of Kodros (see below). On all these Attic kings see Hignett, *Constitution*, 38–46.
6 I.e. the three already mentioned plus the six *thesmothetai* (below).
7 I.e. the relatively late date of their introduction.
8 This symbolic marriage took place each year as part of the Anthesteria festival (see **8** with n.7; not the Great Dionysia, as in von Fritz and Kapp, *Aristotle*, 70, and Moore, *Aristotle*, 212): see Parke, *Festivals*, 112–13, and in general 110–19 on the ceremonial duties of the wife of the *basileus* (*basilinna* or *basilissa*).
9 See **66–67**.

64. Kylon: an unsuccessful attempt at tyranny

By the late seventh century, tyrannies had perhaps been established in several *poleis*, including Athens' southern neighbour Megara (see Ch.4). And Athens, too, was to have its tyrant – but not yet: before the Peisistratidai of the second half of the sixth century (**69–72**) came an Athenian tyranny all the more interesting, to us, because it was a failure. The story was often told (in addition to Herodotus and Thucydides, below, see ?Aristot. *Ath. Pol.* 1 and Plut. *Sol.* 12.1–3); yet none of our sources was in a position to offer real insight into the reasons for Kylon's failure. So as things stand one can hardly better the judicious summing-up in Andrewes, *Tyrants*, 84: 'we know so little of Kylon that we cannot say how far his failure was due to his personal qualities, or to dislike of the support he had from Athens' enemy Megara, but it is evident that Athens had not yet reached a point where it was felt that any alternative was preferable to the continuance of aristocratic government'. See also Forrest, *Emergence*, 145–6; Jeffery, *Archaic Greece*, 87–8.

(A) There was an Athenian called Kylon, an Olympic victor.[1] The man had a high opinion of himself, and of his chances of becoming tyrant; so having formed some of his contemporaries into a body of supporters he made an attempt to seize the Akropolis. When this *coup* failed, he sat as a suppliant for his life at the feet of the statue there, and the presidents of the *naukraroi* – who at that time were the chief executive of Athens[2] – took the whole group, on this understanding, into custody, with a promise to spare their lives. But they were, nonetheless, murdered; and the Alkmaionidai are said to have been responsible.[3] All this took place before the time of Peisistratos.

Herodotus V.71

(B) There was an Athenian called Kylon, an Olympic victor. He belonged to one of the families with a long pedigree of nobility, and was a powerful man in his own right, having married the daughter of the Megarian Theagenes, who at that time was ruling Megara as tyrant. Kylon went to Delphi to consult the oracle, and the response which the god gave him was that he should seize the Akropolis of Athens during 'the greatest festival of Zeus'. He accepted some troops from Theagenes, as well as mobilising the support of his friends, and seized the Akropolis – with a view to setting himself up as tyrant – at the time of the Olympic Games in the Peloponnesos: this, as he saw it, was 'the greatest festival of Zeus', and one with a particular significance for him, as an Olympic victor. Whether this 'greatest festival' might be in Attika, or somewhere else, he did not stop to consider – and the oracle was no help in this. There is in fact an Athenian festival, the Diasia, which is (also) known as the greatest festival of Zeus the Gracious (*Meilichios*); it takes place outside the *polis*, and the whole people make offerings – not blood-sacrifices, but the traditional offerings of Attika.[4] Yet Kylon felt that his own interpretation was the correct one, and so made his attempt. When the Athenians got to hear of it they came in from the countryside in full force to thwart the conspirators, whom they surrounded and besieged (on the Akropolis). As time passed, the Athenians grew tired of the blockade and most

131

of them went away, leaving the nine *archontes* – who were at that time in charge of most of the affairs of the *polis*⁵ – to supervise the siege, with full powers to make whatever settlement they thought best. Kylon and his supporters, meanwhile, were suffering badly from being under siege without food and water. Kylon himself succeeded in escaping, and so did his brother; but the rest, who were in a sorry state and in some cases actually dying of hunger, sat down as suppliants for their life at the altar on the Akropolis. When they saw men dying in the temple, the Athenians who had been posted there as guards took the suppliants into custody with a promise that they would suffer no harm; so they were led away – and murdered. Even those of them who, on their way past, took refuge at the altars of the Dread Goddesses⁶ were killed. It was because of this that the men responsible, and their whole family after them,⁷ were called accursed, and offenders against the goddess.⁸

Thucydides 1.126.3–11

1 His victory was in the thirty-fifth Olympiad, i.e. 640/39. We also know that the *coup* itself was in an Olympic year (see passage B), and before Drakon's legislation (65), the conventional date of which is *c*.621/20.
2 See n.5 below.
3 The Alkmaionidai were a noble Athenian family whose first historically prominent member, the *archōn* Megakles, is made explicitly responsible by sources other than Hdt. (and indeed Thuc.: see B) for the broken promise and the sacrilegious murders: Plut. *Sol.* 12.1–3; Davies, *Families*, 370–1. On the family's wealth see **100**; for a family tree, Fig. 9 on p.133.
4 'The implication is that, if Kylon had chosen this festival he would have found Athens deserted as the populace would have mostly gone outside to take part in the rite of Zeus Meilichios' (Parke, *Festivals*, 120).
5 It is clear that Thuc. is deliberately correcting Hdt. (see A) on this point. The naukraries (*naukrariai*) were primitive local subdivisions of Attika, with, as their name suggests, some sort of responsibility for the provision of ships (see in general Hignett, *Constitution*, 67–74); they, and their officials the *naukraroi*, were largely superseded in the late sixth century by the Kleisthenic demes (see **76**).
6 Otherwise known as the Erinyes (Furies) or Eumenides (Kindly Ones).
7 I.e. the Alkmaionidai (n.3 above).
8 I.e. Athena, to whose statue/altar the suppliants had first turned; compare **92**. See in general J. P. Gould, 'Hiketeia', *JHS* 93 (1973), 74–103.

65. Drakon: the lawgiver

The period of Greek history between *c*.650 and *c*.510 was not only the Age of Tyrants, it was the Age of Lawgivers (*nomothetai*); many *poleis* had a tradition that at this time *nomoi* were given to the community – i.e. committed to a written

The Alkmaionidai

(A simplified stemma; for a full one see Davies, *Families*, 368ff. with Table I)

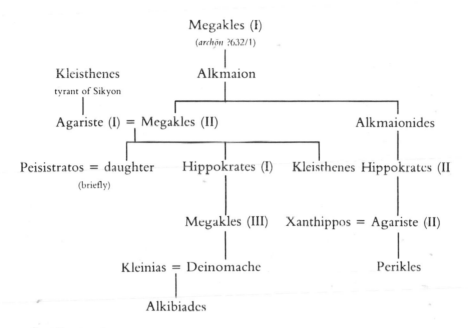

Megakles (I)

(*archōn* ?632/1)

Kleisthenes

tyrant of Sikyon

Alkmaion

Agariste (I) = Megakles (II)

Alkmaionides

Peisistratos = daughter

(briefly)

Hippokrates (I)   Kleisthenes Hippokrates (II

Megakles (III)   Xanthippos = Agariste (II)

Kleinias = Deinomache

Perikles

Alkibiades

y The Alkmaionidai

code – by a lawgiver, so that thenceforth they might be known and accessible to all (see Ch.4 in general, and **40** in particular). In the case of Athens the tradition knew of two such figures, Solon (see **66–68**) and, before him (in *c.*621/20), Drakon. There is no call to doubt the historicity of either of them, though both served, as did the Spartans' Lykourgos (**47**), as convenient names with whom the political propagandists of a later age might associate their anachronistic utopias – or, as the case may be, dystopias: Aristotle (passage A, below) felt obliged to speak out against the tendency to credit Drakon with a full-scale programme of constitutional reform, as opposed simply to a law-code of proverbial severity, and modern scholars widely hold that the 'constitution of Drakon' (passage B) was a product of political pamphleteering in the late fifth century; see for instance Moore, *Aristotle*, 212–14. Nonetheless, the Athenians of 409/8 believed that they were in a position to copy out, and apply, Drakon's law on homicide (passage C).

On the seventh-century context see in general Forrest, *Emergence*, 146–56. On the homicide law (a more elaborate translation of which, giving further detail about the state and layout of the stone itself, may be found as Fornara no. 15), see Hignett, *Constitution*, 305–11; and R. S. Stroud, *Drakon's Law on Homicide* (Berkeley, 1968).

(A) There are *nomoi* of Drakon; but he laid them down for an already-existing *politeia,* and there is no characteristic feature in them which is worth mentioning except their harshness, in the heavy penalties prescribed.[1]

Aristotle, Politics (II) 1274 b 15–18

(B) Not long afterwards,[2] in the archonship of Aristaichmos (621/20), Drakon laid down his statutes (*thesmoi*) in the following manner. A share in the *politeia* had been given (only) to those who provided their own arms and armour. It was they who chose the nine *archontes* and the treasurers, from men who had an unencumbered property-rating of not less than ten minas; the other, lesser officials were drawn from those who provided their own arms and armour;[3] and the *stratēgoi* and cavalry-commanders were men who could declare an unencumbered property-rating of at least 100 minas, as well as legitimate sons, born in wedlock, who were at least ten years of age. The *prytaneis* had to be given sureties for these (newly-elected *stratēgoi* and cavalry-commanders) – and for their predecessors in office as well, until they had come through their audits (*euthynai*)[5] – in the form of four men from the same census-class as themselves. Four hundred and one men, drawn from the citizen-body by lot, were to serve as a *boulē;* everyone aged thirty or over cast lots for membership of it, and for the other offices; and nobody could hold the same office twice until everyone else had held it once – at which point the sortition procedure would start again from the beginning.[6] If any member of the *boulē* failed to attend a session of the *boulē* or *ekklēsia,* he had to pay a fine of three drachmas if he was a *pentakosiomedimnos,* two if he was a *hippeus,* and one if he was a *zeugitēs.*[7] The Council of the Areiopagos was guardian of the *nomoi,*[8] and also supervised the officials to ensure that they discharged their duties in accordance with the *nomoi.* It was open to anyone who was being wronged to lay information before the Council of the Areiopagos, indicating which *nomos* had been infringed in his case. Loans were made on the security of the borrower's person, as stated before,[9] and a few men held all the *chōra.*

?Aristotle, Athenaion Politeia 4

(C) Diognetos of (the deme) Phrearrhioi was secretary; Diokles was *archōn* (409/8). It was resolved by the *boulē* and the *dēmos,* in the *prytaneia* of Akamantis, for which Diognetos was secretary and Euthydikos presided. [. .]e[. .ph]anes proposed: let the Recorders (*anagrapheis*) record the *nomos* of Drakon concerning homicide, when they have received the *nomos* from the king[10] in conjunction with the secretary of the *boulē,* on a stone *stēlē,* and let them set it up in front of the Stoa Basileios. Let the *pōlētai* put this out to contract, as the *nomos* prescribes,[11] and let the Hellēnotamiai provide the money.[12]

First Tablet[13]

Even if without premeditation [someone kills someone, he goes into exile]. The kings[14] are to judge (him) guilty of homicide[15] either [17 letters missing] or him who plotted it; and the *ephetai* are to give the verdict.[16] [Pardon may be granted if the father] is alive, or brothers, or sons, all together; otherwise the one [opposing it shall prevail. If none] of these men is alive, (then by the male relatives) as far as the degree of cousin's son and [cousin, if all] are willing [to pardon.] The one opposing [shall prevail. If not even any of these is alive,] and the killing was involuntary, and it is judged by the (Fifty One,) the *ephetai*, that it was involuntary] homicide, let him be admitted into (Attika) by [ten members of his phratry, if they are willing. These] the Fifty-One [are to choose] according to their merit. [And those also who] were killers in the past [are to be bound by this statute. Let proclamation be made] against the killer [in the] *agora* [(by the male relatives) as far as the degree of cousin's son and cousin. And let the prosecution be mounted jointly by] cousins [and sons of cousins and sons-in-law and fathers-in-law] and members of the phratry [36 letters missing] guilty of homicide [26 letters missing] [the Fifty] One [42 letters missing] of homicide are convicted [35 letters missing]. [If] anyone [kills the murderer or is guilty of (his) homicide, when he has kept away from the *agora*] on the frontier and [(from) the Games and the Amphiktyonic ceremonies,[17] let him be treated on the same terms as he who] has killed an Athenian. The *ephetai* [are to give the verdict.]

Meiggs and Lewis no.86

1 Compare Plut. *Sol.* 17.
2 This presumably means not long after the conspiracy of Kylon – ignoring the intrusion of ch. 3; see **63**.
3 I.e. the citizen-body as a whole, as just defined.
4 Evidently not, at this date, the Kleisthenic tribal committees (see Glossary), but who they are instead is obscure: consult Moore, *Aristotle*, 214.
5 See **52** with n.6; and Hignett, *Constitution*, 203–5.
6 For sortition in fact not fancy see **120**.
7 These census-classes are explained in **67**.
8 Compare **63**.
9 2.2–3; see further **66**.
10 See **63** n.2.
11 Not, of course, the homicide *nomos*. The *pōlētai* were ten officials, one selected by lot from each tribe, whose duties included the contracting out of such services to the community as this: see ?Aristot. *Ath. Pol.* 47.2–3.
12 The Hellēnotamiai: see **130**.
13 At line 56, long after the text has lapsed into illegibility, the rubric 'Second Tablet' can just be made out.

14 It is not certain whether this means the king-archontes (see **63** n.2) of successive years or the *phylobasileis*, 'kings' of the four pre-Kleisthenic tribes (?Aristot. *Ath. Pol* 8.3 and 57.4), or both.

15 Or 'are to decide on the cause of homicide'.

16 The 51 *ephetai* constituted an ancient court of homicide, alongside the Areiopagos: see D. M. MacDowell, *Athenian Homicide Law in the Age of the Orators* (Manchester, 1963), 48–57.

17 Compare Demos. xx.158. On the Amphiktyony see **84.**

66. The economic and political crisis facing Solon

The Athenians seem to have suffered from an economic and political crisis in the last years of the seventh century and the early part of the sixth. What exactly happened is obscure, and one is forced to rely to an uncomfortable extent on extrapolation back from what Solon actually did (see **67**); but with all due caution two central issues can be picked out: pressure, particularly from those who were rich but not noble, for a fresh definition of eligibility for office and power; and discontent, emphasised in the passage given here, with a land-tenure system which kept the poor in a condition, whatever its *precise* nature, little short of slavery.

See in general: Hignett, *Constitution*, 87–9; Forrest, *Emergence*, 147–60; Moore, *Aristotle*, 209–10 and 214–15; and further reading at **67.**

After this[1] there was a long period of *stasis* between the nobles and the masses. This was because the *politeia* was entirely oligarchic – especially so, of course, in that the poor with their children and wives were slaves to the rich. They were known as *pelatai* and *hektēmoroi*, for it was at this rent that they were working the fields of the rich.[2] All the land was in the hands of a few men, and if (the poor) did not pay the rents, they and their children were liable to seizure.[3] Also, all loans were made on the security of the borrower's person – until Solon, that is, who was the first champion of the *dēmos*.[4] So what the majority found the harshest and most intolerable aspect of the *politeia* was their slavery – which is not to say that they did not have other grievances too; for their exclusion was, in a word, total.

(5) So with the *politeia* thus ordered, and the many in slavery to the few, the *dēmos* rose up against the nobles. However, after a long period of *stasis* and confrontation the two sides came together and agreed upon the choice of Solon as mediator and *archōn*, and put the *politeia* into his hands.[5] He had by then written the elegiac poem which begins 'When I watch them killing the most ancient land of Ionia,[6] I see it, and my heart lies stricken within me'. In this poem he fights for each side against the other, debating their respective positions, and then urges them to come together and put an end to their rivalry. By birth and reputation Solon

was one of the leading men, though 'middle class' in terms of his property and business activities.[7] All the evidence confirms this, and he himself bears witness to it in the following poem, urging the rich not to be greedy: 'Restrain your mighty hearts in your breasts, you who have pursued every good thing to excess, and let your pride be in moderation; for we shall not succumb to you, and not everything will turn out as you would like.' He always assigns the fundamental responsibility for the *stasis* to the rich. That is why even at the beginning of the elegy he says that what has alarmed him is (their) 'love of money and excessive pride' – the implication being that these had been the cause of the bad feeling.

?Aristotle, *Athenaion Politeia* 2 and 5

1 I.e. Kylon's conspiracy (**64**).
2 The full significance of these terms is in some doubt. *Pelatai* may possibly have the more general connotation of the two. It later came to be a Greek translation and equivalent of the Latin *clientes*, but there may be no true analogy in that, and it must suffice to say that they were in a dependent state, or states, of some sort. *Hektēmoroi* literally means 'sixth-parters': in addition to any other obligations they presumably had to surrender this proportion of the produce of the land they worked (so Plut. *Sol.* 13.2).
3 I.e. sold into slavery.
4 Champion of the *dēmos* (*prostatēs tou dēmou*) was never an official position in Athens, but it is used in the *Ath. Pol.* almost as if it were (see esp. 28.2–3).
5 Solon was *archōn* in 594/3 (or, less probably, 592/1), and the sources associate his measures (**67**) with this year in high office. For the view that they came later, in the 570s, see **68**.
6 See **3**.
7 'Middle class': for an explanation, and justification, of this translation see von Fritz and Kapp, *Aristotle*, 154 n.14.

67. Solon's measures

There are two substantial accounts of Solon's measures to deal with the Athenian economic and political crisis of his day – in ?Aristot. *Ath. Pol.* 6–12 and Plut. *Sol.* 15–25; we give here, in abbreviated form, that of the *Ath. Pol.* Neither version is satisfactory, and both suffer from the characteristic tendency of the Greek tradition to credit figures like Solon with far more than they can ever have done. Both, however, also have a crucial redeeming feature, in the shape of further quoted extracts (compare **66**) from Solon's own poems.

See in general: Hignett, *Constitution*, 89–107; Forrest, *Emergence*, 160–74; Finley, *Early Greece*, 103–5 and 122–5; Andrewes, *Greek Society*, 66–7, 114–20 and *passim* (and *Tyrants*, ch.7); Moore, *Aristotle*, 216–25; Jeffery, *Archaic Greece*, 90–4 and *passim*; Murray, *Early Greece*, ch.11.

Having been given control of affairs, Solon set the *dēmos* free, both

137

immediately and for the future, by forbidding loans on the security of the borrower's person. He laid down *nomoi* and saw to it that debts, both private and public, were cancelled. This was what they call the 'shaking-off of burdens' (*Seisachtheia*), because they shook off the heavy load (of debt) . . .

(7) He established a *politeia* and laid down other *nomoi*; and (from then on) they stopped using the statutes of Drakon, except for the ones concerning homicide. They recorded the *nomoi* on wooden tablets (*kyrbeis*) and set them up in the Stoa Basileios. Everyone swore to observe them. The nine *archontes*, indeed, used to declare under oath at the Stone that they would set up a golden statue if ever they themselves should break any of the *nomoi*; hence the oath, the same one, that they still swear today. Solon made the *nomoi* binding for a hundred years,[1] and ordered the *politeia* in the following way. He divided (the Athenians) into four census-classes – as they had been divided before: *pentakosiomedimnoi, hippeis, zeugitai* and *thetes*.[2] The higher offices[3] – (i.e.) the nine *archontes*, the treasurers, the *poletai*,[4] the Eleven[5] and the *kolakretai*[6] – he gave to the *pentakosiomedimnoi* and *hippeis* and *zeugitai* to fill, assigning offices to each class in accordance with the size of its census. To those in the class of *thetes* he gave only (membership) of the *ekklesia* and *dikasteria*.[7] In order to be classified as a *pentakosiomedimnos* an individual needed to own property with a yield (annually) of 500 *medimnoi* – taking dry and wet together.[8] In the case of the *hippeis* it was 300, though some say that this class was made up of those men who were able to keep horses . . . but the criterion of measures, as for the *pentakosiomedimnoi*, makes better sense. For *zeugitai* the qualification was two hundred (*medimnoi*), dry and wet together. Everyone else went into the class of *thetes*, and were excluded from all offices. As a result, even now when someone is about to draw lots for an office and is asked for his census-rating, he would never say that he was a *thes*.

(8) He made the procedure for filling the offices that of drawing lots amongst candidates nominated beforehand by each of the (four) *phylai*.[9] For the nine *archontes* each *phyle* put up ten nominees, who then took part in the sortition stage; from this is derived the practice, still in use today, of having each *phyle* choose ten men by lot, who then draw lots again.[10] Proof that Solon had (the offices) filled by sortition amongst men from the census-classes is the *nomos* about treasurers, which is still in force even now: it prescribes that treasurers be *pentakosiomedimnoi*, chosen by lot . . . There were four *phylai*, just as before, and four *phylobasileis*[11] . . . He also created a *boule* of 400 – a hundred from each *phyle*.[12] To the Council of the Areiopagos he assigned the task of guarding the *nomoi*, just as before it had been overseer of the *politeia*. It supervised the majority of the most important aspects of life in the *polis*, and had a special

responsibility for the punishment of wrongdoers: it was fully competent to impose fines, and other penalties; the money exacted as fines was deposited on the Akropolis, and the reason why the fine had been imposed was not recorded. The Areiopagos also sat in judgment upon those who had conspired to subvert (the sovereignty) of the *demos*; Solon had laid down a *nomos* prescribing impeachment in such cases. And seeing that, although the *polis* was frequently subject to *stasis*, some of the *politai* were so apathetic as to be happy to accept any outcome of it, he laid down a *nomos* with precisely such people in mind: it stated that anyone who at a time of *stasis* in the *polis* failed to join in the struggle on one side or the other should be deprived of his citizen rights and shut out from the life of the *polis*.[13]

(9) So much for the offices and what he did about them. And it would seem that the three features of Solon's *politeia* which were of most benefit to the *demos* were: first, and foremost, the prohibition of loans on the security of the debtor's person; second, the provision that anyone who wished to do so could seek legal redress on behalf of those who were being wronged; and third, the right of appeal to a *dikastērion*.[14] It is this last which is said to have strengthened the masses more than anything else – for when the *demos* is master of the courts it comes to be master of the *politeia* . . .

(11) When Solon had ordered the *politeia* in the manner described, people used to come up to him and annoy him with criticisms or queries about the *nomoi* . . . For the *demos* had thought that he would order a complete redistribution of property, while the nobles had imagined that he would give them back their traditional position, or make only minor changes in it. But Solon had not yielded to either side; and although he could have set himself up as tyrant, by joining the faction of his choosing, he preferred to incur the hostility of both sides by laying down the *nomoi* best designed to save his country. (12) That this was his policy is universally agreed, and he himself makes the following observations about it in his poems. 'To the *demos* I gave privilege enough, neither detracting from their status nor enhancing it. Those who had power and were admirable in their possessions I took care, equally, not to injure. I stood firm, protecting both sides with the enveloping strength of my shield, and did not allow either to gain an unjust victory .' He also speaks of the cancellation of the debts, and of the men freed from their former slavery by his *seisachtheia*. 'Which of the aims for which I brought the *demos* together did I abandon unaccomplished? Let my witness to this, before Time's tribunal, be the good black earth, great mother of the Olympian gods: I took up the markers (*horoi*) which were fixed on her everywhere, and now she is no more a slave but free. Many men I brought back to Athens, their motherland founded by the gods, after

they had been sold abroad – some unjustly, others justly – and others whose debts had forced them into exile; they no longer spoke the Attic tongue, so widely had they wandered. And those here at home who had the pain of slavery, cowering before their masters' ways, I made free men. All this I achieved by the power of *nomos*, uniting force with justice, and what I had promised I fulfilled. I drafted statutes for bad men and for good alike, with justice set up straight for each. Another man taking up the spur as I did, a greedy man with evil in his heart, would not have held the *dēmos* in check. If I had been willing to do what their enemies then favoured – or else what they wanted done with these enemies – this *polis* would have known many bereavements! That is why I set up a strong defence on all sides, turning like a wolf caught in a pack of hounds . . .'

?Aristotle, Athenaion Politeia 6–12*

1 So too Plut. *Sol.* 25.1; Hdt. 1.29, however, more plausibly says *ten* years.
2 These terms are defined later in the passage. 'As they had been divided before': see **65B**; it is generally felt, however, that Solon was the creator of these quantitatively calibrated census-classes, even if three at least of them (i.e. except the *pentakosiomedimnoi*) were given names already in use.
3 The papyrus text has a lacuna here, obliterating four letters, but this phrase is what the sense requires (rather than 'the *other* offices').
4 See **65** n.9.
5 The Eleven: a board of officials in charge of prisons and the punishment of offenders.
6 The *kōlakretai*: a board of officials with important financial duties in this early period. They were abolished in 411, and their functions assumed by the Hellēnotamiai.
7 Neither this nor any other passage provides actual evidence for jury courts in Solon's day, though on *a priori* grounds their existence is not unlikely.
8 'Dry' produce meant grain, and 'wet' olive oil or wine.
9 Again (compare n.7, above) sortition *may* be anachronistic as early as this – and if so we need not then accept the author's belief that it lapsed under the Peisistratid tyranny (see **120**). Twice in *Politics* ((II) 1273 b 40 and 1274 a 16–17) Aristotle states that Solon had the officials *elected*. For a fair statement of the issues see Moore, *Aristotle*, 220–1.
10 By the classical period there were of course ten *phylai*, not four: see **76**.
11 See **65** with n.14.
12 For the arguments against the historicity of the Solonic *boulē* see Hignett, *Constitution*, 92–6. Not many modern scholars now share his scepticism: see for instance Murray, *Early Greece*, 187–8.
13 Compare Plut. *Sol.* 20.1, and note also Thuc. II.40.2 (see **149**).
14 See n.7, above.

68. Athens after Solon

By his own admission Solon's measures had been a compromise between the extreme, even irreconcilable, demands of very disparate groups in Attic society; and whatever their merit as 'the bare minimum necessary to stave off an imminent revolution' (Hignett, *Constitution*, 106) and whatever their role in the long-term clarification of status-groups within the *polis* (see Austin and Vidal-Naquet, *Economy*, 72), as a solution to the twin and pressing problems of economic inequality and political instability (**66**) they were hardly adequate in themselves. If a peasant, for example, could no longer borrow on the security of his own person he might have little else to offer. So once again *stasis* and dissension broke out; and after the Solonian pseudo-tyranny, the appearance of a genuine *tyrannos* in Athens grew ever more likely.

See further: Hignett, *Constitution*, 108–13; Forrest, *Emergence*, 175–81; and on the passage given here (with which compare Plut. *Sol.* 29), Moore, *Aristotle*, 225–7.

N.B. As already pointed out (**66** n.5), the sources all assume that Solon's measures were carried in, or in association with, the year of his archonship (probably 594/3), and most modern scholars have always followed them in this. But on various chronological grounds it has been argued with some plausibility that the reforms came *c.*15–20 years later, in the 570s (see for instance Hignett, *Constitution*, 316–21; Davies, *Families*, 323; S. Markianos, 'The chronology of the Herodotean Solon', *Historia* 23 (1974), 1–20). This, if it is correct, would make Solon more of an elder statesman – an ex-*archōn* and (therefore) member of the Areiopagos – when called upon to arbitrate in the crisis; also the *stasis* described in the first paragraph of the passage given here would of course be part of that crisis, and not 'after' Solon at all.

After Solon had left,[1] the polis was still in an agitated state. For four years all was peaceful, but in the fifth year after his archonship[2] they did not appoint an *archōn* because of the *stasis*, and four years after that[3] there was again no *archōn* for the same reason. Then, after the same length of time, Damasias was elected *archōn* and kept the office for two years and two months, before being forcibly stripped of it.[4] Then,[5] because of the *stasis* they made the decision to choose ten *archontes* – five from the eupatridai,[6] three from the farmers and two from the craftsmen; and these men held the office for (the remainder of) the year after Damasias. This shows the enormous power of the *archōn*, for it was always round his office that the *stasis* was most clearly concentrated.

The general domestic malaise, however, continued. Some saw the origin and explanation of this in the cancellation of the debts, a measure which had meant that they were now poor. Others were dissatisfied with the *politeia* and how greatly it had changed. Others still were motivated by personal rivalries. There were three factions. The first was that of the Shore, led by Megakles the son of Alkmaion;[7] their aim seemed to be a middle-of-the-road *politeia*. The second was that of the Plain; what they wanted was oligarchy, and their leader was Lykourgos. The third was that of the Uplands, with Peisistratos at its head – the leader most inclined, so it seemed, towards the *dēmos*. His following had been joined, moreover, by those who had lost money through the cancellation of debts, who were now poor, and those who were not of pure (Athenian) descent, who were now afraid.[8] Proof of this lies in the fact that after the expulsion of the tyrants there was a revision of the registers, on the grounds that many men were sharing in the *politeia* who had no right to do so.[9] Each faction derived its name from the regions (of Attika) in which it farmed.[10]

?Aristotle, *Athenaion Politeia* 13

1 For Egypt, according to 11.1. On his ten years of travels see Hdt. 1.29–33 and 86, 11.177, v.113; Plut. *Sol.* 26–28. In the revised chronology (see introduction) this period is *c.*575–*c.*565.
2 I.e. 590/89.
3 I.e. 586/5.
4 I.e. Damasias was in office for 582/1, 581/0 and the first two months of 580/79. Evidently he was trying to launch himself from this position into that of a *tyrannos*.
5 I.e. for the remaining ten months of 580/79.
6 Literally 'the sons of noble fathers', the collective name for the old ruling aristocracy (who before Solon had of course entirely monopolised the archonships).
7 The successful suitor of Agariste of Sikyon (**26**); he was grandson of the *archōn* in the Kylon affair (**64**), son of Alkmaion (**100**), and father of the reformer Kleisthenes (**71** and Ch.7); see Fig. 9 on p.133.
8 See further, on the rise of Peisistratos, **69**.
9 See **78**.
10 This regional explanation of the three factions, while not without its difficulties, may get nearer to the root of their significance than the political interpretation given earlier in the passage; in addition to the works already cited see Andrewes, *Tyrants,* 102–7, and further **69**.

69. The rise of Peisistratos

The inter-factional strife described in **68** led directly to tyranny. Once firmly in power, the rule of Peisistratos and his sons (**70–72**) lasted for 36 years in all, but initially Peisistratos – like Kylon before him – had encountered opposition and failure, and had succeeded in establishing himself only at the third attempt. We give here the earliest and fullest account, that of Herodotus; compare ?Aristot. *Ath. Pol.* 14–15 and Plut. *Sol.* 30–31.2.

See further: Hignett, *Constitution,* 113–14; Andrewes, *Tyrants,* 100–1; Jeffery, *Archaic Greece,* 94–5.

Attika, Kroisos discovered,[1] was repressed and fragmented under the rule, at that time, of Peisistratos the son of Hippokrates as tyrant in Athens.[2] An extraordinary portent had occurred when this Hippokrates, in a private capacity, had attended the Olympic Games: when he had killed the beasts for his sacrifice, the cauldrons with the flesh and water in them boiled over – before he had lit the fire under them! Chilon the Lakedaimonian happened to be nearby, and when he saw this marvel he urged Hippokrates not to marry a wife who would bear him sons; if he had one already he should divorce her, and if he had a son already he should disown him. But Hippokrates was not prepared to take this advice from Chilon; and subsequently he did have a son, this Peisistratos.[3] And when the Athenians were in a state of *stasis* between the men of the Shore and of the Plain, led respectively by Megakles the son of Alkmaion and Lykourgos the son of Aristolaides, Peisistratos made up his mind to become tyrant and formed a third faction, collecting supporters together and representing himself as champion of the Uplanders.[4] This was the plan he contrived: he gave himself and his mules some cuts and bruises and drove his cart into the *agora*, where he claimed that he had escaped from his enemies who had tried to murder him as he was driving into the countryside. He then asked the *dēmos* to grant him a bodyguard. Since this was the man who had already won a fine reputation in his command against the Megarians, when amongst his great successes had been the capture of Nisaia,[5] the Athenian *dēmos* fell for the trick and granted him a picked citizen bodyguard; they became Peisistratos' Club-bearers, rather than Spear-bearers, because they followed him around armed with wooden clubs.[6] And with their support Peisistratos was able to seize the Akropolis – which of course instantly made him master of Athens. He did not disturb the existing offices or make changes in the statutes but governed the *polis* peacefully, fairly and well on the basis of the *status quo*.[7]

(60) Not long afterwards, however, the supporters of Megakles and of Lykourgos came to an agreement and drove him out. Thus in his first period as tyrant in Athens Peisistratos lost his position because it had not yet firmly taken root. But those who had driven Peisistratos out then began a second, fresh phase of *stasis* between themselves, and when Megakles found himself getting the worst of it he sent messages to Peisistratos proposing to re-establish him as tyrant if he were willing to marry his daughter. Peisistratos agreed to this; and then, to effect his return, the two of them contrived by far the silliest scheme I have ever come across. From earliest times the Greeks have been cleverer and less susceptible to silly foolishness than the *barbaroi*; this is what has set them apart; and yet on this occasion it was on the Athenians, supposedly the wisest of all Greeks, that this trick was played. This is what happened. In

the village of Paiania there was a woman called Phye, almost six feet tall and a great beauty besides. They equipped her with a full set of arms and armour, put her in a chariot, and coached her in gestures and attitudes best suited to the role she had to play; then they drove her into the *astu*. Heralds had meanwhile been sent on ahead to the *astu*, where, as instructed, they made the following announcement: 'Be glad, Athenians, to welcome Peisistratos! Athena herself has honoured him above all mortal men, and she is bringing him home to her own Akropolis!' That is what the heralds went about saying, and very shortly a rumour reached the (rural) demes that Athena was bringing Peisistratos home; so the men of the *astu*, too, became convinced that Phye was actually the goddess, offered this mortal woman their prayers, and took Peisistratos back.

(61) Having recovered his position as tyrant in the manner described, Peisistratos fulfilled his agreement with Megakles and married his daughter. However, as he already had grown-up sons,[8] and also because the Alkmaionidai were said to be cursed,[9] he did not wish to have children by his new wife, and so avoided normal sexual intercourse when he slept with her. At first the wife kept this a secret, but eventually she told her mother – possibly because the mother had asked her straight out – and the mother then told her husband, Megakles. Megakles took Peisistratos' action as an insult, and was so upset and angry about it as to seek out his rivals and put an end to the feuding between them. When Peisistratos got to hear of this measure taken against him, he left Attika altogether and went to Eretria, where he and his sons discussed what was to be done. Hippias' opinion was that they should try to regain the tyranny, and this was the view which prevailed, so they began to collect gifts and contributions from the *poleis* which were at all favourable to their cause. Many offered large sums, with no gifts surpassing those from the Thebans. And finally – to cut a long story short – the time for planning was over and all was ready for the return to Attika: Argive mercenaries had arrived from the Peloponnesos; and a man from Naxos, called Lygdamis, had chosen to turn up with an enthusiastic offer to provide both money and men. (62) So they started off from Eretria and returned to Attika ten years after they had left[10] . . .

(64) Thus Peisistratos gained possession of Athens for the third time; and he now laid firm foundations for his rule as tyrant by hiring (more) mercenaries and by raising revenues – partly in Attika itself and partly from his river Strymon possessions.[11] He also took as hostages the sons of those Athenians who had remained in Attika and not immediately fled, and sent them to Naxos; the island had succumbed to an attack from Peisistratos, who had set up Lygdamis in power there. In addition he fulfilled oracular prescriptions by purifying the island of Delos: all

corpses buried within sight of the temple were dug up and reburied in another part of the island.[12] Thus Peisistratos ruled as tyrant in Athens; and as to (the rest of) the Athenians, some had been killed in the battle,[13] and others left their homes and fled with the Alkmaionidai.

Herodotus 1.59–62.1 and 65

1 See **47** with n.2.
2 This is how it may have been represented to Kroisos. For Hdt.'s own view see below, with n.7 (and compare **70**).
3 Chilon was eponymous *ephoros* at Sparta in *c.*556 (see **58** Intro.). Peisistratos was born in 600 or earlier (Davies, *Families*, 445). It is therefore almost inconceivable (*pace* Jones, *Sparta*, 173) that this story of Chilon and Hippokrates can be true.
4 Hdt.'s word is *hyperakrioi*, whereas the *Ath. Pol* (13.4) and Plut. (*Sol.* 29.1) have *diakrioi*. Any difference in nuance seems less important than the fact – according to Hdt. – that Peisistratos formed his faction when the other two were already in existence. Hignett's statement that Peisistratos and his supporters broke away from the Shore group (*Constitution*, 110) is conjecture.
5 This war against Megara should probably be dated in the mid 560s. It is the usual assumption that Peisistratos was *polemarchos* at the time.
6 Spear-bearers (*doryphoroi*) were the usual bodyguard for a tyrant.
7 This verdict must apply to Peisistratos' rule as a whole, not merely this first short period in power. For the chronology see n.10, below.
8 See **72**, and below. On Peisistratos' marriages and children see Davies, *Families*, 445–50.
9 Because of the Kylon affair; see **64**.
10 The chronology of these years is enormously problematical, chiefly because of dates in *Ath. Pol.* 14–15 which are almost certainly wrongly transmitted; see on this Moore, *Aristotle*, 227–8. We must work backwards from the expulsion of Hippias in 510 (**74**): 36 years of continuous Peisistratid rule (Hdt. v.65.3; ?Aristot. *Ath. Pol.* 17.1 and 19.6; 35 in Aristot. *Pol.* (v)1315 b 30–34) puts the return from Eretria in *c.*546; the quarrel with Megakles is thus *c.*556, and the first and second periods in power between *c.*561/60 and *c.*556. Consult Hignett, *Constitution*, 113–14; Davies, *Families*, 444–5; J. G. F. Hind, 'The "Tyrannis" and the exiles of Peisistratos', *CQ* n.s.24 (1974), 1–18
11 In Thrake. See **132A**.
12 For the more elaborate purification in 426/5 see Thuc. III.104.
13 At Pallene, between Marathon and Athens: see chs.62–63, omitted here.

70. The character and content of Peisistratos' tyranny

Herodotus' view of the behaviour and policies of Peisistratos as tyrant (see **69** with n.7) is confirmed and elaborated by other sources, including Thucydides (see **72** Intro.) and, in the passage given here, the Aristotelian *Ath. Pol.* Although many Greek *tyrannoi* acted hardly at all tyrannically in the modern sense, it was nonetheless true, almost by definition, that a *tyrannos* was a man who, having come to power either unconstitutionally or at least irregularly, continued thereafter to act either unconstitutionally or at least irregularly as a mode of government. The striking thing about Peisistratos, as our sources see it, is that in this respect he behaved not merely unlike a 'tyrant' but unlike even a *tyrannos*. (On the alleged change for the worse, in the second generation, see **72**.) That apart, the concrete evidence that we possess – and in fact there is little enough of it – points to a genuine basis of consensus underlying Peisistratid rule and to real and lasting achievement in two areas above all: public works (compare **32**), and the encouragement of cults and festivals with a significance for the *polis* as a whole.

See further: Hignett, *Constitution*, 114–23; Andrewes, *Tyrants*, 107–14; Forrest, *Emergence*, 181–9; Moore, *Aristotle*, 229–31. On the buildings see particularly J. S. Boersma, *Athenian Building Policy from 561/0 to 405/4* (Groningen, 1970), chs. 2–3, and Murray, *Early Greece*, 229. On the cults see particularly Parke, *Festivals*, 33–50 (the Panathenaia), 125–36 (the Dionysia) and 144 (the Olympeia).

As previously stated,[1] Peisistratos was moderate in his government of the *polis* and its affairs, and acted constitutionally rather than like a tyrant. He was always benevolent and mild, ready to forgive those who did wrong; and what is more he loaned money to the poor to further their work, so that they could make a living by farming. This he did for two reasons: to have them spread around the *chōra*, rather than spending their time in the *astu*, and to make them comfortably off and occupied with their own concerns, so that they would have neither the inclination nor the time to interest themselves with public affairs. And at the same time this cultivation of the *chōra* served to bring him in larger revenues, for he levied a tax of 10 per cent on its produce. It was for this reason also – so that people should not come in to the *astu*, and so neglect their work – that he appointed judges to tour the demes;[2] and he himself used often to go out into the *chōra*, to see what was going on there and to settle disputes. It was during one of these excursions of his, so they say, that there occurred the episode of the man farming on (Mount) Hymettos, and what later came to be known as the Taxfree Estate. What happened was that Peisistratos saw a man who was labouring to dig ground that was nothing but stones. This amazed him, so he told his slave to ask what the estate yielded. 'Aches and pains,' the man replied; 'and Peisistratos ought to take his 10 per cent of *them*!' The fellow gave this answer in ignorance of whom he was speaking to; but Peisistratos was pleased with his frankness as well as his appetite for hard work, and exempted him from all taxes. And in general Peisistratos did not impose heavy burdens on the Athenians while he was in power, but always secured and maintained peace and tranquillity. As a result it became a cliché to call the tyranny of Peisistratos the Golden Age;[3] for later, when his sons succeeded to his position, their rule was much harsher.[4] But of all his qualities which are mentioned, the greatest was his naturally benevolent concern for the *dēmos*. What he wanted was always to govern in accordance with the *nomoi*, and without giving himself an unfair advantage. On one occasion, when he was summoned to appear before the Areiopagos on a charge of homicide, he went in person to defend himself – which so alarmed his accuser that the case was dropped! This explains why he stayed in power so long, and recovered it so easily when he was expelled: the fact was that he was supported by the majority both of the nobles, with whom he naturally associated, and of the *dēmos*, whom he helped in their private affairs; and to both groups he was equally attentive[5] . . . (17) So Peisistratos grew old in office, and then fell ill and died in the archonship of Philoneus (528/7). He had lived for 33 years after first establishing himself as *tyrannos*; nineteen of those years had been spent in power, the rest in exile.[6]

?Aristotle, *Athenaion Politeia* 16.2–9 and 17.1

1 In 14.3.
2 See further **125** and **311**.
3 Literally 'life under Kronos'. The connection of Kronos, father of Zeus, with a Golden Age of happiness for mankind first appears in Hesiod, *Works and Days* line 111.
4 But see 19.1 (**72**) for the view, almost certainly correct, that this change occurred only after one of the sons had been assassinated.
5 Compare Aristot. *Pol* (v)1314 b 36 1315 a 31.
6 See **69** n.10.

71. The archōn-list, 527/6–522/1

According to Thucydides, Athens under the sons of Peisistratos 'generally employed the pre-existing *nomoi*, except in so far as (the tyrants) always saw to it that there was one of their own people in office' (VI.54.6). No corroboration of such an obvious policy would be required in order for us to believe it, but corroboration is in fact strikingly provided by a fragment of the list of eponymous *archontes*, as reconstructed and inscribed in Athens in *c*.425. The fragment in question covers the six years immediately following the death of Peisistratos himself, in 528/7. Its general implications are succinctly discussed by Andrewes, *Tyrants*, 109–11; for the specific individuals concerned see the notes below.

[On]eto[rides][1]	(527/6)
[H]ippia[s][2]	(526/5)
[K]leisthen[es][3]	(525/4)
[M]iltiades[4]	(524/3)
[Ka]lliades[5]	(523/2)
[Peisi]strat[os][6]	(522/1)

Meiggs and Lewis no.6(c)

1 This restoration is to be preferred to the only other alternative to it, [On]eto[r]: see Meiggs and Lewis *ad loc.* (p.11); Davies, *Families*, 421. But the man is in any case unknown.

2 The eldest son of Peisistratos, and now *tyrannos* himself. See further **72, 74, 104, 108.**

3 The alternative [P]leisthen[es] is too rare a name to be seriously entertained, so this must indeed be Kleisthenes, head of the family of the Alkmaionidai in succession to his father Megakles (**68–69**) and ultimately to be a constitutional reformer (Ch.7); see Fig. 9 on p.133. As the commentators have noted, this proof that he was in Athens, and in good odour with the tyrants, in the 520s is little short of spectacular, as Herodotus was led to believe that the Alkmaionidai were in continuous exile between 546 and 510 (1.64.3 (see **69**, end) and VI.123.1).

4 See **101, 106, 108.** Note that this is the chronological anchor for the list, as Miltiades is known to have been *archōn* in the first year of the sixty-fourth Olympiad, i.e. 524/3 (T. J. Cadoux, *JHS* 68 (1948), 110 n.216).

5 This is too common a name – in upper-class circles – for the man to be identified, 'but we may fairly judge his importance from the company in which we find him' (Andrewes, *Tyrants*, 110).

6 If this restoration is correct, the man is Peisistratos, the grandson of his namesake and son (probably the eldest) of Hippias. Thucydides speaks of his archonship, and of a dedication, during his year in office, of two altars; and for one of them, to Apollo, he quotes the dedicatory inscription (VI.54.6–7). As it happens this very stone has survived (Meiggs and Lewis no.11; Fornara no.37). It presents certain difficulties, chiefly in that its letter-forms seem to some epigraphists more suited to the early fifth century than the 520s; but on balance this cannot be decisive. Consult Gomme, *Commentary* IV,330–3; Davies, *Families*, 450–1.

72. The sons of Peisistratos

Peisistratos, like tyrants elsewhere before him, had succeeded in turning his unconstitutional position as *tyrannos* into a hereditary dynasty; and, as we have just seen (**71**), some at least of the men who might have opposed this were, on the contrary, willing enough at first to be associated with the rule of Hippias. However, during what proved to be the last decade of the tyranny, there was perhaps increasing opposition to it: general revulsion was probably felt as a result of the repression which followed the assassination in 514 of Peisistratos' second son, Hipparchos, though an aristocratic attempt against the tyranny still failed at the battle of Leipsydrion (see **74**). We have several accounts of the assassination – chiefly in Herodotus (V.55–56), Thucydides (I.20.1–2 and VI.54–59) and the Aristotelian *Ath. Pol.* (below) – and the ingredient of polemic and controversy, especially in Thucydides' version, stands out clearly. Evidently the story was distorted in transmission, sometimes by sources which themselves no longer survive. Most of the errors in the different versions are fairly easy to correct;

what is less obvious is the reason why so much confusion and obfuscation arose at all. Their ultimate origin may have been a partisan desire to highlight *either* the murder of Hipparchos *or* the expulsion of Hippias, four years later (see **73–74**), as *the* effective end of the tyranny – both versions being pressed all the more insistently not only against each other but also against the unpalatable truth that the decisive role was actually played by the Spartans (see **74**).

See further: Gomme, *Commentary* IV, 317–29; Davies, *Families*, 446–8; Moore, *Aristotle*, 231–3; Jeffery, *Archaic Greece*, 98–9. It is in any case important to remember that Hippias survived in power for nearly twenty years and, without Sparta, might have survived even longer.

After the death of Peisistratos his sons held on to power and managed affairs in the same way. There were two sons, Hippias and Hipparchos, by his Athenian wife, and two by his Argive wife – Iophon and Hegesistratos, who had the surname Thettalos.[1] For Peisistratos had married a woman from Argos, Timonassa, daughter of an Argive called Gorgilos; she had previously been the wife of Archinos of Amprakia, of the family of the Kypselidai.[2] And a result of this marriage was Peisistratos' friendship with Argos: Hegesistratos brought a thousand Argives to fight on his side at the battle of Pallene.[3] According to some accounts he married this Argive woman after he had been expelled for the first time, though others maintain that it was while he was in power.

(18) By virtue of their position and their age, Hipparchos and Hippias were (both) responsible for state affairs. Hippias, however, as the elder of the two and also a natural politician and man of sense, actually presided over the government; Hipparchos preferred to amuse himself with love-affairs and in fostering the arts; he it was who sent for the poets and their entourages – Anakreon and Simonides and the rest.[4] As for Thettalos, he was much younger, and rash and insolent in his life-style; and this was the origin of all their troubles. What happened was that Thettalos fell in love with Harmodios, but was quite unable to win his friendship. This made him uncontrollably angry, and he made his bitterness clear in all sorts of ways, culminating in a refusal to allow Harmodios' sister to be a basket-bearer, as she was intending to be, at the Panathenaia.[5] He also insulted Harmodios by calling him effeminate. So Harmodios and Aristogeiton were provoked into their famous deed, in which many others had a share. During the Panathenaia, as they were lying in wait on the Akropolis for Hippias – for it had fallen to him to welcome the procession there, once Hipparchos had sent it on its way – they saw one of their fellow-conspirators go up and give Hippias a friendly greeting. They thought themselves betrayed at this; and in their wish to accomplish something, at least, before being arrested, they went down and killed Hipparchos as he was organising the procession by the Leokoreion. They did this without waiting for the others, and thereby

ruined the whole enterprise: Harmodios was killed on the spot by the bodyguards; Aristogeiton was captured later and tortured for a long time. Under torture he made accusations against many men who came from well-known families and were friends of the tyrants. Initially his inquisitors had been unable to find any trace of the plot – for the story one hears, that Hippias had disarmed the people taking part in the procession and had searched out those who were carrying daggers, is untrue: it was not until later, under the democracy, that the carrying of arms in the procession was instituted. Why did Aristogeiton accuse the tyrant's friends? Deliberately, says the democratic point of view, so that by killing innocent men who were their own friends they would offend the gods and weaken themselves at the same time. The alternative version has it that Aristogeiton was not inventing his story but really was betraying his accomplices. In the end, when all his attempts to die had failed, he announced that he would reveal many more names; and having persuaded Hippias to give him his right hand as a token of good faith he then abused him for having given his right hand to his brother's murderer. This so infuriated Hippias that in an uncontrollable fit of rage he drew his dagger and killed him. (19) And after this the tyranny became much harsher: to avenge his brother, Hippias killed and exiled many men, and so became universally mistrusted and hated.

?Aristotle, *Athenaion Politeia* 17.3–19.1

1 Not so: Thettalos was a distinct person, and full brother to Hippias and Hipparchos. See Gomme, *Commentary* IV,333; Davies, *Families*, 448–50.
2 The tyrants of Corinth (**27**).
3 See **69**.
4 Anakreon of Teos (born *c.*570), Simonides of Keos (*c.*556–468); both spent periods at the 'courts' of several tyrants and kings. 'The rest' include Lasos of Hermione (Hdt. VII.6). It was a feature of both tyrannies and oligarchies to foster such 'traditional' poetry and other arts; compare **29**.
5 See Parke, *Festivals*, 43–4. According to Thucydides (VI.54–55) the brother who fell in love with Harmodios was Hipparchos.

73. The Harmodios drinking-song

The view that, by murdering Hipparchos, Harmodios and Aristogeiton had not simply killed the tyrant's younger brother but destroyed the tyranny itself (see **72**) gained ground spectacularly in the fifth century, on both the official and the unofficial levels – becoming, and remaining throughout the classical period, what from all points of view can only be called a cult: see C. W. Fornara, 'The cult of Harmodios and Aristogeiton', *Philologus* 114 (1970), 155–80. As far as official public commemoration went, in addition to such things as annual offerings to the two heroes by the *polemarchos* (?Aristot. *Ath. Pol.* 58.1), more concrete recognition came in the form of perpetual maintenance at state expense for their descendants (*IG* I² 77, lines 4–9 (see M. Ostwald, *American Journal of Philology* 72 (1951), 24–46, esp. 32–5); Isaeus V.47 (which also mentions *proedriai* (50n.3) and tax-exemptions); Dinarchus I.101. Note also Plut. *Arist.* 27.4, on Aristogeiton's granddaughter.). And on another level there were the drinking-songs (*skolia*). In the comedies of Aristophanes, staged in the last quarter of the fifth century, there are several references to an evidently well-known song about Harmodios and Aristogeiton (*Ach.* 980 and 1093, *Wasps* 1225, *Lys.* 631–633), and four variants of it survived to be quoted in the late second century A.D. by Athenaeus.

> In a branch of myrtle I shall carry my sword,
> Like Harmodios and Aristogeiton
> When they killed the tyrant
> And made Athens a place of equal rights (*isonomia*).[1]

> Dearest Harmodios, you are surely not dead.
> They say you are in the Islands of the Blest,[2]
> Where swift-footed Achilles (lives)
> And, they say, brave Diomedes, son of Tydeus.[3]

> In a branch of myrtle I shall carry my sword,
> Like Harmodios and Aristogeiton
> When at Athena's festival
> They killed the tyrant Hipparchos.

> Your fame will always live on earth,
> Dearest Harmodios and Aristogeiton,
> Because you killed the tyrant
> And made Athens a place of equal rights.
> Athenaeus 695A–B (=D. L. Page, *Poetae Melici Graeci* nos. 893–6)

1 The *nomos*-element in the word might make 'equality under the law' a better translation. Compare the usage in Hdt. III.80.6 and 83.1 (see **89**), III.143.2, V.37.2; Thuc. III.82.8, IV.78.3. See M. Ostwald, *Nomos and the Beginnings of the Athenian Democracy* (Oxford, 1969), 96ff.
2 See Hesiod, *Works and Days* 171; Hdt. III.26.1.
3 See **5**.

7 Kleisthenes and the demos

The last decade of the sixth century was a momentous one in Athenian history. In 510 two generations of Peisistratid rule came to an end, hastened by the intervention of the Spartans (**74**). In its place, inter-factional politics returned, of a type familiar enough in the first half of the century (**68–69**) but almost forgotten, inevitably, during the period of the tyranny. One of the protagonists, Isagoras, secured a temporary advantage over his rival, the Alkmaionid Kleisthenes, by invoking once again Spartan *force majeure* (**75**). But Kleisthenes' riposte – to widen, unprecedentedly, the entire basis of the political argument – was on a different level altogether; and whether or not he himself realised in full the implications and potential of what he then went on to do (**76–80**), its effect was to mark out these years, for Athens and Attika, as the real pivot between the archaic and the classical periods. The reforms of Kleisthenes, like those of Solon, had their application on several levels, of which the narrowly political, the preoccupation of the ancients them-selves (**80**), is perhaps not the most important. True, the partnership in government between his new *boulē* (**77**) and the *ekklēsia* was to be at the very centre of the evolution of radical Athenian democracy in the fifth and fourth centuries, but it is that extraordinary process itself (charted in Chs. 11, 21 and 31) which calls for a more fundamental explanation than the development of constitutional machinery – which is not so much cause as effect. So in attempting to understand *why*, ultimately, it was so obvious to an observer like Herodotus (see **75**, end) that the Kleisthenic reforms wrought a genuine transformation in the Athenians, one returns to Kleisthenes himself, and to two cardinal points in the 'intellectual coherence' (Murray, *Early Greece*, 258) of his measures: a renewed emphasis on law, *nomos*, as both the guarantee and the expression of equality (see in general M. Ostwald, *Nomos and the Beginnings of the Athenian Democracy* (Oxford, 1969); and **73**, above); and, as the French scholars P. Lévêque and P. Vidal-Naquet have emphasised (*Clisthène l'Athénien* (Paris, 1964)), a restructuring of Attika so rigorous (see **76**) as to be tantamount to a second foundation.

74. The expulsion of Hippias

All our principal sources agree that after the murder of Hipparchos (72–73)
Hippias' rule turned, not altogether surprisingly, into a tyranny in the modern
(and indeed later Greek) sense. We read for instance in the Aristotelian *Ath. Pol.*
19.2 that by 511, three years after the assassination, Hippias had become so
unpopular in Athens itself that he was in the process of building himself a fortress
down at Mounychia, by the sea. This represented the climax, very nearly, of a
military and diplomatic campaign against him which had been mounted for at
least the preceding two years by the family of the Alkmaionidai, and in which, as
this passage of Herodotus makes clear, a crucial role was played by the oracle at
Delphi. For another account see ?Aristotle, *Ath. Pol.* 19.2–6.
    See further: Hignett, *Constitution*, 124–5; Moore, *Aristotle*, 233–5; Jeffery,
Archaic Greece, 99–100; Cartledge, *Sparta*, 146, Murray, *Early Greece*, 250.

I must now resume the story that I was originally about to tell – how the
Athenians were liberated from their tyrants. The murder of Hipparchos
was causing the tyrant Hippias to act harshly towards the Athenians; so
the Alkmaionidai, an Athenian family which had gone into exile under
the Peisistratidai,[1] attempted with the other banished Athenians to force
their way back. But their efforts to return and free Athens, by fortifying
Leipsydrion above Paionia, failed badly.[2] So then, in their search for any
and every scheme to use against the Peisistratidai, the Alkmaionidai
procured a contract from the Amphiktyones to build the temple at
Delphi – the one which is there now but at that time did not yet exist.[3]
Since the family had become a rich one,[4] as well as always having been
held in high esteem, the temple which they built was in many respects
superior to that which the plan had specified, chiefly in that whereas they
had agreed to build the temple of limestone they actually used, for its
front part, Parian marble. (63) Now the Athenians of course maintain
that while these men were based at Delphi they bribed the priestess to
urge any Spartans who came to consult the oracle, whether on private or
public business, to 'liberate Athens'. It was always this same response; so
the Spartans sent out an army under the command of one of their leading
men, Anchimolios the son of Aster, to expel the Peisistratidai from
Athens (c.512). This they did despite the fact that they had particularly
close ties of *xenia* with the Peisistratidai, for they were men for whom
human demands took second place to divine; so the army was put on
board ship and sent off. Anchimolios naturally made his landfall at
Phaleron[5] and disembarked his forces there. The Peisistratidai, however,
had known of this plan in advance and had requested help from the
Thessalians, with whom they had an alliance; the Thessalians had
answered this by joining forces to send a thousand cavalrymen under the
command of their king, Kineas of Konde; and when these allies had

arrived, the Peisistratidai had conceived the plan of cutting down the trees and crops in the plain of Phaleron and so making it good terrain for horses. So now they launched this cavalry against the Spartan army. Many Spartans were killed in the attack, including Anchimolios himself, and the survivors were driven back to their ships.

That then was the end of the first Spartan expedition; and Anchimolios was buried in Attika at Alopeke, near the temple of Herakles in Kynosarges. (64) However, subsequently (510) the Spartans mobilised and sent out against Athens a larger army, appointing their king Kleomenes the son of Anaxandridas to command it. This force did not go by sea, but overland. As soon as it had crossed into Attic territory the Thessalian cavalry was there to meet it – but they were very soon overwhelmed and 40 of them killed; and the remainder promptly set off back to Thessaly. Kleomenes then proceeded to the *astu* itself, accompanied by those Athenians who wanted their freedom, drove the tyrants back behind the Pelargic Wall[6] and besieged them there. (65) Now the Spartans had not come prepared for a blockade, whereas the Peisistratidai had ample stocks of food and drink; so the Spartans would never conceivably have captured them – they would have gone back to Sparta after maintaining the siege for a few days – had it not been for a chance incident which was as helpful to them as it was harmful to the Peisistratidai. What happened was that the children of the Peisistratid family were captured as they were being smuggled out of the country. This threw all their plans into confusion, and to recover the children they had to pay the price which (the rest of) the Athenians set – that of quitting Attika within five days. Later they withdrew to Sigeion, on the (river) Skamandros.[7] They had ruled Athens for 36 years.[8]

Herodotus v,62–65.3

1 Whatever the intended connotation of 'Peisistratidai' (i.e. including or excluding Peisistratos himself), this statement is misleading as it stands, given Kleisthenes' archonship in 525/4 (**71** with n.3). Presumably the family, with others, went into exile again in or after 514.

2 Probably in 513. Leipsydrion is a village in northern Attika on the slopes of Mt Parnes (and north of the better-known Paionia); no doubt the exiles crossed to it from Boiotia. For the drinking-song (*skolion*) lamenting this defeat see Murray, *Early Greece*, 254.

3 Apollo's temple at Delphi had been accidentally destroyed by fire in c.548 (Hdt. II.180). The Amphiktyones: see **84**. For the spectacular growth of Delphi in this period see Fig. 10.

4 See **100**.

5 At this time (before the development of Peiraieus: **159**) the open bay of Phaleron was Athens' principal harbour.

6 On the Akropolis.

7 In Asia Minor, on the Hellespontos; compare Hdt. v.93–94.
8 I.e. the family as a whole, 546–510: see **69** n.10.

75. Kleisthenes and Isagoras

By expelling Hippias (**74**) the Spartans lent substance to their later reputation as opponents of tyranny (see **60**); and they seem to have been prepared at first to allow the Athenians to decide for themselves what mode of government, and of political behaviour, should replace it. Before long, however, Kleomenes felt impelled to intervene again – and by so doing he initiated a turn of events over the next four or five years which Herodotus saw as bringing Athens into the very front rank of Greek *poleis*. Compare the version in ?Aristot. *Ath. Pol.* 20; and see further Hignett, *Constitution*, 125–8; Moore, *Aristotle*, 235–6; Cartledge, *Sparta*, 147.

Athens had been great before, but became still greater once she was freed from the tyrants. Two powerful men were now predominant: Kleisthenes the Alkmaionid – the man who is said to have bribed the priestess at Delphi[1] – and Isagoras the son of Teisandros, who belonged to one of the leading families, which offers sacrifice to Karian Zeus, though I can discover nothing of its origins. These two men began a struggle for power against each other, and when Kleisthenes was getting the worst of it[2] he added the (entire) *dēmos* to his body of supporters. And subsequently he changed the number of *phylai* in Athens from four to ten,[3] doing away with the names deriving from the sons of Ion – the Geleontes, Aigikoreis, Argadeis and Hopletes[4] – and devising (ten) new names, from heroes, all of them native Athenians except for Aias, who as a neighbour and ally counted as a *xenos*.[5] (**69**) Now of course the Athenian Kleisthenes was the grandson and namesake of Kleisthenes of Sikyon;[6] and my opinion is that the grandson imitated his namesake, because he too despised the Ionians and did not wish his *phylai* to be the same as theirs. That is obviously why, when he had secured the support of the *dēmos*, which until that time had had no share in anything at all, he gave the *phylai* new names and increased them in number. And naturally he also created ten tribal presidents (*phylarchoi*) instead of four, and assigned the demes to the *phylai* in ten groups.[7]

(**70**) Having gained the backing of the *dēmos* Kleisthenes was much stronger than his rivals, so it was now the turn of Isagoras to be on the losing side and to plan how to counter it. And what he did was to appeal to Kleomenes the Spartan, who had been his *xenos* since the blockade of the Peisistratidai; in fact the accusation had been made that Kleomenes was seducing Isagoras' wife. Kleomenes began by sending a herald to Athens demanding the expulsion of Kleisthenes and many other Athenians with him – 'the Accursed', as he called them. Isagoras had

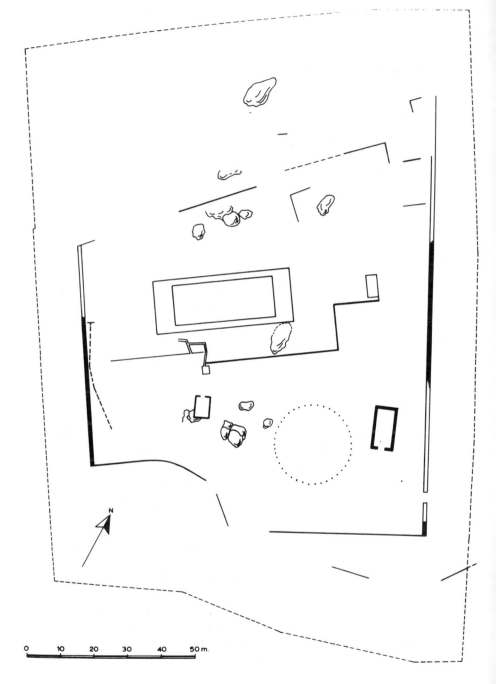

0   10   20   30   40   50 m.

10 The growth of Delphi (*BCH* 93 (1969), 733 and 743)

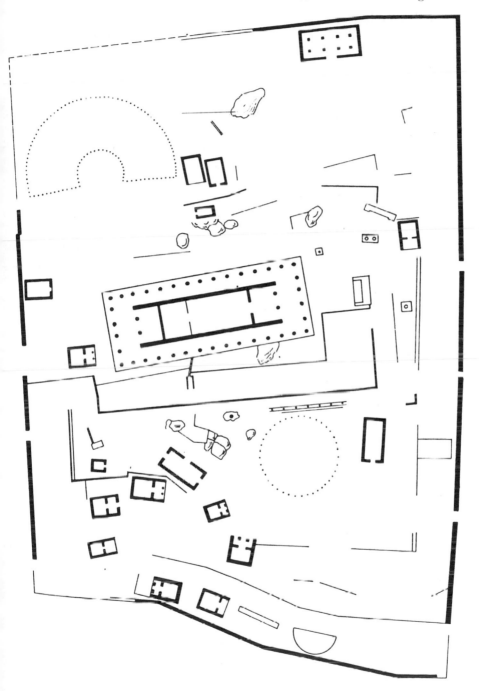

suggested this demand, as the Alkmaionidai and their faction were held responsible for the murder in question, whereas he and his friends had had no part in it.[8] (72) When the demand from Kleomenes arrived for the expulsion of Kleisthenes and 'the Accursed', Kleisthenes himself withdrew from Attika; but this did not prevent Kleomenes, subsequently, from coming to Athens with a small force and driving out 700 Athenian families – as specified for him by Isagoras – who were held to be polluted by murder and sacrilege. This done, he endeavoured to dissolve the *boulē*[9] and entrust the government to 300 of the supporters of Isagoras. The *boulē*, however, stood firm in resistance to him; so Kleomenes, with Isagoras and his faction, occupied the Akropolis. This united the rest of the Athenians against them, and for two days they were besieged there. On the third day a truce was made and they left Attika – the Spartans, that is . . . (73) The others were imprisoned and executed. Then the Athenians recalled Kleisthenes and the 700 families banished by Kleomenes. They also sent messengers to Sardis, in the hope of making an alliance with the Persians: for it was obvious to them that they had provoked the Spartans and Kleomenes to the point of war. When the messengers reached Sardis and said what they had been told to say, Artaphrenes the son of Hystaspes, the governor of Sardis, asked them who on earth they were and where they lived, to wish to become allies of the Persians. The messengers answered these questions, and Artaphrenes' response was brief and to the point: if the Athenians gave King Dareios earth and water,[10] he would make an alliance with them; if not, they should go home. The messengers were eager to make the alliance, and replied that the tokens would be given. They said this on their own initiative – and when they had left Sardis and returned home they were severely censured for it.

(74) As for Kleomenes, he felt that the Athenians had treated him insultingly in both word and deed, and he collected together an army from the entire Peloponnesos. His purpose in doing this – though he did not make it known – was to gratify his wish to punish the Athenian *dēmos* and to set up Isagoras, who had escaped with him from the Akropolis, as tyrant. So Kleomenes and his great army invaded Attika as far as Eleusis; and at the same time, in accordance with a prior agreement, the Boiotians seized the two outlying Attic villages of Oinoe and Hysiai,[11] while the Chalkidians attacked from another direction and raided the Attic countryside. Thus encircled, the Athenians decided to keep the Boiotians and Chalkidians for later and to go and make a stand against the Peloponnesians at Eleusis. (75) However, when the two sides were on the point of joining battle there, the Corinthians were the first to come to the conclusion, amongst themselves, that what they were doing was not right; so they changed their minds and went home. Then

Demaratos the son of Ariston did the same: he was the other Spartan king, and with Kleomenes – with whom he had not previously been at variance – the joint commander of the expedition. It was this disagreement which led to a *nomos* being laid down in Sparta, forbidding both the kings to accompany any army which was being sent out, as had been the previous practice. Now one or the other of them was to stay at home, and one of the Tyndaridai with them – for hitherto, of course, both of these also had had their aid invoked and had accompanied the army.[12] Anyway, on this occasion at Eleusis, when the rest of the allies saw that the Spartan kings were not in agreement with each other and that the Corinthians had already deserted their position, they too gave up and went away. (77) Such was the inglorious dissolution of the Peloponnesian army; and then the Athenians, bent upon revenge, began by mounting an expedition against the Chalkidians. The Boiotians, however, advanced to the Euripos[13] in support of the Chalkidians, and when the Athenians saw this they decided to attack the Boiotians first; so they met the Boiotians in battle and won a great victory over them, killing vast numbers of them and taking 700 alive. And then, on the same day, they crossed to Euboia and fought a battle against the Chalkidians too: this again they won, and followed up the victory by settling 4,000 (Athenians as) cleruchs on the land of the Horse-rearers (*hippobotai*), as the wealthy Chalkidians were called.[14]

(78) Thus the Athenians grew in strength, and demonstrated what a fine thing equality (*isēgoria*) is, not in one respect only but in all: for while they were ruled by tyrants the Athenians were no better in war than any of their neighbours, but once they had got rid of the tyrants they became far and away the best. What this proves is that while they were oppressed they were like men labouring for a master – unwilling to make an effort; but when they had been liberated, each man had his own incentive for working hard.

Herodotus v.66; 69–70; 72.1–2; 73–75; 77.1–2; 78

1 See **74**.

2 Chiefly in that Isagoras was elected *archōn* for 508/7.

3 See further **76**. On precisely how Kleisthenes enacted this and his other reforms see H. T. Wade-Gery, 'The laws of Kleisthenes', *CQ* 27 (1933), 17–29 (reprinted in his *Essays in Greek History* (Oxford, 1958), 135–54); Hignett, *Constitution*, 126–8 and 393–4; A. Andrewes, 'Kleisthenes' reform bill', *CQ* n.s.27 (1977), 241–8.

4 On the Ionic *phylai* see Hignett, *Constitution*, 50–5.

5 The Homeric hero Aias (or Ajax) was connected with the nearby island of Salamis, and Kleisthenes' choice of his name should be seen in the context of a long history of Athenian claims, by arms and propaganda, to Salamis; see for instance Plut. *Sol.* 8–10, and n.14, below.

6 See **26, 30**.

7 See **76**.

8 Here follows, in explanation, the story of Kylon (v.71); see **64A**.

9 This almost certainly means the Areiopagos, rather than either the Solonic *boulē* of 400 or (least likely of all) Kleisthenes' new *boulē* of 500 (**77**): see Hignett, *Constitution*, 93–5; Moore, *Aristotle*, 236.

10 Tokens of complete submission, in Persian eyes: see **107, 109**.

11 Hysiai is actually just on the Boiotian side of the border (**62** with n.5).

12 The Tyndaridai (sons of Tyndareus) were the mythical brothers Kastor and Polydeukes (or Pollux), the Dioskouroi, whose cult was especially associated with Sparta. It was symbolic images of them, the *dokana* (Plut. *Moralia* 478A), which accompanied Spartan expeditions.

13 The strait which separates Euboia (and thus Chalkis) from Attika and Boiotia on the mainland.

14 Cleruchs: compare **139**. A *klērouchos* was the holder of a *klēros*, plot, of land. This Chalkidian cleruchy is the earliest of which we can be certain, though the Athenians *may* have established one on Salamis at about the same time: see Meiggs and Lewis no.14 (Fornara no.44).

   In the passage omitted here (77.3–4) Hdt. goes on to tell how, from the ransom money paid for the Boiotian and Chalkidian prisoners, the Athenians set up various victory monuments, with a dedicatory inscription. Fragments of two copies of the epigram survive: Meiggs and Lewis no.15 (Fornara no.42).

76. Demes, 'trittyes' and 'phylai'

The centrepiece of Kleisthenes' reforms, which brought about a transformation not only in the *politeia* but in the *polis* as such, was his reorganisation (as well as enlargement: see **78**) of the citizen-body; we have already seen what Herodotus thought about it (v.66 and 69; **75**); here is the more colourless account in the Aristotelian *Ath. Pol.* As the basis for a new structure on three levels Kleisthenes took the demes, the natural village units of Attika, and divided up the *astu* on village or suburb lines also. This obviously resulted in entities – *c.*140 of them (see J. S. Traill, *The Political Organisation of Attika*, *Hesperia* Supplement 14 (1975), 73–103) – which varied greatly in size, but at the next level there was some degree of compensation for such inequalities, in that each of the 30 *trittyes* might contain up to eight or nine small demes or only one or two large ones (Traill, 71); and finally three *trittyes*, one each from the *astu*, the 'coast' (*paralia*) and the 'midlands' (*mesogeios*), were brought together to make up one of the ten new *phylai*, which for political and military purposes were to supersede the four original Ionic ones. The effect of all this, as far as the *polis* of Athens was concerned, was a paradoxical one: an unprecedented fragmentation which facilitated an unprecedented unification.

   See further: Hignett, *Constitution*, 129–31 and 134–45; D. M. Lewis, 'Kleisthenes and Attika', *Historia* 12 (1963), 22–40; Forrest, *Emergence*, 192–200; W. E. Thompson, 'The deme in Kleisthenes' reforms', *Symbolae Osloenses* 46 (1971),

72–9; Moore, *Aristotle*, 236–40; Jeffery, *Archaic Greece*, 100–2; Murray, *Early Greece*, 254–8.

It was for these reasons[1] that the *dēmos* put its trust in Kleisthenes, and he became champion of the masses. And then – in the archonship of Isagoras (508/7), three years after the overthrow of the tyrants – he began his measures by dividing everyone into ten *phylai* instead of four. His aim was to mix them up, so that more of them might have a share in the *politeia*.[2] This was the origin of the cry 'No investigation of *phylai*!' when anyone wished to look into family origins. (4) He divided the *chōra*, by demes, into 30 parts – ten in and around the *astu*, ten of the 'coast' and ten of the 'midlands' – which he designated *trittyes*; and three *trittyes* were then assigned by lot to each *phylē*, so that each should consist of territory in all three zones.[3] And he made the men who lived in each of the demes fellow-demesmen; this was in order that they should use their demes as a form of address and not their fathers' names, which would betray the new *politai*.[4] Hence it is that Athenians call one another by their demes. And Kleisthenes also created *dēmarchoi*, with the same duties as the *naukraroi* had previously had; for it was to replace the naukraries that he made the demes.[5] Some of the demes he named after their localities, others after their founders, for not all of them were still connected with specific localities. He did, however, leave the Athenians free to belong, as they had always done, to *genē* and phratries,[6] and to hold priesthoods. He assigned to his *phylai* ten eponymous heroes, chosen by the priestess at Delphi from a preliminary list of a hundred.

> ?Aristotle, *Athenaion Politeia* 21.1–2 and 4–6

1 The role of the Alkmaionidai in ejecting Hippias (20.4–5).

2 See further below, and **78**.

3 This is a crucial sentence for modern study of Kleisthenes' reforms and of the political map of Attika which they produced: *was* this process effected 'by lot'? Some have doubted it, because of the (to them) suspicious fact that areas of particular Alkmaionid influence, far from being broken up in the new and supposedly fortuitous configuration, *seem* on the contrary to have been built into it: see for instance Forrest, *Emergence*, 192–200. But this conspiracy theory is both unprovable – for one could never hope to *prove* that these and other anomalies, real or apparent, did not arise from the luck of the draw – and misdirected. A Kleisthenic deme was not so much a precise subdivision of a (non-existent) map as a concentration of population (see the articles of Lewis and Thompson, cited above), a centripetal focus rather than a centrifugal land-mass; so modern emphasis on the contiguity of *trittyes* or demes may simply be irrelevant. There were apparently no tangible boundaries between demes (nor, *a fortiori*, between *trittyes*), despite the fact that they obviously existed in principle (Traill, *op. cit.* 73 n.6): not a single boundary-stone has survived, and Strabo's remark (1.4.7–8) about the difficulty of deciding where

one deme, Melite, ended and its neighbour Kollytos began applies, significantly enough, to two *city* demes (in the city *trittyes* of different tribes); in the Attic countryside the distinction between one deme and another will have been even more a matter of natural centres, not artificial boundaries.

4 See **78**.

5 Naukraries and *naukraroi*: **64** with n.5. On the functions of the demes and their *dēmarchoi* see Hignett, *Constitution*, 135–40; and below, **78** and **305**.

6 I.e. the smaller units of the kinship structure: Hignett, *Constitution*, 55–67; Forrest, *Emergence*, 50–5 and *passim*; Andrewes, *Greek Society*, ch.5; S. C. Humphreys, *Anthropology and the Greeks* (London, 1978), 193–208. Naturally there was no question of Kleisthenes' abolishing these ancient organisations, or the four Ionic *phylai* which they made up, and their role both official and unofficial remained important through the classical period. Note, however, that despite such conservatism it was probably Kleisthenes who in the prytany system devised a new calendar for the organisation of civil affairs; see, however, **77**, Intro.

77. The new 'boulē'   boulē of 500

Whether or not Solon created a *boulē* of 400 (see **67** with n.12), there can be no doubt at all that Kleisthenes created one of 500. In partnership with the *ekklēsia* it was to prove one of the cardinal features of Athenian radical democracy in the fifth and fourth centuries: see Hignett, *Constitution*, 237–44, and above all Rhodes, *Boule, passim*. There are obscurities surrounding the detail of its original duties (see Hignett, *Constitution*, 145–56) and internal organisation: the prytany system (see Glossary), for example, is not attested with absolute certainty before the constitutional reforms of 462/1 (**123**), and Rhodes (*Boule*, 16–19) questions the usual assumption that it was the work of Kleisthenes. What is not in dispute is that its main work was to be that of *probouleusis*, prior deliberation in advance of a meeting and a decision of the *ekklēsia*. On the bouleutic oath see **119**.

Then he established a *boulē* of five hundred, instead of four hundred, (drawing) fifty men from each *phylē*[1] instead of, as before, a hundred.

?Aristotle, *Athenaion Politeia* 21.3

1 The quotas from each of the ten *phylai* were actually drawn from the demes of that *phylē*, in proportion to their greatly differing sizes: thus – to take the extremes – the largest deme of all, Acharnai, furnished no fewer than 22 of the *bouleutai* for its *phylē* Oineis (of which it constituted the whole midlands *trittys*), whereas almost 40 demes provided only one councillor each; see in detail Traill (cited in **76**), 1–72.

78. The new 'politai'

The centrality of the demes in the Kleisthenic *politeia* is nowhere clearer than in the fact that a *politēs*, henceforth, was to be a man properly registered in the ledgers of his deme; see further **305**. However, we have already seen it stated in the Aristotelian *Ath. Pol.* (**76**) that one of the functions, or at any rate the corollaries, of Kleisthenes' reorganisation of the citizen-body and his emphasis therein on the deme was the more ready absorption and assimilation of 'the new *politai*'. This oblique allusion to Kleisthenic enfranchisements which might otherwise be (and indeed have been) doubted finds some corroboration in two passages of Aristotle's *Politics* – (VI) 1319 b 1–27, and the one translated here.

See further: Hignett, *Constitution*, 132–40; Whitehead, *Ideology*, 143–5; J. K. Davies, 'Athenian citizenship: the descent-group and the alternatives', *Classical Journal* 73 (1977), 115–18; and **128**.

Clearly the criterion[1] of (descent) from a *politēs* or a *politis*[2] is impossible to adapt to the case of the original colonisers or founders (of a city). It may be, though, that a more difficult problem is posed by those who come to share in a *politeia* after a revolution: an example of this is what Kleisthenes did in Athens after the expulsion of the tyrants, when he enrolled in the *phylai* many foreigners and slave immigrants.[3] What is controversial in this instance is not who became a *politēs* but whether they did so rightly or wrongly.

Aristotle, *Politics* (II) 1275 b 32–39

1 As a qualification for citizenship.
2 I.e. a *woman* of citizen family, as the mother.
3 Despite what the next sentence gaily asserts, it is not at all clear exactly who these people were.

79. 'Ostrakismos'

For seventy years in the fifth century (487–417) one of the most striking and characteristic features of Athenian democratic politics was the procedure of *ostrakismos*, whereby a vote of the *ekklēsia* could send a leading public figure into temporary exile; see further **121, 146, 148, 213**. (For the short-lived equivalent at Syracuse, *petalismos*, see Diod. XI.87.) Most of our sources explicitly associate it with Kleisthenes. One of them does not – or at least *appears* not to (passage E, below); and this minority testimony finds support, some scholars argue, in the 15–20 year gap which elapsed between Kleisthenes' reforms (after which we hear nothing more of him) and the first (known) ostracisms, in the 480s. But we know too little about these years to give such a consideration much weight.

See further: Hignett, *Constitution*, 159–66; Meiggs and Lewis no.21; E. Vanderpool, *Ostracism at Athens* (1970); Moore, *Aristotle*, 241–4; Fornara no.41; Murray, *Early Greece*, 262–5; and the references in the notes below. Note the theoretical analysis of Aristot. *Pol.* (V) 1302 b 10–21.

(A) After (Kleisthenes' reforms) the *politeia* became much more inclined towards the *dēmos* than it had been under Solon – and in any case the *nomoi* of Solon had been forgotten under the tyranny, through not being used; so with the aim of pleasing the masses Kleisthenes laid down other, new ones. These included the *nomos* about *ostrakismos* . . . And when two years had passed after the victory at Marathon,[1] and the *dēmos* was already more confident, then it was that they first used the *nomos* concerning *ostrakismos*. It had been laid down because of suspicion of those in power, for Peisistratos had established himself as tyrant when he was a leader of the *dēmos* and a general. And the first man to be ostracised was one of his relatives, Hipparchos the son of Charmos, of (the deme) Kollytos. It had been with the particular aim of driving out this man that Kleisthenes laid down the law: for the Athenians – with the leniency which is the trademark of the *dēmos* – had allowed the friends and relatives of the tyrants to (continue to) live in the *polis*, unless they had taken an active share in crimes during the period of the disturbances; and the leader and champion of these men was Hipparchos. In the year immediately following, the archonship of Telesinos (487/6) . . . they ostracised Megakles the son of Hippokrates, of (the deme) Alopeke. So for three years they ostracised the friends and relatives of the tyrants,[2] on whose account the *nomos* had been laid down, but after that, in the fourth year (485/4), they began to remove anyone else who appeared to be too powerful; and the first man to be ostracised who had nothing to do with the tyranny was Xanthippos the son of Ariphron.[3]

?Aristotle, Athenaion Politeia 22. 1–6★

(B) Kleisthenes introduced the *nomos* of *ostrakismos* into Athens; this is what it was like. The custom was for the *boulē*, having considered the matter for some days, to inscribe on *ostraka* the name of whichever of the *politai* should be banished, and to throw them into the enclosure of the

11 Ostraka (after *The Athenian Citizen* (Princeton, 1960), fig. 27)

bouleutērion. If there turned out to be more than 200 *ostraka* for any one, he had to go into exile for ten years, though he could (continue to) enjoy the income from his property. Later the *dēmos* resolved to lay down a *nomos* stipulating that the *ostraka* were to be more than 6,000 for a man who was to go into exile.[4]

Vaticanus Graecus 1144, fol.222rv[5]

(c) In his third book Philochorus explains *ostrakismos*, writing as follows. *Ostrakismos* was like this. The *dēmos* took a preliminary vote, before the eighth prytany, to resolve whether to hold an *ostrakismos*. When they had resolved to do so, the *agora* was fenced off with planks and ten entrances were left through which the Athenians entered, by *phylai*, and deposited their *ostraka* – keeping hidden the side on which they had written. The nine *archontes* and the *boulē* presided. When the *ostraka* had been counted, whoever received the most – provided it was not less than 6,000 – had ten days in which to settle any lawsuits in which he was privately involved, whether as plaintiff or defendant. After this he was obliged to quit Attika for a period of ten – later five – years, during which he could (continue to) enjoy the income from his property, but could not come nearer to Athens than Geraistos, the promontory of Euboia.[6] Hyperbolos was the only nonentity to be ostracised, and this was because of his personal depravity, not because he was suspected of wishing to be a tyrant; and after him the practice was abandoned.[7] It had begun with a *nomos* laid down by Kleisthenes, when he threw out the tyrants, and wished to expel their friends and relatives as well.

Philochorus, *FGrH* 328 F30

(d) Kleisthenes the Athenian was the first to enact the *ostrakismos* requirement – and also, as it happened, the first to fall victim to its penalty!

Aelian, *Varia Historia* XIII.24.3

(e) In his second book Androtion says of Hipparchos that he was a relative of Peisistratos the tyrant and that he was the first man to be ostracised. The *nomos* concerning *ostrakismos* had been first laid down at that time, because of suspicion of the associates of Peisistratos; for he had been tyrant when he was a leader of the *dēmos* and a general.[8]

Androtion, *FGrH* 324 F6

1 I.e. in 488/7. (For Marathon see **108**.)
2 Evidently a third tyrannophile was ostracised in 486/5.
3 The father of Perikles (Chs.12–19, *passim*).
4 This assertion is also made by Philochorus (passage c) and others, but can hardly be right; it was the quorum for the procedure as a whole which was six thousand (Plut. *Arist.* 7.6 (see **121**); Hignett, *Constitution*, 165–6).

5 A fifteenth-century (A.D.) Byzantine manuscript: see J. J. Keaney and A. E. Raubitschek, *American Journal of Philology* 93 (1972), 87–91.
6 This is a feasible *northern* limit. In *Ath. Pol.* 22.8 (where this provision is dated in 481/0) there is a southern limit also – Cape Skyllaion, the tip of the Argolid – and it may well be that both appeared in Philochorus' original text.
7 See **213**.
8 The similarities in phraseology between this and passage A are self-evident, and they encapsulate the crux of the problem. In the *Ath. Pol.* (A) it is clearly stated that the law was first *used* in 488/7. In Androtion (E) it is apparently claimed that the law was first *enacted* then – though his words may possibly have been wrongly transmitted to us: see K. J. Dover, *CR* n.s.13 (1963), 256; G. V. Sumner, *Bulletin of the Institute of Classical Studies* 11 (1964), 79–86; M. H. Chambers, *JHS* 99 (1979), 151–2.

80. The Kleisthenic 'politeia': democracy or oligarchy?

For the author of the *Ath. Pol.* (22.1 (**79A**) and 41.2) it was obvious that Kleisthenes moved Athens a further stage on towards *dēmokratia*, the rule of the people; and few modern scholars would disagree. Yet however and wherever, precisely, we ourselves choose to locate Kleisthenes in the evolution of radical democracy in Athens (see p.152), it may be salutary to recognise that for the ancients any such assessment was often a relative one, determined by partisan attitudes to that evolution itself.

(A) From their marriage[1] came that Kleisthenes, named after his maternal grandfather the Sikyonian, who instituted the *phylai* and the *dēmokratia* in Athens.

Herodotus VI.131.1

(B) 'Finally Alkibiades and Kleisthenes – both of them my father's great-grandfathers, on the paternal and maternal side respectively[2] – took command of the exiles, restored the *dēmos*, threw out the tyrants, and instituted that *dēmokratia* under which the *politai* were so schooled in bravery that, single-handed, they met and defeated in battle the *barbaroi* who had come to attack the whole of Greece.'[3]

Isocrates XVI (*On the team of horses*). 26–27[4]

(C) So when Kimon returned home he was angry that the authority of the Areiopagos was being treated with contempt;[5] so he endeavoured to revive its powers of jurisdiction and to re-awaken the aristocracy (*aristokratia*) of Kleisthenic times.

Plutarch, *Kimon* 15.2

(D) Kleitophon said that he agreed with the motion of Pythodoros in most respects,[6] but had a rider recorded, to the effect that the men chosen should also search out the traditional *nomoi* which Kleisthenes laid down when he established the *dēmokratia*, so that these too should be taken into account when they discussed what was to be done for the best. This presumably reflected a belief that the *politeia* of Kleisthenes was not inclined towards the *dēmos* but akin to that of Solon.

?Aristotle, *Athenaion Politeia* 29.3

1 Megakles the Alkmaionid and Agariste of Sikyon: see **26**.
2 On this claim see Davies, *Families*, 9–10.
3 At Marathon in 490 (**108**).
4 See also xv.232.
5 On this episode see **123**.
6 On this episode see **227**.

8 Diversity and unity

We have so far observed a number of common features of the archaic period – colonisation, tyrants, lawgivers – within the general theme of the evolution of the institutions of the *polis*; it is essential to recognise, however, that these and other things occurred at different rates (if indeed at all) in different parts of the Greek world, with the result that by the end of the archaic period that world was highly diverse in character. W. G. Forrest writes, for example, of *The Emergence of Greek Democracy*. Democracy certainly did 'emerge', as we have seen (Chs.6–7), in Athens, and in some other places as well (notably in Ionia and Sicily), but elsewhere oligarchy was and always remained a perfectly natural and viable form of government; in certain *poleis* there were good reasons, internal or external, for prolonging the rule of tyrants into the classical period; many aristocracies survived unshaken either by tyranny or by demands for a wider diffusion of power; and in some parts of the Greek world the primitive monarchies of the Dark Ages continued to exist. (On the role of tyrannies (and oligarchies) in the patronage of 'traditional' arts see **29, 72** with n.4.) Admittedly, where social and political development could proceed unimpeded – a crucial proviso – a *polis* was always defined as the collectivity of its *politai*, but that said nothing about how, by what means and to what limits, this collectivity was to take on actual political shape. Yet to talk of *poleis* at all begs a question for much of central and northern Greece, where piracy was still rife (**82**), colonisation late (**86**), and the *ethnos* rather than the *polis* the normal social and political form. (See Ehrenberg, *Greek State*, 22–5 and 120–31; Austin and Vidal-Naquet, *Economy*, 78–81.)

Diversity, then, is obvious and important; but so too are developments which give the period an underlying unity. Thucydides, for example, points to the growth of organised sea-power (**81**), which helped to keep piracy (**82**) temporarily within bounds. Organisation is evident also in the efforts of small communities, whether *poleis* (as in **83**) or *ethnē* (as in **85**), to define their relationships and to seek a *modus vivendi* with each other; and naturally the Delphic Amphiktyony (**84**) brought, for its members, a further measure of unity to the diversity. Thus heterogeneity and uniformity went hand-in-hand by the end of the archaic period, before the fifth-century polarisation of much of the Greek world between the innovating Athens and the reactionary Sparta (**87, cf.88**); reflection upon the different constitutional forms brought forth adherents of each (**89**), but the common factor of Greekness was to come into sharp focus during the 'national' conflict with Persia (Chs.9–10).

81. Thucydides on the archaic period

To back up his belief that the Peloponnesian War of 431–404 would dwarf all its predecessors (see p.11), Thucydides wrote the so-called *Archaeologia* (1.2–21), an excursion into what to him was already ancient history, and a fascinating insight into how an intelligent fifth-century Greek viewed the past. Here is one section of it, concerned particularly with the growth of sea-power; for another see **82**. On sea-power, A. D. Momigliano, 'Sea-power in Greek thought', *CR* 58 (1944), 1–7 (reprinted in *Secondo contributo alla storia degli studi classici* (Rome, 1960), 57–68).

Having with difficulty and over a long period attained a state of secure tranquillity, and being no longer subject to migrations,[1] Greece began to send out *apoikiai*: the Athenians settled Ionia and most of the islands; the Peloponnesians (settled) most of Italy and Sicily, and some places elsewhere in Greece. All these foundations were made after the Trojan War.

(13) As Greece became stronger and acquired even greater wealth than before, tyrannies were established in the majority of the *poleis*; at the time their revenues were increasing, in contrast to the customary dues enjoyed earlier by the hereditary monarchies; and as a result Greece began to build navies and turn more towards the sea. The Corinthians are said to have been the first to involve themselves with naval affairs more or less along modern lines, and it was at Corinth, we are told, that the first triremes were built in Greece. It also appears that a Corinthian shipwright, Ameinokles, built four ships for the Samians; it was about 300 years before the end of this present war that Ameinokles went to Samos. And the earliest sea-battle that we know of took place when the Corinthians fought the Kerkyrans – 260 years ago, on the same reckoning.[2] It should be explained that the Corinthians had their *polis* on the Isthmos, and so obviously possessed a permanent trading-post (*emporion*) there, with the Greeks both from within the Peloponnesos and from outside it – travelling more usually, in the early days, by land than by sea – passing through Corinthian territory in order to make contact with each other. So the Corinthians grew rich, and hence powerful, as has been shown even by the early poets, who called the place 'wealthy'.[3]

And once the Greeks had begun to take more to seafaring the Corinthians acquired (war-)ships and suppressed piracy;[4] and by providing an *emporion* twice over[5] they made their *polis* strong with the wealth which flowed in. Later the Ionians too acquired a large fleet – in the time of Kyros, the first King of the Persians, and of his son Kambyses; when fighting against Kyros they had control for a time of the sea around their territory.[6] Polykrates too, the tyrant of Samos in the time of Kambyses,[7] had a strong fleet and subjected a number of the islands to himself, including Rhenaia, which after capturing it he dedicated to Delian Apollo. And the Phokaians who settled Massalia[8] defeated the Carthaginians in a sea-battle. (14) These then were the most powerful navies; and even these, although they were formed many generations later than the Trojan War, evidently employed few triremes, but were still made up of fifty-oared ships and longboats, just as before. It was not until shortly before the Persian Wars and the death of Dareios, King of the Persians after Kambyses, that triremes appeared in large numbers – in Sicily, with the tyrants there, and in Kerkyra – and these were the last important navies to be established in Greece before the expedition of Xerxes; for the fleets which had been built up by the Aiginetans and the Athenians and others were small, and comprised for the most part fifty-oared ships. It was at this late stage that Themistokles persuaded the Athenians, when they were at war with the Aiginetans and at the same time expecting (an invasion of) the *barbaroi*, to build the ships with which they actually fought the sea-battle (at Salamis);[9] and even these did not yet have decks throughout.

(15) So these were the fleets of the Greeks, both the early ones and those of later times. Nevertheless, those who devoted themselves to their fleets acquired considerable strength from the wealth which flowed in and from their control of others; for they – and particularly those who did not have sufficient *chōra* of their own – sailed against and subdued the islands. On land, however, there was no war which involved the deployment of any significant force: all the wars that did take place were border conflicts between neighbours, and the Greeks did not undertake foreign campaigns, far away from home, designed to subjugate others. This was because not even the largest *poleis* had a galaxy of subjects, nor did communities engage in joint expeditions as equal allies; it was more a case of neighbours going to war with one another as individuals. The war which took place long ago between the Chalkidians and the Eretrians was the one that to the greatest extent involved the rest of the Greek world as allies of one side or the other.[10]

Thucydides I.12.4–15

---

1 Such as the Dorian invasion (**44**), which Thuc. has just mentioned.

2 These two dates are *either* c.721 and c.681 *or* c.704 and c.664, depending upon whether Thuc. is computing by the end of the Peloponnesian War as a whole (404) or its first phase (421) – compare **60** with n.4; but on either count this is before the Kypselid tyranny (**27**).

3 E.g. Homer, *Iliad* II 570; compare Strabo VIII.6.20.

4 See further **82**.

5 I.e. for sea- as well as land routes.

6 See further **92**.

7 See **31**.

8 See **19**.

9 See **112**.

10 This is the so-called Lelantine War, named after the plain between Chalkis and Eretria; compare Hdt. v.99.1, and the later (decidedly inadequate) source-material collected as Fornara no.7. For a conventional modern account see Jeffery, *Archaic Greece*, 63–70; Murray, *Early Greece*, 75–9, is more stimulating. The simple fact of the war is confirmed by archaeological evidence for the destruction, just before 700, of the Eretrian dependency of Lefkandi (excavated in the 1960s), but modern attempts (still influential on Murray) to involve the whole of the Greek world in a major war between rival trading empires have ignored Thuc.'s clear implication that even this conflict, with wider ramifications than usual, amounted only to a border war.

82. Piracy

Despite a strong inclination to locate their Golden Age in the past, Greeks in the classical period had a sense of their greater degree of civilisation (see E. R. Dodds, *The Ancient Concept of Progress* (Oxford, 1973), ch.1). Yet in some areas old habits died hard, if at all: piracy, brigandage and plundering remained endemic, as emerges not only from Thucydides' remarks, below, but also from a small but instructive body of epigraphical evidence: see Meiggs and Lewis no.30 (Fornara no.63; public imprecations at Teos, c.470, against, *inter alios*, pirates or those who receive pirates) and no.42 (Fornara no.89; Argos and two Cretan cities lay down mutual arrangements, c.450, for the division of spoil); and see also **83**. The Athenians' suppression of Aegean piracy during the fifth century was important, but temporary.

See in general: H. A. Ormerod, *Piracy in the Ancient World* (Liverpool, paperback reissue, 1978), chs.1–4.

It should be explained that in early times, once people began to be more in touch with one another by sea, both the Greeks and those *barbaroi* living on the coast of the mainland (of Asia Minor) and in the islands[1] turned to piracy. Their leaders were men who were already powerful, and engaged in piracy for the sake of their own gain and the support of their humble followers. They attacked *poleis* which were unwalled and organised as villages,[2] and plundered and derived most of their livelihood therefrom; as yet their profession carried no stigma, but rather brought its practitioner glory. This is clear from the behaviour even today of some of the inhabitants of the (Greek) mainland, for whom there is honour in being a successful pirate, and also from the poets of old, where the same question always appears, put to travellers who arrive by sea, whether they are pirates; the assumption is that those who are asked will not deny what they do, and those whose business it is to know will not condemn it.[3] Men also plundered each other by land. And to this day much of Greece still lives in the old way – the Ozolian Lokrians, for instance, and the Aitolians[4] and Akarnanians; and the custom of carrying arms still persists among those who live on the mainland in that area, as a result of the plundering which has always gone on. (6) Arms, indeed, were originally carried all over Greece, because places of habitation were unprotected and intercourse with others unsafe; in fact it was quite usual for men to go about their daily business carrying arms, just like the *barbaroi*. An indication of customs which were once common to all may be found in the practice of those parts of Greece which still follow them.

It was the Athenians who first gave up carrying arms and moved on to a more civilised level and relaxed way of life. Until quite recently, in fact, the older members of the wealthy classes there, given over to a luxurious life-style, used to wear linen tunics and tie up their hair in topknots with golden brooches in the shape of a grasshopper; and this explains why the older men among the Ionians also, a related people, for a long time used the same mode of dress. The Spartans were the first to adopt simple clothing like that in use nowadays, with their wealthier men in general taking up habits more or less the same as those of the majority. They were also the first to strip naked and, having taken off their clothes in public, to anoint themselves with oil in the course of their athletic exercises. For originally, even in the Olympic Games,[5] athletes competed with loin-cloths covering their genitals, and it is not many years since this practice ceased. Even now, among some of the *barbaroi*, especially in Asia, there are boxing and wrestling competitions in which the contestants engage wearing a loin-cloth. One could in fact cite many other instances where the customs of the *barbaroi* today are the same as those of the Greeks long ago.

(7) As for the navigation of the seas, as it became more common and *poleis* which were founded relatively recently possessed a greater surplus of wealth,[6] they were built on the edge of the sea and fortified and occupied isthmuses for the sake of trade, as well as for the sake of security vis-à-vis their respective neighbours. By contrast, cities of old were rather settled away from the sea, whether on the islands or the mainland, because of the prevalence of piracy; for everyone plundered

everyone else, including those who lived near the sea but were not actual seafarers; and these old cities still lie inland to this day. (8) Among the worst pirates were the islanders, being Karians and Phoinikians – for of course these were the people who inhabited most of the islands: this can be deduced from the fact that when Delos was purified by the Athenians during this present war and the tombs of all those who had died on the island were removed,[7] more than half were found to be Karian; they were identified as such by the type of weapons buried with them and by the mode of burial itself, which they still use.[8] But navigation became more common once Minos had built his fleet,[9] for in the process of sending settlers to most of the islands he expelled those who were using them as bases for crime. Also, those who lived beside the sea were now in a better position than before to acquire wealth and live in security. Some of them, on the strength of their new riches, even began to build themselves walls. At the same time, in their anxiety for gain the weaker were content to be dominated by the stronger; and those to whom greater resources gave greater power were able to make the lesser *poleis* their subjects. This was still basically the condition that the Greeks were in when they later mounted the expedition against Troy.

Thucydides 1.5–8

1 Phoinikians (see **2**) and Karians are mentioned later.
2 A contradiction in terms, strictly speaking: what Thuc. must mean is communities which were identifiable as such but had not undergone *synoikismos* (**7** and **8**).
3 See for instance Homer, *Odyssey* III 69–74, IX 252–55.
4 On the backwardness of the Aitolians compare Thuc. III.94.3–5 (Austin and Vidal-Naquet, *Economy* no. 53).
5 See **11** and **12**.
6 Compare **81**.
7 In the winter of 426/5: Thuc. III.104.
8 For the development of Greek historiography it is of great interest that Thuc. thought to appeal to archaeological evidence in this way; on the point at issue, however, he seems to be wrong, misinterpreting Geometric Greek culture as Karian.
9 See 1.4.

83. Treaty between Oiantheia and Chaleion

As we have just seen (**82**), Thucydides considered the Ozolian (or Western) Lokrians to be among the more backward peoples of Greece. Yet by his day they had evolved *poleis*; and we have a bronze tablet which records (I) a treaty of *c*.450 between two of them, Oiantheia and Chaleion, followed by (II) a domestic law of Chaleion (or so we must assume, as the inscription was found there). The

173

document provides, *inter alia*, evidence of piracy and of measures taken to control it, and also of how these little-known communities regulated their internal and external relations.

For commentary on points not covered here see Austin and Vidal-Naquet, *Economy* no. 54.

(I) No one shall carry off the Oiantheian *xenos* from the territory of Chaleion nor the Chaleian from the territory of Oiantheia, nor his property, even if (someone) is making a seizure; if someone does make a seizure, he may himself be seized with impunity.[1] (But) the property of *xenoi* may be carried off from the sea without liability to seizure, except from the harbour of either *polis*. If anyone does make unjust seizure, (the penalty is) four drachmas; but if anyone holds what he has seized for more than ten days, he shall owe one and a half times what he seized.

If a Chaleian sets up home[2] for more than a month in Oiantheia, or an Oiantheian in Chaleion, he shall use the legal procedure of that place.

(II) The *proxenos*, if he acts falsely as *proxenos*, shall pay double. If the judges for *xenoi* are in disagreement, the *xenos* who brings the suit shall choose additional jurors, excluding his *proxenos* and personal guest-friends, from the best men – fifteen men for cases involving a mina or more, nine men for lesser cases. If a citizen (*astos*) brings suit against another citizen in accordance with the treaty, the *dāmiourgoi* shall select the jurors from the best men, after they have sworn the five-fold oath.[3] The jurors shall swear the same oath. The majority shall prevail.

Tod. no. 34

1 'The seizure of a pledge to enforce payment of a claim' (Ormerod, *op. cit.* (p. 171), 64–5). The Greek word for such reprisals is *sylē*.
2 The verb used is *meta(w)oikein*, cognate with the noun *metoikos* (immigrant). For the relatively well-attested status of *metoikos* in Athens see **160**.
3 Presumably an oath invoking five gods.

84. The Delphic Amphiktyony

Amphiktyonies (or amphiktionies – see below) were religious leagues, often of early and obscure origin, connected with temples and the maintenance of their cults. We hear of several, in various parts of the Greek world (for the Ionian Panionion see **92**), but the Amphiktyony *par excellence* was that of Delphi, which in conjunction with the Delphians themselves administered the temple and property of Apollo and conducted the Pythian Games. And as the Panhellenic stature of Delphi increased, so did the political as well as religious character of the Amphiktyony, with internal dissension between members sometimes spilling over into a Sacred War (declared in the name of Apollo on the grounds of sacrilege against him). For the first of these, in the early sixth century, see

Fornara no.16 (though note that N. Robertson, 'The myth of the First Sacred War', *CQ* 28 (1978), 38–73, argues at length for dismissing the war as an invention of the fourth century); there was a second Sacred War in *c*.448 (see **173** Intro.), and a third between 356 and 346 (see **336**).

See in general Ehrenberg, *Greek State*, 108–11.

Some think that it was Amphiktyon the son of Deukalion who established the synod of the Greeks at Delphi, and that the name *Amphiktyones* for those assembled derived from him. But Androtion in his *Atthis*[1] declared that originally the delegates came to Delphi from the neighbouring communities, and were (therefore) given the name *Amphiktiones* (Neighbours),[2] before in the course of time their present name prevailed. They say that it was Amphiktyon himself who gathered together into the common synod the following peoples of Greece: Ionians, Dolopians, Thessalians, Ainianes, Magnetes, Malians, Phthiotians, Dorians, Phokians, (and) Lokrians bordering on Phokis beneath Mount Knemis.[3]

Pausanias X.8.1–2

1 See p.15.
2 The point here is not so much the different spelling of *Amphiktyones/-iones* as that Androtion evidently wished to use it to debunk the aetiological derivation and press a rational one.
3 This list omits the northern (Perrhaibians) and southern (Boiotians) extremes of what was in fact a geographically compact league of twelve ethnic groups; the emergence of the *polis* had little or no impact here.

85. Treaty between Elis and Heraia

A bronze tablet found at Olympia in 1813 is inscribed with the record of a 100-year alliance, concluded in *c*.500 (or possibly earlier), between two peoples of the Peloponnesos, the Eleians and the Heraians. Neither community, at that time, had become a *polis* (Strabo viii.3.2)

This is the covenant[1] between the Eleians and the Heraians. There shall be an alliance for a hundred years. It shall begin from this (year). If there is need of anything, either word or deed, they shall stand by each other in all things, and especially in war. If they do not stand by each other, the wrongdoers shall pay a talent of silver to Olympian Zeus, for use in his service. And if anyone harms this writing, whether private individual or official or community (*dāmos*), he shall be liable to the sacred fine here written.

Meiggs and Lewis no.17

1 The word is *wrātra* (*rhētra*): compare **38, 49**.

86. The settlement of new territory

A law (apparently from the last quarter of the sixth century) of an unidentified community of west Lokris, inscribed on bronze, follows many of the precedents and preserves many of the practices of the main period of Greek colonisation (see Ch.2; and compare Meiggs and Lewis no.20 (Fornara no.47), a law of the eastern Lokrians relating to their colony at Naupaktos).

For commentary on points not covered here see Austin and Vidal-Naquet, *Economy* no.46

(I) This law concerning the land shall be valid for the division of the plain of Hyla and Liskara, for both the individual and the public plots. Inheritance[1] shall be the right of both parents and son; if there is no son, of the (unmarried) daughter; and if there is no daughter, of the brother. If there is no brother, let the inheritance be the right of a relative, according to what is just. Failing that, (the owner) shall have the right to bestow his property on whomever he chooses.[2] Whatever a man plants, he shall be immune from (its) seizure. Unless under the pressure of war it is resolved by a majority of one hundred and one men, chosen as the best, to bring in at least 200 fighting-men as additional settlers,[3] anyone who proposes a division (of the land) or puts it to the vote in the council of elders or the *polis* or the select committee (*apoklēsia*),[4] or creates *stasis* about land-division, he himself and his family shall be accursed for all time, and his property shall belong to the *dēmos*, and his house shall be demolished in accordance with the law on murder. This law shall be sacred to Pythian Apollo and the gods who dwell with him. May destruction be the fate of him who transgresses it, and of his family and property; but may (the god) be kind to him who observes it.

And the land shall belong[5] half to the original settlers and half to the additional settlers.

(Addendum:) Let them distribute the valley portions. Exchange of plots shall be valid, but let it take place in the presence of an official.

(II)[6] If the *dāmiourgoi* gain more than what is prescribed, let them dedicate a statue of Apollo Echetos within nine years, and it shall not be set down as gain (of the *dēmos*).

Meiggs and Lewis no.13

1 The more common meaning of *epinomia* is 'right of pasturage', but it does not seem to fit here.
2 This is the isolated line from the top of the reverse side of the bronze; we follow the interpretation of the text which inserts it here, as an omission.
3 For reinforcement of a colony compare 14B.
4 For differentiated institutions in small communities see in general Ch.4.
5 Presumably in the eventuality mentioned above.

6 The meaning of this second law and its relationship, if any, with the first is obscure.

87. The Athenian and Spartan characters

Perhaps the most influential element in the Greeks' vision of their world which emerged from the archaic period was the picture of a radical opposition between the Spartan and Athenian characters, here vividly described by a speaker in Thucydides. For another extract (set in its proper historical context, just before the Peloponnesian War) see **182**.

'The Athenians are innovators, quick to make plans and quick to put what they have planned into execution. You (Spartans), by contrast, like to keep what you already have; you never devise anything new, and when you do take action it stops short even of its most essential objectives. Then again, the Athenians are bolder than their strength warrants and they run risks against their better judgment; yet their confidence surmounts these dangers. Your way, on the other hand, is to do less than you could have done, to mistrust your own judgment even on matters of certainty, and to imagine that when dangers come you will never be free of them. What is more, while you wait before acting they do not hesitate, and while you are stay-at-homes *par excellence* they are always abroad; for their attitude is that leaving home is the way to add to their possessions, whereas you are afraid that going out after something else might jeopardise what you already have. If they win a victory over their enemies they press home the advantage to the utmost; if they are beaten they scarcely give ground at all. Furthermore, their bodies they use in the service of the *polis*, as if they were the bodies of other men altogether; it is their minds that they treat as wholly their own, even though here too their aim is to accomplish something for their city. If they plan to do a thing but fail, they see themselves as robbed of their own property; if they succeed, the deed is deemed as nothing by comparison with what they will do next. If some project of theirs is a failure they compensate themselves with hopeful plans of some other sort: for what is unique about them and their plans is that hoping for something amounts to the same as possessing it, so quickly do they put into effect whatever they have decided to do. And so they toil on, through hardships and dangers, all their lives – deriving little or no pleasure from what they already have because they are perpetually adding to it. Their only idea of a holiday is to do what needs doing, and they respond to peace and quiet more badly than to hard labour. Consequently one would best describe them, in a nutshell, as men congenitally incapable either of living a quiet life themselves or of allowing the rest of humanity to do so!'[1]

(71) Such is the character of the *polis* which is your opponent, Spartans – yet even so you hesitate, refusing to recognise that those who best preserve their tranquillity are men who employ their resources for just ends, yet are resolute, when they are wronged, in showing clearly that they will not tolerate it. Your idea of how to behave fairly, on the other hand, is to avoid injury to others and, even in self-defence, to yourselves. It would be difficult to make this policy a success even if you had as neighbour a *polis* just like yourselves; but as things stand we have just shown you how archaic your ways are by comparison with theirs. And what is true of the arts and crafts must be true here too: the new always supersedes the old. For a *polis* at peace it may be best to make no changes in how things are done, but men who are obliged to face many new situations need to be highly inventive in dealing with them. This is why, because of their varied experiences, the Athenians have a political system which has seen so many more changes than yours.'[2]

Thucydides 1.70.2–71.3

1 On this Athenian characteristic see further **175**.
2 The immutability of the Spartan system: compare **60** (end).

88. Relationship between the institutions of Crete and Sparta

We have already observed (in Ch. 5) the many peculiarities of Spartan society and institutions, which sealed the 'archaic' character of that *polis* even in the classical period. (On the 'archaic' and 'modern' Greek state as a distinction of type, not of period, see Austin and Vidal-Naquet, *Economy*, 80–1.) There were, though, a number of obvious similarities between the institutions of Sparta and Crete, which led in antiquity to a belief that Lykourgos had made use of Cretan models. In point of fact the similarities are best explained as common inheritances from a common Dorian past (Forrest, *Sparta*, 53); and there are clear differences to balance the resemblances (see Bury and Meiggs, *Greece*, 99–101, rightly stressing the importance, in Sparta's case, of the subject population). At all events the conflicting claims for the priority of either Cretan or Spartan institutions were discussed by Ephorus (see p. 14) in his *Constitution of the Cretans*, of which Strabo preserves a resumé.

It is said by some (according to Ephorus) that the bulk of the institutions which are regarded as Cretan are in fact Lakonian; the truth is, however, that they were invented by the Cretans and the Spartans perfected them, while the Cretans neglected military matters after the disasters which befell their *poleis*, especially Knossos; but some of the institutions survived at Lyktos and Gortyn[1] and certain other little towns to a greater extent than at Knossos. Indeed the institutions of the Lyktians are used as evidence by those who assert that the Lakonian institutions are the earlier: the argument is that as *apoikoi* (from Sparta) they preserve the customs of the mother-*polis*; for on the other hypothesis one has to argue against all reason that those (like the Knossians) who were well organised and had a good *politeia* deliberately adopted a bad one. But this argument is false, for two reasons. Firstly, one should not infer how things were long ago from how they are now, for the two situations have been completely reversed: the Cretans, for instance, once ruled the sea, which gave rise to the proverb 'The Cretan does not know the sea', applied to those who claim not to know what they in fact know; yet now they have abandoned naval affairs. And in the second place it does not follow that because some of the *poleis* in Crete were founded by Spartan *apoikoi* they were bound to keep to Spartan institutions. At any rate, many *apoikiai* do not preserve their ancestral institutions[2] – and many of the communities in Crete which are not *apoikiai* have the same institutions as those which are. (18) Also, Lykourgos the Spartan lawgiver (*nomothetēs*)[3] was five generations later than Althaimenes, the man who took the *apoikia* to Crete; and Althaimenes, the historians say, was the son of Kissos, the man who founded Argos about the same time as Prokles brought about the *synoikismos* of Sparta,[4] whereas it is universally agreed that Lykourgos was sixth in descent from Prokles. Imitations cannot be earlier than their originals, or the newer come before the older! (Ephorus advances further reasons for believing in the priority of Cretan institutions, and records the Cretan tradition that Lykourgos visited Crete.) (19) . . . When he arrived he met Thales, a poet and *nomothetēs*, and learned from him the way in which first Rhadamanthys and later Minos had laid down *nomoi* for mankind, representing them as coming from Zeus. He also spent some time in Egypt, studying the institutions there also; then, some say, he met Homer on Chios before returning to his own land, where he found that Charilaos, the son of his brother Polydektes, was now king. He therefore set about laying down his *nomoi*, going to the god (Apollo) at Delphi and bringing back the ordinances with him, just as Minos and his associates had brought back ordinances – most of them very like those of Lykourgos – from the cave of Zeus.[5]

Strabo x.4.17–19* (Ephorus *FGrH* 70 F149)

---

1 Chance has preserved for us a copy of the civil law-code of Gortyn, from *c*.450: see Tod no.36 (text and commentary on column I) and Meiggs and Lewis no.41 (text and commentary on columns IV.23–VI.1, with translation; and references to full texts, translations and commentaries), also Austin and Vidal-Naquet, *Economy* no.62, and Fornara no.88 for translation and commentary on selected passages.

2 The facts hardly support this contention: see Graham, *Colony*, esp. 211–17.

3 See **47**.

4 *Synoikismos*: see **7** and **8**.
5 Note the rationalising view of the role of religion; compare Plut. *Lyk.* 4 (on
  Sparta) and Polybius VI.45 (on Rome).

89. The different constitutions

In III.80–83 Herodotus presents a debate on the relative merits of democracy,
oligarchy and monarchy. The setting is a Persian one, between the assassination
of a pretender and the accession to the throne, in 521, of Dareios; and Herodotus
was at pains to insist (see below, and VI.43.3) that it really took place; but it is
very hard to believe him. Whatever its precise origins, the debate as we read it
here clearly reflects *Greek* discussion, in the second half of the fifth century, of the
constitutional developments of the preceding three centuries and their relevance
to contemporary circumstances (see for instance Connor, *Politicians*, 199–206); it
can therefore serve here to remind us that the heterogeneity of the archaic and
classical Greek world lent viability to a whole range of constitutional forms.

When the tumult had died down and five days had passed, the conspirators began to discuss the situation as a whole, and speeches were made
which some of the Greeks find incredible; nevertheless, what was said
was said. Otanes urged that control of affairs be placed in the hands of
the Persians as a whole, speaking as follows. 'In my opinion no one man
amongst us should become sole ruler any longer; it would be neither a
pleasant thing nor a good one. I say this because you know the lengths to
which the insolent pride (*hybris*) of Kambyses went; and as for that of the
Magos, you have tasted it for yourselves.[1] How can monarchy be an
acceptable thing, when it gives a man the power to do whatever he likes
without being called to account for it? Even the best man imaginable,
once put in such a position, would abandon the habits of a lifetime: *hybris*
arises whenever good things are at hand, and jealousy is an inborn
human weakness anyway. And once a man is both insolent and jealous,
he is as bad as can be, for he will perpetrate many outrages when full of
insolence, and many more when full of jealousy. Absolute power ought,
of course, to free a man from jealousy, as he already possesses every
good thing. But in fact his behaviour towards the *politai* is quite the
reverse: he resents the fact that the best of them are alive and well, and
takes pleasure in the worst of his citizens (*astoi*); and no one is readier than
he to listen to slanderous accusations. He is the most inconsistent of men:
show him respect in moderation, and he is angry at not receiving your
abasement; abase yourself, and he hates you for a flatterer! But of course
you have yet to hear the worst of it: a king disturbs ancestral customs,
rapes women, and puts people to death without trial. If on the other hand
the whole populace rules, in the first place it has a name that is the most
beautiful of all – *isonomia*;[2] and secondly it does none of the things that a

king does. The choice of officials is by lot,3 office is held subject to rendering account, and all discussions are carried on in public. So my view is that we should abandon monarchy and put the people in power; for everything resides in the will of the majority.' This was the advice put forward by Otanes.

(81) Megabyxos, by contrast, argued, as follows, for a change to oligarchy. 'In so far as Otanes spoke in favour of getting rid of tyranny, I quite agree with him, but in proposing that we confer power on the masses his judgment has let him down; for there is nothing more stupid or more insolent than a useless mob. Indeed, for men to escape the *hybris* of a tyrant only to succumb to that of an unruly *dēmos* is quite unbearable. At least if a tyrant does something he does it wittingly, whereas the *dēmos* is incapable of comprehension – for how could someone who has neither been taught nor knows for himself his own good comprehend anything? Such a one rushes on with things mindlessly, like a river in flood. So let those who wish the Persians harm opt for the *dēmos*; but as for ourselves, let us select a group of the best men and confer the power on them. We ourselves will obviously be part of it; and it is reasonable to suppose that the best men will produce the best deliberations.' This was the advice put forward by Megabyxos. The third man to speak his mind was Dareios. (82) 'What Megabyxos said in relation to the people seems to me correct, but not what he had to say about oligarchy. There are three possibilities before us – democracy, oligarchy and monarchy – each of them supposedly the best of its kind; and I say that the last of them is by far the best. Nothing could be better than one man who is the best: such a man, with judgment to match, would be beyond reproach in his control of the masses, and the best keeper of secret plans against enemies. But in an oligarchy, with many men publicly competing to display their excellence (*aretē*), there is a likelihood of strong private enmities developing. This is because everyone wants to be at the top and to see his own proposals prevail; this leads to bitter internecine enmities, then to *stasis*, and from *stasis* to bloodshed – and the outcome of bloodshed is monarchy, which is thereby shown to be the best solution. Then again, with the *dēmos* in power it is impossible to stop the spread of evil. Once this is happening it leads the bad men not into public enmities but close friendships, for those out to harm the state do so in collusion with one another. And this sort of thing then goes on until the point where somebody stands up on behalf of the *dēmos* and puts a stop to it all; he is then of course courted by the *dēmos*, until their idol becomes their king – proof again that monarchy is best! Let me sum up the whole question in a word: from where did we get our freedom, and from whom? Was it from the *dēmos*, from an oligarchy, or from a king? We gained our freedom thanks to one man;4 so I consider that monarchy

is what we should stick to. In any case we should not do away with ancestral *nomoi* which are still functioning well; that is not the way to make things better.'

(83) These were the three opinions put forward – and the remaining four men out of the seven agreed with this last one. And when Otanes, who wished to create *isonomia* in Persia, was thus defeated, he spoke openly to them as follows. 'Fellow-conspirators, it is perfectly clear that one of us must become King, whether by lot, or by our asking the Persian people to choose, or in some other way. I shall not join in the contest with you, for I wish neither to rule nor to be ruled. I therefore withdraw from the contest for the throne – on this condition: that neither I myself nor my descendants in perpetuity shall be subject to any of you.' When he had said this, and the six had agreed to his conditions, he did not join the contest with them but withdrew from the ring. And to this day his family remains the only free one in Persia, not violating the *nomoi* of the Persians, but obeying the King only so far as it chooses.

Herodotus III.80–83

1 Kambyses: see **93**. After his madness and death in 522, one of the priestly Magoi (the Biblical Magi) usurped the throne until assassinated by Dareios and his fellow-conspirators. See in general Hdt. III.61–79.
2 Equality before the law: compare **34, 73** (with n.1), **102** (end). Note that in VI.43.3 Hdt. describes Otanes' favoured system as *dēmokratia*.
3 Election by lot is barely attested outside Athens.
4 I.e. Kyros, the first King of an independent Persia (see **91**).

9 The Persian empire

The Greek *poleis* in Asia Minor soon found that they had to live with powerful empires based in the interior, first Lydia, then Persia; after the defeat of Lydia, Persia indeed controlled the entire seaboard of the eastern Mediterranean, from the Bosporos to Pelousion; the conquest of Egypt and Kyrene in the south and of Thrake in the north soon followed. But the empire which in 490 and 480 set out to conquer Greece was not only vast, it was also from the reign of Dareios onwards relatively highly organised, compared with other ancient empires of the Mediterranean area.

The Greeks were fascinated by Persia (see in general Momigliano, *Alien Wisdom*, ch.6), and Herodotus (partly no doubt because he was born in Halikarnassos) was able to describe Persian religion and social structure with a fair degree of accuracy; but despite his often accurate perception of the alien nature of Persia (see **99**), Herodotus chose to place a quintessentially Greek constitutional debate in a Persian setting (see **89**). Greek fascination with Persia did not prevent the perpetuation of substantial ignorance and, during the century and a half in which the two worlds co-existed, endless difficulties over their mutual relationships (see, for instance, **231**, as well as **99**); and the Greeks never really understood the functions of *proskynēsis* (obeisance, see **98**) or of 'gifts' in an absolute monarchy.

Before 490 the Greeks were presumably to the Persians simply one of their subjects and neighbours and there is no evidence that even after 480 the clash between Persia and Greece had the importance in Persia which it had in Greek and Western tradition. Yet the Greeks *were* unlike the other peoples with whom the Persians had to deal and their unlikeness was perceptible; their cultural aggressiveness was quite unique and the evidence of archaeology reveals the use of Greek artefacts and the creation of works of art in a Greek style deep in Asia Minor. The Phrygians had adopted an alphabet based on the Greek alphabet before 700; as early as 700–650, an organised city using Greek pottery existed on the site which later became Daskyleion, the capital of the Persian satrapy of north west Asia Minor. Greek architectural terracottas have been found at a large number of sites in western Asia Minor (see Fig. 12); the

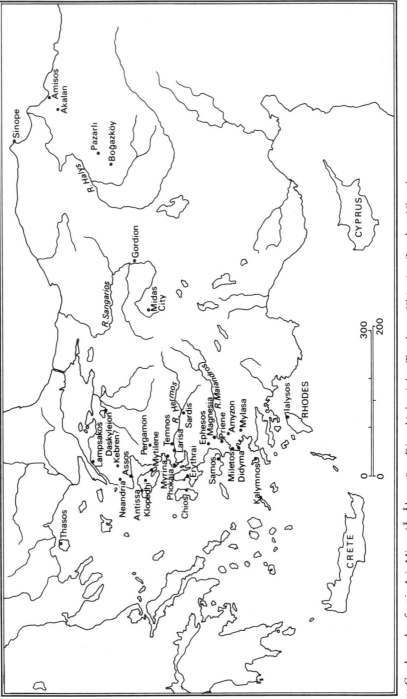

Sinope

Amisos
Akalan

Pazarlı
Boğazköy

R. Halys

R. Sangarios

Gordion

Midas
City

Lampsakos
Daskyleion
Kebren?
Pergamon
Neandria Assos
Antissa
Klopedhi
Myrina
Phokaia
Chios
Mytilene
Temnos
Larisa
Erythrai
Samos
Ephesos
Magnesia
Priene
Amyzon
Miletos
Didyma
Mylasa
Kalymnos
Ialysos
RHODES
R. Hermos
Sardis
R. Maiandros

Thasos

CYPRUS

CRETE

300
200
0
0

12 Greek works of art in Asia Minor (Å. Åkerström, *Die architektonischen Terrakotten Kleinasiens* (Lund, 1966), xx)

sculptured tombs of Xanthos or the painted tombs of Elmalı (also in Lykia) are equally revealing of Greek influence; Greeks had been established in Egypt as traders and mercenaries before the Persian conquest and remained after it; Greeks helped to build the capital city of Persepolis. Even if (as with the native communities in the west) Hellenisation only touched the élite, it was they who dealt with the Greeks in the years after 480. And, if nothing else does, their interest in hiring Greek mercenaries to the exclusion of all others (see H. W. Parke, *Greek Mercenary Soldiers* (Oxford, 1933), chs.3–5) suggests that the Greeks were now more than just another foreign people.

90. The empire of Kroisos

The first eastern empire with which the Greeks came into close and prolonged contact was that of Kroisos of Lydia.

Kroisos was a Lydian by race and son of Alyattes, and ruler of the peoples this side of the Halys river which flows northwards between the Syrians and the Paphlagonians, into the so-called Pontos Euxeinos (Black Sea). This Kroisos was the first of the barbarians of whom we know who compelled some of the Greeks to pay tribute and made others his friends. For he subdued the Ionians and the Aiolians and the Dorians who live in Asia, and made the Spartans his friends. But before the reign of Kroisos the Greeks were all free. For the expedition of the Kimmerians which came as far as Ionia, before the time of Kroisos, did not involve the subjugation of the *poleis,* but was a plundering raid. (Herodotus now narrates the earlier history of the dynasty.) (26) The first of the Greeks whom he attacked were the Ephesians; and when they were besieged by him they dedicated their *polis* to Artemis, fixing a rope from the temple to the wall; the distance from the original site of the *polis,* which was then being besieged, and the temple is seven stades.[1] So Kroisos attacked them first and afterwards each of the Ionians and Aiolians in turn, using various pretexts, substantial grounds when he could find them, otherwise trivial. (27) And when he had forced the Greeks in Asia to pay tribute, he then decided to build ships and attack the islanders. And when everything was ready for the shipbuilding to begin, Bias of Priene according to some, Pittakos of Mytilene[2] according to others, came to Sardis and when Kroisos asked what news there was from Greece, he made a speech which put an end to the project of building ships: 'Your majesty, the islanders are raising ten thousand horse, and have it in mind to march against Sardis and attack you.' Kroisos, hoping that he was speaking the literal truth, said, 'Would that the gods *would* put this into the heads of the islanders, to come against the Lydians on horseback!' But his interlocutor replied, 'Your majesty, you seem to me very eager to catch the islanders on horseback on land, reasonably so. But what do you think the islanders want more than to set out and catch the Lydians at sea, now that they have heard that you intend to build a fleet against them? For thus they will take revenge on you for the Greeks on the mainland, whom you have enslaved to your rule.'³ Kroisos was delighted at the way this was put and, since the man seemed to be talking sense, he followed his advice and abandoned the project of building ships. And instead he established a relationship of *xenia*⁴ with the Ionians on the islands. (28) In the course of time almost everyone living this side of the Halys river was subjected to Kroisos, in fact everyone except for the Kilikians and the Lypians: Lydians, Phrygians, Mysians, Mariandynoi,⁵ Chalybes, Paphlagonians, Thrakians – both Thynians and Bithynians – Karians, Ionians, Dorians, Aiolians, Pamphylians. (Herodotus now tells of the alleged visit of Solon and of the death of Kroisos' son.) (46) Kroisos remained deep in mourning for two years for the loss of his son; but then the fact that the reign of Astyages son of Kyaxares⁶ had been ended by Kyros son of Kambyses and that the Persian empire was growing put a stop to his mourning and made him think if there was some way in which he could check the growth of Persian power before it became too great.

Herodotus 1.6; 26–28; 46.1

1 The site of the city was moved after its capture.
2 See **23–24**.
3 See **81** for the role of sea-power in early Greek history.
4 See **5B**.
5 See **19**.
6 The core of the Persian empire had been ruled initially by a dynasty belonging to the Median race, related to the Persian race; Astyages was its last king.

91. Kroisos and Kyros

Contact with the Greeks of Asia and of the islands had led Kroisos to take an interest also in the mainland, establishing relationships with its *poleis* and in particular with its great shrines. Faced now with the growing power of Persia, it was to the Greeks of the mainland that Kroisos turned.

So when Kroisos had found out all this,¹ he sent messengers to Sparta with gifts to ask for an alliance, after instructing them what to say. And when they arrived, they spoke as follows: 'Kroisos the king of the Lydians and other peoples has sent us with this message, "Lakedaimonians, the oracle² instructed me to make the Greek my friend and since I gather that you are the leaders of Greece I ask for your help according to the oracle; I want to be your friend and ally without subterfuge or deceit.''' This was the proposal Kroisos made through his messengers; the Spartans had already heard about the oracle and were glad when the Lydians arrived and swore oaths of *xenia*[3] and alliance; indeed they were already beholden as a result of earlier benefactions of Kroisos to them; for the Spartans had sent to Sardis to buy gold, wanting it for the image of Apollo which now stands in Thornax in Lakonia, but Kroisos had given it for nothing.

(70) This then was the reason why the Spartans accepted the alliance, and no doubt also because Kroisos had chosen them from among all the Greeks to be his friends . . . (71) Kroisos now, misunderstanding the oracle,[4] mounted an expedition against Kappadokia,[5] expecting to destroy Kyros and the power of Persia . . . (73) These were the reasons for Kroisos' expedition against Kappadokia: a desire to get more territory in addition to what he had, and especially trust in the oracle and a wish to punish Kyros for his treatment of Astyages[6] . . . (75) Kroisos held it against Kyros that he had deposed Astyages; so he sent to the oracles[7] to ask if he should march against the Persians and when the ambiguous reply came back, thinking that it was in his favour, he marched against the land of the Persians. And when Kroisos reached the Halys river, in my view he proceeded to put his army across it by the existing bridges; but the common view among the Greeks is that Thales of Miletos organised the crossing.[8] According to this view, Kroisos did not know how his army would cross the river, for at that time the bridges in question did not exist; Thales was present in the camp and made the river flow not only on the left side of the army,[9] but also on the right side; this is how. Beginning upstream from the camp, he dug a deep trench, making it crescent-shaped, so that he might thus turn the rear of the camp where it lay, diverting the river from its original bed and then returning it below the camp; the result then was the river was divided and each part was crossable. Some people even say that the original bed was completely dried up; but I cannot accept this; for how could the army have crossed the new bed on its return? (76) So Kroisos crossed with his army and reached that place in Kappadokia known as Pteria; Pteria is indeed the strongest site in this area and lies more or less on a line with the *polis* Sinope on the Black Sea. Kroisos encamped there and attacked the lands of the Syrians.[10] He captured the *polis* of the Pterians and enslaved the inhabitants and captured all its dependent communities and uprooted the Syrians, who were quite innocent of any offence against him.

Meanwhile, Kyros gathered his own army and set off against Kroisos, picking up contingents from everyone on his path. Before he set his army on the march he sent messengers to the Ionians and tried to detach them from Kroisos; they did not listen, however. In due course Kyros arrived and camped opposite Kroisos and there in the land of Pteria there was a trial of strength between them. There was a tough fight and many fell on both sides, but in the end neither side was victorious and the two armies separated when night fell. (77) That was the result of the battle between the two sides, but Kroisos blamed the size of his own army, for when it joined battle it was much smaller than that of Kyros. And when on the next day Kyros did not come out to the attack, Kroisos set off for Sardis, intending to summon the Egyptians according to his treaty with them, and the Babylonians,[11] and bidding the Spartans come on an agreed date; for he had made an alliance with Amasis king of Egypt even earlier than with the Spartans, and there was also an alliance with the Babylonians, whose king at that time was Labynetos. His intention was to collect all these allies and summon his own army and, when winter was over, at the beginning of spring march against the Persians. With this in mind, as soon as he reached Sardis, he sent messengers bidding his allies to gather at Sardis four months later. As for the existing army, a mercenary one, which had fought the Persians, he dismissed it and let it all break up, never expecting that Kyros would move on Sardis after so close a battle.[12]

Herodotus 1.69–77*

1 The power of Sparta.
2 Of Delphi.
3 See 5B.
4 On war with Persia, see below.
5 The area east of the Halys river, the home of the Syrians of 90.
6 See 90 n.6; in deposing Astyages, Kyros had deposed Kroisos' brother-in-law.
7 Of Delphi and of the Amphiareion, in Boiotia. The oracle at Delphi told Kroisos that he would destroy a great empire if he attacked Persia; it turned out to be his own.
8 For Thales, see Murray, *Early Greece*, 234.
9 The army, attempting to cross to the east of the Halys, was presumably facing south at the time.
10 See n.5.
11 For the eventual conquest of Egypt by Persia, see 93; Babylonia also succumbed to Persia after the defeat of Kroisos.
12 In fact, Kyros marched on Sardis and captured it, along with Kroisos, in 546.

92. The Persian conquest of Ionia

Kyros, after the defeat of Lydia, moved on to deal with the Greek *poleis*.

As soon as the Lydians had been captured by the Persians, the Ionians and Aiolians sent messengers to Kyros at Sardis, offering to be his subjects on the same terms as they had had under Kroisos. When he had heard what they offered, he told them a story: 'A flute-player once saw some fishes in the sea and played to them, thinking that they would come out on to the land. But when he was deceived in his hope, he took a net and picked up a large number of them and dragged them in, and when he saw them jumping about he said to the fishes, "Stop dancing in front of me, since you were unwilling to come out and dance for me when I played to you."' Now the reason why Kyros told this story to the Ionians and the Aiolians was that, when the Ionians were earlier requested by Kyros' own messenger to abandon Kroisos, they had not done so, but now when matters were settled they were ready to be Kyros' subjects.[1] So it was in anger that he spoke to them in this way; but the Ionians, when the news was brought back to the *poleis*, all fortified themselves and all met at the Panionion,[2] with the exception of the Milesians; for they were the only people with whom Kyros reached an agreement on the same terms as Kroisos. The rest of the Ionians agreed to send messengers to Sparta to ask for help. (Herodotus briefly discusses the *poleis* of Ionia.) (143) Of these Ionians then, the Milesians lived protected from fear, having reached an agreement with Kyros, while the islanders among them[3] had nothing to fear; for the Phoinikians were not yet subject to the Persians, nor were the Persians themselves sailors. The only reason why the Milesians had abandoned the other Ionians was that in a period when the whole Greek people was weak, by far the weakest and least important element of all was the Ionian;[4] for apart from Athens they had no significant settlement. The other Ionians, including the Athenians, avoided the name, not wishing to be called Ionians; in fact even now I think most of them are ashamed of the name. Only the twelve *poleis*[5] rejoiced in the name and founded a shrine exclusively for themselves, which they called the Panionion; and they agreed not to give any share in it to any of the other Ionians, though in fact only the Smyrnaians ever asked to belong. (Herodotus compares the twelve with the group of Dorian *poleis* in south-west Asia Minor, speculates on the reason for the number twelve and gives an account of early Ionian history.) (148) The Panionion is a sacred place on the north side of Mykale, chosen by the Ionians in common and dedicated to Poseidon Helikonios;[6] Mykale is a promontory of the mainland running west towards Samos and it is here that the Ionians from the various *poleis* always gathered to celebrate the festival which they called Panionia . . . (151) The remaining *poleis*[7] agreed to follow the Ionians as a group wherever they led. (152) They acted with speed and Ionian and Aiolian messengers were sent to Sparta; when they arrived they chose a man of

Phokaia, called Pythermos, to speak on behalf of all of them. He put on purple clothing, so that as many of the Spartiatai as possible should come together and hear him, and got up and made a long speech asking for help. But the Lakedaimonians paid no heed, but decided not to help the Ionians; so they went away, but the Lakedaimonians, although they had rejected the messengers of the Ionians, nonetheless sent some men in a fifty-oared ship, presumably to act as spies on the affairs of Kyros and of Ionia. When they reached Phokaia, they sent the leading man among their number, who was called Lakrines, to Sardis to deliver the message of the Lakedaimonians to Kyros, bidding him harm no *polis* in Greek territory – or they would take action. (153) When the herald had spoken in these terms, it is said that Kyros asked some Greeks who were present who the Lakedaimonians were and how many, thus to address him; and when he heard he said to the Spartiate herald, 'I am not afraid of men who have a special place in the middle of the *polis* where they gather to swear oaths to and cheat each other; if I am spared, I shall see that it is not the sufferings of the Ionians that are their concern, but their own.' Kyros in fact had all the Greeks in mind when he delivered these remarks, since they establish an *agora* and buy and sell there; for the Persians are not in the habit of using an *agora* and none exists in their country.

After this Kyros handed over Sardis to a Persian, Tabalos, but entrusted a Lydian, Paktyes, with the task of collecting the gold of Kroisos and of the other Lydians; he himself set off for Agbatana (Ekbatana), taking Kroisos with him and not at first supposing that the Ionians were of any importance. For Babylon stood out against him and the Baktrian people and the Sakai and the Egyptians; he planned to march against them in person, but to send another commander against the Ionians. (154) But as soon as Kyros had set off from Sardis, Paktyes detached the Lydians from Tabalos and Kyros and, going down to the sea, since he had all the gold from Sardis, hired mercenaries and persuaded the people living in the west to join his cause. Moving on Sardis he shut Tabalos up in the *akropolis* and besieged him . . . (157) Kyros adopted these measures while on the march and continued towards Persian territory; but when Paktyes heard that an army to oppose him was at hand, he took fright and fled to Kyme, while Mazares the Mede marched on Sardis with the detachment of Kyros' army which he had been given. When he found that Paktyes and his men were no longer at Sardis, his first step was to compel the Lydians to obey the measures of Kyros;[8] as a result they changed their whole way of life. Mazares then sent messengers to Kyme ordering them to surrender Paktyes. But the Kymaians decided to take the matter to the god (Apollo) at Branchidai for advice; for there was an ancient oracle there, which all the Ionians and Aiolians often used. The place is in the territory of Miletos by the harbour Panormos. (158) So the Kymaians sent sacred messengers to Branchidai to ask about Paktyes, what they should do to please the god; and when they put the question the oracle bade them surrender Paktyes to the Persians. When the Kymaians back at home heard the reply, they prepared to give him up; but when the majority had already agreed on this, Aristodikos son of Herakleides, a man of repute among the townspeople (*astoi*), held the Kymaians back from going ahead, not trusting the reply and thinking that the sacred messengers had not spoken the truth; finally, another group of sacred messengers, among them Aristodikos, set off once more to ask about Paktyes. (159) When they arrived at Branchidai, Aristodikos as the representative of the group put the following question: 'My lord god, Paktyes the Lydian has come to us as a suppliant, fleeing a violent death at the hands of the Persians; but they demand his person, bidding the Kymaians to hand him over. Although we fear the power of the Persians, we have not so far dared to hand the suppliant over, before your advice on what we should do is clearly given to us.' This was his question, but the god gave him the same answer once more, bidding him surrender Paktyes to the Persians. In response, Aristodikos, who had thought the possibility over beforehand, acted as follows: he went right round the temple, and threw out the sparrows and the young of whatever other kinds of birds there were there. As he was doing this, it is said that a voice came from the inmost shrine, addressed to Aristodikos and pronouncing these words: 'Most impious of mortals, how do you dare to do this? Do you destroy the suppliants in my temple?' Aristodikos was not at a loss and replied, 'My lord god, how is it that you come to the aid of these suppliants, but bid the Kymaians give a suppliant up?' And the god replied in turn, 'I bid you do it, in order that you may the quicker be destroyed for your impiety, so that you may not in future come to consult my oracle about the surrender of a suppliant.'[9] (160) When the Kymaians heard this back at home, they wished neither to give the suppliant up and be destroyed nor to be besieged because they had him among them; so they sent him to Mytilene (on Lesbos). But when Mazares sent a messenger, the Mytilenaians prepared to give up Paktyes, in return for a certain amount of money; but I cannot say exactly what this part of the bargain was, because it was never carried out. For when the Kymaians heard what was going on among the Mytilenaians they sent a boat to Lesbos and moved Paktyes to Chios. But he was given up by the Chians, after being dragged from the sanctuary of Athena Poliouchos;[10] the Chians gave him up in return for Atarneus, the site of which is in Mysia, opposite Lesbos. Anyway, the Persians now received Paktyes into custody, intending to bring him before Kyros. But it was some considerable time before any Chian made an offering to any of the gods of barley meal from Atarneus or made (sacred) cakes from the produce of that place; in fact everything from the territory was banned for religious purposes.

(161) So the Chians had given up Paktyes; and after this episode, Mazares marched against those who had joined in besieging Tabalos; he first sold into slavery the Prienians and then plundered the whole of the plain of the (river) Maiandros for his army, and the territory of Magnesia likewise. But immediately afterwards he died of disease. (162) After his death, Harpagos came down as successor in the command; he was also a Mede . . He was now appointed *stratēgos* by Kyros and as soon as he arrived in Ionia he set to work to capture the *poleis* by means of earthworks; once he had got the inhabitants inside the walls, he next built mounds against the walls and captured the towns. The first place in Ionia he attacked was Phokaia. (163) The men of Phokaia had been the first of the Greeks to go on long sea voyages, and had shown the way to the Adriatic, Tyrrhenia (Etruria), Iberia and Tartessos. And they travelled not in merchant vessels, but in fifty-oared ships[11] . . . (164) The fortifications of the Phokaians, then, were built in the way I have described; and as soon as Harpagos had brought his army up he opened the siege, proclaiming that it would suffice as far as he were concerned if the Phokaians demolished no more than one bastion on the walls and consecrated one house (to Persia). But the Phokaians, indignant at the prospect of slavery, said that they wanted a day to consider the matter and would then give their reply. And while they were considering, they bade him withdraw his army from the fortifications. Harpagos replied that he knew perfectly well what they intended to do, but that nonetheless he would let them deliberate. So while Harpagos and his army were no longer before the walls, the Phokaians made for their fifty-oared ships, put their children, wives and property aboard, together with the statues from the temples and the other offerings, apart from bronze or stone objects or paintings, and going on board themselves sailed for Chios; so the Persians captured a deserted Phokaia. (165) The Phokaians wished to buy the islands known as the Oinoussai from the Chians, but the latter were unwilling to sell, fearing lest the islands become an *emporion* and their own island be cut off as a result;[12] so the Phokaians sailed for Corsica. For twenty years earlier they had founded a *polis* on Corsica, called Alalia, following the direction of an oracle;[13] at that stage Arganthonios[14] was already dead. In the course of sailing for Corsica, they first sailed back to Phokaia and killed the Persian garrison, which was guarding the city, having received it from Harpagos, and once they had done this, laid powerful curses on anyone who abandoned their expedition. In addition, they sank a lump of iron in the sea[15] and swore not to return to Phokaia before this lump reappeared. But while they were actually *en route* for Corsica, over half of the people (*astoi*) were

seized with such longing and regret for their *polis* and for the ways of their home that they forswore themselves and sailed back to Phokaia.[16] The others, however, kept their oath and, leaving the Oinoussai, sailed off. (166) When they reached Corsica, they lived alongside the earlier arrivals for five years and built temples. In fact they lived by robbing and plundering all their neighbours; so the Etruscans and Carthaginians got together and sailed against them, each with sixty ships. The Phokaians manned their own ships, also sixty in number, and met them in the so-called Sardinian sea; battle was joined and the Phokaians won what might be called a Kadmeian victory;[17] for forty of their ships were sunk and the remaining twenty rendered unfit for combat, since they had lost their rams. So they sailed back to Alalia and took on board their children and their wives and such other property as their ships would carry and, leaving Corsica, sailed to Rhegion. (167) Those of the Phokaians who escaped to Rhegion set out again and acquired a *polis* in the land of Oinotria which is now known as Hyele (Velia). They founded it after learning from a man of Poseidonia that the oracle at Delphi had instructed them not to settle the island of Kyrnos, but to establish the hero Kyrnos in a shrine.[18] So much then for Phokaia in Ionia . . .

(169) The Phokaians and the Teians[19] then were the only ones of the Ionians who could not bear slavery and left their homes; the other Ionians, except the Milesians, opposed Harpagos, it is true, in battle just like those who eventually left their homes and behaved bravely as each of them fought for their own homes; but they were defeated and captured and remained on the spot, each of them doing what they were bidden. The Milesians, as I have mentioned earlier, came to an agreement with Kyros himself and lived in peace. So Ionia was enslaved for the second time; and when Harpagos had subjected the Ionians on the mainland, the Ionians on the islands were frightened and gave themselves up to Kyros. (170) The Ionians were in a bad way, but they continued to meet nonetheless at the Panionion; and I gather that Bias, a man of Priene, propounded a most profitable project to the Ionians; if they had followed his advice, it would have resulted in their becoming the most prosperous of the Greeks; his proposal was that the Ionians should set off in a single expedition and sail to Sardinia and then found a single *polis* of all the Ionians; they would thus be free of slavery and prosperous, living in the biggest of the islands (of the Mediterranean) and ruling over others;[20] but, he said, if they remained in Ionia he did not see that they would ever be free. This was the advice of Bias of Priene to the Ionians when their cause was already lost; but good advice was also given by Thales, a man of Miletos, before the ruin of Ionia;[21] he was a Phoinikian in ultimate origin. He suggested that the Ionians have a single *bouleutērion* and that it should be at Teos, for Teos was in the middle of Ionia; the other

poleis should continue to be inhabited and regarded as if they were demes.

(171) These then were the projects which they suggested. Having subjected Ionia, Harpagos led an expedition against the Karians and Kaunians and Lykians, including Ionians and Aiolians in his army. (Herodotus goes on to discuss the Karians, Kaunians and Lykians and their respective subjections, also that of Knidos.)

Herodotus I.141–171*

1 See **91**.
2 See below.
3 Samos and Chios.
4 Herodotus has in general a low opinion of the Ionians, compare **101** (for the tribes of Greece in general see **3**).
5 The twelve were Miletos, Myous, Priene, Ephesos, Kolophon, Lebedos, Teos, Klazomenai, Phokaia, Samos, Chios, Erythrai.
6 The reason for the name is uncertain.
7 Of Aiolis – just listed by Hdt. – with the exception of the island *poleis*.
8 Prohibiting them from carrying arms.
9 For the sacred status of a suppliant, compare **64**.
10 The defender of the *polis*.
11 The Phokaians doubtless engaged in piracy as much as in trade, see Intro. to Ch.2, and below.
12 This is a rare example of what we should call economic considerations affecting policy; the reason may be that Chios was an early centre of the slave trade (see **99** and **232**), and presumably dependent on proximity and access to Asia Minor; for the slave trade in general see M. I. Finley, 'The Black Sea and Danubian regions and the slave trade in antiquity' *Klio* 40 (1962) 51.
13 Compare **16**.
14 Who had welcomed them at Tartessos, see above.
15 Compare **129**.
16 The whole episode illustrates two major themes of the history of the *polis*, the deep attachment to it of its members and the way in which they *were* the *polis*, independent of physical location, compare Intro. to Ch.2.
17 Kadmos, the founder of Thebes, sowed a crop of a dragon's teeth; the armed men who sprang up fought each other until only five remained.
18 Kyrnos is the Greek for Corsica and the Greek word *ktizein* may mean 'to settle' a place or 'to establish' (a person in a place).
19 See **18**B.
20 Note the early occurrence of the awareness of the correlation between freedom for oneself and rule over others (and see Ch.12).
21 See **91** n.8.

93. The Persian conquest of Egypt

We have already seen that the Greeks of Asia Minor were at once forced to provide contingents for the Persian army in its career of further conquest (see **92**);

when Persia conquered Egypt in 525 they went along too, thus acquiring a new role in a country where they had long been known as traders and mercenaries (see **94**). The long-standing Greek knowledge of and fascination with Egypt lies behind Herodotus' account, which forms his longest digression, filling Book II.

Kambyses,[1] the son of Kyros and the Kossandane whom I have just mentioned, regarded the Ionians and Aiolians as his inherited slaves and so when he mounted an expedition against Egypt he took with him those of the Greeks whom he controlled and the rest of the peoples over whom he ruled.

Herodotus II.1.2

1 The second Persian King (530–522).

94. The Greeks in Egypt

Alone of the countries round the Mediterranean with which the Greeks came into contact, Egypt was a centrally organised state with a bureaucracy which controlled not simply settlement, but ingress and egress; it was thus closed to colonisation in the normal sense (see Intro. to Ch.2); but Greeks served its kings as mercenaries from an early date and many settled in Egypt (for their inscriptions, analogous to that of Lord Byron on a column of the temple at Sounion, see Meiggs and Lewis no.7 = Fornara no.24); and in due course the Egyptian monarchy encouraged the creation of an *emporion*, under close supervision (see M. M. Austin, *Greece and Egypt in the Archaic Age*, PCPhS Supp. vol. 2, 1970). With the *emporion* at Naukratis, compare that at Gravisca in Italy (Boardman, *Greeks Overseas*, 206).

(A) Psammetichos[1] gave two pieces of land for settlement, facing each other across the river Nile and called the Camps, to the Ionians and Karians who had helped him gain the throne; he also gave them everything else which he had promised. He even put some Egyptian boys among them to learn the Greek language; the interpreters who now exist in Egypt are the result of their having done so. The Ionians and Karians lived on these pieces of land for a long time; they lie a little below Boubastis towards the sea on the so-called Pelousian branch of the Nile. At a later stage king Amasis moved them and settled them in Memphis, as his garrison against the Egyptians. When these people had once settled in Egypt, we Greeks were in contact with them and so know what happened in Egypt from the time of Psammetichos onwards; for they were the first men of foreign tongue to settle in Egypt. In the places from which they were moved, the slips where they drew up their ships and the ruins of their houses were still visible in my time.[2]

Herodotus II.154

(B) Amasis[3] was someone who was attached to the Greeks, and among the privileges which he granted to certain of them was the gift of the *polis* of Naukratis for those who visited Egypt to settle in; he also gave places for the building of altars and sacred enclosures for the gods to those of them who did not wish to settle but voyaged there. The biggest, best-known and most frequented of the sacred enclosures at present is known as the Hellenion. These are the *poleis* which together built it: of the Ionians, Chios and Teos and Phokaia and Klazomenai; of the Dorians, Rhodes and Knidos and Halikarnassos and Phaselis; of the Aiolians, only the *polis* of the Mytilenaians. These are the people to whom the sacred enclosure belongs and these are the *poleis* which provide *prostatai*[4] of the *emporion*; any other *poleis* which claim a share claim something which does not belong to them;[5] the Aiginetans, however, built a sacred enclosure of Zeus all by themselves, the Samians one of Hera and the Milesians one of Apollo. (179) Originally Naukratis was the only *emporion* in Egypt and there was no other; if anyone arrived at any of the other mouths of the Nile, he had to swear that he did not do so from choice and having sworn sail with his ship to the Kanopic mouth; if he were unable to sail because of contrary winds, he had to carry his cargo in barges around the Delta until he reached Naukratis; such was the position of Naukratis.

(180) When the Amphiktyons[6] put the temple which now stands at Delphi out to contract, offering a sum of 300 talents for its reconstruction after the earlier temple there had been destroyed by an accidental fire,[7] it fell to the Delphians to provide a quarter of the sum; and when the Delphians were wandering from *polis* to *polis* asking for contributions, they were helped to a very significant extent by Egypt. For Amasis gave them 1,000 talents of alum[8] and the Greeks living in Egypt 20 minas.[9]

Herodotus II.178–180

1 The first king of the so-called Saïte dynasty, 664–610.
2 See the discussion by A. M. Snodgrass in M. H. Crawford (ed.), *Sources for Ancient History* (Cambridge, 1982).
3 Ruling from 569 to 525.
4 A non-technical term, normally, for which compare **66** n.4; it was no doubt used at Naukratis partly because it was initially not a true *polis*.
5 For the problematic relationship between a share in the control of the chief shrine and a share in the government of Naukratis see Austin, *op. cit.* 22–33.
6 See **84**.
7 See Fig. 10.
8 Note the gift in kind and compare **96** and **188**.
9 There follows an account of Amasis' gifts to Greek temples, analogous to those of Kroisos, including one to the temple of Hera on Samos.

95. Persian kingship

We are fortunate in possessing a number of documents emanating from the King of Persia, which well illustrate the absolute nature of his monarchy; for a story illustrating the Greek view of this absolute monarchy see Hdt. viii.118–120 (and compare **96** on the Behistun inscription). For the nature of Persian kingship in general see R. N. Frye, in G. Walser (ed.), *Beiträge zur Achaemenidgeschichte* (Wiesbaden, 1972).

(A) I am Dareios the Great King, King of Kings, King of (many) countries, son of Hystaspes, descendant of Achaimenes. Saith Dareios the King: 'By the favour of Ahuramazda[1] these are the countries which I got into my possession with the help of the Persian folk, (countries) which felt fear of me (and) bore me tribute: Elam, Media, Babylonia, Arabia, Assyria, Egypt, Armenia, Kappadokia, Sardis, Ionians who are of the mainland and (those) who are by the sea, and countries which are across the sea,[2] Sagartia, Parthia, Drangiana, Aria, Baktria, Sogdiana, Chorasmia, Sattagydia, Arachosia, Sind, Gandara, Skythians, Maka.'[3] Saith Dareios the King:[4] 'If thus thou shalt think, "May I not feel fear of (any) other," protect the Persian people; if the Persian people shall be protected, thereafter for the longest while happiness unbroken – this will from Ahura come down upon the royal house.'

R. G. Kent, *Old Persian*, p. 136
(inscription from Persepolis, between 516 and 509)

(B) The King of Kings, Dareios son of Hystaspes, says this to his slave Gadatas:[5] 'I find that you are not obeying my commands in all respects; insofar as you are cultivating my land and planting the furthest parts of Asia with the fruit-trees from across the Euphrates,[6] I praise your design and as a result great favour will lie in store for you in the house of the King; but insofar as you are flouting my disposition with respect to the gods, I shall make you experience the wrath of my spirit unless you change your course; for you are exacting tribute from the sacred gardeners of Apollo and ordering them to cultivate profane land,[7] ignorant of my ancestors' attitude to their god, who enjoined strict uprightness on the Persians and . . .'

Meiggs and Lewis no.12[8]

1 The chief god of the Persians, also called simply Ahura.
2 I.e. Mediterranean islands.
3 See **96** Intro. for this list of peoples.
4 Addressing himself.
5 Perhaps satrap (governor) of Ionia; note the terminology.
6 I.e. from the area known to the Romans and to us as Syria.
7 For Persian religious toleration see Burn, *Persia*, ch.4.

8 The inscription comes from Magnesia on the Maiander; it was originally inscribed between 522 and 486, and was re-inscribed in the second century A.D. Meiggs and Lewis discuss the authenticity of the document and the parallels to its language and content.

96. The Persian empire

We have remarked briefly that the Persians made sure that the resources in terms of manpower of their empire were at their disposal; they also in due course drew tribute from it. An inscription of Dareios from Behistun (R. G. Kent, *Old Persian*, p. 119, written in a new monumental script) provides both another example of Persian kingly style and an outline account of the organisation of the empire; we print the account of Herodotus (arranged on rather different principles) both as giving more detail and as illustrating the Greek view of the power whom they had defeated.

The whole world felt his power. And first he had made and put up a stone relief; on it there was a representation of a man on horseback and he added an inscription which read, 'Dareios, son of Hystaspes, by the virtue of his horse – giving the name – and of his groom Oibares gained the throne of Persia.'[1] (89) Having done this in Persia itself, he set up twenty governorships, which they call satrapies; and having set up the governorships and appointed the governors he laid down the tributes which were to come in, either by nation or sometimes joining smaller neighbours to a nation; sometimes going beyond neighbours he joined those far away to one nation or another. This then was the way in which he divided up the governorships and the yearly tribute; those of them which paid in silver were instructed to pay according to the Babylonian talent weight, those in gold according to the Euboic;[2] the former weighs $1\frac{1}{10}$ of the latter. Now under Kyros and again under Kambyses nothing was fixed over tribute, but the various nations brought offerings. As a result of his organisation of tribute and other similar activities,[3] the Persians say that Dareios was a huckster, Kambyses a despot, Kyros a father; for the first was mercenary over everything, the second was harsh and selfish, the third was gentle and always contriving good things for the Persians.

(90) From the Ionians and Magnesians in Asia, and Aiolians and Karians and Lykians and Milyans and Pamphylians – for a single assessment covered them all – there came in 400 silver talents; this was the first division which he established.

From the Mysians and Lydians and Lasonians and Kabalians and Hytennians, 500 talents; this was the second division.

From those on the right of the Hellespontos as one sails in, and

Phrygians and Thrakians in Asia, and Paphlagonians and Mariandynoi[4] and Syrians[5] the tribute was 360 talents; this was the third division.

From the Kilikians 360 white horses, one for each day[6] and 500 talents of silver; of this 140 (talents) went to the cavalry which guarded the territory of Kilikia,[7] the remaining 360 went to Dareios; this was the fourth division.

(91) From the *polis* of Poseideion,[8] which Amphilochos son of Amphiaraos founded on the borders of the Kilikians and the Syrians,[9] as far as Egypt, except for the territory of the Arabians, which was untaxed, the tribute was 350 talents; in this division lies the whole of Phoinikia and that part of Syria known as Palestine and Cyprus; this is the fifth division.

From Egypt and the Libyans who border on Egypt, and Kyrene and Barke, which had been assigned to the Egyptian division, there came in 700 talents, in addition to the money coming from Lake Moeris, which came from the fish, and indeed in addition to the corn which was exacted; for the Egyptians provide 120,000 *medimnoi* of corn for those of the Persians who live in the White Tower at Memphis and their servants;[10] this is the sixth division.

The Sattagydai and Gandarians and Dadikai and Aparytai, who are placed together, provide 170 talents; this is the seventh division.

From Sousa and the rest of the territory of the Kissians 300 talents; this is the eighth division.

(92) There came in to him from Babylon and the rest of Assyria 1,000 talents of silver and 500 castrated boys;[11] this is the ninth division.

And from Agbatana (Ekbatana) and the rest of Media and the Parikanians and Orthokarybantians 450 talents; this is the tenth division.

And the Kaspians and Pausikai and Pantimathoi and Darcitai contributing together brought in 200 talents; this is the eleventh division.

From the Baktrians as far as the Aigloi the tribute was 360 talents; this is the twelfth division.

(93) From Paktyia and the Armenians and their neighbours as far as the Black Sea 400 talents; this is the thirteenth division.

From the Sagartians and Sarangai and Thamanaians and Outians and Mykoi and those living in the islands in the Red Sea (Persian Gulf), where the King settles those who are known as deportees, from all these the tribute was 600 talents; this is the fourteenth division.

And the Sakai and Kaspians[12] paid 250 talents; this is the fifteenth division.

And the Parthians and Chorasmians and Sogdians and Areians paid 300 talents; this is the sixteenth division.

(94) The Parikanians[12] and Ethiopians in Asia brought in 400 talents; this is the seventeenth division.

The tribute of the Matienoi and Saspeires and Alarodians was fixed at 200 talents; this is the eighteenth division.

The tribute of the Moschoi and Tibarenoi and Makrones and Mossynoikoi and Mares was laid down as 300 talents; this is the nineteenth division.

The number of the Indians is by far the greatest of all the races known to us and they paid by far the largest tribute compared with all the others, 360 talents of gold dust. This is the twentieth division.

(95) If silver in Babylonian talents is reckoned in Euboic talents (of silver), the sum is 9,880 talents; and if gold is reckoned at 1:13 in silver, the gold dust comes out at 4,680 talents; so when all this is added up, the yearly tribute collected for Dareios in Euboic talents totals 14,560; I have ignored some small sums in reaching this total. (96) This was the tribute which came in to Dareios from Asia and a bit of Libya;[13] but as time went on, more tribute came in from the islands and from the peoples of Europe as far as Thessalia. This is how the King of Persia keeps this tribute – he melts it and pours it into earthenware jars and when the vessel is full he breaks it open; and when he needs money he cuts off as much as he needs on each occasion. (97) These then were the governorships and the levels of taxation; Persia is the only country which I have not mentioned as paying tribute, for the Persians hold the land free of tribute. And some peoples did not have tribute levied from them, but brought offerings, firstly the Ethiopians who are neighbours of Egypt; Kambyses subdued them while marching on the long-lived Ethiopians – they live round Nysa the sacred mountain and celebrate festivals in honour of Dionysos. They and their immediate neighbours use the same grain as the Kallantian Indians and live underground; these two peoples brought and still bring every third year two *choinikes* of unrefined gold and 200 logs of ebony and five Ethiopian children and 20 big elephants' tusks. As for what the Kolchians and their neighbours as far as the Kaukasos mountain were expected to give, they still in my time brought every four years 100 boys and 100 girls; the Persian empire extends as far as the Kaukasos mountain, but what lies to the north of it knows nothing of the Persians. And the Arabians brought 1,000 talents of frankincense every year. This is what the King received as gifts, apart from the tribute.

Herodotus III.88–97

1 See Hdt. III.85–87.
2 Note that the tribute was paid by weight and not in coin; the so-called Euboic talent was also that on which the Athenian coinage system was based.
3 It is interesting that the existence of a unified system of taxation in the Persian empire had ensured by the fourth century that payments by the Lykian city of

Xanthos to its own sanctuary, the Letoon, were expressed in Persian units of reckoning.

4 See **19**.
5 See **91** n.5.
6 The Greek year had 360 days.
7 A crucial hub in the Persian communications network.
8 Al Mina, see Intro. to Ch.2.
9 Here used to cover the area known to the Romans and to us as Syria.
10 The administrators and garrison of the Persian capital of Egypt.
11 See **99**.
12 Presumably different groups from those in the tenth and eleventh divisions.
13 I.e. Africa.

97. The religion of Persia

On Persian religion, Herodotus is both an interested commentator and a relatively well-informed one; see in general Burn, *Persia*, ch.4; Momigliano, *Alien Wisdom*, ch.6; **95**B.

These, I know, are the sorts of *nomoi* which are observed in Persia; they do not regard it as proper to dedicate statues or temples or altars, but consider it folly to do so; I suppose it is because they do not think that the gods have the shape of men, as the Greeks do. It is their *nomos* to go up onto the highest mountains and sacrifice to Zeus,[1] calling the whole circle of the heavens Zeus; and they sacrifice to the sun and the moon and the earth and fire and water and the winds. Originally, these were the only gods to whom they sacrificed, but they later learnt from the Assyrians and Arabians to sacrifice to Ourania; the Assyrians call Aphrodite Melitta, the Arabians Alilat, the Persians Mitra.[2] (132) This is the form which sacrifices to the gods whom I have mentioned takes among the Persians: they do not build an altar or light a fire when they intend to sacrifice, nor do they use libations, or flute music or garlands or barley-meal;[3] but when a man wishes to sacrifice to any of the gods he takes the victim to an open place and calls upon the god, after garlanding his tiara,[4] usually with myrtle. It is not possible to ask for benefits for the single individual actually sacrificing, but he prays for success for all the Persians and for the King; for he is himself included in all the Persians. When he has cut up the victims into joints and cooked the flesh, he puts it all on a prepared bed of green stuff, as soft as possible, usually clover. When he has made his arrangements, a Magos[5] standing by sings a hymn to the gods, which they say is an account of their coming into being; for it is not the custom to sacrifice without a Magos. Then after waiting a short time the sacrificer takes the flesh away and does what he wishes with it.

Herodotus I.131–132

1 Herodotus uses the Greek name for the chief of the gods to characterise the chief of the Persian gods.
2 Herodotus has gone badly astray here, since Mitra was firmly male (Ourania was one form of the Greek goddess Aphrodite).
3 This 'negative' account of Greek sacrifice is one of the fullest that we have; see W. Burkert, 'Greek tragedy and sacrificial ritual', *GRBS* 7 (1966), 87.
4 A felt hat, the characteristic Persian headdress.
5 Persian priest.

98. The Persian aristocracy

Persia was not only ruled by an absolute monarchy; its governing class was a warrior aristocracy, most of the rest of the population, briefly mentioned by Herodotus, presumably peasants working the estates of the aristocracy in a state of dependence defined by custom rather than by law or economic forces; they were in due course known to the Greeks who conquered the Persian area by such terms as *laoi*, people, not readily fitted into the fairly clear-cut Greek categories of slave and free (see **162**). It is ironic that Kyros in expressing Persian contempt for mercantile activity, did so à propos of Sparta (see Herodotus 1.153 = **92**). The aristocratic ethos of Persia found in the fourth century idealised expression in Xenophon's *Education of Kyros*.

One can tell, when Persians meet each other in the street, whether they are of the same social level, for instead of greeting each other they kiss mouth to mouth; but if one is a lesser man than the other, they kiss on the cheek; and if one is far inferior, he falls down and reveres the other.[1] After themselves, they respect most those who live nearest to them, then the next and so on; they respect least those who live furthest from them, thinking that they themselves are by far the finest of people and that others have some merit, in proportion to their position, with those furthest away being the least meritorious.

Herodotus 1.134.1–2

1 The act known as *proskynēsis*.

99. A eunuch at the Persian court

Despite Greek contact with and knowledge of Persia, an isolated incident could sometimes produce a sense of shock at what was alien in the Persian way of life; the story of Hermotimos is such a case.

Hermotimos of Pedasos exacted the most signal vengeance for a wrong once done of any one of whom I have heard. He was captured in war and when he was sold as a prisoner he was bought by Panionios, a man of

Chios,[1] who made his living by the most revolting means; for whenever he got hold of boys who had an attractive appearance, he castrated them and brought them to Sardis or Ephesos and sold them for a great deal of money. For eunuchs are more esteemed among the *barbaroi* than normal men for their complete trustworthiness; and Panionios castrated a great many boys, since he made his living in this way, including Hermotimos. But *he* was not entirely without a breath of good fortune; he was sent from Sardis, along with other gifts, to the King, and in the course of time he came to be the most esteemed of all the eunuchs of Xerxes.[2] (106) Now when the King was in Sardis and was launching the Persian expedition against Athens,[3] Hermotimos went down on some business to a part of Mysia which the Chians possess and which is called Atarneus;[4] there he met Panionios and, recognising him, spoke for a long while in a friendly fashion, first of all telling of the success which he had had as a result of what Panionios had done and then promising to gain him all sorts of rewards if he brought his household and settled there (in Persia); so Panionios gladly accepted his offer and brought his children and his wife. But when Hermotimos had him and his household in his power, he spoke as follows: 'You have made your living by the most revolting means open to mankind; what evil had I or any of mine done you or any of yours, for you to make me a nothing instead of a man? You expected that the gods would not notice what you did then; but they have delivered you whose behaviour was so revolting into my hands, following the precepts of justice; so you will not complain at the punishment which I am going to inflict.'[5] After speaking these reproaches, he brought his sons before him and compelled Panionios to castrate all four of them; when he had done, his sons were forced to castrate him. So Hermotimos got his revenge on Panionios.

Herodotus VIII.105–106

1 See **92** n.12.
2 See **109** n.2.
3 Note Herodotus' Athenocentric viewpoint, see **107**.
4 See **92**.
5 Compare Hesiod's view of justice in **10**.

100. The wealth of the east

Not the least of the reasons for the Greek fascination with the east was a purely mercenary interest in its wealth; Alkmaion's visit to Sardis was only an early example of something which was a recurring feature of Greek history.

The Alkmaionidai[1] were a distinguished family at Athens from very early times, but after Alkmaion and later Megakles they became extremely distinguished. For Alkmaion son of Megakles[2] adopted the role of helper to the Lydians who came from Kroisos at Sardis to the oracle at Delphi and carried out the task with enthusiasm, and when Kroisos heard from the Lydians who had visited the oracle of his beneficence towards him he invited him to Sardis and when he arrived offered him as much gold as he could carry out on his own person at one go. Given the nature of the offer, this was the plan which Alkmaion thought up: he put on a large tunic with a deep fold and put on the largest boots he could find and thus dressed went into the treasury to which he was led. Falling on the heap of gold dust he crammed down his legs as much gold as the boots would hold, then filled the entire fold of his tunic with gold and finally scattered gold dust over the hairs on his head and took some more in his mouth; he left the treasury scarcely able to drag his feet along, looking quite unlike a human being; for his mouth was full and his whole body swollen. Kroisos could not help laughing when he saw him and gave him everything which he had and as much more besides. So his house (*oikia*) was enormously enriched and Alkmaion himself was able to run a four-horse chariot, and won at Olympia.[3]

Herodotus VI. 125

1 See **64**.
2 See family tree, Fig. 9 on p. 133.
3 See **11–12** and **265**.

10 Persia and the Greeks

The Persian and the Greek worlds met along the coast of Asia Minor. There, the Greek (and particularly the Ionian) *poleis* found themselves, after the fall of Lydia, as the western seaboard of the Achaimenid empire – the dominant military and territorial power of the Near and Middle East. But the Asiatic Greeks never fully reconciled themselves to Persian suzerainty; and their efforts, under energetic and ambitious leaders, to enlist the support of the Balkan and Aegean Greeks in throwing off Persian rule brought the two worlds into direct conflict with each other. The confrontation – chronicled by the West's first true historian, Herodotus – saw the Persians twice beaten back; while at the other end of the Mediterranean the Greeks of Sicily withstood a scarcely less weighty assault from Carthage. See in general Burn, *Persia*, and Hignett, *Xerxes*.

101. The tyrants sponsored by Persia

The Persians no doubt found it easy to deal with a single person in each of the *poleis* under their control, as well as in accord with their belief in the propriety of monarchy, and few Greeks were able to resist the temptation offered by the position of tyranny or quasi-tyranny which resulted (see Andrewes, *Tyrants*, 123–4). In the course of Dareios' Skythian expedition, the Greek leaders guarding the bridge over the Danube were invited by the Skythians to remove it; their response was not automatic and was, in the end, negative.

The opinion of Miltiades the Athenian, who was the tyrant of the Chersonesitans on the Hellespontos[1] and commander of their contingent, was that they should follow the advice of the Skythians and thereby free Ionia; but Histiaios the Milesian[2] held the opposite view, saying that each one of them was tyrant of his *polis* by the agency of Dareios, and that if the power of Dareios were removed he would not be able to rule over the Milesians and none of the others would be able to rule over their communities either. For all the *poleis* would prefer to be democracies rather than tyrannies. When Histiaios put forward this opinion everyone immediately went over to it, despite the fact that they had supported the view of Miltiades earlier. (In order to satisfy the Skythians, the Greeks removed a section of the bridge, but repaired it when the Persians appeared.) (142) This then was how the Persians escaped, while the Skythians failed for the second time in their attempt to make contact with them; and they reckon that, considered as free men, the Ionians are the most worthless and cowardly of all, but that, considered as slaves, they are the most fond of their masters and the least likely to run away.[3]

Herodotus VI.137 and 142

1 See 106.
2 See 102.
3 Compare 92 n.4.

102. The early stages of the Ionian revolt

Despite failing to seize the opportunity of stranding the Persian army north of the Danube (101), the Ionians in the end did attempt to throw off the Persian yoke. See Burn, *Persia*, ch.10.

Naxos and Miletos were the places where the second round of troubles for the Ionians began; Naxos now, on the one hand, was the richest of the (Aegean) islands, and Miletos, on the other hand, was at this very time at the height of her fortunes and was the glory of Ionia, although earlier she had suffered very badly from *stasis* for two generations, until the Parians settled things . . . (30) At Naxos, some of the wealthy had been exiled by the *dēmos* and as a result had come to Miletos. As it happened the man in charge of Miletos was Aristagoras son of Molpagoras, son-in-law and cousin of Histiaios son of Lysagoras, whom Dareios was detaining in Sousa.[1] For Histiaios was actually tyrant of Miletos and simply happened to be at Sousa at the moment when the Naxians, who were his *xenoi*, arrived. So when they arrived they asked Aristagoras if he could manage to give them some troops so that they could get back to their own country. He calculated that if they got back to their *polis* by his agency he would be ruler of Naxos; so he spoke to them as follows, using the *xenia* with Histiaios as a pretext, 'I am not in a position to guarantee you enough troops to get you back against the will of the Naxians who control the *polis*; for I understand that they have 8,000 soldiers[2] and many warships. But I will make every effort to find a way; what I suggest is this: Artaphrenes[3] happens to be my friend and, as you know, he is son of Hystaspes, brother of Dareios the King, and he controls all the peoples in Asia who live by the sea[4] and has a large army and many ships. So I think that *he* will do what we want.' When the Naxian exiles heard this they agreed with Aristagoras that he should act as best he could and bade him offer bribes and the entire cost of the army; they intended to pay this themselves, having great hopes that when they appeared before Naxos the Naxians would do everything they commanded, and the other islanders likewise; for none of these islands[5] was yet under Dareios. (31) So when Aristagoras arrived at Sardis he said to Artaphrenes that, although Naxos was not a large island, it was a fine and fertile one and near Ionia, and full of property and slaves. 'So,' he said, 'mount an expedition against this country and restore its exiles. If you do this, I have available for you, first and foremost, a large sum of money quite apart from the cost of the army, for it is right that we who summon it should pay this; and then it will fall to the King to add to his dominions Naxos itself and the other islands which depend on it, Paros and Andros and the other so-called Kyklades. And with these as a jumping-off point you will be able without difficulty to attack Euboia, a large and fertile island, as big as Cyprus and very easy to seize. A hundred ships are quite sufficient to subdue all these islands.' To which Artaphrenes replied, 'Your advice is such as is profitable to the *oikos* of the King and these plans are sound in every respect, except over the number of ships. Not a hundred, but two hundred will be ready for you in the spring. There is no chance of all this failing to get the approval of the King himself.' (The King does approve and the expedition is mounted; but its commander quarrels with Aristagoras and betrays its approach to the Naxians, who repel the expedition.)

(35) So Aristagoras was unable to keep his promise to Artaphrenes; he was at the same time in difficulties because of the demand for the cost of the army, and afraid because of the failure of the expedition and his quarrel with its commander, and apprehensive of losing his position in Miletos. With all these worries he began to plot revolt; and as it happened there arrived at the same time a messenger from Histiaios at Sousa, with a message pricked on his scalp instructing Aristagoras to revolt from the King . . . Histiaios had done this, regarding his detention at Sousa as a great disaster; he hoped that if there were a revolt he would be sent down to the coast, whereas if Miletos remained tranquil he did not expect ever to go back there. (36) So Histiaios sent his messenger with these plans in mind and everything coincided for Aristagoras. He took counsel with his associates, expounding his own view and the instructions from Histiaios. Everyone expressed the same opinion, for revolt, except for Hecataeus the historian;[6] he first urged them not to make war on the King of the Persians, drawing attention to all the peoples over whom Dareios ruled and to his power; but when he failed to persuade the others, he then advised them to see that they gained control of the sea. But he said that he did not see how on earth they would achieve this, for he knew that the power of Miletos was not great,

except by seizing the treasure in the temple at Branchidai which Kroisos of Lydia had dedicated;[7] if they did this, there was a good chance of controlling the sea and they would have the treasure to use and their enemies would not plunder it. As I have explained in the first of my *logoi*,[8] the treasure was substantial. The advice of Hecataeus was not taken, but they decided nonetheless to revolt . . . (37) And Aristagoras began by pretending to surrender his tyranny in favour of *isonomia*[9] at Miletos, so that the Milesians should associate themselves willingly with him in revolt, and then went on to do the same in the rest of Ionia . . .

Herodotus v.28–37★

1 See Hdt. v.23–25.
2 Certainly a wild exaggeration.
3 Satrap of Ionia.
4 Aristagoras means the peoples of western Asia Minor.
5 Of the central Aegean.
6 See p.9.
7 See **92**.
8 Book 1.92.
9 See **73** n.1.

103. Aristagoras at Sparta

Aristagoras, in desperate need of help, turned to Sparta; recently humiliated at Athens (see **75**), hampered thereafter by the formal constitution of a Spartan League with a voting assembly, the Spartans were hardly in a position to intervene.

So Aristagoras the tyrant of Miletos came to Sparta during the reign of Kleomenes;[1] according to the Lakedaimonians, he came to negotiate with him with a bronze plaque in his hands, on which was engraved a map of the whole world with every sea and all the rivers. And opening the negotiations, Aristagoras made the following speech to him: 'Kleomenes, do not be surprised at my anxiety to come here; for this is the situation: it is a matter of reproach and a great grief that the Ionians are slaves rather than free men, both to ourselves and, among everyone else, especially to you, who are the leaders of Greece. So now I beg you by the gods of the Hellenes to save the Ionians from slavery, for they are related to you by blood. It is easy for you to accomplish this, for the *barbaroi* are not warlike, whereas you have reached the peak of perfection in the field of martial valour. They fight with the bow and the short spear and go into battle wearing trousers, and hats on their heads. So they are easy to get the better of.' (Aristagoras goes on to compare the wealth of Persia with the poverty of the land for which Sparta now fights rivals equal in strength.) 'When you can easily rule over the whole of Asia, how can you choose otherwise?' This was the plea of Aristagoras, but Kleomenes replied as follows: '*Xenos* of Miletos, I will put off replying to you till two days from now.' (50) That was as far as they got for the moment; and when the appointed day arrived for Kleomenes to reply and they had met at the agreed rendezvous, he asked Aristagoras how many days' journey it was from the sea by the land of the Ionians to the King. At this point, Aristagoras, although in general quick-witted and hitherto successful in misleading Kleomenes, made a mistake; for when he should have told a lie, at any rate if he wished to get the Spartiatai[2] over to Asia, in fact he said that it was a journey of three months. And Kleomenes cut off the rest of the speech which Aristagoras was on the point of making about the journey and said, '*Xenos* of Miletos, leave Sparta before sunset; for your proposal to take the Lakedaimonians three months' journey from the sea is quite improper.' (51) Having said this, Kleomenes returned home; but Aristagoras took the olive-branch of a suppliant in his hand and went to the house, and going in as a suppliant bade Kleomenes send his daughter away and listen; she happened to be standing by – she was called Gorgo and was his only child, now about eight or nine. But Kleomenes told him to say what he wanted and not hold back because of the child. So Aristagoras began by offering ten talents, if Kleomenes did what he wanted. When Kleomenes refused, Aristagoras went on offering more and more money, until he was promising 50 talents, at which point the child said, 'Father, the *xenos* will corrupt you, unless you leave him and go away.' Kleomenes was glad of his daughter's warning and went into another room and Aristagoras left Sparta for ever, without managing to say any more about the journey to the King.

Herodotus v.49–51*

1 See **61**.
2 See **53**.

104. Aristagoras in Athens

Thwarted at Sparta (**103**), Aristagoras turned to Athens for help.

When he had got back to Asia from Sparta, Hippias[1] adopted every expedient he could think of, traducing the Athenians to Artaphrenes and doing everything possible to bring Athens into subjection to himself and Dareios. But the Athenians learnt that Hippias was engaged on this course of action and sent to Sardis, urging the Persians not to heed exiles from Athens. But Artaphrenes ordered them to take Hippias back, if they wished to remain unscathed. Now the Athenians refused to accept the instructions which their envoys brought back and, in doing so, they had agreed on open hostility with the Persians. (97) At this point, while they were in this state of mind and were in any case *personae non gratae* with the Persians, Aristagoras of Miletos arrived at Athens, having been driven from Sparta by Kleomenes; for, after Sparta, Athens was the most powerful *polis* in Greece. Coming before the *dēmos*, Aristagoras made the same speech as in Sparta about the wealth of Asia and about the Persian manner of fighting, about how they used neither shields nor spears and were easy to defeat; he also added that the Milesians were colonists of the Athenians[2] and that it was right for them to use their great power to save them; in his need, there was nothing which he did not promise them, and finally he persuaded them. For it seems to be easier to impose on a crowd than on one man, if Aristagoras failed with the one man, Kleomenes, and succeeded with the 30,000 Athenians.[3] Anyway, the Athenians were persuaded and voted to send twenty ships to help the Ionians, appointing as their commander Melanthios, an outstanding man in every respect. But these ships were the beginning of trouble for the Greeks and the *barbaroi.*

Herodotus v.96–97

1 See **72**.
2 The Ionians of Asia Minor were universally regarded as colonists from Athens (see also **92**); in fact many of the Greeks who settled Asia Minor at the end of the Mycenaean Period, in waves of migrations unlike the later colonising movement, probably did come from Athens.
3 A widely attested conventional figure for the population of Athens.

105. The Ionian revolt

When the Ionians finally rebelled, they were, despite some successes, quickly defeated; the whole episode was probably most important for the later attitudes which it engendered. See in general Murray, *Early Greece*, 243–5.

(A) The Athenians arrived with twenty ships, accompanied by five triremes of the Eretrians; these had not joined the expedition in deference to the Athenians, but for the sake of the Milesians themselves; in fact they were repaying a debt, for the Milesians had earlier helped the Eretrians in the war against the Chalkidians,[1] when the Samians helped the Chalkidians against the Eretrians and the Milesians. Anyway, when the two groups had arrived and the other allies had gathered, Aristagoras mounted an expedition against Sardis. He himself did not join the expedition, but remained in Miletos and appointed others as commanders of the Milesians, his own brother Charopinos and from outside his family Hermophantos. (100) The Ionians reached Ephesos with the expedition and left the ships at Koresos in the territory of Ephesos while they marched up-country with the Ephesians as their guides, a substantial force. They marched along the river Kaystrios, then crossed the Tmolos mountains and when they arrived they captured Sardis without opposition, everything, that is, except the *akropolis*; Artaphrenes himself held the *akropolis* with a sizeable force. (The city was accidentally fired and the Greeks retreated.) (102) And so Sardis was burnt to the ground, including a temple of the local goddess Kybebe (Cybele), which the Persians later used as a pretext when they burnt in return the temples in Greece.[2] At that point, however, the Persians stationed this side of the river Halys, on hearing what had happened, assembled and went to the aid of the Lydians. As it turned out, they found that the Ionians had left Sardis and following on their tracks they caught up with them at Ephesos. The Ionians drew themselves up against them, but were decisively defeated in the battle. And the Persians killed many of them, including men of repute, among them Eualkides the *strategos* of the Eretrians, who had won a number of crowns in athletic contests and often had his praises sung by Simonides of Keos.[3] Those who escaped from the battle scattered to their respective *poleis*. (103) This then was the result of the battle; and the Athenians now abandoned the cause of the Ionians and, though Aristagoras frequently sent envoys to summon them, they refused to help him. But although the Ionians were now deprived of the alliance of the Athenians, they continued all the same to prepare for war against the King, for their actions against Dareios left them no choice. Sailing to the Hellespontos they got control of Byzantion and all the other *poleis* in the area, and outside the Hellespontos they won over the bulk of Karia to their side. This even included Kaunos, which had earlier been unwilling to join them; but when they burnt Sardis, she also came over to them. (104) The Cypriots all gladly joined them with the exception of the Amathousians; for they also thus rebelled from the Persians . . . (105) So Onesilos[4] was besieging Amathous; meanwhile it was reported to King Dareios that Sardis had been captured and burnt by the Athenians and the Ionians and that the leader of the conspiracy to bring this about was Aristagoras of Miletos. It is said that as soon as he heard this he was not bothered about the Ionians, since he knew well that they would not escape punishment for their revolt, but that he asked who the Athenians were; when he had found out, he called for his bow, took it, fitted an arrow and shot it up to heaven and as he did so said, 'Zeus,[5] grant that I may punish the Athenians!'; having said this, he instructed one of his servants to repeat three times before every meal, 'Lord, remember the Athenians'. (106) Having given these instructions,

Dareios summoned before him Histiaios of Miletos, whom he had had at Sousa for some time (and accused him of involvement in the revolt. Histiaios cleared himself for the time being and was sent down to Ionia. Meanwhile the Persians recovered Cyprus and defeated the Karians and recaptured Klazomenai and Kyme.) (124) After the *poleis* had been taken, Aristagoras of Miletos emerged as a poor-spirited creature; for he had disturbed the peace of Ionia and stirred up a great deal of trouble, but now that he saw what was happening he planned to flee; it came to seem impossible to him to overcome King Dareios. With this in mind, therefore, he called together his fellow-conspirators and began to plan, saying that it would be better for them if they had some place of refuge, if they were driven from Miletos; he could take them either to found an *apoikia* in Sardinia or to Myrkinos in the land of the Edonians, which Histiaios had had as a gift from Dareios[6] and had fortified. This was the choice which Aristagoras offered. (125) The advice of Hecataeus son of Hegesandros, the historian, was not to go to either of these places, but to build a fortress on Leros and lie low, if he (Aristagoras) were expelled from Miletos; in due course he could use this as a base for a return to Miletos. (126) This was the advice of Hecataeus, but Aristagoras himself felt on the whole that he should go to Myrkinos. So he entrusted Miletos to Pythagoras, a man of repute though not of his family, and himself sailed with anyone who wished to come to Thrake and got control of the territory which was his objective. But while using it as a base, he and his followers were killed by the Thrakians, while he was besieging a town, which the Thrakians had made a compact to leave under the terms of a truce.

Herodotus v.99–126*

(B) This, then, was how Aristagoras, the originator of the Ionian revolt, died; meanwhile, Histiaios, the tyrant of Miletos, arrived at Sardis after his release by Dareios. When he arrived from Sousa, Artaphrenes the governor of the Sardians asked him why he thought the Ionians had revolted; he claimed not to know and expressed surprise at what had happened, as if he knew nothing at all of the state affairs were in. But Artaphrenes, seeing that he was making it up and knowing his complicity in the revolt, said, 'This is how things are, Histiaios: you made the shoe and Aristagoras put it on.' (2) This is what Artaphrenes said in relation to the revolt; and Histiaios, afraid of him as knowing everything, fled down to the sea during the first night after his arrival, breaking his trust with Dareios; for he had promised to subject to him the biggest of all the islands, Sardinia,[7] and in fact took up the *hēgemonia* of the Ionians in the war against Dareios . . . (7) The Persians now mounted an expedition against Miletos and the rest of Ionia; and when the Ionians learnt of this they sent their representatives to the Panionion.[8] After they had come together there and debated the question, it was agreed not to collect a land army to oppose the Persians, but that the Milesians should defend their walls themselves and that a fleet should be manned down to the last ship and that as soon as it had been manned it should gather at Lade and there fight on behalf of Miletos; Lade is a small island lying just off Miletos. (8) Shortly after this the Ionians arrived with the ships which they had manned and along with them those of the Aiolians who live on Lesbos . . . (The Ionians were defeated, Miletos captured and Didyma sacked.) (20) Then those of the Milesians who had been taken alive were removed to Sousa. And King Dareios did them no further harm, but settled them on the Red Sea (Persian Gulf), in the *polis* of Ampa,[9] past which the river Tigris flows out to the sea. The Persians themselves held that part of the *chōra* of Miletos which is by the *polis* and the coastal plain, while they assigned the frontier region to the Pedasans of Karia.[10] (21) The Sybarites, who lived in Laos and Skidros after the loss of their *polis*, did not show the same feeling for the Milesians who had suffered thus at the hands of the Persians as the Milesians had shown them; for when Sybaris was captured by the Krotoniates, all the Milesians from the young men upwards shaved their heads and went into deep mourning; for of all the *poleis* which I know about these two were the most closely related to each other.[11] The Athenians behaved very differently from the Sybarites; for they made it very clear how much they were grieved by the capture of Miletos in all sorts of ways; in particular, when Phrynichus put on the capture of Miletos as a play,[12] the theatre was moved to tears and the Athenians fined him 1,000 drachmas for having revived the memory of what was in fact a domestic disaster[13] and forbade anyone ever again to use this theme. (22) Miletos was thus emptied of its inhabitants (and the revolt was virtually at an end; Histiaios held out for a time as a *condottiere*, but the various mainland and island communities were quickly subjected; the process was at least *remembered* as a brutal one).

Herodotus VI. 1–32★

1 See **81** n. 10.
2 See **108**.
3 Like Pindar (see **12**), a man who wrote odes to celebrate victories in the great games, he wrote for the tyranny at Athens and for one of the great aristocratic families of Thessaly, but also composed the epitaph for the Athenians who fell at Marathon and the Spartans who fell at Thermopylai.
4 Of Salamis in Cyprus.
5 Herodotus has Hellenised the supreme Persian god Ahura(mazda), compare **97**.
6 In Thrake, see Hdt. v.11.

7 See Hdt. v.106–107.
8 See **92**.
9 In fact, obviously not a *polis* in the full sense of the word.
10 The archaeological evidence suggests that Herodotus' picture of the fate of
   Miletos is exaggerated.
11 Perhaps as a result of trade.
12 In 494; for Attic tragedy see Ch.14 Intro.
13 See **104** n.2.

106. Miltiades

The hero of the Greek resistance to the first Persian invasion of Greece was
Miltiades (**108**); as a result his prestige was such that he was allowed a fleet to
attack Paros without having told the Athenian assembly that that was what he
was going to do (see Hdt. vi.132–136; R. Develin, 'Miltiades and the Parian
expedition', *L'Antiquité Classique* 1977, 571–7). But before 490, he had spent
much of his life on the marches of the Greek and Persian worlds (compare
Hdt. v.94–95 for Peisistratos and Sigeion).

The ruler[1] up to this point had been Miltiades son of Kimon and
grandson of Stesagoras; Miltiades son of Kypselos had earlier acquired
this position, in the following way.[2] The Thrakian Dolonkians originally
held the Chersonesos, but when they were getting the worse of a war
against the Apsinthians they sent their kings to Delphi to consult the
oracle about the war; and the oracle ordered them to acquire as founder
(*oikistēs*) for the land[3] the person who first offered them hospitality after
they had left the sanctuary. So the Dolonkians followed the sacred way
through Phokis and Boiotia; but no one offered them hospitality and so
they turned off to Athens.[4] (35) In Athens at that stage Peisistratos held
supreme power, but Miltiades son of Kypselos was also important; he
came from a family which kept a four-horse chariot; his line descended
ultimately from Aiakos son of (the nymph) Aigina, but later became
Athenian; Philaios son of Aias was the first of the family to be Athenian.
The elder Miltiades happened to be sitting on his porch and saw the
Dolonkians passing, with their foreign dress and their spears, and called
out to them and when they came up offered them shelter and *xenia*. They
accepted and were entertained by him and revealed the whole oracle, and
having revealed it asked him to obey the command of the god. When
Miltiades had heard what they had to say, he was at once persuaded,
since he was resentful of the rule of Peisistratos and wanted to be out of
the way. So he at once sent to Delphi to ask the oracle if he should do
what the Dolonkians asked him. (36) When the oracle confirmed that he
should, he then set sail with the Dolonkians and gained control of the
Chersonesos, having taken with him any Athenian who wished to share

in the venture; he had already won the four-horse chariot race at Olympia and now those who had brought him to the Chersonesos made him tyrant. The first thing he did was to build a wall across the isthmus of the Chersonesos from the *polis* of Kardia to Paktye, in order that the Apsinthians should not be able to invade the land and harm them. . . . (39) After Stesagoras[5] had been killed, the sons of Peisistratos sent Miltiades son of Kimon and brother of the dead Stesagoras by sea to take over affairs in the Chersonesos; even in Athens they treated him well, in order to give the impression that they had not been involved in the death of his father Kimon, the manner of which I shall narrate elsewhere[6] . . . (41) When he now learnt that the Phoinikians[7] were at Tenedos, he filled five triremes with his moveable goods and sailed for Athens. Starting from Kardia, he sailed across the Black Gulf; as he rounded the Chersonesos, the Phoinikians fell in with the ships. Miltiades with four of the ships escaped to Imbros, but the Phoinikians pursued and captured the fifth. Now in command of this ship, as it happened, was the eldest son of Miltiades, Metiochos, born not to the daughter of the Thrakian Oloros, but to another woman. The Phoinikians captured him along with the ship and, learning that he was the son of Miltiades, they took him to the King, expecting that they would be substantially rewarded; for it had been Miltiades who had expressed the opinion among the Ionians that they should obey the Skythians, when they bade them break the bridge[8] and sail back home. But when the Phoinikians brought Metiochos son of Miltiades to Dareios, he did him no harm, but rather the reverse; for he gave him a house and land and a Persian wife, who bore him children regarded as Persian.[9] Meanwhile Miltiades arrived at Athens from Imbros.

Herodotus VI.34–41*

1 Of the *poleis* in the Thrakian Chersonesos.
2 For a family tree see Fig. 13 on p.216.
3 For *oikistēs* as founder of a colony see **18**; Miltiades was as it were a second founder, and after his death the inhabitants of the Chersonesos 'sacrificed to him as is done for an *oikistēs* and established a horse-race and an athletic contest in his honour' (VI.38.1).
4 For Athenian openness to foreigners see **158**.
5 The rule had passed in due course to Stesagoras, the son of Miltiades' uterine brother Kimon. The relationships emerge clearly from the family tree (Fig. 13 on p.216), as does the connection of the historian Thucydides with the family.
6 See VI.103.3.
7 The Phoinikians were the Persian fleet and were in the course of suppressing the Ionian revolt.
8 See **101**.
9 Compare the case of Themistokles, at **168**.

The Philaïdai
(A simplified stemma; for a full one see Davies, *Families*, 293ff. with Table I)

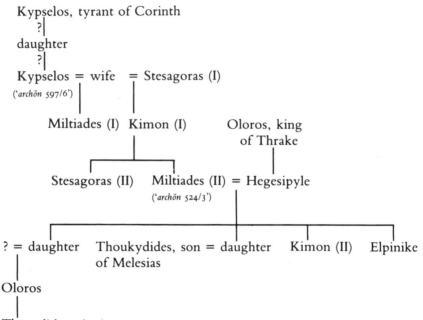

For Miltiades, son of Kypselos, see Hdt. VI. 34

Hippokleides, son of Teisandros (**26**), was also descended from the tyrant family of Corinth, but whether Hippokleides or Teisandros was brother of Kypselos the *archōn* is unknown.

On the problematical relationship of Thucydides the historian to this family see Davies, *Families*, 233–6.

For the list of *archontes*, see T.J. Cadoux, *JHS* 68 (1948), 70; for acutely expressed scepticism as to its worth, W.H. Plommer, *CR* n.s. 19 (1969), 126.

13 The Philaïdai

107. The first Persian invasion of Greece

In 492, the King was at last ready to seek revenge for the sack of Sardis (**105**).

It was at the beginning of spring that the King dismissed his other *stratēgoi* and Mardonios the son of Gobryes came down to the sea, bringing with him a large force, particularly of infantry, but also a large fleet. He was still a young man and had just married Artozostre the daughter of King Dareios. When Mardonios reached Kilikia at the head of this force, he himself went aboard ship and voyaged with the other ships while other commanders led the infantry to the Hellespontos. Sailing along the coast of Asia, Mardonios arrived in Ionia and there something very remarkable happened, at least I think so, for those Greeks who do not believe that Otanes propounded the view to the seven Persians[1] that they should establish a democracy; for Mardonios put down all the tyrants of the Ionians and established democracies in the *poleis*. Having done this he hastened on to the Hellespontos. And as soon as a large fleet and a large force of infantry had been assembled, they crossed the Hellespontos in the ships and began the march through Europe, heading for Eretria and Athens. (44) These places at any rate were the pretext for the expedition, but it was in their minds to subdue as many as possible of the Greek *poleis*; so with the fleet they took Thasos, without meeting any resistance, and with the army they added the Makedonians to the subjects they already had; for all the peoples up to the Makedonians had already come under their sway. (The fleet failed to round Athos and Mardonios was wounded in a skirmish, and the expedition turned back; Thasos, however, remained loyal.) (48) After this Dareios attempted to find out what was in the minds of the Greeks, whether they would go to war with him or surrender. So he sent heralds hither and thither throughout Greece, bidding them ask for earth and water[2] for the King. At the same time as he sent these men to Greece he sent others to the *poleis* by the sea which paid tribute to him, bidding them prepare warships and horse transports. (49) While they were in the process of making these preparations, the heralds were in Greece; many of the mainlanders gave what the Persian demanded and all the islanders whom they visited with their request, including the Aiginetans.[3]

Herodotus VI.43–49.1*

1 See **89**.
2 Symbols of submission.
3 Compare **115A** for the hostility of Herodotus to the Aiginetans.

108. The Marathon campaign

Expecting little opposition in Greece, the Persian armada finally reached the coast of Attika in 490. See Hignett, *Xerxes*, 55–75; Burn, *Persia*, ch. 12.

The Athenians and the Aiginetans were thus at war with each other; meanwhile the King of Persia was at work. His servant regularly reminded Dareios 'Remember the Athenians', and the Peisistratids were at hand to traduce them;[1] at the same time Dareios wished to take advantage of this pretext to subdue those peoples in Greece who had not given him earth and water. He dismissed Mardonios from his command, since he had performed badly on the previous expedition,[2] and appointing other *stratēgoi* despatched them against Eretria and Athens; they were Datis, who was a Median, and Artaphrenes the son of Artaphrenes, his own nephew; he sent them off bidding them to reduce Athens and Eretria to slavery and to bring the population before him as slaves.

(The expedition sailed directly for Greece from Samos, touching at Naxos,[3] where the population fled and the *polis* and the temples were burnt, and at Delos, which was ostentatiously spared;[4] there was an earthquake at Delos, which marked for Herodotus more ills for Greece during the reigns of Dareios, Xerxes and Artaxerxes than for twenty generations before Dareios, 'some of them inflicted on her by the Persians, some by the leading powers themselves fighting for supremacy'; the expedition first met resistance, which was overcome, at Karystos.[5])

(100) When the Eretrians learnt that the Persian expedition was sailing against them, they asked the Athenians to help them; the Athenians agreed, and designated the 4,000 men who held the land of the *hippobotai* of Chalkis[6] as their protectors. But the counsel of the Eretrians was evil, for they had sent for the Athenians while entertaining other ideas; for some of them proposed to abandon the *polis* for the backwoods of Euboia, while others among them prospecting their own gain from the Persians meditated betrayal. (The Athenians were warned and escaped by crossing to Oropos in Attika; Eretria was attacked, in due course betrayed and burnt along with its temples in revenge for the sack of Sardis. Led by Hippias the son of Peisistratos, the expedition landed at Marathon.) (103) As soon as the Athenians heard this, they too set off for Marathon to oppose the Persians, commanded by the ten *stratēgoi*; one of the ten was Miltiades, whose father Kimon the son of Stesagoras had, as it happened, been banished from Athens by Peisistratos the son of Hippokrates . . . (104) As for Miltiades, his enemies had waited for him on his return from Chersonesos[7] and had brought him before a court and prosecuted him for his tenure of the tyranny there. But he escaped from

these enemies also and so was appointed *stratēgos* of the Athenians, elected by the *dēmos*.[8]

(A message to Sparta brought a promise of help after the full moon;[9] meanwhile the Athenians at Marathon were joined by the Plataians.)[10] (109) Two contrary opinions were held by the *stratēgoi* of the Athenians, some of them being opposed to an attack because of their weakness compared with the Persian expedition, some of them being in favour, including Miltiades. Given the (even) division of opinion, the more passive approach prevailed; but there was an eleventh person entitled to vote, the man who was chosen by lot[11] to be *polemarchos* of the Athenians; for originally the Athenians had a *polemarchos* whose vote was equal to that of a *stratēgos*. Kallimachos of (the deme) Aphidna was *polemarchos* that year and so at that point Miltiades approached him and said, 'It rests with you now, Kallimachos, either to reduce Athens to slavery or to set her free . . .' (110) Thus Miltiades won over Kallimachos and with the vote of the *polemarchos* the decision to attack was taken. Then the *strategoi* who had been in favour of an attack, as each one's daily presidency of the board of *stratēgoi* came round, handed it over to Miltiades; he accepted, but did not launch the attack until his own presidency came round.

(After the Athenian and Plataian victory, (115) the Persian force boarded the ships) and sailed round Cape Sounion, aiming to arrive at the city (*astu*) before the Athenians; among the Athenians, the Alkmaionidai were blamed for a plot which suggested this plan to them; they were believed to have come to an agreement with the Persians and to have raised a shield (as a signal) when they were again aboard ship.[12] Anyway, they sailed round Cape Sounion; but the Athenians came to the rescue of the city (*astu*) as fast as they could and got there before the *barbaroi* arrived; when they got there, having camped at Marathon in the precinct of Herakles, they camped in another precinct of Herakles at Kynosarges.[13] The *barbaroi* rode at anchor in their ships off Phaleron, which was then the harbour of the Athenians,[14] and after doing this for a while sailed back to Asia. (117) In the battle at Marathon about 6,400 of the *barbaroi* were killed and 192 of the Athenians.

Herodotus VI.94–117*

1 See **104**.
2 See **107**.
3 See **102**.
4 'For I myself am thus inclined and this is the command of the King to me,' said Datis; for Persian attitudes to other religions compare **95** with n.7; there is another example of Datis' piety at Hdt. VI.118.
5 Naxos and Karystos were clearly inclined to independent action; the latter had to be coerced into the Delian League, the former was its first rebel, see Ch.12.

6 See **75**.

7 See **106**.

8 See **119**.

9 For Spartan religious scruples and their conduct of war see Pritchett, *War* I, ch.9; a Spartan force came post-haste after the full moon.

10 See **62**.

11 The *polemarchos* was not chosen by lot till 487/6 (see **120**) – and then lost his effective military function.

12 Herodotus returns to this story at VI.121–124 and expresses disbelief.

13 A quarter of Athens.

14 See **159** Intro.

109. Preparations for a renewed attack

See Hignett, *Xerxes*, 77–96.

(A) When the news of the battle which had been fought at Marathon reached King Dareios the son of Hystaspes, he took it even harder still – he was already extremely angry with the Athenians because of the attack on Sardis – and was even more determined to mount an expedition against Greece. So he immediately sent messengers round to each city and prescribed the preparation of an expedition, commanding everyone to produce a much larger force than before, whether of ships or of cavalry, and a much bigger supply of food and transports. Whereupon Asia was turned upside down for three years, as the best men and equipment were got together for the expedition against Greece. But in the fourth year the Egyptians, who had been enslaved by Kambyses,[1] rebelled from the Persians; at this Dareios simply became even more eager to march, against both enemies.

Herodotus VII.1

(B) Arriving at Sardis, he (Xerxes)[2] first of all sent heralds to Greece to ask for earth and water and to order the preparation of meals for the King; he sent the heralds everywhere except Athens and Sparta. He sent for the second time to ask for earth and water because he was quite sure that those who had not given them earlier when Dareios had asked would now be terrorised and give them;[3] anyway he wished to find this out and so sent the heralds.

Herodotus VII.32

(C) Of those who gave (earth and water) there were the following, Thessalians, Dolopians, Ainianes, Perraibians, Lokrians, Magnetes, Malians, Achaians of Phthiotis and Thebans and the other Boiotians except for the Thespians and Plataians. The Greeks who were proposing to make war on the *barbaroi* swore an oath against them, that any Greeks who gave themselves up to the Persians without being compelled to should be required to give up a tenth of their property to the god of Delphi, if things went well for the Greeks. This was the oath which the Greeks swore.[4] (133) As for Athens and Sparta, Xerxes did not send heralds there to ask for earth, because when Dareios had sent for this very purpose, the former had thrown the messengers into a pit, the latter into a well, bidding them take earth and water thence to the King.[5]

Herodotus VII. 132–133.1[6]

1 See **93**.
2 Dareios had died in 486 and was succeeded by his son Xerxes, who promptly quelled the revolt of Egypt; Xerxes was then persuaded by Mardonios to continue with the expedition against Greece. A huge army was collected, a canal dug through Mount Athos and Xerxes conveyed to Sardis.
3 See **107** n.2.
4 See **115**.
5 Herodotus goes on to consider the consequences of such acts of impiety; for heralds were sacred.
6 Compare **117** for medism.

110. The Greek response

See Hignett, *Xerxes*, 96–104.

(A) The expedition mounted by the King had as its pretext an attack on Athens, but in fact aimed at the whole of Greece. The Greeks, however, although long aware of this fact, did not all work together. For some of them, having given earth and water to the Persian, were emboldened to think that they would suffer nothing untoward from the *barbaroi*; but those who had not given were most apprehensive, since there was not a large enough number of ships in Greece to meet the invader in battle, and the majority of Greeks were unwilling to go to war but were gladly going over to the other side. (139) At this point I am compelled to express an opinion which will be resented by the majority of men, but I shall not restrain myself, since it seems to me to be correct. If the Athenians had taken fright at the coming danger and abandoned their country, or had not abandoned it but remained and surrendered to Xerxes, no one would have tried to resist the King by sea. And if no one had resisted Xerxes by sea, the same would have happened by land. Even if many protecting walls had been built across the Isthmos by the Peloponnesians, the Lakedaimonians would have been abandoned by their allies as each saw its *polis* taken by the fleet of the *barbaroi*; they would not have wished to give in, but would have been forced to do so.

And the Lakedaimonians would have been isolated and then have performed great deeds and died bravely. That is what would have happened, or else they would have seen the other Greeks medising[1] and come to an agreement with Xerxes before the end came. And so in either case the Greeks would have been subject to the Persians. For I cannot imagine what use walls built across the Isthmos would have been if the King controlled the sea. As it is, anyone who claimed that the Athenians were the saviours of Greece would be quite right. For whichever way they turned, that side was bound to win; and having chosen that Greece should remain free, it was they who roused the rest of the Greek world, which had not medised, and played a role second only to that of the gods in repelling the King. Not even the fearful oracles coming from Delphi and striking fear into their hearts persuaded them to abandon Greece; they remained and prepared to receive the invader of their land.[2]

Herodotus VII.138–139

(B) The Greeks who were loyal to the Greek cause now met and exchanged promises and guarantees, and concluded in their discussions that the most important thing of all was to patch up their quarrels and put an end to the wars between them; there were a number of wars going on, but the most serious was that between Athens and Aigina.[3] Later, when they heard that Xerxes and his army was at Sardis, they decided to send spies to Asia to find out what the King was doing and envoys to Argos to conclude an alliance against the Persians; they also decided to send other envoys to Sicily to Gelon the son of Deinomenes,[4] and others to Kerkyra and others to Crete, to bid them come to the rescue of Greece. They hoped in fact that the Greek world would be united and that everyone would join together and pursue the same course of action, since the same dangers threatened all Greeks alike. The power of Gelon was said to be very great, greater than that of all the other Greeks.

Herodotus VII.145

1 Compare **117**.
2 Delphi produced two oracles, one uniformly gloomy, the other stating *inter alia* that a wooden wall would remain intact; Themistokles then persuaded the Athenians to put their trust in their fleet. At 144.3 Herodotus repeats his statement of Athenian determination, 'Discussing things after their consultation of the oracle, they determined to receive the barbarian invader of Greece with their entire naval strength, along with any Greeks who wished to join them, in obedience to divine command.' This relates again, in our view, to the general attitude of the Athenians, not to the particular decision to attempt to block the Persian fleet at Artemision (for which see **111**).
3 See **108**.
4 Tyrant of Syracuse, compare **118**.

111. Thermopylai and Artemision

The Greeks first held the pass at Tempe, between Makedonia and Thessalia, but on the advice of Alexandros of Makedon fell back to the pass at Thermopylai, with the fleet nearby at Artemision (the contingents are listed at Hdt. VII.202–203; each was under its own commander and the whole army was under king Leonidas of Sparta). See Hignett, *Xerxes*, 105–92; Burn, *Persia*, chs.18–19.

(A) Leonidas came then to Thermopylai, having picked three hundred men, all in their prime and all with living sons;[1] and he arrived having picked up from the Thebans the contingent the size of which I have already given, whose commander was Leontiades the son of Eurymachos. These were the only ones whom Leonidas was particularly anxious to take along, since they were under considerable suspicion of intention to medise;[2] so he summoned them to fight, wishing to know whether they would send a contingent or would openly abandon the Greek alliance. As it was, they sent troops, but with disloyal intentions. (206) The Spartiatai[3] had sent the men with Leonidas off ahead, in order that seeing them arrive the other allies might join the expedition and not themselves medise, as they might if they realised that the Spartiatai were holding back; afterwards, when the Karneia (festival), which was at that moment in the way,[4] had been celebrated, they intended, leaving only a garrison in Sparta, to march out at full speed with all their forces. The rest of the allies also intended to do the same themselves; for the Olympiad happened also to coincide with the events so far narrated. And because no one expected the war at Thermopylai to be decided so quickly, they sent only advance contingents. (207) This then was their intention; meanwhile, the Greeks at Thermopylai, when the Persians approached the entrance to the pass, became frightened and began to discuss withdrawal. The Peloponnesians in general wished to retreat to the Peloponnesos and guard the Isthmos; but since the Phokians and Lokrians were indignant at this proposal, Leonidas determined to wait there and send messengers to the various *poleis* bidding them send further help, since they themselves were too few to resist the invading army.

Herodotus VII.205.2–207

(After a short delay, Xerxes attacked, but was repulsed; he was then told of a way to turn the Greek position by a Malian, Ephialtes; the Greeks withdrew, except for the Spartans and the Thespians, of their own volition, and the Thebans, under compulsion. This tiny defending force was eventually overwhelmed; but the heroic deaths of Leonidas and the men with him clearly had a tremendous effect on Greek morale for the rest of the war. Meanwhile a detachment from the Persian fleet at Aphetai was sent off round Euboia in an attempt to take the Greek fleet also in the rear; but it was wrecked on the way and a reinforced Greek fleet successfully raided the Persian position.)

(B) The commanders of the *barbaroi* took it ill that so few ships were able to inflict such damage on them and were also afraid of what might befall them at Xerxes' hands; so on the third day they gave up waiting for the Greeks to begin the fighting, fitted out their ships and put to sea about midday. As it happened, the sequence of sea-battles took place about the same time as the fighting on land at Thermopylai; and the struggle at sea was over the strait of the Euripos, just as those with Leonidas were guarding the pass. The cry of the Greeks was not to let the barbarians through into Greece, of the Persians to wipe out the Greek forces and gain control of the route . . (18) When the two sides parted (after an inconclusive battle), both were glad to get back to their bases. The Greeks, when they broke away and got clear of the battle, were able to pick up the dead and gather in the wrecks; but they had suffered considerably, not least the Athenians, half of whose ships were damaged, and they planned withdrawal into territory under Greek control.

Herodotus VIII. 15–18*

1 See Cartledge, *Sparta*, 204.
2 See **110A**.
3 See **53**.
4 Compare **108**.

112. Salamis

The Greek fleet fetched up at Salamis, in order to cover the Athenian evacuation of non-combatants, rendered necessary by the evident intention of the Greeks of the Peloponnesos to retire beyond the Isthmos. A recently discovered inscription is relevant (A); it once formed part of a complex at Troizen not inscribed until the third century B.C.; attitudes towards it range from the view that it represents what was actually decided as the Persian force moved south, to the view that it is a late reconstruction from literary sources with no documentary basis whatever. See in general Hignett, *Xerxes*, 193–239; Burn, *Persia*, ch.21.

(A) Gods
It was resolved by the *boulē* and the *dēmos*:
Themistokles the son of Neokles of (the deme) Phrearrioi proposed: To place the *polis* in the hands of Athena who [watches over] Athens and of all the other gods, to guard and to keep the *barbaroi* from the *chōra*; and that [all] Athenians and *xenoi* living in Athens should place their children and wives in Troizen [?in the care of Theseus] the *archēgetēs*[1] of the *chōra*; and that they should place the old men and the moveable property on Salamis; and that the treasurers and priests should remain on the *akropolis* guarding the belongings of the gods; and that all other Athenians and the

xenoi of military age should board the two hundred ships which have been made ready and resist the *barbaroi* in defence of their own freedom and that of the other Greeks, along with the Lakedaimonians and Corinthians and Aiginetans[2] and the others who are willing to face the danger together; and that the *stratēgoi* in command should tomorrow appoint 200 *triērarchoi*,[3] one for each ship, from among those who hold land and house in Athens and who have legitimate children and who are not older than 50, and allot the ships to them; and that they should choose ten marines for each ship from those who are between 20 and 30, and four archers; and that they should choose the officers[4] for the ships by lot when they allot the *triērarchoi*; and that the *stratēgoi* should list the [oarsmen] by ship on whiteboards,[5] the Athenians according to the deme registers, the *xenoi* according to the registers with the *polemarchos*; and that they should list them, having divided them into 200 units of a hundred men each,[6] and write up for each unit the name of the trireme and of the *triērarchos* and the names of the crew so that they may know which trireme each unit should board; and when all the units have been divided up and allotted to the triremes, the *boulē* and the *stratēgoi* are to man all the 200 ships after sacrificing in appeasement of Zeus Pankrates and Athena Nike and Poseidon Asphaleios;[7] and when the ships are manned, they are to send 100 to Artemision in Euboia and keep 100 around Salamis and the rest of Attika and guard the *chōra*; and so that all Athenians may be united in resisting the *barbaroi*, those who have removed themselves for ten years[8] are to go to Salamis and to wait there until the *dēmos* decides about them; and those [who have been deprived of civic rights . . .]

Meiggs and Lewis no.23

(B) The others then put in at Salamis, the Athenians on their own territory. After their arrival, they proclaimed that every Athenian was to place his children and slaves in safety where he could.[9] Thereupon the majority sent them to Troizen, but some to Aigina and some to Salamis. They hastened to do this, wishing to obey the oracle,[10] but also for another pressing reason: according to the Athenians, a large snake lives in the temple as guardian of the *akropolis* and furthermore they worship it and place food out for it every month on the assumption that it is really there, food in the form of honey-cake; now earlier this honey-cake was always consumed, but that month remained untouched; and when the priestess reported this, the Athenians were even readier to leave their *polis*, since the goddess herself had abandoned the *akropolis*. And when they had transferred everything, they sailed to rejoin the Greek force.[11]

Herodotus VIII.41

(The temple treasurers and a few men who had not possessed the resources to organise their transfer to Salamis barricaded themselves on the *akropolis*, thus trusting a 'wooden wall';[12] they were eventually overwhelmed, the temple plundered and the *akropolis* fired.[13] At this, the allied fleet determined to withdraw to the Isthmos, but Themistokles got the decision reversed, in a debate which involved a remarkable exchange.)

(C) After Themistokles had spoken, the Corinthian Adeimantos weighed into him once more, bidding a man without a country remain silent and urging Eurybiades not to allow a man without a *polis* to put a question to the vote; he added that if Themistokles could produce a *polis* then he could offer advice. He took this line of course because Athens had fallen and was in enemy hands. In reply Themistokles abused both him and the Corinthians, and made it clear that he and his fellow-countrymen possessed both a *polis* and a land more substantial than theirs, as long as they manned 200 ships;[14] for none of the Greeks would be able to resist them if they attacked.

Herodotus VIII.61

1 Compare **16** for the term.
2 Compare **110B**.
3 See **144** Intro.
4 Their precise identification is disputed.
5 See p.21.
6 The normal figure for a ship's complement was 200, Hdt. VIII.17.
7 Zeus All-powerful, Athena Victory, Poseidon Safety-bringer; the stone actually reads 'Athena *and* Nike'.
8 The ostracised, see **79**.
9 Compare Plut. *Them.* 10.2.
10 And trust their ships, see **110** n.2.
11 In which they formed the largest and finest part, despite the arrival of other contingents; the commander was a Spartan, Eurybiades the son of Eurykleides, as at Artemision.
12 See **110** n.2.
13 Xerxes, like Datis (see **108**), made a pious gesture, ordering the Athenian exiles in his entourage to go up onto the *akropolis* and sacrifice in the traditional manner.
14 We have an early and a dramatic example of the fact that to the Greeks a *polis* was its men (compare **17**).

113. From Salamis to Plataiai

Themistokles foiled a last attempt by the Greek fleet (see **112C**) to withdraw by sending a secret message to Xerxes to send part of his fleet round Salamis and cut off the Greek fleet; battle was joined and the Persian fleet routed; what was left withdrew to guard the bridges over the Hellespontos and the army withdrew to Thessaly; Xerxes returned thence to Persia, while Mardonios remained with a large army to carry on the fight in the spring of 479. Early in 479, the Persian fleet, which had wintered at Kyme and Samos, mustered at Samos, but proceeded no further west. The Athenian fleet mustered at Aigina. See Hignett, *Xerxes*, 240–88; Burn, *Persia*, ch.23.

When all the ships had reached Aigina, messengers from the Ionians arrived at the Greek camp, having shortly before this gone to Sparta and asked the Lakedaimonians to free Ionia; among them was Herodotos the son of Basileides.[1] Being embroiled in *stasis*, they had plotted to assassinate Strattis the *tyrannos* of Chios,[2] being originally seven in number; but when their plot was exposed, one of their group carried out the deed and the remaining six left Chios and went to Sparta and then to Aigina, urging the Greeks to sail to Ionia; but they barely got them to go as far as Delos. For everything beyond held terrors for the Greeks, since they themselves did not know the area well and they thought that it was full of enemy forces; they thought that Samos and the Pillars of Herakles[3] were about the same distance away. The result was that the *barbaroi* were afraid to sail west of Samos, the Greeks to sail east of Delos, despite the request of the Chians; fear stood guard over the water which lay between them.

Herodotus VIII.132

1 No relation of the historian.
2 Compare 101.
3 The Straits of Gibraltar – the alleged state of Greek ignorance is incredible.

114. Plataiai

On land, Mardonios sent Alexandros of Makedon to Athens with an offer of alliance, which was rejected (see 25A); he then captured Athens for a second time, but withdrew when the Spartans marched north after concluding the celebration of the Hyakinthia (compare 108) and took up a position near Plataiai in Boiotia. For both sides, the omens were good for a defensive action, bad for an attack; but the Persians attacked. See Hignett, *Xerxes*, 289–344; Burn, *Persia*, ch.24.

Where Mardonios himself was, fighting on a white horse and surrounded by a picked band of the thousand best Persians, that was where they inflicted the most damage on their enemies; and as long as Mardonios was alive, they held their ground and laid low many of the Lakedaimonians in doing so; but when Mardonios fell together with the band surrounding him, which was the strongest element in the army, then the rest turned and fled from the Lakedaimonians. They suffered most from the fact that their equipment did not include defensive armour; for they were as a result engaged in a contest (*agōn*) of men without protection against hoplites. Thus Mardonios paid the Lakedaimonians the price for the death of Leonidas as the oracle foretold, and Pausanias the son of Kleombrotos the son of Anaxandridas won the greatest of all known victories; I have already mentioned the names of his other ancestors in dealing with Leonidas;[1] for they are the same in the two cases. Mardonios was killed by Arimnestos, a leading man of Sparta; some time after the Persian Wars he joined battle at Stenyklaros when Sparta was at war with all the Messenians;[2] he had 300 men under him and he and they were all killed.

Herodotus IX.63–64

1 VII.204.
2 See **169**.

115. The serpent column

The Greeks had vowed to Delphi a tenth of the property of those who medised (see **109**); this extreme measure was abandoned in the hour of victory and a more conventional tithe of the booty won was offered.

(A) Pausanias now issued a proclamation that no one was to touch the booty, and ordered the helots to collect everything together. So they scattered over the encampment and found tents full of gold and silver, gilded and silver couches, golden mixing-bowls and cups and other vessels; and they found wagons loaded with sacks full of gold and silver basins; and they stripped golden bracelets and collars and swords from the dead, since no attention was paid even to richly decorated clothing; in fact the helots stole a great deal and sold it to the Aiginetans, but they brought in a great deal too, anything in fact which they could not conceal; that was when the great riches for which the Aiginetans are known first fell into their hands; for they bought the gold from the helots as if it was bronze.[1] (81) When they had collected everything, they set aside a tithe for the god at Delphi, with which they dedicated the golden tripod on the bronze three-headed snake,[2] which stands just beside the altar; they also set aside a tithe for the god at Olympia, with which they dedicated a bronze statue of Zeus ten cubits high, and for the god at the Isthmos, from which a bronze statue of Poseidon seven cubits high was made; afterwards they divided up the rest and each man took his due, including the concubines of the Persians and their gold and silver and other objects and beasts of burden.

Herodotus IX.80–81.1

(B) These fought the war[3] –
Lakedaimonians, Athenians, Corinthians, Tegeates, Sikyonians, Aiginetans, Megarians, Epidaurians, Orchomenians, Phleiasians, Troizenians, Hermionians, Tirynthians, Plataians, Thespians, Mykenaians, Keians, Melians, Tenians, Naxians, Eretrians, Chalkidians, Styrians, Eleians, Poteidaians, Leukadians, Anaktorians, Kythnians, Siphnians, Amprakiots, Lepreates.

Meiggs and Lewis no.27

1 For other evidence of a hostile attitude to Aigina see **107** and Hdt. IX.85; for Athens and Aigina in the fifth century see **178**.
2 In fact on three snakes intertwined. The golden tripod was melted down by the Phokians in the fourth century (see **336**), the stone base survives at Delphi; the bronze column six metres high, made of the three intertwined snakes, was taken to Constantinople by Constantine the Great and may be seen in the Hippodrome there; one of the heads is in the Istanbul Archaeological Museum. The ethnics are inscribed one above another, normally three to a coil; but the Tenians are a late addition to the seventh coil (see Hdt. VIII.82.1), the Siphnians to the tenth coil (perhaps at the instance of the Athenians). Among early references to the monuments erected after Plataiai note Thuc. I.132.
3 Up to and including the battle of Plataiai; Kroton, Pale in Kephallenia, Seriphos and the Opountaian Lokrians, all mentioned by Herodotus, are missing.

116. Mykale and Sestos

The last stage, the pursuit of the Persian armada to Asia, was finally undertaken.

(A) So Artabazos (with the rest of the Persian army) returned to Asia; meanwhile it so happened that they suffered a further defeat at Mykale in Ionia on the same day as that at Plataiai. For while the Greeks in the ships who had come with Leotychidas of Sparta lay off Delos, three messengers came to them from Samos, Lampon the son of Thrasykles and Athenagoras the son of Archestratidas and Hegesistratos the son of Aristagoras, sent by the Samians without the knowledge of the Persians or of the *tyrannos* Theomestor the son of Androdamas, whom the Persians had put in control of Samos.[1] When they came before the commanders, Hegesistratos made a long and appealing speech, arguing that if the Ionians merely saw the Greek force they would rebel from the Persians and that the *barbaroi* would not resist, but that if they did the Greek force would find such a prey as they would never find again; and calling on the gods whom they shared he urged them to save fellow-Greeks from slavery and drive away the *barbaroi*.

Herodotus IX.90.1–2

(The Greek fleet sailed for Samos and the Persian force retired to Mykale on the mainland, beached its ships under the cover of a Persian army and was overwhelmed along with it.)

(B) When the Greeks had killed the majority of the *barbaroi*, either in the battle or in the flight afterwards, they burnt the ships and the whole palisade, having first dragged the booty out onto the beach; in the process they found a number of hoards of money. Having burnt the palisade and the ships they sailed away. When they reached Samos, they debated whether to remove Ionia elsewhere and where in that part of Greece which they controlled they should settle the population, abandoning Ionia itself to the barbarians. For it seemed impossible that they themselves should occupy the borders of the Ionians and guard them for ever,[2] and if they did not do this they had no hope that the Ionians would get off with impunity at the hands of the Persians. In the face of these problems the commanders of the Peloponnesians proposed to confiscate the *emporia* of the Greek peoples who had medised and to give the land to the Ionians to settle;[3] but the Athenians did not at all approve of the idea of removing Ionia nor did they think that the Peloponnesians should have any say in what happened to their own *apoikiai*.[4] So when they opposed the project the Peloponnesians readily gave way. And so they included the Samians and Chians and Lesbians and the other islanders who had joined the Greek force in the alliance, binding them by promises and oaths to remain loyal and not revolt.[5] They then sailed to break the bridges (over the Hellespontos), which they expected to find still intact.[6]

Herodotus IX.106

1 See **101**.
2 In fact the history of the next 50 years is in large measure that of the successful Athenian attempt to do just this.
3 Compare **92** n.12.
4 See **104** n.2.
5 Compare **129–130**.
6 When the Greeks found the bridges already dismantled, the Spartans returned home, while the Athenians invested Sestos, where the remaining Persian forces in the area had concentrated, capturing it at the very end of the year and returning in triumph to Athens.

117. Medism

We have already had a number of occasions in this Chapter to observe the fact of medism (see also Hdt. IV.144.3; 165.3; VII.172.1; VIII.92.2; Thuc. I.95.5; 135.2; III.62.1–2; Bury and Meiggs, *Greece*, 144); Herodotus here comments on the phenomenon in terms which are still illuminating for events a century and a half later, when the Greek *poleis* divided into supporters and opponents of Philippos II of Makedon (see Ch.34). For the treatment meted out to the medising group at Thebes see Hdt. IX.86–88.

Now the Phokians were the only ones of the peoples hereabouts who did not medise; their only reason, I infer, was their hatred of the Thessalians; if the Thessalians had joined the Greek ranks, in my opinion the Phokians would have medised. As it was, when the Thessalians made this proposal,[1] they declined to give any money and said that they could medise as well as the Thessalians, if they were so minded; but they would not of their own volition betray the Greek cause.

Herodotus VIII.30

1 To intercede with the enemy in return for a fee.

118. Carthage and Syracuse

Herodotus reports that Gelon of Syracuse (see **110**) declined to help the Greeks unless he was made supreme commander, and indeed that he was prepared to submit to Xerxes in the event of a Persian victory (VII.157–164); but he also reports an alternative version which we give here. See also Diodorus XI.20–26, who claims that the Carthaginians and Persians were acting in concert, that the battle of Himera was fought on the same day as Thermopylai, and that Gelon heard the news of Salamis when on the verge of departing to help against the Persians; Diodorus also gives a highly eulogistic account of Gelon as ruler of Syracuse. For Gelon see Andrewes, *Tyrants*, 131–6.

But those who live in Sicily claim that even though he would have had to be subordinate to the Lakedaimonians Gelon would still have come to the help of the Greeks, were it not for one thing; Terillos the son of Krinippos had been *tyrannos* of Himera, but had been driven out by Theron the son of Ainesidemos, the ruler of the Akragantines; at about this time he (Terillos) brought against Sicily an army of 300,000 Phoinikians, Libyans, Iberians and Ligurians and Elisykans and Sardinians and Corsicans, and their general Amilkas the son of Annon, king of the Carthaginians. Terillos had persuaded him, partly in recognition of his own *xenia* with him, but largely as a result of the enthusiasm of Anaxilaos the son of Kretines, the *tyrannos* of Rhegion, he gave his own children as hostages to Amilkas to induce him to come to Sicily and so protect the interests of his father-in-law. For Anaxilaos had married the daughter of Terillos, who was called Kydippe. It was as a result of this sequence of events that Gelon was unable to help the Greeks, but sent the money to Delphi.[1] (166) Further, those who live in Sicily claim that it so happened that Gelon and Theron defeated Amilkas of Carthage in Sicily and the Greeks defeated the Persians at Salamis on the same day.

Herodotus VII. 165–166

1 Which the other version of events regarded as a *douceur* for Xerxes if he won.

Part II

The Fifth Century

11 The development of Athenian democracy

Although Kleisthenes can be seen to have been the creator of many of the cardinal features of radical, participatory democracy in Athens (Ch 7), his creation was in many ways no more than a blueprint for the future, and the development of the system in practice – whether or not as envisaged by him – was left for the fifth century. On one level this was a matter of changes in political attitudes, and consequently in political behaviour, on the Athenians' part, changes hastened on their way by such practical corollaries of the Kleisthenic machinery as the institution of salaries attached to all the new public offices (see 137 and 141); and evidence selected to illustrate the character of public life and politics in the period is presented in Ch.13. But on the purely constitutional plane there was still to come after Kleisthenes a half-century of development, most of it pithily documented in the Aristotelian *Ath. Pol.* It is impossible to say whether those responsible for each part of the process, known or anonymous, saw themselves primarily as tinkering with the past or mapping out the future; nonetheless the various individual developments did go to make up a more or less coherent and linear evolution, to a point where Athens in the second half of the fifth century displayed a set of political institutions and practices corresponding almost exactly with those which Aristotle – looking back from the fourth century – declared to be characteristic of a democratic constitution (126). And there is some evidence which shows the Athenian *dēmos* in the generation after 480 as possessing a clear consciousness of its achievements and its distinctiveness (127–128), when Aeschylus in *The Suppliant Women* talks of 'the ruling hand of the *dēmos*' (line 604), it seems very likely that he has Athens in mind.

It is also worth remarking that once the *dēmos* had achieved complete power, it set about imposing limits on the exercise of that power, chiefly by way of procedural restrictions on the conduct of business in the *ekklēsia*. 'It is not possible for the *dēmos* to vote on anything which has not been discussed beforehand by the *boulē* and which the *prytaneis* do not list beforehand (for debate)' (?Aristot. *Ath. Pol.* 45.4, perhaps exaggerating), and 'in general the *ekklēsia* was prepared to let the *boulē* decide what it should debate' (Rhodes, *Boulē*, 57). In addition, a preliminary vote of *adeia* (literally 'immunity'; in fact a prior decision to debate something) was necessary for certain kinds of business, notably the raising of an *eisphora* (a capital levy–see **144** n.2, **197** n.7, and **312**); a quorum was also sometimes necessary. And it is possible that the procedure attested by Aeschines (II.60) for the fourth century for making treaties existed in the fifth: debate without vote on one day, vote without debate the next day (for the treaty with Kerkyra, see **176**); two meetings were also necessary to confer citizenship. It is also significant that the first step taken by the oligarchs in 411 was the abolition of the *graphē paranomōn* (see **227**); this was the challenge of a measure as illegal and its testing in the courts (we do not know how it functioned in the fifth century; for the fourth century see **310**). In general, the *dēmos* was impressively aware of the awfulness of power: rash advocacy of a proposal by a demagogue could lead to prosecution, and rash action by the *dēmos*, as over Mytilene (see **197**) or the *stratēgoi* after Arginousai (see **237**), was rare.

119. The measures of 501/0

In ch.22 of the *Ath. Pol.* we have brief notices of two measures, dated in the year 501/0, which were evidently ancillary to the main Kleisthenic reforms, though apparently not enacted by Kleisthenes himself. Beyond that, their exact significance is obscure – especially so in the case of the *stratēgia*, an office which the author believed (**65B**) to have existed in the seventh century; for the issues here see n.3, below.

See further: Hignett, *Constitution*, 166–73; Moore, *Aristotle*, 244–5.

First of all, in the fifth year after this establishment (of Kleisthenes' *politeia*, which is to say) during the archonship of Hermokreon,[1] they devised the oath for the *boulē* of five hundred which its members still swear today.[2] Furthermore they began to choose the *stratēgoi* by *phylai*, one from each *phylē*[3] – though the *polemarchos* was (still) in command of the army as a whole.[4]

?Aristotle, *Athenaion Politeia* 22.2

1 'The fifth year after this establishment (of Kleisthenes' *politeia*)' might naturally suggest 504/3, but (*a*) we have another name, Akestorides, for the *archōn* of that year and (*b*) it is not in any case eleven years before the battle of Marathon in 491/90 (22.3). This latter criterion produces 501/0; and it is in fact plausible enough that Kleisthenes' complex reforms were *completed* in 506/5.

2 For detailed discussion of the oath and its history see Rhodes, *Boulē*, 190–9.

3 If we believe, as the author did, that this statement does *not* mean that the office of *stratēgos* was newly created now, in 501/0, we must take it to mean either (*i*) that the ten new *phylai*, not the four old ones, from now on provided a general apiece, or (*ii*) that the *dēmos* as a whole (i.e. the *ekklēsia*) from now on elected

them, not each *phylē* its own *stratēgos*. The main objection to (*i*) is the difficulty of supposing that at least five years elapsed between the creation of the new tribal system and this essential adjustment in consequence of it. The main objection to (*ii*) is that it puts an unnatural construction upon the Greek; certainly we should conclude that from 501/0 the body which chose the *stratēgoi*, on a tribal basis, was the *ekklēsia*, but there is no compelling indication *in this passage* that any earlier procedure was thereby being superseded. So it may be best to suppose that the author was a prisoner of his anachronistic belief that the 'constitution of Drakon' (65B) had included provisions for a board of *stratēgoi*, and that the *stratēgoi* were in fact a creation of this year 501/0.

   Note also that by the author's own day the *stratēgoi* were still directly elected, but irrespective of their *phylai* (61.1). Scholars have for long tried to establish the date of this change; we find convincing the arguments of C. W. Fornara, *The Athenian Board of Generals from 501 to 404* (*Historia* Einzelschriften 16 (Wiesbaden, 1971)), that it was as early as the 460s.

4 This is clearly correct, and important, until the appointment of the nine *archontes* by lot from 487/6: see **120**. On the relationship between the *polemarchos* and the *stratēgoi* at the battle of Marathon note Hdt. VI.109–111 (see **108**), who incorrectly asserts that the *polemarchos* was already by then appointed by lot.

120. 'Klērōsis ek prokritōn' (487/6)

Even without the explicit testimony of Herodotus (III.80.6: see **89**) and Aristotle (**126**, below), it would be obvious that appointment to office by lot was central to democratic theory and practice. In origin, sortition may perhaps have reflected a desire to leave the choice of appointee to the gods or providence, but there is reason to doubt whether it was ever employed in Athens before Kleisthenes (see **67** with n.9), and by the early fifth century the overriding rationale must have been a secular, political one – the egalitarian idea that whoever was appointed would do a competent and honest job. Not unnaturally, however, it took quite some time (and degree of association with other developing practices, such as the rotation of office) before the doctrine was carried through to its logical conclusion, which entailed a massive diminution in the prestige of the offices involved. But even so the adoption from 487/6 of a sort of half-way procedure – sortition (*klērōsis*) amongst a body of candidates (*prokritoi*) whose quality was guaranteed by prior selection – meant an immediate loss of status for the *archontes* and a gradual one for the Areiopagos (**122, 123**); the measure also opened the way to the political as well as military primacy of the board of *stratēgoi*.

   See further: Hignett, *Constitution*, 226–32; Moore, *Aristotle*, 245.

In the year immediately following, the archonship of Telesinos,[1] they cast lots for the nine *archontes*, by *phylai*, from amongst the 500 men previously selected by the demesmen[2] – this for the first time since the tyranny; the earlier ones had all been elected.[3]

?Aristotle, Athenaion Politeia 22.5

1 In 487/6, 'immediately following' the *ostrakismos* of Hipparchos (**79A**).
2 This seems an implausibly large pool of candidates both *per se* and in terms of the proportion of the citizen-body in the two highest census-classes (see **67**); we should probably accept Kenyon's emendation to *one* hundred.
3 Unless this is taken to refer only to the period after 510, it ignores the author's own earlier statement that *klērōsis ek prokritōn* was originally introduced by Solon. It is tempting to reject that statement, and the consequent need to assume that the practice then lapsed under the tyranny. See **67** with n.9.

121. Aristeides the Just

From 488/7 onwards, prominent Athenians began to find themselves the victims of *ostrakismos* (**79**). Since the *ostrakismos* procedure required, theoretically, every participant to be sufficiently literate to scratch a name on a potsherd, it – and indeed radical democracy as a whole, as it was now developing – appears to presuppose a high level of literacy, at least among adult males, in classical Athens: see p.21 and the careful study of F. D. Harvey, 'Literacy in the Athenian democracy', *REG* 79 (1966), 585–635. We should nonetheless footnote, so to speak, the point that not every voter necessarily inscribed his own *ostrakon*. A political clique might hand them out to its adherents and others ready-prepared: this must be the explanation of the deposit of 190 *ostraka* found in a well on the Akropolis, all of them votes against Themistokles (**112, 159, 166, 168**, etc.) – and written in only fourteen hands! (See O. Broneer, *Hesperia* 7 (1938), 228–43; Meiggs and Lewis no.21, at p.43; Murray, *Early Greece*, 263.) Alternatively, as the following anecdote illustrates, practical assistance might be sought in a way less sinister but more ironic.

At first Aristeides found himself the object of love because of this surname of his,[1] but this subsequently turned into jealous hatred, especially when Themistokles began to spread a tale amongst the masses that Aristeides had (in effect) abolished the *dikastēria* by his practice of judging cases and pronouncing the verdicts himself, and that without anyone noticing it he had set himself up in a monarchy – the only thing he now lacked was a bodyguard! Also, because of the victory,[2] the *dēmos* must by now have been in a mood of exhilaration, thinking nothing too good for itself, and hating those whose name and reputation made them stand out from the crowd. So they came together in the *astu* from all over Attika and ostracised Aristeides,[3] invoking 'fear of tyranny' as the name for their jealousy of his reputation. For the fact was that the sentence of *ostrakismos* was no punishment of individual depravity, and it was merely specious to call it a humiliation and curtailment of a man's self-importance and power: what it was really was a way of relieving feelings of jealousy humanely, in that they did not express their malignant desire to cause injury in something irreparable but simply in prescribing a

238

change of residence for ten years. And when the procedure did come to be employed against low-born rascals, that was the finish of it: there were no more ostracisms after that of Hyperbolos[4] . . . Anyway, on the occasion of the *ostrakismos* of Aristeides, the story goes that, as the voters were writing on their *ostraka*, an illiterate and thoroughly boorish fellow handed his to Aristeides – as if to any ordinary Athenian – and asked him to write 'Aristeides' on it! Aristeides was amazed, and asked the man how on earth Aristeides had ever injured him. 'He has not – not at all,' was the reply. 'I don't even know the man. But I do know that I'm sick and tired of always hearing him called The Just!' On hearing this Aristeides made no answer but simply wrote his name on the *ostrakon* and gave it back.

Plutarch, *Aristeides* 7*

1 The Just (*Dikaios*): see 6.1. On Aristeides see further **129**.
2 Over the Persians at Marathon (**108**), presumably.
3 In 483/2 (?Aristot. *Ath. Pol.* 22.7).
4 See **79**c, **213**.

122. The Areiopagos after 480

Although *klērōsis ek prokritōn* (**120**) will have entailed a loss of prestige for the *archontes* themselves, its effect on the Areiopagos, as a body of *ex-archontes*, will necessarily have been more gradual, and one sees nothing which might be considered a direct consequence of it for 25 years, until 462/1 (**123**). On the contrary we read in the *Ath. Pol.* (below) that the prestige of the Areiopagos actually *increased* for a time after 480; but this disconcerting claim should be viewed with suspicion. Herodotus surely ought to have known of any payments made by the Areiopagos – usurping, in this, the functions of the *stratēgoi* – before the battle of Salamis; and in general it is not too difficult to see why *either* side in the propaganda war of 462/1 itself might have sought to inflate, retrospectively, the Areiopagos' position in these years – the radicals to explain and justify their attack, the conservatives to make it appear all the more outrageous. The tone of this particular passage perhaps points to the latter source of distortion (though see further **123**); the view may well have been cemented in the fourth century, when at least one political commentator depicted the great days of the Areiopagos with nostalgic regret (Isoc. vii (*Areopagitikos*). 37–55).

See further: Hignett, *Constitution*, 147–8; Moore, *Aristotle*, 246.

So until the Persian Wars the gradual advance and growth of the *polis* went hand in hand with that of its democracy, but after them the Council of the Areiopagos became strong again and governed the *polis*. It assumed this *hēgemonia* not by virtue of any decree (to that effect) but because it had been responsible for the sea-battle at Salamis: when the *stratēgoi* had proved unable to control the situation and had ordered every man to see to his own safety, the Areiopagos provided for a distribution of eight drachmas to each man and so manned the ships. This explains why the Athenians treated the Areiopagos with respect, and why in this period they had a fine government.

?Aristotle, *Athenaion Politeia* 23.1–2

123. Reform of the Areiopagos (462/1)

Even if we are right to suspect that the story of the resurgence of the Areiopagos after 480 is propaganda (see **122**), it is nonetheless true that that ancient body was at the centre of the constitutional reforms of 462/1. We give here the bald account from the *Ath. Pol.*; compare Plut. *Per.* 9.3–4 and 10.6–7. In the 40 years since Kleisthenes the position of the Areiopagos must increasingly have come to be regarded as anomalous, given the direction in which the *politeia* was heading, and the essence of what happened in 462/1 was that its powers of (mainly) jurisdiction were taken away from it and given to the principal organs of democracy. Aeschylus' *Eumenides*, performed four years later, is usually taken as reflecting these events; see especially lines 704–706. For the many problems of detail and nuance beyond that, see Hignett, *Constitution*, 193–213; Forrest, *Emergence*, 209–20; Moore, *Aristotle*, 251–2; Davies, *Democracy*, ch.4.

For about seventeen years after the Persian Wars the *politeia* remained (the same), under the supervision of the Areiopagos. Little by little, however, it was declining; and as the masses grew in strength, Ephialtes the son of Sophonides – a man reckoned to be incorruptible and upright in his attitude to the *politeia* – became champion of the *dēmos*, and attacked the (Areiopagos) Council. He began by eliminating many of its members individually, through prosecutions for misconduct in office. Then, in the archonship of Konon (462/1), he deprived the Council of all its additionally-acquired (powers),[1] which made it the guardian of the *politeia*, and gave some of them to the Five Hundred,[2] some to the *dēmos*[3] and the *dikastēria*[4] . . . And Ephialtes too died,[5] not long afterwards, murdered by Aristodikos of Tanagra.[6]

?Aristotle, *Athenaion Politeia* 25*

1 This phrase may well reflect the radicals' propaganda: if the Areiopagos had usurped *extra* powers, all the more reason to take them away; see Hignett, *Constitution*, 198. The traditional powers of the Areiopagos are as unclear to us as they were to the author of *Ath. Pol.* (see **63**), but they surely included vetting of officials.

2 I.e. the Kleisthenic *boulē*.

3 I.e. the *ekklēsia*.

4 This should not be taken as proof that the *dikastēria* already existed, even though the author himself certainly thought so (see **67** with n.7).

5 There seems to be a gap in the papyrus test just before this point, and the commentators conjecture that it contained a reference to the death of Themistokles, since he is associated – absurdly (see **168**) – with Ephialtes in the passage omitted here (25.3–4).

6 The man was presumably an assassin in the pay of Ephialtes' conservative opponents, the extent of whose alarm is hereby made clear; political murder was most uncommon in Athens.

124. Extension of archonships to the 'zeugitai'

A further stage in the democratisation of the government and its machinery came in 458/7 or 457/6 (for the doubt see nn.1 and 2, below), when eligibility for appointment to the archonships was extended to the third of the Solonian census-classes, the *zeugitai*. See Hignett, *Constitution*, 225. N.B. We are explicitly told by the *Ath. Pol.* (below) that the method of appointment was still, for the time being, to be the 487/6 *klērōsis ek prokritōn* (**120**); but by the time *Ath. Pol.* was being written, the process was double sortition (8.1). The change *may* be datable to the 430s or 420s, if one is prepared to press hard the implication in [Xen.] *Ath. Pol.* 1.2 that election and sortition were at that time the only two methods in use.

They made no change in the choice of the nine *archontes*, except that in the sixth year after the death of Ephialtes[1] they decided that the *zeugitai* should be included in the preliminary selection of candidates who would draw lots to become the nine *archontes*; and the first *zeugitēs* to hold office as *archōn* was Mnesitheides.[2] His predecessors had all come from the *hippeis* and *pentakosiomedimnoi*, while the *zeugitai* had held only the lesser offices – except on occasions when the stipulations in the *nomoi* may have been disregarded.

?Aristotle, *Athenaion Politeia* 26.2

1 Inclusive Greek reckoning from 462/1 would make this 457/6; but see n.2.
2 Mnesitheides is known to have held office in 457/6, so there is a small anomaly in the fact that the reform itself is put in that year. With Hignett we assign the reform to 458/7.

125. Re-establishment of the 'dikastai kata dēmous' (453/2)

Peisistratos had created circuit-judges for the country districts of Attika (**70**), but the office had evidently lapsed at some later (unknown) date, for we read in the *Ath. Pol.* that in 453/2 it was revived. (On its subsequent history, in the fourth century, see **311**.)

See further: Hignett, *Constitution*, 218–19; Moore, *Aristotle*, 253.

Four years later,[1] in the archonship of Lysikrates (453/2), they established again the thirty judges, the so-called deme judges.

?Aristotle, *Athenaion Politeia* 26.3

1 I.e. later than the archonship reform (**124**).

126. The fundamentals of democracy

In Book VI of the *Politics* Aristotle sets out in summary form what he saw as the characteristic institutions and practices of a democracy. If these are found to correspond closely to what we actually find in operation in fifth- and fourth-century Athens, that need occasion no surprise and no disappointment. What we are given, clearly, is not an entirely abstract, theoretical analysis but something much more like an intelligent observer's extrapolation from the particular mechanisms and rationales which the Athenians – and, in whole or in part, some other *poleis* too – had evolved in the actual process of giving the *dēmos* political sovereignty. And this is to be achieved, as the passage abridged below makes clear, by both negative and positive means: strict controls upon the holders of public office (and their areas of competence) and the channelling of power to the *ekklēsia*, the *boulē* and the popular courts.

See further: Hignett, *Constitution*, 214–15, and more generally 215–51. For the fourth century see Ch.31.

The principles of democracy are these: that the officials be chosen by all and from all; that each be ruled by all, and all by each in turn; that the offices be filled by lot – either all of them or (at least) those which call for no experience or skill;[1] that there be no census-qualification, or only the very lowest one, for holding office; that no office be held twice, or more than a few times, by the same man – or (at least) not many offices besides the military ones; that the tenure of all offices, or as many as possible, be short; that judgment in the courts be given by all or bodies drawn from all, and concerning all matters or (at least) most, and the greatest and most important, such as *euthynai*[2] and *politeia*[3] and private contracts; and that the *ekklēsia* be sovereign over all things, or (at least) the greatest, and no official over anything, or (at least) as few things as possible. A *boulē*, in fact, is the most democratic of official bodies, in places where there is not an abundance of state salaries (*misthos*) for everybody, though where there is, on the other hand, such an abundance, even this body is deprived of its power; for when the *dēmos* has an abundance of *misthos*, as has been remarked before in the treatise preceding this one,[4] it draws all the trials to itself. At all events, the key principle is this: that there be a *misthos* for everyone – for attending the *ekklēsia*, sitting on the *dikastēria* and holding office;[5] failing that, for (at least) the offices and the *dikastēria* and the *boulē* and the *ekklēsiai kuriai*;[6] or (at least) to those officials who are obliged to take their meals together[7] . . . Furthermore, none of the officials should hold office for life. If any office tenable for life has been left after an ancient revolution, it should at least have its power removed and be filled by lot instead of election.[8]

Aristotle, *Politics* (VI) 1317 b 18–1318 a 3*

1 As the passage goes on to make clear, this crucial exception at the heart of egalitarian theory and practice is chiefly to accommodate the military posts, and the board of *stratēgoi* above all; compare [Xen.] *Ath. Pol.* 1.3. (But it also covered envoys and technical experts such as architects.)
2 See **52** with n.6, **65B** with n.5.
3 Here this probably means 'grants of citizenship'
4 (IV) 1299 b 38–1300 a 4. (Books IV and V are evidently regarded as a unit.)
5 See **137, 141** and (for the *ekklēsia*) **304**.
6 At the *kuria ekklēsia* in each prytany, i.e. ten times a year, there was – at least in the fourth century – a fixed and formal agenda (**308**) and, ultimately, a higher attendance-allowance than for other meetings (**304**).
7 The prime example of this would be the *prytaneis* (?Aristot. *Ath. Pol.* 43.3).
8 It is a reasonable supposition that Aristotle had the Areiopagos in mind here (see **120, 123**).

127. The 'dēmos' and its dead

Athens, alone among Greek *poleis*, organised collective burial at home for the bones of those who died in battle (see **149** and **154** for Thucydides' account of the ceremony of 431 and the speech of Perikles); the date at which the custom originated is uncertain, but it seems to have been formalised in the early years of the Pentekontaëtia (see F. Jacoby, '*Patrios nomos*: state burial in Athens and the public cemetery in the Kerameikos', *JHS* 64 (1944), 37; Gomme, *Commentary* II, 94–8; Thucydides wrongly supposes the custom to be ancient). The names of the dead of all ten *phylai* were normally inscribed on a single *stēlē* or on a group of *stēlai* with a single heading. For a campaigning season which is probably that of 460, a single *phylē* inscribed its 177 dead on its own *stēlē*.

OF (THE *PHYLĒ*) ERECHTHEIS
These died in the war in Cyprus, in Egypt, in Phoinikia,
at Halieis, on Aigina, at Megara[1]
IN THE SAME YEAR
Of the *stratēgoi*
Ph[. . . .]chos[2]
(The names follow, in three columns, of one other *stratēgos*,
one seer, four archers and 170 others.)

Meiggs and Lewis no. 33[3]

1 Note the combination of campaigns serving the interests of the Delian League (see Ch. 12) and campaigns against Athens' immediate neighbours.
2 Perhaps Ph[ryni]chos.
3 Compare no. 48, a casualty list of the 440s.

128. The Athenian citizenship law

In 451/0 'because of the number of *politai*, on the proposal of Perikles, they decided that no-one should be a member of the *polis* who was not born of two *astoi*' (?Aristot. *Ath. Pol.* 26.4). The reason given is inadequate and the significance of the law is hard to comprehend; the problem is exacerbated by the fact that even if we regard the notices of citizenship measures of Solon (see **68–69**) and Kleisthenes (see **78**) as trustworthy, the complete absence of any historical context for *them* leaves us more or less where we started. It seems clear from Herodotus' account of Lykia (1.173.4–5) that he thought it normal in the Greek world for citizenship to be that of the father; it is also clear that the rule at Athens after 451/0 was in marked contrast to the practice of aristocrats in general (such as Kimon) and tyrants in particular (see **26**) and that because it limited Athenian citizenship the rule was one of the factors which emphasised the privileged nature of this citizenship in the fifth century (J. K. Davies, 'Athenian citizenship: the descent group and the alternatives', *Classical Journal* 73 (1977–78), 105–21, well discusses the tensions which the system generated and the methods used to bolster it). One may also surmise that part of what lay behind the measure was a desire on the part of the imperial *dēmos*, having arrived in a position of power, to define itself. (Considerations of 'racial purity' (so Hignett, *Constitution*, 343) may safely be excluded.)

Long before this,[1] when Perikles was prominent in the state and had legitimate sons, he proposed a law that only those who were born of two Athenians should be Athenians. And then when the king of the Egyptians sent 40,000 *medimnoi* of wheat as a gift to the *dēmos*, it was necessary for the *politai* to divide it among themselves; and many suits were revived against people who were illegitimate under the law in question, suits which had been overlooked and neglected, and many people fell victim to informers. In fact just under 5,000 were convicted and sold into slavery, while those who remained and were adjudged Athenians amounted to 14,040 in number.[2] So it was a serious matter for the law which had been enforced against so many to be broken now by the man who had proposed it; but the present disaster which had befallen the house of Perikles[3] broke down the objections of the Athenians, since he seemed to have paid the penalty for his arrogance and well-known pride; so thinking that he had suffered retribution and was asking what a man should, they agreed that he should inscribe his illegitimate son among the members of his *phratria*[4] and give him his name. And this was the man whom the *dēmos* later put to death along with his fellow *stratēgoi* after he had fought at Arginousai against the Peloponnesians.[5]

Plutarch, *Perikles* 37.2-end

1 The occasion is the grant of citizenship to Perikles' illegitimate son by his Milesian mistress Aspasia.

2 Philochorus (*FGrH* 328 F 119) reports that 30,000 *medimnoi* of corn were offered, 4,760 men deprived of citizenship and 14,240 men given corn; the difference between this figure and the 14,040 of Plutarch presumably results from a manuscript error and the ascription of the number to those who received corn rather than to those who were adjudged Athenians may well be correct. Few will believe either Plutarch or Philochorus on the number deprived of citizenship; it may also be doubted whether there was a systematic revision of the list of citizens (*diapsephismos*) on the occasion of the distribution, which occurred in 445/4.

3 The deaths of his two legitimate sons, the second in the plague (for which see **196**).

4 See **16** n.6.

5 See **237**; also Meiggs and Lewis no. 84 for the younger Perikles as Hellēnotamias.

12 The Athenian empire

In the immediate aftermath of the Persian Wars, the Athenians showed themselves more eager than anyone else to carry the war into enemy territory and before long replaced the Spartans as the *hēgemones* of the allied forces; and a new alliance was created to prosecute the war (**129–130**). Much modern debate centres round an alleged transformation of this Delian League into an Athenian empire (for instance, Meiggs, *Empire*, ch.9). It is of course clear that practice hardened into precedent as the years went by, and that the Athenians took various coercive measures as they became necessary to ensure their hegemony; it is also clear that the phrase used by the Athenians 'the *poleis* over which the Athenians rule' (e.g. Thuc. v.47.2) is not conceivable in 477, and that allied perceptions of their position changed between then and 431; but it is not clear that Thucydides is wrong to hang his general account of the Athenian empire on the *first* revolt and largely ignore the detailed mechanisms by which the Athenians ensured their hegemony (**134–135**). What is important is that it was an Athenian organisation from start to finish (compare VIII.68.4 = **227B**, and see M. I. Finley, 'The fifth-century Athenian empire: a balance sheet', in P. D. A. Garnsey and C. R. Whittaker (eds.), *Imperialism in the Ancient World* (Cambridge, 1978), ch.5).

The acquisition of an empire of course went hand in hand with the emergence of the *dēmos* in control at Athens itself, a fact of which the *dēmos* took advantage. From the foundation of the Delian League, the activities demanded by the decisions of the *ekklēsia* relating to foreign policy were largely paid for by the tribute of the allies. But not only were Athens' own considerable resources now largely freed for internal purposes (see **137–138**); some of the tribute was used for the building programme of Athens, and her *politai* also profited individually from the creation of the empire; the result was the partial democratisation of the traditional aristocratic ideal of living off the work of others (for the fourth century see **286**). Use of the resources of the empire for internal Athenian purposes naturally attracted aristocratic opposition; Thucydides provides (see **227**) a cooler estimate of the link between democracy and empire, perhaps somewhat paradoxical in modern eyes.

If we turn to the allies, there is a problem and a paradox. The problem is posed by the remarkable degree of 'loyalty' of the allies to Athens; on the political reasons for this the most sensible remarks seem to us to be those of J. de Romilly, 'Thucydides and the cities of the Athenian empire', *Bull. Inst. Class. Stud.* (1966), 1–12; note also de Ste Croix, *Origins*, 34–43, discussing work since his article of 1954 posing this question. Finley, *op. cit.* 124–5, remarks that the tribute was probably not actually paid by the lower orders in the allied *poleis*, but by the rich; one might add that many poor men from the allied *poleis* earned substantial sums of money by serving in the Athenian fleet.

The paradox is that, of the areas within the empire, Ionia, the principal beneficiary of the crusade against Persia, suffered in the fifth century a marked decline in material well-being (J. M. Cook, 'The problem of classical Ionia', *PCPhS* n.s.7 (1961), 9–18).

129. The formation of the alliance

Once the Persians had been expelled from Greece proper, the problem arose of what to do next; unlike the Athenians, the Spartans had no wish to prosecute the war (see **116** n.6). In addition, Pausanias, the Spartan king who was sent across the Aegean as commander-in-chief, proceeded to behave more arrogantly than the Persians towards the eastern Greeks under his command.

So (Aristeides and Themistokles) organised the building of the walls together[1], although they were political opponents, but it was Aristeides who urged the Athenians to detach the Ionians from the alliance of the Lakedaimonians, watching for the moment when they were in bad odour because of Pausanias. As a result it was he who determined the first instalment of tribute from the *poleis*, in the third year after the sea-battle at Salamis, in the archonship of Timosthenes (478/7) and swore the oaths to the Ionians to have the same enemies and the same friends (as the Athenians), a ceremony at which they also sank the usual lumps of iron in the sea.[2]

?Aristotle, *Athenaion Politeia* 23.4–5

1 See **166**.
2 The lumps of iron perhaps symbolised the fate of those who broke the oaths; see H Jacobson, 'The oath of the Delian League', *Philologus* 119 (1975), 256–8.

130. The early years

Thucydides' account of the period between the Persian Wars and the Peloponnesian War is intended to document his view that the Spartans voted for war in 432 because of their fear of the growth of Athenian power (see Ch. 17). That power of course depended on the empire, whose development is here chronicled and analysed by Thucydides (c.f. 1.115.2–117 on the revolt of Samos).

Now this was the way in which the Athenians arrived at the situation in which they had become so powerful. When the Persians had retreated from Europe after their defeat by the Greeks by land and sea and those of them who had escaped by sea to Mykale had been wiped out, Leotychidas the king of the Lakedaimonians, who was the commander of the Greeks at Mykale, returned home with the allies from the Peloponnesos, while the Athenians and the allies from Ionia and the Hellespontos who had already rebelled from the King remained and besieged Sestos, which was held by the Persians;[1] after wintering there they took it when the *barbaroi* evacuated it and then sailed out of the Hellespontos, each to their own *poleis*. (The Athenians meanwhile began to reconstruct their *polis* and its walls, see **166**.) (94) Pausanias, however, the son of Kleombrotos from Lakedaimon, was sent out as commander of the Greeks with twenty ships from the Peloponnesos; and the Athenians also joined him with thirty ships, as did a large number of the other allies. They sailed on Cyprus and won over the greater part of it and then to Byzantion, which was in the hands of the Persians, and captured it while Pausanias was *hēgemōn*. (95) But he was already overbearing in manner, which the other Greeks resented, in particular the Ionians and those who had just been freed from the King; so going to the Athenians they asked them to be their *hēgemones*, being their kinsmen,[2] and not leave them in Pausanias' hands if he tried anything violent. The Athenians were receptive to these suggestions and turned their minds to the problem, proposing not to stand idly by and in general to organise things as seemed best for themselves. Meanwhile, however, the Spartans recalled Pausanias to investigate the stories which they had heard; for he was accused of many unjust dealings by the Greeks who came to Sparta and his behaviour seemed to be imitating that of a tyrant rather than being that of a commander. It so happened that he was summoned back at the very moment that the allies, from hatred of him, went over to the Athenians, except, that is, for the forces from the Peloponnesos. Anyway, on his return to Lakedaimon he was found guilty of some misdemeanours towards private individuals, but was found not guilty on the major counts; in particular, he was accused of medism,[3] of which he certainly seemed guilty. Now the Spartans did not send him out as commander again, though they did send Dorkis and some others with him, with a small force; but the allies were no longer prepared to accept them as *hēgemones*. Realising this, they went home, and the Lakedaimonians did not send anyone else to succeed them, fearing that those of them who went out would be corrupted, as they had seen happen in the case of Pausanias, and at the same time wishing to be relieved of the burden of the war against Persia and thinking that the Athenians were quite capable of conducting it and supposing at that moment that they were their friends. (96) So this was the way in which the Athenians took over as *hēgemones*, with the consent of the allies and as a result of their hatred for Pausanias; and they laid down which of the *poleis* were to provide money and which ships for the war against the *barbaroi*; for the pretext for the war was revenge for what they had suffered, to be achieved by ravaging the *chōra* of the King.[4] And this was when the office of Hellēnotamiai was first established for the Athenians, to receive the *phoros*; for this was what the contributions of money were called.[5] And the *phoros* as first laid down amounted to four hundred and sixty talents.[6] Delos was their treasury and the revenues came in to the temple. (97) The Athenians then were *hēgemones* of allies who were originally autonomous and who planned operations on the basis of their common revenues;[7] these were some of the things they did, in the course of their wars and of their general conduct of affairs, between the war against Persia and the war which forms my subject matter; they were involved in action against the *barbaroi* and against their own allies who revolted and against those of the Peloponnesians whom they came across in one way or another. I have written about this and provided this digression from my theme because this material is not covered by any of my predecessors; they have dealt either with Greek affairs before the Persian Wars or with the Persian Wars themselves; Hellanicus, who did deal with these matters in his *Attic History*, did so briefly and with mistakes over dates.[8] At the same time my exposition contains an account of the way in which the rule (*archē*) of the Athenians became established. (98) Their first action, under the command of Kimon the son of Miltiades, was to besiege and take Eion on the (river) Strymon; it was held by Persians, who were sold into slavery. Then they took Skyros, the island in the Aegean, which was inhabited by Dolopians, who were also sold into slavery; they then settled the island themselves. Next they became involved in war against the Karystians, who were acting without the other Euboians, who came to terms eventually.[9] After this they went to war against the Naxians, who had revolted, and besieged them and brought them over; this was the first allied *polis* to lose its freedom contrary to the prevailing custom;[10] later it happened to the others one by one. (99) There were various reasons for the revolts, but the most important were failure to provide *phoros* or ships, and desertion, which sometimes occurred; for the Athenians made no allowances in their demands and were severe in applying pressure to those who were not used to it and were unwilling to make sacrifices. And in a variety of other ways too the Athenians came no longer to enjoy the same popularity as *hēgemones*; and they did not participate in campaigns as equals and found it easy to subdue those who revolted. For these developments the allies were themselves responsible; for the majority of them, because of their reluctance to go on campaign, let it be laid down that they should contribute money up to a sufficient level instead of ships, so as not to have to leave home; thus they increased the size of the Athenian navy with the money which they themselves contributed, while at the same time rendering themselves unprepared and incompetent for war when they revolted.

Thucydides 1.89–99*

1 See **116**.
2 See **116**.
3 See **117**.
4 See A. H. Jackson, 'The original purpose of the Delian League', *Historia* 18 (1969), 12–16.
5 The accounts which record the $\frac{1}{60}$ of each payment of tribute which was offered to Athena (see Meiggs and Lewis no. 39; J. K. Davies, *Democracy*, 78) imply that only from 454/3 did the Hellēnotamiai form an Athenian office; Thucydides here apparently implies that the office was Athenian from the start, and if that is so the contradiction is irremovable – Thucydides has presumably retrojected the institution.
6 It is often supposed that this figure includes a notional value for the ships contributed by some *poleis*, since it is higher than that attested for the years after 454/3 by the tribute quota lists, by which time many *poleis* had presumably converted from ships to tribute; but it is equally plausible to supposed that the tribute was reduced, perhaps after Eurymedon (see **131**), when the threat from Persia was temporarily eliminated. See M. H. Chambers, 'Four hundred sixty talents', *CPh* 1958, 26–32.
7 Here and in the previous sentence we adopt a translation suggested by R. I. Winton, in place of the more usual 'the assemblies took place at the temple' and 'on the basis of their common assemblies'.
8 See p. 14.
9 See **108** n. 5; one of the men who figures in a casualty list of *c*.447 (Meiggs and Lewis no. 48), is called Karystonikos – his father clearly named him to celebrate the victory (*nikē*) over Karystos, in which he perhaps participated.
10 Thucydides uses the metaphor of enslavement, compare **136**.

131. The Eurymedon campaign

The greatest victory of the alliance came in 470/69 when Kimon sailed round the coast of Lykia to attack a Persian fleet and army based in Pamphylia (the event is briefly narrated by Thuc. 1.100.1, lengthily and inaccurately by Diod. XI.60–62); a contemporary vase provides a stunning visual expression of the impact made by the victory (see K. J. Dover, *Greek Homosexuality* (London, 1978), 105).

Wishing to act before they[1] arrived, Kimon set sail, prepared to force the issue, if they[2] were unwilling to fight. To begin with, however, in order not to be compelled to fight, they anchored in the river (Eurymedon), but then when the Athenians bore down on them sailed out to meet them, with 600 ships according to Phanodemus, 350 according to Ephorus.[3] At any rate by sea they achieved nothing worthy of the force at their disposal, but immediately made for the land; those in the front got ashore and fled to the army which was stationed nearby, but some were caught and killed when their ships were destroyed. This makes it clear that the number of ships originally manned by the *barbaroi* was very large, since it appears that many escaped and many were destroyed, but the Athenians nonetheless captured 200 [4] (13) (After some hesitation, Kimon landed and after a hard fight defeated and destroyed the Persian army and captured its camp, going on to destroy the reinforcing squadron also.) This achievement so humbled the will of the King, that he made the peace which everyone talks about, undertaking to keep a day's journey on horseback away from the Greek sea (the Aegean) and not to sail past the Kyaneai or the Chelidoniai[5] with a warship equipped for battle. Callisthenes indeed denies that the *barbaroi* made this peace, but simply observed these limits in practice as a result of the terror caused by this defeat, and indeed kept so far away from Greece that Perikles sailed past the Chelidoniai with only 50 ships and Ephialtes with only 30 and no fleet came to meet them from the barbarians. There is, however, a copy of the treaty as having been made laid out in the collection of *Psēphismata* which Craterus made.[6] It is also recorded that the Athenians set up an altar of peace as a result and voted special honours to Kallias who was the ambassador.[7] When the spoils which had been captured had been sold, the *dēmos* had a plentiful supply of money for all its needs, and fortified the south wall of the *akropolis* from the resources made available by that campaign.[8]

Plutarch, Kimon 12.6–13.5

1 Eighty ships in reinforcement.
2 The main Persian fleet.
3 See p.14.
4 Plutarch here attempts to justify the patriotic fictions of Phanodemus the Atthidographer (author of a history of Attika) and Ephorus on the size of the Persian force, given by Thucydides as 200 ships in all. See Meiggs, *Empire*, 75–7.
5 The entrance to the Black Sea and the promontory between Lykia and Pamphylia respectively; see Map 1.

6 Callisthenes was the nephew of Aristotle and a historian of Alexander the Great, Craterus a third-century researcher in the tradition of the Atthido-graphers, see p.14.

7 The controversy over the authenticity of the Peace of Kallias continues unabated: did it exist or was it invented by Athens in the fourth century to point the contrast with the disgraceful relationship between Sparta and Persia? For a favourable view, see Meiggs, *Empire*, ch.8; for a sceptical view, see D. Stockton, 'The peace of Kallias', *Historia* 8 (1959), 61–79. We note that at Thuc. III.10.2–6(=**136**), where the existence of a peace would have strengthened the argument, the historian is silent, a fact that no believer in the peace has satisfactorily explained (away). It must be admitted that the problem is basically historiographical, since it is not in dispute that Athens and Persia largely stopped fighting each other after the middle of the century.

8 Plutarch goes on to talk of the contributions made by Kimon as a private individual to the building of the Long Walls and the beautification of the city; compare Ch.14 Intro. and for Kimon in Athens immediately after the victory, see **142A**, **150**.

132. Imperial enterprise

In the first generation of its existence, the empire under Athenian leadership was astonishingly active: two ventures may be taken to exemplify this activity, the attempt to colonise Ennea Hodoi (Nine Ways) in Thrake on the river Strymon and the involvement in Egypt. The first venture ended in failure and probably provoked the revolt of Thasos; but this was rapidly suppressed and the chosen site later settled with the name of Amphipolis (see **192**). Athenian involvement in Egypt likewise failed in the end in its immediate objective; but it doubtless contributed, along with the Athenian campaigns in Cyprus, to persuade Persia to withdraw from the Aegean and the west coast of Asia Minor (see **131**). For Thucydides, both ventures illustrated Athenian capacity to bounce back in the face of disaster.

(A) Some time later,[1] it came about that the Thasians rebelled from the Athenians, being at loggerheads over the *emporia* on the coast of Thrake opposite which they owned and over the mine which they worked.[2] And the Athenians sailed to Thasos with their fleet, won a sea-battle and landed, while at about the same time they sent 10,000 settlers drawn from themselves and their allies to the Strymon to settle the place then called Ennea Hodoi, but now Amphipolis; they gained control of Ennea Hodoi, which was held by the Edonians, but when they advanced into the interior of Thrake they were wiped out at Drabeskos in the territory of the Edonians by all the Thrakians in concert, who viewed the foundation of the place with hostility.[3] (101) Meanwhile, the Thasians, defeated in battle and under siege, turned to the Lakedaimonians and urged them to come to their rescue by invading Attika. This they promised to do, unknown to the Athenians, and indeed intended to do, but they were prevented by the earthquake which occurred then, which was the occasion on which the helots as well as the Thouriatans and Aithaians among the *perioikoi* revolted against them and congregated in Ithome.[4] The bulk of the helots were the descendants of the Messenians of old who were then enslaved,[5] as a result of which the entire category was known as Messenians. So the Lakedaimonians were at war with those in Ithome, and the Thasians were forced to come to terms with the Athenians in the third year of the siege, pulling down their wall and handing over their ships, accepting an assessment of how much they were to pay at once and (as yearly tribute) in the future and giving up the mainland and the mine.

Thucydides I.100.2–101

(B) Now Inaros the son of Psammetichos, of Libya, king of the Libyans who live near Egypt, starting from Mareia, the *polis* beyond Pharos, detached the bulk of Egypt from King Artaxerxes and becoming its ruler brought in the Athenians. They happened to be on an expedition to Cyprus with 200 ships drawn from themselves and their allies; they left Cyprus and came to Egypt and sailing up the Nile from the sea they gained control of the river and of two thirds of Memphis; they then set to to attack the third part which is known as the White Tower, where those of the Persians and Medes who had escaped as well as those of the Egyptians who had not revolted were confined . . . (109) (After an unsuccessful attempt to persuade the Spartans to invade Attika, the King sent a large army to Egypt.) (Megabyxos) arrived and defeated the Egyptians and their allies in a land-battle, drove the Greeks out of Memphis and finally shut them up in the island of Prosopitis; there he besieged them for a year and six months, finally draining the channel round the island and diverting the water elsewhere, thus leaving the ships high and dry and converting the bulk of the island into mainland; he then crossed and took the island on foot. (110) In this way the Greek venture failed after six years of fighting; a few of the many involved got through Libya to Kyrene and escaped, but the majority was lost . . . Meanwhile 50 triremes drawn from Athens and the rest of the alliance sailed to Egypt to relieve the force there and put in at the Mendesian mouth of the river, in complete ignorance of what had happened;[6] they were attacked by the infantry on land and by the fleet of the Phoinikians at sea and the bulk of the ships was lost, though some got away. So ended the great expedition of the Athenians and their allies to Egypt.

Thucydides I.104 and 109–110*

1 Than Eurymedon, see **131**.

253

2 It is doubtful if the Athenians set out to deprive the Thasians of *emporia* or mine; they doubtless argued that the land on which they wished to found Ennea Hodoi was not Thasian but Thrakian, whatever claims the Thasians might make; in the event, of course, they were proved right.

3 Both here and at IV.102.2 Thucydides allows us to suppose that all the colonists were killed, which is clearly impossible.

4 For the *perioikoi* see **44** n.4; for the siege of Mount Ithome, in central Messenia, see **169**.

5 See **45**.

6 The 50 triremes were presumably intended to replace a similar number left out of the 200; Thucydides again allows us to suppose very high losses. See Meiggs, *Empire*, 104–8.

133. Samians in Egypt

Not the least of all the benefits which the Athenians derived from their empire was allies to fight in their wars, highlighted by an epigram on the Samian dead in the most ambitious venture of all, the attempt to free Egypt from Persian dominion (see **132**).

[Of this] deed many [are witnesses . . . when] around lovely Memphis fierce Ares brought about a battle between the ships of the Medes and the Hellenes [and the Samians] captured fifteen ships of the Phoinikians . . .[1]

Meiggs and Lewis no. 34

1 Compare the single memorial for all the dead of the Erechtheid *phylē* in a group of campaigns, including that in Egypt, belonging to one year (**127**).

134. Athens and Chalkis

Even if one shares, as we do, Thucydides' view that the alliance was always an *empire*, the mechanisms by which the Athenians ruled it at its height are nonetheless of considerable interest. We possess from the dossier dealing with the Chalkidians after their revolt in 446/5 (Thuc. 1.114) the oath to be sworn by Athens and Chalkis and a decree dealing with queries raised by the Chalkidians, documents which reveal much of the general principles according to which Athens regulated her relationship with an ally who had revolted (compare **135** for some of the practical measures).

It was resolved by the *boulē* and the *dēmos*, in the *prytaneia* of (the *phylē*) Antiochis, for which Drakontides presided. Diognetos proposed: that the *boulē* and the *dikastai* of the Athenians should swear the oath in these terms: 'I will not expel the Chalkidians from Chalkis, nor will I destroy the *polis*, nor will I deprive any individual of his rights, nor will I punish him with exile, nor will I arrest him, nor will I kill him, nor will I confiscate the property of anyone, unless with the approval of the *dēmos* of the Athenians; I will not introduce a vote without due summons either against the *koinon* (community) or against any individual, and if an embassy comes I will introduce it to the *boulē* and *dēmos* within ten days, if I am *prytanis*, as far as I am able. I shall guarantee this to the Chalkidians as long as they obey the *dēmos* of the Athenians.' (It was further resolved) that an embassy coming from Chalkis should administer the oath to the Athenians along with the *horkōtai*[1] and record those who swore; and that the *stratēgoi* should see that everyone swears.

(It was resolved) that the Chalkidians should swear in these terms: 'I will not rebel from the *dēmos* of the Athenians by any means or artifice, or be disloyal in word or deed, nor will I obey anyone who does revolt, and if anyone does revolt I will tell the Athenians, and I will pay the tribute (*phoros*) to the Athenians, at such level as I may persuade the Athenians (to accept), and I will be as good and as true an ally as I can and I will help and defend the *dēmos* of the Athenians, if anyone wrongs the *dēmos* of the Athenians, and I will obey the *dēmos* of the Athenians.' (It was resolved) that of the Chalkidians all those of age should swear, and that if anyone did not swear he should be deprived of his rights and his property should be confiscated and a tithe of this property should be consecrated to Zeus Olympios (in Chalkis); and that an embassy of the Athenians coming to Chalkis should administer the oath along with the *horkōtai* in Chalkis and record those of the Chalkidians who swore.

Antikles proposed: that Athenians and Chalkidians should arrange the oath, (in the hope of) good fortune for the Athenians, according to the same procedure as the *dēmos* of the Athenians prescribed for the Eretrians;[2] and that the *stratēgoi* should see that it take place as soon as possible; and that the *dēmos* should at once choose five men who would go to Chalkis and administer the oath; and that concerning the hostages reply should be made to the Chalkidians that for the moment the Athenians had decided to leave things as they had voted, but that when it seemed good they would take counsel and organise the exchange[3] as seemed good and expedient for the Athenians and the Chalkidians; and that the *xenoi* in Chalkis, who living there do not pay taxes to Athens, even if any of them (does not pay because he) has been granted exemption from taxes by the *dēmos* of the Athenians, should pay taxes to Chalkis just as the other Chalkidians do;[4] and that this *psēphisma* and the oath should be inscribed, at Athens by the secretary of the *boulē* on a stone *stēlē* to be placed on the *(akro)polis*, at the expense of the Chalkidians, at Chalkis in the temple of Zeus Olympios by the *boulē* of the Chalkidians; this should be the decision for the Chalkidians. As for the sacrifices prescribed by the oracles about Euboia, Hierokles[5] and three others should carry them out as soon as possible, the three to be chosen by the *boulē* from among its own members; and the *stratēgoi* should see that they take place as soon as possible and provide the money for them.

Archestratos proposed: that everything else should be as Antikles proposed; but that the Chalkidians should have the control of law-suits in their own hands in Chalkis just as the Athenians do at Athens, except for cases involving exile or death or loss of rights; and that concerning these cases there should be reference to Athens to the Heliaia of the *thesmothetai*[6] according to the *psēphisma* of the *dēmos*;[7] and that the *stratēgoi* should see to the defence of Euboia to the best of their ability, so that everything might turn out as well as possible for the Athenians.

OATH (not inscribed)

Meiggs and Lewis no. 52

1 Officials in charge of administering oaths (*horkoi*).
2 Who had also rebelled.
3 Probably the replacement of one group of hostages by another.
4 The identity of the *xenoi* in Chalkis who did pay taxes to Athens is a puzzle – probably Athenians living there as *metoikoi*.
5 Who appears as an oracle-monger in Aristophanes, *Peace* 1047.
6 See **63**.
7 For Athenian control over jurisdiction in the empire see Meiggs, *Empire*, ch. 12. If Athens had not reserved judgment on certain cases to herself, the life expectancy of pro-Athenian politicians in the empire would have been very short indeed.

135. Methods of control

Athenian methods of control were both formal and informal. Among the former, the imposition of a garrison was perhaps the most drastic of the measures available to Athens, though the sending out of a *klērouchia* or *apoikia* (the nature of the distinction is not altogether clear, see **75** n. 14) was probably just as effective; the latter approach had the added benefit of providing a livelihood for the settlers involved (see **198**, end); in addition or by way of alternative, Athenian *archontes* (officials), *epimelētai* (supervisors) and *episkopoi* (inspectors – the institution may owe something to an institution of the Persian empire, see J. M. Balcer, 'The Athenian *episkopos* and the Achaemenid King's eye', *American Journal of Philology* (1977), 252–63) could also spend periods in the *poleis* of the empire. But there were also informal methods of control, local men who acted as Athenian *proxenoi* (see **43**; it was the Athenian *proxenoi* on Mytilene who warned of the impending revolt in 428, see **197**), pro-Athenian politicians and even the establishment of constitutions on the Athenian model (see Meiggs, *Empire*, 208–11); it was of course to protect supporters of Athens that she reserved law-suits involving extreme penalties to herself (see **134** n.7).

(A) This was how savage the *stasis*[1] was as it progressed, and it seemed even more so, since it was the first of this kind of event; while later almost the whole of the Greek world was disturbed, as everywhere quarrels arose between the *prostatai* of the *dēmos* wishing to bring in the Athenians and the few wishing to bring in the Lakedaimonians. In time of peace they would not have had an excuse or felt able to bring them in, but in time of war, with an alliance available to either side to help harm its enemies and at the same time to gain strength for itself, those who wished to engage in revolutionary activity found it easy to call others in.

Thucydides III.82.1

(B) As far as the allies are concerned, there is the fact that they (the Athenians) sail out and lay charges as they please and disdain the *chrēstoi*;[2] in fact they recognise that a ruler is bound to be hated by the ruled anyway, and that if the rich and the *chrēstoi* are powerful in the *poleis* the rule of the *dēmos* at Athens will not last for long; so this is why they deprive the *chrēstoi* of rights and take away their money and kill them and exile them, and put the *ponēroi*[3] in power. But the *chrēstoi* among the Athenians protect the *chrēstoi* in the allied *poleis*, recognising that it is in their interests always to protect the best people in the *poleis*. (15) One might argue that this is where the strength of the Athenians lies, in the ability of the allies to contribute money; but the leaders of the *dēmos* regard it as better if any individual among the Athenians has the money of the allies[4] and they have only enough to live off and are rendered unable to plot.[5]

Old Oligarch (=[Xenophon], *Athenaion Politeia*) I.14-15

1 On Kerkyra in 427, just described by Thucydides.
2 The good, i.e. the upper classes, see **143**.
3 The bad, i.e. the lower classes, see **143**.
4 As a reward for initiating a successful prosecution.
5 Compare **32B**.

136. The allied view

We have suggested that the reality underlying the Athenian empire was unchanged from the beginning; but the relationship between the Athenians and their allies clearly became increasingly formalised as regulations were devised to deal with one problem or another, and this may have encouraged resentment (note the swift development of resentment against the relatively formalised fourth-century Spartan empire, see Ch.26). At the same time, such things as the removal of the treasury from Delos to Athens probably in 454/3 (see **138**), though at the proposal of the Samians, presumably made the nature of the relationship increasingly clear; the Athenians ceased to talk of their allies and talked instead of the *poleis* which the Athenians ruled (as in Thuc. v.47.2); and they imposed on these cities a religious obligation previously only applicable to Athenian *apoikiai*, the offering of a cow and suit of armour at the Panathenaia festival (Meiggs and Lewis no.46). Finally the Athenians went so far as to impose the use of Athenian silver coinage and weights and measures on the empire (Meiggs and Lewis no.45), thus in a sense almost making it part of Attika (compare Hdt. VI.139–140, where the Chersonesos (see **106**) is regarded as part of Attika). Just as Thucydides, in the Athenian speeches of 431, gives us an account of the Athenian view of their empire, so too he uses the Mytilenaian speech at Olympia in 428 to portray allied feelings.

'The alliance between ourselves and the Athenians came into being when you (Spartans) withdrew from the war against the Persians and they stayed on to see what remained to be done.[1] We became allies, however, not to enslave the Greeks to the Athenians, but to free the Greeks from the Persians. And as long as they led in an equitable fashion, we were glad to follow; but when we saw that they were abandoning their war with the Persians and pursuing the enslavement[2] of their allies, our apprehensions were aroused. In due course,[3] the allies were all enslaved apart from ourselves and the Chians; for each one was isolated because of the multiplicity of conflicting voices[4] and they were unable to protect themselves; we (and the Chians) continued to fight with the Athenians, nominally as free and autonomous peoples. And so it was that we no longer trusted the Athenians as *hēgemones*, bearing in mind what had happened; for there was no likelihood that men who had subdued those whom they had accepted into a treaty relationship along with us would not, if they were able, do the same to those who remained.'

Thucydides III.10.2–6

1 See **129–130**.
2 See **130**.
3 After the revolt of the Samians, Thuc. I.115, 2–117.
4 We take Thucydides' expression, *dia polypsēphian* (literally 'because of the multiplicity of votes'), as metaphorical.

137. Empire and 'misthos'

The most crucial use of the resources made available to Athens as a result of the existence of the empire was the introduction of pay (*misthos*) for state service, first for jury service (see **141**); the step had of course symbolic as well as practical importance, as with pay for serving in the fleet; not only did many ordinary Athenians earn part of their living as a result, they were also now visibly the backbone of the *polis*, rather than the cavalry or the hoplites.

After this,[1] now that the *polis* was growing bolder and a great deal of money had been collected, Aristeides advised them to lay claim to the *hēgemonia* and leaving their fields to live in the town; for there would be a livelihood for all, some in the army, some on guard duty, some on public business; furthermore this would be the way to ensure the *hēgemonia*. Obeying this advice and seizing their empire, they treated the allies more like subjects, except for the Chians, Lesbians and Samians – them they used as guards for their empire, allowing them to keep their own *politeiai* and rule their existing subjects. And they established a plentiful livelihood for the many, as Aristeides had proposed; for it came about that more than 20,000 men were supported from the tribute and the taxes and the allies. For there were 6,000 jurors and 1,600 archers and in addition 1,200 horsemen and a *boule* of 500 and 500 guards of the docks and in addition 50 guards in the *polis* and as many as 700 officials at home[2] and 700 abroad; and in addition to all these, when later they entered the war, there were 2,500 hoplites, twenty guard ships and further ships conveying the guards chosen by lot, to the number of 2,000 men; and furthermore there was the *prytaneion*[3] and the orphans and the prison guards; for all these were maintained from public funds.

?Aristotle, *Athenaion Politeia* 24

1 The foundation of the Delian League, see **129–130**.
2 See M. H. Hansen, *GRBS* 21 (1980), 151–73, for defence of this figure.
3 See **41**.

138. The argument over the building programme

It was one thing to use Athenian resources, no longer needed for the fleet, to introduce pay for performing public duties; it was quite another to use the tribute itself for internal purposes; and the debate that began in 447 (see Meiggs and Lewis nos. 54 and 59) still continues: see Meiggs, *Empire*, chs. 14–15; M. I. Finley (cited on p. 246).

The thing that provided most pleasure and adornment to Athens, and most astonishment to other men, and is the only one which now bears witness in Greece that her much discussed power and her ancient prosperity are not fictional, the construction of sacred buildings – this was the policy of Perikles which his enemies most maligned and attacked in the meetings of the *ekklēsia*. They claimed that the reputation of the *dēmos* was being ruined and that it was being slandered, for bringing into its own care from Delos the common funds of the Greeks; Perikles had destroyed the best and most plausible excuse it had in the face of its accusers, that it had removed the common funds from Delos and was keeping them in a safe place from fear of the *barbaroi*;[1] Greece was seen to be suffering a grievous insult and to be ruled by an open tyranny,[2] as it watched the Athenians gilding their *polis* with the moneys which it had been compelled to contribute for the war and beautifying it like a wanton woman, decorated with precious stones and statues and thousand-talent temples.[3]

Plutarch, Perikles 12.1–2

1 See **136** Intro.
2 For the theme of the *tyrannos polis* compare Thuc. 1.122.
3 For the actual programme see **151**.

139. Land in the empire

According to Herodotus (1.126), Kyros had encouraged the Persians to revolt from the Medes by drawing attention to the material benefits to be expected; the Athenians were also perfectly conscious of the material benefits of empire and the behaviour of the Athenian *dēmos* should not have surprised those Athenians who chose to oppose it (see **138**); one may suspect jealousy as a motive rather than a tender concern for the Athenian allies. The possibility of organised settlement on allied land was the major opportunity available to the *dēmos*, but was far from unique; see especially M. I. Finley (cited on p.246) for ownership of allied land by individuals.

(A) They say that one of these (friends of Perikles) was Ephialtes[1] who destroyed the power of the Areiopagos, giving unlimited and undiluted liberty to the *politai*, according to Plato;[2] the comic poets say[3] that the *dēmos* was made as wild as an unbridled horse by this liberty and 'no longer had the patience to obey, but bit off Euboia[4] and trampled on the islands'.

Plutarch, Perikles 7.8

(B) In addition to this, he sent 1,000 *klērouchoi* to the Chersonesos, 500 to Naxos, half that number to Andros, 1,000 to Thrake to live among the Bisaltans,[5] and others to Italy, when Sybaris was being resettled; they named it Thourioi.[6] And in doing this he relieved the *polis* of an idle and, because of its leisure, interfering mob,[7] and provided a remedy for the poverty of the *dēmos*, and placed among the allies garrisons to instil fear and prevent revolt.

Plutarch, Perikles 11.5–6

1 As long as he lived Ephialtes was more important than Perikles, contrary to what Plutarch suggests; see **123**.
2 *Republic* (VIII) 562C.

3 The author of the quotation which follows is unknown.

4 See **134**.

5 See Meiggs and Lewis no.49 = Fornara no.100 for the *apoikia* at Brea; also **192**. It is not possible to identify the occasions of all the *klērouchiai* mentioned by Plutarch. For a definition of a *klērouchos* see **75** n.14.

6 See **172**.

7 The apparent motivation is no doubt an attribution of Plutarch or his source.

140. The economic consequences of thalassocracy

The Athenian empire brought other benefits than tribute and land, graphically described in the passage below; for comment see M. I. Finley (cited on p.246); compare also **154**.

They are the only people among the Greeks and the *barbaroi* who are able to accumulate resources; for if some *polis* is rich in shipbuilding timber, where will she sell it, if she cannot persuade the mistress of the seas (to take it)? Similarly, if a *polis* is rich in iron or copper or flax; for these are the things from which ships are made, timber from one source, iron from another, copper from another, flax from another, wax from another.[1] (12) Furthermore, they will not allow our enemies to convey these materials anywhere else – or at any rate such people will not be users of the sea. The result is that although they get none of these things from their land they get them all by sea; while there is no other city which has even two of them, say wood and flax, rather where there is a plentiful supply of flax the countryside is bare and treeless; nor are iron and copper to be got from the same *polis* or any other two or three things in one *polis*, but one here and one there.

Old Oligarch (=[Xenophon], Ath. Pol.) II.11–12

1 So far, the author has discussed not control of trade, but simply the fact that since Athens was the only naval power in the Greek world she was the only market for shipbuilding material (he obviously exaggerates, and Athenian interest in Makedonia and courtship of its monarchy suggests that getting timber was not all that easy); in the next sentence he makes the obvious point that the Athenians could prevent strategic material reaching their enemies, at any rate by sea, which is not in any sense control of trade either; the 'Megarian Decree' (**178**) belongs in a very different context.

For fourth-century Athenian interest in another shipbuilding material, red ochre, see **282**.

13 Athenian political life

As we saw in Ch. 11, during the first half of the fifth century Athenian political institutions developed from the basic form given them by Kleisthenes to a stage where, from the 450s onwards, they provided the means for the *politai* of Athens to govern themselves in a fully participatory democracy: *ekklēsia, boulē* and *dikastēria*; a multiplicity of boards of officials, great and (especially) small; and close control of all holders of office. This was the institutional structure, documented for us by such sources as the Aristotelian *Ath. Pol.* But when it comes to understanding how the dynamics of political life and practice animated this structure, the *Ath. Pol.* has little to offer, and one turns instead to a variety of sources which, when used with care, add to our constitutional facts the further and vital dimension of political insights: Thucydides (**149**), the Old Oligarch (**143**), Lysias (**144**), Plato (**141B**), and above all – given his access to so much material which no longer survives – Plutarch. Here we can learn of such matters as the mobilisation of political support, and the relationship (at all levels of society) between income, expenditure and political activity. Yet the conceptual frameworks employed by the ancients themselves must always be understood for what they are, too often naive and preoccupied with personalities, and our own notions from the world of organised party-politics must not intrude. Fortunately these two sources of possible distortion in perspective are absent from the best of modern work on the subject (e.g. M. I. Finley, 'Athenian Demagogues', *Past and Present* 21 (1962), 3–24; Connor, *Politicians*), and with its help we can appreciate both the unique position, *de facto*, attained during this period by Perikles son of Xanthippos (**148**) and the basic facts of political life in democratic Athens which made his ascendancy very much the exception rather than the rule.

141. 'Misthos'

If one thing above all others enabled the political machinery set up by Kleisthenes and his successors to become a fully operative reality in the second half of the fifth century, it must surely have been the introduction – and the extension, to virtually all parts of the system – of state salaries (*misthoi*); this was essential if theoretical eligibility for service on (chiefly) the juries and the *boulē* was to become, for the mass of ordinary Athenians, practical eligibility. Exact dates elude us, but it is reasonable to suppose (with Hignett, *Constitution*, 220) that all officials appointed by lot were receiving payment for their duties before *c*.430. *Misthos* is known in some other cities too (see G. E. M. de Ste Croix, 'Political pay outside Athens', *CQ* n.s.25 (1975), 48–52), but it was especially associated with radical democracy in the Athenian style (see **127**) and with the profits which the Athenians drew from their empire (**137**) – two facts which naturally made it a subject inviting partisan differences of opinion.

See further: Hignett, *Constitution*, 216–21; Jones, *Democracy*, 3–19 and 49–50 (arguing against the view embodied in the texts translated here); M. H. Hansen, 'Misthos for magistrates in classical Athens', *Symbolae Osloenses* 54 (1979), 5–22.

(A) Initially, as has been said,[1] pitted as he was against the reputation of Kimon, Perikles endeavoured to ingratiate himself with the *dēmos*. But he was at a disadvantage in terms of wealth and property – and these were what Kimon was using to win over the poor: he was providing a dinner every day to any needy Athenian, clothing the elderly men, and allowing anyone who wished to pick the fruit on his estates, from which he had had the fences removed.[2] It was because Perikles found himself outdone in these demagogic techniques that he turned to the distribution of public funds. His advisor in this, as Aristotle reports, was Damonides of (the deme) Oa.[3] And very soon he had bribed the multitude, one and all, with theatre tickets (*theōrika*)[4] and fees for *dikastai* and other forms of *misthos* and largesse, so that he could use their support in his attack on the Areiopagos Council.[5]

Plutarch, Perikles 9.2–3

(B) Sokrates: 'But tell me this as well: are the Athenians said to have become better because of Perikles, or exactly the opposite – to have been ruined by him? What I have heard, myself, is that Perikles has made the Athenians idle and cowardly and greedy for money, because he was the first to bring in state salaries.'

Kallikles: 'You (must) have heard *that* from the men with battered ears,[6] Sokrates!'

Plato, Gorgias 515E

1 In 7.3 Plutarch's source here is ?Aristot. *Ath. Pol. 27*.
2 Compare *Kimon* 10.1–2 – where, however, Plutarch notes that in the *Ath. Pol.* (27.3) it is only Kimon's fellow-demesmen to whom these facilities are offered.
3 *Ath. Pol.* 27.4, where we are told that Damonides was later ostracised. In Plut. *Per.* 4.1–2, Perikles' teacher, later ostracised, is called Damon. The two *may* be one, but they are perhaps more probably father and son, given the existence of a Damon Damonidou *ostrakon* (see Meiggs and Lewis no.21); if so, the two men and their activities and attributes are hopelessly conflated.

4 *Theōrika*, and the fund which provided them, became centrally important to Athenian financial management in the fourth century (see **313**), but their origins are obscure. Despite Plutarch's assertion here, they may not have existed in the fifth century at all; or if they did, their purpose and scope may have been much narrower than the general poor-relief functions which were later served by the *diōbelia* (see **216**) and eventually by the *theōrika* as we see them in the fourth century.

5 See **123**. The implied chronology here, i.e. all these measures supposedly pre-dating 462/1, is highly improbable, but the association with Perikles is firm in our sources: see further, B below, and Aristot. *Pol.* (II)1274 a 8–9.

6 I.e. those who admired Sparta, and were therefore excessively fond of boxing (see Plato, *Protagoras* 342A–C).

142. The political use of wealth: public relations and private expectations

As we have just seen (**141**), an institution such as *misthos* might be represented as unscrupulous bribery – but only by those unable or unwilling to accept the very idea of a participatory democracy. It is clear enough, however, that quite apart from any political advantage which might be gained from the manipulation of *public* money, prominent Athenian politicians were very far from blind to the uses to which they could put their own resources in creating a reputation for conspicuous consumption (or possibly conspicuous frugality: see B, below) and operating the 'politics of largesse' (Connor, *Politicians*, 18–22). As well as the three cases illustrated here see that of Alkibiades (**219**), a particularly spectacular example. It is also worth observing that during the Peloponnesian War the *dēmos* persistently elected as *stratēgos* a man called Hipponikos, not obviously recommended by anything except his wealth (see **161B**).

(A) *Kimon*

When the captured spoils had been sold the *dēmos* found itself in a strong financial position and went ahead with various projects, including the southern wall on the Akropolis, which was built from the ample proceeds of that expedition.[1] And it is said that, whereas the complete construction of the Long Walls – the ones they call 'Legs' – was not until later,[2] the initial foundations for them, where the work met the obstacle of wet and marshy ground, were laid safe and sound by Kimon; what he did was to arrange, at his own expense, for masses of rubble and boulders to be dumped in the marshes. And Kimon was also the first to beautify the *astu* with the so-called liberal and elegant haunts which were excessively popular a little later: he planted the *agora* with plane-trees, and turned the Academy[3] from a waterless, parched place into an irrigated grove, furnished by him with clear running-tracks and covered walks in the shade.

Plutarch, *Kimon* 13.6–8

(B) *Perikles*[4]

Perikles took care not to succumb to bribery, although in point of fact he was not wholly indifferent to money-making either. As regards the wealth which he had legally inherited from his ancestors, he did not wish to see this vanish through neglect, yet he was equally unwilling for it to be a serious and time-consuming concern to him when he was occupied with other things. He therefore had to operate a system of household management (*oikonomia*) which was intended to combine the maximum of ease with the maximum of frugality; and this was to sell all his annual produce in bulk, and then, to provide the wherewithal for daily life and subsistence, to buy in the *agora* each thing as it was needed. This made him unpopular with his sons when they grew up, and their wives found him no lavish provider; they criticised him for organising his expenditure on such a thoroughly parsimonious, hand-to-mouth basis, and for the fact that there were never the sort of surpluses which were appropriate to a great household that wanted for nothing – every expense and every receipt being a matter of precise count and measure. And the man who supervised all this frugality for him was a single household slave (*oiketēs*), Euangelos, whose unrivalled mastery of *oikonomia* was the result either of natural gifts or else of Perikles' training.

Plutarch, *Perikles* 16.3–5

(C) *Nikias*

So Perikles led the *polis* by virtue of genuine excellence (*aretē*)[5] and power of speech and argument, and thus had no need to secure mass appeal by any plausible posturing. Nikias, by contrast, lacked these (natural attributes) – but he was extremely rich,[6] and used this as his means of influencing the *dēmos*. He had no confidence in his ability to compete in the same sort of irresponsible buffoonery by which Kleon catered to the pleasures of the Athenians,[7] so he endeavoured to win over the *dēmos* with expenditure on theatrical productions and games and other such lavish and ambitious outlays; and in the costliness and the elegance of these he outdid all his predecessors and contemporaries. Two of his dedicatory offerings have remained *in situ* until my own day: the statue of Pallas (Athena) on the Akropolis – the one which has lost its gilding – and the temple, situated within (the precinct) of Dionysos, which has a display of the tripods that he won as *choregos*.[8] For he won many victories as *chorēgos*; indeed, he was never defeated . . .

We also have on record how splendid – and worthy of the god – his lavish outlays at Delos were.[9] The choirs which the *poleis* used to send there to sing in praise of Apollo would sail in to the island unceremoniously, and at once a crowd would meet them at the ship and urge them to sing, not in an orderly fashion but as they were disembarking, enthusiastically and chaotically, and putting on their garlands and robes. But when Nikias led the festal embassy, he landed first on (the nearby island of) Rheneia with his choir and sacrificial victims and other equipment; then, during the night, with the bridge of boats which he had had made to measure in Athens and brilliantly adorned with gilding and dyestuffs and garlands and curtains, he bridged the strait – not an especially wide one – between Rheneia and Delos. This done, at daybreak he led his procession in honour of the god across the bridge to the island, with his choir lavishly decked out and singing as it went. And after the sacrifices and the choral contest (*agōn*) and the feasts he set up, as an offering to Apollo, the (famous) bronze palm-tree, and he consecrated to him an estate which he had bought for ten thousand drachmas; with the revenues from this the Delians were to hold sacrificial feasts and pray to the gods to send him, Nikias, many blessings. This stipulation was actually engraved on the *stēlē* which he left on Delos – to stand guard, so to speak, over his benefaction . . .

Plutarch, *Nikias* 3*

1 Eurymedon (**131**).
2 See **171**.
3 Later the site of Plato's philosophical school.
4 See **146, 148**, etc.
5 *Aretē*: see **5**B, **33** n. I. Perikles' predominance: **148**.
6 See further **161**B.
7 Kleon: see **210, 212**.
8 The *chorēgia* was the liturgy (see **144**) of equipping, paying and training a festival chorus: see in brief Parke, *Festivals*, 131–2.
9 On Peisistratos and Delos see **69** with n.12. Presumably the episode which Plut. now goes on to describe belongs in 426/5, when the Athenians purified Delos again and inaugurated a quadriennial festival there (Thuc. III.104).

143. The moral vocabulary of politics

The vocabulary of political life in fifth-century Athens sprang from the application of three sets of criteria – political (i.e. ability and competence to govern), economic and moral – which from a partisan standpoint were deemed to be convergent; and in view of the largely conservative bias of our surviving sources (Jones, *Democracy*, 41–3), it is no surprise that the standpoint from which we generally see this convergence expressed is an anti-democratic one. In other words we find a schematic opposition between the *dēmos*, whose constituent members are poor (*penētes*) and worthless (*ponēroi, phauloi, cheirous*), and the 'best men' (*beltistoi, aristoi*), who are well born (*gennaioi*), rich (*plousioi*) and competent (*chrēstoi*) – in short, *kaloi k'agathoi*, literally 'beautiful and good' but with quite untranslatable nuances: see Connor, *Politicians*, 88–9; de Ste Croix, *Origins*, 371–6; W. Donlan, 'The origin of *kalos k'agathos*', *American Journal of Philology* 94

266

(1973), 365–74, and 'The role of *eugeneia* in the aristocratic self-image during the fifth-century B.C.', *Essays . . . R. E. Dengler*, E. N. Borza and R. W. Carrubba (eds.) (University Park, Pa., 1973), 63–78.

There could be no better, or balder, illustration of this than some passages from the so-called Old Oligarch, whose *Athenaion Politeia*, once mistakenly attributed to Xenophon, was written at some time between 445 and 415 – probably, in our view, during the early years of the Peloponnesian War. Although it shares the title of the Aristotelian *Ath. Pol.* it would be classified today as a political pamphlet. Its author was apparently an Athenian oligarch in exile, moved to explain to non-Athenians how the *dēmos* in Athens maintained and justified its political supremacy. For a full introduction, translation, commentary and bibliography see Moore, *Aristotle*, 19–61.

As regards the *politeia* of the Athenians, I do not applaud this way that they have chosen to have it, because in choosing it they have preferred to let the *ponēroi* do better than the *chrēstoi*; so for this reason I do not applaud it. Since, however, this is what they decided, I shall demonstrate how well they keep their *politeia* safe and manage the other things in which, as the other Greeks see it, they go wrong.[1]

(2) So first I shall say this: it is right that the *penētes* and the *dēmos* there (in Athens) have more than the *gennaioi* and the *plousioi*, for the reason that it is the *dēmos* which rows the warships and (thereby) gives the *polis* its power. The helmsmen, the boatswains, the petty officers, the look-out men, the ships' carpenters – these are the men who give the *polis* its power much more than the hoplites and the *gennaioi* and the *chrēstoi*. So, since this is the case, it seems right for everyone to share in the holding of offices, whether filled by lot or by election,[2] and for any of the *politai* to be permitted to speak if he wishes.[3]

(4) Some people are amazed that the Athenians everywhere assign more to the *ponēroi* and the *penētes* and the men of the *dēmos* than to the *chrēstoi*, yet in this very thing they manifestly keep the democracy safe: for if the *penētes* and the men of the *dēmos* and the *cheirous* do well and grow numerous they will strengthen the democracy, whereas if it is the *plousioi* and the *chrēstoi* who do well, the men of the *dēmos* create a strong opposition for themselves. (5) It is, after all, a fact of life that the best element is opposed to democracy. This is because the *beltistoi* are least prone to unruliness and injustice and most intent upon pursuing what is good and useful, whereas in the *dēmos* one finds the extremes of ignorance and disorder and wickedness; their poverty leads them more towards the disgraceful (than the good and useful), and it is their lack of money which in some cases renders them uneducated and ignorant. (6) The point may be raised that the Athenians ought not to let everyone speak on equal terms or serve on the *boulē*, but only the ablest men and the *aristoi*, yet even in this – in allowing even the *ponēroi* to speak – their

267

reasoning is excellent: for if the *chrēstoi* (only) were to speak and make policy,[4] that would be good for the likes of them but not good for the men of the *dēmos*. As things are now, any *ponēros* who wants to can stand up and speak and obtain what is good for him and his kind. (7) Again, an objection might be raised here: how would such a fellow know what is good for him or for the *dēmos*? Well, the Athenians recognise that this man's goodwill, ignorant and wicked though he is, profits them more than the hostility of the *chrēstoi*, for all their *aretēs* and wisdom. (8) So although this is not a recipe for producing the best *polis*, it is certainly how one preserves democracy. The *dēmos* does not want to see *eunomia*[6] in the *polis* at the price of its own servitude; it wants to be free and to rule; and if this means the opposite of *eunomia*, what does it care? What for you is the opposite of *eunomia* is exactly what makes the *dēmos* strong and free.

Old Oligarch (= [Xenophon], Athenaion Politeia) 1.1–2 and 4–8

1 Here, and throughout, our translation attempts to convey something of the author's odd, awkward style.
2 1.3 (omitted here) goes on to concede, however, that the *dēmos* is shrewd enough to fill important *military* offices (by election) with the ablest men available; compare **126** with n.1.
3 This means, above all, speaking in the *ekklēsia*, and this important issue recurs later in the passage. Equal freedom of speech, *isēgoria*, was a central concept in Athenian radical democracy; it is indeed the word that Herodotus uses (rather than *dēmokratia*) to describe the outcome of the Kleisthenic reforms (Hdt. v.78; see **75**, end), and inscriptions furnish ample evidence in practice of the fact that when the herald proclaimed the invitation 'Who wishes to speak?', it was the absolute right of any and every Athenian to respond (see for example the amendment moved by Phantokles in Meiggs and Lewis no.49, lines 32–42; the amendment in **152**; and general discussion in Jones, *Democracy*, 111–18). See further G. T. Griffith, 'Isegoria in the assembly at Athens', in *Ancient Society and Institutions: Studies . . . Ehrenberg* (Oxford, 1966), 115–38; J. D. Lewis, 'Isegoria at Athens: when did it begin?', *Historia* 20 (1971), 129–40. There is a very remarkable eulogy of *isēgoria* in Euripides, *Suppliant Women* 399–455.
4 Or, as Moore has it (*Aristotle*, 38), speak in the *ekklēsia* and serve on the *boulē*.
5 See **5B**.
6 See **45** with n.4. It is of course highly significant that this word, with its Spartan associations, is part of the political vocabulary of the Oligarch and his friends.

144. Politics, liturgies and the courts

Liturgies (*leitourgiai*) were an integral part not only of the fiscal and administrative systems in Athens but of the whole psychology and practice of radical democracy. The Athenians – indeed, the Greeks in general – had a pronounced distaste for taxing themselves directly, except *in extremis*, yet the proceeds of indirect taxation (sales taxes, harbour dues, etc; see **42**) fell far short of meeting all the city's financial needs; so many important functions, recurrent or occasional, were imposed, as a combination of duty and privilege, upon the wealthiest of the individual citizens (and, to a limited extent, non-citizens also: see Whitehead, *Ideology*, 80–2). Much the most onerous of them was the *triērarchia* – equipping, maintaining and (usually) commanding a trireme in the Athenian war fleet; but equally important in their way, and far more numerous (*c.*100 a year: J. K. Davies, *JHS* 87 (1967), 33–40, corrected on one point by J. M. Moore, *JHS* 91 (1971), 140–1), were the festival liturgies such as the *chorēgia* (see **142** with n.8). The Old Oligarch represents the liturgy system quite simply as soaking the rich ([Xen.] *Ath. Pol.* 1.13), but this was only half the story, if that: in the general context of the political deployment of individual wealth (**142**), the discharging of liturgies was a *quid pro quo*, a recognised act of political investment which could look for its return either in further advancement or else, as in the passage translated here, in the protection and justification of a position already achieved. See further: Davies, *Families*, xvii–xxxi, and *Democracy*, 109–10.

'Now as for me, gentlemen of the jury, I never suffered any misfortune at that time,[1] private or public, as a result of which, through eagerness to be relieved of the ills of the moment, I would have sought a change in the political system. I have performed the *triērarchia* five times; I have fought in four sea-battles; I have contributed to many *eisphorai* during the war;[2] and I have discharged my other liturgies as well as the (other) *politai*. (13) Indeed I spent more than the *polis* required of me. And why? In order that you should think the better of me, and so that if any misfortune should happen to befall me, I might put up a better fight in court. Under the oligarchy[3] all this went for nothing: instead of considering those who had bestowed some benefit upon the *dēmos* as worthy recipients of their favour, they preferred to give the honour of office to the men who had done you most harm – as if this were their guarantee of our good behaviour! You should all bear this in mind, and refuse to believe what my accusers allege: every man ought to be assessed on the record of his achievements.'

Lysias xxv (*Defence against a charge of subverting the democracy*) 12–13

1 The years 410–404.
2 *Eisphorai* were extraordinary capital levies on all but the poorest free residents of Attika, to raise money during or for a war (in this case the latter part of the Peloponnesian War); see Intro to Ch.11
3 The régime of the (so-called) Thirty Tyrants, 404/3: see **244**.

145. Political organisation

Although political parties of the modern sort did not exist in fifth-century Athens, it does not follow that the political leaders of the time were ignorant of methods of mobilising support beyond their natural circle of relatives and friends (*philoi*: see Connor, *Politicians*, 9–32 and *passim*). In Plutarch's *Perikles* we read that Perikles' opponent Thoukydides son of Melesias, probably the grandfather of the historian Thucydides, went some way towards organising a body of support for himself in the *ekklēsia*. It is not quite clear whether the main object of the exercise was that of sitting together (Connor, *Politicians*, 24 with n.36) or voting together (H. T. Wade-Gery, *Essays in Greek History* (Oxford, 1958), 243), and in any case the basic credibility of the information has been called into question (by A. Andrewes, *JHS* 98 (1978), 2); but here is the story, for what it is worth. On Thoukydides and Perikles see further **146**.

The aristocrats saw even before this[1] that Perikles had already become the greatest of the *politai*, but they wished nonetheless that there should be someone in the *polis* who could stand up to him and blunt the edge of his power, to stop it becoming a thoroughgoing monarchy; so as an opponent for him they put up Thoukydides, from (the deme) Alopeke. Thoukydides was a moderate man, and a relative of Kimon's,[2] though less of a military man than Kimon: law and politics were his preferred spheres, and by acting as a watchdog in the *astu* and getting to grips with Perikles on the speaker's rostrum[3] he soon brought the *politeia* into equilibrium. For he did not allow the so-called *kaloi k'agathoi*[4] to be scattered about and mixed up, as before, with the *dēmos*, and their prestige thus swamped by force of numbers: he separated them out, brought them together in one unit, and created a sort of counterpoise in the balance by the weight and power that this gave them collectively. Right from the start, in fact, there had been a kind of hidden flaw, just as in a piece of iron, which pointed to a divergence between the policies of the *dēmos* and of the aristocrats, but now the ambitious rivalry between Perikles and Thoukydides cut the deepest of gashes in the *polis*: one section of it now came to be called the *dēmos*, the other the few (*oligoi*).

Plutarch, *Perikles* 11.1–3

1 The death of Kimon, *c*.450. (It should be noted, however, that Plut. often disregarded chronology when arranging his material, and the location of any episode within one of his Lives may tell us nothing at all about its date.)
2 The precise relationship is problematical: consult Davies, *Families*, 232.
3 On the wrestling metaphor applied here and elsewhere to Thoukydides see further **146** (and Davies, *Families*, 231).
4 See **143** Intro.

146. Perikles versus Thoukydides

The central section of Plutarch's *Perikles* contains further anecdotal material relating to the opposition between Perikles and Thoukydides (**145**), before its culmination in *ostrakismos* for the latter in 444/3. Despite the general doubts cast recently on this source of information (by A. Andrewes, 'The opposition to Perikles', *JHS* 98 (1978), 1–5) and the undeniably over-schematic representation – both here and elsewhere – of the power-struggle between the two men, the material is of some interest. On Thoukydides in general see H. T. Wade-Gery, *Essays in Greek History* (Oxford, 1958), 239–70.

(6) It is said that once upon a time the head of a one-horned ram was brought to Perikles from the countryside, and that Lampon the seer, when he saw how the horn had grown strong and firm from the middle of the beast's forehead, declared that although two power-groups existed in the *polis*, those of Thoukydides and Perikles, the power was going to devolve upon one man – the man to whom this sign had been given. Anaxagoras,[1] however, cut the skull open and demonstrated how the brain had not filled out its position but had compressed itself sharply together, just like an egg, at that very place in the entire cavity where the root of the horn began to grow out. And at the time, the story goes, it was Anaxagoras who won the admiration of the onlookers; but soon afterwards it was Lampon – for Thoukydides was overthrown,[2] and all the affairs of the *dēmos* came entirely under the control of Perikles.

(8) We have on record too a certain saying of Thoukydides son of Melesias, a humorous remark about Perikles and his cleverness; Thoukydides was one of the *kaloi k'agathoi*,[3] and a long-standing political opponent of Perikles'. When Archidamos, the king of the Spartans,[4] asked Thoukydides whether he or Perikles was the better wrestler, he replied, 'Whenever we are wrestling and I throw him, he denies that he has fallen – and convinces of this the very men who have seen him fall!'[5]

(14) Thoukydides and his supporters kept denouncing Perikles for squandering public money and ruining the revenues; so Perikles asked the *dēmos* in the *ekklēsia* whether too much money seemed to have been spent. Much too much, was the verdict, to which Perikles replied, 'In that case let the expenditure be credited not to you but to me; then it will be my own name, as a private individual, which I shall have on the dedicatory inscriptions!' When he had said this the Athenians cried out and urged him to take the money from public funds, and to spare no expense: either they had been impressed by his magnanimity, or else they were eager to stake their claim against his for the glory of the projects.[6] And eventually, when he took the risk of setting up a contest (*agon*) of *ostrakismos* with his rival, Perikles brought about the expulsion of Thoukydides and the dissolution of the faction which had been set up in opposition to himself.

Plutarch, Perikles 6.2–3; 8.3–4; 14

1 The philosopher and scientist Anaxagoras of Klazomenai (*c.*500–*c.*428), who

spent most of his working life in Athens and whom Plut. represents (*Per.* 4. –6.1) as a major formative influence on the young Perikles. See further **157**.
2 By *ostrakismos*: see below. On Lampon see further **174**.
3 See **143** Intro., and **145**.
4 Archidamos: see further **183A**, **186**.
5 While it is not impossible that Thoukydides and Perikles really did wrestle together, this story more probably springs from the wrestling metaphor of their political rivalry (**145** with n.3).
6 This story is obviously 'financially impossible' (Davies, *Families*, 459 n.1), but perhaps a distorted reflection of a real event – the offer of Perikles' family to pay for the Springhouse: see **152**.

147. Restriction upon comic licence, 440/39–437/6

The Old Oligarch (**143**) declares that the Athenians 'do not allow the *dēmos* to be attacked in comedies, so as to avoid hearing criticism of themselves; against individuals, on the other hand, they encourage it . . .' ([Xen.] *Ath. Pol.* II.18). The second part of this statement is amply born out by the whole history of Old Attic Comedy – which in terms of what survives is tantamount to saying the whole *oeuvre* of Aristophanes. As to the first part, some have seen here an allusion to a short-lived decree of 440/39 which we hear of in a chance reference by a scholiast (annotator), commenting on a passage in the first of Aristophanes' surviving plays, *Acharnians*. However, despite what various scholars assert (e.g. V. Ehrenberg, *Sophocles and Pericles* (Oxford, 1954), 86 n.2, 'Pericles' law of censorship'; Bury and Meiggs, *Greece*, 241; Moore, *Aristotle*, 55; contrast the proper scepticism of Gomme, *Commentary* I, 387), we do not know who was responsible for the measure, what gave rise to it, and what precisely it prohibited; and the trouble which Aristophanes met over his (now lost) *Babylonians* of 426 (see *Ach.* lines 377–8 with scholiast; G. Norwood, *CPh* 25 (1930), 1–10) suggests that there were more general and long-lived constraints upon the comic poets in this respect. The particular restrictions imposed during the early 440s thus remain obscure. See in general M. Radin, 'Freedom of speech in ancient Athens', *American Journal of Philology* 48 (1927), 215–30.

Herald: The envoys from the King![1]
Dikaiopolis: King? What King? Me, I'm sick of envoys, and their peacocks and their humbug!
Herald: Silence! (*The envoys appear*)
Dikaiopolis: Blimey, what an Ekbatana of a get-up![2]
Envoy: You sent us to the Great King, at a salary of two drachmas a day, in the archonship of Euthymenes.
   (*Scholiast:* This is the *archōn* in whose year of office (437/6) the decree prohibiting ridicule in comedy was repealed. It had been enacted in the archonship of Morychides (440/39) and was in force for that year and the next two, the archonships of Glaukinos and Theodoros, after which, in the archonship of Euthymenes, it was repealed.)

Dikaiopolis: Oh, those drachmas!

Envoy: And of course we wore ourselves out, wandering about in tents through the Kaystrios plains,[3] and dying of luxury as we lolled in our covered carriages.

Dikaiopolis: And there was I on the battlements, lolling on a pile of shavings – what a narrow escape!

Envoy: As to hospitality, we were positively forced to drink sweet, unmixed wine from crystal and gold goblets.

Dikaiopolis: O *polis* of Kranaos,[4] do you see the mockery of the envoys?

Envoy: The *barbaroi*, you understand, hold only those with the greatest capacity for food and drink to be real men.

Dikaiopolis: Whereas with us it's wenchers and debauchees.

Envoy: Anyway, after three years of this we got to the palace; but he had taken his army and gone off for a crap – and for eight months he was relieving himself up in the golden mountains.

Dikaiopolis: How long was it before he pulled himself together again?

Envoy: At the full moon; and then he returned home. Then he entertained us, and served us whole oxen, baked in a pot.

Dikaiopolis: Who ever saw oxen baked in a pot? Humbug!

Envoy: And then, by Zeus, he served us with a bird three times the size of Kleonymos; a 'cheat', its name was.[5]

Dikaiopolis: It's you who were the cheat, taking those two drachmas!

Aristophanes, Acharnians 61–90, with the scholiast on line 67

1 The scene is the Athenian *ekklēsia*. This excerpt should illustrate the flavour of Aristophanic humour in general and, in this particular instance, the sort of caricature of Persia which would amuse ordinary Athenians.

2 Ekbatana, the old Median capital, and summer residence of the Great King.

3 The river Kaystrios flows down from the mountains of Lydia to meet the sea at Ephesos.

4 Kranaos was one of the mythical early kings of Athens.

5 Kleonymos, a radical politician prominent in the 420s, much vilified by Aristophanes. Two surviving decrees were proposals of his: see Meiggs and Lewis nos.65 (lines 32–60) and 68.

148. Perikles supreme

Between the *ostrakismos* of Thoukydides in 444/3 and his own death in 429, Perikles commanded a degree of supremacy in Athenian political life such as no one had attained before him, or was to attain after him. This had a formal basis in his repeated re-election to the board of *stratēgoi* (see the passage below), but almost certainly nothing more than that, *de iure* (see further **181**); and in any case the *stratēgia* had to be fought for afresh every year round. So 'Periklean Athens' is a term to be used with caution, for it can lead us to forget (*a*) the extent to which the Athenian democratic system demanded that even a Perikles continually re-earn his supremacy and (*b*) 'the inadequate surviving accounts of so many political figures, our ignorance of so many men of the second rank, the inevitable tendency for the unsuccessful rival to disappear from the pages of history' (Connor, *Politicians*, 69). However, if the picture which the sources present or suggest to us is a distorted one it is still of value and interest in its own terms; and this is especially true of the testimony of Plutarch, which as always represents a digest of more, and more varied, opinions than have survived to us in their own right. In this instance the views of his authorities were so disparate that he could only solve them by postulating a change (*metabolē*) in Perikles' behaviour and policies after 444/3 – a change from demagogue (first in opposition to Kimon, then later to Thoukydides) to statesman.

See further: Gomme, *Commentary* I, 65–70; A. B. Breebaart, 'Plutarch and the political development of Pericles', *Mnemosyne* 24 (1971), 260–72.

Thucydides writes of the *politeia* of Perikles as somewhat aristocratic – 'nominally a democracy, but in fact the rule of the first man'.[1] Many others, however, maintain that it was he who first led the *dēmos* on into cleruchies,[2] theoric distributions[3] and *misthoi*,[4] things which accustomed them to bad habits and made them extravagant and unruly instead of sensible and self-supporting. Let us therefore look at the events themselves for the explanation of the *metabolē* in him.

Initially, as has been said, pitted as he was against the reputation of Kimon, he sought to ingratiate himself with the *dēmos* . . . (Which he succeeded in doing for 25 years, until the *ostrakismos* of Thoukydides.) (15) Then, when the political differences had been completely resolved and the *polis* had become smooth, so to speak, and thoroughly united, he brought under his own control Athens and everything which was dependent upon the Athenians: tributes, armies, triremes, islands, the sea – the enormous power which derived from Greeks and *barbaroi* alike, and a *hēgemonia* bolstered up by subject nations, royal friendships and dynastic alliances. Now, however, he was no longer the same man as before: he was not as amenable to the *dēmos* as he had been, ready to yield and submit to the desires of the masses as if blown by the breeze; instead, putting aside his free and sometimes wanton demagogy like some soft, flowery melody, he struck the keynote of an aristocratic and regal *politeia*. This he employed, with perfection as his goal, and he led the *dēmos* – willingly, for the most part – by a combination of persuasion and instruction . . . Great as it was already, he made the *polis* the greatest and richest of all, and he himself grew to be more powerful than many a king and tyrant . . . (16) The power that he had is clear enough both from what Thucydides recounts and from what is incidentally and maliciously revealed by the comic poets when they call him and his friends 'the new

Peisistratidai' and urge him to take an oath not to set himself up as tyrant – on the grounds that his pre-eminence was too weighty, and threw the democracy out of balance[5] . . . And this was no flash in the pan, nor even the gratifying culmination of a *politeia* which bloomed for a season only: for forty years (469–429) he stood first amongst men like Ephialtes, Leokrates, Myronides, Kimon, Tolmides and Thoukydides; and after the fall and *ostrakismos* of Thoukydides, for no fewer than fifteen of those years, he possessed a rule and a power that was continuous and unbroken, by virtue of being a *strategos* every year.

Plutarch, Perikles 9.1–2*; 15–16.3*

1 Thuc. II. 65.9: see **209**.
2 See **137**.
3 See **141** with n.4, **313**.
4 See **141**.
5 Compare **25**.

149. The Funeral Speech

To illustrate the aspirations of the Athenian *demos* in the second half of the fifth century, some extracts from the Periklean Funeral Speech in Thucydides (II.35–46) are virtually self-selecting. (For more of it see **154** and **163B**.) Whether or not what is said here corresponds in any detail to what Perikles actually said to his fellow-citizens in the winter of 431/0, when he was chosen to deliver the *epitaphios* over the Athenian war dead (II.34; and see **139**), is indeterminable, and for most purposes irrelevant: what we have here is the essence of the radical democracy at its height.

'We live under a *politeia* which does not copy the *nomoi* of our neighbours; it would be truer to say that we ourselves are a model for others than that we imitate anyone else. And its name – because the majority share in it, not just a few – is democracy. As far as the *nomoi* go, everyone is equal when private disputes are being settled; and as regards the criteria by which anyone is picked out for public office, what matters is not his membership of a particular class but how distinguished he is in anything – his own personal qualities. Even to be poor is no impediment: as long as he can be of value to the *polis*, no man is barred from public life simply because his poverty has made him obscure. Freedom is the hallmark of our common political life, freedom in particular from suspicion of one another as we go about our daily business: we do not become angry with our neighbour if he does as he pleases; we do not even vex him with the sort of looks which, although harmless, will hurt his feelings. In our private relationships, then, we avoid giving offence; and in our public lives we are kept from breaking the *nomoi* above all because we respect them. We obey those who, at any given time, are the holders of public office, and we obey the *nomoi* themselves[1] – particularly those which exist to help the oppressed, and those unwritten *nomoi* which all would concede as bringing disgrace upon those who break them.[2]

(40) Our love of good things is compatible with economy, and our love of discussion does not involve cowardice.[3] Wealth we use rather as an opportunity for action than as something to boast about; and as for poverty, there is no disgrace in admitting it – the greater shame is in not taking steps to escape from it. In the same individuals one finds a concern for their own affairs and for the affairs of the *polis* at the same time, and those who are otherwise preoccupied with their own doings are not deficient in their knowledge of the affairs of the *polis*. We Athenians are unique, in fact, in considering the man who has no share in the affairs of the *polis* not as someone who minds his own business but as good for nothing at all. We take our own decisions and give due consideration to what we do: this is because we believe that it is not discussion which is detrimental to action but rather having to act before there has been consideration of what to do for the best. Here again, no doubt, we are something special, in that we not merely take risks but calculate what their effects will be . . . (41) All in all, then, I declare that our whole *polis* has something to teach the Greeks, and that in my opinion each individual Athenian, with grace and dexterity, shows himself to be self-reliant in a multiplicity of ways. Is this a boast for the present occasion? No, it is the factual truth; and the power of our *polis*, which we have built up by these very means, is the proof of it . . . We have given impressive demonstrations of this power – at any rate, they can hardly have gone unnoticed! – and we shall be the wonder not only of our own times but of posterity . . .'

Thucydides II.37; 40–41*

1 Compare **237** with n.4.
2 On unwritten laws compare Sophocles, *Antigone* 450–461, and *Oidipous Tyrannos* 863–870.
3 This is the translation of these two paradoxes proposed by A. E. Wardman, 'Thucydides 2.40.1', *CQ* n.s.9 (1959), 38–42.

14 The culture of Athens

Just as the creation of the empire was an enterprise of the *polis*, so the wealth from the empire, public and private, facilitated the visual transformation of Athens by the construction of magnificent sacred and secular buildings and the lavish celebration of the festivals of the *polis* with their associated dramatic contests (for an early tragedian, Phrynichus, see **105**). The artistic and literary achievements of the fifth century are indeed so stunning that it is hard for us to remember that to an Athenian they were an essential and inseparable aspect of the religion of the *polis*. It is also important to remember that it was the *dēmos* which chose and paid its architects (as in the accounts for the building of the Erechtheion, see **242** Intro.), the *dēmos* which channelled the resources of the wealthy into, for instance, the training of choruses for the dramatic festivals (see **144**); it was not only the scale of activity which led to advance, but also the fact that for the first time a *dēmos* was patron of the arts. The contrast with the tyrants and aristocrats for whom Pindar continued to write traditional odes celebrating victory in the Olympic and other games (see **11–12**) could not be more striking. For a large selection of texts in translation see J. P. Sabben-Clare and M. S. Warman (eds.), *The Culture of Athens* (Lactor 12, 1978).

150. The 'stratēgoi' after Eurymedon

Empire and drama come together in the context of the *polis* in 469/8, with the entry of Kimon and his colleagues into the theatre on their return from the great victory of Eurymedon (see **131**).

To increase his fame, they also conferred on him, by name, the power of judging between the tragedians. For when Sophocles, still young, was presenting his first set of plays, the *archōn* Apsephion did not draw the judges by lot for the contest, since there was a great deal of quarrelling and taking of sides among the audience; but when Kimon and his fellow *stratēgoi* came into the theatre and made the customary offerings to the god (Dionysos), he did not let them go away, but bound them by oath (to judge fairly) and made them stay and judge; they were ten in number, one from each *phylē*.[1] So the contest, because of the reputation of the judges, escaped from the quarrelling of the audience. And it is said that when Sophocles won, Aeschylus took it very ill and was very upset and did not remain much longer in Athens, but in his anger went off to Sicily, where indeed he died and is buried near Gela.

Plutarch, Kimon 8.7–9

1 See **119**.

151. The building programme

Contemporary sources do not even begin to provide a continuous account of the buildings erected at Athens in the fifth century and we are forced to rely in part on much later accounts, such as that of Plutarch, and in part on a combination of snippets in other sources, epigraphical evidence and archaeological discoveries. We view with scepticism the report in Plut. *Per.* 17 that Perikles attempted to convene a congress of representatives from all the Greek *poleis* in order to discuss the reconstruction of the temples burnt by the Persians and with even greater scepticism the modern suggestion that the failure of this initiative was the prelude to a systematic use of the tribute from the empire for the building programme of Athens. One may suspect also that progress was more halting than appears from the account by Plutarch given below. See in general J. S. Boersma, *Athenian Building Policy* (Groningen, 1970), chs. 1, 6 and 8; Meiggs, *Empire*, ch. 14; Fig. 14.

Pheidias managed everything and was overseer of everything for him (Perikles), although the different projects had great architects and craftsmen in charge of them; for Kallikrates and Iktinos built the hundred-foot Parthenon, while the building of the *telestērion*[1] at Eleusis was begun by Koroibos; it was he who placed the columns on the foundations and joined them to the architraves, and when he died Metagenes of (the deme) Xypete added the cornice and the upper columns, while Xenoklēs of (the deme) Cholargos finished the lantern in the circular roof of the temple. As for the Long Wall,[2] for which Sokrates says that he himself heard Perikles introducing the proposal, Kallikrates was the contractor. Cratinus deals with the project in one of his comedies because of its slow execution, 'Perikles has been pressing on with it in his speeches for a long time, but no action ensues'. (Plutarch goes on to the building of the Odeion.) And in his ambition Perikles then first introduced a contest in music as part of the Panathenaia and, having himself been chosen as organiser, laid down how the contestants should play the flute or sing or play the lyre. And the population then and later watched the musical contests in the Odeion. And the Propylaia of the Akropolis were built in five years with Mnesikles as the architect . . .

And Pheidias created the golden statue of the goddess (Athena) and is recorded as the *dēmiourgos*[3] who made it on the inscription . . .

Plutarch, *Perikles* 13 6–14*

1 Sanctuary for the secret rites.
2 See **171**.
3 Worker for the community.

152. The Springhouse decree

This decree, the main outlines of which are secure despite its fragmentary state, illustrates both the minute attention given by the *dēmos* to building works and its jealous refusal of private munificence on the traditional pattern – from Perikles and his family (see **142B**). See Fornara no. 117.

. . . [Nikomachos proposed]: that everything else should be as [the *boulē* proposed; and that attention should be paid to the fountains in the town] so that they may flow [. . . and so that the works may be completed] as cheaply as possible [the *prytaneis* who] draw the first lot to serve [are to introduce the architect in the first] of the *kuriai ekklēsiai*[1] immediately [after the sacrifices, doing what seems] good to the *dēmos* of the Athenians; [and they are to see that delay] is avoided and things turn out for the Athenians [. . . ?] proposed: that everything else should be as Nikomachos proposed; [and that thanks should be offered to Perikles and] Paralos and Xanthippos[2] and their sons; [but that expenditure should be made from the money] which belongs to the tribute (*phoros*) of the Athenians [after the goddess (Athena)] has received the customary portion [thereof].

SEG X.47

1 See **126** n.6.
2 The sons of Perikles, see **128**.

153. Liturgies and culture

Although, as we have seen (**152**), private financing of public buildings was rare in classical Athens, the system of liturgies (**144**) was used for other cultural purposes; and the phenomenon was explicitly analysed by Aristotle. It is important that Aristotle gives considerable prominence to those liturgies associated with cult activity.

Within the general field of outlays there are some which we regard as honourable, such as those relating to the gods, offerings and buildings and sacrifices, and indeed anything connected with the whole divine sphere; also those which are the mark of a proper ambition for the good

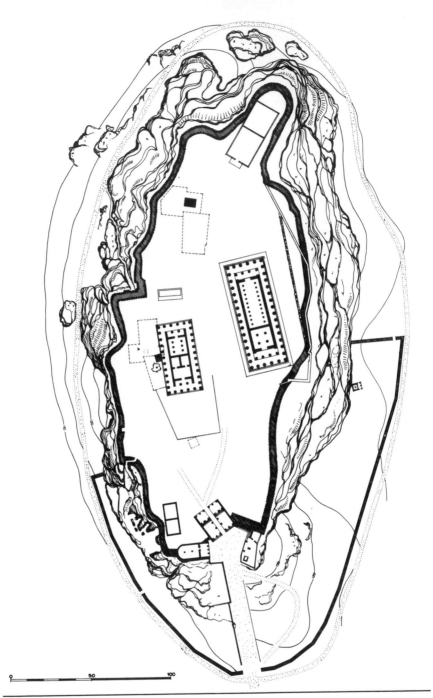

a The *akropolis ca* 480

14 The growth of Athens (J. Travlos, *Pictorial Dictionary of Ancient Athens* (London, 1971), pp.61,71.

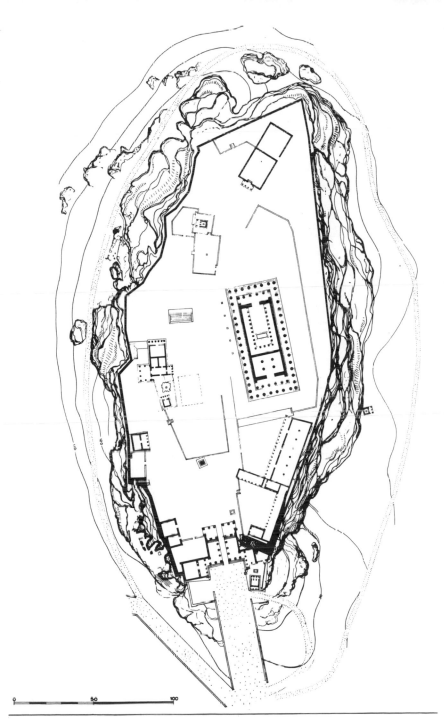

0   50   100

b The *akropolis ca* 404

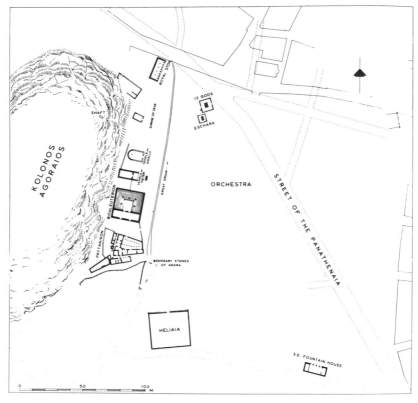

c The *agora ca* 500

The growth of Athens (H. A. Thompson and R. E. Wycherley, *The Agora of Athens*
(Princeton, 1972), pls. 4 and 5)

of the community, for instance if people think one should go to town in
training a chorus or fitting out a trireme or feasting the *polis*.

Aristotle, *Nicomachean Ethics* (IV)1122 b 19–23

154. Athens and Greece

The culture of Athens, in its widest sense, was readily to be observed by the rest
of the Greek world – and emulated; the *poleis* of the empire were indeed closely
and deliberately associated with the great public and religious festivals of the
hēgemōn: already in the 450s Erythrai was required to send representatives to the
Great Panathenaia (Meiggs and Lewis no.40), and in due course the obligation on
Athenian *apoikiai* to offer a cow and suit of armour was extended to all the *poleis*
of the empire (see the Kleinias decree, Meiggs and Lewis no.46); by perhaps 422
they were required to offer first-fruits at Eleusis (Meiggs and Lewis no.73);

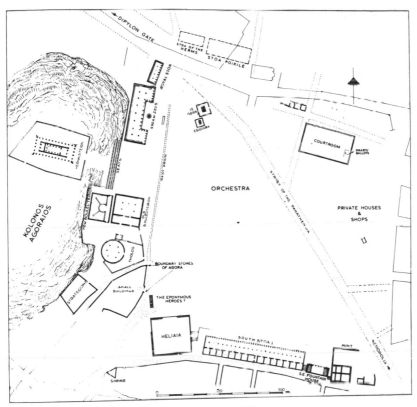

d The *agora ca* 400

delegates of the *poleis* brought their tribute (*phoros*) on the occasion of the Dionysia, when also honours conferred by the *dēmos* were proclaimed and embassies often arrived. It is entirely in character that the Funeral Speech put into the mouth of Perikles should be addressed *urbi et orbi* (the presence of *xenoi* is explicitly mentioned at II.36.4; for further sections of the speech see **149**). Nor is it surprising that in the fourth century there was at Athens much nostalgic praise for the period before the Peloponnesian War (see Meiggs, *Empire*, ch.22).

'And indeed we have provided for our minds frequent occasions of rest from our labours, doing so by means of the contests and festivals which occur throughout the year as well as by appropriate private arrangements, daily delight in which banishes gloom. And because of the size of the *polis* every kind of ware is imported from all over the earth,[1] the consequence of which for us is that the enjoyment of the good things which grow here is not more familiar than that of the things which other men produce.'

Thucydides II.38

1 Compare **140**.

155. The education of a politician

Athens increasingly became in the fifth century the cultural centre of the Greek world and there were few of the great intellectuals of the period who did not spend a longer or shorter period there; one of them, Protagoras, evolved a philosophical theory of democracy, presented (how accurately cannot be said) by Plato as the 'Great Speech' in *Protagoras* 320C–328C. At a humbler level, the complexity and diversity of the subjects on which public speakers had to give advice and the growth in legal business generated by the empire created a demand for teachers of rhetoric and political argument, the Sophists, who took money for their services and with whom neither Protagoras and other visitors nor Sokrates (see **248**) wished to be confused. See in general W. K. C. Guthrie, *The Sophists* (Cambridge, 1971), and G. B. Kerferd, *The Sophistic Movement* (Cambridge, 1981). The training required by a man who wished to be a politician at Athens is amusingly illustrated by a story from among the recollections of Sokrates compiled by Xenophon.

When Glaukon the son of Ariston set out to become a speaker before the *dēmos*, ambitious to be *prostatēs*[1] of the *polis* although not yet twenty years old, none of his family or friends could stop him, although he was getting dragged from the *bēma*[2] and was becoming an object of mockery, with one exception; this was Sokrates, who was inclined to help him for the sake of Charmides, son of Glaukon, and of Plato.[3] (Sokrates engages Glaukon in conversation and persuades him that he knows nothing of the revenues of the *polis*, its expenditure, its military position, its defence, the silver mines, the grain supply.) 'Take care, Glaukon, that in your ambition to be famous you do not become infamous. Do you not see how dangerous it is to speak or act in a field of which one knows nothing? Think of other people, whom you know to be the sort of person who is known for speaking or acting in a field of which he knows nothing; do you think they are praised rather than blamed for this sort of conduct, or admired rather than despised? Then think of those who understand what they say and do; I think you will find that in every case those who have a good reputation and are admired fall among those who have a good knowledge, while those who have a bad reputation and are despised belong to the ignorant. So if you are ambitious to have a good reputation and to be admired in the *polis*, try to see that you know as much as possible of what you wish to do; for if you attempt to involve yourself in the affairs of the *polis* with this to distinguish you from the others, I should not be surprised if you achieve your ambition quite easily.'

Xenophon, *Memorabilia* III.6*

1 See **66** n.4.
2 Speakers' platform.

3 The philosopher – the family tree is

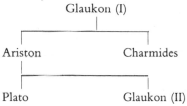

156. The popular reaction

Not surprisingly, the intellectual activities of some members of the élite aroused suspicion among ordinary Athenians, who in the end voted to condemn Sokrates (see **248**); it must be remembered that the 'enlightened' views of Perikles or the historian Thucydides and the sacrilegious behaviour of Alkibiades (see **214**) were always less typical than the Athenian interest in oracles at the outbreak of war in 431 or the reaction to the mutilation of the Hermai in 415 (see **214**). The whole of Aristophanes' play *Clouds* (staged in 423) is an interesting reflection of popular views of the Sophists (though it must be remembered that willingness to laugh at something does not necessarily imply deep hostility to it); we present one short section.

Pheidippides, the son: Tell me, what is your bidding?
Strepsiades, the father: Will you obey?
Ph.: I will, by Dionysos.
Str.: Look over there. Do you see that gate and the house?
Ph.: Yes; what is it, father?
Str.: That is the power-house of learning of wise men, where there live people who can persuade us that heaven is a furnace all around us who are the coals. And what is more, if one pays them, they teach one how to win a case, just or unjust.
Ph.: Who are they?
Str.: I can't remember what they call themselves, but they're deeply learned and *kaloi k'agathoi*.[1]
Ph.: I know who the scoundrels are – you mean those whey-faced, barefoot windbags, the evil Sokrates and Chairephon.

Aristophanes, Clouds 90–104

1 See **143** Intro.

157. The friends of Perikles

Popular suspicion of the Sophists was apparently exploited by the enemies of Perikles to attack him by way of his friends; there is little evidence for the dates of these attacks, and some modern scholars are sceptical of their very existence (see **146** Intro.).

At about the same time, Aspasia[1] was acquitted on a charge of impiety; the prosecutor was Hermippos the comic poet and he threw in the additional accusation that she received free women who also visited Perikles for immoral purposes.[2] And Diopeithes proposed a *psēphisma* that summonses should be issued against those who did not believe in the divine or gave lessons about the heavens, hoping to fix suspicion on Perikles by way of Anaxagoras.[3] And when the *dēmos* turned out to be receptive of the slanders and to listen to them, Drakontides actually succeeded in getting a *psēphisma* passed that Perikles should deposit his accounts of financial dealings with the *prytaneis* and that the jurors should judge the case on the Akropolis, drawing the ballots from the altar. Hagnon managed to get that part withdrawn and proposed that the case be heard by 1,500 jurors, whether one wanted to call the prosecution one for embezzlement and bribe-taking or one for general wrong-doing. Now Perikles got Aspasia off, by a travesty of justice, as Aeschines says, by shedding tears on her behalf and imploring the jurors to be lenient; but in the case of Anaxagoras he feared the outcome of the trial and snatched him away and sent him abroad.

Plutarch, *Perikles* 32

1 The Milesian mistress of Perikles.
2 See **180**.
3 See **146**.

15 Economic and social developments in Athens

The economic foundations of Athens, as of all *poleis*, lay in land, the land of Attika. The Athenians claimed to be 'sprung from the soil' (auto-chthonous), and whatever alternative sources of community supply and of personal affluence might arise, cultivating the *chōra* of Attika pre-served the *polis* as an agricultural state, and owning a part of it was and always remained the traditional, basic and best source and index of wealth. Yet the foundations of Athens' robust economic position in the fifth century had been set down, by Solon and then the Peisistratidai, principally by fostering the non-landed sectors of the Athenian eco-nomy. By about the time of the Persian Wars three interconnected areas were clearly emerging as important: a large and energetic immigrant community (**160**); a thriving commercial traffic through the Peiraieus (**159**) – these two linked by a policy of welcoming foreigners, whether as residents or visitors (**158**); and the optimisation of Attika's supreme natural asset, the silver mines (**161**). These three areas were still seen as crucial in the mid-fourth century, when Xenophon came to write his treatise *Ways and Means (Poroi)*; in addition he proposed acquisition by the state of a slave labour force (see **277**, and Ch.29 in general). The bulk of chattel-slaves were in fact in private ownership, however; and their contribution to the economy was vital (**162**). Had this not been so, the economic burdens upon *women* would have been much greater (see Austin and Vidal-Naquet, *Economy* no.15); as it was, the economic and social role of women in Athens was something which varied consider-ably from one sector and level of society to another (**163**).

158. 'Philoxenia'

As Athenian society, with the evolution of the *polis*, moved from aristocracy towards democracy, so *xenia* (**5B**) was increasingly – though never completely – superseded by *philoxenia*; that is to say, beside the interrelationships of hospitality and mutual benefit at the individual (and élite) level, the community itself was obliged to formulate a general attitude and policy towards *xenoi* in the mass. And here as elsewhere Sparta and Athens came to occupy polarised positions: at Sparta, outsiders were to stay out (**56**), whereas at Athens a tradition of *philoxenia* (literally 'the love of *xenoi*') came down from – or else was projected back into – early times (see passages A and B, below), as a backcloth for a policy during the classical period which nicely combined altruism with economic self-interest. See Whitehead, *Ideology*, 140–2; and on one crucial aspect of this subject, the immigrant population, **160**.

(A) Because of the lightness of the soil, Attika has generally been free from *stasis*, and therefore always inhabited by the same men. This indeed is an excellent illustration of my view that it was because of expulsions that the rest of Greece did not develop at an even rate: for when they were driven out of their own communities by war or *stasis*, the most powerful men from elsewhere felt that they would find safety in taking refuge with the Athenians. They became (Athenian) *politai*[1] – and this had the immediate effect, from earliest times, of making the (Athenian) *polis* still more densely populated. And as a result Attika later became insufficient for them all, which is why they sent out *apoikiai* to Ionia.[2]

Thucydides 1.2.5–6

(B) Wishing to enlarge the *polis* still further, Theseus used to invite everyone (to Athens) on equal terms; and the phrase 'Come hither all ye people' is said to have originated as his proclamation when he established a sort of all-embracing populace.[3]

Plutarch, *Theseus* 25.1

(C) *Oidipous:* What is the use, I wonder, of reputation and a good name when they go to waste? None at all – if this is what they call the supreme piety of Athens, the only place which is reckoned to offer the suffering *xenos* safety and help.[4]

Sophocles, *Oidipous at Kolonos* 258–262

(D) Just as the Athenians continue in other respects to show *philoxenia*, so too in their dealings with the gods: they accepted many foreign rites, and were ridiculed for it by the comic poets. Good examples of this are the cults from Thrake – the rites of Bendis, which Plato mentions – and from Phrygia, referred to by Demosthenes.[5]

Strabo x.3.18

---

1 For one example of this, the Aiakidai from Aigina, see Hdt. vi.35.1. Compare in general Isoc. iv.41, Paus. vii.1.9. It should be noted, however, that the actual incorporation of outsiders into the citizen-body (see also B) was only one, though obviously the most conclusive, manifestation of *philoxenia*; by the classical period it had more usually become a matter of welcoming and catering to the needs of outsiders who remained *xenoi* – see **160**.

2 See **3**.

3 Plutarch's source here is the lost opening of the Aristotelian *Ath. Pol.*
4 Oidipous, banished from Thebes, has been refused refuge in Attika.
5 Plato, *Republic* 327A and 354A; Demos. XVIII.260. See in general, on non-Hellenic cults in Attika, Whitehead, *Ideology*, 88–9; Parke, *Festivals*, 149–52.

159. Themistokles and the Peiraieus

Until the early fifth century, what served Athens (which is four or five miles from the coast) as a principal harbour was the open beach of the Bay of Phaleron; see Map 4. Yet a much more promising harbour-site lay only a little to the west, enclosed by the promontory of Peiraieus; and it may well have been the establishment of complete Athenian control over the island of Salamis by the end of the sixth century (see Meiggs and Lewis no.14) which made a move from Phaleron to Peiraieus not merely desirable and possible but to some extent inevitable. All our sources attribute responsibility for the scheme to Themistokles: as well as Plutarch, below, see Diod. XI.41–43, Isoc. IV.42 and Paus. I.1.2. There can be little doubt that his chief objective was a military one; but it is equally true that what he did had enormous economic and political implications.

See further: Bury and Meiggs, *Greece*, 204–5 and (on later developments) 235–6; M. Amit, *Athens and the Sea* (Brussels, 1965), 73–94; Isager and Hansen, *Aspects,* 62–4; R. J. Lenardon, *The Saga of Themistocles* (London, 1978), 87–97.

Note on chronology: both Plutarch (implicitly) and Diodorus (explicitly) place the Peiraieus project in the early 470s, after Xerxes' invasion. Both writers, however, are notoriously indifferent to exactitude in matters of chronology – and Diod. XI.43.2 speaks of a Persian invasion which is still to come. Thucydides (1.93.3) represents the scheme as the completion of something begun in Themistokles' archonship, which is itself a problem: the documented date is 493/2, but some scholars have seen reason to doubt this and to locate Themistokles' term of office in the vacant year 482/1 (see Gomme, *Commentary* I, 261–2). Yet a perfectly good case can still be made for 493/2 (see for instance A. J. Podlecki, *The Life of Themistocles: a critical survey of the literary and archaeological evidence* (Montreal, 1975), 6–8 and 196; Lenardon, *op. cit.* 35–9). It seems clear that the project was accomplished in two stages at least.

After this[1] (Themistokles) equipped the Peiraieus; he had noticed the excellent shape of its harbours, and he wanted to marry the entire *polis* to the sea. In this his policy was somewhat at variance with that of the ancient kings of the Athenians: they, we are told, in their efforts to tear the *politai* away from the sea and accustom them to live not by sailing but by cultivating the *chōra*, spread the story about Athena – how when Poseidon was contending with her for possession of Attika she defeated him by showing the *dikastai* her sacred olive-tree.[2] But Themistokles did not, as Aristophanes the comic poet states, 'knead the Peiraieus on to the *polis*';[3] on the contrary, it was the *polis* that he fastened to the Peiraieus, and the land to the sea. And through this he strengthened the *dēmos* at the expense of the *aristoi*, and filled men with boldness, since power was now coming into the hands of sailors and boatswains and helmsmen.[4] Also this explains why the speakers' rostrum on the Pnyx,[5] which had been made so as to look towards the sea, was later turned round by the Thirty[6] and made to face the *chōra*: their belief was that a sea-based empire brought about democracy, whereas oligarchy was less hateful to men who farmed the land.

Plutarch, *Themistokles* 19.2–4

1 The rebuilding of the city walls (see **166**) after Xerxes' invasion – but see introductory note on chronology.
2 Compare Hdt. VIII.55.
3 Aristoph. *Knights* 815.
4 Compare **143**.
5 The Pnyx hill, where the *ekklēsia* met.
6 See **244**.

160. The 'metoikoi'

Athenian *philoxenia* did not necessarily imply or involve the simple absorption of immigrants into the citizen-body (see **158** with n.1). As the nature of the *polis* became clearer, during the seventh and sixth centuries, so extension of membership to outsiders grew ever less tolerable; yet, in a city with developing commercial aspirations and opportunities such as Athens, immigration could not but increase willy-nilly, and by the beginning of the classical period the Athenians were ready to channel it into a legally recognised and defined status-category – the *metoikia*. (Other *poleis* had their immigrants too, but we know little or nothing of them in detail.) As the Athenian economy came increasingly to rely, in certain areas, upon the presence and activities of this free non-citizen community, special incentives (temporary or permanent) to the *metoikoi* were from time to time offered – see for instance passage A, below; for the most part, though, the assumption was that they would come, and stay, anyway; and so they did. And as to the attitude of the Athenians towards their *metoikoi*, this was every bit as ambivalent as attitudes to immigrants in other societies and periods. See in general – for the evidence, and a tentative reconstruction of the history of the *metoikia* – Whitehead, *Ideology*.

(A) (Themistokles) also persuaded the *dēmos* to build and add, every year, twenty triremes to the fleet that they already had, and to make the *metoikoi* and the craftsmen exempt from tax, so that a great multitude would come to the *polis* from everywhere and would readily establish many crafts; for both these things he judged to be most useful in the establishment of naval power.[1]

Diodorus XI.43.3

(B) Next, son of the huntress Atalante, Parthenopaios, of peerless beauty. He was an Arkadian, but came to Inachos' streams and grew up in Argos. Reared there, he avoided – as befits the immigrant *xenos* – making trouble or arousing jealousy in the *polis*;[2] contentious argument, by which the man of the *dēmos* and the *xenos* alike makes himself most vexatious, he eschewed. He stood in the ranks like a native Argive and defended the *chōra*. He rejoiced when the *polis* did well, and sorrowed when any adversity befell it. Many, men and women, loved him, but he took care not to cause offence.

Euripides, *Suppliant Women* 888–900

(C) *Dikaiopolis:* This time at least, Kleon will not accuse me of speaking ill of the *polis* in the presence of *xenoi*.[3] For we are by ourselves: the festival is the Lenaia,[4] and there are no *xenoi* here yet; for the tribute is not yet come in, nor the allies from their *poleis*. So, for the moment at least, we ourselves are winnowed clean – for the *metoikoi* I call bran of the citizens.[5]

Aristophanes, *Acharnians* 502–508

(D) Now among the slaves and the *metoikoi* in Athens there is the greatest unruliness: you cannot strike (them) there, nor will the slave stand aside for you. And I will tell you the reason for this local peculiarity. If it were customary for the slave – or the *metoikos* or the freedman – to be beaten by the free man, you would often strike an Athenian in the belief that he was a slave; for the *dēmos* there is no better dressed than the slaves and the *metoikoi*, nor at all superior in appearance. (11) And if anyone is surprised that they allow the slaves there to live in luxury, and some even in great splendour, it should be clear that even this they do for a reason. The point is that for any naval power financial considerations make it necessary to be slaves to the slaves – so as to take a portion of their earnings – and ultimately to let them go free.[6] And where there are rich slaves it is no longer profitable for my slave to be afraid of you. In Sparta my slave would fear you, but if (in Athens) your slave fears me he is likely to spend his own money in order to escape the danger. (12) For this reason we established equal freedom of speech as between slave and free, and as between *metoikoi* and citizens also; for the *polis* needs *metoikoi* because of the multiplicity of crafts and because of the fleet. So because of this it was reasonable for us to establish equal freedom of speech even for the *metoikoi*.[7]

Old Oligarch (=[Xenophon], *Athenaion Politeia*) 1.10–12

1 On the problems in this description of Themistokles' measure see Whitehead, *Ideology*, 148–9.
2 On this blueprint for the ideal *metoikos* see Whitehead, *Ideology*, 37 and 58.

3 See **147** Intro.
4 The Lenaia: see Parke, *Festivals*, 104–6.
5 This is intended as a compliment to the *metoikoi* – and of course it shows that they, unlike other *xenoi*, were present at the festival. (Parke, *Festivals*, 105, is wrong on this.)
6 The Greek text of this sentence is very garbled, but this is what it is normally taken to mean.
7 On this passage and its paradoxes see Moore, *Aristotle*, 27–8; Whitehead, *Ideology*, 54 and *passim*; Austin and Vidal-Naquet, *Economy* no.74.

161. The silver mines

If the soil of Attika was not of the best (**158A**), it harboured a non-agricultural asset which offered the Athenians, as they were well aware, ample compensation: in the Laureion area of southern Attika there were deposits of silver – or, to speak strictly, silver-bearing lead ore (*galēnē*) – which were rivalled within the Greek world only by the mines of the Thrakian coast and Thasos, far away in the north. These Attic deposits had been discovered in the Bronze Age but were not exploited by genuine mining techniques until the second half of the sixth century, presumably on the initiative of the Peisistratidai; at any rate, the characteristic Athenian coins issued from the last quarter of that century onwards became famous as the 'owls of Laureion' (Aristoph. *Birds* 1106). With the opening of the rich new veins at Maroneia in 483/2 (A, below) there began a seventy-year heyday of Laureion mining until its curtailment by the Spartan occupation of Dekeleia (**229**). In the fourth century the industry was slow to pick up again, but had certainly done so by the time that Xenophon wrote *Poroi* (passages B and C); see further, **277**, and Ch.29 in general. For further reading see Isager and Hansen, *Aspects*, 42–5 with bibliography at p.244.

(A) *Themistokles and the mining revenues*

On an earlier occasion too, and a most opportune one,[1] Themistokles had been successful with one of his policies. This was when the Athenians had a great deal of money in their treasury, which had accrued to them from the mines at Laureion,[2] and they were on the point of sharing it out amongst themselves at ten drachmas a man.[3] Themistokles persuaded them, however, not to distribute the money like this but to use it to build 200 ships[4] 'for the war'. The war which he meant by this was the one against the Aiginetans – a war which, by arising at that time and obliging the Athenians to become men of the sea, was the salvation of Greece: the ships were not employed for the purpose for which they had been built, and were thus at the disposal of Greece when the need arose.[5]

Herodotus VII.144.1–2

(B) *The mining magnates*

It is very surprising that although the *polis* is aware that many private individuals are enriching themselves at public expense, she herself does not follow their example. Those of us who are concerned about this subject have doubtless heard long ago that Nikias the son of Nikeratos once owned 1,000 men in the silver-mines, whom he hired out to Sosias the Thrakian on condition that Sosias paid him back, after tax, an obol per man per day, as well as making sure to keep up their numbers.[6] (15) Hipponikos, also, had 600 slaves leased out in the same way, and derived a net profit of a mina a day;[7] Philemonides had 300, which brought him in half a mina; and there were others too who presumably owned as many as their resources allowed. (16) But why speak of the past? There are many men in the mines here and now[8] who are hired out in this way.

Xenophon, *Poroi* iv.14–16

(C) *The theory and practice of the mining industry*

It is obvious to everybody that mining (in Attika) is old established; nobody, at any rate, tries to estimate when the workings began; and yet, although the digging and extracting of the silver-bearing ore is of such antiquity, one notices how small the present slag-heaps are by comparison with the hills in which the silver is still untouched. (3) It is evident, indeed, that the silver-producing area, so far from contracting at all, extends ever wider and wider. In the period when the maximum number of men was employed in the industry, nobody ever wanted for a job; on the contrary, there were more jobs than workers. (4) And even today nobody who owns slaves in the mines reduces their number; no, they always take on as many extra men as possible. No doubt the explanation of this is that when only a few men are digging and searching they find, I imagine, only a small amount of silver, whereas when many men are at work the amount of silver ore discovered is multiplied accordingly. Hence this is the only industry that I know of where nobody is jealous of those who achieve greater productivity! (5) What is more, any farmer can tell you how many yoke of oxen his land needs, and how many labourers; and if anyone brings in more than sufficiency requires, this is accounted as loss. But in mining operations, of course, the constant complaint is a *shortage* of labour. (6) The situation, you see, is not the same as if there occurred a glut of coppersmiths, which would lead to copper work being cheap but would put the smiths out of business – or ironmongers, for the same reasons. Similarly, when there is a lot of grain and wine about, the crops are cheap but there is no profit in growing them, so that many men give up farming and turn to commerce or shop-keeping or money-lending. But no matter how much silver ore is discovered and how much silver comes from it, there will always be a commensurate increase in the numbers of those who come to mine it. (7) Let me put it this way: when a man has acquired enough furniture for his house he does not keep on buying it; but no man has ever yet acquired so much silver as to want no more of it, and those who come into possession of a great deal of it derive just as much pleasure from burying the surplus as from spending it. (8) And another point: whenever a *polis* is doing well, silver is in great demand – for the men want to spend money on fine armour and good horses and houses with suitably grand fixtures and fittings, while their wives turn to expensive clothes and gold jewellery – (9) and when, by contrast, a *polis* is stricken by crop failure or war, its land goes out of cultivation and the demand for coined money, to pay for food and mercenaries, is even greater![9] (10) And if it should be suggested that gold is every bit as useful as silver, I would not dispute this; but I know one thing, that when gold is plentiful it is silver which rises in value while gold falls.

(11) Why am I pointing out all this? So as to give us the confidence to bring as many men as possible to work in the silver-mines – confidence that the silver ore will never be exhausted and that silver itself will never lose its value. (12) And the *polis*, I believe, has anticipated me in recognising these facts; at any rate, it is made open to foreigners to take up a concession in the mines on the same fiscal terms (as citizens).[10]

Xenophon, *Poroi* IV.2–12

1 In 483/2, according to ?Aristot. *Ath. Pol.* 22.7. (Hdt. is dealing with 480.)
2 ?Aristot. *Ath. Pol.* 22.7 specifies Maroneia.
3 For the *viritim* distribution of mining profits, compare the case of the island of Siphnos: Hdt. III.57.2 (see Austin and Vidal-Naquet, *Economy* no.20).
4 ?Aristot. *Ath. Pol.* 22.7 and Plut. *Them.* 4.1–2 both say one hundred.
5 I.e. to face the invasion of Xerxes.
6 An important consideration, as the mortality rate in the mines was high.
7 On Hipponikos and his family see Davies, *Families*, 254–70, esp. 260–1; **142**, Intro.
8 I.e. the 350s.
9 Mercenaries: a very telling detail, which betrays the period – see Chs.27 and 30.
10 The translation of this last clause follows D. Whitehead, *Eirene* 16 (1978), 13–15.

162. Slaves

'At all times and in all places the Greek world relied on some form (or forms) of dependent labour to meet its needs, both public and private' (M. I. Finley, 'Was

Greek civilisation based on slave labour?', *Historia* 8 (1959), 145–64 at p. 145). This dependent labour, which largely filled the role that wage labour does in the society and economy of the modern world, fell into various different categories, and despite the all-embracing and unsystematic terminology used by the Greeks themselves it is important that we distinguish between three categories in particular. The helots of Lakonia and (subsequently) Messenia are the best-known example of a *subjugated indigenous* (or at any rate pre-existing) *population*, a ready-made labour force of either other Greeks, as in the Spartan case, or *barbaroi*, such as the Mariandynoi of Herakleia (**19A**); see in general Austin and Vidal-Naquet, *Economy*, 86–90. Most *poleis*, however, were unwilling or unable to adopt such a brutally simple solution to their labour needs; and if we may judge from the Athens of Solon (**66–67**), one of the obvious alternatives to it, *debt-bondage*, came to be seen as socially unacceptable for different reasons, and did not in most cases outlast the archaic period. So a new 'invention' was called for (see Theopompus, *FGrH* 115 F122, which is Austin and Vidal-Naquet, *Economy* no.50B): *chattel-slavery*, involving the forced labour of men and women, some of them other Greeks but predominantly *barbaroi*, imported as prisoners-of-war (*via* a slave trade), sold on the open market, and bought and owned to a small extent by the *polis* itself but chiefly by private individuals. The importance of chattel-slavery in the society and economy of Greece in general and classical Athens in particular has been a source of profound disagreement amongst scholars during the last 25 to 30 years. Those who have seen it as minimal include W. L. Westermann (*The Slave Systems of Greek and Roman Antiquity* (Philadelphia, 1955)), A. H. M. Jones (*Democracy*, 11–20 and 76–90) and C. G. Starr ('An overdose of slavery?', *J. Econ. Hist.* 18 (1958), 17–32, reprinted in A. Ferriria and T. Kelly (eds), *Essays on Ancient History* (Leiden, 1979), 43–58). But in our judgment the evidence proves exactly the opposite – that chattel-slavery was a basic and integral feature of Greek, and especially Athenian, life: see G. E. M. de Ste Croix, *CR* n.s.7 (1957), 54–9 (review of Westermann); M. I. Finley, *op. cit.*; M. H. Jameson, 'Agriculture and slavery in classical Athens', *Classical Journal* 73 (1977), 122–45; Austin and Vidal-Naquet, *Economy*, 18–19, 101–3 and *passim*. We have already encountered Perikles' household slave Euangelos (**142B**), and the less fortunate slaves in the silver-mines (**161B** and, by implication, C), and **244C** will provide an example of a slave-run 'factory'; but in fact slaves were to be found, to a greater or lesser extent, in virtually every area of Athenian economic life: Jones, *Democracy*, 11–17, cites much of the literary evidence, though he distorts its implications. It is vital to understand that the issue here is not whether *either* the Athenians *or* their slaves put in a hard day's work but the extent to which slave labour was usual and important *as well*: see A, below. Kephisodoros (B) doubtless owned more slaves than the average, but it seems equally certain that all but the poorest families will have had one or two.

For a large selection of sources in translation see T. E. J. Wiedemann, *Greek and Roman Slavery* (London, 1980).

(A) Those who are able to do so buy slaves, in order that they may have fellow-workers (*synergoi*).[1]

Xenophon, *Memorabilia* II.3.3

(B) (Property) of Kephisodoros, *metoikos* (living) in Peira[ieus][2]

2 drachmas	165 drachmas	Thrakian woman
1 dr. 3 obols	135 dr.	Thrakian woman
[2 dr.]	170 dr.	Thrakian
2 dr. 3 obols	240 dr.	Syrian
[1 dr.] 3 obols	105 dr.	Karian
2 dr.	161 dr.	Illyrian
2 dr. 3 obols	220 dr.	Thrakian woman
1 dr. 3 obols	115 dr.	Thrakian
1 dr. 3 obols	144 dr.	Skythian
1 dr. 3 obols	121 dr.	Illyrian
2 dr.	153 dr.	Kolchian
2 dr.	174 dr.	Karian boy
1 dr.	72 dr.	Karian child
[3 dr.] 1 obol	301 dr.	Syrian
[2 dr.]	151 dr.	Melitt[enian][3]
1 dr.	8[5 dr. 1 obol?]	Lydian woman

Meiggs and Lewis no.79 A, lines 33–49

(C) The Athenians were deprived[4] of the whole of their *chōra*, and more than twenty thousand slaves deserted, the majority of whom were men with manual skills (*cheirotechnai*).[5]

Thucydides VII.27.5

1 Note that E. C. Marchant's translation in the Loeb edition ('. . . to relieve them of work') is not merely inaccurate but dangerously misleading.

2 This is part of the lists of the confiscated property of the Hermokopidai, auctioned off by the *pōlētai* in 414 (see **214**). Of the 45 slaves in the lists as a whole the largest single holding is that of this man Kephisodoros, who had at least 16 (the list appears to be incomplete); the fact that he was a *metoikos* rather than an Athenian citizen is, however, unimportant in this connection. The central column in this list indicates the purchase price, and the left-hand column the sale-tax (*epōnion*). For further commentary, as well as Meiggs and Lewis *ad loc.* (pp.240–7, esp.247) see Fornara no.147 and Austin and Vidal-Naquet, *Economy* no. 75.

3 Probably Melitene (*sic*) in Kappadokia; alternatively Melite (Malta). It cannot be determined whether the slave is male or female.

4 By the Spartan occupation of Dekeleia between 413 and 404 (**229**). For another example of the disruption of slave labour during the Peloponnesian War see Thuc. III.73 (Kerkyra).

5 Compare Xen. *Poroi* IV.25; and note that this effect of the (or any similar) occupation is foreshadowed in Thuc. I.142.4 and (especially) VI.91.7. According-ing to the '*Hellenica Oxyrhyncia*' (see p.13) the prosperity of the Thebans in the early fourth century was attributable to their having purchased these slaves (etc.) at knock-down prices (XII.4). See in general Gomme, *Commentary* IV, 405–6; Austin and Vidal-Naquet, *Economy* no.76.

163. Women

An important fact about Greek *polis* society will have emerged clearly enough by now, but should nonetheless be explicitly stated: it was a society dominated, in most significant respects, by men – on the simple grounds that they were the superior sex (see for instance **7**; and Austin and Vidal-Naquet, *Economy* no. 14). A story from the Roman antiquarian writer Varro, quoted by St Augustine, claimed that in the case of Athens at least this domination had resulted from the loss, by women, of an original position of equality (see Austin and Vidal-Naquet, *Economy* no. 16; S. G. Pembroke, 'Women in charge: the function of alternatives in early Greek tradition and the ancient idea of the matriarchy', *Journal of the Warburg and Courtauld Institutes* 30 (1967), 1–35); and whatever credence we may give to such rationalisation it is undeniable that what we see of the 'archaic' Greek woman – that is, in the archaic period itself and in places like Sparta which in many ways never lost their archaic character – shows her with wider social scope and influence than her classical counterpart; witness, for example, Kimon's sister Elpinike in Plut. *Kim.* 4, and, on Spartan women, Lacey, *Family*, 203–6. And the contrast between an Elpinike and the modest wife and mother envisaged by Perikles in the Funeral Speech (B, below) is plain to see. Yet in all periods it will have been the case that the position of women varied enormously between different areas of life, and different social levels; and it is only in fifth- and fourth-century Athens that we have any insight into the middle and lower levels at all. So within an all-pervading ethos of 'male chauvinism' (see for instance [Demos.] LIX.122), and communal laughter at the idea of a female revolution (Aristophanes' *Lysistrata* and *Ekklesiazousai*), each sector of female society, Athenian or alien, had its own functions, fears and aspirations.

See further: A. W. Gomme, 'The position of women in Athens', *CPh* 20 (1925), 1–25 (reprinted in his *Essays in Greek History and Literature* (Oxford, 1937), ch.5); H. D. F. Kitto, *The Greeks* (Harmondsworth, 1967), 219–36; Lacey, *Family*, ch.7, G. E. M. de Ste Croix, 'Some observations on the property rights of Athenian women', *CR* n.s.20 (1970), 273–8; Sarah B. Pomeroy, 'Selected bibliography on women in antiquity', *Arethusa* 6 (1973), 127–57, esp. 140–3; Sarah B. Pomeroy, *Goddesses, Whores, Wives and Slaves* (New York, 1975), chs.4–6; D. M. Schaps, *Economic Rights of Women in Ancient Greece* (Edinburgh, 1979).

(A) [– –]kos proposed: [for Athena Ni]ke a priestess who [. . . .] [12 letters missing][1] from all Athenian women shall be [appointed],[2] and the sanctuary shall have whatever doors Kallikrates designs; the *pōlētai*[3] shall let the contract out for hire during the prytany of (the *phylē*) Leontis. The priestess shall be paid fifty drachmas (a year) and the legs and the hides from the public (sacrifices).

Meiggs and Lewis no.44, lines 2–11[4]

(B) 'I ought perhaps to say something about the *aretēs* appropriate to a wife – or rather a widow, as some will now be. A short piece of advice is all I shall give: your glory will be great if you do not behave more feebly than is natural to your sex – and if men, whether praising your *aretē* or deploring your lack of it, talk about you least'.[6]

(c) *First landlady:* Plathane, Plathane, come here: here's the villain who came into our lodging-house once and ate up sixteen loaves!
Second landlady (Plathane): Yes, by God, that's him all right.
Xanthias (a slave): (aside) Here comes trouble for *somebody*!
First landlady: Yes, and as well as that, twenty pieces of boiled meat, at half an obol each.
Xanthias: (aside) It's paying-up time – for *somebody*!
First landlady: And all that garlic, too.
Dionysos: You're talking rubbish, woman; you don't know what you're saying.
First landlady: So you thought I wouldn't know you again, with those boots on? Hah! And we haven't even got on to all that dried fish you had.
Second landlady: No, by God, nor that fresh cheese which the wretch gobbled up, baskets and all.
First landlady: And then, when I asked him for the money, he gave me a dirty look and started bellowing.
Xanthias: Yes, that sounds like him; he does that all the time.
First landlady: And he drew his sword, too. I thought he'd gone mad!
Second landlady: You poor dear!
First landlady: Yes, terrified, weren't we? We ran off upstairs, right away, while he grabbed the mattresses and left.
Xanthias: Yes, that's always his way.
Second landlady: So we ought to *do* something about it.
First landlady: (to an attendant) Go and fetch my friend Kleon.[7]
Second landlady: (to another attendant) And you see if you can find Hyperbolos,[8] for me; then we'll sort him out!
First landlady: Look at his horrible gullet! How I'd love to take a stone and smash those molars of his, the ones he used to gobble up all our wares!
Second landlady: Me, I'd chuck him into the Pit![9]
First landlady: And I'd take a sickle to you and slit your throat, the one that all my tripe went down!
Second landlady: I'll go and get Kleon, then; he'll have him in court and screw it all out of him this very day!

(d) 'They have used my mother too to slander me, so I shall speak of her also, and call witnesses in support of what I want to say. And yet, men of Athens, the slanders which Euboulides laid against us contravene not only the *psēphisma* which regulates the *agora* but also the *nomoi* which prescribe that anyone who reproaches a citizen, male or female, with the work that he or she does in the *agora* is liable to prosecution for slander. (31) For our part, we admit that we sell ribbons, and live in a way that we would not choose. And if for you, Euboulides, this is a sign that we are not Athenians, I will show you that it is precisely the opposite, that it is a *xenos* who is not permitted to work in the *agora*[10] . . . (32) . . . So the duty of you the jury is to defend the *nomoi*, and to hold not that those who work for their living are *xenoi* but that those who act as informers are wicked men. What is more, Euboulides, there is another *nomos*, dealing with idleness, under which you are liable when you slander those of us who work for our living.[11] (33) Yet our luck is so bad at the moment that our opponent can tell irrelevant lies about us and do everything he can to ensure that justice is denied to me on every count; and if I were to tell you how *he* goes about the *polis* earning his living, you would quite possibly criticise me for it – and rightly so, for what need is there to tell you what you already know? So look at it this way, if you will: I personally think that our earning our living in the *agora* is the best proof of the falsity of the accusations which our opponent has brought against us. (34) When he claims, you see, that my mother is a ribbon-seller, and universally known as such, surely he ought to bring forward witnesses who all know her personally, and what she is, not just by hearsay. And if (his claim is that) she was a foreign woman (*xenē*), they ought to have examined the taxes paid in the *agora*, to see whether she was paying the foreigners' taxes, and where she came from. If, however, (his claim is that) she was a slave woman, the man who bought her, or failing that the man who sold her, ought to have come forward as a witness – or at least someone else to testify that she had indeed been a slave, or had been given her freedom. But as it is, Euboulides has proved none of this; he has simply, as I see it, abused us in every conceivable way. How like an informer – to claim everything but prove nothing! (35) And what of that claim of his that my mother was a wet-nurse? Well, we do not deny it; it was when the *polis* was down on its luck, and *everybody* was doing badly.[12] How and why she became a wet-nurse I shall explain to you, in detail, and you, men of Athens, must not, any of you, hold it against us: for you will find many citizen-women working as wet-nurses; I could give you their names, if you liked! If of course we had been rich, we would not have been selling ribbons, or in a position of such utter destitution. But what has that to do with my family origins? Nothing at all, I believe. (36) Gentlemen of the jury, do not deny all honour to the poor, for whom poverty itself is dishonour enough, nor to those, at any rate, who have chosen to earn their living by honest, hard work . . .'[13]

Demosthenes LVII. 30–36*

1 As the epitaph of the first priestess (see next note) shows that she was appointed by lot, suggested restorations have a provision for that here.

2 'It is to be a democratic priesthood, not confined to an aristocratic family as so many of the traditional priesthoods had been' (Meiggs and Lewis *ad loc.*). The first incumbent was in fact a woman called Myrrhine, whose epitaph survives (*SEG* xii.80), and who seems to have been a well-known figure in the *polis* over many years – if, as scholars have assumed, she is the Myrrhine who appears as a character in Aristophanes' *Lysistrata* (of 411).

3 See **65** with n.11.

4 The inscription is conventionally dated to the first half of the 440s: for the arguments involved see Meiggs and Lewis *ad loc.* On the reverse of the *stēlē* is a decree of 424/3, also dealing with the priestess (Meiggs and Lewis no.71).

5 See **5B**.

6 'His explanation of the whole matter is not only brief and priggish, but advice, not consolation, and advice that is most of it not called for by the occasion' (Gomme, *Commentary* ii, 143). Whether or not we share Gomme's reaction to these sentiments, the irony of them is worth noting: Perikles, author of the 451/0 citizenship-law (**128**), was also the man who, at some time in the 440s, divorced his Athenian wife and began a liaison, lasting until his death in 429, with a foreign woman about whom there was more 'talk' than any in Athens – Aspasia of Miletos (on whom see Davies, *Families*, 458–9; Meiggs, *Empire*, 279; de Ste Croix, *Origins*, 235–43; Fornara no.96).

7 As the scene is in the Underworld (and the play staged in 406) it is a nice touch to bring in Kleon, who had died in 422 – and an indication, of course, of how much comic mileage Aristoph. still felt there was in him. See also next note.

8 See **213**. (Hyperbolos had died in 411.)

9 Compare **109C**.

10 A 'Solonian' *nomos*, to this effect, is now read out to the jurors. However, it emerges later in the passage that *xenoi* need only pay a special tax to circumvent it.

11 This is possibly the *nomos* mentioned by Hdt. ii.177.2.

12 The last years of the Peloponnesian War.

13 For another woman like the speaker's mother see Aristoph. *Thesmophoriazousai* 443–458.

16 Athens and Sparta in the Pentekontaëtia

In the Pentekontaëtia – the period of almost fifty years between the Persian and Peloponnesian Wars – the single most important theme, as regards the interrelationships between Greek *poleis* large and small, is clearly the one dealt with in Ch. 12: the establishment and history of the anti-Persian alliance, which was in effect the Athenian empire. This organisation can be seen as, and (more important) was at the time seen as, a power bloc in ideological opposition at virtually every turn to the Peloponnesian League headed by Sparta. It was Sparta and Athens, in the van of their respective alliances, who polarised the Greek world between them and who were to fight out the great Peloponnesian War of 431–404 (see Part III); and it was the most intelligent of contemporary observers of that war, the Athenian aristocrat and *stratēgos* Thucydides, who perceived that its origins stretched back right through the Pentekontaëtia, in the form of the reaction of the Greeks at large to the presence and the potentiality of the Athenian empire – specifically (as he saw it), the growth of Athenian power and the fears to which this gave rise in Sparta (**165**). So these two elements, separately and in combination, form the subject of this chapter.

It should be noted that the chronology of the Pentekontaëtia presents severe problems. The fullest account surviving, that of Diodorus, is unreliable in this as in other respects (see Meiggs, *Empire*, 452–7), and Thucydides deals with these years only incidentally, in the form of an extended explanation of how in his judgment the Peloponnesian War arose (Thuc. 1.89–118.2) – an excursus without a single absolute date in it. It is therefore unlikely that certain controversies here (e.g. the dates of the helot revolt: **169**) will ever be solved to universal satisfaction, despite the prodigious efforts expended on them. But it would be generally conceded that Thucydides presents us with the events in the correct *relative* order (as he criticises a predecessor for chronological inaccuracy: 1.97.2); and beyond that, the best discussion of particular problems is arguably still that of Gomme, *Commentary* I, 361–413.

164. The size of Sparta and Athens

In the course of his excursus (1.2–19) designed to prove that no earlier war in Greek history had been on the scale of the (then beginning) Peloponnesian War, Thucydides was moved to argue, a little paradoxically in this context, that it would be wrong to consider the Trojan War unimportant and the accounts of it (therefore) exaggerated – as some of his contemporaries evidently did – simply because in the fifth century Mykenai and some of the other places involved had declined into insignificance; and to emphasise the impossibility of drawing inferences of this sort he points to the strikingly contrasting cases of the two principal powers of his own day – Sparta and Athens.

Because Mykenai was small, and some of the towns of that period do not seem to be places of importance today, it would be a mistake to deduce that what the poets have said – and indeed what general tradition holds – about the great size of the expedition (against Troy) is not to be trusted. Imagine what would happen if the *polis* of the Lakedaimonians were to become deserted, leaving only the temples and the foundations of the (other) buildings: I think that the people of that time, far ahead in the future, would be very reluctant to believe that the power of Sparta had been as great as its fame suggested. Of course *we* know that the Spartans inhabit two-fifths of the Peloponnesos and have a *hēgemonia* over the whole of it,[1] as well as over many allies further afield;[2] and yet one would suppose Sparta itself an inferior place, not only because it lacks costly temples and (other) buildings but because it has not undergone *synoikismos* into a *polis* but remains a collection of separate villages (*kōmai*) in the early Greek manner.[3] However, if the same thing were to happen to Athens, one would conjecture from the visible remains that it had been a *polis* twice as powerful as in fact it is.

Thucydides 1.10.1–2

1 This is not quite true: Argos constantly repudiated Spartan hegemony.
2 E.g. the Boiotians.
3 See **7** and **8**. On ninth-century Sparta see Cartledge, *Sparta*, 93–100.

165. The 'truest cause' of the Peloponnesian War

As stated above (p.301), Thucydides believed that a satisfactory explanation of the origins of the Peloponnesian War of 431–404 called for a consideration, to some extent, of virtually the entire Pentekontaëtia. The war's immediate, proximate causes – what he calls the *aitiai* and *diaphorai* – were obvious enough, to him at least, and he is naturally the principal source of what we know about them: see Ch.17. But over and above such things he saw also a single explanatory theme – the 'truest cause' (*alēthestatē prophasis*) – which had attracted, consciously or subconsciously, much less attention to itself and which he was therefore all the more determined to make explicit: the long-term relationship between the Athenians and the Spartans. The main expression of this, and its role in bringing on the war, is in the famous passage 1.23.4–6, but the succinct phraseology of these few sentences is such that we can be glad to turn also to 1.118.2, as (in a sense) further commentary. See also 1.88–89.1 and 1.97.2.

The fullest modern discussion of the *alēthestatē prophasis* is that of de Ste Croix, *Origins*, 50–63 and *passim*, whose treatment of most of the topics and problems of the Pentekontaëtia is brilliantly stimulating; the student should be warned, however, that the book's general thesis – that the Spartans were primarily responsible for the war, in both the short and the long term – is controversial, and in our view misleading. A more neutral study is D. Kagan, *The Outbreak of the Peloponnesian War* (Ithaca, N.Y., 1969).

(A) The Athenians and the Peloponnesians began the war when they broke the Thirty Years' Peace which had been made after the (re)capture of Euboia.[1] As to why they broke it, I have put on record first of all their (respective) grounds of complaint and disputes – this in order that nobody need ever ask why such a great war came upon the Greeks: for its truest cause, albeit the one least publicised, was in my opinion the fact that the Athenians, by growing great and making the Spartans afraid, obliged them to go to war. Each side's openly-expressed complaints, on the other hand, which led them to break the Peace and begin the war, were as follows.

Thucydides 1.23.4–6

(B) All these actions of the Greeks,[2] against both each other and the *barbaroi*, took place in a period of approximately fifty years, between the retreat of Xerxes and the beginning of this present war. They were years in which the Athenians increased the strength of their empire, as well as greatly adding to their domestic power and resources. The Spartans were aware of this but did little or nothing to stop it, preferring for most of the time not to interfere: even before this they had never been quick to go to war unless compelled to do so, and in any case they were hindered by wars on their own doorstep.[3] But eventually, of course, the power of the Athenians clearly reached a peak, and they began to encroach upon the Spartans' own alliance;[4] and then it was that the Spartans felt their position to be no longer tolerable, and decided, by starting this present war, to direct all their energies into attacking and if possible destroying Athenian strength.

Thucydides 1.118.2

1 In 446/5: see **173**.
2 Just described in 1.89–118.1.
3 See **169**.
4 Particularly Corinth: see Ch.17.

166. Themistokles and the walls of Athens

In the context of the general brevity of Thucydides' account of the Pentekontaëtia, almost five chapters devoted to the rebuilding of the walls of Athens has to
be counted lavish treatment. No doubt the main reason for it is that its twin
themes – Athenian enterprise and Spartan fear of it – were to serve as the
keynotes for the excursus as a whole. With the (abbreviated) account of
Thucydides, below, compare Diod. XI.39–40 and Plut. *Them.* 19.1–2.

When the *barbaroi* had retreated from their *chōra* the Athenian people at
once began to bring back their children and wives and such property as
they had left from the places where they had taken them for safe
keeping,[1] and made preparations for the rebuilding of the *polis* and its
walls. Only short stretches of their surrounding wall were still standing
and most of the houses were in ruins, the few remaining ones being those
which Persian dignitaries had used as their quarters. (90) However, when
the Spartans got to hear of what was being planned they sent an embassy
to Athens. This was partly because they themselves would not have been
pleased to see either Athens or anywhere else with fortifications, but
principally because they were urged on by their allies, who were
frightened both by the size of the Athenians' fleet – which had not even
existed before the war – and of the daring which the Athenians had
shown in fighting the Persians. So the Spartans made two proposals: not
only should the Athenians refrain from fortifying their own city but they
should join Sparta in demolishing all city walls which still existed outside
the Peloponnesos. They did not, however, reveal to the Athenians the
wishes and suspicions which really lay behind this policy: their argument
instead was that if the *barbaroi* were to invade again they should not have
a stronghold from which to operate, as they had been able to do this time
from Thebes; and as to the Greeks, all of them would find the
Peloponnesos adequate both as a place of refuge and as a base from which
to counter-attack. After this speech from the Spartans, the Athenians, on
the advice of Themistokles, packed them off at once with the reply that
Athenian envoys would be sent to Sparta to discuss these questions.
Themistokles then proposed that he himself be sent to Sparta without
delay, but not the other envoys who had been elected to go with him;
they instead should stay in Athens until such time as the wall had been
raised to a level where its lowest point could be defended. Meanwhile, he
said, the entire manpower of the *polis* was to work at building the wall:
no building, private or public, which would be of any use in the task was
to be spared, but everything dismantled.

(93) This was the way in which the Athenians fortified their *polis*, in no
time at all. And even today it is clear that the building took place in a
hurry: the foundations are laid in stone of all sorts, not fitted together

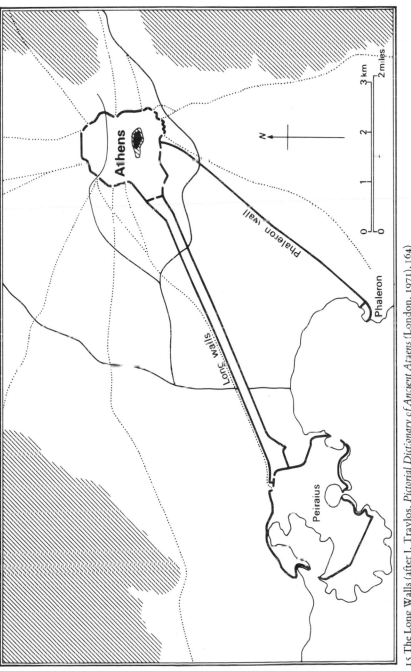

15 The Long Walls (after J. Travlos, *Pictorial Dictionary of Ancient Athens* (London, 1971), 164)

into place but deposited, each block, as it was brought forward; and lots of *stēlai* from tombs and pieces of sculpture were mixed in with the rest. It should be explained that the boundaries of the *polis* were extended in all directions[2] – hence their readiness to uproot anything and everything that came to hand.

Thucydides 1.89.3–90.3; 93.1–2

1 Troizen, Aigina and Salamis (Hdt. VIII.41.1).
2 The boundaries of the *astu*, more properly speaking.

167. The debate in Sparta

Thucydides records that the Spartans were 'secretly vexed' (1.92) over the affair of the walls; but after this tantalising comment he says nothing more, directly, about the relationship between the Athenians and the Spartans until the revolt of Thasos (see 169). If, however, we are prepared to accept the testimony of Diodorus we can gain a valuable insight into the mood in Sparta in the early 470s, when the Spartans needed to adopt a public attitude to the existence and early successes of the Delian League (129–130). The authenticity of this episode is argued, and matters arising discussed, by de Ste Croix, *Origins*, 170–1.

In this year[1] the Spartans, having unaccountably lost the *hēgemonia* at sea, began to resent the fact, and this led them to be angry with the Greeks who had deserted them and to threaten to exact the appropriate punishment from them. And when the *gerousia* had been convened they discussed whether to make war upon the Athenians to determine who should have the *hēgemonia* at sea. Likewise when the general assembly had been convened the younger men and most of the others were ambitious to recover the *hēgemonia*: if this could be done, it was felt, they would acquire great wealth, make Sparta as a whole greater and more powerful, and give the *oikoi* of its private citizens a great bonus in prosperity. They also kept calling to mind the ancient oracle in which the god (Apollo) told them to take care that their *hēgemonia* should not become 'lame'. This oracular utterance, it was maintained, could refer to nothing other than their present circumstances, since their rule would certainly be 'lame' if they were to lose half of their dual *hēgemonia*.[2]

Since virtually all the *politai* were enthusiastic about this proposal – and it was in any case what the *gerousia* was in session to deal with – nobody expected that anyone would be so bold as to advocate any other course of action. However, there was one member of the *gerousia,* called Hetoimaridas, who was descended from the Herakleidai[3] and whose *aretē* made him highly esteemed by his fellow-*politai*; and he attempted to convince everybody that the *hēgemonia* should be left with the Athenians.

It was not, he argued, in Sparta's interests to lay claim to the sea; and with the wealth of (other) pertinent considerations which he adduced in support of his surprising proposal he was able, quite unexpectedly, to win over both the *gerousia* and the *dēmos*. In the end, then, the Spartans decided that what Hetoimaridas was saying was in their best interests, and they abandoned their impulse to make war upon the Athenians. As for the Athenians, they had initially been expecting to have a great war with the Spartans over the *hēgemonia* at sea, and had therefore begun to build more triremes, raise a large sum of money, and behave reasonably towards their allies; however, when they got to hear of what the Spartans had decided they were relieved of their fear of such a war and began to busy themselves instead with increasing the power of their own *polis*.

Diodorus XI. 50

1 In 475/4 – but Diodorus' dates are notoriously inexact.

2 I.e. on land and at sea. This 'lame' *hēgemonia* metaphor, as de Ste Croix comments (*Origins*, 170), occurs also in Plut. *Kim*. 16.8 (taken from the fifth-century poet Ion of Chios, said to be quoting Kimon himself), in connection with the Ithome affair in 462 (see **169**). There, however, there is a crucial difference: it is Greece as a whole which will be 'lame' if deprived of the (single) *hēgemonia* of Sparta, leaving only that of Athens.

3 See **44**.

168. The last years of Themistokles

Despite Themistokles' service to his fellow-Athenians in the affair of the walls (**166**), it is significant that 480/79 was apparently his last year on the board of *stratēgoi* – which meant that the inauguration and the early successes of the Delian League (**129–130**) shifted the limelight to others, first the returned exiles Aristeides and Xanthippos, and then, throughout the 470s and on into the 460s, Kimon. And as Kimon's stock rose ever higher, Themistokles' sank ever lower. The precise chronology of his decline is no clearer than its precise cause or causes, but in or around 471 he was the chosen victim of the *ostrakismos* procedure. This meant ten years in exile (see **79**), and should have meant also his political impotence during that time, but, as Thucydides relates in the passage below, he himself had other ideas. The effectiveness of the anti-Spartan activities that he was orchestrating from Argos until *c*.467 is shown by the Spartans' concern to discredit and persecute him and the extent to which the Athenians in the mid 460s still wanted good relations with Sparta is shown by *their* readiness to join in with this; so for Themistokles there was the final irony, in *c*.465, of flight to his old enemies the Persians, with whom he lived in safety and esteem until his death in *c*.459.

With Thucydides' account, below, compare Diod. XI. 54–59 (with J. F. Barrett, *GRBS* 18 (1977), 291–305) and Plut. *Them.* 22–31. On the problems, especially chronological, see Gomme, *Commentary* I, 397–401; G. L. Cawkwell, 'The fall of

307

Themistocles', in B. F. Harris (ed.), *Auckland Classical Essays presented to E. M. Blaiklock* (Auckland, 1970), 39–58; de Ste Croix, *Origins*, 173–8; A. J. Podlecki, *The Life of Themistocles: a critical survey of the literary and archaeological evidence* (Montreal, 1975), 197–9; R. J. Lenardon, *The Saga of Themistocles* (London, 1978), 98–153; Davies, *Democracy*, 61–2.

On the matter of the medism of Pausanias,[1] the Spartans sent ambassadors to Athens and, on the basis of what they had found when looking into the Pausanias affair, accused Themistokles of the same crime; they urged the Athenians to punish him in the same way, and the Athenians agreed to this. Indeed already, as it happened, he had suffered *ostrakismos* and was living in Argos, as a base for journeys into the rest of the Peloponnesos.[2] So the Athenians sent back with the Spartans – who offered to help in catching him – some men with orders to track him down, wherever he might be, and bring him back (to Athens). (136) Themistokles, however, was warned of this and hurriedly left the Peloponnesos for Kerkyra, where he was honoured as a benefactor; but the Kerkyrans told him that they were afraid to take him in and incur thereby the hostility of both the Spartans and the Athenians, so they sent him across to the mainland opposite. By now his pursuers were hot on his heels, following up information about his movements whenever they could get it, and he himself was running so short of ideas that he was forced to turn to the king of the Molossians, Admetos, who was no friend of his . . . (137) . . . What Themistokles wanted was to go to the King (of Persia); so Admetos sent him overland to Alexandros' city of Pydna,[3] on the other sea,[4] where he found and took passage in a merchant vessel bound for Ionia. During the voyage, however, a storm carried the ship towards the Athenian fleet which was besieging Naxos.[5] This alarmed Themistokles: the men on the ship did not know who he was, but now he went to the *nauklēros* to disclose his identity and the reason for his flight – threatening that if the man were to hand him over he would accuse him of having accepted bribes to bring him along on the voyage. There would be no danger, according to Themistokles, as long as nobody left the ship until they set sail; and if the *nauklēros* did as he was told he would be suitably rewarded. The latter did so, and after riding at anchor for a day and a night at a distance from the fleet they subsequently reached Ephesos. There Themistokles rewarded the man with a gift of money, once it had reached him there from his friends in Athens and also from what he himself had saved at Argos, and he then set off inland accompanied by one of the Persians from the coastal region. A new King had recently come to the throne – Artaxerxes, the son of Xerxes[6] – and Themistokles sent ahead a letter to him which ran as follows. 'I, Themistokles, have come to you. I did more harm to your *oikos* than any other Greek, during the time when I was obliged to defend myself against your father's invasion, but this is far outweighed by the good I did during his retreat, when I was safe but he in danger. My benefaction deserves repayment' – here he wrote of how he had given advance warning of the (Greeks') retreat from Salamis, and of how the bridges (over the Hellespontos) had not been destroyed, which he falsely pretended was his doing[7] – 'and now, chased here by the Greeks because of my friendship for you, I am in a position to be of great service to you. But I want to wait a year before showing you, in person, why I have come.' (138) The King, so it is said, was impressed by the determination of the man and told him to carry out what he had planned. So during the time he was waiting, Themistokles learned as much as he could of the Persian language and way of life. Then, when his year was up, he went to Artaxerxes, who made him a great man – greater than any Greek (in Persia) before him. This was partly on account of the reputation which he already had and partly because of the hope which he held out to Artaxerxes of subjugating Greece; but the main reason was that his behaviour was always a proof of his intelligence.[8]

Thucydides 1.135.2–138.2*

1 Medism: see **117**. Pausanias, the Spartan regent: see **114** and (esp.) **130**.
2 On his activities in this period see W. G. Forrest, 'Themistocles and Argos', *CQ* n.s. 10 (1960), 221–40, and *Sparta*, 100–1; Cartledge, *Sparta*, 215–16.
3 Pydna was a Euboian *apoikia* on Makedon's Thermaic Gulf coastline (see Map 1), so it is not at all clear in what sense Thuc. could call it 'Alexandros'' (referring to king Alexandros I of Makedon: see **111, 321**).
4 I.e. the Aegean – 'other' in contradistinction to the Ionian-Adriatic, upon which Molossian territory bordered.
5 See **130**; but the siege of Naxos belongs in the late 470s, Themistokles' flight in 465 or later (see next note); we cannot explain this.
6 A firm chronological peg: we know that Artaxerxes succeeded his father late in 465.
7 For Themistokles' two messages to Xerxes see Hdt. VIII. 75.2 and 110.3; and on the interpretation of his two claims consult Gomme, *Commentary* I, 440–1.
8 Here follows (138.3) a short but concentrated eulogy of Themistokles' intelligence and foresight – one of the very rare occasions when Thuc. allowed himself the indulgence of so personal an assessment.

169. The revolt of the Messenian helots and the rift between Athens and Sparta

Whether the Hetoimaridas debate (**167**) took place or not, the Spartan 'hawks' (see de Ste Croix, *Origins*, 169ff.) were evidently unable to initiate any definite anti-Athenian policy decisions during the remainder of the 470s and the first half of the 460s; however, by the time of the revolt of Thasos from Athens in *c*.465

(**132**), the prevailing mood in Sparta does seem to have changed – given their undertaking to invade Attika (see **132**) – and Thucydides records a rapid sequence of events, over the next four years, which marked an open rift between the two hegemonial powers and set the stage for the 'First Peloponnesian War' (**170**). Ever since the crisis of the seventh century (**45**), another helot revolt had been a possibility; there *may* have been one in c.490 (see Cartledge, *Sparta*, 153–4); at all events there was undoubtedly one now. With Thucydides' account, below, compare Diod. xi.63–64 and 84.7–8. And see further: de Ste Croix, *Origins*, 178–80; Cartledge, *Sparta*, 217–22.

(The Thasians surrendered since they were not supported by the Spartans, who were occupied by a helot revolt: see **132A**.)

(102) For the Spartans, on the other hand, the war against the men on Ithome was dragging on interminably, so they appealed for help to their allies, including the Athenians, who arrived with a considerable force[1] under the command of Kimon. The main reason why the Athenians were asked was that they were thought to have expertise in siege operations,[2] which from the length of the siege already was evidently something that the Spartans themselves lacked, or they would already have taken the place by storm. And it was from this campaign that there arose the first open dispute between the Spartans and the Athenians. It did so because when the Spartans found themselves (still) unable to take the enemy position by storm they became afraid of the Athenians' boldness and love of innovation. They reflected, too, that the Athenians were not of the same nationality as themselves,[3] and they feared that if they stayed on at Ithome they might be won over to the rebel cause and stage some sort of revolution. So, while keeping the rest of their allies there, they sent the Athenians away – not making their suspicions known but simply saying that they had no further need of Athenian help. The Athenians, however, realised that this reason for their dismissal was a shabby pretext to hide the fact that they had somehow become suspect, and they took offence: this was not, they felt, the sort of treatment they deserved from the Spartans; and as soon as they were back in Athens they repudiated the old anti-Persian alliance (with the Spartans) and became allies instead of Sparta's enemy Argos. Also, at the same time, both the Athenians and the Argives swore oaths of alliance, on the same terms, with the Thessalians.[4] (103) The men on Ithome, however, were unable to hold out any longer, and in the tenth year of the siege they came to terms with the Spartans,[5] who allowed them to leave the Peloponnesos unmolested on condition that they never set foot in it again; if any of them were caught there he was to be the slave of whoever captured him. (The Spartans did this because) they had once been told by the Delphic oracle to 'let the suppliant of Zeus leave Ithome'. So they left, with their children and wives – and because of the hostility which they now felt for

the Spartans, the Athenians took them and settled them at Naupaktos, which they happened to have recently taken from the Ozolian Lokrians.[6]

Thucydides 1.102–103.3

1 Four thousand hoplites, according to other sources.
2 See the long and excellent note on this in Gomme, *Commentary* I, 301–2.
3 I.e. they were Ionian rather than Dorian Greeks.
4 A further consequence, it is generally held (e.g. de Ste Croix, *Origins*, 179), was the *ostrakismos* of Kimon in 461.
5 This is a notorious chronological crux: it seems to be best to emend the text to read 'sixth year' (so that the revolt lasted from 465/4 until 460/59), but the problems are complex; see Gomme, *Commentary* I, 401–11 and Fornara no.67.
6 Naupaktos is on the northern coast of the Corinthian Gulf, and effectively commands the entrance to it. The Athenians were to make good use of this base during the 420s.

170. The outbreak of the 'First Peloponnesian War'

'When Athens formally renounced the anti-Persian alliance of 480 and allied with Argos and Thessaly, war could be expected sooner or later. It could be expected sooner when Megara, attacked by Corinth, appealed to Athens and Athens accepted her into the alliance' (Meiggs, *Empire*, 92). Thucydides' summary narrative moves directly from the conclusion of the helot revolt (**169**) into the opening events of what modern scholars conventionally call the First Peloponnesian War, which lasted sporadically from *c*.460/59 until 446/5. A brief chronological outline is provided by de Ste Croix, *Origins*, 196, with a discussion of its outbreak at 180–3; as to his insistence (50–1 and *passim*) that we do wrong to follow Thucydides in not counting the wars of 460 and 431 as a single entity, the point may have some validity, though de Ste Croix himself offers the best explanation of why *Thucydides* saw it this way – that the 'First Peloponnesian War' centred upon Sparta's allies rather than the Spartans themselves.

Next the Megarians repudiated their alliance with the Spartans and came over to the Athenians; their reason was that the Corinthians were attacking them in a war about boundary land (between them). Thus the Athenians held both Megara and Pegai,[1] and they built for the Megarians the long walls stretching from the *polis* itself to Nisaia,[2] garrisoning them with Athenian troops. It was particularly from this episode that the intense hatred of the Corinthians for the Athenians[3] first began to exist.

Thucydides 1.103.4

1 Megara's western port, on the Corinthian Gulf.
2 Megara's eastern port, on the Aegean (Saronic Gulf). For the Athenians' own Long Walls see **171**.
3 See Ch.17.

171. The Long Walls at Athens, and the battles of Tanagra and Oinophyta

After the Megara episode (**170**), Thucydides' account of the campaigning in the First Peloponnesian War continues in 1.105–106. No absolute dates are given, as usual in the excursus, but it is made clear that between 460 and 458 the Athenians were very active (see also **127**) and very successful – chiefly at the expense of the Corinthians. The narrative then continues as follows.

At about this time the Athenians also began to build their Long Walls to the sea, one to Phaleron and one to Peiraieus.[1] And the Phokians started a campaign against Doris, the original homeland of the Spartans, (which consisted of the towns of) Boion, Kytinion and Erineos.[2] When they had captured one of these places, the Spartans came to the assistance of the men of Doris with an army of 1,500 hoplites of their own and 10,000 from their allies; its commander was Nikomedes the son of Kleombrotos, standing in for the king, Pleistoanax the son of Pausanias, who was still a minor.[3] The Spartans duly compelled the Phokians to come to terms and give back the captured *polis*, and then they started on their journey home. If they went by sea, crossing the Gulf of Krisa,[4] the Athenians would be likely to sail up with their fleet and stop them. On the other hand they did not think it safe to march over Geraneia, with the Athenians in possession of Megara and Pegai:[5] Geraneia was difficult to cross anyway, and was now under constant guard by the Athenians, who on this occasion the Spartans knew to be intending to prevent them from passing through. They therefore decided to stay in Boiotia and see what the safest line of march might be. Apart from anything else, they were urged, in secret, to do this by a group of Athenians who had hopes of suppressing the (rule of the) *dēmos* and (preventing) the building of the Long Walls.[6] However, the Athenians marched out against them in full force, together with 1,000 Argives and contingents from their other allies too[7] – a total of 14,000 men. They did so partly because it occurred to them that the Spartans had no idea how to get home and partly because they had some suspicions of the plot to overthrow the *dēmos*. Some Thessalian cavalry also arrived and joined the Athenians, in accordance with the alliance,[8] though in the event they deserted to the Spartan side. (108) And a battle was fought at Tanagra in Boiotia: the losses were heavy, on both sides, but the Spartans and their allies emerged victorious.[9] The Spartans were thus able to pass into the Megarid, cutting down trees as they went, and journeyed home again across Geraneia and the Isthmos. The Athenians, however, on the sixty-second day after the battle marched (back) into Boiotia, under the *stratēgos* Myronides: they defeated the Boiotians in a battle at Oinophyta and thereby gained control of the whole *chōra* of Boiotia and Phokis.[10] The walls of Tanagra were demolished, and a hundred of the richest men taken as hostages from Opountian Lokris. The Athenians then completed their own Long Walls.

Thucydides 1.107–108.3

1 A second wall to Peiraieus, south of and parallel to the first, was built later, perhaps *c.* 444–442: see Gomme, *Commentary* 1, 312–13; Fornara no.79; Fig. 15 on p.305; and **151**.

2 See **3** with n.2, **45** with n.5.

3 Nikomedes was the younger brother of the disgraced Pausanias (**130**), therefore uncle to Pleistoanax. For the Agiad family tree in the fifth century see Gomme, *Commentary* 1, 370.

4 I.e. crossing the Corinthian Gulf at Krisa – the direct route, virtually due south from Doris. It seems clear, in view of the Athenian occupation of the Megarid (which Thuc. goes on to mention), that this was how the Spartans had reached Doris in the first place: see de Ste Croix, *Origins*, 190–5.

5 Geraneia was the mountainous interior of the Megarid, to the west of Megara and Pegai.

6 The two things were evidently seen to be interdependent: compare **143**.

7 The Thessalians are mentioned later, but as well as (possibly) the Megarians we must take this to mean contingents from the members of the Delian League.

8 See **169**.

9 For the Spartan thank-offering see Meiggs and Lewis no.36 (Fornara no.80).

10 Myronides: see **148** (end). This was his second brilliant victory within two or three years: see Thuc. 1.105.3 106.2, Gomme, *Commentary* 1, 308–9.

172. Athens and Sicily

Something which will have contributed to the Athenians' reputation for enterprise and 'Themistoklean' far-sightedness is the fact that from the early 450s onwards – at the same time, that is, as the First Peloponnesian War – they showed signs of a sporadic but nonetheless clear interest in Sicily and southern Italy. The few hints of an earlier 'Western policy', appropriately linked with the name of Themistokles himself, are marshalled and discussed by de Ste Croix, *Origins*, 378–9, though he rightly emphasises that they add up to very little: what we are talking about here is, principally, the alliance with Egesta (B, below), the foundation of Thourioi (**174**), and the alliances with Rhegion and Leontinoi (Meiggs and Lewis nos.63 and 64, generally taken to be renewals in 433/2 of treaties made in the 440s). Sicily in the mid-fifth century was in a troubled state – see A, below – and it is not easy to see what the Athenians hoped to gain, concretely, from alliances with minor Sicilian cities; however, as de Ste Croix points out (*Origins*, 220–2), it was probably the Sicilians rather than the Athenians who initiated the contacts and expected most from them, at a time years before the Athenians were moved to intervene directly (Ch.22).

(A) In Sicily the Syracusans, in their war with the mercenaries who had revolted,[1] were mounting constant attacks against both Achradine and the Island: they defeated the rebels in a sea-battle, but on land they were unable to expel them from the *polis* because the positions they held were so strong. Subsequently, though, a pitched battle took place on open ground: the participants on both sides met the dangers of battle with courage and there were heavy casualties all round, but victory went in the end to the Syracusans. After the battle the élite troops, 600 in number, who were responsible for the victory, were crowned and given each a mina of silver as a prize for valour.

While all this had been going on, Douketios, the leader of the Sikels,[2] angry at the way in which the settlers of Katane had robbed the Sikels of their land, led an army against them. And since the Syracusans, too, had sent an army against Katane, they and the Sikels jointly shared out the land in allotments and made war upon the men who had been settled there by the tyrant Hieron.[3] The people in Katane put up a fight, but after they had been beaten in battle many times they were expelled from Katane and took possession of the place which is now called Aitne, the former Inessa. As for the original inhabitants of Katane, after a long period of time they recovered their native city. And after these events the (other) peoples who had been expelled from their own *poleis* under the rule of Hieron, now that they had assistance in their struggle, returned to their native cities and expelled from them the men who had unjustly taken for themselves *poleis* which belonged to others; those who did this included the men of Gela and Akragas and Himera. Similarly the people of Rhegion, with the help of those of Zankle, expelled the sons of Anaxilas who were ruling over them,[4] and liberated their native cities. Later the men of Gela, who had been the original settlers of Kamarina, shared out its land in allotments. Virtually all the *poleis*, moreover, eager to see the end of the wars, made a common decision and came to terms with the mercenary settlers; they then received back the exiles and restored the *poleis* to their original *politai*. As for the mercenaries who because of the tyrannies were in possession of *poleis* not their own, they were given permission to take their possessions and go and settle all together in (the territory of) Messana (Zankle). It was in this way, then, that the *stasis* and disturbances in the *poleis* of Sicily were brought to an end; and the *poleis* not only threw out the *politeiai* which others had imposed upon them but also, in practically all cases, divided out their own *chōra* in allotments amongst all their *politai*.

Diodorus XI.76

(B)   [The alliance and] oath [of the Athenians and] Egestaians.[5]
[It was resolved by the *boulē* and] the [*dēmos*, . . . is] held the prytany, [--

– was secretary, – –]o[– presided, Ha]b[r]on was *archōn*,[6] Ar[– – proposed:] (five lines in which the general sense is obscure, beyond reference to sacrificial victims and an oath) That (the oath) [be] sworn [by everyone] is to be the responsibility of the [*strat*]*ēgoi* [– – –] with the *horkōtai*,[7] so that [– – –]. This *psēphisma* and the [oath are to be inscribed on a stone *stēlē* on the] (Akro)polis by the secretary of the *boulē*; [let the *pōlētai*[8] put this out for contract,] and let the *kōlakretai*[9] provide [the money. Invitation is to be made for] hospitality (*xenia*) to the embassy of the E[gestaians in the *prytaneion* at the] customary time.

Euphem[os said that in most respects he agreed with the] *boulē*, but in future, when [envoys come from the Egestaians, the] herald shall introduce [– –]

(*lacuna*)

[As envoys of the] Egestaians, [the following men swore the oath: – – –] son of [– –]ikinos, Ap [34 letters missing]

D. W. Bradeen and M. F. McGregor, *Studies in Fifth-Century Attic Epigraphy* (1973), pp. 71–72, with modifications[10]

1 As Diod. has already related in XI 72–73, the democratic régime set up in Syracuse in 466 had disfranchised the mercenaries who had been admitted to citizenship by the former tyrant Gelon; the mercenaries had then revolted and occupied fortified positions in the quarter of Syracuse called Achradine and also on the offshore (but linked) island of Ortygia.

2 With the Sikans and Elymians, the pre-Hellenic native people of Sicily: see Thuc. VI.2.

3 See Diod. XI.49.

4 See Diod. XI.48.

5 Egesta (as the Greeks rendered it; more properly Segesta) was a Hellenised Elymian foundation in the north-west corner of Sicily.

6 The *archōn* of 458/7 – but the traces of his 'b' have been disputed, and without it the *archōn* of 454/3, Arist]on, is an alternative restoration. Only by contesting the ruling orthodoxy about epigraphical letter-forms (for which see R. Meiggs, 'The dating of fifth-century Attic inscriptions', *JHS* 86 (1966), 86–98) can one argue for a date as late as 418/17 (the *archōn* Antiphon), as did H. B. Mattingly, *Historia* 12 (1963), 267–9 (supported by J. D. Smart, *JHS* 92 (1972), 128–46, and T. E. Wick, *JHS* 95 (1975), 186–90).

7 *Horkōtai*: see 134.

8 *Pōlētai*: see 65 with n.11.

9 *Kōlakretai*: see 67 with n.6.

10 The stone is extremely worn, which accounts for the small differences in both readings and restorations between the various published texts; for a marginally more conservative one see Meiggs and Lewis no.37.

173. The Thirty Years' Peace

After the Athenian campaigns briefly described by Thucydides in 1.108.5 and 111.2–3, the First Peloponnesian War drifted into stalemate with the five years' truce (Thuc. 1.112.1) of 451, which from the Athenian viewpoint provided the opportunity for Kimon's last expedition to Cyprus (Thuc. 1.112.2–4). But in Greece the five years did not run their course: both the Spartans and the Athenians took initiatives in the Sacred War of *c.*448 (Thuc. 1.112.5; Plut. *Per.* 21); and then, as Thucydides recounts, there occurred a rapid concatenation of events, from which the Athenians must be held fortunate to have emerged, in the Thirty Years' Peace of 446/5, in such a strong position – with the admitted loss of their short-lived 'Land Empire' but with their Aegean *hēgemonia* intact.

Some time after this[1] the Athenians mounted an expedition against the Boiotian exiles[2] who had gained control of Orchomenos, Chaironeia and some other Boiotian towns. The *stratēgos* was Tolmides the son of Tolmaios, in command of 1,000 Athenian hoplites with contingents from the allies. The enemy strongholds were attacked, and Chaironeia was taken and its inhabitants sold as slaves; the Athenians then left a garrison there and began to make their way home. However, as they were on the march they were attacked, at Koroneia, by the Boiotian exiles from Orchomenos, with the help of some Lokrians and exiles from Euboia and others who were of the same way of thinking: a battle took place in which the Athenians were defeated, and those of them not killed were taken alive. And in order to recover these men the Athenians made a treaty under which they withdrew from the whole of Boiotia. The Boiotian exiles then returned home, and recovered their independence – as indeed did all the rest of the Boiotians. (114) Next, and not long after this, Euboia revolted from the Athenians; and Perikles had already crossed to the island with an Athenian army when he was given the news that Megara (too) had revolted and that the Peloponnesians were on the point of invading Attika. It was also reported that the Megarians had killed the Athenian garrison troops, except for some who had succeeded in escaping to Nisaia; and in staging the revolt the Megarians had enlisted the support of the Corinthians, the Sikyonians and the Epidaurians. So Perikles made haste to bring the army back again from Euboia; and the Peloponnesians subsequently did invade Attika, led by the Spartan king Pleistoanax the son of Pausanias, and laid it waste as far as Eleusis and Thria. They did not, however, advance any further than that, but went off home.[3] The Athenians, (still) with Perikles as *stratēgos*, then crossed back into Euboia and subdued the whole island. With most of the cities a settlement-treaty was drawn up,[4] though in the case of Hestiaia the inhabitants were driven out and the Athenians took possession of the land themselves.[5]

(115) And soon after their return from Euboia the Athenians made peace with the Spartans and their allies, to last for thirty years. The Athenians therefore gave up Nisaia, Pegai, Troizen and Achaia – all places which they had taken from the Peloponnesians.[6]

Thucydides I.113–115.I

1 I.e. after the Sacred War.

2 Presumably oligarchs expelled by the Athenians after Oinophyta (**171**).

3 It was believed – in both Athens and Sparta – that Pleistoanax and his advisor Kleandridas had been bribed by Perikles to withdraw: see Gomme, *Commentary* I, 341; de Ste Croix, *Origins*, 197–9; Fornara no.104; Cartledge, *Sparta*, 230.

4 For part of the settlement with Chalkis see **134**.

5 According to Plut. *Per.* 23.2, the Hestiaians were singled out because 'they had captured an Attic ship and killed its crew'.

6 For a reconstruction of the Peace (which survived for Pausanias to see it at Olympia: v.23.4) see de Ste Croix, *Origins*, 293–4.

174. The foundation of Thourioi

In 444/3 the Athenians' interest in the far west (**172**) took another step forward with the establishment of the *apoikia* at Thourioi, in the 'instep' of southern Italy. As Diodorus (lamentably, our principal source) explains, the new city was located near the site of Sybaris, and was to some extent intended to be a reincarnation of that foundation whose history since 510 (as Diodorus relates) was so troubled and such a contrast with its earlier peace and proverbial prosperity. Diodorus' account is, however, unsatisfactory in various ways, not all of them his fault: in particular, the supposedly Panhellenic spirit of the enterprise is highly doubtful, and Thourioi was surely 'meant to serve strictly Athenian interests' (A. Andrewes, 'The opposition to Perikles', *JHS* 98 (1978), 1–8 at p.1).

See further: V. Ehrenberg, 'The foundation of Thurii', *American Journal of Philology* 69 (1948), 149–70; de Ste Croix, *Origins*, 381; Andrewes, *op. cit.* 5–8.

In Italy the *polis* of Thourioi came to be founded, for the following reasons. When, in an earlier period, Greeks had founded in Italy the *polis* of Sybaris,[1] the excellence of its *chōra* had led to its rapid growth: since it lay midway between two rivers, the Krathis and the Sybaris, from which it took its name, the settlers, who cultivated a large and fruitful *chōra*, came to possess great riches. Furthermore they were so lavish with grants of citizenship that the extent of their growth led to their being considered far and away pre-eminent amongst the inhabitants of Italy; in fact they so excelled in population that the *polis* possessed 300,000 *politai*[2] . . . (But after a dispute with Kroton, in the late sixth century, Sybaris is plundered and laid waste.) (10) . . . Fifty-eight years later, some

Thessalians joined in settling the place, but after only a short time they were driven out by the men of Kroton, in the period we are now considering. And before very long the city was moved to another site and received another name, with (the Athenians) Lampon and Xenokritos as its founders.[3] What happened was that when the Sybarites had been expelled from their homeland a second time they sent envoys to Greece, to the Spartans and the Athenians, requesting that they help their repatriation and join in the *apoikia*. The Spartans paid them no attention, but the Athenians undertook to take part in the venture, and they manned ten ships and sent them out to the Sybarites under the command of Lampon and Xenokritos. They also sent heralds round the *poleis* of the Peloponnesos, offering a share in the *apoikia* to anyone who cared to join it. Many people took up the offer, and an oracular response was procured from Apollo, who declared that they must found a *polis* in the place where they could live 'drinking water in due measure, but eating bread without measure'. So they sailed off to Italy, arrived at Sybaris, and began to search for the spot where the god had told them to settle. And not far from Sybaris they discovered a spring called Thouria, which had a bronze pipe known locally as a 'measure': this, they felt, was the place which the god was showing them, so they built a wall round it and founded a *polis* named, after the spring, Thourion[4] . . .

(11) For a short time the men of Thourioi lived together in peace, but then they fell into serious *stasis* – and with every reason: the former Sybarites were assigning the most prestigious offices to themselves and the unimportant ones to those *politai* who had been enrolled later; they also thought that their wives should take precedence among the citizen women, above the wives of those newly enfranchised, in offering sacrifices to the gods; and as if that were not enough, the *chōra* near the *polis*[5] they were apportioning out amongst themselves and the more distant plots to the newcomers.[6] And when a dispute had arisen because of all this, those *politai* who had been registered later than the rest, having the power of the majority, killed virtually all the former Sybarites and settled the *polis* themselves. In view of the large and fine *chōra* at their disposal they sent for settlers in large numbers from Greece and assigned parts of the *polis* and its *chōra* on equal terms. Those who continued to live there became extremely prosperous; they established friendly relations with the men of Kroton, and their own *politeia* – a democracy – was an admirable one. They divided the *politai* into ten *phylai*, assigning to each a name derived from the ethnic origin of its members. Thus, three (*phylai*) of men gathered from the Peloponnesos they called the Arkadian, the Achaian and the Eleian; the same number from related peoples outside the Peloponnesos they named the Boiotian, the Amphiktyonian[7] and the Dorian; and the remaining four, drawn from other peoples, were

the Ionian, the Athenian, the Euboian and the Islander.[8] As for a lawgiver (*nomothetēs*), they chose the best man from amongst those of the *politai* who were admired as teachers – Charondas. After a comprehensive study of other legislation Charondas picked out the best points and incorporated them into his own *nomoi*, as well as reasoning out many legal principles for the first time[9] . . .

Diodorus XII.9–11*

1 In *c*.720.
2 The figure is frankly incredible.
3 For Lampon see **146**. Xenokritos appears in the anonymous ancient *Life of Thucydides* as a successful prosecutor of Thoukydides son of Melesias, so although this source is generally garbled it seems proper to think of Xenokritos, as well as the better-known Lampon, as an associate of Perikles.
4 Or Thourioi.
5 Near the *astu*, strictly speaking.
6 Compare the allocation of plots in **86**.
7 See **84**.
8 On the significance of this tribal organisation see the articles of Ehrenberg (esp. pp.158–9) and Andrewes (esp. pp.7–8), cited above.
9 Diod. goes on to outline the *nomoi* of Charondas in XII.12–18 (see also **7, 40A**); and he reports the subsequent history of Thourioi in XII.23.2 and 35.1–3.

175. Athenian 'polypragmosynē'

If one wanted a single Greek word to encapsulate Thucydides' description of the Athenian character in 1.70–71 (see **87, 182**) – and indeed to sum up his *alēthestatē prophasis* (**165**) – it would be *polypragmosynē*. As V. Ehrenberg's classic study made clear ('Polypragmosyne: a study in Greek politics', *JHS* 67 (1947), 46–67), *polypragmosynē* is a concept of psychology as reflected in behaviour: a *polypragmōn* – whether an individual (as in Aristoph. *Ach*. 833) or a whole *polis* – must always be active, interfering in the affairs of others, neither keeping quiet themselves nor allowing others to be quiet. Its opposite is *apragmosynē*, or, better, *hēsychia* (peace and quiet), lauded by Pindar in his last *epinikion*, Pythian VIII, of 446; this may not indeed be a direct criticism of the Athenians, but possibly a reflection of a feeling that they were, temperamentally, *polypragmones* whose dynamic imperialism disrupted everyone else's lives. To Thucydides such a quality gave the Athenians their greatness – so long, that is, as a leader of the moral and intellectual stature of a Perikles was there to keep it under control. (See in general A. W. H. Adkins, 'Polypragmosynē and minding one's own business: a study in Greek social and political values', *CPh* 71 (1976), 301–27.) To the Greeks at large, however, it was necessarily a nuisance, or worse. As regards the Peloponnesians in particular, A. H. M. Jones' careful study of Thuc. 1.40–43 ('Two synods of the Delian and Peloponnesian Leagues', *PCPhS* n.s.2 (1952–53), 43–6) demonstrated that in 440, during the revolt of Samos (Thuc. 1.115.2–117), the Spartans had taken a formal decision to go to war with Athens; they discovered, however, that the majority of their allies, including the Corinthians, were unwilling to support them. This suggests in general that the Corinthians' 'intense hatred' for Athens (**170**) had abated since 460, and in particular that they had not felt unduly upset or threatened by the foundation of Thourioi. Yet from 433 onwards it was the Spartans who held back while Corinth lobbied for war (Ch.17). Can this be explained solely in terms of the *aitiai* and *diaphorai* of the years after 435? They were undeniably important, as we shall see – but before them, in the *first* half of the 430s, we catch glimpses of other acts of Athenian *polypragmosynē* which must have been significant also. As well as the two given here, note also the re-foundation of Ennea Hodoi (**132**) as Amphipolis, which is securely datable to 437/6; for others see the footnotes below.

(A) (Perikles) also sailed into the Black Sea, with a large and splendidly equipped expeditionary force. There he made arrangements in accordance with what the Greek *poleis* wanted and dealt with them benevolently; and as for the neighbouring nations of *barbaroi* with their kings and dynasts, to them he displayed both the magnitude of his power and the fearless courage of men who were sailing wherever they liked and bringing the whole sea under their control. At Sinope he left Lamachos with thirteen ships and some soldiers, to fight the tyrant Timesileos; and when the tyrant and his friends had been driven out, Perikles moved a *psēphisma* providing that 600 Athenian volunteers should sail to Sinope and settle there with the Sinopians, dividing amongst themselves the houses and *chōra* once owned by the tyrants.[1]

In other matters, however, he did not yield to the impulses of the *politai*, nor was he swept along with the tide when, elated by their strength and good fortune, they wanted to get their hands on Egypt again[2] and to disturb the (Persian) King's coastal dominions. Many, too, were already possessed by that disastrous and ill-starred passion for Sicily which was later inflamed by the rhetoric of Alkibiades and his supporters.[3] There were even some who dreamed of Etruria and Carthage – and not hopelessly, either, given the great size of their *hēgemonia* already and the momentum of success in their undertakings. (21) Perikles, however, endeavoured to restrain this impulsiveness, keep their *polypragmosynē* in check, and channel the bulk of their resources into guarding and securing what they already had[4] . . .

Plutarch, *Perikles* 20–21.1

(B) Many generations later (than the Trojan War), when (the men of Amphilochian Argos) were experiencing difficulties, they invited the Amprakiots, who shared a frontier with them, to join their settlement. And it was from these Amprakiots who became their fellow-settlers that the Amphilochian Argives first learned to speak Greek – as they still do;

the rest of the Amphilochians are *barbaroi*. After a time, however, the Amprakiots threw out the Argives and held the *polis* themselves. This led the Amphilochians to put themselves in the hands of the Akarnanians; and the Akarnanians together then sought further help from the Athenians. The Athenians sent them the *stratēgos* Phormion with 30 ships, and when he arrived they captured Argos by storm and sold the Amprakiots (there) into slavery; the Amphilochians and Akarnanians then lived in the place together. And it was after this that the alliance between the Athenians and the Akarnanians was first concluded.[5]

Thucydides II.68.5–8

1 On this expedition, its date, and other events possibly associated with it, see Gomme, *Commentary* I, 367–8; D. Kagan, *The Outbreak of the Peloponnesian War* (Ithaca, N.Y., 1969), 387–9.
2 For the first attempt see **132B**.
3 See **219**.
4 Compare Perikles' reported advice to the Athenians in Thuc. II.65.7 (**209**).
5 On the criteria for dating this expedition to north-west Greece, and the alliance, see Gomme, *Commentary* I, 367 and II, 416; de Ste Croix, *Origins*, 85–8.

17 The prelude to the Peloponnesian War

Thucydides has left us a long account of the immediate antecedents of the Peloponnesian War from 435 onwards, which presumably represents material collected soon after the events; in its finished form, however, his text presents a further complex of factors for consideration, and distinguishes between 'each side's openly expressed complaints' and the 'truest cause, albeit the one least publicised' (see **165**). A further problem is posed by the fact that the speeches which Thucydides attributes to the various actors in the drama are redolent of this allegedly least publicised truest cause (see, e.g., **176**); these speeches raise, in fact, in its acutest form the problem of the speeches in Thucydides (see p.11). It is also necessary to observe that the jokes made about the outbreak of war by Aristophanes and others have hopelessly contaminated the later historical tradition (see, for instance, **180**).

In looking at the contrast between the 'truest cause, albeit the one least publicised' and 'each side's openly expressed complaints', there are likely to be as many different views as there are scholars; one may remark, however, that it is not possible to fuse the two Thucydidean accounts by arguing that the Spartans and their allies were always disposed to go to war with the Athenians and saw an occasion in the complaints made at the meeting of 432. For in 440, the Corinthians had blocked a Spartan proposal to help Samos (see **176**) and (apparently subsequently) the Spartans had refused to help Lesbos when it wished to revolt (Thuc. III.2.1); they had also attempted to prevent the split between Corinth and Kerkyra. One can perhaps suggest that in Sparta and among her allies there were hard-liners and soft-liners, and that an oscillating centre was persuaded in the late 430s to join the former; they will have observed that Athens had never been stronger in terms of men and money and they may have known of the Lesbians' view that nothing now prevented the Athenians treating their allies as they wished (see **136**; also **175**, and note the inference of F. A. Lepper, 'Some rubrics in the Athenian quota-lists', *JHS* 82 (1962), 25–55, that a great deal of quiet tidying-up of the *archē* went on during these years); the Kerkyra and Poteidaia affairs will only have provided further evidence of Athenian ambition, great as ever.

176. The Kerkyra affair

In 435 a quarrel between Kerkyra and Corinth arose over Epidamnos. Epidamnos was an *apoikia* of Kerkyra, which was in turn an *apoikia* of Corinth, and had been founded, according to custom, by an *oikistēs* (see 18) drawn from Corinth; the *dēmos* at Epidamnos drove out the leading men and then, suffering from their attacks, appealed unsuccessfully to Kerkyra and successfully to Corinth; her attempt to help, however, ended in defeat at the hands of Kerkyra, protecting what she saw as her sphere of influence. See in general de Ste Croix, *Origins*, 66–79.

Nursing their anger at the outcome of the war with the Kerkyrans, the Corinthians spent the whole of the year after the sea-battle (of Leukimme in 435) and the one after that building ships and preparing a naval expedition of as great a strength as possible; they collected oarsmen from the Peloponnesos itself and from the rest of Greece, enticed by the pay offered. When the Kerkyrans learnt of their preparations they were afraid; they did not have treaty relations with any Greek *polis* and had not concluded any kind of agreement with either the Athenians or the Lakedaimonians; so they decided to go to the Athenians and become their allies and try and get some support from them. When the Corinthians heard of this they also came on an embassy to Athens, so that the Athenian navy might not join the Kerkyran navy and prevent them settling the war as they wished. An *ekklēsia* was held and both sides of the case were put; the Kerkyrans spoke as follows: '. . . (33.3) If any of you supposes that the war in which we may be useful to you is not on the way, he is wrong and does not realise that the Lakedaimonians will be inclined to go to war from fear of you,[1] and that the Corinthians are influential with them and hostile to yourselves. They have made a preliminary attack on us now in order to go on and attack you, so as to prevent us standing together because of our common enmity with them and so as not to fail in getting one or other advantage, harming us or strengthening themselves. *Our* task, then, is to take the first step, for you to grant and for us to accept an alliance, to plan ahead against them rather than to face their plans. (34) And if they claim that it is not right for you to receive their *apoikoi* into your arms, they should realise that any *apoikia* will honour its *mētropolis* if it is treated well, but that if it is wronged it will be alienated; for men are sent out not to be the slaves, but to be the equal of those who remain. As it is, it is clear that they are in the wrong; for when they were summoned to accept arbitration over Epidamnos, they chose to pursue their grievances by war rather than by an equitable procedure . . . (36.3) This should convince you why you should not abandon us – both the general and the particular arguments can be expressed with extreme brevity: there are three navies of any size in the Greek world, yours and ours and that of the Corinthians; if you stand by and watch two of these merged into one and the Corinthians get control of us first, you will fight against the Kerkyrans and the Peloponnesians together, but if you take us onto your side you will be able to fight against them with your forces increased by our ships.' (The Corinthians replied.) (40.4) 'So you will be in the right most clearly if you avoid hindering either side or otherwise if you join us against them; for you have a treaty with the Corinthians, but you have never even made a truce with the Kerkyrans; and you should not establish the custom of accepting onto your side those who abandon others. For when the Samians rebelled we did not cast a vote which was inimical to your interests; the other Peloponnesians had already voted the other way on the question of whether to help them,[2] but we explicitly put the opposite view that anyone might punish the allies who belonged to them. For if you accept onto your side and protect those who are engaged in wrongdoing, it will turn out that people on your side will come over to us to no less an extent and you will establish a custom which will hurt you yourselves more than us . . .' (44) This was the speech of the Corinthians. The Athenians heard them both, an *ekklēsia* being convened twice; on the first day they were no less receptive to the arguments of the Corinthians, but on the second day they changed their minds; they did not agree to make a *symmachia*[3] with the Kerkyrans on the basis of having the same friends and enemies, for if the Kerkyrans had bidden them sail with them against Corinth, their treaty with the Peloponnesians would have been broken; but they did conclude an *epimachia*[3] on the basis of helping each other if anyone attacked the Kerkyrans or the Athenians or the allies of the latter. For it seemed clear that the war against the Peloponnesians would after all come upon them and they did not wish to abandon Kerkyra to the Corinthians with such a large navy; the Athenians did wish the two as far as possible to fight each other, so that they might go to war if occasion arose against the Corinthians and the others with these hostile navies in an already weakened state. The island also appeared to them to be very conveniently situated for the passage to Italy and Sicily.[4] (The Athenians offered modest help to the Kerkyrans and beat off a Corinthian attack.) (55.2) So Kerkyra survived in her war with the Corinthians and the ships of the Athenians withdrew from the island; but this was the first occasion which led to war between the Corinthians and the Athenians, because these had fought on the side of the Kerkyrans against the Corinthians, who had a treaty (with Athens).

Thucydides 1.31–55.2★

1 Thucydides here makes the Kerkyrans refer very clearly to the 'truest cause' of the war.

2 See **175** Intro.

3 A *symmachia* was a full alliance with aggressive intent, an *epimachia* merely a defensive alliance.

4 See **172** and **174**.

177. The Poteidaia affair

As ill-luck would have it, the Athenians aroused the ire of the Corinthians not only over Epidamnos (**176**), but also over Poteidaia. See in general de Ste Croix, *Origins*, 79–85.

And immediately after this the following events occurred which also provided the Athenians and the Peloponnesians with grounds for war. For since the Corinthians were trying to get their revenge, the Athenians, divining their hostility, issued a series of instructions to the Poteidaians, who inhabit the isthmus of Pallene and are *apoikoi* of the Corinthians, while being at the same time allies of the Athenians bound to pay tribute (*phoros*); they bade them pull down the wall on the side of Pallene[1] and give hostages and dismiss the *epidēmiourgoi*[2] whom the Corinthians had sent out and not admit them in future years;[3] for the Athenians were afraid that the Poteidaians would rebel, urged on by Perdikkas and the Corinthians, and that they would lead the other allies in Thrake to rebel also. (57) The Athenians took these precautions over the Poteidaians immediately after the sea-battle off Kerkyra; for the Corinthians were now clearly at odds with them and Perdikkas the son of Alexandros the king of the Makedonians had become their enemy, although an ally and a friend earlier; this had happened because the Athenians had made an alliance with his brother Philippos and with Derdas, who were engaged in joint action against him. Thus alarmed, Perdikkas both tried to stir up war between the Athenians and the Peloponnesians by sending embassies to Lakedaimon and approached the Corinthians over a revolt by Poteidaia; and he also encouraged the Chalkidians in Thrake and the Bottiaians to join in the revolt, calculating that if he had these places which were his neighbours on his side he would find it easier to carry on the war with their help. (Despite Athenian precautions, the Poteidaians rebelled, along with the Chalkidians[4] and the Bottiaians, when promised Spartan help.)

Thucydides 1.56–57.5

1 And thus not needed for defence against the barbarians in the hinterland (see Map 1).

2 We have no information on the functions of these officials.

3 For this and other examples of the relationship between the Corinthians and their *apoikoi* see Graham, *Colony*, ch.7; and compare **176**.

4 Urged on by Perdikkas, the Chalkidians synoikised (see **7–8**) and made Olynthos their centre; it was eventually destroyed by Philip II (see **344–345**).

178. The allies of Sparta meet

Provoked over Epidamnos and Poteidaia, Corinth set out to orchestrate a demand for war among the allies of Sparta.

These then were the grounds of complaint which the Athenians and the Peloponnesians so far had against each other. The Corinthians objected to the fact that the Athenians were besieging both Poteidaia, which was their *apoikia*, and the men from Corinth and the Peloponnesos who were inside; the Athenians to the fact that the Peloponnesians had caused to revolt a *polis* which was their ally and bound to pay tribute, and had gone and openly fought against them alongside the Poteidaians. The war, however, had not yet actually broken out and the peace was still in force; for the Corinthians had taken their action on their own account. (67) But they did not abate their efforts now that Poteidaia was under siege, since their own men were inside, and they were at the same time afraid for the safety of the place; they immediately set about urging the allies to go to Sparta, and coming themselves denounced the Athenians for breaking the peace and wronging the Peloponnesos. And the Aiginetans, although they did not openly send an embassy, for fear of the Athenians, nonetheless in secret joined the Corinthians in urging on the war, claiming that they were not allowed the autonomy guaranteed by the peace.[1] So the Spartans summoned those of their allies and indeed anyone who claimed to have suffered any wrong at the hands of the Athenians and, convening their usual assembly, bade them speak. Various peoples came forward and made their several complaints, including the Megarians, who expounded a number of substantial grievances and complained in particular that they were excluded from the harbours in the empire of the Athenians and from the *agora* of Athens, contrary to the terms of the peace.[2] Finally the Corinthians came forward and, having allowed the others first of all to arouse the indignation of the Lakedaimonians, made their speech.

Thucydides 1.66–67

1 Of 446/5.

2 See de Ste Croix, *Origins*, ch.7, arguing correctly that the 'Megarian decrees' were of no importance 'until Sparta cleverly chose (them) as a test case of Athenian willingness to yield'.

179. The Athenian case

That the Athenians did not seek war emerges very clearly from their offer to go to arbitration, an offer refused by Sparta; but they were, equally, not prepared to yield, as Thucydides makes clear in a speech attributed to an Athenian envoy in Sparta. Whether he actually dared to speak the words attributed to him by Thucydides is doubtful; but the portrayal of the attitude is presumably authentic.

Now as it happened there was an embassy of the Athenians which had come to Sparta earlier on other business; and when they gathered the nature of the speeches which were being made, they thought that they ought to appear before the Spartans, not in any way to answer the charges which the *poleis* were bringing against them, but to deal with the entire issue and suggest that they should not come to a hasty decision, but consider the matter fully. And they wished at the same time to indicate how powerful their *polis* was, and to remind the older men of things they knew and to tell the younger men about things of which they were ignorant; they supposed that the Spartans would as a result of reckoning things up turn rather to peace than to war. So they approached the Spartans and said that they too wished to speak to their assembly, unless there was some obstacle; but the Spartans bade them come forward, so they came forward and made their speech. (73) (In addition to attempting to deter the Spartans from making a hasty decision, the embassy set itself a second objective, of showing 'that it is not unreason- able that we hold what we do'; the embassy set about achieving the first objective by drawing attention to the Athenian role in the Persian Wars – at the same time making much of Athenian services to Greece.) (75) 'Is it right, Lakedaimonians, that the zeal and intelligent forethought which we showed then should be repaid by such a hostile attitude on the part of the Greeks to the empire which we possess? For we did not gain it by force, but gained it when you were unwilling to continue with the end of the war against the barbarian and the allies approached us and themselves asked to have us as *hēgemones*; and it was the logic of events which forced us to develop it to its present state, first motivated mostly by fear for our safety; later we took into account the reputation which possession of the empire gave us, finally the profit derived from it. And then it no longer seemed safe to run the risk of letting it go; for we were hated by the majority of our allies, some of whom had indeed already revolted and been suppressed, you yourselves were no longer so friendly to us, but were suspicious and hostile; and in fact any revolt would have involved (our allies) going over to you. No one should be begrudged the right of taking whatever steps are most expedient where very great dangers are involved. (76) At any rate, Lakedaimonians, you control the *poleis* in the Peloponnesos and have arranged matters there as suits yourselves. And if

327

you had gone on taking an active part in the war against the *barbaroi* and been hated by your followers, like us, we are sure that you would have been just as harsh to your allies and would have been forced to rule firmly or yourselves be in danger. So neither have we done anything remarkable or contrary to human nature in accepting an empire which was handed down to us and in refusing to give it up, swayed by three of the most powerful motives imaginable – concern for our reputation, fear and desire for profit – nor again were we the first to pursue this line of conduct; rather it has always been the rule that the weaker is controlled by the stronger. What is more, we regard ourselves as worthy of our position and seemed so to you until you reckoned up what was expedient for yourselves and took to your present talk of justice, a thing which no one in a position to get something by force has ever rated above aggrandisement, turning away from his objective as a result. Those who are deserving of praise are those who follow human custom in ruling over others, but behave with greater respect for justice than their actual strength demands. So we are certain that anyone who acquired our power would show very well whether we behave with moderation; as for us, it is precisely our reasonableness which surprisingly has brought us blame rather than praise. (77) In fact, in cases between ourselves and our allies regulated by judicial agreements we tend to come off worse, and when we hold trials at Athens we do so under the same laws as bind us, yet our only reward is a reputation for litigiousness.[1] And none of them considers why this reproach is never made against those who possess an empire elsewhere and behave less reasonably towards their subjects than we do; the reason is that those who can use force do not need to go to law (as we in fact do). As it is, those who are accustomed to deal with us on a basis of equality, if they do come off worse in any respect contrary to what they think right, either because of the reputation or because of the power which we derive from the empire, are not pleased because they have not lost everything, but grieve over what they *have* lost more than if we had ignored the law from the start and gone for open aggrandisement. Under those circumstances, not even they would have objected that the weak should not give way to the strong. In fact, it seems that men become more angry at losing in court than at being coerced; for if one starts from a basis of equality one feels that someone has got the better of oneself, rather than merely suffering the compulsion of a superior.' (The peroration reverts to themes already raised and makes clear the Athenian view that if the Spartans went to war they would have broken the peace.)

Thucydides 1.72–77.4*

---

1 For the two kinds of cases, (commercial) cases regulated by agreements

between the *poleis* to which the two parties belonged and cases relating to the running of the empire (tried at Athens), see Meiggs, *Empire*, ch.12, and **134** n.7. The sentence can only be understood in relation to what follows; the Athenians expected praise for using the judicial process at all.

180. The people of Athens

We shall never know in detail what moved the Athenian *dēmos* to accept war; presumably it hesitantly accepted the Periklean analysis (see **181**) or, on a more straightforward level, did not accept that the Spartans could tell the Athenians what to do about their empire. But that did not prevent them from laughing at two stories told by the comic poet Aristophanes, stories which illustrate to perfection the dangers involved in using the evidence provided by his plays (see p.8); the motives suggested in the stories are attributed to Perikles in all seriousness in the account given by Diodorus XII.38–40, derived from the fourth-century historian Ephorus.

(A) 'Now it's true that I really hate the Lakedaimonians and wish that Poseidon of Tainaron[1] would cause an earthquake and bring all their houses down; for I too have had my vines cut down. But only friends are here to listen to what I say;[2] so I ask why we blame this on the Lakedaimonians. For some among us – I do not mean the whole *polis*, remember that, I do not mean the whole *polis* – wretched little men, misbegotten, worthless half-foreign miscreants, took to denouncing cloaks from Megara;[3] and if they saw a cucumber or a hare or a piglet or garlic or coarse salt, it was taken as Megarian and confiscated and sold the same day. All this was a mere trifle and just the way we do things here; but then some young players at *kottabos*[4] got drunk and went to Megara and stole Simaitha from a brothel; and then the Megarians, infuriated by the loss, stole two of Aspasia's girls in return.[5] And *that* was how the war began, involving all the Greeks – with three whores. For then Perikles the Olympian[6] in his anger thundered and lightened and turned Greece upside down; he passed laws which sound like drinking songs 'that the Megarians be expelled from land and *agora* and sea and sky'.[7] Then the Megarians, since they were slowly starving, asked the Lakedaimonians to get the *psēphisma* passed because of the whores revoked; although they kept on asking us, we refused; the clash of shields followed at once.'

Aristophanes, Acharnians 509–539

(B) (Hermes explains how Peace departed.) 'Pheidias, guilty of misconduct, was the original cause of the trouble; for Perikles then became frightened lest he share his fate, dreading your instinct (to punish) and your fierce manner; so before he himself came to any harm, he stirred the *polis* up. With the one little spark of the Megarian *psēphisma* he set this war ablaze . . .'

Aristophanes, *Peace* 605–610

1 Poseidon, god of earthquakes as well as of the sea, had a famous shrine on Mt Tainaron in Lakonia.
2 See **160C**, from which this passage follows on.
3 For the process of denunciation, with its reward to the informer (*sykophantēs*) see **214**. For the 'Megarian decrees' see **178** n.2.
4 A game of chance.
5 As Aspasia was Perikles' mistress, the accusation that she kept a brothel was an understandable piece of abuse, compare **157**.
6 The epithet reflects Perikles' position, see **181**.
7 The absurdity of this list prevents its use to reconstruct the terms of the *psēphisma*.

181. The position of Perikles

The crucial nature of the decision taken by the Athenians in 432 and the way in which Aristophanes took it for granted that the responsibility for that decision lay with Perikles (**180**) forces us to consider again (see **148**) his position and his relationship with the *dēmos* in these years (compare the famous characterisation of that position by Thucydides at II.65, **209**). K. J. Dover, *'Dekatos autos'*, *JHS* 80 (1960), 61–77, has shown that he occupied no position of formal authority within the college of ten *stratēgoi* either earlier or after he was re-instated in 430 (Thuc. II.65.4); and when 'he did not call an *ekklēsia* or any other gathering of the Athenians' in 431 (II.22.1), he was merely refraining from exercising a right to action and not avoiding doing something he should have done (compare Meiggs and Lewis no.65 (Methone decree), lines 55–6, for the right of the *stratēgoi* to raise matters ahead of business otherwise given priority). More important, even the picture of *de facto* pre-eminence which emerges from the sober words of Thucydides at I.127.3 (below), 139.4 (see **194**) and II.59.2 requires modification; despite the fact that acceptance of the Kerkyran appeal must have been Periklean policy, Thucydides thought that the *ekklēsia* which heard the appeal was going to reject it and in the end it only voted for an *epimachia*, a defensive alliance (see **176**). And the *sort* of speech which Thucydides puts into Perikles' mouth implies that a great deal of hard reasoning was necessary to convince the *ekklēsia*; certainly the Spartans thought that the position of Perikles was vulnerable and worth attacking in the propaganda war which preceded the outbreak of hostilities; that they were not wholly wrong is shown by the response of Perikles himself (II.13.1).

Meanwhile, they sent embassies to the Athenians with various complaints, so that if they failed to pay attention to any of them they themselves would have the best possible grounds for going to war. And the first embassy which the Spartans sent instructed the Athenians to drive out 'the abomination of the goddess'; the abomination came about in this way.[1] (127) This then was the abomination which the Spartans instructed the Athenians to drive out, posing in the first place as defenders of the gods, but knowing that Perikles the son of Xanthippos was tainted through his mother's family[2] and thinking that if he were exiled they would find everything easier as far as the Athenians were concerned. They did not, however, really expect that he would suffer exile so much as that they would bring him into ill-repute with the *polis* on the grounds that the war was in part the result of his position. For he was the most powerful man of his generation and in exercising political leadership he opposed the Lakedaimonians at all turns and allowed no concessions, but encouraged the Athenians to go to war. (The Athenians countered with similar demands of a religious nature.)

Thucydides 1.126.1–2 and 127

1 See **64**.
2 See family tree on p.133.

Part III

The Peloponnesian War

Whether we lay the greater stress on issues and events from 435 onwards (Ch. 17) or on the long-term problems of co-existence between the Athenians and the Spartans (Ch. 16), the plain fact is that in 431 the two blocs went to war against each other; and 27 years later, in 404, after 'the greatest upheaval to affect the Greeks and, in part, the *barbaroi* as well – in short, the majority of the human race' (Thuc. I.1), the Spartans finally achieved their declared objective and the Athenian *hēgemonia* was in ruins. The very term 'Peloponnesian War' (on which see de Ste Croix, *Origins*, 294–5) is coined, obviously enough, from an Athenian stand-point, though apparently not until several centuries afterwards; and in fact our knowledge and understanding of the events which give it substance is conditioned, to an extent hardly paralleled by any other war before or since, by one man, one Athenian, above all – Thucydides. Thucydides was a great and admirable historian in any company, and our problem in seeing the war through his eyes (until 411, at any rate, where his account breaks off unfinished) is certainly not one of having to eliminate crude bias in favour of his own side and against the enemy, but the more subtle difficulty of escaping – if and when we feel the need to – from his overall interpretation of events and their significance. It is, for example, at his insistence (v.26) that 431–404 is regarded as a single war at all, rather than ten years of the so-called Archidamian War (431–421) and nine of the Ionian or Dekeleian War (413–404), linked by a period of uneasy peace. The latter view, evidently, was the more common in his day, and persisted into the fourth century despite him; and modern scholars, while taking a long-term perspective of which Thucydides himself would have approved, sometimes use it to argue that 'there is a very real break in the years 413–411, when Athenian superiority had been broken, Persia entered the war, and Sparta became a sea-power. Thereaf-ter the new configuration of international politics remained stable for a generation until the 370s' (Davies, *Democracy*, 129). Yet, illuminating though it can be to make fresh assessments in this way, the validity of Thucydides' periodisation, at least in a formal sense, can scarcely be contested, and we are content to follow it here.

There is not the scope in this book to document the war as it unfolded year by year; and in any case that task has already been done, with diligence and acumen, by Thucydides himself. Instead we give here a chronological table of the main events, and then pick out for documentation eight topics illustrating important thematic threads within a general diachronic framework.

431 Thebans attack Plataiai (spring)
    First Peloponnesian invasion of Attika (summer)
    Athenian naval raid (*periplous*) round the Peloponnesian coast
    Athenian army and fleet ravage the Megarid (autumn). (This repeated yearly (Thuc. II.31.3), later twice yearly (VI.66.1), until 424)
Winter 431/0 Perikles' Funeral Speech
430 Second Peloponnesian invasion of Attika (summer)
    Outbreak of the Plague in Attika
    Second Athenian *periplous*
Winter 430/29 Poteidaia, besieged since 432, surrenders to the Athenians
                 Phormion and an Athenian fleet based at Naupaktos
429 Peloponnesians lay siege to Plataiai
    Naval victories of Phormion in the Corinthian Gulf (continuing into winter 429/8)
    Death of Perikles (autumn)
428 Third Peloponnesian invasion of Attika (summer)
    Revolt of Mytilene from the Athenians
427 Fourth Peloponnesian invasion of Attika (summer)
    Surrender of Mytilene to the Athenians, and of Plataiai to the Peloponnesians
    Stasis in Kerkyra
    First Athenian expedition to Sicily
Winter 427/6 Recurrence of the Plague (Thuc. III.87)
426 (Fifth Peloponnesian invasion of Attika turned back by earthquakes, but:)
    Peloponnesians establish an *apoikia* at Herakleia in Trachis
    Demosthenes' Aitolian expedition
Winter 426/5 Athenians purify Delos
            Battle of Olpai
425 Aristophanes' *Acharnians* staged (January)
    Fifth Peloponnesian invasion of Attika (spring), abandoned at news of Pylos (below)
    Athenian reinforcements sent to Sicily
    Athenian occupation of Pylos and capture of the Spartiates on Sphakteria
    Extraordinary reassessment of tribute in the Athenian empire
424 Athenians capture Kythera, Nisaia, and Megara's Long Walls
    Peace in Sicily: Athenian forces withdraw, and *stratēgoi* punished
    Athenian invasion of Boiotia
    The Spartan Brasidas in Thrake: Akanthos and Stagiros revolt from Athens

Winter 424/3 Athenian defeat at Delion (Boiotia)
    Brasidas captures Amphipolis, Torone, etc.
    Megarians recover their Long Walls
423 One-year armistice begins (spring)
  Revolts of Skione and Mende. The Athenians recover Mende and besiege
  Skione
422 (Expiry of the armistice (spring))
  Battle of Amphipolis: deaths of Kleon and Brasidas
Winter 422/1 Peace negotiations begin
421 'Peace of Nikias' concluded (spring), followed by defensive alliance between
  the Athenians and the Spartans
420 Alkibiades engineers a quadruple alliance between Athens, Argos, Elis and
  Mantineia
418 Spartan victory in the Battle of Mantineia: end of the quadruple alliance
Winter 418/17 Alliance between Sparta and Argos
416 Athenians besiege and (in winter 416/15) capture Melos
Winter 416/15 Egestaian embassy to Athens, and debate on a (second) expedi-
    tion to Sicily
415 Mutilation of the Hermai. The expedition sails, but Alkibiades is recalled
Winter 415/14 Athenian victory at Syracuse
    Alkibiades in Sparta
414 Athenians begin blockade of Syracuse
  The Spartan Gylippos sent out to help the Syracusans
Winter 414/13 Another Peloponnesian invasion of Attika prepared
413 Peloponnesians invade Attika (early spring) and fortify Dekeleia
  Athenian reinforcements sent to Sicily
  Athenians defeated in the Great Harbour at Syracuse, and at Epipolai
  Total destruction of the Athenian expeditionary forces
Winter 413/12 (continuing into 412) The allies of Athens begin to revolt
    The Persian satraps Tissaphernes and Pharnabazos negotiate with
    the Spartans
412 Revolts of Chios, Klazomenai and Miletos
  First treaty between Sparta and Persia
Winter 412/11 Second treaty between Sparta and Persia
411 Further revolts of Athenian allies
  Third (and definitive) treaty between Sparta and Persia
  Oligarchic *coup d'état* in Athens: the rule of the Four Hundred (May–
  September)
  Revolt of Euboia
  Deposition of the Four Hundred, in favour of moderate oligarchy
  Athenian victory at Battle of Kynossema
410 Athenian victory at Battle of Kyzikos
  Radical democracy restored
409 and 408 Athenians recover some of their allies
407 Alkibiades returns to Athens
  Kyros becomes super-satrap of coastal Asia Minor, and begins a fruitful
  relationship with the new Spartan admiral Lysandros

406 Athenians defeated at the Battle of Notion; Alkibiades deposed
   Battle of Arginousai; trial of the Athenian *stratēgoi*
405 Athenians defeated at the Battle of Aigospotamoi (late summer)
Winter 405/4 Athens blockaded
404 The Athenians capitulate (spring)
   Rule of the 'Thirty Tyrants' (until September 403)

18 Spartan strategy during the Archidamian War

As the climax of the interchange of demands and counter-demands which Thucydides represents as filling the period between the Spartan and the Athenian votes for war (**181**), the Spartans insisted that the Athenians 'let the Greeks be autonomous' (see **194A**) in other words, relinquish their Aegean *hēgemonia*. The Athenians, despite what Perikles is made to say in Thuc. 1.144.2 (**194A**), had no aggressive objective corresponding to this. It is therefore obvious that whereas the Athenians could have settled for simple survival in the war (see Thuc. 1.144.1, II.13.9 and II.65.7), the Spartans needed to win it outright. Unfortunately – for them – they turned out to be ill-equipped to do so, at least during the Archidamian War. The theoretical basis of Peloponnesian strategy was necessarily well known to all concerned (see **183**), but since the same must have been true of the Athenian counter-strategy there was every possibility of stalemate unless one side or the other could make a really telling move, or else capitalise on their opponents' mistakes or bad luck. It was undeniably bad luck for the Athenians that in 430 they fell victim to the Plague (**196**), but the Spartans found no way to take advantage of this, and for the first seven years of the war their basic strategy – annual invasions of Attika (**186**) – proved increasingly and embarrassingly ineffective. However, from a position perilously close to rock bottom in 425/4 (**190–191**), Spartan fortunes did revive significantly before the peace of 421, partly because the Athenians were beginning to have severe financial problems (see **200** and **201**) and partly because the Spartans themselves had at last turned to a more productive tactic: fostering revolt within the Athenian empire (**192**); so both sides were ready for the peace (**193**) when it came.

See further: P. A. Brunt, 'Spartan policy and strategy in the Archidamian War', *Phoenix* 19 (1965), 255–80; Forrest, *Sparta*, 110–14; I. S. Moxon, 'Thucydides' account of Spartan strategy and foreign policy in the Archidamian War', *Rivista Storica dell'Antichità*, 8(1978), 7–26; Cartledge, *Sparta*, 234–49.

182. Spartan psychology

Thucydides puts into the mouth of some Corinthian delegates speaking at Sparta in 432 a speech which contains a sharp delineation of the psychological contrast between the Spartans and their opponents the Athenians; for one extract already given see **87**. In its reflection in the practice of strategy, this contrast took some time to emerge, in the Athenians' case, thanks to the authoritative caution of Perikles (see **194**); for Sparta, however, it provides the keynote for much of this chapter. See also Archidamos in Thuc. 1.80–85 (including **183A**, below).

'You Spartans are the only Greeks who remain passive, defending yourselves not by exercising your power but by threatening to exercise it; and you alone attack an enemy's strength not in its initial stage but when it has grown and doubled. You used, of course, to have the reputation of being safe and reliable – but surely actions speak louder than words: the Persians, as we (Corinthians) well know, came from the ends of the earth and reached the Peloponnesos before you mounted any decent sort of opposition to them. Well, unlike the far-off Persians the Athenians are your neighbours, yet still you disregard them, and instead of attacking them yourselves you choose rather to defend yourselves when an attack comes from them – thereby taking on a hazardous struggle with opponents who have become far more powerful. And yet you are aware that it was the *barbaroi* themselves who contributed most to their own defeat, and that most of our successes, so far, against the Athenians themselves have been more the result of their mistakes than of your assistance to us. Indeed it might be said that, in pinning their hopes on you, certain states came to ruin because their trust led them into action unprepared.'[1]

Thucydides 1.69.4–5

1 E.g. Thasos (see **169**) and, arguably, Euboia (**173**).

183. The speeches of 432

In three further speeches, all set in 432, Thucydides pieces together the theory and practicalities of Spartan strategy. The cautious old king Archidamos (A) and the fiery *ephoros* Sthenelaidas (B) speak at the same conference as the Corinthians of **182**, and its result is that the Spartan assembly votes for war (see B); the Corinthians speak again (C) at a second congress later in the year. (On the difficult chronology of the year 432 consult de Ste Croix, *Origins*, 317–28.)

(A) *Archidamos*
'I have had personal experience of many wars, Spartans, and I see amongst you men of the same age as myself – who are therefore not

likely to be naively enthusiastic for a war, as most men might be, or to think it a good or a safe thing. Anyone examining the matter sensibly would conclude that this war which you are now discussing is not likely to be a trifling one. When, you see, our opponents are (other) Peloponnesians and our neighbours, our strength is of the same sort as theirs and we can speedily attack them at every point. But to fight the Athenians means taking on men whose territory is far away,[1] who besides have great experience of the sea and are well equipped in all other respects, with wealth both private and public, ships, horses, arms, and a population larger than that of any other place in the Greek world, and who moreover possess many allies who pay them tribute. How can we think nothing of starting a war against these men? On what do we rely if we rush into one unprepared? Our ships? But our navy is inferior to theirs; and if we are to train it properly and prepare ourselves to match them, that will take time. Our wealth? Here their superiority is far greater still. we have no public funds, and cannot readily raise money from private sources.[2] (81) Perhaps some see grounds for confidence in our superiority in arms and in numbers, which means that we can invade their land and lay it waste. Yet there is other land, a great deal of it, which they control, and they can import what they need by sea. And if we attempt to induce their allies to revolt, we shall have in addition to support them with a fleet, since most of them are islanders.[3] What sort of a war will it be, then, from our point of view? Unless we can either gain the upper hand at sea or else deprive them of the revenues upon which their navy depends for support, we shall be the ones who get the worst of it; and what will happen then is that we shall not even be in a position to make an honourable peace – particularly if it is believed that we were the ones who began the quarrel. Let us not, for heaven's sake, bolster ourselves up with the hope that if we devastate their land the war will soon be over. My fear is that we shall instead be bequeathing it to our sons, so unlikely is it that the Athenians' spirit will permit them either to become slaves in their own land or to be panic-stricken by the war as if they were men of no experience. (83) Nobody should think it cowardice if we, many as we are, do not rush into an attack upon a single *polis*: for they too have allies, as many as we have, and their allies pay them tribute.[4] Particularly when a land-power is fighting a sea-power, war is a matter, for the most part, not of arms but of the expenditure of money which gives arms their usefulness. So let us first of all set about acquiring some money, before we are carried away by what our allies have to say. It is we who will bear most of the responsibility for what happens, good or bad, so they must allow us the leisure to assess the situation before we act.'

Thucydides 1.80–81; 83

(B) *Sthenelaidas*

'Others may well have money and ships and horses, but we have good allies, and we ought not to betray them to the Athenians. Nor are the issues here to be settled by law-suits and speeches, for it is not words which are doing us harm; what we must do is to exact retribution speedily and with all our might. I do not care to be told that when we are being wronged what we ought to do is *talk* about it; lengthy deliberations are more suited to those who are planning to do wrong themselves. So, Spartans, cast your votes for the honour of Sparta and for war! Do not allow the Athenians to grow stronger still, and do not leave your allies utterly in the lurch, but with the gods' help let us strike at those who do us injury.' (87) After speaking in this vein, he himself, as *ephoros*, put the matter to the vote. Now the assembly of the Spartans actually reaches decisions by shouting, not casting votes;[5] and Sthenelaidas declared that he could not tell which shout was the louder. What he wanted was to make them show their verdict openly and thus create more enthusiasm for going to war, so he made an announcement: 'Spartans, those of you who think that the treaty has been broken and that the Athenians are in the wrong, get up and stand there' – and he showed them the spot – 'and those who do not think so, on the other side.' So they rose and divided; and the great majority were of the opinion that the treaty had been broken.

Thucydides 1.86.3–87.3

(C) *The Corinthians*

'There are many reasons why we are likely to win. First of all we are superior in numbers and military experience; secondly we all, one and all, obey orders; and thirdly, as regards a fleet, where they are so strong, we shall be able to equip one not only from the resources which we each possess at present but also by using the (temple) funds at Delphi and Olympia. Such loans, you see, will enable us to offer higher wages and tempt away their foreign rowers: for the power of the Athenians is not so much home-grown as bought for cash. We, on the other hand, would be less affected in this way, as our strength lies in men rather than money. (122) And there are other ways, too, in which we can wage this war. We can make their allies revolt – the best means, this, of depriving them of the revenues which are their strength; and we can plant forts in their *chōra*.[6] And there will be all sorts of other measures unforeseeable at the moment: for war is not something that runs on pre-planned lines, but generally calls for skills to meet changing circumstances.'

Thucydides 1.121.2–3; 122.1

1 Compare the Old Oligarch ([Xen] *Ath. Pol.*) II.5.
2 See **188**.

3 The Corinthians (c, below) see no such difficulties.
4 Sparta's allies paid no tribute (Thuc. 1.19).
5 Compare **51**.
6 For the implementation of this plan – 20 years later – see **228** and **229**.

184. The fighting begins: Plataiai

After the structural complexity of his Book I, Thucydides starts in Book II a comparatively straightforward narrative account of the Peloponnesian War itself, from spring 431. (Note the elaborate chronological references here, to pinpoint its beginning.) We read that hostilities were actually initiated not by the Spartans but by the Thebans, who seized this opportunity to attack their *bête noire* (see **62**), Plataiai.

This is the point from which the war between the Athenians and the Peloponnesians – and their respective allies[1] – actually begins; from now on the two sides had no further communication with each other except through heralds,[2] and once they had begun the war they continued it without intermission. I have recorded its events as they occurred each summer and winter.[3]

(2) For fourteen years the Thirty Years' Peace, concluded after the (re)capture of Euboia,[4] remained unbroken; but in the fifteenth year – which was the forty-eighth year of the priestess-ship of Chrysis at Argos, when Ainesias was *ephoros* in Sparta and Pythodoros still had four months to serve as *archōn* in Athens,[5] in the tenth month after the battle at Poteidaia,[6] and just as spring was beginning – a body of rather more than 300 Thebans, with the *boiōtarchoi*[7] Pythangelos son of Phyleidas and Diemporos son of Onetorides in command, came at about the first watch of the night and made an armed entry into Plataiai, a Boiotian town which was an ally of Athens.[8] They had been called in by a party of Plataians, Naukleides and his supporters, who opened the gates to them. The aim of these men, in their pursuit of power, was to destroy those of their fellow-*politai* who were their opponents and to bring the *polis* over into Theban control; they had therefore put this plan into effect through the agency of one of the most influential Thebans, Eurymachos son of Leontiades. The fact was that the Thebans realised that the war was on the way and wanted to get their hands on Plataiai – which had always been hostile to them – while it was still peace-time and the war had not yet been openly declared. This indeed was why they were not seen as they entered the town, because no sentries had been posted.

Thucydides II.1–2.3

1 See **185**.
2 Who were safe from attack.

3 Thuc. briefly explains the rationale of this system in v.20.

4 In 446/5: see **173**.

5 The transmitted texts say *two* months but this cannot be right: at the beginning of spring (see below), i.e. in early March, the *archōn* of 432/1 had *four* months still in office.

6 Another problematical figure: the texts have the *sixth* month, but chronology seems to demand the tenth (or possibly ninth); see Gomme, *Commentary* I, 421–4.

7 The eleven chief civil and military executives of the Boiotian League; see the note in Gomme, *Commentary* III, 560.

8 See **62**.

185. The Spartans and their allies

After completing his account of the Theban attack on Plataiai (II.2–6), Thucydides devotes three chapters to a general description of the preparations undertaken by the two sides, and lists their respective alliances.

Once the affair at Plataiai had occurred and the Peace had been demonstrably violated, the Athenians began their preparations for war, and so did the Spartans and their allies. Both sides had it in mind to send embassies to the King (of Persia) and to any other *barbaroi* from whom they might hope to obtain support, and they were already trying to make alliances with those *poleis* not yet committed to one side or the other. The Spartans, in addition to the ships that they could already muster, ordered more to be built by those states in Italy and Sicily which had chosen their side; the number was to be commensurate with the size of each *polis*, and this was to produce a fleet totalling 500 ships in all.[1] These *poleis* were also to make ready a prescribed sum of money; and until all these preparations were completed they were to remain generally neutral, allowing Athenians access to their harbours in single vessels only . . . (8) None of this planning – on either side – was on a small scale; both sides put all their strength into the war effort. And this was only natural: everyone tackles a project with more enthusiasm at the beginning, and on this occasion there were plenty of young men, both in the Peloponnesos and in Athens, who knew nothing of war and who were therefore willing participants in this one. As for the rest of Greece, it hung in total suspense, as its leading *poleis* came into conflict with one another . . . For the most part, though, it was the Spartan side which attracted the greater goodwill, especially since their claim was to be liberating Greece. Everyone, individuals and *poleis* alike, was determined to support them in every possible way, verbal and practical,[2] and everyone felt that unless he himself took an active role the whole cause would suffer a setback. This shows the extent of the anger which the

Athenians brought out in most people, some of whom wished to rid themselves of Athenian rule, while the rest were afraid that they might come under it.

(9) . . . The Spartans had as their allies all the Peloponnesians south of the Isthmos apart from the Argives and the Achaians, who at this stage had friendly relations with both sides; one Achaian state, Pellene, did in fact join the Spartans from the outset and fight with them – and ultimately the rest did the same. Outside the Peloponnesos the Spartans could call on the Megarians, the Boiotians,[3] the Lokrians, the Phokians, the Amprakiots, the Leukadians and the Anaktorians. Of these, the Corinthians, the Megarians, the Sikyonians, the Pellenians, the Eleians, the Amprakiots and the Leukadians supplied ships, while cavalry was contributed by the Boiotians, the Phokians and the Lokrians; the other *poleis* provided infantry. This was the Spartan alliance.

Thucydides II.7–9.3*

1 An absurdly large figure: in 412 the Sicilians sent a mere 22 ships (Thuc. VIII.26.1)! See the note in Gomme, *Commentary* II, 7.
2 See **188**.
3 Except, of course, Plataiai.

186. The first Peloponnesian invasion of Attika

The mainstay of Spartan strategy in the Archidamian War will have come as no surprise to anyone: annual invasions of Attika. The first, in summer 431, was repeated in 430 (Thuc. II.47.2). In 429 the siege of Plataiai took precedence (II.71.1), but the Peloponnesians were back in Attika in 428 (III.1) and 427 (III.26). In 426 the invasion force was turned back by earthquakes at the Isthmos (III.89.1) and the Spartans had to content themselves with planting their *apoikia* in Trachis (see **189**). The year 425 saw a fifth invasion (IV.2.1), but it was abandoned after fifteen days (IV.6) at the news from Pylos (see **190**). The ineffectuality of the policy, 'foreseen' by Archidamos (**183A**), is self-evident.

Immediately after the episode at Plataiai the Spartans sent messengers through the Peloponnesos and to their allies outside it, with instructions to the *poleis* to prepare the troops and supplies necessary for a foreign expedition – their intention being to invade Attika. When everything was ready they met together at the Isthmos at the appointed time, each *polis* bringing two thirds of its forces.

(18) The first place in Attika that the Peloponnesian army came to as it advanced was Oinoe, from where they planned to launch the invasion. And while they were making camp there they also began to prepare for attacks upon its walls, by various means including siege-engines; this was because Oinoe, by virtue of its position on the border between

Attika and Boiotia, had been made into a fortified stronghold and was used as such by the Athenians in time of war. So the Peloponnesians prepared to mount these attacks, and in all sorts of ways wasted a lot of time over it . . . (19) Then, when despite all their various assaults on Oinoe they were unable to capture it, and the Athenians were making no moves towards negotiation, they set off at last from Oinoe – about 80 days after the events at Plataiai – and invaded Attika just as summer was ripening the grain. In command was Archidamos son of Zeuxidamos, king of the Lakedaimonians. What they did first was to make camp and begin to ravage the territory round Eleusis and the Thriasian plain. They also defeated the Athenian cavalry, near the so-called Streams. Then, keeping Mount Aigaleos on their right, they advanced through Kropia until they reached Acharnai, the largest of what are known as the demes of Attika;[1] here they stopped to make camp, and stayed for a long time ravaging the area. (20) The reasoning behind Archidamos' decision to keep his army on stand-by for battle at Acharnai instead of continuing the invasion by descending to the plain was, so it is said, that he hoped that the Athenians, who were at their peak in terms of a large population of young men and who were also prepared for war as never before, would perhaps come out and fight him rather than allow their land to be devastated . . . (21) . . . And indeed when the Athenians saw this army at Acharnai, a mere seven miles from their *polis*, they were unable to bear it any longer: they were horrified, naturally enough, to watch their land being ravaged before their very eyes – something that the younger men had never seen before, and their elders only during the Persian invasion – and it was generally felt, particularly by the young, that instead of letting this happen they should go out and fight . . . (22) Perikles, however, saw that for the moment they were so angry that they were not thinking properly. He himself was convinced that his own view, about not going out to fight, was the right one; so he summoned no *ekklēsia* or any (other) gathering,[2] for fear that if they did meet together they would be influenced by anger rather than good judgment and so make a mistake; all he did was to see to the defences of the *polis* and keep it as calm as he could . . . (23) And since the Athenians did not come out and face them in battle, the Peloponnesians left their camp at Acharnai and began to ravage some of the other demes which lie between Mount Parnes and Mount Brilessos[3] . . . They remained in Attika for as long as their supplies lasted and then withdrew by a different route – through Boiotia – from that by which they had come. This took them past Oropos, where they laid waste the so-called Graian land, which was cultivated by the men of Oropos as subjects of the Athenians.[4] Then, once back in the Peloponnesos, they were sent back to their various *poleis*.

Thucydides II. 10. 1–2; 18–23★

1 The demes: see **76**. Acharnai was indeed the largest of them, by far; on the test of how many men each deme sent annually to the *boulē*, it made up almost half the *phylē* to which it belonged.

2 This he did almost certainly by means of personal influence, not special powers: see **181**.

3 Brilessos is more generally known as Pentelikon. It was the source of Attika's best marble.

4 In terms of natural topography Oropos was part of Boiotia rather than Attika, albeit appropriated by the Athenians in (probably) the sixth century, and it was never incorporated into Attika proper. See the note in Gomme, *Commentary* II, 80–1.

187. Unsuccessful Peloponnesian attack on Peiraieus

In 429 came one of the Spartans' rare moments of tactical initiative – a surprise attack on the Athenian port of Peiraieus; and we may think it no great surprise that, according to Thucydides, one of the prime movers in the venture was Brasidas, the man who a few years later was to be responsible for Sparta's greatest successes in the Archidamian War (see **192**). On this earlier occasion, however, a daring plan was spoiled by timid execution.

Before dispersing the fleet which had retired to Corinth and the Gulf of Krisa,[1] Knemos and Brasidas and the other Peloponnesian commanders decided, on the advice of the Megarians, to make an attempt, as winter was beginning, upon the Athenians' harbour, Peiraieus. It had been left open and unguarded – and reasonably so, given the Athenians' great naval superiority. The plan was that each sailor should take his oar, his mat and his thong[2] and go on foot from Corinth to the sea on the Athenian side (of the Isthmos); once there, they were to hurry to Megara, launch from the dockyard at Nisaia 40 ships of theirs which happened to be there, and sail straight for Peiraieus. It was known that no fleet was on guard there, and that the Athenians did not at all anticipate such a sudden enemy attack; the Athenian view was that either their opponents would not have the courage to make their preparations at leisure and mount an open assault, or else, if they did have such a thing in mind, there would certainly be advance warning of it.

So that was the plan, and it was put into effect without delay. Reaching Nisaia at night they launched the ships and set sail – not, however, to Peiraieus, in accordance with their original intention, for the danger in that made them afraid, apart from the fact that the wind is said to have been against them; they sailed instead to the promontory of Salamis that faces Megara. Here there was an (Athenian) guard-post and three ships on watch to prevent entry to and exit from Megara. The Peloponnesians attacked this post, towed away the vessels empty and began to ravage the rest of Salamis, falling upon its people unawares. (94) The Salaminians did manage to light beacons nonetheless, to warn Athens of an enemy attack, and a panic erupted there which was as great as any in the course of the war:[3] those in the *astu* thought that the enemy had already sailed into Peiraieus, while in Peiraieus it was believed that they had taken Salamis and were all but sailing into Peiraieus too. And in fact they might easily have done so, wind or no wind, if only they had made up their minds not to be timid. But as it was, next morning the Athenians went in full force to defend Peiraieus: they launched their ships, embarked in haste and great confusion and sailed for Salamis; meanwhile the infantry was set to guard Peiraieus. The Peloponnesians had by now overrun most of Salamis, and when they realised that this relief expedition was on its way they hastily sailed off back to Nisaia, taking with them what they had captured – men, booty, and the three ships from the Boudoron guard-post. Apart from anything else they feared for the condition of their own ships, which had not been launched for so long and were by no means watertight. From Megara they made their way back to Corinth overland. As for the Athenians, having failed to intercept the enemy on Salamis they too sailed away; and after this episode they were more careful in future to keep Peiraieus safe, by closing up the harbour entrance and taking other precautions.

Thucydides II.93–94

1 After defeats at the hands of the Athenian fleet under Phormion: see Thuc. II.79–92.
2 See the notes on this equipment, especially the 'thong', in Gomme, *Commentary* II,237–8.
3 The Archidamian War only, we must presume: later passages (VII.71.7, VIII.1 and VIII.96.1) refer to apparently more serious panics after 421.

188. Contributions to the Spartan war-fund

The financial weakness of the Peloponnesians in general and of the Spartans in particular, emphasised by three speakers in Thucydides (see **183A**, **183C** and **194A**), is strikingly documented by one of the extremely few Spartan inscriptions. It records contributions – some in cash, some in kind, some from states and some from individuals – to the Spartan war-effort; and the contrast that it offers with the Athenian tribute-lists, reflecting massive and regular cash revenues and a financial administration to match them, is obviously enormous. The inscription is in fact impossible to date with any precision: it could be placed during the Archidamian War, but equally it could belong twenty or thirty years later; see the commentary in Meiggs and Lewis *ad loc.* For details see, as well as Meiggs and Lewis (and the notes below), Fornara no. 132.

(Front)

[————— to the Lak]edaimonian[s—]
[————] hundred darics.[1] [——]
[————— to the L]akedaimonians, for the
[war,] nine minas and ten staters.[2]
[Gave to the Lak]edaimonians Lykeidas' son
[—————]os of Ole[n]os[3] gave [to the Lake] –
[daimonians] for the war, trireme [——————][4]
[——— in silver,] thirty-two minas. [Gave]
[——————] friends amongst the Chians who [———]
[——————] Aiginetan staters. [———]
[————— to the] Lakedaimonians for the [war,]
[*medimnoi*][5] four thousand, and another
[*medimnoi*] four thousand, and of raisins
[————— tal]ents
[———————]son gave [to the Lakedaimo] –
[nians ———] in abundance, and eight hundred darics
[—— and in] silver three talents.
[————] gave, for the war,
[a silver] talent, thirty minas [and]
[————] three thousand *medimnoi*, and [another]
[*medimnoi* ——]ty,[6] and, in silver, sixty
[minas. Gave] the Ephesians to the Lakedaim[o] –
[nians, for the] war, one thousand dar[ics.]

(Side)

The Melians gave to the Lakedaimonians twenty minas in silver.
Molokros[7] gave to the Lakedaimonians talents of silver.[8] The Melians
gave to the Lakedaimonians [———]

Meiggs and Lewis no.67

1 Persian gold pieces.
2 Large silver coins – presumably, as in another donation mentioned later, of the
   Aiginetan weight-standard.
3 In Achaia. Ole[r]os, in Crete, is an alternative.
4 Possibly trireme[s' pay].
5 Of grain, presumably (here and throughout).
6 Some multiple of ten between thirty and ninety.
7 Or perhaps Molobros, cf. Thuc. IV.8.9. In either case, possibly an individual
   Spartan.
8 The line is evidently corrupt, and should perhaps read a (single) talent.

189. The Spartan 'apoikia' at Herakleia

With the Peloponnesian invasion of Attika scheduled for summer 426 turning back *en route* (Thuc. III.89.1), the main Spartan initiative of that summer was something different, and potentially much more enterprising: the establishment of an *apoikia* at Herakleia in Trachis, a few miles north west of the pass at Thermopylai. The motives for the foundation, and the reasons for its ultimate ineffectuality and failure, are fully brought out in Thucydides' account.

See further: A. Andrewes, 'Two notes on Lysander', *Phoenix* 25 (1971), 217–26, and 'Spartan imperialism?' in P. D. A. Garnsey and C. R. Whittaker (eds.), *Imperialism in the Ancient World* (Cambridge, 1978), 95–9; Cartledge, *Sparta*, 238–9.

It was about this time that the Lakedaimonians established an *apoikia* at Herakleia in Trachis. The reasoning behind it was as follows. There are, altogether, three divisions amongst the Malian people: the Paralians, the Irieans and the Trachinians; and it was the Trachinians who, after faring badly in a war with their neighbours the Oitaians, planned at first to become allies of the Athenians. Subsequently, however, they began to fear that the Athenians were not to be trusted, and so, having chosen Teisamenos as their spokesman, they sent him to Sparta instead. And the embassy was joined by the men of Doris, the Spartan homeland,[1] who had the same request to make, for they too were suffering at the hands of the Oitaians. When they had heard the envoys, the Spartans resolved to send out the *apoikia*, as they wished to help both the Trachinians and the Dorians; and at the same time they felt that such a *polis*, once established, would be well placed for the war against the Athenians, in that a fleet could be prepared there for an attack on Euboia, just a short crossing away, and also by virtue of its useful position on the way to Thrake.[2] So all in all they were eager to found the place, and they began by consulting the god (Apollo) at Delphi. His command was that they should proceed, so they sent out the settlers, some of them Spartans, others *perioikoi*,[3] with an invitation for volunteers to join in from the rest of Greece – excluding the Ionians and the Achaians[4] and certain other peoples. The leaders and *oikistai*[5] were three Spartans, Leon, Alkidas and Damagon. So they established and fortified afresh the *polis* which is now called Herakleia, situated about five miles from Thermopylai and two-and-a-half from the sea. They also began to build dockyards and, to make it easier to guard the place, blocked off the side facing Thermopylai with a wall across the pass itself.

(93) At first, as this *polis* was taking shape, the Athenians were alarmed, thinking that the foundation was aimed particularly at Euboia; it is only a short passage across to (Cape) Kenaion in Euboia; but subsequent events turned out unexpectedly different and the place did

them no harm at all. The reason was that the Thessalians, who were the dominant power in those regions and whose land was threatened by the settlement, were frightened at the thought of having powerful neighbours; they therefore attempted constantly to harass and make war upon the new settlers, until what had begun as a very numerous population – all emboldened to go there by the idea that the *polis* would be safe because it was being founded by Spartans – was worn down to nothing. Yet the people who did most to spoil the enterprise and reduce the population were the officials sent out by the Spartans themselves: their arrival served to frighten away the majority of the settlers, who found themselves harshly and in some respects unjustly governed; and this made it all the easier for their neighbours to gain the advantage over them.

Thucydides III.92–93

1 See **3**.
2 See **192**.
3 See **44** n.4.
4 Achaians: see **185**.
5 See **18**.

190. Pylos and Sphakteria

In the summer of 425 came an episode which Thucydides recounts at great length (IV.2–41), as a measure of its central importance in the Archidamian War as a whole. It began when an Athenian fleet on its way to Sicily (see **217**) stopped off to fortify a position at Pylos in Messenia, leaving a small garrison there under the *stratēgos* Demosthenes. The news of this cut short the Peloponnesians' invasion of Attika (Thuc. IV.6), and initiated a train of events which brought the Spartans almost to their knees (see **191**).

See further: H. D. Westlake, 'The naval battle at Pylos and its consequences', *CQ* n.s.24 (1974), 211–26; and in general J. B. Wilson, *Pylos 425 B.C.* (Warminster, 1979).

When the Peloponnesians had withdrawn from Attika, the Spartiatai themselves and the *perioikoi* who were nearest at hand marched immediately to the relief of Pylos; the other Lakedaimonians, having only just returned from the other expedition, were slower in setting out.[1] Orders were also sent round the Peloponnesos for troops to go to the aid of Pylos as quickly as possible, and the Spartans sent as well for their 60 ships in Kerkyra,[2] which were hauled across the Isthmos of Leukas and thus reached Pylos without attracting the attention of the Athenian fleet at Zakynthos.[3] By this time the land forces had also arrived there. However, while the Peloponnesian ships were still on their way Demosthenes had anticipated them by sending out, in secret, two ships to inform Eurymedon and the (other) Athenians in the fleet at Zakynthos that Pylos was in danger and that they were to come to his aid; and in accordance with Demosthenes' summons the fleet had immediately set sail. The Spartans, meanwhile, were making ready to assault the fortifications both by land and by sea, in the hope that it would be easy to capture a structure which had been so hastily built and had so few occupants. They did anticipate, though, that the Athenian fleet would come from Zakynthos to defend it; and in case it should do so before they had taken the place they conceived the idea of blocking up the entrances to the harbour, so as to make it impossible for the Athenians to have an anchorage inside it. For the island called Sphakteria stretches along the mainland and lies quite close to it, which therefore makes the harbour safe and its entrances narrow: at the end opposite Pylos and the Athenian fortifications there is room for only two ships abreast, and for eight or nine at the other end, near the rest of the mainland.[4] The whole island was wooded and, being uninhabited, pathless – and almost two miles long.[5] The Spartans' plan was therefore to seal off the entrances with ships anchored[6] stem to stem. As for the island itself, they were afraid that the Athenians might use it as a base for campaigning against them, so they ferried some hoplites across to it, as well as posting others along the mainland. Thus, they reasoned, the Athenians would meet opposition both on the island and on the mainland too – where in any case they would be unable to land because, apart from this entrance behind Sphakteria, the coast around Pylos has no harbours; so the Athenians would have no base of operations from which to relieve their garrison. The Spartans accordingly thought that without running the risk of a sea-battle they could reasonably expect to capture the place by siege, since it had no food and had been occupied on the spur of the moment. And once they had reached this conclusion they began to convey the hoplites across to the island, having chosen them by lot from each of the divisions (*lochoi*). Several detachments had been over to serve their turn before the final group, the one that was caught there – 420 (Spartiatai), with helots to attend them, under the command of Epitadas son of Molobros. (This happens because the Athenian garrison holds out against the amphibious assault, and the Athenian fleet then arrives and defeats the Peloponnesian navy – leaving the men on the island stranded.)

(15) When the news of what had happened at Pylos reached Sparta it was regarded as such a major catastrophe that the authorities decided to visit the camp, see the situation for themselves and determine on the spot what to do about it. And when they realised that it was impossible to relieve the men on the island, they decided, as they were not prepared to risk the troops' being starved out or else obliged by superior

numbers to surrender, to approach the Athenian *strategoi* to see if they were willing to conclude a truce at Pylos; this done, they would then send envoys to Athens to discuss a peace-treaty under which they could recover their men without delay.

(A local armistice is indeed agreed on, and Spartan envoys do sue for peace in Athens, but Kleon sees to it that the negotiations come to nothing; so at Pylos the blockade continues.) (26) At Pylos the Athenians continued to besiege the Lakedaimonians on the island, and the Peloponnesian army remained where it was on the mainland. For the Athenians, lack of food and water made the blockade difficult: there was no spring, apart from the single one on the *akropolis* of Pylos itself, and that was small, so most of them scraped around in the shingle by the sea for such water as could be expected there. They were cramped for room, too, encamped in a confined space, and with no anchorage for the ships they had to take it in turns to eat ashore while the rest were at anchor out at sea. And the most disheartening thing of all was the surprisingly long time that the operation was taking, when what they had expected was to spend a few days blockading and capturing some men on a deserted island who had only brackish water to drink. What had happened, in fact, was that the Spartans had called for volunteers to bring in to the island ground corn and wine and cheese and other food useful in a siege. A large cash reward had been offered for this, and any helots who managed it were promised their freedom as well. So many men, and helots particularly, were engaged in the dangerous task of provisioning the islands. What they did was to put to sea from wherever they happened to be in the Peloponnesos and sail under cover of night to the side of the island which faced the open sea. They found it best to wait for a wind to bring them in to the shore, because when the wind blew in from the sea it was easier to escape the notice of the patrolling (Athenian) triremes, which were not then able to anchor all round the island. And the provisioners could make their landings as reckless as they liked, for the boats which they ran up on to the beach had been insured; besides, the hoplites would be watching out for them at the landing-places. But the Athenians intercepted anyone who risked the landing on a calm day. Underwater swimmers were also involved: they would swim through the harbour towing behind them, by a cord, skins filled with honeyed poppyseed and crushed linseed. At first the Athenians knew nothing of these swimmers, though later they posted guards to watch out for them. Both sides were operating every scheme they could think of – the Spartans to bring in the food and the Athenians to catch them at it.

(Eventually Kleon and Demosthenes make a landing on Sphakteria, by now denuded of its trees after a fire, and after a hard fight the surviving Spartans receive authorisation to surrender.)

(38) The numbers of those killed and taken alive on the island were as follows. In all, 420 hoplites had crossed to Sphakteria, and 292 of them were captured alive; the rest died. A hundred and twenty of the prisoners were Spartiatai. Athenian casualties, on the other hand, were minimal, as there had been no pitched battle. (39) The total time of the siege, from the sea-battle until the fight on the island, was 72 days. For about twenty of those days – the period during which the (Spartan) envoys were away (in Athens) at the peace-talks – the men on the island were allowed normal provisions, but for the rest of the time they lived on what could be smuggled in. Some grain and other food was in fact found on the island; this was because the commander, Epitadas, had been giving each man smaller rations than his stocks would have permitted.

Anyway, the Athenians and the Peloponnesians withdrew their forces from Pylos and each returned home; and as regards Kleon's promise, mad though it was, it had been fulfilled – he had indeed brought the men back, as he had undertaken to do, within twenty days.[7] (40) And of all the events of this war none came as a greater surprise to the Greeks than this: nobody had supposed that hunger or any other constraint would make the Lakedaimonians surrender, instead of fighting on for as long as they could and dying with their weapons in their hands; and it was difficult to believe that those who capitulated were the same sort of men as those who had died. Indeed, when a certain ally of the Athenians, some time afterwards, taunted one of the prisoners from the island by asking him whether the dead had been *kaloi k'agathoi*,[8] he was told in reply that 'Spindles would be invaluable if they picked out only the brave.' By 'spindles' the man meant arrows; and the point of his remark was that the casualties were simply those who had happened to be killed by the stones and bow-shots.

(41) When the prisoners had been brought to Athens, the Athenians decided to keep them imprisoned until some settlement could be reached – and if, before that, the Peloponnesians invaded Attika, to take them out and execute them. A garrison was sent to protect Pylos itself; and the Messenians from Naupaktos,[9] regarding the area as their own homeland – for Pylos is part of the territory that was once Messenia – also despatched some men, the best that they had, who began to send raiding parties into Lakonia and did a great deal of damage there, being able to speak the local dialect. The Lakedaimonians had never before experienced this sort of guerilla warfare, and with the helots beginning to desert they feared the further spread of revolution in their *chōra*. These were worries that they did not wish to make obvious to the Athenians, though they were still sending embassies to Athens in an attempt to recover Pylos and the prisoners. The Athenians, however, made more and more demands, and however often the Spartan envoys made the

journey they were always sent away empty-handed. So much for the events at Pylos.

Thucydides IV.8; 15; 26; 38.5–41

1 Note the precise terminology here: 'the Lakedaimonians', a broader term than 'the Spartiatai', covers the *perioikoi* also; see **44** with notes 4 and 5.
2 See Thuc. IV.2.3.
3 I.e. *en route*, still, for Sicily.
4 This is generally taken to be one of Thuc.'s few important topographical errors, for the southern entrance is almost a mile wide (see Gomme, *Commentary* III, 443), but it is possible that Thuc. meant, and indeed wrote, 'eight or nine stades' (not ships): see R. A. Bauslaugh, 'The text of Thucydides IV.8.6 and the south channel at Pylos', *JHS* 99 (1979), 1–6.
5 Three, actually.
6 Or, as Gomme believed (*Commentary* III, 444), sunk.
7 See **212**.
8 See **143**, and Gomme, *Commentary* III, 480.
9 See **169**, end.

191. Spartan despondency in 424

The summer of 424 marked the lowest ebb of Spartan morale in the Archidamian War. The Athenians had recently occupied Methana (Thuc. IV.45) and Kythera (IV.53–54) as well as Pylos, and would soon take Nisaia also (IV.66–69); so, with Naupaktos, Aigina (II.27), and allies in the north west, they had the Peloponnesos almost completely ringed.

The Spartans now saw the Athenians in possession of Kythera, and they expected other landings of this sort in their territory. But at no point did they muster to face their enemies in full force; instead they sent hoplite garrisons all over the *chōra* – their size determined by the needs of each particular area – and in general stayed very much on the defensive, afraid of some revolution occurring against their government. After the great and unexpected disaster which they had suffered on Sphakteria, Pylos and Kythera were now in Athenian hands, and they themselves were embroiled on all sides in a war where events moved so swiftly that no precautions could be taken against them. So what they did, most unusually, was to organise a force of 400 cavalry and a contingent of archers, and to proceed with the war more timidly than ever before – a war which defied their existing military organisation by being contested at sea, and a war, besides, against the Athenians, who believed that whenever they were not attacking they were sacrificing something of what they had expected to achieve.[1] At the same time, too, the Spartans were very greatly perplexed by the many reverses of fortune which they had so rapidly and unexpectedly suffered, and afraid that some other

353

catastrophe might befall them like the one on the island. Hence they had no confidence when they went into battle, and believed that everything they tried would fail. They had lost faith in themselves, having never before been used to adversity.

Thucydides IV. 55

1 Compare **87** and **182**.

192. Brasidas in Thrake

Just when the Spartans so badly needed a miracle (**191**), they got one. After several fleeting appearances in Thucydides' narrative (II.25.1, II.85–86, II.93 (see **187**), III.69–79, IV.11–12 and IV.70–74), Brasidas son of Tellis now, in the summer of 424, moves to centre-stage, as the leader of a Spartan expedition to Thrake – its object being to fulfil the plan (see **183**C) of inducing the Athenians' allies to revolt. The policy, in the hands of the shrewd and moderate Brasidas, was to prove spectacularly successful, and was arguably the only thing which allowed the Spartans to salvage as much as they did (see **193**) out of the Archidamian War.

At about the same time of the summer[1] Brasidas was on his way to the Thrakian regions, with 1,700 hoplites. When he reached Herakleia in Trachis[2] he sent a messenger ahead to his friends in Pharsalos, requesting an escort for himself and his army . . . It was no simple matter in any circumstances to go through Thessaly unescorted, and especially not with an armed force; indeed, to go through a neighbour's territory without his permission is something that all Greeks alike view with suspicion. Also, the mass of the Thessalians had always been well disposed towards the Athenians. All in all, if the Thessalians had been under a constitutional government (*isonomia*), as usual, instead of the rule of a powerful clique, Brasidas would never have been able to proceed . . . (79) It was in this way that Brasidas hurried through Thessaly before any preparations could be made to stop him, and reached Perdikkas[3] and Chalkidike. The reason why the Thrakian towns in revolt from the Athenians had, in conjunction with Perdikkas, summoned this army from the Peloponnesos was because the Athenians' successes were filling them with alarm. The Chalkidians (of Olynthos), for their part, believed that the Athenians would give priority to mounting an expedition against them; and the *poleis* nearby, which had not revolted, joined secretly in the move to have the Spartans intervene. As to Perdikkas, although he was not ready to come out into the open as an enemy of Athens, he was nonetheless nervous, on his own behalf, about the long-standing disputes between himself and the Athenians, and he was particularly keen to crush Arrhabaios, the king of the Lynkestians.

And what made it all the easier to procure this army from the Peloponnesos was the fact that at this time the Spartans were faring so badly. (80) The Athenians were now harassing the Peloponnesos in general and Spartan territory in particular, and the Spartans hoped that the best way of diverting them would be to give them a similar problem, by sending out an army against their allies – especially since the allies in question were ready to provision the army, and since revolt was what they had in mind in asking for it. Besides, the Spartans were glad of an excuse to send away some of the helots, whom they were afraid might seize the opportunity, with Pylos in enemy hands, to start some sort of revolution. Most of Spartan policy towards the helots has been framed with security in mind.[4] Indeed, fear of how mischievous as well as how numerous the helots were had once led the Spartans to issue a proclamation to the effect that the helots should choose out of their own number those who claimed to have done outstanding service for Sparta in time of war. The implication was that those chosen would be given their freedom; in fact, however, the Spartans were conducting a test, as they believed that the ones with spirit who came forward first to claim their freedom would also be the ones most likely to turn against their masters. So about 2,000 were picked out, who crowned themselves with garlands and made the rounds of the temples as if they were now free men; but shortly afterwards the Spartans did away with them, and nobody ever found out how each of them died. Thus it was, on this occasion (in 424), that the Spartans were glad to send out 700 helots to serve as hoplites with Brasidas – the rest (of the 1,700: see above) being mercenaries raised from the Peloponnesos. (81) As for Brasidas himself, it was largely at his own wish that the Spartans sent him, but in any case he was the man the Chalkidians wanted. In Sparta his reputation was that of someone who was constantly active, and who had proved invaluable to the Spartans when they sent him to do anything; and as regards this present venture it was by behaving with justice and moderation towards the *poleis* that he caused so many of them to revolt, apart from the few he took by treachery. And the result was that when the Spartans wanted to make peace, as they eventually did, they had places to offer in exchange (for those held by the Athenians), and could thus relieve the Peloponnesos of its burden of war.[5] Furthermore, in the later period of the war, after the events in Sicily, it was the *aretē*[6] and the intelligence of Brasidas on this occasion which did most to create a pro-Spartan feeling amongst the Athenians' allies,[7] whether they had experienced these qualities for themselves or knew of them by hearsay. He was in fact the first (Spartan) sent abroad who gained the reputation of being a wholly good man; thus his legacy was the firm belief that the rest were like him.

(Brasidas soon wins over Akanthos and Stageiros (IV.84–88), and his activities culminate in the winter of 424/3 – despite the best endeavours of Thucydides himself, the Athenian *stratēgos* in the area – in the capture of the key *polis* of Amphipolis (IV.102–107), on the river Strymon.) (108) The capture of Amphipolis caused great alarm amongst the Athenians, chiefly because that *polis* was useful to them as a supplier of timber for shipbuilding and as a source of revenue. There was also the fact that (hitherto) the Spartans could, with a Thessalian escort, reach the Athenians' allies as far as the Strymon but could not get beyond it without controlling the bridge, because of the great lake which the river formed above the town and because, in the direction of Eion, there would be (Athenian) triremes on patrol; now, however, the problem seemed much simpler. And the Athenians were also afraid that their allies would revolt, as Brasidas was behaving with such all-round moderation and declaring, in particular, in his speeches everywhere that he had been sent out to liberate Greece. Indeed, when the *poleis* which were subject to the Athenians heard the news of the capture of Amphipolis and of what Brasidas had had to say there, as well as the mild behaviour of the man himself, they did of course become very enthusiastic for revolution, and sent secret messages urging him to come to them next; each of them wished to be the first to rise in revolt . . . They were influenced more than anything else by the sheer pleasure of the moment, as well as by the fact that for the first time they were likely to see the Spartans acting with urgency, and so they were ready to take whatever risks might arise. When news of all this reached the Athenians they started, as far as was possible at short notice and in winter, to send off garrisons to the various *poleis*. As for Brasidas, he sent a message back to Sparta with a plea for reinforcements, in addition to beginning to make his own preparations for building triremes on the Strymon. But the Spartans ignored him – partly because their leading men were jealous of him and partly because they were more concerned with recovering the men captured on Sphakteria and ending the war.

Thucydides IV.78*; 79–81; 108*

1 I.e. at about the same time as the Athenians' plans to gain control of Boiotia (IV.76–77).
2 See **189**.
3 King of Makedonia: see **177**.
4 This important parenthetical remark is so construed by Gomme, *Commentary* III, 547–8. The broader interpretation argued by de Ste Croix, *Origins*, 92 ('Spartan policy is always mainly governed by the necessity of taking precautions against the helots'), however true as a fact (compare Cartledge, *Sparta*, 246), does not appear to be what is actually said here.

5 See **193**.
6 See **5B**.
7 See **226**.

193. The 'Peace of Nikias'

Brasidas followed up his success at Amphipolis with further gains during the winter of 424/3 (Thuc. IV.109–116), and by the spring of 423 both the Athenians and the Spartans saw ample reason to conclude an armistice for twelve months (IV.117–119). Events in Thrake, however, went on largely unimpeded (IV.120–135), and as soon as the armistice expired in 422 Kleon sailed north in an attempt to make good the Athenian losses (V.1–3); but at the battle of Amphipolis both he and Brasidas were killed (V.6–11).

What happened immediately after the battle at Amphipolis and the withdrawal of Ramphias from Thessaly[1] was that neither side carried on with the war but were inclined, on the contrary, towards peace. In the Athenians' case this was because of the blows they had suffered at Delion and now again, shortly afterwards, at Amphipolis, and because they no longer had that same confidence in their strength as had induced them to reject previous offers of peace in the belief that their good luck at that time would lead them to victory. At the same time they were afraid that their allies might take heart from these defeats to step up their revolts; and they regretted that they had not taken the golden opportunity of making peace after the episode at Pylos. As for the Spartans, the war was turning out very differently from what they had imagined when they thought that they could destroy the power of the Athenians within a few years simply by laying waste their land. Far from it: the disaster on Sphakteria had been something never before known in Sparta; their own *chōra* was being raided from Pylos and Kythera; the helots were deserting; and there was always the likelihood that the ones who stayed behind might gain confidence from the deserters and turn the situation to their advantage, as they had done once before, by starting a revolution.[2] Also, as it happened, the thirty years' truce with the Argives was on the point of expiring,[3] and the Argives were not willing to negotiate another one unless the Kynourian territory was restored to them;[4] and to be at war with the Argives and the Athenians simultaneously seemed impossible. Besides, the Spartans suspected that some of the *poleis* in the Peloponnesos might revolt from them and join the Argives – as indeed happened.

(15) With these considerations in mind, then, both sides were keen to reach an agreement – the Spartans especially, because of their anxiety to recover the men from Sphakteria, some of whom were Spartiatai, men

of high rank with relations in the government. This was why negotiations had begun immediately after their capture; but the Athenians had not been prepared, when they were doing so well, to make a fair settlement then. After the defeat at Delion, however, the Spartans realised at once that the Athenians would be more likely to come to terms, and so they had concluded the one year's armistice, during which the two sides were to come together and discuss the longer-term issues. (16) Now the Athenians had been defeated again, at Amphipolis, and Kleon and Brasidas were both dead – the two men, one on each side, who had been most opposed to peace, Brasidas because of the success and honour which the war had brought him, and Kleon because he thought that with the return of peace and quiet his own villainy would be more blatant and his accusations of others less credible.[5] So this was naturally the moment when peace was sought even more eagerly by the two men who each aimed at being the leading statesman in his own *polis*: Pleistoanax son of Pausanias – one of the Spartans' kings – and Nikias son of Nikeratos.[6] Nikias had been a more successful *stratēgos* than any of his contemporaries, and wanted to preserve this good luck of his before failure could damage his reputation: his immediate aim was to see an end of toil and hardship both for himself and for his fellow-*politai*, and then to leave for posterity the name of one who, to the end, had never done his *polis* harm; and his belief was that this could be achieved by trusting himself as little as possible to chance and by avoiding all risks – which was possible only in peace. Pleistoanax, by contrast, wanted peace because he was being slandered by his enemies in connection with his return from exile: whenever anything went wrong in the Spartans' affairs they always brought up his name, as if what had happened was because he had been illegally restored. Their claim was, in fact, that he and his brother Aristokles had bribed the priestess at Delphi to give this reply to the various official Spartan delegations which came to consult the oracle: 'Bring back the seed of the demi-god, the son of Zeus, from abroad to your own land – or else you will plough with a silver ploughshare.'[7] And so finally, in the nineteenth year of his exile (427/6), he had induced the Spartans to bring him back, with the same dances and sacrifices as they had originally used when first founding Lakedaimon and instituting the monarchy; he had spent his exile, after supposedly taking bribes to withdraw from Attika, at Lykaion,[8] where through fear of the Spartans he had built half of his house inside the sanctuary of Zeus. (17) So now these slanders angered him and he became eager for peace to be made, his reasoning being that in peace, with no disasters occurring and with the Spartans recovering the prisoners, he would no longer be vulnerable to the attacks of his enemies, whereas during a war the leading men are always and inevitably blamed when things go wrong.

Talks went on throughout this winter (422/1); and as spring approached there was a threat that the Spartans were preparing another invasion, sending orders round the allied *poleis* to make ready to plant a fort in Attika.9 The object of this was to make the Athenians more responsive. At the discussions many claims were put forward by both sides before agreement was reached that peace should be made on the basis of each side's restoring what it had captured during the course of the war. The exception to this was that the Athenians were to keep Nisaia: this was because the Thebans, in demanding back Plataiai, had maintained that they had acquired it not by force but by agreement, without treachery, with the Plataians; so the Athenians claimed to have obtained Nisaia in the same way. At this point the Spartans called their allies together, all of whom voted in favour of peace except for the Boiotians, the Corinthians, the Eleians and the Megarians, who were displeased about what was being done. The treaty was then (nonetheless) concluded and peace made between the Lakedaimonians and the Athenians, with each side solemnly swearing to the following terms:10

(18) 'The Athenians and the Lakedaimonians and their (respective) allies made a treaty and swore to it, *polis* by *polis*, as follows:
(i) As regards the temples which are common to all,11 anyone who wishes may, in accordance with ancestral custom, offer sacrifice in them, consult the oracle, and attend the festival, travelling there with impunity by land or sea. The precinct and temple of Apollo at Delphi, and the people of Delphi, shall be independent, in accordance with ancestral custom, with control of their own taxes and their own courts – both the people and the territory.
(ii) The treaty is to be in force between the Athenians and their allies and the Lakedaimonians and their allies for 50 years, without fraud or hurt, both by land and by sea.
(iii) It shall not be permitted to take up arms with harmful intent, either for the Lakedaimonians and their allies against the Athenians and their allies or for the Athenians and their allies against the Lakedaimonians and their allies, in any way or by any means whatsoever. If any dispute should arise between them they shall resolve it by such legal process and oaths as may be agreed between them.
(iv) The Lakedaimonians and their allies shall return Amphipolis to the Athenians. But in the case of any *polis* which the Lakedaimonians hand over to the Athenians it shall be permissible for the inhabitants to leave and go wherever they like, taking their property with them; and so long as these *poleis* pay (to the Athenians) the tribute as fixed in the time of Aristeides,12 they shall be independent; once the treaty has come into force it shall not be permitted for the Athenians or their allies to take up arms against them, so long as they pay the tribute. The *poleis* in question

are Argilos, Stagiros, Akanthos, Skolos, Olynthos, and Spartolos. They are to be allies of neither side, neither the Lakedaimonians nor the Athenians; if, however, the Athenians can persuade them, of their own free will, to be made allies of the Athenians, this shall be permitted.

(v) The people of Mekyberna and Sane and Singos shall live in their own *poleis*, like the Olynthians and Akanthians.

(vi) The Lakedaimonians and their allies shall return Panakton to the Athenians.[13]

(vii) The Athenians shall return to the Lakedaimonians Koryphasion (Pylos), Kythera, Methana, Pteleon (in Thessaly) and Atalante (in Lokris). They shall also return all Lakedaimonians who are in prison either in Athens or anywhere else under Athenian rule. They shall also release the Peloponnesians besieged in Skione and all others in Skione who are allies of the Lakedaimonians, and the men that Brasidas sent in there, and any other allies of the Lakedaimonians who are in prison either in Athens or anywhere else under Athenian rule.

(viii) Likewise the Lakedaimonians and their allies shall return all Athenians and allies of the Athenians who are in their custody.

(ix) As regards Skione, Torone, Sermyle and any other *polis* held by the Athenians, the Athenians shall determine what is best done with them.

(x) The Athenians shall take an oath to the Lakedaimonians and their allies, *polis* by *polis*. Seventeen men shall take the oath for each *polis*, of the most solemn and binding character that each recognises. The wording of the oath shall be: "I shall abide by this agreement and treaty honestly and sincerely". Likewise the Lakedaimonians and their allies shall take an oath to the Athenians. Both sides shall renew the oath every year; and *stēlai* (inscribed with the treaty) shall be set up at Olympia, Delphi, the Isthmos, on the (*akro*)*polis* in Athens, and at the temple at Amyklai in Lakedaimon.

(xi) If either side has overlooked any point about any subject whatsoever, it shall be consistent with the oath for both sides to discuss it honestly and make a change wherever they both, the Athenians and the Lakedaimonians, see fit.

(19) The treaty comes into effect in Lakedaimon on the 27th (day) of the month Artemision, with Pleistolas as *ephoros*, and in Athens on the 25th (day) of the month Elaphebolion, with Alkaios as *archōn*. The men who took the oath and poured the libations were as follows. For the Lakedaimonians: Pleistoanax, Agis,[14] Pleistolas, Damagetos, Chionis, Metagenes, Akanthos, Daithos, Ischagoras, Philocharidas, Zeuxidas, Antippos, Tellis,[15] Alkinadas, Empedias, Menas, Laphilos. For the Athenians: Lampon,[16] Isthmionikos, Nikias, Laches, Euthydemos, Prokles, Pythodoros, Hagnon, Myrtilos, Thrasykles, Theagenes, Aristokrates, Iolkios, Timokrates, Leon, Lamachos, Demosthenes.'

(20) This treaty was made as winter was ending and spring beginning, immediately after (the Athenians had celebrated) the City Dionysia – just ten years and a few days since the first invasion of Attika and the start of this war.

Thucydides v.14–20.1

1 Ramphias had been bringing – at last – reinforcements for Brasidas (Thuc. v.12–13).
2 I.e. in the 460s: see **169**.
3 Not to be confused with the comprehensive Thirty Years' Peace of 446/5 (**173**); this Sparta/Argos treaty had evidently been made earlier, in 451 or 450.
4 See Thuc. iv.56.2.
5 On Kleon (and Thuc.'s attitude to him) see further **210** and **212**.
6 Pleistoanax: see **173**. Nikias: see **142C**, **161B**, and Ch.22.
7 I.e. (as a scholiast explains) plague and famine would make food a luxury.
8 In Arkadia.
9 See **183C** and **228–229**.
10 Clearly Thuc. saw an official copy of what follows, so we give it within quotation marks. We also separate out, and number, what to a modern eye are the various clauses of the document; note, however, that other texts or translations may do so differently.
11 Principally Delphi (specified below) and Olympia.
12 See **129**. This provision nullified the punitively high rates set by the 425 reassessment (**200**).
13 See Thuc. v.3.5.
14 The two kings.
15 Generally taken to be the father of Brasidas (see Thuc. ii.25.2).
16 Presumably the well-known seer (**146, 174**). On the 34 'signatories' in general see A. Andrewes and D. M. Lewis, 'Note on the Peace of Nikias', *JHS* 77 (1957), 177–80. Also D. J. Mosley, 'Who "signed" treaties in ancient Greece?', *PCPhS* n.s.7 (1961), 59–63.

19 Athenian strategy during the Archidamian War

Perikles held that all Athens had to do was to retain the empire and to avoid any defeat. (Note the remarks of the Mytilenians on the dependence of the Athenians on their empire, Thuc. III.13.5–7.) It was not as easy as he supposed, however, to retain control of the empire and simultaneously to fight even a limited war against Sparta, and it is reasonable to surmise that among the Athenians there were those who held that as long as Sparta remained potentially hostile Athens and her empire were necessarily insecure. Did the Athenians, if they made peace after achieving stalemate, have to fear another war in the future when their reserves of men and money were still depleted? Did they have to *defeat* Sparta before making peace? Certainly attempts were made to tip the balance decisively against Sparta; the recovery of Megara would have achieved this, as well as rendering Attika immune to invasion; and as early as 426, a raid on Tanagra in Boiotia was mounted (Thuc. III.91.3–6). This was the prelude to a full-scale attempt in 424 to recover Boiotia, which ended in defeat at Delion (Thuc. IV.76–101.2).

With none of these moves is Kleon associated; his strategy is that of Perikles; his interest in the occupation of Pylos and the capture of Sphakteria (**190**) and in the recovery of the *poleis* in Thrake detached by Brasidas (**193**) is wholly Periklean. It is also desirable to posit a serious motive for his advocacy of the rejection of peace in 425 (Thuc. IV.21 – before the capture of Sphakteria; IV.41 – after the capture) and 422; did the terms of any peace need to include the explicit acceptance by Sparta of the Athenian empire, since she had demanded its abolition in 431 (a demand repeated – and rejected – in 411, ?Aristot. *Ath. Pol.* 32.3 = **227A**)? Although the Athenians were in some ways weaker in 421, when they made peace, than in 425 they extorted from Sparta the return of Amphipolis and a recognition of the Athenian right to collect the tribute (**193**).

For an extended critique of the strategy of Perikles see D. Kagan, *The Archidamian War* (Ithaca, N.Y., 1974).

194. The advice of Perikles

Just as Thucydides uses speeches made at Sparta to analyse the Spartan position (**183**), so he deploys speeches made by Perikles to analyse the Athenian position; the echoes in the two sets of passages are of the highest importance, as are also the common themes in the speeches of Perikles on the one hand and the monograph of the Old Oligarch ([Xen.] *Ath. Pol.*) on the other.

(A) These then were the demands which the Spartans made on the occasion of their first embassy[1] and these were the counter-demands, in both cases for the expulsion of religious abominations; later the Lakedaimonians came to the Athenians and demanded that they raise the siege of Poteidaia and allow Aigina to be autonomous, but they proclaimed most insistently and most explicitly that if they revoked the *psēphisma* concerning the Megarians in which they were forbidden to use the harbours in the empire of the Athenians and the *agora* of Athens there would be no war.[2] But the Athenians paid no attention to the other demands and did not revoke the *psēphisma*, instead accusing the Megarians of cultivating sacred land and unassigned boundary land and of harbouring runaway slaves. Finally the last embassy came from Lakedaimon, consisting of Ramphias, Melesippos and Agesandros, and spoke of none of the things which they had normally raised earlier, but said only that 'the Lakedaimonians wish the peace to remain, and it would remain if you would let the Greeks be autonomous'; the Athenians summoned an *ekklēsia* and propounded a number of views to each other and agreed to take counsel and reply once and for all on every issue. And a lot of people came forward and spoke, taking one side or the other in the debate, arguing that war was necessary or that the *psēphisma* should not stand in the way of peace and should be revoked; then Perikles the son of Xanthippos, the leading Athenian of that period and a powerful speaker as well as a capable man of action, came forward and gave the following advice. (140) 'I am still of the same opinion, Athenians, that we should not give in to the Peloponnesians, although I know that men do not preserve the zeal with which they agree to fight when they are actually involved, but change their minds in the light of events. Nonetheless, I see that the advice which I must give is the same as always and I ask those of you who are persuaded to stand by what we have decided together, even if we suffer some reverses; for I expect you otherwise not to claim any credit for the wisdom of the decision if we succeed. The course of events may be just as random as the plans of men, which is why we tend to blame chance whenever anything happens contrary to our expectations.

The Lakedaimonians were clearly involved in plotting against us before and their activity has not diminished. For although it is laid down that both sides should offer and accept arbitration of their differences and that otherwise we should each continue to hold what we now hold, they have never offered arbitration and have not accepted it when we have offered it. They prefer to resolve their complaints by war rather than by discussion, and they are now here with orders rather than with complaints as earlier. For they bid us raise the siege of Poteidaia and allow Aigina to be autonomous and revoke the Megarian *psēphisma*: and this latest embassy to come proclaims that we should let the Greeks be autonomous. But none of you should suppose that we should be fighting for something unimportant if we refused to revoke the Megarian *psēphisma* – they lay most emphasis on the suggestion that if it were revoked the war would not break out – nor should you allow the view to linger among yourselves that you went to war over a trifle. For this supposed trifle involves the testing and confirmation of your entire purpose. If you give in, you will immediately be confronted with a further and more substantial demand, as having accepted this one through fear; but if you stand firm, you will make it clear to them that they have rather to deal with you as equals. (141) So now you must decide either to obey them before suffering at their hands or to go to war; and if we go to war, as it seems to me at any rate we should, we must be determined not to yield for great or little cause alike and not to hold what we have in fear. For the most substantial and the most trifling demand, made by an equal on a neighbour without resorting to arbitration, may equally bring slavery.

As far as the war is concerned, you will realise as I deal with everything in turn that the resources available to us will be no weaker than those of the other side. For the Peloponnesians cultivate their own land themselves and possess funds neither as individuals nor as communities; furthermore they have no experience of long wars or overseas wars, since because of their poverty they only fight short wars against each other. And such men cannot often man naval expeditions or often despatch armies by land, since that would mean at the same time absence from their own property and expenditure from their own resources; and in any case we have control of the sea. It is availability of resources rather than sudden levies which supports a war effort. And those who cultivate their own land themselves are readier to contribute their strength than their money to a war; for they are convinced that they will survive the dangers, but are not at all certain that they will not use up their money before the end, especially if the war goes on longer than expected, as may well happen. The Peloponnesians and their allies can stand up to the whole of Greece in a single battle, but they are incapable of fighting a war against any power unlike themselves; for they lack a single deliberative body[3] and so cannot engage in rapid and sudden action; they all have an equal voice[4] and they belong to different peoples, so that each pursues his own objective. All these things are fatal for decisive action; for some of them want nothing so much as revenge on someone, others nothing so much as to conserve their own resources. They meet infrequently and spend a short time considering some aspect of their common business, but for the most part they concern themselves with their own affairs; no one supposes that any harm will come of his own lack of involvement, and everyone thinks that it is for someone else to exercise forethought on his behalf, so that while everyone has the same opinion in private no one notices that their entire common enterprise is headed for disaster.

(142) But the most important thing is that they will be hindered by lack of money, when they dally in order to find time to procure it; in war, opportunities do not wait. And furthermore, neither their threat to build fortifications in Attika nor their navy need be feared. For even in peace-time it is difficult to build a *polis* strong enough to counterbalance another, let alone build one in enemy territory, and at a time when our fortifications pose no less of a threat. And if they build a guard-post, they may damage part of our land by raids or by encouraging slaves to desert, but such action will be insufficient to stop us sailing to their territory to build fortifications there and defending ourselves with our navy, wherein lies our strength. For as a result of our naval activity we have more experience of land operations than they have of naval operations as a result of activity on land; and it will not be easy for them to add skill as seamen to their other accomplishments, for even you, when you took to the sea, did not reach perfection immediately after the Persian Wars. How can men who are farmers and not sailors and who will also be prevented from practising by the fact that you will be lying in wait with a large navy, how can such hope to get anywhere? They might run the risk against a few blockading ships, taking courage in their numbers despite their lack of skill, but if they are blockaded by a large force they will remain inactive and become even less competent as a result of lack of practice and therefore even more reluctant to act. Seamanship, just like anything else, is a matter of skill and it is not possible to learn it casually, when occasion arises; rather, nothing else can be *its* casual accompaniment.

(143) They might take some of the treasures at Olympia or Delphi and try to draw away those of our sailors who are foreigners (*xenoi*);[5] this would be serious if we were not able to equal them by boarding the ships ourselves along with the *metoikoi*; as it is, not only is this the case, but, what is most important, we have among our own *politai* both helmsmen and other members of the crew[6] in greater numbers and of better quality than the whole of the rest of Greece. And none of those who are foreigners (*xenoi*) would agree to fight with them, for the sake of

365

receiving extra pay for a few days, but at the risk of exile and with less expectation of victory.

This then seems to me more or less what one can say about the affairs of the Peloponnesians; our own position seems to me to have none of the weaknesses which I have attributed to them and other strengths of even greater significance. If they invade our territory by land, we shall invade theirs by sea; and then it will be a very different matter for even a part of the Peloponnesos to be devastated compared with the devastation of the whole of Attika. For without fighting they will not be able to get any other land in compensation, while we already possess a great deal of land both on the islands and on the mainland; for control of the sea is all important. Consider the position: if we were islanders, who would be less vulnerable? As it is, we must think of ourselves as much as possible as islanders, abandon our land and our houses and keep control of the sea and the *polis*; we must not in our distress over land and houses fight it out with the Peloponnesians, who are much more numerous than we; for even if we win, we shall have to fight on another occasion against a force no less numerous and if we lose, we shall lose also the support of our allies from whom we derive our strength; for they will not remain inactive once we are no longer strong enough to campaign against them; we must not lament the loss of houses and land, but of men; for the former cannot create men, it is men who acquire them. Indeed, if I thought I could persuade you, I should have bidden you go out yourselves and destroy them, in order to show the Peloponnesians that fear for them will not make you obey.

(144) I have many other reasons for hoping that we shall come through, if you are prepared not to attempt to increase your empire while the war is on and not to bring on yourself dangers of your own making; for I fear more our own mistakes than the plans of our enemies.[7] But I shall deal with all this in another speech when it is a question of action. Let us now send the ambassadors back, having replied to them that we shall let the Megarians use our *agora* and harbours if the Lakedaimonians will abandon *xenēlasiai*[8] of ourselves and our allies – for the peace treaty mentions neither the one practice nor the other – and that we shall allow the *poleis* to be autonomous if they were so when we made the peace and if they too grant to their own *poleis* the right to be autonomous not as suits them, but as each of the *poleis* wishes;[9] also that we are willing to offer arbitration according to the terms of the peace and that we shall not begin the war, but shall resist those who do begin it. For this reply is both a just one and one which is appropriate for our *polis*. We must realise that we are being compelled to fight;[10] and if we accept the challenge readily rather than reluctantly, we shall find that our enemies are less aggressive; we must realise also that it is the greatest dangers

which bring the greatest credit to both *polis* and individual. Our fathers at any rate withstood the Persians, not only without the resources which we possess, but having abandoned even those which they did possess; and it was by intelligence rather than luck, and daring rather than sheer strength, that they repelled the *barbaroi* and brought things to their present state. We must not be lesser men than they, but resist our enemies at every turn and try to hand on to the next generation no less than we received.'

(145) This was Perikles' speech, and the Athenians, thinking that he had offered them the best advice, voted for what he had suggested; they replied to the Spartans according to his proposal, both on individual points and on the entire issue, that they would take no action under duress, but were ready to come to an agreement about the complaints against them by means of arbitration according to the terms of the peace treaty, on a fair and equal basis. (146) And the Spartans went home and sent no further embassies. And these were the complaints and quarrels of the two sides before the war, beginning with the business of Epidamnos and Kerkyra; but in the course of it all they continued to have dealings with each other and went to each others' territory without heralds,[11] though not without mutual suspicion; for what was happening was destroying the peace and providing a ground for war.

Thucydides 1.139–146

(B) (On the eve of the Spartan invasion of Attika Perikles) gave the same advice on the present situation as he had earlier, namely to prepare for war and to bring in things from the countryside, not to go out to fight, but to come into the *polis* and guard it, to fit out the fleet, which was where their strength lay, to keep a firm control over the allies; he pointed out that their strength came from them and from the revenue which they provided and that victory in war came for the most part from good judgment and availability of resources. And he told the Athenians to take courage from the fact that the *polis* drew virtually 600 talents a year in tribute from the allies, without taking into account other forms of revenue;[12] also from the fact that there were at that moment on the *akropolis* still 6,000 talents in coined silver. When it was at its largest, the reserve had stood at 9,700 talents, from which payments had been made for the Propylaia of the *akropolis* and the other buildings and for the siege of Poteidaia.[13] In addition to the 6,000 talents, there was uncoined gold and silver in the form of private and public dedications, and the sacred furnishings used for processions and festivals, and the Persian spoils and other things of the same kind, worth at least 500 talents. And Perikles also reckoned in the substantial possessions of the other shrines, which they could use,[14] and they could also use the golden ornaments of the statue of Athena herself, if absolutely nothing else was available to them; Perikles pointed out that the statue carried 40 talents' weight of pure gold and that it was all removable; if they used it to save themselves they must of course put back at least the same amount afterwards. These were the facts which Perikles deployed to give the Athenians courage as far as money was concerned; he went on to say that there were 13,000 hoplites, as well as 16,000 used for garrison purposes[15] and the defence of the *polis*; for this was the number which was on guard whenever an enemy attack began, drawn from the oldest and youngest and from those of the *metoikoi* who were hoplites. (Thucydides goes on to give an account of the walls to be defended.) Perikles also said that there were 1,200 cavalry, including mounted bowmen, 1,600 bowmen, and 300 seaworthy triremes. This at least was what the Athenians had in each category, on the eve of the first Peloponnesian invasion and of the outbreak of war. Perikles also made the other points he usually made to show that they would come through the war.

Thucydides II.13.2–end

1 See **181**.
2 See **178**.
3 This implies that the *Athenians* took unilateral decisions on behalf of *their* allies.
4 *Isopsēphoi*, literally 'with an equal vote', is perhaps here used metaphorically.
5 In fact probably used here and below to refer to the allies of Athens.
6 Presumably the officers, as opposed to the oarsmen, compare **112** with n.4.
7 It is hard not to believe that Thucydides wrote this after the defeat of Athens.
8 See **56**.
9 One wonders if Thuc. is here referring to the members of the Peloponnesian League or to the *perioikoi*.
10 Compare 1.23.6 (**165A**).
11 See **184** n.2.
12 The 600 talents must include such things as revenue from Amphipolis, not strictly tribute (*phoros*); 'other forms' no doubt includes such things as revenue accruing to individuals from property owned in the *poleis* of the empire (see **269** for the prohibition of this practice in the fourth-century alliance).
13 The history of Athenian imperial finances is a matter of uncertainty and dispute; see, briefly, Meiggs, *Empire*, ch.13.
14 For loans to Athens from temple treasuries see Meiggs and Lewis no.72.
15 Presumably in the *chōra*; see **186** for the fort at Oinoe.

195. The Athenian reaction to invasion

In the first year of the war, everything went according to plan for the Athenians; they despatched a fleet to raid the Peloponnesos, and in due course expelled the

Aiginetans from Aigina and raided the territory of Megara; having taken the measure of the first Peloponnesian invasion, they also made plans for the rest of the war.

When (the Spartans) had retreated, the Athenians established guard points at sea and on land, according to the pattern which they intended to adopt for the rest of the war. And they agreed to segregate 1,000 talents of the money on the *akropolis* and keep it separate and not spend it,[1] but use their other resources for the war; and they sanctioned the death penalty for anyone who proposed or put to the vote a proposal to touch the money for any purpose except the defence of the *polis* against a naval expedition by the enemy. And alongside the money they each year kept in reserve the hundred best triremes, together with their *triērarchoi*,[2] none of which was to be used except along with the money and for the same purpose, if need arose.

Thucydides II.24

1 It was used in 406 for the fleet that fought at Arginousai, see **237**.
2 See **144** Intro.

196. The plague

The second year of the war brought the first disaster for Athens, a mysterious epidemic, followed before long by the discovery that the empire was neither as subservient nor as financially productive as was desirable. The effect of the plague on Athenian morale is incalculable; what is known is that by the time it had recurred in 427/6 (see also Thuc. VI.26.2) it had caused the total loss of 4,400 hoplites and 300 cavalry and that Thucydides held that 'nothing else did the Athenians so much harm or so reduced their strength for war' (III.87).

And after the Peloponnesians had been in Attika for only a few days, the disease made its first appearance among the Athenians; it was said that it had earlier affected many other places including Lemnos,[1] but there was no record of its having been so severe or of its having caused so many deaths anywhere else. For initially the doctors were unable to treat it because of unfamiliarity with it and indeed themselves suffered a higher mortality rate because they came more into contact with it; and no other device of which men could think was of any use either. Going as a suppliant to a shrine or consulting an oracle or doing anything like that, it was all quite useless; and in the end people were so overcome by the disaster that they gave such things up. (Thucydides goes on to describe whence the disease came and its symptoms.)[2] (51.4) The worst aspect of the whole disaster was the despair which came over anyone who realised that he was ill; for people at once gave up hope, met their end first and foremost by this loss of will and did not fight back. Another terrible aspect was the way in which those who looked after others caught the disease and died like sheep; this was the cause of most of the deaths. For if people in their fear were unwilling to approach other people, these died uncared for, and many households were wiped out without anyone going to attend to them; and if people did visit, they themselves were lost, and in particular those who tried in any way to behave properly. For they would have been ashamed to spare themselves and visited their friends, when even the relatives, overcome by the scale of the disaster, had finished by abandoning the lamentations for the dying. On the whole, though, those who had come through the illness were those who were more ready to take pity on the dying and the suffering, since they already knew the illness and were themselves now confident; for it did not affect the same person for a second time, at any rate fatally. And such people were congratulated by the rest and themselves in their sudden joy cherished the unfounded hope that they would never die from any other diseases. (52) The existing disaster was made much worse for people by the fact that the transfer from the fields to the *astu* had taken place; those who had come in were particularly affected. For since there were no houses for them and they lived in the summer season in badly ventilated huts, the disease killed without hindrance; corpses lay on other corpses as they had fallen and the dying tottered around the streets and around all the wells in their desire for water. The temples in which they were living were full of the corpses of those who had died there; for as the disaster overwhelmed them, men turned to contempt of sacred and holy things alike, not knowing whether they would continue to exist.[3] All the funeral customs which had obtained hitherto were abandoned and people were buried in any way that lay to hand. In their lack of relatives, because of the number of those who had already died, many turned to shocking means of disposal of the dead; for arriving at other people's pyres ahead of those who had built them, they placed their own dead thereon and set them alight; or when someone else was being burnt, they threw on the corpse which they were carrying from above and made off. (53) The disease was also in large part the origin of other sorts of lawlessness (*anomia*) in the *polis*. For when men saw the abrupt change in fortune of those who were rich and died suddenly and of those who previously had nothing and then all at once inherited what the others had had, they were readier to venture on acts of self-indulgence which they had previously kept a secret. So they decided to go in for quick enjoyment and making merry, regarding their bodies and their wealth as equally ephemeral. And no one was prepared to undergo hardship for the sake of what was regarded as honourable, since everyone regarded it as uncertain whether he would survive to acquire a good reputation therefrom; anything that was pleasurable in the present circumstances or brought pleasure, this was what was regarded as good and valuable. Neither fear of the gods nor laws of men acted as a restraining influence; for when men saw everyone equally facing destruction they regarded piety and impiety as the same; and no one expected to live long enough for a trial to take place and punishment to be exacted for their wrongs; rather indeed they thought that punishment had already been decreed and now hung over them and that it was reasonable to enjoy life a bit before the time came. (54) This then was the oppressive disaster which had befallen the Athenians, with their men dying within and their land being ravaged outside. In their suffering, as one might expect, they remembered this oracle, which the old men said had been proclaimed long ago: 'A Dorian war will come and a *loimos* (plague) along with it.' There had been a controversy among some people as to whether it was not *loimos* (plague) which was mentioned in the oracle, but *limos* (famine); but in the present circumstances it was not surprising that the view which favoured *loimos* prevailed; for men moulded their memories to suit what they were suffering. But I think that if another Dorian war ever comes after this one and it happens that a *limos* (famine) occurs as well, then probably men will repeat the oracle in this version.

Thucydides II.47.3–4 and 51.4–54

1 An Athenian island possession.
2 Much has been written about the identification of the disease, without agreement being reached; it is not in any case certain that the disease is one known to modern medicine.
3 Note the combination in Thucydides of respect for established religious practice with scepticism over oracles (below); compare v.26.

197. The revolt of Mytilene

In the fourth year of the war (428) the first major crack appeared in the edifice of the Athenian empire, with the revolt of Mytilene; the slowness of the Athenian reaction suggests that the Mytilenians had chosen the right moment to act; and in the course of the suppression of the revolt the weakness of the finances of Athens became apparent. The text of Thucydides as we have it contains a long digression on Athenian resources, at the point where he has described the Athenian measures taken in response to the threatened second invasion of Attika (III.17): even more ships had been deployed at the beginning of the war than now, and naval activity, along with the siege of Poteidaia (which had cost 2,000 talents, II.70.2), had been particularly expensive. The authenticity of the passage is disputed, but the siege of Mytilene is clearly an appropriate moment for a glance at the early stages of the decline in Athenian reserves. We see no way of deciding whether the passage is Thucydidean material, not fully worked in (the text is in any case imperfect) or the work of a later commentator.

See J. Wilson, 'Strategy and tactics in the Mytilene campaign', *Historia* 30 (1981), 144–63.

(A) Immediately after the invasion of the Peloponnesians, Lesbos apart from Methymna rebelled from the Athenians; they had wanted to do so before the war, but the Spartans had not accepted their overtures; and they were now forced to rebel before they had intended to. For they were waiting for the completion of work on narrowing the mouths of the harbours, repairing the walls and building ships and also for the arrival of consignments of bowmen and grain from Pontos[1] and of other things which they were in the process of getting. What happened was that the Tenedians, who were hostile to them, and the Methymnians and some individuals among the Mytilenians themselves, who were at odds with the generality and were *proxenoi* of the Athenians,[2] informed the Athenians that the Mytilenians were in the process of synoecising Lesbos into a single *polis* – their own[3] – by force and that all the preparations in which they were engaged involved the Lakedaimonians and the Boiotians, who were related to them,[4] and were intended to lead to revolt; unless they were caught and stopped, the Athenians would lose Lesbos. (3) The Athenians had been weakened by the plague and by the war, which was of recent origin and was still being conducted energetically; so, thinking that it would be extremely difficult to subdue Lesbos, which had a fleet and whose strength was intact, they at first refused to believe the accusations, giving greater weight to their wish that they were untrue. But when they had sent ambassadors and failed to persuade the Mytilenians to abandon the *synoikismos* and their preparations, they took fright and determined to try and stop them. They immediately sent out forty ships, which happened to have been got ready to sail round the Peloponnesos; Kleïppides the son of Deinias and two others were *stratēgoi*. For the Athenians had been told that there was a festival of Apollo of Malea outside the *polis*, which the entire body of the Mytilenians celebrate, and that there was hope if they made haste and if the plan worked of falling on them by surprise; otherwise, they were to order the Mytilenians to surrender their ships and pull down their walls and to make war on them if they refused. So the ships set off; and meanwhile the Athenians seized the ten ships of the Mytilenians, which happened to be on the spot serving according to the terms of the alliance,[5] and kept their crews under guard. But someone crossed from Athens to Euboia and then went on foot to Geraistos, where he found a merchant ship setting off; setting sail and arriving at Mytilene on the third day out from Athens, he informed the Mytilenians of the despatch of the expedition. As a result they did not go out to the festival of Apollo of Malea, but strengthened the half-finished parts of their walls and harbour defences and mounted guard.[6]

Thucydides III.2–3

(B) (The Lakedaimonians planned a second invasion of Attika, but called it off and planned a naval expedition to Lesbos instead; meanwhile the Athenians reinforced their army there.) But since the Athenians needed additional finance for the siege, even though they had just for the first time levied an *eisphora* of 200 talents,[7] they also sent out twelve ships to collect money among the allies, with Lysikles and four others as *stratēgoi*. He sailed round various places and collected money, and then went inland from Myous in Karia across the plain of the Maiandros as far as the hill of Sandios; at that point he was attacked by the Karians and the Anaitans and was killed along with a large part of his army.

Thucydides III.19

1 The Mytilenians thus copied the Athenians, who drew Scythian bowmen to form a sort of police force and – notoriously – corn from the Black Sea area.
2 See **135**.
3 For *synoikismos* see **7–8**; note that freedom from Athens and local aggrandisement go hand in hand.
4 Lesbos and the mainland opposite regarded themselves as settled from central Greece.
5 See **133** Intro.
6 The Athenians arrived and delivered their ultimatum, which was rejected; after some fighting, the Mytilenians attempted to negotiate, sending 'one of those who had denounced them, who had already changed his mind'; the Mytilenians also sent to Sparta, wisely, since negotiations broke down and fighting resumed; see **136** for their speech to the Lakedaimonians and their allies at Olympia. The Mytilenians attempted little, but waited for help from Sparta; the Athenians were much encouraged and summoned further allies, 'who came much more readily since they saw no sign of decisive action on the part of the Lesbians'.
7 Thucydides cannot mean that this was the first *eisphora* (for which see Intro. to Ch.11) ever; did he mean the first of the war or the first of two hundred talents? See, most recently, J. G. Griffith, 'A note on the first eisphora at Athens', *Am. Journ. Anc. Hist.* 2 (1977), 3–7.

198. The control of the empire

The second debate after the suppression of the revolt of Mytilene (see **210**) gave Thucydides the opportunity to present at some length a picture of post-Periklean political conditions in Athens; but although both speeches cover an enormous range of issues, both return at the end to the crucial problem of the war, how to retain control of the source of Athenian strength.

(A) (Kleon speaks.) 'It is to try and stop you behaving like this¹ that I now argue that the Mytilenians have wronged you more than any other single *polis*. For I can forgive those who have always been unable to stand your empire or those who have revolted under the compulsion of our enemies; but they live on an island and have walls and needed to fear our enemies only if they attacked by sea, in which case they had their own force of triremes to defend themselves against them, they were autonomous and enjoyed the highest degree of respect from us – and yet they have done this; what else is it but a deliberate attack rather than a revolt? For one can only talk of a revolt in the case of those who have suffered some outrage. What else have they done but joined our enemies and sought to destroy us? This is something far worse than if they had made war on us simply to aggrandise themselves. The fate of their neighbours, who had already revolted from us and been subdued, did not serve as a warning to them and their state of prosperity did not make them ashamed to resort to extreme measures. On the contrary, they became unduly confident about the future, hoping for more than they could achieve, though still less than they would really have liked, and went to war, regarding force as meaning more than justice. Choosing the moment when they thought they would win, they attacked us although we had done them no wrong. Any *polis* which suddenly enjoys considerable and unexpected success is likely to become arrogant; reasonable prosperity is usually safer for men than an excess of it and it is, I imagine, easier to avert disaster than to preserve prosperity. We should all along have accorded the Mytilenians the same degree of respect as the others; they would not then have become so arrogant; for in general men naturally despise someone who goes out of his way to cultivate them, while they look up to someone who does not make concessions. So let them now pay the penalty which fits their crime; do not let the blame fall on the few, but allow the *dēmos* to get off. For they all without distinction attacked you, including those who could have come over to us and would now be once more in control of their *polis*; but they joined in the revolt, thinking it safer to run the risk along with the few.² Now think of your allies; if you punish in the same way those who are coerced by the enemy and those who revolt of their own volition, do you not suppose that they will all revolt on the slightest pretext, since freedom attends success and no unpleasant consequences attend failure? We shall have to risk our resources and our lives against every *polis*; if we succeed we shall gain control of a *polis* incapable of producing in the future the revenue on which we depend, if we fail we shall be confronted with new enemies in addition to those we already have and at a time when we should be fighting against these existing enemies we shall be making war on our own allies.'

Thucydides III.39

(B) (Diodotos speaks.) 'But think what a major mistake you would make if you followed Kleon on this point. For, as it is, the *dēmos* in every *polis* is well disposed to you; either it does not join the few in revolt or, if it is forced to do so, it is from the start hostile to those who have revolted and you go to war against the *polis* concerned with the majority on your side. But if you execute the *dēmos* of the Mytilenians, which did not participate in the revolt and which of its own free will handed over the *polis* to you when it got weapons into its hands,[3] in the first place you will do wrong by killing your benefactors and in the second place you will do exactly what the leading men in any group want; for when they incite a *polis* to revolt they will have the *dēmos* on their side from the start, since you will already have made it clear that the same punishment awaits those who are in the wrong and also those who are not. In fact, even if the *dēmos* is in the wrong, it is necessary to dissimulate the fact, so that the one element which is still on our side does not become our enemy. What is more, I think that it is much more conducive to the retention of the empire to allow ourselves to be wronged than to execute with every justification those who are better left alive. In fact the combination of justice and expediency to which Kleon points in the punishment which he proposes is simply inconceivable.' (Diodotos proposes that the men identified as guilty and sent home by the Athenian *stratēgos* on Lesbos be tried, the rest let off; his proposal just passes and the ship countermanding the order to execute all the adult male Mytilenians arrives just in time.) (50) But the Athenians executed, on the proposal of Kleon, the others whom Paches had sent home as the ringleaders of the revolt, just over 1,000 in number, and pulled down the walls of the Mytilenians and took over their ships. For the future, they did not assess the Lesbians for tribute but divided up the land, except that of the Methymnians, into 3,000 plots (*klēroi*);[4] they set aside 300 as sacred to the gods and sent out *klērouchoi* chosen by lot from among themselves to take over the rest. The Lesbians agreed to pay two minas of silver a year for each plot (*klēros*) and themselves worked the land.[5] The Athenians also took over the settlements on the mainland which the Mytilenians controlled, and the Mytilenians thereafter were the subjects of the Athenians. This was how affairs at Lesbos turned out.

Thucydides III.47 and 50

1 See **210B** at end.
2 There has been in recent years a long and irresolvable controversy over what the *dēmos* of Mytilene really felt; certainly it provoked the end of the revolt, but only after the Spartan commander in Mytilene had armed it, in the absence of

help from the Peloponnesos, *and* after it had objected to the lack of food (III.27–2.8). See Intro. to Ch.12.

3 See above.

4 See **17** and **139**.

5 Thucydides allows us to suppose that the *klērouchoi* did not remain on Lesbos; there is certainly no sign of them in 424 (IV.52). It is remarkable that despite their financial difficulties (see **197**) the Athenians chose not to draw tribute from Lesbos, but to send *klērouchoi* instead; presumably relief for those afflicted by the invasions of Attika seemed more urgent (compare **241**); such relief was of course less necessary after the last invasion of the Archidamian War in 425, a factor which may also be invoked to explain the apparent absence of *klērouchoi* in 424.

199. Athens and Chios

One immediate consequence of the Mytilenian revolt was Athenian suspicion of their one remaining autonomous ally.

In the same winter also the Chians pulled down their new wall at the bidding of the Athenians, who suspected them of plotting something; nonetheless they got from the Athenians guarantees and as much assurance as they could that they would not contemplate any changes in their relationship with them. And the winter ended and along with it the seventh year of the war of which Thucydides wrote the history (425/4).

Thucydides IV.51

200. The reassessment of the tribute

The early years of the war made it clear that the empire both was vulnerable and did not produce enough revenue to provide for its policing as well as for the prosecution even of the limited war advocated by Perikles; the natural reaction was to demand more from the empire (see also **201**). The lists at the end of the decree of 425/4 which follows show that between 1,460 and 1,500 talents were now expected; the amount collected is likely to have been substantially less, since apparently every *polis* which had ever paid is listed and many *poleis* which are never known to have paid are listed; one *polis* known never to have paid is listed – Melos (for which see **206**). The near-contemporary *Knights* of Aristophanes contains a series of allusions to the obsession of Kleon with getting in the tribute: lines 311–312, 326, 1070–1071.

(i)   Gods

Assessment of *phoros*

It was decided by the [*boulē* and the *dēmos*, ?] held the *prytaneia* [?] was secretary, [?] presided, Thoudippos[1] [proposed: that heralds be sent] from among [?those present, whomsoever the *boulē*] shall choose, to the *poleis*, two [to Ionia and Karia], two [to Thrake, two] to the Islands, [and two to] the Hellespontos; let them [announce in] public [in each *polis* that ambassadors are to arrive (in Athens) in the month of] Maimakterion (November–December). (The ill-organised and badly preserved text goes on to establish assessors to assess the new *phoros*, a new court to hear disputes and *eisagōgeis*[2] to oversee the cases.) (The *dikastai*) are to draw up in consultation with the *boulē* the [new assessments of the *phoros*,] since this has turned out to be inadequate; (they are to draw up the assessments)[according to the procedure used in the] preceding year, (?) in turn, [all] within the month of Poseideion (January–February) [They are to deal with business every day] from the new moon, according to [the same principles in order that] the *phoros* [may be assessed within the month of] Poseideion; [and a full *boulē*] is also to deal with business continuously in order that the assessments may take place unless [the *dēmos* decrees otherwise.] And they may not [assess the new] *phoros* for any [*polis* at a lower level than they paid before] unless [there appears to be some obstacle, as of the] *chōra* being incapable of [producing more.] (The text continues with provisions for publication, future assessments every four years on the occasion of the Great Panathenaia, urgent despatch of the later stages of the present assessment and the activities of the heralds; then, increasingly fragmentary, with collection of the *phoros*, some kind of budgeting for its use, another procedure for disputes; finally, an amendment to this last clause.)[3]

(ii) It was decided by the *boulē* and the *dēmos*, (the *phylē*) Aigeis held the *prytaneia*, Philippos was [secretary, ?] presided, Thoudippos proposed: that all the *poleis* which [were assessed] for *phoros* [during the tenure of the *boulē* of which Pleistias] was the first secretary, during the tenure of Stratokles as *archōn*, [should bring] a cow and panoply to the Great Panathenaia; and that they should take part in the procession in the same way as *apoikoi*.[4]

(iii) The *boulē* of which Pleistias [of ? was the first secretary] assessed the *poleis* for *phoros* [thus], during the tenure of Stratokles as *archōn*, during the tenure of the *eisagōgeis* of whom Ka [? of ? was secretary.]

(The list of *poleis* and assessments follows.)

Meiggs and Lewis no. 69, lines 1–22*; 54–60

1 There is some evidence to suggest that he may be a son-in-law of Kleon.
2 Officials who bring cases into court.
3 Given the fragmentary state of the text, we think it less misleading to summarise its content than to attempt a translation; in particular, we doubt, *contra* Meiggs and Lewis, whether the decree entrusts the *stratēgoi* with collection of the *phoros* or with budgeting for its use, and we see no reason

whatever to believe that 'it seems to provide for extraordinary assessments of individual cities by the Boule in the light of an annual review by the generals of the anticipated military and naval expenses of the year'.

4 The obligation with which this section deals is mentioned casually in the Kleinias decree (see **154** Intro); if this is to be dated in the 440s, one must suppose that the second decree of Thoudippos applies an existing rule to all the cities now assessed, and does not, as might appear, create the rule.

201. The taxation of the rich

As well as leading to an increase in the *phoros*, the war also led to substantial levies of *eisphorai* (see **197**B); that they were seen as a burden emerges clearly from a passage of Aristophanes in a play of 424. Despite the *phoros* and *eisphorai*, however, the Athenians were forced to borrow heavily from the possessions of their temples (see Meiggs and Lewis no. 72, covering 426/5–423/2; and compare Thuc. II.13.5 = **194**B).

(Kleon addresses the chorus of wealthy *hippeis* who have just insulted him.) 'You'll pay me back good and proper when you're weighed down by *eisphorai*; for I'll see that you're listed among the rich' (thus with the heaviest obligations).

Aristophanes, Knights 923–926

20 The uneasy peace

Of the allies of Sparta, the Boiotians, Corinthians, Eleians and Megarians had voted against the peace of 421 (see **193**); in the uncertain atmosphere of the period, the Spartans seem to have attempted to restore the unity between themselves and the Athenians which had obtained at the time of the Persian Wars. The Argives, fearing the Spartans, sought first to ally themselves with Sparta's disgruntled allies, then to bring in an Athens suspicious of Sparta; and 'traditional' alignments at once asserted themselves once more – Sparta and her allies (except for Elis and Mantineia) on the one side, Athens and Argos on the other.

202. The problems of peace

One factor which had no doubt encouraged some Spartans to vote for war in 431 was the fear that their allies would otherwise abandon them (and the defensive ring round the vulnerable Spartan *politeia* disappear); Spartan hopes in 421, however, that they would not be forced to choose between peace with Athens and the satisfaction of their allies, turned out to be ill-founded.

It fell by lot to the Spartans to be the first to give back what they held, and so they at once released the men whom they held as prisoners and sent Ischagoras and Menas and Philocharidas as ambassadors to the area of Thrake to order Klearidas to hand over Amphipolis to the Athenians and everyone else to implement the terms of the treaty as they applied to them. But they refused, regarding the terms as unacceptable; and even Klearidas refused to hand over the *polis*, thereby gratifying the Chalkidians,[1] saying that he could not hand over the *polis* if they were opposed . . . (22) Meanwhile, the allies also happened to be at Sparta, and the Spartans also ordered those of them who had not implemented the terms of the treaty to do so; but they used the same pretext on which they had rejected similar orders before and refused, unless the Spartans made a treaty which had more regard for justice than the present one. So the Spartans sent them away since they would not obey them, and themselves made an alliance with the Athenians; now that the Argives

379

had refused to come to an agreement in response to the embassy of Ampelidas and Lichas, the Lakedaimonians thought that if the Athenians were allies the Argives would pose the least possible threat to them; they also thought that the rest of the Peloponnesos would be most likely to remain quiet; for if it had been able to, it would have turned to the Athenians. So since there were ambassadors of the Athenians present, discussions took place and they came to an agreement and swore to an alliance. (There follow the terms and the names of those who swore on behalf of the two sides.) (24.2) This alliance was made not long after the peace treaty and the Athenians then returned to the Lakedaimonians the men captured on the island;[2] it was the beginning of summer of the eleventh year.[3]

This then is the account of the ten years which the first war occupied.[4] (25) And after the treaty and the alliance of the Spartans and the Athenians, which occurred after the ten-year war, when Pleistolas was *ephoros* at Sparta and Alkaios was *archōn* at Athens, there was peace between those who accepted their terms; but the Corinthians and some of the *poleis* in the Peloponnesos were trying to overturn what had been agreed, and the immediate consequence was another quarrel, this time between her allies and Lakedaimon. And furthermore, as time went on, the Spartans became objects of suspicion to the Athenians also, since they failed to do some of the things which were laid down in what had been agreed;[5] and for six years and ten months they refrained from invading each others' land, but elsewhere they did each other as much harm as possible, at peace, but close to war; finally, however, they were actually compelled[6] to break the treaty made after the ten years (of war) and once more went openly to war.

Thucydides v.21–25*

1 The people of Olynthos (see **192**), concerned at the prospect of the re-establishment of Athenian power.
2 Of Sphakteria, see **190**.
3 Of the war, thus 421.
4 This sentence and the final version of the chapter which follows were clearly written after the outbreak of the Dekeleian War in 413, perhaps even after the defeat of Athens in 404.
5 This theme recurs at v.32.5.
6 Compare **165**A and **194** n.10.

203. The rise of Alkibiades

We have seen (**202**) that the Athenians came to suspect the intentions of the Spartans because of their failure to keep some of the terms of the peace treaty;

their suspicion was increased as Sparta began to attempt to restore her credibility with her allies. As it became clear that the 'Peace of Nikias', although it had left the Athenians their empire, had not precipitated the dissolution of the alliance under the control of Sparta, an increasing number of Athenians turned their thoughts to a more aggressive policy; their spokesman was Alkibiades.

Since the Spartans were at odds with the Athenians in this way, those in Athens also who wished to break the peace treaty at once set to work. There were a number of them, but they included Alkibiades the son of Kleinias, a man who was then still young in years, at any rate in the estimation of any other *polis*, but who commanded respect because of the reputation of his ancestors. He did indeed believe that it was better to turn rather to the Argives, but he was also hostile to the peace treaty because of his own ambitious attitude; he resented the fact that the Spartans had made the treaty through Nikias and Laches and had overlooked him because of his age and had not respected him because of the *proxenia* which had once existed in the past. His grandfather[1] had given this up, but he had cultivated the Spartan prisoners from the island with a view to taking it on again. Thinking therefore that he was accorded less than his due in every respect, he opposed the treaty from the beginning, saying that the Spartans were unreliable and only wished to make peace with them in order, having done so, to destroy the Argives and so once more attack the Athenians, now isolated. Now, when the quarrel had taken place, he at once sent to Argos in his private capacity, bidding them as quickly as possible send ambassadors to Athens, in conjunction with the Mantineians and the Eleians, to advocate an alliance; now was the time and he would help them as much as possible.

Thucydides v.43

1 See Fig. 9 on p.133.

204. The quadruple alliance

Alkibiades' efforts (see 203) were crowned by success and what was an anti-Spartan league in all but name came into being. See in general H. D. Westlake, 'Thucydides and the uneasy peace', CQ 65 (1971), 315–25; R. Seager, 'After the peace of Nikias: diplomacy and policy', CQ 70 (1976), 249–69.

These then were the terms of the treaty and the alliance (between the Athenians, Argives, Mantineians and Eleians); the treaty with the Lakedaimonians was not as a result revoked, not by either party. On the other hand, the Corinthians, although they were allies of the Argives,[1] did not become a party; furthermore, they had not been a party to the earlier alliance between the Eleians and Argives and Mantineians, who had agreed to have the same friends and enemies; they had said that they were satisfied with the existing *epimachia*,[2] having agreed to help each other, and would join in hostile action against no one. So the Corinthians detached themselves from the allies and inclined once more to the Spartans.

Thucydides v.48

1 As a result of earlier Argive diplomatic activity.
2 See **176** n.3.

205. The battle of Mantineia

Helped along by Alkibiades, the quadruple alliance finally lurched into battle with Sparta, at Mantineia in 418; Sparta won.

This then at least in broad outline was the course of the battle, the greatest of those in Greece for a very long time and fought by the most important *poleis*. The Lakedaimonians, displaying the weapons of the enemy dead, immediately set up a trophy[1] and stripped the dead; they also collected their own dead and took them to Tegea, where they buried them, and they returned the dead of the enemy under a truce. Seven hundred of the Argives and Orneatans and Kleonaians had died, 200 of the Mantineians and 200 of the Athenians and Aiginetans,[2] including both the *stratēgoi*. The allies of the Lakedaimonians did not even suffer enough for it to be worth mentioning; as far as they were concerned, it was difficult to find out the truth,[3] but it was said that about 300 had died. (75) When it was clear that there was going to be a battle, the other king Pleistoanax had also set out to bring help with the oldest and youngest, and had come as far as Tegea; but when he heard of the victory, he returned. And the Lakedaimonians sent word to the allies from Corinth and beyond the Isthmos to turn back and themselves retreated and dismissed the allies (who had fought); they turned to religious celebration, for it happened to be the time of the Karneia festival.[4] And by this one achievement they dispelled the view of them then current among the Greeks which censured them for their weakness because of the disaster on the island[5] and their senselessness and slowness in other respects; it seemed that they had been done down by fate, but that in spirit they were the same as ever.

Thucydides v.74–75.3

1 See Pritchett, *War* II, ch.13.
2 The men settled on Aigina in 431 when the original inhabitants were expelled.

3 See **56**.
4 See **108** n.9.
5 See **190**.

206. Athens and Melos

Assessed for tribute in 425/4, but never paying it and never part of the Athenian empire, Melos by its independence was the living exception to the assumption that the Athenians could do what they liked with the islands. Just as the Athenians chose to demonstrate their power by subjecting Melos, so Thucydides chose to analyse the position of Athens by staging a debate between the Athenians and the Melians: clearly fictional, since the Melian participants were later executed and no Athenian is likely to have been inclined to divulge to Thucydides remarks such as they are alleged to have made, when he returned from exile at the end of the war. The passage below conveys, we hope, something of the nature of the analysis attempted by Thucydides. See, most recently, D. Gillis, 'Murder on Melos', *Rend. Ist. Lomb.* 112 (1978), 185.

Athenians: Then we shall not use fine phrases saying, for instance, that we have a right to rule because we defeated the Persians or that we are attacking you now because of injuries received – a speech as time-consuming as it would be incredible. And we expect you not to suppose that you will influence us by saying that, although *apoikoi* of the Spartans, you have not served with them or that you have never done us any harm. Rather we urge that you should aim for what is feasible, taking into consideration what we both really think; for you know as well as we do that in human reckoning the standard of justice depends on equality of power to compel and that the strong do what they can and the weak obey.

(90) Melians: Then in our view – our choice is limited, since you have now set us the task of discussing expediency in contrast to justice – it is desirable for you not to undermine a principle that is to the general good of all men, namely, that in the case of all who fall into danger there should be such a thing as fair play and just dealing and that people should be allowed to profit by arguments that are not absolutely decisive. And this affects you as much as anybody, since your own fall would be visited by the most terrible vengeance and would be an example to others.

(91) Athenians: As for us, even if our empire does come to an end, we are not despondent about that end. For powers which rule over others, as the Spartans do – not that we are concerned with the Spartans now – are not severe to the defeated, unlike the subjects of a ruling power who attack it and defeat it. So far as this point is concerned, leave it to us to face the risks. What we shall do now is to show that we are here to negotiate for the good of our own empire and that our remarks are

383

directed to the salvation of your *polis*. We prefer to rule over you without any special effort and we prefer you to be spared for the good of yourselves as well as of ourselves.

(92) Melians: And how could it be just as desirable for us to be enslaved as for you to dominate us?

(93) Athenians: You, by giving in, would save yourselves from disaster; we, by not destroying you, would be able to profit from you.

(94) Melians: So you would not agree to our remaining at peace as friends instead of enemies, but as allies of neither side?

(95) Athenians: It is not that your hostility injures us; rather, if we were on friendly terms with you, our subjects would regard that as a sign of weakness in us, whereas your hatred is evidence of our power.

(96) Melians: Is that your subjects' idea of what is reasonable – to assimilate men who are unconnected with you and men who are mostly your own colonists and in some cases rebels whom you have subdued?

(97) Athenians: They suppose that neither has a worse case in law, but that those who preserve their independence do so by force and that if we fail to attack them it is because we are afraid. So by conquering you we shall increase not only the size but also the security of our empire. We rule the sea and you are islanders, and weaker islanders, too, than the others.

Thucydides v.89–97

21 Athenian politics during the war

The nuances of Spartan politics can no more be observed during the Peloponnesian War than at any other time; with Athens one can, on the other hand, piece together some evidence for the character and problems of war-time political life. The basic context for it was the fact that the entire population of Attika was evacuated to the *astu* itself (**207**). On an abstract view this might have been no bad thing, with decision-making in the *ekklēsia* thus more fully representative of 'the Athenians' as a whole than ever before (and ever again), and general political awareness profitably increased thereby. In fact however the outcome seems to have been at best apathy (**211**) and at worst the development of symptoms of stress and strain within the very fabric of a radical democratic system, now left (as Thucydides, at any rate, saw it: **208–209**) with inferior and unstable leaders to guide it through the war; the competence of the *dēmos* to sustain a consistent strategy was called into question (**210**), and a gulf began to open between those advising a course of action and those who had the job of implementing it (**212**). After 421 there was an opportunity for these problems to diminish, but instead they grew worse: the gifted but flawed young aristocrat Alkibiades dominated Athenian politics, present and absent, between then and the end of the war; there was a succession of unedifying political scandals (**213, 214, 237**); and, most seriously of all, the *débâcle* in Sicily (**219–226**) and the consequent resumption of the war brought to a head the feeling amongst many Athenians, including that crucially important group of *chrēstoi* (see **143**) who had hitherto been prepared to accept the democracy on its own terms and pursue a career of leadership within it, that a different *politeia* might have its advantages. And from there it was only one small step to an oligarchic revolution (**227, 244**).

See further: Connor, *Politicians*, 87–198.

207. The evacuation of Attika

In the Periklean strategy for the Archidamian War (**194**), the *chōra* of Attika itself was expendable; indeed it simply had to be expended, so as to deny the Spartans the opportunity of fighting and overcoming Athenian hoplites who were vainly attempting to defend their lands. Consequently, as Thucydides describes, the rural population was brought inside the *astu* and the Long Walls. In purely strategic terms the idea was sound, even though it was to offer more scope to the chaos and devastation brought by the Plague (**196**). However, its more general social and political effects – such as the unaccustomed juxtaposition of city and country so vividly depicted in Aristophanes' *Acharnians* – were more complex, and the inevitable stresses of such a situation must go some way towards explaining many of the war-time political phenomena documented in the rest of this chapter.

The Athenians took Perikles' advice and brought in from the countryside their children and wives and household belongings, bringing away even the woodwork of the houses themselves; their sheep and cattle they sent across to Euboia and the (other) islands nearby. But they found it difficult to uproot themselves, as most of them had always been used to living in the countryside.[1]

(16) So for a long time the Athenians had lived in independent communities throughout the *chōra*, and this persisted even after the *synoikismos*,[2] with most of them – both in early times and latterly too, right down to this present war – being habitually born in the countryside and continuing to live there. Thus they did not find it easy to be uprooted like this and migrate with their entire households, particularly as they had only recently re-established themselves after the Persian Wars.[3] They were dejected and aggrieved at having to leave their homes and their ancestral holy places which were a constant reminder of their origins as a community: what lay before them now was a new way of life, as each man left behind what was, to him, nothing less than his own *polis*.[4] (17) When they arrived in the *astu*, a few found refuge in the houses of friends or relatives but most of them settled down in the uninhabited quarters of the city and in the temples and the shrines of heroes – all except the *akropolis* and the Eleusinion[5] and anywhere else that could be closed off securely. As for the area of land called the Pelargikon, at the foot of the *akropolis*, it was under a curse forbidding anyone to live there, and this was also prohibited by a fragment of a Pythian oracle which said 'better the Pelargikon empty'; nonetheless in this emergency there was no option but to build there as well. And the oracle did, it seems to me, come true, though in a sense contrary to what was expected: what I mean is that it was not because of the unlawful occupation (of the Pelargikon) that the *polis* suffered her misfortunes, but it was thanks to the war that the occupation was necessary, and although the oracle did not mention the war it did foresee that if such occupation ever occurred it would be at a bad time for the Athenians. Many people also established themselves in the towers along the walls, and anywhere

else they could, for the fact was that the *polis* did not have room for them in such numbers – not until later, when they shared out and occupied the (space between the) Long Walls, as well as most of Peiraieus.

Thucydides II.14; 16–17.3

1 Here follows the passage (II.15) translated as **8**.
2 See **8**.
3 An indication of the long and slow-moving memories of the Greeks: compare the 'Marathon-fighters' who appear in the comedies of Aristophanes (e.g. *Acharnians* 181, *Clouds* 986), 65 years and more after that battle.
4 Compare Aristoph. *Ach.* 32–33: 'looking out into the country, longing for peace, hating the *astu*, yearning for my own deme'. It was of course true that the *ekklēsia* had taken a democratic decision to approve Perikles' proposal, but the rural population actually affected by it will have been in a minority at this as at all other (pre-431) *ekklēsia* meetings: see in brief J. A. O. Larsen, *CPh* 44 (1949), 175 with n.28; and, further, **211**.
5 The temple of Demeter.

208. Perikles' policy under stress

Perikles must have been well aware that his evacuation policy was a risk – not in purely strategic terms but because of the heavy demands which it made upon the Athenians' self-restraint and long-term optimism. And with the second Peloponnesian invasion coinciding with the Plague (**106**) he found himself, as he must have anticipated, bearing the brunt of their anger and disappointment.

After the second Peloponnesian invasion (in 430), the Athenians had had a change of heart, as for a second time their land had been devastated, and the plague had come upon them simultaneously with the war; and they began to blame Perikles, as the man who by persuading them to go to war had brought about all their misfortunes. They also became eager to reach an agreement with the Spartans, to the extent even of sending them some envoys, but nothing came of it. They were in fact utterly at a loss, and it was upon Perikles that they turned their frustration. He could see how they were reacting badly to their present circumstances and doing everything exactly as he had expected; so as he was still one of the *stratēgoi*, he called together a meeting with the aim of putting fresh heart into them and of making them, if he could dispel their anger, more calm and confident. This is the sort of thing he said when he came forward to speak. (60) 'As I anticipated, you are angry with me, and I understand your reasons: that is why I convened the *ekklēsia* – to remind you (of what was decided), and to rebuke you, if there is any injustice either in your vexation with me or in your wallowing in your misfortunes . . .
(61) . . . Personally, I am the same as ever; I do not change. It is you who

387

have changed. What has happened is that you took my advice before you came to any harm and you regret it now that things are turning out badly for you, so that it is the weakness of your resolve which makes my words appear mistaken. This is because each of you has already experienced the hardship (which my policy entails), whereas proof – for all of you – of its benefits is still a long way off; so now that a great disaster has suddenly come upon you, you do not have the strength of purpose to stick to your decisions. When something happens suddenly, unexpectedly and entirely incalculably it makes a slave of a man's spirit. This is what has happened to you, for all sorts of reasons – the plague being the last straw. Nevertheless you live in a great *polis* and have been brought up in a way of life appropriate to its greatness, so you must be prepared to face major calamities without detriment to your reputation. All mankind alike claims the right to censure those whose faintheartedness causes them to fall short of their reputation, as well as to abhor those whose presumption leads them to pretend to a reputation which was never theirs. So what each of you must do is to put aside your private sorrows and join in the communal effort to survive. (62) As to the hardships involved in this war, you may fear that they will increase to such an extent that we will be bound to succumb in the end, but what I have said on many other occasions ought to be quite enough to convince you that such fears are groundless. Here though is another point – something which, it seems to me, you have never yet realised as an advantage, which belongs to you from the great size of your empire. I myself have never mentioned this before in my speeches, and I should not have done so now, in a claim which gives the appearance of boasting, if I had not seen that you are discouraged beyond all reason. The point is this: you imagine that your empire consists only of your allies, but I declare that of the two parts of the useful and visible world – the land and the sea – you are absolute masters of the whole of one of them, in terms both of the area which you already control and of what, if you wanted, you could go on to add to it. At the moment, with your navy as strong as it is now, neither the King (of Persia) nor any other nation can stop you from sailing wherever you choose. Thus this power of yours brings an advantage quite different from that of houses and land, which you prize so highly once they have been taken away from you. It is unreasonable of you to react so badly to the loss of what by comparison with our sea-power are no more than rich men's pleasure parks. You must make light of it, and recognise that if we are determined to work to preserve our freedom we shall easily recover such things, whereas to submit to the will of others is just the way to lose our heritage altogether. Be the men that your fathers were! They won an empire by their own labours, not by inheritance from others, and then went on to preserve it and bequeath it to you; and there is more shame in being robbed of an empire that one already has than in trying to acquire one and failing in the attempt. When you come to grips with your enemies, do so not simply with spirit but with the knowledge that they are inferior to you: even a coward, if his ignorance does not bring him bad luck, may boast that he is confident, but a sense of superiority over one's opponents comes only to those who like ourselves have good reason to believe that the enemy can be beaten. And when fortune favours both sides equally, what makes boldness so much stronger is the intelligence which comes from this sense of superiority, and which puts its trust not so much in hope – a desperate resort for desperate circumstances – as in rational thought about the facts of the situation and, on that basis, a safer prediction of what is to come. (63) And it is reasonable that you should support the dignity which the *polis* has gained through its empire. This is something in which you take pride, all of you, and you must not seek to evade its burdens unless you also forgo its honours. Do not imagine, either, that this is a simple struggle about slavery or freedom: it is also about the loss of our empire, and the dangerous hatred we have incurred in ruling it. The empire is something from which it is no longer possible for you to withdraw – however much this appeals to those whose immediate fears may lead them to sit back and do nothing, calling their conduct manliness. By now your empire is like a tyranny:[1] it may seem wrong to have acquired it, but letting it go means danger.'

Thucydides II.39 60.1, 61.2–63.2

1 This phrase is echoed – though with the crucial omission of 'like' – by Kleon in III.37.2: see **210B**.

209. Perikles and his successors

With speeches such as the one just excerpted (**208**), Perikles defended his war strategy against criticism and disillusionment; nonetheless, as Thucydides describes, the issue soured the last years of his long and distinguished career in the forefront of Athenian political life (and he died not long after it, in the autumn of 429). The episode prompted Thucydides, in a passage written with post-404 hindsight, to reflect upon what he saw as the disastrous contrast, for Athens, between the statesman Perikles and his unworthy, irresponsible and demagogic successors. Tendentious and overdrawn though it is, this judgment has exerted a fundamental influence upon subsequent views of Athenian political life in these years, and it retains some residue of validity even today.

These were the sort of arguments that Perikles used in his attempt to make the Athenians less angry with him and to divert their thoughts

389

from their immediate sufferings. And as far as official policy was concerned they took his advice and sent no more envoys to Sparta, becoming instead more enthusiastic about the war. On an individual level, though, their misfortunes were a great burden to them. The *dēmos*, with little enough to begin with, was deprived even of that; the upper classes (*dunatoi*) had lost their fine estates in the *chōra* and their expensive, lavishly-furnished country houses; and worst of all, they were at war, not peace. So the anger against Perikles was universal, and it did not abate until he had been condemned to pay a fine.[1] But not long afterwards – as is the way with crowds[2] – they elected him *stratēgos* again and put all their affairs into his hands; by then they were feeling their individual sufferings less keenly, while as regards the needs of the *polis* as a whole they regarded him as invaluable. This was because for the whole period of peace-time when he presided over the *polis* his moderate policies kept it safe;[3] it was indeed under him that Athens was at her greatest; and when the war came it was clear that here again he was estimating in advance the city's strength. He lived on for two years and six months after it had begun, and when he died his foresight with regard to it became even more evident. For he had said that the Athenians would win through if they bided their time and looked after their navy, without trying to extend the empire while the war was in progress, and avoiding anything which put the *polis* at risk. But what they did was the exact opposite, both in these respects and also in others which had no apparent connection with the war; and the pursuit of personal ambition and private profit led to policies which were bad for themselves and their allies alike – policies which if successful brought honour and advantage mainly to individuals but impaired the war-effort of the whole *polis* when they failed. And the reason for this was that Perikles, by dint of his position of esteem, his intelligence and his obvious and utter incorruptibility, was able to hold the masses in check without taking away their liberty. It was not a question of their leading him but of his leading them: since he did not seek to acquire power for improper reasons he had no need to flatter them; and once the power was his, his standing was such that he could contradict them and provoke their anger. At any rate, whenever he realised that arrogance was leading them to initiate something at the wrong moment his words would give them a sharp reminder of what they had to fear, and when, conversely, they were unreasonably afraid he would restore their confidence. And what resulted was nominally a democracy, but in fact the rule of the first man.[4] His successors, on the other hand, were more on a level with one another, and as each of them strove for supremacy there was resort to demagogic methods and thus surrender of control over the conduct of affairs. This, in a great *polis* with an empire to govern, led to many blunders, including the expedition to Sicily – though there the error, while to some extent one of judgment, an underestimate of the opposition to be expected, was more one of management, with those at home making decisions later which were not in the best interests of the expeditionary forces: in their fight for the leadership of the *dēmos* they were so busy abusing each other that they allowed the expedition to lose its impact, and their squabbling brought the affairs of the *polis* for the first time into real confusion.[5] And yet, after being crushed in Sicily, where they lost most of their fleet and all their other forces, and with *stasis* already breaking out in the *polis*,[6] the Athenians nonetheless held out for eight years[7] against their original enemies (the Peloponnesians), joined now by the Sicilians, against their own allies, most of whom had revolted, and – later on – against Kyros, son of the King (of Persia), who joined the Peloponnesians and provided them with money for their fleet;[8] and it was not until they had ruined themselves by their own internal strife that, in the end, they had to capitulate. So overwhelmingly great and numerous were the grounds for Perikles' initial forecast that, as regards the war against the Peloponnesians themselves, the *polis* would quite easily win through.

Thucydides II.65

1 And, necessarily, dismissed from office. On the fine and possible grounds for it see Gomme, *Commentary* II, 182–3.
2 By such casual asides as this Thuc. betrays his distaste for democracy *per se* – without someone like Perikles there to 'rule' it (see below); compare IV 28 3 (**212**).
3 Compare and contrast the arguments of Alkibiades in Thuc. VI 18.
4 See **148**.
5 See Ch.22.
6 See **227**.
7 Shilleto's textual emendation must surely be right here; the MSS reading 'three' makes no sense.
8 See **233**.

210. Political aspects of the Mytilene debate

The suppression of the revolt of Mytilene (**197–198**) gave Thucydides the opportunity to present at some length a picture of post-Periklean political conditions in Athens. Naturally the debate which actually took place will have been much less formalised than is suggested here, where only two opposing speeches are given, and it may well have also concentrated more upon the immediate strategic and tactical issues which the revolt raised; nevertheless, as Thucydides presents it to us it becomes an analysis, from two contrasting standpoints, of the current problems both of Athenian imperialism and of Athenian radical democracy.

(A) When Salaithos[1] and the others arrived (in Athens), the Athenians immediately put Salaithos to death, despite his offer, amongst other things, to have the Peloponnesians withdrawn from Plataiai, which they were still besieging. They then discussed what to do with the other prisoners, and in their anger they decided to put them to death – not only them, indeed, but all the adult male Mytilenians; and the women and children were to be sold into slavery. What they held against the Mytilenians was the fact that they were not, like the others, subject-allies, yet they had still revolted; and much of their bitterness arose from the fact that the Peloponnesians' fleet had dared to venture across to Ionia to support the revolt – a point which showed, it seemed to them, that the revolt had been long premeditated. So they sent a trireme to Paches,[2] to tell him what had been decided and to order him to kill the Mytilenians without delay. On the following day, however, there was a sudden change of heart, and people began to reflect upon the gravity and the cruelty of this decision, to destroy a whole *polis* rather than simply the men responsible for the revolt. When this became clear to the Mytilenian envoys who were there in Athens, and also to their Athenian supporters, the authorities were approached with a view to having the matter debated a second time; and they succeeded in this all the more easily because the authorities too plainly recognised that the majority of the *politai* wanted to be given a second opportunity to consider the question. So the *ekklēsia* was convened without further ado. Several speeches were made, taking differing points of view, and then Kleon son of Kleainetos came forward and spoke again. He it was who on the previous occasion had successfully pressed the view that the Mytilenians should be put to death. Indeed he was in general the most violent of the *politai*, and the man who at that time had by far the most influence with the *dēmos*.

Thucydides III.36

(B) *Kleon*

'On many other occasions before now I have seen for myself that a democracy is not competent to rule others, but this has never been clearer than it is now, with your change of heart about the Mytilenians. The fact is that because your own daily relations with one another are not prey to fear and intrigue you imagine that the same goes for your allies, and you do not see that whenever you let them persuade you into an error or you yield to them out of pity you are being weak, in a way which is dangerous to you and does not even make them any more grateful to you. What you fail to appreciate is that your empire is a tyranny,[3] imposed upon people who intrigue against you and who do not enjoy being ruled. Their obedience to you is a result not of any favours you may do them – to your own detriment – but of your own superiority; it is a matter of your strength, not their goodwill. And what is worst about this whole situation is the thought that we cannot stick to any of our decisions, or recognise that a *polis* with inferior *nomoi* which are always observed is better off than if good ones are constantly disregarded; that ignorance combined with self-control is more helpful than unbridled cleverness; and that, by and large, ordinary folk, with all their limitations, make a better job of running a *polis* than those with more brains. The trouble with intellectuals, you see, is that they want to appear wiser than the *nomoi* and to dominate all public discussions, as if there could never be other, more important occasions for them to display their opinions; and the usual result of this sort of thing is that they ruin their *poleis*. Ordinary men, on the other hand, without such confidence in their own intelligence, are content to be more ignorant than the *nomoi* and do not mind their comparative inability to criticise a speech made by a good speaker; and in this role of impartial judges – rather than competitors – they generally do well. And that is how we (politicians) too ought to behave, instead of being led by cleverness and the desire to win a contest of wits to give you people advice against our better judgment.

(38) As for me, I am the same as ever;[4] my view has not changed, and I am amazed at those who proposed a second discussion about the Mytilenians. It is a waste of time, and more advantageous to the criminals than to us: for this is the way to dull the edge of the victim's anger when he takes action against the offender, whereas reprisals are best, and best suited to the offence, if they are dealt out as soon as possible. I also wonder who will undertake to contradict me and try to prove that the Mytilenians have helped us by hurting us, or that our misfortunes are injurious to our allies as well. Clearly anyone who attempted to convince you of this would be a man who either had such confidence in his powers of speech as to struggle to persuade you that the previous resolution was not resolved at all, or else someone motivated by personal gain to lead you astray with some polished piece of plausible rhetoric. And in contests of this sort the *polis* gives the prizes to others but runs the risks alone. It is you who are to blame for this, for staging these disastrous competitions. You have become spectators at a speech-festival; an audience for action. When something is to be done, you examine how feasible it will be by hearing fine speeches on the subject; when something has already been done, your assessment of it relies not so much upon what you have seen for yourselves as upon what you are told by accomplished – and critical – speakers. In your capacity for being deceived by some novel argument you are second to none, yet you do not like to follow one which is tried and tested; you disdain the normal,

enslaved as you are to every new paradox. Each one of you, in fact, wishes above all else to be able to speak himself, or, failing that, to compete with those who can and do make such speeches, by not appearing to lag behind in your comprehension of the views put forward, by applauding a good point even before it is made, and by being as eager to guess where an argument is leading as you are slow to foresee what its consequences will be. One might say that you are looking for some sort of different world from the one in which we actually live. Certainly you do not put your minds adequately to the situation facing you at the moment. You are quite simply victims of your own pleasure in listening, and more like an audience sitting and listening to sophists[5] than men deliberating about the affairs of the *polis*.'

Thucydides III. 37–38

(c) *Diodotos*[6]

'I have no fault to find with those who proposed a second discussion about the Mytilenians, and I do not applaud those who say that it is bad to deliberate many times about important issues. In my opinion the two things which are most inimical to good counsel are haste and anger, the one being regularly accompanied by folly and the other by ignorance and narrowmindedness. And as to speeches, whoever contends that they are not to be the instructors of actions is either stupid or has some personal axe to grind: he is stupid if he thinks that there is any other possible way to assess the uncertainties of the future, and he must have an axe to grind if, in his wish to persuade you to do something discreditable, he realises that although he cannot make a good speech in a bad cause he can spread some fine slanders instead, thus intimidating both his opponents and his hearers. Most intolerable of all, though, are those who claim, *before* their opponent has spoken, that he has been paid to put on a rhetorical display. If their charge was simply that of ignorance, the speaker who failed to convince his hearers would go away with the reputation of being more stupid than his opponents but no less honest, but if dishonesty is what he is accused of, the speaker who wins his case becomes suspect, and the one who does not is regarded as dishonest and stupid at the same time! And there is no advantage to the *polis* in this sort of thing, but a loss – a loss of her advisers, who are afraid to open their mouths; and it would in fact be the best thing for the *polis* if the sort of *politai* I have been describing were incompetent speakers, for then we should be much less likely to be talked into making mistakes. The good *politēs* ought to prove his case not by intimidating the opposition but in fair argument, while the sensible *polis*, without giving extra honours to its best counsellors, should not deprive them of the honours that they already have; and if a man's advice is not taken he should not be disgraced, let alone punished. In this way the successful speaker would be least likely to pursue still greater rewards by making some popular but insincere speech; nor would the unsuccessful speaker, for his part, strive to win over the masses by the same sort of ingratiating methods. (43) Yet what we do is the opposite. And what is more, if a man is so much as suspected of having been bribed to speak, however excellent his advice may be, we are so resentful of him because of the dubious suspicion that he has made a profit that we rob the *polis* of the undubitable benefit of his opinion. The state of affairs now is such that good advice honestly given is no less suspect than bad, and the result of this is that just as the speaker with highly dangerous proposals in mind resorts to deceit to win over the masses, so also the man with better suggestions has to tell lies if he is to be believed. And thanks to this excess of subtlety we live in the only *polis* where it is impossible to perform a public service openly and without deception, for anyone who does so is rewarded with the suspicion that he is out for some secret profit. Yet even so, in view of the great importance of matters such as the one we are now facing, we the advisers have to resolve to look further ahead than you who view things only superficially, especially since we are accountable for the advice we give you, whereas you are not accountable for how you take it.[7] Indeed if those giving advice and those following it ran the same risks you would take decisions which were more sensible; but as it is, there are times when failure leads you to punish on an angry impulse the one man who originally advised you – forgetting that you all agreed with him and were therefore equally mistaken.'

Thucydides III.42–43

1 The Spartan adviser to the revolt: see Thuc. III.25–27.
2 The Athenian *stratēgos* there (Thuc. III.18.3).
3 Compare Perikles in **208** (with n.1).
4 Another echo of Perikles in **208**.
5 See **155**.
6 All that Thuc. tells us about this speaker (III.41) is that he too, like Kleon, was repeating his views of the previous day. For the sum total of what can be said or surmised about Diodotos see M. Ostwald, *GRBS* 20 (1979), 5–13.
7 'Accountable' in various ways – by the *euthynai* audits for those in office (**65B**) and such procedures as the *graphē paranomōn* (see **310**) for others. This issue of who was ultimately responsible for action proposed, necessarily, by an individual but endorsed by the *ekklēsia* as a whole was clearly a difficult one: see also Old Oligarch (= [Xenophon], *Ath. Pol.*) II.17; and further **212** and **226**.

211. The red rope

Every Athenian citizen was eligible to attend the *ekklēsia* – but how many actually did so? The 'electorate' as a whole probably numbered more than 40,000 in this period (Ehrenberg, *Greek State*, 31), yet before its reconstruction in *c*.400 the Pnyx auditorium seated a maximum of 6,000; see M. H. Hansen, 'How many Athenians attended the *ekklesia*?', *GRBS* 17 (1976), 115–34, at pp.130–2; so particularly given the presence in the *astu*, during the Peloponnesian War, of the large rural population of Attika (207) it might be thought that full houses were assured. Yet on the contrary we have some evidence, presented here, that attendance figures were falling, to a level where action was needed to attempt to improve them.

On this 'red rope' see also Aristoph. *Ekkles.* 376–379 (with Hansen, *loc. cit.* 123–4 and 132–3); and on positive incentives, in the fourth century, to attend see **304**.

Dikaiopolis: Never since I was old enough to wash myself have I been so tormented in my eyebrows by dust as now, the morning of the *kuria ekklēsia*,[1] with the Pnyx here empty, while the men in the *agora* gossip and shift up and down to avoid the red-soaked rope.

(*Scholiast*:[2] In view of the necessity that they should meet together in the *ekklēsia* they contrived this and many other things. For they used to open out the wattle screens, shut off the roads which do not lead into the *ekklēsia* and remove the goods for sale in the markets, so that people would not waste time round about them; then encompassing them with a rope soaked in red ochre they would drive them together into the *ekklēsia*. This they did to prevent loitering – for whoever they touched had a penalty to pay.)

Aristophanes, *Acharnians* 17–22, with the scholiast on line 22

1 The principal, formal meeting, ten times a year; see **309**.
2 Compare **147**.

212. Nikias and Kleon: the rift between politicians and generals

The Pylos and Sphakteria affair (190) has a significance quite unconnected with Archidamian War strategy – a significance in Athenian internal politics: for Kleon's boast that he could outdo Nikias (see below) marks, symbolically at any rate, the early stages of a gulf between speakers and doers; orators and politicians on the one hand, *stratēgoi* and other office-holders on the other. For the time being it remained bridgeable, as Kleon demonstrated. The fourth century, however, was to be a different story; see **314**.

Kleon realised that he had become a suspect figure for having prevented the two sides from reaching an agreement, so he declared that the men who had brought the news were not telling the truth. The response of the messengers to this was to suggest that if the Athenians did not believe their reports they should send out some inspectors; and Kleon himself was chosen for this, together with Theagenes. Kleon now realised that he would be obliged either to bring back the same report as the men whom he had been calling liars or else be shown to be a liar himself if he said the opposite. He also saw that the Athenians had become somewhat more inclined to send out an(other) expedition, so he told them that they ought not to be sending out inspectors and wasting time while opportunities slipped by: if they believed what the messengers said to be true they should sail to Pylos and tackle the men on the island. He then pointed at Nikias son of Nikeratos, the *stratēgos* involved, and a man he hated; and he put the blame on him, by declaring that if only the *stratēgoi* were real men it would be easy to equip a force to sail and capture the men on the island; certainly he himself would have done it – had he been in command. (28) At this the Athenians began to make a certain amount of clamour against Kleon, demanding to know why, if he thought the operation so easy, he was not already embarked and on his way. Nikias noticed this – as well as the fact that he was being baited – and said that as far as the *stratēgoi* were concerned Kleon could take out whatever forces he liked and try his luck. Kleon thought at first that this offer to relinquish the command was purely a debating point, and as such he was ready to take it up; however, once he realised that Nikias was genuinely handing over to him he tried to back out, saying that Nikias, not he, was the *stratēgos*. He was now frightened, having never imagined that Nikias would have the nerve to resign in his favour. But Nikias again urged him to go, calling the Athenians to witness that he was offering to relinquish the Pylos command. As for the Athenians, they behaved in the way that crowds always do:[1] the more Kleon tried to avoid the expedition and take back what he had said, the more they urged Nikias on to give up his command and shouted to Kleon to sail. Consequently, seeing no longer any way of backing out of what he had said, Kleon came forward and agreed to lead the expedition: he was not afraid, he declared, of the Spartans, and he would sail without taking a single man from Athens, but only the Lemnians and Imbrians who were available,[2] together with the peltasts from Ainos[3] who had come to help and 400 archers from elsewhere; with these forces, added to those already at Pylos, he said that within twenty days he would either bring the Lakedaimonians back alive or else kill them where they were. This airy claim caused a certain amount of laughter, though the sensible men were cheered by it, thinking to themselves that its result would be a good thing either way: either they would be rid of Kleon, which was what they rather expected,

397

or else, if they were wrong about this, they would have the Lakedaimonians in their power.⁴

Thucydides IV.27.3–28

1 See **209** with n.2.
2 Not, in all probability, native Lemnians and Imbrians but Athenians living as *klērouchoi* there: see Meiggs, *Empire*, 424–5.
3 In eastern Thrake. Peltasts: see **257**.
4 For Kleon's success see **190**.

213. The 'ostrakismos' of Hyperbolos

The Peloponnesian War also saw, in 417 (or possibly one or two years later), the *reductio ad absurdum* of the *ostrakismos* procedure (**79**) – for reasons made clear enough by Plutarch in this passage. (For shorter versions of the story see Plut. *Arist.* 7.3–4 and *Alk.* 13.3–4.) On Alkibiades see further **214–215**. On Hyperbolos, B. Baldwin, 'Notes on Hyperbolos', *Acta Classica* 14 (1971), 151–6; and on the episode in general Connor, *Politicians*, 79–84.

Alkibiades' quarrel with Nikias¹ became so intense that a vote about *ostrakismos* was held. This is the procedure which the *dēmos* used to employ from time to time when they wished, by the *ostrakon* vote, to remove for ten years any individual who was an object of general suspicion because of his reputation or jealousy because of his wealth.² This involved both men in a lot of confusion and danger, since one or the other of them would clearly fall victim to the *ostrakismos*. In the case of Alkibiades, people detested the way he lived and dreaded his boldness – as is made clear elsewhere, in my biography of him. With Nikias, on the other hand, it was to some extent his wealth³ which made him an object of envy but above all his life-style, which seemed anti-social and unpopular and made him appear stand-offish, anti-democratic and peculiar; and since he often opposed what the masses wanted and tried to force them to do what he, though not they, thought was good for them, he was considered a nuisance.⁴ To tell the simple truth, though, this was a contest between the young men who wanted war and their elders who wanted peace, with the former voting against Nikias and the latter against Alkibiades.⁵ However, 'in seditious times even the villain gets his share of honour';⁶ and on this occasion too, by splitting into two, the *dēmos* gave scope to the worst sort of reckless mischief-makers. One of them was Hyperbolos, of (the deme) Perithoidai, a fellow whose boldness derived not from any power but whose power, as he acquired it, derived from his boldness; and it was the very credit which he gained in the *polis* which led to his being a discredit to the *polis*. Hyperbolos thought himself, at this time, beyond the reach of the *ostrakon* – he would indeed have been a more suitable candidate for the pillory! – and he expected that when one or the other of his rivals had been banished he would himself be a match for whichever one of them was left; so everyone knew that their quarrel was a source of pleasure to him and that he was inciting the *dēmos* against both of them. Accordingly, when his rascally behaviour became known to the two sides, the supporters of Nikias and of Alkibiades, they held secret talks with one another, combined and unified their two factions into one, and thus brought it about that the victim of the *ostrakismos* was neither Nikias nor Alkibiades but Hyperbolos himself.[7]

The immediate reaction of the *dēmos* to this was delight and laughter, but afterwards they were vexed to think that the procedure had been insulted by its application to so unworthy a man. This was because they considered that even punishment is a matter of some dignity, or rather they regarded *ostrakismos* as a punishment for men of the likes of Thoukydides and Aristeides but as an honour for Hyperbolos, and an excuse for him to boast that being a villain had brought him the same fate as the best men. Hence Plato the comic poet[8] somewhere said of him: 'what befell him was worthy indeed of the men of old, *too* worthy for slaves like him; not for his sort was the *ostrakon* devised'. And the outcome was that nobody was ever ostracised after Hyperbolos: he was the last, just as Hipparchos of (the deme) Cholargos, a relative of Peisistratos, had been the first.

Plutarch, *Nikias* 11.1–6

1 See **203**, **219**.
2 See **79**.
3 See **142**C.
4 Evidently he had failed to learn from Perikles (see **209**).
5 See further **219**.
6 A proverb in hexameter verse attributed to the Hellenistic poet Callimachus (*c.*305–*c.*240).
7 For his ultimate fate see Thuc. VIII.73.3; Fornara no.145.
8 I.e. not the philosopher. Plato Comicus lived and wrote in the late fifth century and the early fourth, his plays including a *Hyperbolos* from which Plut. took the quotation which now follows.

214. The Hermai and the Mysteries

The departure of the Athenian expedition to Sicily in 415 (**219**) coincided with the war's most serious scandal in Athens itself. The two primary sources for it (i.e. apart from Plut. *Alk.* 18–23.2) are Thuc. VI.27–29, 53 and 60–61, translated here, and the speech *On the Mysteries* by the orator Andocides, one of the men personally involved. Our difficulties in establishing exactly what happened arise to some extent from the inevitable divergences between these two very different authorities, but more particularly from the inherent obscurity and irrationality of the episode itself. Fundamentally it was a religious scandal, with two overlapping components: the mutilation of the small stone effigies of Hermes which were a common sight throughout the city, and the profanation by parody of the secret and solemn ceremonies of the Eleusinian Mysteries, with *c*. 100 men implicated in the two episodes taken together (list in Gomme, *Commentary* IV, 276–80). It would be an error to suppose that many Athenians would not have been sufficiently appalled at such things, at such a time, on religious grounds alone; nevertheless, with the *enfant terrible* Alkibiades at the centre of the accusations (as regards the Mysteries, at least), the political dimension of the affair was inescapable also. D. M. MacDowell (*Andokides: On the Mysteries* (Oxford, 1962), 192) makes the cogent point that as profanation of the Mysteries took place in secret it is unlikely to have been a political act in intent; once brought to light, however, it was clearly given a political interpretation. The mutilation of the Hermai is harder to understand, except as an attempt (ineffective, if so) to stop the Sicilian expedition. Overall it seems safe to say that 'the impieties prompted in the Athenians the thought that a whole section of their society had demonstrated the will to do as it pleased and, if not resisted, would have demonstrated also the power to do so' (Gomme, *Commentary* IV, 285). For the detailed problems see MacDowell, *op. cit.*, and the fundamental discussion of K. J. Dover in Gomme, *Commentary* IV, 264–88, esp. 282–8.

Meanwhile, and in a single night, nearly all the stone Hermai in the *polis* – those characteristically Athenian ones with the square pillars, which are so numerous in the doorways of private houses and in temples – had their faces mutilated.[1] Nobody knew who had done it, but large public rewards were offered for informants, and it was further decreed that there should be a guarantee of immunity for anyone – Athenian, foreigner or slave – who knew of any other act of impiety which had taken place and who cared to give information about it. Thus the matter was taken very seriously: as well as being an omen for the expedition it gave the impression at the same time of being part of a revolutionary conspiracy to overthrow the *dēmos*. (28) Accordingly information was lodged by certain *metoikoi*[2] and slaves – not about the Hermai at all but about other statues which they claimed had been defaced on an earlier occasion by some young men as a drunken joke, and also about mock celebrations of the Mysteries in private houses.[3] Amongst those accused was Alkibiades, and this fact was taken up by those who hated him most, as an obstacle in the way of their securing the leadership of the *dēmos*, and who thought that if they could drive him out they would occupy first place; so they exaggerated the affair with noisy allegations that both the (profanation of the) Mysteries and the mutilation of the Hermai were part of a plan to overthrow the *dēmos*, and that proof of the fact that

Alkibiades was behind it all could be found in the other instances of his lawless and undemocratic way of life. (29) Alkibiades denied these charges straight away, and was prepared before sailing – the preparations for the expedition being now completed – to stand trial to determine whether he had done any of the things alleged: if, he said, he were found guilty he would pay the penalty, but if acquitted he should continue in his command. He urged the Athenians too not to listen to slanders made against him in his absence but, if he had done wrong, to have him executed without more ado, instead of being so foolish as to send him out in command of such an important expedition with an accusation of this sort still unsettled. But his enemies were afraid that if he were brought to trial then and there he would have the goodwill of the army, while a lenient *dēmos* might wish to protect him because he had persuaded the Argives and some of the Mantineans to join in the expedition. So they were anxious that things should not yet be brought to a head, and produced some more speakers who insisted that Alkibiades ought not to delay the departure of the expedition; he should sail now, but come back and stand trial within a prescribed period of days. Their object in this was to find even more slanderous charges – something which they could do more easily while he was away – and then to send for him and bring him back to stand trial. So it was decided that Alkibiades should sail.

(And so he did; but while the Sicilian campaign gets under way (vi.30–52) his enemies prepare their ground.) (53) At Katane they found that the Salaminia[4] had arrived from Athens for Alkibiades, with orders that he should sail home to defend himself against the charges which the *polis* was bringing, and also for certain other men in the army against whom information had been laid, either – like Alkibiades – in connection with the profanation of the Mysteries or, in some cases, the Hermai affair. The fact was that after the expedition had set off the Athenians had been every bit as anxious as before to investigate what had happened with both the Mysteries and the Hermai, but instead of testing the suitability of their informants they took everything they heard as grounds for suspicion and so, putting their trust in villains, imprisoned some of the very best of the *politai*. To their way of thinking it was preferable that the affair should be ruthlessly dissected and the truth discovered than that any of the accused, of however good repute, should avoid interrogation merely because the man informing against him was a villain. The *dēmos*, it should be explained, had heard tales of the tyranny of Peisistratos and his sons, and of how harsh it had become at the end; they also knew that it had been brought to an end not by themselves and Harmodios but by the Spartans;[5] so they were in a constant state of fear and suspicion (of another tyranny).

401

(60) With these events in mind, and recollecting everything they had heard about them, the Athenian *dēmos* at this time was in an ugly mood, suspicious of the men who had been accused in connection with the Mysteries; and it was believed that the whole thing had been arranged in furtherance of a conspiracy to set up an oligarchy or a tyranny. Because of these suspicions and the anger resulting from them, many leading men were already in prison and there seemed no end to it all; on the contrary, each day saw an increase in savagery, as well as more and more arrests. Eventually, however, one of the prisoners, and the man regarded as the most guilty,[6] was persuaded by one of his fellow-detainees to lodge information, which may or may not have been the truth; some guess that it was and others that it was not, but nobody, either at the time or since, has been able to say for certain who did the deed. Still, this one prisoner talked to the other and persuaded him that even if he had not done the deed himself he should secure a guarantee of immunity and so save himself and also put an end to the prevailing suspicion in the *polis*; he would have a better chance of saving his own skin, he was told, if he made a confession with immunity than if he denied the charges and stood trial. So the man laid information which incriminated both himself and others in the affair of the Hermai. The Athenian *dēmos* was delighted to think that the facts were now out in the open, after all the earlier fears and worries that the anti-democratic conspirators might not be discovered: the informer was immediately set free, together with other prisoners not named in his statement, while the men whom he had accused were brought to trial and executed – the ones, that is, who had been arrested; those who had escaped were condemned to death in their absence and a price put on their heads.[7] It was not clear, in all this, whether the victims deserved their punishment or not, but the short-term benefit to the *polis* at large was obvious enough. (61) As for Alkibiades, the men who had been attacking him even before he set sail were still doing so, and the Athenians began to turn against him: since they believed that the facts about the Hermai affair were now established they were all the more inclined to think that the episode of the Mysteries too, in which he was implicated, had been committed by him with the same end in view, that of conspiring against the *dēmos*. (So, as stated, the Salaminia had been sent to fetch him (and others) back to stand trial; but they evaded the escort – Alkibiades himself making for the Peloponnesos – and were condemned to death by default.)

Thucydides VI.27–29; 53; 60–61.1

1 And also, apparently, their most prominent feature, the phallos, knocked off: see Gomme, *Commentary* IV, 288–9.

2 See **160**.

3 On the Mysteries see Parke, *Festivals*, 55–72.

4 One of the two Athenian 'state' triremes (the other being the Paralos), used to carry messages at high speed: compare, for instance, Thuc. III.33.
5 See **72, 73, 74.** (The story of Harmodios and Aristogeiton now follows: VI.54–59.)
6 The orator Andocides; see above, Intro.
7 Also, and necessarily, their property was confiscated and publicly auctioned: see Meiggs and Lewis no.79 (part of which is **162B**) = Fornara no.147.

215. The charisma of Alkibiades

Many incidents and anecdotes, in Plutarch and elsewhere, testify to the potent charm and charisma of Alkibiades, and the use to which he put these assets during his chequered political career. A telling example is one reported by his sober contemporary Thucydides, who probably knew him personally (see P. A. Brunt, *REG* 65 (1952), 59–96) and who was certainly well aware (see **219**) of how such personal magnetism was more likely to have bad results than good.

The delegates[1] had much more to say, but the army was no more disposed to listen to them; instead, in their anger, the soldiers began to voice all sorts of proposals, with the majority view being that they should sail against Peiraieus. And now it was – seemingly for the first time – that Alkibiades did something which was of enormous benefit to the *polis*: for when these Athenians at Samos were set upon sailing against their fellow-citizens – which, it is quite clear, would have enabled the enemy immediately to take control of Ionia and the Hellespontos – it was he who stopped them. No other single individual would have been capable of restraining the mob in that situation. Alkibiades, however, not only stopped them from making the voyage but also rebuked those who were showing their anger against the envoys for personal reasons, and put a stop to that too. And it was also he himself who gave the delegates their reply when he sent them away: he said that he had no objection to the rule of the Five Thousand but that the Four Hundred should be deposed and the (Kleisthenic) *boulē*, of five hundred, appointed as before; and he would give his full support to any measures of economy which resulted in better pay for the armed forces. In general his message was that they should stand firm and make no concessions to the enemy: for as long as the *polis* was kept safe there was every chance of coming to an agreement with their fellow-citizens there, but it needed only a single defeat for either party – those in Samos or those in Athens – for there to be nobody left with whom to be reconciled.

Thucydides VIII.86.4–7

1 From the government of the Four Hundred in Athens, speaking (in 411) to the Athenian forces at Samos: see in full **227.**

216. The later demagogues

If the distorting effects of Thucydides' view of post-Periklean Athenian politics are subtle ones (see **209**), there is little or no subtlety at all in the picture presented by the Aristotelian *Ath. Pol.*: following in succession from Solon, Peisistratos, Kleisthenes and the leading figures of the early and mid fifth century (28.2), pairs of 'champions' – one of the *dēmos*, one of the upper classes – are passed in review, until the whole sequence supposedly degenerates into undiluted demagogy. Even the author's oligarchic bias (see 28.5) does not excuse such a palpably inadequate model.

After the death of Perikles, Nikias, who later died in Sicily, was the champion of the upper classes, while Kleon son of Kleainetos led the *dēmos*. And Kleon seems to have been the man who did most to corrupt the *dēmos*, by the violence of his methods:[1] he was the first man who shouted when he came to the speaker's rostrum, who used abusive language (there) and who addressed the *dēmos* with his garments tucked up, not with the decorum of the other speakers.[2] Then, after them, Theramenes son of Hagnon[3] led the others, and Kleophon the lyre-maker[4] the *dēmos*. Kleophon was also the man who first provided the two-obol payment (*diōbelia*). This was paid out for some time but subsequently abolished by Kallikrates of (the deme) Paiania, who was the first to promise to raise the payments from two obols to three.[5] Both (Kleophon and Kallikrates) were later condemned to death: for even if the masses have been deceived, for a time, they tend later to hate the men who induced them to do something improper. And after Kleophon there was a continuous succession of demagogues whose main aim was to act outrageously and please the majority, with no thought for the future.

?Aristotle, *Athenaion Politeia* 28.3–4

1 Compare Thuc. in **210A**.
2 Moore, *Aristotle*, 256, suggests that this made Kleon look like a labourer at work. It would thus be the Athenian equivalent of ostentatiously rolling up one's shirt-sleeves.
3 See **227, 237, 244**.
4 See also (e.g.) ?Aristot. *Ath. Pol.* 34.1; Aristoph. *Frogs* 679; Lysias XIII.8 and XIX.48; Aeschin. II.76 and III.150; Connor, *Politicians*, 139–70, *passim*. As regards his being (in the common tradition) a 'lyre-maker', that is the same sort of snobbish misrepresentation that made Kleon a tanner: see Connor, *Politicians*, 151–5.
5 On the *diōbelia* see further **237, 241**. Its history and nature have been matters of some controversy: we follow Meiggs and Lewis (in their commentary on an inscription, no.84, which shows it in existence, and a major item of annual expenditure, in 410/09) in taking it as identical neither with pay for juries (**141**) and assembly (**304**) nor with the contentious fourth-century *theōrika* (see **141**

with n.4, **313**) but as 'a measure of poor relief' in its own right. Kleophon must have introduced it very soon after the fall of the Four Hundred (**227**). It was still in existence in 406 (**237**), but exactly when Kallikrates did away with it in this strange manner is indeterminable.

22 Athens and Sicily

As we saw in Ch. 16 (**172, 174**), the Athenians had a long-standing interest in the far west. They had entered into alliances with various cities of Sicily and southern Italy, presumably out of a desire to exert some general influence in this important grain-producing area but probably not in any expectation that it would come under their direct *hēgemonia*. During the Archidamian War however we see the desire for influence turning into a desire for conquest (**217**), and a consequent feeling that such conquest was a real possibility; so when an opportunity arose to remedy the 'failure' of 427–424 it was eagerly seized. Between 415 and 413, with the Peloponnesian War in a state of uneasy truce, the Athenians mounted a second expedition to Sicily – shorter in length than the first, therefore, but incomparably larger in its scope and its (for Athens) disastrous consequences. It is an episode which finds Thucydides' narrative powers, in Books VI and VII, at their zenith, and this chapter can give no more than the barest bones of his detailed account of the despatch, the fortunes and the ultimate annihilation of the Athenian forces. As an explanation of the fiasco he asserts in II.65.11 (see **209**, end), written after the war was finally over in 404, that to some extent it was simple military underestimation of the opposition – which was evidently the conventional verdict – but chiefly the fact that back in Athens decisions were made which put domestic political advantage above the interests and requirements of the campaign itself. (For this interpretation of the passage and its difficulties see Westlake, *Essays*, ch. 11.) Unfortunately neither he nor any other source gives us enough information to be able to assess this claim. What is clear enough, though, is that the reverberations of the Athenian disaster spread far and wide through the whole Greek world (**226**), and that amongst the Athenians themselves it paved the way for revolution (**227**).

217. The first Sicilian expedition

In Books III and IV of his History Thucydides chronicles, piecemeal, an Athenian expedition to Sicily which lasted from 427 until 424. Sicily, as he explains, had become by now firmly divided between Dorians and Ionians, and it was this which formed the basis (together with a formal alliance with one of the *poleis* involved) of the call to the Athenians to intervene. As to the Athenians' side, we can see the scope of their ambitions enlarging before our very eyes, until their buoyant mood of 424, with the three *stratēgoi* penalised for failing to bring home a victory for which they had never been equipped, clearly prefigures that of 416 (see **219**).

See further: Westlake, *Essays*, chs.6 ('Athenian aims in Sicily, 427–424 B.C.') and 12 ('Hermocrates the Syracusan'); Meiggs, *Empire*, 320–1; de Ste Croix, *Origins*, 221–2.

Towards the end of this same summer (427) the Athenians sent twenty ships to Sicily with the *stratēgoi* Laches son of Melanopos and Charoiades son of Euphiletos. This was because the men of Syracuse and of Leontinoi were at war with each other. With the exception of Kamarina, the other Dorian *poleis* were allies of the Syracusans; these were the *poleis* which originally, at the start of the (Peloponnesian) war, had joined the Spartan alliance,[1] but had not in fact taken an active part in the fighting. On the side of the men of Leontinoi were the *poleis* of Chalkidian origin, together with Kamarina. As regards Italy, Lokroi joined the Syracusans, while the men of Rhegion supported their kinsmen of Leontinoi. Anyway, the allies of Leontinoi sent a delegation to Athens,[2] to appeal both to the ancient alliance[3] and to their common Ionian origin: the Syracusans, they said, were shutting them out from land and sea alike, and the Athenians should send them some ships. And the Athenians did send them ships. Their pretext for doing so was kinship; in fact, though, their aim was to prevent any imports of grain from there into the Peloponnesos, and also to make a preliminary test as to whether Sicily and its affairs could be brought under their control.[4] Accordingly they established themselves at Rhegion, in Italy, and began, with their allies, to carry on the war. And so the summer ended.

(The somewhat desultory campaigning is reported by Thuc. in III.88, 90, 99, 103 and 115. Forty more ships and three new *stratēgoi* are sent out (III.115, IV. 1–5), and the campaigning intensifies (IV.24–25); but at a conference at Gela in the summer of 424 the Syracusan Hermokrates speaks out against Athenian involvement.)

(IV.59) 'Each of us went to war in the first place with the aim, no doubt, of making decisions best suited to our own interests; and now here we are attempting by claim and counter-claim to reach agreement with one another on a settlement. If it should turn out that each one of us does not leave here with a fair deal, we shall go to war again. (60) Yet we ought to recognise, if we have any sense, that when we came together (again) in conference we would be discussing not simply our own individual concerns but the question of whether we would still be able to save Sicily as a whole – for it is Sicily as a whole, in my judgment, that the Athenians are scheming to take over. And it is the Athenians also, far more than any words of mine, who ought to be making us come together and settle our differences. They have the greatest power of any Greeks, and they have come here with a few ships to wait until we make mistakes; in the name of a normal, lawful alliance they are turning our natural hostility towards each other to their own profit. If, you see, we start a war ourselves and invite them into it – though in fact they are men who join in a fight whether they are invited or not – and if we use up our own resources in weakening ourselves and at the same time doing the preliminary spade-work for their empire, what is likely to happen is that when they realise that we are worn out they will one day come here with a larger force and try to bring everything here under their control. (61) Yet, if we have any sense, our purpose – each of us on behalf of his own state – in calling in allies and in running these extra risks ought to be to gain possession of what is someone else's, not to damage what we already have at hand. We must realise too that *stasis* is the greatest destroyer of *poleis* – and of Sicily as a whole, when we its inhabitants respond to a common threat by standing aloof in our individual *poleis*. This is what we must recognise, and then reach agreement, individual with individual and *polis* with *polis*, so as to make a united attempt to save Sicily as a whole. Nobody should suppose that, while the Dorians amongst us are enemies to the Athenians, those of Chalkidian stock are safe because of common Ionian kinship: the Athenians are not here out of hatred of one of the two races into which we are divided but because they want the good things of Sicily which we possess in common.'

(65) When Hermokrates had spoken like this, the Sicilians took his advice and came to an agreement between themselves to end the war. Each state was to keep what it had, except that Kamarina was to take Morgantine, on payment of a stated sum of money to the Syracusans. Those who were allies of the Athenians then summoned the Athenian commanders and told them that they were going to make peace, and that the treaty would apply to the Athenians also; and when the agreement had been made, with the approval of the Athenian commanders, the Athenian fleet then sailed away from Sicily. However, on their return home the *stratēgoi* were punished – Pythodoros and Sophokles by a sentence of exile and the third man, Eurymedon, by a fine – on the grounds that they had been bribed to leave Sicily at a time when they could have taken control of it. Such was the effect upon the Athenians of their good fortune at that moment that they expected never to be thwarted in anything, and believed that the possible and the difficult were equally attainable – whether the forces they used were large or inadequate. And the reason for this was that they *were* surprisingly

successful in most of what they did, which backed up their hope with strength.

Thucydides III.86; IV.59.4–61.3; 65

1 See **185**.
2 Headed by the famous rhetorician and sophist Gorgias (on whom see W. K. C. Guthrie, *The Sophists* (Cambridge, 1971), 269–74).
3 See Meiggs and Lewis nos. 63–64; and **172** Intro.
4 This second reason seems to betray post-416 hindsight; Thuc.'s actual narrative of 427–424, and his final verdict on it (see below), keeps the scale of the forces and their operations in proper proportion.

218. Phaiax in Sicily

After the 'failure' of the 427–424 expedition (**217**) the Athenians turned, in their Sicilian policy, from warfare to diplomacy; but the attempt of Phaiax and his colleagues in 422 to rally support against the ever-increasing power of Syracuse produced little solid result. (On Phaiax see Connor, *Politicians*, 80–4.)

About the same time, Phaiax son of Erasistratos was sent out by the Athenians with two ships and two colleagues as a delegation to Italy and Sicily. This came about because, after the Athenians had withdrawn from Sicily following the peace-agreement, the men of Leontinoi had enrolled large numbers of new *politai*, and the *dēmos* there was planning a redistribution of the land; and when the leading men had got to hear of this they had called in the Syracusans and thrown the *dēmos* out. Thus the *dēmos* was dispersed in all directions. The leading men, however, came to an arrangement with the Syracusans by which they left Leontinoi empty and went to live in Syracuse with citizen-rights there; later, though, some of them grew dissatisfied, left Syracuse and took over an area of the *polis* of Leontinoi known as Phokaiai, and also Brikinniai, a stronghold in Leontine territory; the majority of the exiled *dēmos* came to join them there and were carrying on a war from these two fortified places. This was what the Athenians discovered to lead them to send out Phaiax, to see whether they could somehow persuade their own allies there and, if possible, the other Sicilians too to make a united assault upon the growing power of the Syracusans, and thus save the *dēmos* of Leontinoi. And Phaiax, on his arrival, did win over the men of Kamarina and Akragas. At Gela, however, events went against him, and he did not approach the other states, realising that he would not succeed with them; instead he withdrew through Sikel territory[1] to Katane, taking the opportunity *en route* to visit Brikinniai and encourage the people there, and then sailed back home. (61) On his voyage out to Sicily and also on

409

the return voyage he negotiated with some of the Italian *poleis* too, so as to make them friendly towards the Athenians.

Thucydides v.4–5.1

1 The Sikels: see **172A**.

219. Preparations for the second expedition

By their willingness to mount the expedition of 427–424 (**217**) the Athenians had shown themselves both ready and able to fight in Sicily while the Peloponnesian War was in progress; but the suspension – temporary, in the event – of that domestic conflict by the Peace of Nikias denied them, for a few years, a major outlet for their *polypragmosynē* (**175**), and with the ambitious Alkibiades steadily advancing in persuasive influence a second expedition to Sicily was resolved as soon as the first solid opportunity arose.

In that same winter (416/15) the Athenians began to wish to sail again against Sicily – with larger forces than those which Laches and Eurymedon had taken – and, if possible, to conquer it. They were ignorant, most of them, of the great size of the island and large number of its inhabitants, both Greeks and *barbaroi*; nor did they realise that they were taking on a war hardly at all smaller in scope than the one against the Peloponnesians. (6) The truest cause[1] of the expedition was that the Athenians were set upon ruling the whole of Sicily, though they wanted to be under the plausible cover of assisting their kinsmen and newly-acquired allies[2] there. And they were particularly urged on by envoys from Egesta who were in Athens at the time and who were most eager that the Athenians be called in. This was because the Egestaians had gone to war with their neighbour Selinous over certain problems in inter-marriage rights and disputed territory; the men of Selinous had then called in the Syracusans as their allies and were pressing Egesta hard in the war both by land and by sea. So the Egestaians reminded the Athenians of the alliance made in the time of Laches, during the earlier, Leontine war;[3] and they urged the Athenians to send a fleet and come to their aid. Their chief argument, amongst many, was that if the Syracusans, after depopulating Leontinoi, were to go unpunished and continue destroying the remaining allies (of Athens) until they had acquired control of the whole of Sicily, there was a danger that at some time or other they might, as Dorians, send a large expedition to join their fellow-Dorians the Peloponnesians – who had indeed sent them out as *apoikoi* – in destroying the Athenians' power. So it would make sense, they argued, for the Athenians to combine with those allies they still had in making a stand against the Syracusans – particularly as the Egestaians would supply enough of their own money to finance the campaigning. These were the arguments which the Athenians heard many times at meetings of the *ekklēsia*, from both the Egestaians and those Athenians who supported them; and finally a vote was taken in favour of first sending envoys to Egesta to see whether the money which they claimed to be in their treasury really existed, and at the same time to find out what the situation was with regard to the war against Selinous.

(8) Next year (415), at the beginning of spring, the Athenian delegation returned from Sicily, and with them came the Egestaians, bringing 60 talents of uncoined silver bullion – a month's pay for 60 ships,[4] which was the number they planned to ask the Athenians to send. The Athenians held a meeting of the *ekklēsia* and listened to what the Egestaians and their own envoys had to say. On matters such as the money said to be available in large quantities in the temples and the treasury there, the reports were encouraging – though untrue.[5] So they voted to send 60 ships to Sicily, with Alkibiades son of Kleinias, Nikias son of Nikeratos and Lamachos son of Xenophanes as *stratēgoi* with full powers (*autokratores*);[6] their task was to help the Egestaians against Selinous, to join in (re-)establishing Leontinoi – if things were going well for them in the war – and in general to settle matters in Sicily in the way best suited to Athenian interests. Four days later the *ekklēsia* met again, to decide the quickest way to prepare the fleet and to vote any extra supplies that the *stratēgoi* might need for the expedition.[7] Nikias had been chosen for the command against his will, and his opinion was that the polls had not made a wise decision – to aim, on a slight and specious pretext, at such a massive undertaking as the conquest of the whole of Sicily; so he came forward to speak in the hope of persuading the Athenians to change their minds. (The speech of Nikias follows, chs.9–14, of which the following is an extract.) 'What we have to realise is that the Spartans, because of the disgrace they have suffered, think of nothing else than how even now they can restore their tarnished reputation by defeating us; and this is natural enough, as for so long now they have been schooling themselves in military excellence to the exclusion of all else. If we have any sense, then, we must recognise that the issue before us is not the fate of the Egestaians in Sicily – a set of *barbaroi*[8] – but how best to be on our guard against an oligarchical *polis* which is plotting our downfall. (12) We must bear in mind also that only recently have we been enjoying some small relief from a great plague and from war, so as to rebuild our resources of money and manpower; and the right place to deploy these resources is here at home, on ourselves, not on these exiles who are begging for assistance and who find it advantageous to tell plausible lies while others are running their risks for them – words being the only thing they have to offer. Success in this venture would not make them

411

decently grateful; failure, if that should be the outcome, would spell ruin for their friends as well as themselves. And if a certain person,[9] elated at having been chosen for the command, urges you to sail – looking only at his own interests, which are above all those of a man not old enough for such a position, and wanting to be admired for his horse-breeding as well as to recover from this command some of the expenses it entails – do not grant him the opportunity for personal display when this puts the whole *polis* at risk. Men like him exploit public resources as criminally as they waste their own; and this is an important matter – too important to be decided and acted upon by a young man on the spur of the moment.'

(15) After such a speech from Nikias, most of the Athenians who came forward spoke in favour of the expedition and of not revoking the decisions which had already been voted through; only a handful spoke against; and the most eager advocate of the expedition was Alkibiades son of Kleinias. He was perfectly willing to oppose Nikias, who was his constant adversary in public life and whose own speech had made a personal attack on him. Above all, though, he had set his heart on holding the command, as *stratēgos*, and had hopes thereby of conquering both Sicily and Carthage too. Success in this would make him rich as well as famous: for a man held in such esteem by his fellow-citizens tended to be more enthusiastic about horse-breeding and other expensive activities than his finances warranted. And all this, in point of fact, was primarily responsible, later, for destroying the Athenians' *polis*.[10] What happened was that the majority grew frightened at the extent both of the lawlessness of his personal life-style and of the frame of mind in which he tackled every single thing in which he became involved: they therefore became hostile towards him, in the belief that his aim was tyranny; and although in a public capacity his conduct of the war was excellent, universal distaste for his private life led them to entrust their affairs to others, which before long brought the *polis* to ruin. On this occasion, anyway, he came forward and advised the Athenians as follows. (16) 'I, Athenians, have a better right to command than others – this must be my starting-point, as it is the point on which Nikias attacked me – and I believe too that I am worthy of it. The things for which I am criticised bring not only glory to my ancestors and myself but also advantage to my motherland. At one time the Greeks believed that our *polis* had been ruined by the war, but later they concluded it to be even greater than it actually is, thanks to the magnificent showing I put up at the Olympic festival:[11] I entered seven chariots – more than any single individual had ever done before – and won the first, second and fourth prizes; and I saw to it that everything was done in a manner worthy of this victory. Our custom is that such things bring honour, and to do them at all gives an impression of power. And whatever display I make within the *polis*,

when I provide choruses and so forth, makes my fellow-citizens envious, naturally enough, but again it suggests to the outside world that we are strong. So it could hardly be called useless folly when a man's private expenditure benefits not simply himself but the *polis* as well; equally, though, it is not unfair that a man who has a high opinion of himself should refuse to be on a level with others. One's misfortunes, after all, are never shared out amongst other people, and nobody wants to know a failure; by the same token, then, one must either put up with being despised by the successful or else deserve equal treatment by giving it. But I am aware that men like this – anyone, in fact, whose illustriousness in any field has given him prominence – are the objects of troublesome envy during their lifetime, particularly from their peers but also from others with whom they come into contact, whereas what happens after they are dead is that people claim to be related to them even when they are not, and their motherland, whichever it happens to be, boasts about them not as strangers or criminals but as fine and successful fellow-countrymen.' (He goes on to press, again, for the expedition to be sent out. Nikias replies (chs.20–23) by arguing that larger forces are needed.) (24) In saying this sort of thing Nikias imagined that either the Athenians would be deterred by how much (extra) needed to be done or else, if he was obliged to make the expedition, he would in this way do so as safely as possible. But the Athenians were by no means diverted from their enthusiasm for the voyage because of the burdensomeness of preparing for it; on the contrary they were far more eager about it than ever, and what happened was quite the opposite of what Nikias had expected, for it was decided that he had given good advice and that now everything was bound to be safe and well provided-for. Everyone alike was in the grip of a passion for the expedition: the older men believed that they would either conquer the places against which they were sailing or at any rate, with so great a force, come to no harm; those in the prime of youth yearned for the sights and the experiences of far-away places, and were confident of a safe return; and the general masses serving as soldiers saw the chance not only of money for the time being but of so extending Athenian power as to ensure perpetual paid employment ever afterwards. And so, because of this excessive majority enthusiasm, those few who were opposed to the expedition were afraid that if they voted against it they would appear ill-disposed towards the *polis*, so they kept quiet. (25) Finally one of the Athenians came forward and addressed Nikias personally, saying that he ought not to be making excuses and causing delays but should say then and there, in front of everybody, what forces he wanted the Athenians to vote him. Nikias was reluctant to do this and said that he would prefer to discuss the matter with his colleagues at their leisure; as far, though, as he could judge then and there, they ought to sail with at least a hundred Athenian triremes – of which as many as they thought fit would be troop-transports, to be joined by others provided by the allies – and a total hoplite force, Athenian and allied, of not less, and preferably more, than 5,000; and the rest of the force should be made ready and taken along in proportion – archers from Athens and Crete, slingers, and whatever else was thought proper and necessary. (26) On hearing this the Athenians voted at once that the *stratēgoi* should have full powers, with regard both to the size of the expeditionary force and to the voyage as a whole, to act as they saw fit in the Athenians' best interests. And after this the preparations began: orders were sent to the allies, and in Athens itself lists (of those to be levied) were made. It was all the easier to provide for everything as the *polis* had just recovered from the Plague and the years of continuous warfare, with large numbers of young men having now reached maturity and money having accumulated because of the truce.

Thucydides VI.1.1; 6; 8; 11.6–12; 15–16.5; 24–26

1 This is the phrase more famous in 1.23.6 (see **165**).
2 A small textual variant in some manuscripts gives exactly the opposite meaning – their *pre-existing* allies; but it hardly matters which is right.
3 I.e. the 427–424 expedition. Dover's arguments (in Gomme, *Commentary* IV, 221) to the effect that what the Egestaians cited was an alliance made *by Leontinoi* are unconvincing, but he may well be right in suggesting that the noun *symmachia* refers, here and sometimes elsewhere, not to a specific act (or renewal) of alliance but to allied activity.
4 That it cost a whole talent to keep a trireme at sea for one month is a fact of crucial importance for our understanding of the economics of sea-power in the fifth century. (With a crew of *c.*200, each man received a drachma a day.)
5 Thuc. of course means that this was later (VI.46) found to be the case.
6 I.e. they were authorised to take decisions without reference back to the *ekklēsia*. Note that we have an epigraphical record (Meiggs and Lewis no. 78 = Fornara no. 146) of this meeting and of others which followed it, from which we learn that at first the Athenians seriously considered sending one *stratēgos* only – Alkibiades, no doubt.
7 On this meeting see Gomme, *Commentary* IV, 229–30.
8 Strictly true (**172** n. 5), but tendentious; compare the Egestaian 'exiles', below.
9 Alkibiades.
10 This, and what follows, refers to the years 406–05: see the exhaustive note in Gomme, *Commentary* IV, 242–5.
11 In 416. Compare Isoc. XVI.34, Plut. *Alk.* II.

220. The Sicilian response

The great expedition finally set sail in midsummer 415, as graphically described by Thucydides in VI.30–32.2 (see also VII.57–59.1 for a list of the forces engaged on both sides); he then turns at once to Sicily itself, to analyse the reaction and response of the Syracusans to the news of an invasion in which, as they well knew, they would be the principal Athenian target.

News of the expedition was reaching Syracuse from all sides, though for a long time none of it was believed. And when an assembly was convened and speeches such as those which follow were made, some declared that the story of the Athenian expedition was to be credited while others maintained the opposite. However, Hermokrates son of Hermon[1] believed that he knew the truth of the matter and came forward to deliver the following advice. (Speech of Hermokrates, chs. 33–34, urging defensive preparations.) (35) Yet despite such a speech from Hermokrates, the Syracusan *dēmos* was still split into several conflicting views: some believed that the Athenians would not come at all and that the reports were untrue; others felt that even if they did come they would be given at least as good as they gave; others still scorned the whole matter and turned it into a joke. Those who believed Hermokrates and were fearful of what was to come were in the minority; and the next man who came forward to speak was Athenagoras, champion of the *dēmos* and, at that time, highly influential with the masses.[2] (Speech of Athenagoras, chs. 36–40, belittling the dangers.) (41) When Athenagoras had spoken in this vein, one of the *stratēgoi* got up and forbade anyone else to come forward. His own speech on the matter was as follows 'It is senseless both for speakers to make these attacks upon one another and for their hearers to put up with them, when, in view of the reports that are coming in, we ought rather to be seeing how the *polis* as a whole and every individual in it can best prepare a defence against the invaders. And even if it should turn out not to be needed there is no harm in having the state adorned with horses and arms and all the other things which give war its glory – all of which we ourselves shall take charge of providing and inspecting – and in sending men round the (other) *poleis* for reconnaissance and for any other purposes thought to be useful. We have in fact seen to some of these matters already, and whatever we discover we shall bring to your attention.' That was what the *stratēgos* had to say, after which the Syracusans ended the assembly and went away. (The Athenian armada crosses from Greece to Italy, chs. 42–44.) (45) Meanwhile news was reaching the Syracusans from all sides, and their own reconnaissance clearly established and reported that the (Athenian) fleet was at Rhegion; so they had to believe it at last, and applied themselves fully to making preparations. These included sending men round the Sikel areas – garrisons in some cases, embassies in others – and manning the outlying guard-posts in their own *chōra*. Within the *polis* itself, arms and horses were examined to see whether everything was in order, and all other measures were taken for a war which was all but upon them.

Thucydides IV.32.3; 35; 41; 45

1 See **217**, and note Thuc.'s opinion of the man in VI.72.2 (**221**).
2 Compare the description of Kleon in III.36.6 (**210A**); if Hermokrates is depicted as the Syracusan equivalent of Perikles, Athenagoras is clearly the Kleon figure.

221. Athenian victory before Syracuse, winter 415/14

The financial resources of the Egestaians proving to be illusory (VI.46), the three Athenian *stratēgoi* took counsel together and engaged in various preliminary operations (VI.47–52). Alkibiades was then recalled to Athens to stand trial for his alleged part in the Hermai and Mysteries scandal (see **214**), and absconded to the Peloponnesos. Further campaigning completed the summer of 415 (VI.62), after which it was time for an attack on Syracuse itself.

At the very beginning of the following winter (415/14) the Athenians began preparations for an attack on Syracuse, while the Syracusans themselves made ready to move against the Athenians. For the fact was that once the Athenians had failed to make an immediate assault upon them, as they had been fearing and expecting, the Syracusans grew in confidence with each successive day; and now that it was clear that the Athenians were sailing far away from them, on the other side of Sicily, and had failed in their attempt to storm Hybla,[1] the Syracusans were even more contemptuous of them than ever, and – typically of mobs when they feel confident[2] – they kept urging their *stratēgoi* to lead them out against Katane,[3] since the Athenians would not come out against them. In addition, Syracusan cavalry on reconnaissance were constantly riding up to the Athenian army and finding ways to insult it, such as asking whether their purpose in coming was not so much to resettle the men of Leontinoi in their own land as to settle down themselves in someone else's.

(Eventually, however, a battle does take place (chs.64–71) – and the Syracusans are beaten.) (72) After burying their dead the Syracusans held an assembly, at which Hermokrates son of Hermon came forward and spoke. He was a man whose intelligence was in every respect second to none, and who in the war had been showing himself to be experienced, able, and outstandingly brave. And he now spoke encouragingly, refusing to let them be gloomy about what had happened. It was not their spirit, he declared, that had let them down; what had done the harm was their lack of discipline. And even so they had not been so far outclassed as might have been expected – particularly as they were, so to speak, amateurs who had been pitted against skilled craftsmen in the art, the most experienced in all Greece.[4] Another thing, in his view, which had done great harm was the large number of the *stratēgoi* – there were fifteen of them – which meant a multiplicity of people giving orders, while the mass of the troops were in disarray and chaos: if, instead, they had only a few *stratēgoi*, men of experience, who could spend the winter preparing the hoplite force, maximising the size of the army by providing arms for those without them, and stepping up the rest of the training, he thought it likely that they would defeat their opponents; they were already courageous enough to do it, and by working hard they would be disciplined enough as well. Both things would improve, in fact, of themselves: their discipline would be learned in the school of danger, and their courage would be all the more steadfast once they had the assurance that comes from a professional skill. As to the *stratēgoi*, they should elect a small number and give them full powers,[5] including a solemn assurance under oath that they would be allowed to carry out their command in whatever way they saw fit; this, said Hermokrates, would mean better security for those matters which ought to be kept secret, and more orderly and straightforward preparations in general. (73) When the Syracusans had heard what he had to say they voted in favour of all his proposals, choosing as *stratēgoi* Hermokrates himself, Herakleides son of Lysimachos and Sikanos son of Exekestes – these three only. They also sent delegations to Corinth and to Sparta, to enlist the help of an allied force and also to attempt to persuade the Spartans, for their sake, to be more frank and positive in their prosecution of the war against the Athenians,[6] so that the Athenians would either have to withdraw their army from Sicily or else be less able to send out reinforcements to it.

Thucydides VI.63; 72–73

1 See VI.62.5.
2 Compare **209** with n.2, **212** with n.1.
3 The Athenians' base (VI.50–51).
4 For the *Spartans* (more aptly) as craftsmen in the art of war see **50B**, **270**.
5 Compare **219** with n.6 (the Athenian *stratēgoi*).
6 I.e. not even to *pretend* that the Peace of 421 had ended it!

222. Both sides seek more allies

In that same winter of 415/14 there was another success for Hermokrates, that of thwarting the Athenians' attempts to secure help from Kamarina (VI.75–88.2), after which both sides redoubled their efforts to find more allies.

While the Syracusans were busy with their own preparations for the war, the Athenians, encamped at Naxos, began negotiations with the Sikels, in the hope of winning over as many of them as possible. Those of them who lived mainly in the (coastal) plains, and were subjects of the Syracusans, were mostly uninterested; but the Sikels of the interior, whose settlements were and always had been independent, immediately, with a few exceptions, joined the Athenians, bringing grain and in some cases money too down to the coast for the army. Against those who did not come over the Athenians mounted expeditions and compelled some of them to change sides, though in other instances they were thwarted by the Syracusans, who sent out garrisons and came to the Sikels' assistance. The Athenians also moved their winter-quarters from Naxos to Katane, where they rebuilt the camp burned by the Syracusans and spent the rest of the winter. They sent a trireme on a mission of goodwill to Carthage, to see whether they could secure any assistance, and they sent also to the Etruscans, some of whose *poleis* were offering of their own accord to join them in the war.[1] Messengers were sent round to the Sikels too, and to Egesta, with orders to send as many horses as possible; and in general they were making ready for the blockade (of Syracuse) – preparing bricks, ironwork and everything else that was necessary – with a view to proceeding with the war at the beginning of spring. Meanwhile the Syracusan envoys who had been despatched to Corinth and Sparta took the opportunity of their voyage along the coast to try to persuade the Greeks of Italy to resist what the Athenians were doing, which was aimed, they argued, just as much against Italy as against Sicily. And when they reached Corinth and made their speeches there, kinship was the basis of their appeal that the Corinthians should give them aid. The Corinthians lost no time in voting to give them, unstintingly, all the help that they could themselves, and then joined in the delegation to Sparta, to help persuade the Spartans to carry on more openly the war at home, against the Athenians, and also to send some help out to Sicily.[2]

Thucydides VI.88.3–8

1 Compare VII.57.11.
2 The delegation then moved on to Sparta, where Alkibiades also added his weight to it: see **228**.

223. Nikias' letter

In Sparta the Syracusan–Corinthian proposals received the support of the exiled Alkibiades (see **228**), who contributed the specific suggestion that the Spartans send out a commander to Syracuse. They chose (VI.93.2) Gylippos son of Kleandridas; and his arrival in summer 414 had the desired effect of revitalising the Syracusans' resistance (VII. 1–7). By this time the Athenians had moved south to Syracuse itself and were in possession of the crucial heights of Epipolai (VI.97–103) – but with Lamachos dead (VI.101.6) the cautious Nikias was left in sole command.

Nikias could see that as each day passed both the enemy's strength and his own perplexity were increasing, so he sent a personal message to Athens. He had often done this before, to report on each development as it was happening, but the urgency of his despatch on this occasion reflected how gravely he viewed the situation: his opinion was that unless, without delay, the expedition was either recalled or else massively reinforced, all would be lost. He was afraid, however, that the messengers might not report the facts as they really were – either through incompetence in speaking, or even forgetfulness, or out of a wish to please the crowd in what they said. He therefore wrote a letter, in the belief that this would be the best way to tell the Athenians what he thought, unobscured by any messenger's report, and to have them make up their minds on the basis of the truth. So his picked men set off, with the letter and the necessary verbal instructions, while he himself turned his attention to the army, his objective now being more that of defence than of voluntarily running risks.

(The letter arrives in Athens in the winter of 414/13 (VII.10), and Thucydides purports to reproduce it in full (11–15).[1]) (16) That was what Nikias' letter had to tell, but when the Athenians heard it they did not relieve him of the command;[2] they (merely) chose two of the men on the spot, Menandros and Euthydemos, to share it with him so that, until the arrival of other (*stratēgoi*) elected to be his colleagues in command, he should not suffer alone and in ill health. Then a vote was taken to send out another force, a fleet and an army, to be drawn from Athenians on the call-up lists and from the allies; and as joint commanders with Nikias they chose Demosthenes son of Alkisthenes and Eurymedon son of Thoukles.[3] Eurymedon was sent out to Sicily at once, around the time of the winter solstice, with ten ships and 120 talents of silver – and a message to the men there that help was on its way and that their interests would be taken care of. (17) Demosthenes stayed behind to prepare for the departure of the expedition, which he planned for the beginning of spring (413); he was telling the allies what contingents they had to provide, and making ready money and ships and hoplites in Athens itself.

Thucydides VII.8; 16 17.1

1 As noted in Gomme, *Commentary* IV, 385, the actual letter must surely have been more specific than Thuc. makes it appear here.
2 As he had wanted (VII.15.1), largely on the grounds of a kidney complaint.

3 On these two men see Gomme, *Commentary* IV, 392–3; and note that Eurymedon is the same *stratēgos* thought to have mismanaged Sicilian affairs in 424 (**217**).

224. Nikias versus Demosthenes

By the time the Athenian reinforcements arrived (VII.42.1) the Syracusans too had received further support, from the Peloponnesos and from the rest of the Sicilians; the Athenians had lost the heights of Epipolai and been defeated in the Great Harbour of Syracuse (VII.36–41), and the whole Athenian position was looking increasingly vulnerable. Demosthenes quickly appreciated the necessity for action, but his assault on the Syracusan position on Epipolai was a failure (VII.42.3–46); and the Athenian commanders now needed to be decisive, one way or the other.

The Athenian *stratēgoi*, meanwhile, were discussing the situation in the light both of the defeat which they had suffered and of the general gloom now prevailing in the army. They saw that they were not succeeding in their endeavours and that the soldiers hated staying where they were. This was because they were ill, for two reasons: this was the season of the year when men are most prone to fall sick, and at the same time the place in which they were encamped was marshy and unhealthy. And over and above everything else, the situation seemed utterly without hope. Demosthenes therefore was of the opinion that they should stay no longer, and, in accordance with his plan of risking the attack on Epipolai – which had now failed – he cast his vote for leaving without delay, while it was still possible to cross the sea and to have naval superiority, at least with regard to the newly-arrived ships, over the enemy. And from the point of view of the *polis*, he maintained, it was more profitable for them to carry on the war against the men who were building fortifications in the *chōra* (of Attika)[1] than against the Syracusans, who could no longer be easily conquered; and it was in any case unreasonable for them to be spending so much money on the siege to no purpose.

(48) Such was the assessment of Demosthenes. But although Nikias agreed that their situation was bad he did not want their weakness to be expressly revealed, or to have it reported to the enemy that the Athenians in full council were openly voting to retreat; for they would then be far less likely, when they did wish to retreat, to do it in secret. Furthermore his sources of information about the enemy's affairs were better than those more generally available, and gave some grounds for hope, still, that if they persisted with the siege the Syracusans' position would be worse than their own. How they would wear them out would be by cutting off their supplies of money, especially since now with the ships at

their disposal they had better control of the sea. Also there was a group of men in Syracuse who wanted to betray the place to the Athenians and who were sending messages to him urging him not to withdraw; and it was his awareness of this – despite the fact that in reality he was still pondering the question and hesitating between the two alternatives – which led him in his speech on this occasion to make a clear declaration that he would *not* lead the army away. He was sure, he said, that the Athenians (at home) would not accept a withdrawal without having decreed it themselves; and those who would be voting would not be forming a judgment as they themselves had, from seeing the facts with their own eyes and without listening to hostile criticism, but would be ready to credit any slander from a clever speaker. And of the soldiers now present in Sicily and crying out about their desperate plight, many, indeed most, would change their tune, he said, once they were back in Athens, and claim that the *strategoi* had been bribed to betray them and withdraw. Thus, for his part at least, knowing the Athenian character as he did, he had no wish to be unjustly executed by the Athenians on a disgraceful charge but preferred to take his chance and, if necessary, die on his own terms, at the hands of the enemy. In spite of everything, bad as their own situation was, that of the Syracusans was, he claimed, worse: with payments to mercenaries and expenditure on guard-posts coinciding with the maintenance, for a year now, of a large fleet they were already short of money and would soon not know where to turn; they had already spent 2,000 talents and had borrowed still more, and if failure to pay wages were to mean the loss of even a small proportion of their present forces their cause would be ruined – for unlike the Athenians they depended more upon mercenaries than upon their own (conscripted) men. He therefore urged that they stay where they were and continue the siege, and not go away defeated by money, in which they were actually far superior.

(49) Nikias said all this so forcibly because he was receiving accurate information about the state of affairs inside Syracuse – of their shortage of money, and of the existence there of a substantial group which wanted the Athenians to be successful and which was sending him messages urging him not to withdraw; and at the same time he had more confidence than before that he would be victorious, at any rate with the fleet.[2] Demosthenes, however, was utterly opposed to the continuation of the siege. His view was that if it was necessary to stay where they were, with withdrawal of the army impossible without a *psēphisma* of the Athenians (at home), they ought to move to Thapsos or Katane, which would serve as a base from which the army could overrun a wide area of territory, provision itself by ravaging it, and so do the enemy harm; and as for the fleet, it would not be fighting in a confined space, which

favoured the enemy, but on the open sea, where there would be plenty of room for them to take advantage of their experience and where they would not have to advance from and retreat back to a small and circumscribed base. In short, then, he was altogether against staying any longer where they were, and urged that they should waste no more time but get away at once. Eurymedon thought the same, and said so. But with Nikias still against this, some hesitation and delay ensued – together with a suspicion that in adhering to his view so strongly Nikias might be privy to extra information; so the upshot was that the Athenians delayed and stayed where they were. (Further reinforcements arrive for the Syracusans, 50.1–2.) (50.3) As soon as the reinforcements had arrived the Syracusans made ready for another two-fold assault, by sea and land, on the Athenians. The Athenian *stratēgoi* saw that the enemy had been reinforced with another army, while their own position, so far from improving, was daily deteriorating in all respects, particularly as regards the distress caused by sickness amongst the troops; and they regretted not having withdrawn earlier. And since even Nikias was no longer so strongly opposed to this – simply arguing, now, against an open vote – they sent out orders as secretly as possible for everyone to be prepared to sail out from the camp when the signal to do so was given. However, when everything was ready and they were on the point of leaving, there was an eclipse of the moon, which happened to be at the full.[3] Most of the Athenians took this so seriously that they began to urge the *stratēgoi* to wait; and Nikias – who was rather too given to divination and suchlike – declared that until they had waited for the 'thrice nine days' prescribed by the seers he was not even prepared to discuss any further how the move could be made. And this was how the Athenians delayed and stayed on.[4]

Thucydides VII.47–49; 50.3–4

1 I.e. the Peloponnesians: see **229**.
2 An alternative manuscript reading produces a slightly different sense: '. . . despite the earlier defeat he had more confidence, at any rate in the fleet'.
3 This dates the episode securely to 27 August 413.
4 On Nikias' superstition compare Plut. *Nik.* 4.1–2, but see also the note in Gomme, *Commentary* IV, 428–9, and (more generally) C. A. Powell, 'Religion in the Sicilian expedition', *Historia* 38 (1979), 15–31.

225. Total destruction of the Athenian forces

During the delay brought about by the eclipse (**224**) the Athenian position deteriorated still further: after more defeats, one of which saw the death of

Eurymedon (VII.52), their exit from the Great Harbour was blocked (VII.59.2–3), and in a naval battle inside it they were again defeated (VII.70–71). So they withdrew from Syracuse by land, but were caught and overwhelmed at a nearby river-crossing (VII.72–84).

Finally, when the many dead were already heaped upon each other in the river, and with part of the army destroyed there by the river and the few who succeeded in escaping killed by the cavalry, Nikias surrendered himself to Gylippos, whom he trusted more than he did the Syracusans; and he told him and the (other) Spartans to do whatever they liked with him personally but to stop slaughtering the rest of the army. So Gylippos then gave the order that prisoners be taken alive, and all the rest – apart from a large number concealed by their captors – were brought in alive. They also sent men in pursuit of three hundred who had broken through the guards during the night, and caught them too. So the proportion of the army taken *en masse* into public custody was not large,[1] but many captives had been stolen away (by individual Syracusans); in fact the whole of Sicily was full of them, for they had not, as had Demosthenes' men, formally agreed to surrender.[2] Substantial numbers, besides, were killed: for this was without doubt a very great slaughter – greater, indeed, than any other that took place in this war; and many had also died in the frequent attacks made upon them during the march. Nonetheless many did escape – some at the time and others later, when they had been slaves – and ran away to refuge in Katane. (86) The Syracusans and their allies then joined forces, took up the spoils and as many of the prisoners as they could, and returned to Syracuse, where they put the prisoners, the Athenians and their allies, in the stone-quarries, having decided that this was the safest place for them. Nikias and Demosthenes, however, were put to death – against the wishes of Gylippos, who thought that it would be a fine achievement for him if he could crown his other successes by bringing the enemy *stratēgoi* back to the Spartans. Coincidentally, one of them, Demosthenes, was Sparta's greatest enemy, because of what had happened at Sphakteria and Pylos;[3] while the other, for the same reasons, was a very good friend. This was because by persuading the Athenians to make peace Nikias had done his utmost to have the Lakedaimonians captured on the island released; this led the Spartans in return to be well disposed towards him, and for his part it was chiefly this which had given him the confidence to surrender himself to Gylippos. However, those Syracusans who had been in contact with him[4] were afraid, so it was said, that this fact might lead to his being examined under torture, which would spell trouble for them in the midst of success. Others, and particularly the Corinthians, feared that because he was rich he might well bribe his way to freedom and do them some harm again in the future; so they secured the agreement of their allies and had him executed. So these were the reasons, as near as can be discovered, why he died – a man who of all the Greeks of my time least deserved so unfortunate an end, having regulated the whole of his life in accordance with *aretē*.[5]

(87) The men in the stone-quarries were at first treated badly by the Syracusans. Crowded together as they were in a deep, narrow cavity they suffered first from the sun and the stifling heat of the air, for there was no roof over their heads; and then, by contrast, the ensuing nights were autumnal and cold and the change in temperature fostered illness. Besides, space was so confined that they had to do everything in the same place, and there were in addition the corpses heaped together, one on top of another – some men dying from their wounds, others from the change in temperature and allied causes. This led to an intolerable stench, to add to their sufferings from hunger and thirst: for over a period of eight months the daily allowance for each man was one *kotylē* of water and two of food.[6] So, of all the miseries and evils likely to fall upon men thrown into such a place, there was not one that did not afflict them. For about seventy days they lived like this, all the prisoners together, and then, with the exception of the Athenians and any Greeks from Sicily or Italy who had joined the expedition, the rest were sold as slaves. It is difficult to be exact about it but the total number of the prisoners must have been at least 7,000.

And this event turned out to be the greatest in this whole war – indeed, in my view, the greatest that we know of in Greek history. To the victors it was the most dazzling of successes, and to the vanquished an utter calamity: for their defeat was total and absolute, and they suffered to the limit in every respect. As to their losses, these certainly added up, as the saying goes, to annihilation: army, fleet, absolutely everything was destroyed, and those who returned home were few out of many. So ended the events in Sicily.

Thucydides VII.85–87

1 See below for the actual figure. The fact (which Thuc. now reiterates) that so many prisoners were taken as private booty by individual soldiers helps to explain, together with the heavy casualties, why it is so low.
2 Demosthenes: see VII.82.
3 See **190**.
4 See **224**.
5 *aretē*: see **5B**; and on this verdict the remarks of Gomme, *Commentary* IV, 461–4.
6 Approximately half a pint of water and a pint of food. The harshness of this can be appreciated by comparing it with the truce at Pylos, where even the helots were allowed four *kotylai* of flour (Thuc. IV.16.1). It is in fact likely that most of the prisoners were eventually ransomed: see D. H. Kelly, 'What happened to the Athenians captured in Sicily?', *CR* n.s. 20 (1970), 127–31.

226. Athenian reaction to the catastrophe

Although the Spartans had already established their fortified position within Attika (see **229**), it was the Athenian disaster in Sicily which really inaugurated the final and (for the Athenians) fateful phase of the Peloponnesian War. Thucydides here describes the initial reaction to the news, in Athens itself and the Greek world at large, in the autumn and winter of 413/12.

When the news reached Athens it was a long time before it was credited that the expedition could have been so totally and completely destroyed, even though there were clear reports from the actual soldiers who had been there and had escaped. And when the Athenians did recognise the facts they were angry with those politicians who had combined to support the expedition – as though they themselves had not voted for it[1] – and they were enraged also at the oracle-mongers and seers and all the rest who had originally led them to believe, by divination, that they would conquer Sicily. So they had nothing but troubles and woes on every side, and after what had now happened they were not only afraid but also, and not surprisingly, utterly dumbfounded. For it was a great sorrow, to individuals and to the *polis* alike, to think of all the many hoplites and cavalrymen and all the military manhood which had been irreplaceably lost; and at the same time they saw that there were insufficient numbers of ships in the docks, no money in the treasury, and no crews for the fleet. So for the moment they had little hope of survival: they thought that their enemies from Sicily, especially after their great victory, would at once sail with their fleet against Peiraieus; that their enemies at home, now doubly prepared in all aspects, would naturally now mount an offensive against them from both land and sea with all their might; and that their own allies would revolt and join them. Nevertheless they resolved, as far as present circumstances permitted, not to give in, but to equip a fleet – getting the timber from wherever they could – and raise money and keep a safe watch on their allies, particularly Euboia. They also decided, as regards expenditure within the *polis*, to make some sensible economies, and to appoint a board of older men whose task would be to give preliminary advice on the situation, whenever the occasion required it.[2] And all in all, as is always the way with a *dēmos*, the terror of the moment made them ready to behave in an orderly manner. What they had decided was put into effect; and so ended that summer (413).

(2) But in the following winter (413/12), because of the great calamity which had befallen the Athenians in Sicily, all the rest of the Greeks suddenly turned against them. Those who were allies of neither side thought that even if they were not invited to join in they should no longer hold aloof from the war but should attack the Athenians of their

own accord; for they believed, each of them, that they would have been the target for the Athenians to attack if they had succeeded in Sicily, and they thought at the same time that the remainder of the war would be short and that it would be a fine thing to participate in it. As for the allies of the Lakedaimonians, they were all even more eager than before to be freed quickly from their many sufferings. The prime movers, though, were the subjects of the Athenians, who were ready – if not always able – to revolt: this was because they were not judging the situation dispassionately and would not even countenance the idea that the Athenians might be able to survive the coming summer. All this gave great encouragement to the Spartans, particularly the likelihood that in the spring their allies from Sicily would be joining them in force, and with the additional asset of the navy that they had been obliged to build. So they were optimistic from all points of view and made up their minds to throw themselves wholeheartedly into the war: they calculated that once it had been brought to a successful conclusion they would be free in future from the sort of dangers which the Athenians would have posed to them if they had added the resources of Sicily to their own, and that destroying the Athenians would leave Sparta safely with the *hēgemonia* of all Greece.

(4) During this same winter the Athenians too were making preparations, as they had planned, for shipbuilding, having now procured the timber for it. They had also fortified (Cape) Sounion, to give protection to the grain-ships on their voyage round (Attika into Peiraieus); but the fortress in Lakonia, built during the voyage out to Sicily,[3] they abandoned, and they introduced economies wherever else they saw useless expenditure to be curtailed. Their chief concern, however, was to watch what their allies were doing and to try to forestall revolts.

Thucydides VIII. 1–2; 4

---

1 On this refusal of the *ekklēsia* to acknowledge collective responsibility, after the event, for its decisions compare **210C** with n.7 (Diodotos). In this case Thuc. has particularly emphasised the *general* enthusiasm for the venture (see **219**).
2 On these ten *probouloi* see further **227A**; and Rhodes, *Boule*, 216.
3 See VII.26.2.

227. The rule of the Four Hundred

If the Athenian disaster in Sicily inaugurated the final and decisive phase of the war, it was the aftermath of Sicily and the resumption of open war together which paved the way within Athens for the revolution of the Four Hundred. Supporters of oligarchy had always existed amongst the Athenians, implacably opposed to the aims and methods of radical democracy (one may imagine that something like the oligarchs' oath in Aristot. *Pol.* (v)1310 a 6–12 was frequently sworn behind closed Athenian upper-class doors; note also the personification of Oligarchy mentioned by de Ste Croix, *Origins*, 370) and willing, if given the opportunity, to try to replace it with a more palatable alternative; see for instance **171**. What was different about 411 was that instead of these isolated minorities of grumblers (like the 'Old Oligarch': **143**), it was upper-class Athenians in increasingly large numbers who were beginning to withdraw, disillusioned, from active participation in democratic political life (see Connor, *Politicians*, 175–206), and still larger numbers of more ordinary citizens – not the poor, by and large, but those who fought as hoplites – who were ripe for persuasion, by fair means or foul, that political change was desirable and possible. So between June and September 411 a revolutionary Council of 400 men ruled Athens, in the name of a wider (and genuinely oligarchical) 'electorate' of 5,000; thereafter this larger group assumed supremacy in fact as well as in name, until by July 410 full radical democracy had been restored. We give here two accounts of these startling events: the Aristotelian *Ath. Pol.* (A), with what purport to be contemporary documents (see n.2, below) and with a political bias which tones down conflict and highlights consent, and Thucydides (B), rich in contemporary impressions and sharp political insights.

See further: Hignett, *Constitution*, 268–80 and 356–78; A. Fuks. *The Ancestral Constitution* (London, 1953); Finley, *Use and Abuse*, ch.2; Davies, *Democracy*, 148; Gomme, *Commentary* v, 184–256.

(A) Now as long as fortunes in the war were equally balanced, (the Athenians) preserved their democracy; after the disaster in Sicily, however, and the increase in Lakedaimonian strength because of their alliance with the King (of Persia),[1] they were obliged to remove the democracy and to establish the *politeia* of the Four Hundred. Melobios made the speech introducing the *psēphisma*, and the motion itself was drafted by Pythodoros of (the deme) Anaphlystos; and what chiefly persuaded the masses to support it was the belief that the King would be more likely to take their side in the war if they made the *politeia* an oligarchic one. The *psēphisma* of Pythodoros was as follows:[2] that the *dēmos* should elect, to join the already-existing ten *probouloi*,[3] twenty other men from those over 40 years of age; that these (thirty) men should swear on oath to draft such proposals as they might consider to be in the best interests of the *polis*, and should then, with a view to its safety, draft them; and that anyone else who wished to do so should also be free to draft proposals, in order that the best of all the proposals put forward might be selected.[4]

The first proposal drafted by these men, once they had been elected, was that it should be obligatory for the *prytaneis* to put to a vote all resolutions made with a view to (public) safety. Then, in order that all Athenians who wished could join in making suggestions about these proposals, they abolished the *graphē paranomōn*[5] and the procedures for impeachments and summonses; and if any man punished, summonsed or brought before a *dikastērion* anyone (for making suggestions), he was to be arrested and indicted before the *stratēgoi*, who were to hand him over to the Eleven[6] for execution. And after this they arranged the *politeia* in the following manner: the money coming in as a revenue was to be spent exclusively on the war, (so that) for the duration of the war all officials were to be unpaid – all except the nine *archontes*, and the *prytaneis* as they held office, who were each to receive three obols a day; all the rest of the *politeia*, for the duration of the war, was to be put in the hands of those Athenians best fitted to serve the state with their persons and their property, to the number of not less than 5,000; these 5,000 men were to be empowered to conclude treaties with anyone they wished; and ten men over 40 years of age were to be elected from each *phylē*, with the task of swearing an oath over unblemished sacrificial victims and then drawing up a list of the 5,000.

(All these arrangements were ratified, and ch. 30 then outlines alleged constitutional proposals 'for the future': see Moore, *Aristotle*, 260–2.) (31) So this was the *politeia* that they drafted for the future, but in the interim it was to be this: that there should be a *boulē* of four hundred, in the traditional manner,[7] with forty men aged 30 or more elected from each *phylē* out of candidates preselected by their fellow-tribesmen; that this *boulē* should appoint the officials, draft the oath that they were required to swear, and take such action as they saw fit with regard to the *nomoi* and the *euthynai*[8] and other matters; that such *nomoi* as might be laid down about political matters should be observed with no possibility of changing them or of laying down others; that there should be an interim election of *stratēgoi* from the 5,000 as a whole, with the *boulē*, once it had been established, holding an inspection under arms and choosing ten men, with a secretary for them, elected to hold office for the ensuing year with full powers and to consult with the *boulē* if the need arose; that (the 5,000) should elect one cavalry-commander, also, and ten tribal commanders (of cavalry) – though in future their election would be by the *boulē*, in accordance with the drafted proposals; that in the case of all offices except the *boulē* and the *stratēgoi* it should not be permissible for either these officials or anyone else to hold the same office more than once; and that, for the future, the hundred men should allot the four hundred amongst the four sections so that they might take part when the (rest of the) citizens join the others in membership of the *boulē*.[9]

(32) So this was the *politeia* drafted by the hundred men who had been elected by the 5,000; and when it had been put to a vote by Aristomachos and ratified by the mass of the people, the *boulē* of (the year of the archonship of) Kallias (412/11) was dissolved on the 14th of the month Thargelion[10] – before the end of its term of office – and the Four

428

Hundred entered into office on Thargelion 22nd. The regular *boulē* chosen by lot ought to have entered into office on the 14th of Skirophorion.[11] So this was how the oligarchy was established, during the archonship of Kallias – and about a hundred years after the expulsion of the tyrants.[12] Chiefly responsible for it were Peisandros, Antiphon and Theramenes, who were men of good birth and had the reputation of being outstanding in intelligence of judgment.[13] Once this *politeia* had been established the 5,000 were chosen – but only nominally: it was the Four Hundred who entered the council-house who, together with the ten (*stratēgoi*) with full powers, ruled the *polis*. They also sent an embassy to the Spartans with a proposal of peace on the basis, for both sides, of the *status quo*, but they abandoned this once the Spartans proved unwilling to negotiate unless the Athenians surrendered their rule of the sea. (33) At all events, the *politeia* of the Four Hundred lasted for about four months, and Mnasilochos – one of them himself – was *archōn* for (the first) two months of the year of the archonship of Theopompos (411/10), who held office for the remaining ten months. But when the Athenians were defeated in the sea-battle near Eretria, and the whole of Euboia revolted except for Oreos, they took the disaster more badly than any previous one, for Euboia was of more use to them at this time than Attika; so they abolished the Four Hundred and handed everything over to the 5,000 – the men who provided their own arms and armour.[14] They also voted that all officials should (continue to) be unpaid. Chiefly responsible for the overthrow were Aristokrates and Theramenes, who did not approve of what the Four Hundred had been doing, in handling everything themselves and never referring it to the 5,000. And it would appear that the constitutional arrangements were excellent in this period, with a war in progress and the *politeia* comprising those who provided their own arms and armour.[15]

?Aristotle, *Athenaion Politeia* 29.1–2 and 4–5; 31–33

(B) This movement began in the army (at Samos) and later spread from there to Athens. Various people began to cross over from Samos and have talks with Alkibiades, who was holding out the prospect of friendship initially with Tissaphernes and then with the King (of Persia) also, if only the Athenians did not have a democracy – for this would give the King more confidence in them.[16] So the most influential of the *politai*, the very men who are apt to bear the heaviest burdens, began to have high hopes of bringing affairs under their own control, as well as of overcoming the enemy; and once they were back in Samos they brought together the right people to form a conspiracy. What they said openly, to the masses, was that the King would be their friend and provide money on two conditions, the recall of Alkibiades and the abolition of the democracy.

The immediate response of the multitude to these developments was somewhat unfavourable, but then the pleasant thought of being paid wages by the King kept them quiet; and once they had made this general statement the oligarchic conspirators again discussed Alkibiades' proposals amongst themselves and with the majority of their party. Most felt the scheme to be practicable and trustworthy. Phrynichos, however, who was still *stratēgos*, declared that he was not at all satisfied. His opinion was that Alkibiades cared no more for oligarchy than for democracy – which was quite true – and that his sole objective was, somehow or other, to change the existing order in the *polis* and so secure his return at the invitation of his friends, whereas for the (rest of the) Athenians it was of paramount importance to guard against *stasis*. As to the King, Phrynichos felt that, with the Peloponnesians now just as much a naval power (as the Athenians) and in possession of some of the most important *poleis* in his empire, it was not at all 'practicable' for him to take on the problems of joining the Athenians, whom he did not trust, when he had the opportunity of making friends with the Peloponnesians, who had never done him any harm . . .[17] (49) However, the assembled conspirators went on as they had originally determined and accepted the present proposals, and they began preparations to send Peisandros and others as envoys to Athens, where they were to work towards the recall of Alkibiades and the overthrow of the *dēmos* there, and so make Tissaphernes friendly towards the Athenians.

(53) When Peisandros and the other Athenian envoys sent from Samos arrived in Athens they spoke to the *dēmos*, summarising some of their many proposals and stressing in particular that if they recalled Alkibiades and changed their form of democracy the Athenians could have the King as their ally and beat the Peloponnesians. However, as regards the democracy, many others spoke against what was being suggested, and at the same time the enemies of Alkibiades loudly protested that it would be a terrible thing to recall a man who had done violence to the *nomoi*. In addition the Eumolpidai and the Kerykes[18] invoked the affair of the Mysteries, the reason why Alkibiades had been exiled, and solemnly forbade his recall in the name of the gods. In the face of all this opposition and abuse Peisandros then came forward, took each of the objectors aside one by one and asked him what hope he had of salvation for the *polis*, now that the Peloponnesians had just as many ships as the Athenians waiting to fight at sea, as well as many *poleis* in alliance with them, and money – of which they themselves now had none – supplied to them by the King and Tissaphernes, unless someone could persuade the King to change sides and join the Athenians; and when of course they answered that they had no such hope, Peisandros then spoke plainly. 'Very well then, we cannot achieve this unless we adopt a more sensible *politeia* and

put the government in the hands of fewer men, so that the King may have faith in us. Besides it is not our *politeia* that we ought to be discussing here and now but our survival; we can always change a *politeia* later if we do not like it. So let us recall Alkibiades, who is the only man alive who can bring all this about.' (54) At first the *demos* reacted unfavourably to this talk of oligarchy, but once Peisandros had made it quite clear that there was no other means of survival, fear – together with the expectation that a change could be made later – won the day, and they voted that Peisandros and ten others with him should sail back and make whatever arrangements with Tissaphernes and with Alkibiades that they thought best. At the same time, since Peisandros had also been spreading slanders about Phrynichos, the *demos* deposed both Phrynichos and his colleague Skironides from office and sent out Diomedon and Leon as *strategoi* in charge of the fleet. Peisandros believed that Phrynichos was (still) not in favour of the deal with Alkibiades, and so spread the false tale that he had betrayed Iasos and Amorges.[19] Peisandros also visited all the political clubs which already existed in the *polis* and were active in law-suits and elections,[20] urging them to unite and formulate a plan in common to overthrow the *demos*. Then, after making whatever other arrangements the circumstances required so that there should be no further delay, he and the ten others made their voyage to Tissaphernes.

(But thanks to the ambiguous position of Alkibiades the compact with Tissaphernes fails to materialise. Nonetheless the conspirators' plans proceed, and having consolidated their position in Samos they set out again for Athens.) (65) During the voyage, in accordance with what had been decided, Peisandros and his associates did away with the democracies in the *poleis* (on their way) and from some places took hoplites who were friendly to their cause. Upon their arrival in Athens they found that their friends in the clubs had already done most of the work: some of the younger men had banded together and surreptitiously murdered a certain Androkles, one of the principal champions of the *demos* – and the man largely responsible for the banishment of Alkibiades;[21] they did it for two reasons, because he was a demagogue and more particularly because they thought it would please Alkibiades, whom they believed to be returning from exile and preparing to secure the friendship of Tissaphernes. Certain other opponents were also disposed of in the same way, without detection. Furthermore they had already openly proclaimed that nobody should be paid a wage except the armed forces and that no more than 5,000 men should have a share in the conduct of affairs – these being the men best able to be of use in terms of both their property and their person. (66) This however was a piece of propaganda for mass consumption, for it was the conspirators themselves, once they had changed things, who planned to have control of the *polis*. The *dēmos* and the lot-appointed *boulē* continued to meet, despite all this, but they discussed only what the conspirators saw fit to let them; everyone who spoke came in fact from their number, and what they had to say had been previously vetted by the party. Opposition to them from other quarters was non-existent, because of the fearful realisation of how many were involved. Anyone who did venture to object was soon conveniently dead, and there was no attempt to seek out the culprits or take legal action against any suspects; instead the *dēmos* kept quiet, and people were in such a state of terror that they considered themselves lucky not to be molested even if they had never opened their mouths. They imagined that the conspiracy was much more widespread than it actually was, and so were dismayed – and unable to find out the true facts because of the great size of a *polis* in which men did not know each other. For this same reason it was impossible also for anyone with a grievance to complain about it to anyone, with a view to planning how to defend himself: for the person to whom he turned would either be a stranger or else, if a friend, a faithless one; and amongst the *dēmos* everyone approached everyone else with suspicion, as if they might be party to what was happening. And in fact the conspiracy did include some people whom one would never have imagined turning to oligarchy; and it was they who were chiefly responsible for making the masses distrust each other – and for keeping the Few safe – by establishing this mutual suspicion within the *dēmos*.

(67) It was at this juncture then that Peisandros and his associates arrived and at once set about doing what remained to be done. First they convened the *dēmos* and proposed that ten men be elected[22] as commissioners with full powers, and that when they had done their work these commissioners should put before the *dēmos*, on a prearranged day, proposals for the best way of governing the *polis*. Then when the day came they convened the *ekklēsia* at Kolonos, where, rather more than a mile from Athens, there is a temple of Poseidon.[23] Here the commissioners made just one proposal: that any Athenian be allowed, with impunity, to state whatever opinion he liked – heavy penalties being prescribed for anyone who attempted to thwart such a statement, either by a *graphē paranomōn* or by any other means. And then of course came the time for plain speaking, with a proposal immediately that the holding of office and drawing of salaries under the present constitutional order should end and that five men should be elected as presiders (*proedroi*) with the task of choosing a hundred men;[24] each of this hundred was then to choose three colleagues, and the resulting four hundred was to enter the council-chamber with full powers to govern as they saw fit and to convene the 5,000 whenever they thought it necessary. (68) It was

432

Peisandros who proposed all this, and who in general was the most prominent and eager in the overthrow of the *dēmos*. However, the man who had planned how to bring the whole thing to this point and had devoted most thought to it was Antiphon. Antiphon was second to none in ability amongst the Athenians of his time and supreme in analysing an issue and then expressing what he thought about it; but he never came forward, if he could help it, to speak in the assembly or compete in any other area of public life. His reputation for cleverness thus made him suspect to the masses; yet to men contesting with each other in a *dikastērion* or in the assembly he was uniquely able to give helpful advice to anyone who asked for it. And on his own behalf, when, later, the democracy had been restored and the acts of the Four Hundred – which the *dēmos* had rescinded – were being roughly treated, Antiphon's speech in his own defence was clearly the best made by any man up to my time; the charge was that he had helped to establish the Four Hundred, and he was on trial for his life. Phrynichos too showed himself outstandingly enthusiastic for the oligarchy. He was afraid of Alkibiades, who, he realised, knew of his intrigues at Samos with Astyochos,[25] and his opinion was that Alkibiades was never likely to be recalled by an oligarchy; so once he had joined the movement Phrynichos proved to be utterly reliable in facing danger. Theramenes the son of Hagnon was also prominent amongst those joining forces to overthrow the *dēmos*, and he was both a competent speaker and a man of judgment. Consequently, carried out as it was by many intelligent men, it was hardly surprising that the enterprise succeeded, for all its magnitude: for it *was* a difficult task, virtually a hundred years after the expulsion of the tyrants, to deprive of its liberty the Athenian *dēmos* – a people not only unused to subjugation but also, for more than half of this period, accustomed itself to rule others.

(However, the Athenian forces in Samos have other ideas, and Alkibiades come down on the side of the *dēmos*: see **215**. In Athens Theramenes and Aristokrates begin to orchestrate moderate opposition.)
(89) They did not go as far as to advocate stopping the progress towards extreme oligarchy, but they did maintain that the 5,000 should be appointed, so as to exist in fact as well as in name, and that the *politeia* should be made more equitable. But this was mere political propaganda on their part, for in fact most of them were motivated by personal ambition in pursuing the sort of course that is always most apt to ruin any oligarchy which replaces a democracy: what happens is that each and every man is not only immediately unwilling to think of himself as his fellows' equal but regards himself as unequalled by anyone at all; in a democracy, on the other hand, it is easier for someone who is not chosen for office to maintain that the odds were stacked against him. However,

what had the most obvious effect in spurring the dissidents on was the strength of Alkibiades' position in Samos, together with their own opinion that the oligarchy would not last; so each one of them was striving to become the principal champion of the *dēmos*. (90) Those of the Four Hundred who were most opposed to such a (moderating) course had several spokesmen: Phrynichos – the man who as *stratēgos* in Samos had quarrelled with Alkibiades; Aristarchos, a particularly extreme opponent of the *dēmos*; Peisandros, Antiphon, and other very influential men. Even before this time – in fact as soon as they had come into power, and the Athenian forces in Samos had set themselves up as a breakaway democracy[26] – they had been sending their own envoys to Sparta and pressing eagerly for a peace-agreement, as well as building the wall at the place called Eetioneia;[27] and now, when their delegation had returned from Samos, they became still more active than ever, by far, as they could see that not only the masses but also some of their own following, who had previously seemed trustworthy, were turning against them. The situation both in Athens and in Samos was a source of alarm to them, so they made haste to send Antiphon and Phrynichos with ten others to the Spartans, with instructions to make peace on any sort of terms that would be at all tolerable. They also put more effort still into building the wall at Eetioneia. Theramenes and his associates maintained, however, that the purpose of the wall was not to prevent the men from Samos from making an armed entry into Peiraieus but rather to let in the enemy fleet and army whenever they liked.

(The split within the revolutionary party intensified over this issue of the wall, and after the assassination of Phrynichos (VIII.92.2) Theramenes and his adherents had it demolished. Further chaos was then interrupted by the news of a general revolt in Euboia.) (96) When the Athenians received the news of what had happened in Euboia, the consternation was undoubtedly greater than on any previous occasion. The disaster in Sicily had seemed great enough at the time, but neither it nor anything else before this caused as much panic. And was their despair not perfectly understandable? The army in Samos was in revolt; they had no more ships, or crews to man them; they themselves were in a state of *stasis*, in which there was no telling when actual fighting might not break out; and now there was this great catastrophe in which they had lost their fleet and, worst of all, Euboia too, which had been more useful to them than Attika itself. But their most serious worry, and the one which struck closest to home, was the thought that the enemy might follow up their victory by venturing to make a direct and immediate attack on Peiraieus, which now had no ships to defend it; indeed they were convinced that this was going to happen at any moment. (97) At all events the Athenians responded to the news by manning twenty ships and convening the *ekklēsia*: the first of a series of meetings was called immediately, and, for the first time again, on the hill called Pnyx, where they had been in the habit of meeting before;[28] there they deposed the Four Hundred and voted to entrust the conduct of affairs to the 5,000 – who were defined as all those who provided their own arms and armour. They also decreed that nobody, on pain of being put under a curse, was to receive a salary for holding any office. Later the *ekklēsia* met again, many times, to vote upon the choice of lawgivers (*nomothetai*) and other arrangements for the *politeia*. And it is perfectly clear that this was the first time, at any rate in my lifetime, that the Athenians had a good *politeia*:[29] there was a moderate blending of the Few and the Many, and it was this in the first instance which allowed the *polis* to recover from the wretched state into which its affairs had fallen. They also voted to recall Alkibiades and others with him, and they sent to him and to the forces in Samos urging them to make an active response to these events. (98) Another, immediate consequence of the change in regime was that Peisandros and Alexikles and their supporters, and all the leading oligarchs, made off to Dekeleia . . .

Thucydides VIII.48.1–4; 49; 53–54; 65–68; 89.2–90.3; 96.1–3; 97–98.1

1 See **230**.
2 On the authenticity of this and the other documents in *Ath. Pol.* 29–31 see A. Andrewes, 'Androtion and the Four Hundred', *PCPhS* n.s.22 (1976), 14–25.
3 See **226** with n.2.
4 Here follows Kleitophon's rider about the *nomoi* of Kleisthenes: see **80D**.
5 The public prosecution of an illegal proposal: see **310**.
6 See **67** with n.5.
7 I.e. on the Solonian (**67**) rather than the Kleisthenic (**77**) model.
8 See **52** n.6.
9 We construe this clause, which is certainly obscure and probably corrupt, in the same way as Moore, *Aristotle*, 264. The 'hundred men', it has been alleged in ch.30, had been chosen by and from the 5,000 to draft the future *politeia*; see also below.
10 Approximately the beginning of June, 411.
11 The next month, and last of the twelve.
12 See **74**.
13 On these three men see further, B.
14 If we can believe Lysias (XX.13), there were in fact as many as 9,000 men in this category.
15 For the *politeia* of the 5,000 see further, B (with n.29).
16 On the Persia/Alkibiades dimensions of these events see Ch.23.
17 For what follows here (48.5–7) see **235**.
18 The two most prestigious priestly families in Athens: see in brief Parke, *Festivals*, 57–8.

19 See Thuc. VIII.28.
20 See Connor, *Politicians*, 25–9 and 197.
21 See Plut. *Alk.* 19.
22 More probably thirty: see A, above.
23 I.e. rather than on the Pnyx hill in Athens (see below). It is usual to believe (see for instance Moore, *Aristotle*, 260) that with the Spartans at Dekeleia this move was intended to restrict attendance at the meeting *de facto* to hoplites, but A. Andrewes (in the article cited above (n.2), at p.24 n.18) casts reasonable doubts on this – without, however, offering another explanation for why Kolonos was chosen. The existence of a shrine of Poseidon Hippios there perhaps suggests a wish to give prominence to the cavalry (*hippeis*).
24 In fact 95, or 100 including themselves.
25 See Thuc. VIII.50–51.
26 See Thuc. VIII.75.
27 Overlooking the main Peiraieus harbour-basin (as Thuc. explains in VIII.90.4, omitted here).
28 The meeting at Kolonos had intervened (see above); and another had been scheduled for, though never actually held in, the theatre of Dionysos (VIII.93–94).
29 An alternative understanding of the Greek here makes Thuc.'s verdict less extreme: '. . . that during the first period of this *politeia* it was the best that the Athenians ever had, at any rate in my lifetime'; however, either way his enthusiasm for the constitution of the 5,000 is plain, and it is a pity that he did not see fit to tell us more about it (and the author of the *Ath. Pol.* evidently knew little more: see A, above). G. E. M. de Ste Croix, 'The constitution of the Five Thousand', *Historia* 5 (1956), 1–23, pressed a heterodox interpretation – that the 5,000 (i.e. hoplites) were not the basic 'electorate', which in his view was restored to its fully democratic, pre-411 basis, but a group from whom all office-holders were to be drawn; see however the reply of P. J. Rhodes, 'The Five Thousand in the Athenian revolutions of 411 B.C.', *JHS* 92 (1972), 115–27.

23 The Spartan offensive

Despite the battle of Mantineia in 418 (see **205**), the Spartans and the Athenians remained formally at peace with each other and the Spartans made no attempt to come to the help of Melos (see **206**). But the Sicilian expedition clearly induced a majority at Sparta to believe that Athens must and could be attacked and defeated; and this time, there was none of the feeling which had dogged Sparta in the Archidamian War, that she had been guilty of starting the war and therefore enjoyed no success. The exile Alkibiades found a ready hearing and the Spartans moved to fortify Dekeleia in the heart of Attika.

But even after the defeat of the Sicilian expedition, Athens was far from being down; and the Spartans were even now only able to make headway by persuading Persia to provide them with the money for a fleet. The long-term effect of the Spartan offensive was to make Persia once more a major factor in Greek affairs.

See in general Lewis, *Sparta and Persia*

228. Alkibiades in Sparta

Choosing exile rather than trial (see **214**), Alkibiades arrived in Sparta in the winter of 415/14; he there set out to disarm opposition generated by his earlier activities inimical to Spartan interests and his democratic leanings, and then proceeded to make himself indispensable by terrifying the Spartans with an account of Athenian plans to conquer Sicily, Italy and Carthage and deploy the forces so acquired against Sparta.

'You have now heard about the expedition which is under way and about what we planned, from the man who was in the best position to know; and the *stratēgoi* who are left, if they can, will still attempt the same goals. But you must now realise that unless you send help it will be all over with the situation there. For the Sicilians are less experienced than their enemies; even so, if they all got together, they might still survive. But the Syracusans fighting alone have already seen their entire levy defeated in battle,[1] and since they are at the same time hemmed in by sea they will be unable to resist the force of the Athenians which is now there. And if this *polis* is captured, they will have the whole of Sicily, and Italy immediately afterwards. And the resulting danger which I mentioned just now would not be long in threatening you. So let none of you imagine that you will be concerned with Sicily, rather than with the Peloponnesos, if you do not at once do what I recommend; you must send out there by sea a force so organised that the men will get themselves there as oarsmen and then immediately serve as hoplites; and you must send out a Spartiate[2] as commander, something which I regard as even more desirable than the force just mentioned; for he will need to organise those who are ready to fight and dragoon those who are unwilling. For if you act on these lines, those who are your friends will be the more eager and those who are hesitating will be the less reluctant to come over. And at the same time it is necessary to be more open about carrying on the war here, in order that the Syracusans may realise that you are serious and hold out more vigorously, and that the Athenians be less able to send any further support to their men. And it is necessary to fortify Dekeleia in Attika, something of which the Athenians have always been most afraid and which they realise to be the only thing of which they so far have no experience in the war.[3] For this is the surest way to harm one's enemies, if one realises that there is something of which they are particularly afraid, when one is clear about this, to act; for it is likely that they will best know their own weaknesses and, knowing them, be afraid of them. As for the ways in which you would yourselves benefit and would disadvantage your enemies by fortifying a base against them, I shall leave aside most of the reasons and talk briefly of the most important. For most of the property and slaves which there is in the *chōra* would come to you, partly by capture, partly of its own free will.[4] And they will at once be deprived of the revenues from the silver mines at Laureion, also of the income which they now derive from rents for land and fees for legal facilities, and most notably of the revenue from the allies, as less is handed over;[5] for they will look down on the Athenians when they realise that the war is already being prosecuted energetically from your side. (92) It is up to you, Lakedaimonians, whether any of these projects is carried out quickly and with enthusiasm, since I am entirely confident that they are feasible – and I do not think that I am wrong in my opinion.'

Thucydides VI.91–92.1

1 See **221**.
2 See **53**.
3 See **183** and **229**.
4 Thucydides does not mention slaves in so many words, but 'things with which

the *chōra* is furnished' which will come over of their own free will can hardly be anything else.

5 We think that rents for land relate to land owned in the empire by individual Athenians; for fees for legal facilities see **179**. Thucydides assumes that allied disloyalty will have an immediate practical effect.

229. The fortification of Dekeleia

The Spartans took the advice of Alkibiades, sending Gylippos to Syracuse (see **223**) and also fortifying a base in Attika.

(A) And the Spartans also made ready for the invasion of Attika, as they themselves had already proposed, urged on also by the Syracusans and the Corinthians; their aim, since they had heard of the reinforcements planned by the Athenians for Sicily, was that they might be stopped if an invasion took place. And Alkibiades also pressed home his point and said that they should fortify Dekeleia and not abandon the war. But the chief reason for a certain access of energy among the Spartans was that they thought that if the Athenians had two wars on their hands, against themselves and against the Sicilians, they would be easier to defeat; the Spartans also reflected that it was the Athenians who had been the first to break the treaty. For in the earlier war they thought that theirs had been the greater transgression, both because the Thebans had attacked Plataiai in time of peace and because they had refused to submit to arbitration when the Athenians suggested it, although there was a provision in the earlier treaty forbidding resort to arms if the other party was willing to go to arbitration. And so they thought it was right that they had fared ill and took to heart the disaster at Pylos and any other that had happened to them. But since the Athenians, using the thirty ships based on Argos, had ravaged some of the territory of Epidauros and Prasiai and other places, and at the same time were engaged in raids from Pylos and since, whenever disagreement occurred about anything arising out of the disputed points in the treaty and the Spartans suggested arbitration, the Athenians refused to submit to it, the Spartans now became convinced that the transgression of which they had been guilty earlier was now being perpetrated by the Athenians; as a result they became eager for war. And so in the course of this winter (414/13), they sent round to their allies for iron[1] and collected the other equipment necessary for their proposed fortification; and at the same time they themselves prepared a force which they planned to send to join those in Sicily in the merchant ships which were available, and compelled the other Peloponnesians to join in. And the winter ended and with it the eighteenth year of this war of which Thucydides wrote the history. (19) As soon as the following spring arrived, at the earliest possible moment, the Spartans and their allies invaded Attika; Agis the son of Archidamos, king of the Lakedaimonians, was in command. And first of all they ravaged that part of the *chōra* which lay around the plain, then they fortified Dekeleia, assigning the work by *poleis*. Dekeleia lies about 120 stades[2] from the *polis* of the Athenians and is about the same distance or slightly more from Boiotia. The fort was built to threaten the plain and the best parts of the *chōra* and was visible from the *polis* of the Athenians.

Thucydides VII.18–19.2

(B) And there arrived in Athens in the course of this same summer (of 413) 1,300 peltasts,[3] from the tribe of the Dians, Thrakians who use the short sword; it had been intended that they should sail to Sicily with Demosthenes. The Athenians, however, since they arrived too late, planned to send them back to Thrake, whence they had come; for it seemed too expensive to keep them for the war against the enemy based on Dekeleia, since they were each paid a drachma a day. For from the moment in the course of the summer when Dekeleia had been fortified by the entire army (of the Peloponnesians), thereafter to be occupied by contingents from the different *poleis* in succession as a base from which to attack the *chōra*, it had done a great deal of harm to the Athenians; the worst damage to their position had been due to the destruction of property and the loss of manpower. For before, the invasions had been short and had not prevented the farming of the land for the rest of the time; but now the enemy were there continuously; at times an even larger force was involved, at times the existing garrison raided the *chōra* and seized what there was to obtain supplies; furthermore, Agis the king of the Lakedaimonians was there and prosecuted the war with energy; as a result, the Athenians suffered a great deal of damage. For they were deprived of the whole of their *chōra*, and more than 20,000 slaves deserted, the majority of whom were men with manual skills (*cheirotechnai*),[4] and they lost all their flocks and draught animals; and, since the cavalry rode out every day to attack Dekeleia and guard the *chōra*, some of the horses were lamed by the rough ground and the continuous exertion, some were wounded.[5] (28) And the transport of necessities from Euboia, which had been speedily carried out by land from Oropos past Dekeleia, now took place by sea round Sounion and involved great expense.[6] The *polis* still needed to import everything and in fact became a garrison rather than a *polis*; for by day the Athenians stood guard on the walls in turn, by night all of them were on duty except the cavalry, some of them resting under arms, some of them (on duty) on the walls, and their sufferings lasted the whole year round.

Thucydides VII.27–28.2

1 It is paradoxical that a community which displayed its contempt for wealth by using raw iron as currency (see **53**) had none for construction purposes; compare also **222** and **259A**.
2 About 24 miles; for the stade see p. xvii.
3 See **257**.
4 Probably mostly from the mines at Laureion, see **161**.
5 The depressing experience of the cavalry in these years should be borne in mind in assessing the declining loyalty of the wealthy to the Athenian democracy in the closing years of the war.
6 Presumably not because of the basic cost of water transport, which was relatively low in antiquity, but because merchant fleets had to be convoyed by warships.

230. Persia and Greece

For those who were unwilling to accept the verdict of a struggle conducted in a Greek context or simply found Greece too restricting a field, there was always Persia, unlikely ever to have been averse to avenging her defeats at the hands of Athens from 478 onwards (see Ch. 12); something of the fascination of Persia for a Greek may be glimpsed in Aristophanes (see **147**), as well as in the careers of Pausanias and Themistokles (see **130** and **168**); and Persia or Persian-controlled territory was in due course to provide a refuge for the Athenians Andokides and Konon, just as she now provided help for Sparta. Both sides had courted Persia in the early stages of the Peloponnesian War, perhaps more than the text of Thucydides in its unfinished form allows us to see (A Andrewes, 'Thucydides and the Persians', *Historia* 10 (1961), 1–18). But it was only with the decline of Athenian power that the efforts we observe here were successful.

(A) And at the end of the same summer (430) Aristeus of Corinth and, as ambassadors of the Lakedaimonians, Aneristos and Nikolaos and Prato-damos, and also Timagoras of Tegea and, in a private capacity, Pollis of Argos were on their way to Asia to the King, to try to persuade him to provide money and join in the war on their side (but were captured by the Athenians).

Thucydides II. 67. 1

(B) And during the following winter (425/4) Aristeides the son of Archippos, a *stratēgos* with the money-collecting ships of the Athenians, which had been sent out around the allies, captured at Eion on the Strymon Artaphernes, a Persian on his way from the King to Lake-daimon. And when he was brought in, the Athenians translated the letters from the Assyrian[1] and read them; among many other points the chief as far as the Spartans were concerned was that the King did not understand what they wanted; for although many ambassadors came, none of them ever said the same thing; so if they wanted to deliver an

unambiguous message, they should send some men to him with the
Persian ambassador. As far as Artaphernes was concerned, the Athenians
later sent him by ship to Ephesos, accompanied by some ambassadors;
but when they heard there that King Artaxerxes the son of Xerxes had
just died – for he died about this time – they returned home.[2]

Thucydides IV.50

1 Thucydides uses the term simply to indicate an oriental language, in fact
  Aramaic, used by the Persians for the day-to-day administration of their
  empire.
2 But did not give up the attempt, see **233** Intro. For the chaotic nature of the
  succession to Artaxerxes, see Lewis, *Sparta and Persia*, 69–73.

231. The legacy of distrust

In contrast with their behaviour in 425/4 (see **230**), the Spartans after 413 knew
well how to go about getting Persian help, approaching Tissaphernes the satrap
of Ionia rather than the King; nevertheless, all did not go smoothly.

During the winter which followed (412/11), when Tissaphernes had put
a garrison into Iasos, he went to Miletos and provided upkeep for all the
ships for a month, as he had promised at Sparta, at the rate of an Attic
drachma per man;[1] but for the future he proposed to provide half a
drachma, until he could consult the King; and if the King so ordered he
said that he would give the full drachma. But Hermokrates the Syracusan
general[2] objected; for Therimenes was not admiral (*nauarchos*), but was
simply sailing with the ships to hand them over to (the admiral)
Astyochos, and did not stand firm over the problem of pay; nonetheless
it was agreed to give each man more than half a drachma by providing in
addition the pay of five ships; for Tissaphernes provided 30 talents for a
month for 55 ships; and he provided for the rest according to this same
formula, in so far as there were more ships than the total of 55.

Thucydides VIII.29

1 The normal rate for an oarsman in the Athenian fleet; the Attic drachma is
  treated as a unit of account – we do not know what coinage was actually used.
2 See **185** with n.1.

232. The illusion of Athenian weakness

The Athenians had been suspicious of Chios after the revolt of Lesbos (see **199**),
but down to 413 the Chians remained loyal; their behaviour now was symptomatic of a belief in Athenian weakness, universal in the Greek world – and wrong.

Indeed, the Chians are the only people apart from the Lakedaimonians, as far as I know, who have attained prosperity[1] and still not turned to excess; in fact, the further their *polis* advanced in well-being, the more firmly they were governed. Nor indeed, in case they seem here to have acted in a way that was less than prudent, did they dare to begin this very revolt before they had the prospect of sharing the danger with many good allies and saw that not even the Athenians themselves continued to deny after the disaster in Sicily that their affairs were certainly in a very bad way. And if they were somewhat in error in the unpredictable field of human behaviour, they realised their error in the company of many who held the same opinion, that the power of the Athenians would soon be destroyed. Now, when they were cut off from the sea and their land was being ravaged, there were some who tried to bring the *polis* over to the Athenians; when the *archontes* got wind of their action, they themselves did nothing, but brought in Astyochos the (Spartan) admiral from Erythrai with four ships which he had with him, and planned how to put a stop to the plot in as restrained a way as possible, either by taking hostages or by some other means.

Thucydides VIII.24.4–6

1 See Austin and Vidal-Naquet, *Economy*, no. 50B, for slavery on Chios. Compare also the reputation of the Chians as evidenced by 92 n.12 and the remark of Alkibiades at VIII.45.4.

233. Persia helps Sparta

In the speech *On the peace with Sparta* attributed to Andocides, it is claimed (III.29) that Athens and Persia agreed to become friends 'for ever' after an embassy undertaken by Epilykos, the uncle of the speaker, but that Athens threw away this friendship by supporting the rebel Amorges (see Meiggs and Lewis no.70 for a decree, perhaps of 424/3, relating to the initial agreement); it was not the last time that the ambiguous relationship between centre and periphery in the Persian empire caused problems for the Greeks, and on this occasion their action was fatal for the Athenians (see Lewis, *Sparta and Persia*, 76–7). A desire to recover lost territory and outrage at Athenian support for Amorges combined with a belief in Athenian weakness to bring Persia firmly back into Greek affairs. Thucydides reports three treaties between Persia and Sparta, the first of which (VIII.18) would have restored the whole of Greece as far as the Isthmos of Corinth to Persia without embodying any specific provisions for Persian help to Sparta; the second treaty rectified the latter defect (VIII.37); but only in the third treaty was the Persian empire limited to Asia. We see no way of deciding if all three treaties were actually made or whether Thucydides has interpreted drafts as the first two treaties, but incline (with Lewis, 90–107) to the former view. What seems to us important is that the treaties must have come into Thucydides' hands because they had been circulated by some person or persons who wished to represent the alliance between Persia and Sparta in as unfavourable a light as possible.

(A) All the ships of the Peloponnesians were now together at Knidos; they were being fitted out in any way that was necessary and the eleven representatives of the Lakedaimonians were negotiating with Tissaphernes, who was present, about what had already been done, raising anything with which they disagreed, and about the future conduct of the war; they were concerned that it should be prosecuted as efficiently as possible and to the greatest advantage of both sides. Lichas[1] paid particular attention to what had been done and said that neither of the agreements, whether that of Chalkideus or that of Therimenes, was acceptable and that it was outrageous if the King now claimed to rule over all the land over which he or his ancestors had once ruled; for that would involve all the islands once again being reduced to slavery, as well as Thessaly and the Lokrians and indeed everything as far as the Boiotians; and the Spartans were imposing a Median empire on the Greeks instead of bringing them freedom. So he urged the conclusion of a more acceptable agreement, or at any rate not the implementation of the existing agreements; he wanted no pay on these terms. Provoked in this way, Tissaphernes left the Spartans in a fit of anger and without achieving anything.

Thucydides VIII.43.2–4

(B) While this was going on and indeed even earlier, before they moved to Rhodes, the following intrigues were taking place. After the death of Chalkideus and the battle at Miletos, Alkibiades became an object of suspicion to the Peloponnesians; and when a letter came from them from Lakedaimon ordering Astyochos to put him to death, as a result of his having aroused the enmity of Agis and seeming in general untrustworthy, he first fled in fear to Tissaphernes and then began to damage the cause of the Peloponnesians as much as he possibly could in Tissaphernes' eyes. Then, becoming his adviser in everything, Alkibiades cut down the amount of pay being provided, so that instead of an Attic drachma half a drachma was provided and that not regularly;[2] he bade Tissaphernes say to the Spartans that the Athenians, who had long experience of naval affairs, were giving their men half a drachma, not so much from lack of resources as in order that their sailors might not become insubordinate as a result of their wealth, some of them reducing their fitness by spending their money on the sorts of things which cause illness, others of them deserting their ships, since they were not leaving behind the pay which was owing them as security.

Thucydides VIII.45.1–2

(c) In the thirteenth year of King Dareios, when Alexippidas was *ephoros* at Sparta, agreement was reached on the plain of the Maiandros between the Lakedaimonians and their allies on the one side and Tissaphernes and Hieramenes and the sons of Pharnakes[3] on the other side, concerning the affairs of the King and of the Lakedaimonians and their allies. The land of the King, as much as is in Asia, is to belong to the King; and the King is to decide as he wishes about the land which is his. And the Lakedaimonians and their allies are not to enter the land of the King with evil intent, nor is the King to enter the land of the Lakedaimonians or their allies with evil intent. And if any of the Lakedaimonians or their allies enter the land of the King with evil intent, the Lakedaimonians and their allies are to stop them. And if anyone from the side of the King goes against the Lakedaimonians or their allies, the King is to stop them. Tissaphernes is to provide upkeep for the ships which are now present according to the existing agreement until the ships of the King arrive. And it shall be for the Lakedaimonians and their allies to provide upkeep themselves for their own ships, if they wish, when the ships of the King arrive. And if they wish to receive upkeep from Tissaphernes, Tissaphernes is to provide it, but the Lakedaimonians and their allies are to repay to Tissaphernes at the end of the war as much money as they receive. And when the ships of the King arrive, the ships of the Lakedaimonians and of their allies and of the King are to prosecute the war together as seems best to Tissaphernes and the Lakedaimonians and their allies. And if they wish to make peace with the Athenians, they are to do so together.

Thucydides VIII.58

1 For the wealth of Lichas, perhaps the source of his self-assurance, see **265**.
2 See **231** n.1.
3 Hieramenes is perhaps a representative of the King or an associate of Tissaphernes as satrap of Ionia; the sons of Pharnakes control the satrapy to the north, the oldest, called Pharnabazos, being satrap.

234. Lysandros and Kyros

It was only when the Spartans placed a new commander, Lysandros, in control of the Spartan war effort in Asia and Tissaphernes was superseded by a son of the King that effective collaboration began.

Not long before this the Spartans had sent out Lysandros as admiral since the term of office of Kratesippidas was over. When he reached Rhodes, he took the ships which were there and sailed to Kos and Miletos and then to Ephesos, where he waited with 70 ships until Kyros reached Sardis. (2) When he had arrived, he went up to see him with the ambassadors from Lakedaimon. There he accused Tissaphernes of his various misdeeds, and begged Kyros to be as energetic as possible in the prosecution of the war. (3) Kyros replied that this was what his father had instructed him to do and that he himself had no other intention, but would do just that; he had come with 500 talents; if they ran out, he would use his own resources, which his father had granted him; if even they ran out, he would melt down the throne on which he sat, made of silver and gold. (4) The Spartans expressed their approval and urged him to establish an Attic drachma as the rate for a sailor, saying that if this were the pay the sailors of the Athenians would desert their ships and he would in the end spend less money. (5) He replied that they were right, but that he could not do anything except what the King had instructed; and there were agreements which laid down that he should give 30 minas (half a talent) to each ship for a month,[1] for as many ships as the Lakedaimonians wished to keep. (6) Lysandros said nothing at that stage, but after dinner, when Kyros was drinking his health and asked him what action of his would give him the most pleasure, he replied, 'If you would add an obol (a sixth of a drachma) to his pay for each sailor.' (7) From then onwards the pay was four obols, having previously been three obols (half a drachma). He also paid what was in arrears and even gave pay in advance for a month, so that there was a surge of energy in the army. (8) When the Athenians heard of this, they were downcast, but sent ambassadors to Kyros through Tissaphernes. He, however, declined to receive them, although Tissaphernes asked him to and said that he should see if he could ensure that none of the Greeks were strong, but that they were all weak, as a result of fighting among themselves; this was the policy which he had adopted at the instance of Alkibiades.[2]

Xenophon, *Hellenika* 1.5.1–9

1 Thus one mina, or 100 drachmas, a day for 200 men.
2 See **233**, and note that the Athenian *dēmos* could be persuaded to believe that Persia might help Athens, Thuc. VIII.48.3 (= **227B**); 54.1 (= **227B**).

24 The defeat of Athens

Having taken the decision after the defeat in Sicily to fight on (see **226**), the Athenians were remarkably successful; the last years of the war, however, saw the balance of power shifting steadily against them. Internal dissension affected their ability to control the empire (see **235**) and the cohesion of the fleet (see **236**), culminating in the trial of the *stratēgoi* who fought at Arginousai (**237**). Finally, failure to perceive that Persia had definitely decided to back Sparta led to inevitable defeat. But not the least interest of these years lies in the deliberate attempt to preserve *homonoia*, concord, in the *polis* (**241–243**); the fatal mistake of the democracy was perhaps not to realise that the loyalty of the rich was as crucial as that of the poor.

235. Phrynichos and the empire

Given the absolute dependence of Athens on her empire in the last stages of the war (see **215** for the service rendered by Alkibiades in this sphere), it is not surprising that problems arising out of the relationship between Athens and the *dēmos* in each *polis* should be prominent in this period, with a *dēmos* favourable to Athens at Chios and Samos, an oligarchy hostile to Athens at Rhodes, Thasos and Methymna (in this last case with the help of mercenaries, Thuc. VIII. 100); nor is it surprising that the period should evoke reflection on the problems, here attributed by Thuc. to Phrynichos (for whom see **227**).

But as for the *poleis* which were allies, to whom they had promised oligarchy, since they themselves were no longer to be a democracy, Phrynichos said that he was quite sure that this would have no effect on making those which had revolted come over to them or those which remained more reliable. For they would not accept slavery, accompanied by oligarchy or democracy according to individual taste, in preference to freedom accompanied by either at random; nor would they suppose that the so-called *kaloi k' agathoi*[1] would cause them any less trouble than the *dēmos*, since it was they who were the instigators and proposers of the crimes which the *dēmos* had perpetrated, crimes from which they had been the more important gainers. And it was at the hands of the *kaloi k'*

447

agathoi that men would die without trial and by violence, while the *dēmos* defended the *poleis* and controlled the *kaloi k' agathoi*. Phrynichos said that he knew very well that this was the view of the *poleis* and that they held it as a result of their experience of what had actually happened. So he at any rate did not hold with any of the ideas of Alkibiades or the current intrigues.

Thucydides VIII.48.5–7

1 Of Athens, see **143**.

236. Athenian morale

Desperately short of money in the last years of the war (see **241**), the Athenians were hampered by other factors as well; it is hard to be impressed by the general level of competence of her *stratēgoi* in this period and the crews of her ships were no longer the envy of other powers – Konon was forced at one point to select only a proportion of the total available to him as fit to serve, and the performance of the fleet at Aigospotamoi left much to be desired (see **239**); lack of bases for repair work also reduced the efficiency of the ships themselves. But perhaps the most paralysing factors were fear of treachery and lack of unity; the oligarchic coup of 411 and its aftermath surely had a catastrophic effect on morale among the *dēmos*, the heavy losses among the cavalry (Xen. *Hell.* 1.6.24) at Arginousai no doubt affected *their* morale, and the way in which Theramenes saved his own skin by ruining the *stratēgoi* at that battle (see **237**) no doubt did little to restore confidence. The climate of opinion at the end of the war may be imagined when we observe that already before the battle of Kyzikos fear of treachery was a central factor.

(At Prokonnesos) they learnt that Mindaros was at Kyzikos together with Pharnabazos and the army. So they remained there for that day, and the next day Alkibiades summoned an assembly and told them that they had to fight by sea and on land and before the walls (of Kyzikos). 'For', he said, 'we have no money, but the enemy have an unlimited supply from the King.' (15) And on the next day, when they had anchored, he gathered all the ships including the small boats close to himself, so that no one might inform the enemy of the size of the fleet, and announced that if anyone was caught sailing over to the other side the penalty was death.

Xenophon, *Hellenika* 1.1.14–15

237. Arginousai and the 'stratēgoi'

The final, and from most standpoints the least edifying, political scandal of the Peloponnesian War was reserved for its very last years. In the summer of 406 the

Athenians won their last victory at sea, near the Arginousai islands (east of Lesbos), but after the battle the crews of 25 Athenian triremes had been left to drown. Had weather conditions made their rescue impossible? The Athenian people did not think so – and neither did their leading politicians.

With Xenophon's full account, abridged below, compare the short notice in ?Aristotle, *Ath. Pol.* 34.1. For the technical details of the trial see M. H. Hansen, *Eisangelia* (Odense, 1975), 84–6.

The Athenians deposed all the *stratēgoi* involved except for Konon, and elected two other men, Adeimantos and Philokles, to be his colleagues. (2) Two of the *stratēgoi* who had taken part in the sea-battle, Protomachos and Aristogenes, did not return to Athens; the other six – Perikles,[1] Diomedon, Lysias, Aristokrates, Thrasyllos and Erasinides – did When they had done so, Archedemos, who at that time was the champion of the *dēmos* in Athens and also in charge of the *diōbelia*,[2] had Erasinides fined and brought before a *dikasterion* on a charge, first, of being in possession of public money from the Hellespontos and, second, of misconduct as *stratēgos*; and the court decided that Erasinides should go to prison. (3) Then the (other) *stratēgoi* made statements in front of the *boulē*, about the sea-battle and the great storm which had sprung up after it. Timokrates then proposed that these others too should be imprisoned and handed over to the *dēmos* (for trial). This the *boulē* did, (4) and at a subsequent meeting of the *ekklēsia*, a number of speakers, with Theramenes prominent amongst them, attacked the *stratēgoi* on the grounds that they should rightly be held responsible for not picking up the shipwrecked sailors . . . (7) It was decided, however, to postpone any decision to another meeting of the *ekklēsia*, as by then it was late, and too dark to see the hands raised in any vote; and the *boulē* was instructed to discuss the matter in advance and bring in a proposal about what sort of trial the men should have.

(8) However, there then occurred the festival of the Apatouria, at which fathers and their families meet together;[3] and Theramenes and his supporters made arrangements that large numbers of men should appear at this festival dressed in black and with shaven heads – purporting, of course, to be relatives of those who had died – and should then go on to attend the *ekklēsia*. They also persuaded Kallixenos to make accusations against the *stratēgoi* in the *boulē*. (9) They then summoned a meeting of the *ekklēsia* at which the *boulē*, on the proposal of Kallixenos, laid down the following motion . . . (to vote on the fate of the *stratēgoi* then and there). (11) Then a man came forward and claimed that he had survived only by clinging on to a meal-tub, and that as his comrades were dying they had said to him that if he were to be saved he should tell the *dēmos* that the *stratēgoi* had abandoned men who had been giving their all for their mother-city.

(12) Euryptolemos son of Peisianax and some others were for bringing Kallixenos to court on a charge of having made an illegal proposal, and part of the *dēmos* expressed its support for this – but the majority cried out that it was a terrible thing if the *dēmos* was to be prevented from doing what it liked; (13) and this prompted Lykiskos to propose that unless the sponsors of the summons withdrew it they too should be judged by the same vote as the *stratēgoi*. So, amid mob uproar once again, they were obliged to withdraw the summonses. (14) Next some of the *prytaneis* declared that it would be illegal for them to put the motion to the vote, and so they would not do it; but when Kallixenos had come forward again and made the same charges against them, and the crowd had started to shout that refusal would mean summonses, (15) the *prytaneis* were intimidated into agreeing to put the motion to the vote – all except Sokrates son of Sophroniskos, who said that he would never do anything at all which was contrary to the law⁴ . . . (A lengthy speech by Euryptolemos follows, chs. 16–33.) (34) After making this speech Euryptolemos put forward a motion to the effect that the men be tried in accordance with the decree of Kannonos⁵ and one at a time, whereas the motion from the *boulē* was that they be all tried together, by a single ballot. When a vote was taken on these motions the decision went at first in favour of that of Euryptolemos; but a second vote, after Menekles had lodged a formal objection under oath,⁶ passed the motion from the *boulē*. So they then voted on the eight *stratēgoi* who had taken part in the sea-battle: they were found guilty, and the six who were present were put to death.

(35) Yet it was not long afterwards before the Athenians began to regret what they had done, and voted that formal complaints (*probolai*) be lodged against those who had deceived the *dēmos*, and that these men be required to put up bail until they could stand trial. Kallixenos was explicitly mentioned in this connection, though in fact the *probolai* named four others as well, and they were all kept in confinement by those who had stood surety for them. Later, however, during the disturbances in which Kleophon was killed,⁷ they escaped, before they could be brought to trial. Kallixenos did come back, at the time when the men from Peiraieus returned to the city,⁸ but he was universally detested, and died of starvation.

Xenophon, Hellenika 1.7.1–15,* 34–35

---

1 The bastard son of *the* Perikles and his Milesian mistress Aspasia. He had been specially exempted from his father's citizenship law (see **128**).

2 See **216** with n.5.

3 See Parke, *Festivals*, 88–92.

4 This is the famous philosopher: see **248**. For the role of *nomos* in political debate

in this period compare Xen. *Hell.* II.4.42, for the attitude of Sokrates compare the whole of Plato, *Kriton*; note also the analysis in Aristot. *Pol.* (IV)1292 a 2–6.

5 E. has referred to this in his speech (ch.20); it prescribed, for those accused of 'wronging the *dēmos*', a humiliating trial in chains as well as a gruesome (death-)penalty.

6 Against the vote.

7 In 404.

8 See **244–245**.

238. The refusal of peace terms

Despite their weak position, the Athenians were determined to fight on; our sources deride the decision (see Diodorus XIII. 52–53 – after the battle of Kyzikos; Androtion, *FGrH* 324 F44 – in 408; and below), but one must attempt to understand the reasons behind it. The Athenians no doubt underestimated the Persian threat (see **234**) and no doubt also thought that to accept the loss of some *poleis* was to invite the secession of the rest; but it is hard not to suppose that after the oligarchic coup of 411 advocacy of peace was associated with oligarchic leanings; and in an atmosphere where treachery was readily suspected few could afford even the slightest appearance of disloyalty.

Then (in 406/5), when the Lakedaimonians were willing to evacuate Dekeleia and to make peace on the basis that each side hold what it had, some were in favour, but the majority did not approve, deceived by Kleophon,[1] who prevented the conclusion of the peace, coming into the *ekklēsia* drunk and wearing a breastplate, saying that he would not accept it, unless the Lakedaimonians surrendered all the *poleis*.

?Aristotle, *Athenaion Politeia* 34.1

1 See **216**.

239. The battle of Aigospotamoi

The account of Xenophon (*Hell.* II.1.15–32) presents the Athenians and the Spartans facing each other across the Hellespontos, both sides anxious for battle, and makes the Spartans victorious when Lysandros pretended to decline battle, allowed the Athenians to return and disembark and then attacked. Only from the account in Diodorus (deriving from another fourth-century historian, Ephoros) do we discover why the Athenians were desperate for battle – the Spartans controlled Lampsakos and therefore the Hellespontos and the Athenians were starving – and find a credible account of the battle (so rightly C. Ehrhardt, *Phoenix* 24 (1970), 225). On the rejected initiative of the exiled Alkibiades, the truth will probably never be known – the advice to retire to Sestos, according to Xenophon, the offer of help from two kings of the Thrakians in return for a share in the command, according to Diodorus (XIII.105).

When the enemy continued to be unwilling to fight at sea and the army had no food, Philokles (the *stratēgos*),[1] in command on that day, ordered the remaining trierarchs to man their triremes and follow him, and set sail himself in advance with the 30 triremes which were ready. Lysandros, however, on learning of this from some deserters,[2] weighed anchor with all his ships, routed Philokles and pursued him towards the other ships. Since the triremes of the Athenians were not yet manned, they all fell into confusion with the unexpected appearance of the enemy. And when Lysandros saw the disarray of his opponents, he at once landed Eteonikos with the men who normally fought on land; he made good use of the momentary advantage and seized a part of the palisade; Lysandros himself sailed up with all his triremes ready, fixed iron grappling hooks and dragged away the ships moored by the shore. The Athenians were shattered by the surprise and had neither time to put out with their ships nor possibility of fighting on land; so they resisted for a while and then gave way and fled, some of them abandoning the ships, some the palisade, in whatever direction each man hoped for safety. Of the triremes only ten escaped; Konon the *stratēgos* had one of them and, abandoning any thought of return to Athens in fear of the anger of the *dēmos*, he fled to Euagoras who was in control of Cyprus and whose friend he was; of the soldiers, the majority fled by land and escaped to Sestos. The rest of the ships Lysandros took captive and, having taken Philokles the *stratēgos* alive, he took him to Lampsakos and executed him.

Diodorus XIII.106

1 See **237**.
2 Compare **236**.

240. The fall of Athens

After Aigospotamoi, the allied *poleis* except for Samos (which murdered its upper classes and remained loyal) fell away from Athens; king Pausanias summoned the allies of Sparta and besieged Athens, Lysandros blockaded the Peiraieus.

But the Athenians, under siege by land and sea, did not know what to do, since they had neither ships nor allies nor food; and they thought that there was no escape from suffering what they had done to others, not in revenge, but wrongly and arrogantly to men from small *poleis* for the sole reason that they were fighting with the Lakedaimonians. (11) So they held out, having restored political rights to the *atimoi*,[1] and although many were dying of hunger in the *polis* they did not enter into discussions about terms. (The Athenians then attempted to come to terms, retaining their walls and the Peiraieus, but were rebuffed; they in turn rejected terms involving the destruction of a section of each Long Wall, terms which were apparently on offer.) (16) In this situation, Theramenes said in the *ekklēsia* that if they were willing to send him to Lysandros he would return after finding out whether the Spartans were holding out over the walls because they wished to enslave the *polis* or in order to obtain a guarantee of good faith. But when he was sent he wasted time in the company of Lysandros for three months or more, waiting for the Athenians to be ready to agree to whatever anyone said because of the lack of food. (17) And when he returned during the fourth month, he announced in the *ekklēsia* that Lysandros had kept him for a long time, but had then told him to go to Sparta; for he was not in a position to answer his request, only the *ephoroi*. Theramenes was then chosen as one of a team of ten plenipotentiary ambassadors to Sparta. (18) Meanwhile, Lysandros sent one Aristoteles, an Athenian exile, along with others who were Spartans, to tell the *ephoroi* that he had told Theramenes that they were empowered to discuss war and peace.

(19) When Theramenes and the other ambassadors had reached Sellasia[2] and were asked in what capacity they came, they replied that they were plenipotentiary ambassadors for the conclusion of peace; thereupon, the *ephoroi* issued orders to summon them. And when they arrived, the Spartans summoned an assembly, in which the Corinthians and the Thebans in particular, but many others of the Greeks also, opposed them and urged them not to make peace, but to destroy the Athenians. (20) But the Lakedaimonians refused to enslave a Greek *polis* which had performed great services at the moment of greatest peril for Greece, but offered peace on condition that they pull down the Long Walls and the walls of the Peiraieus, hand over their ships apart from twelve, receive back the exiles,[3] have the same friends and enemies as the Spartans and follow them by land and sea wherever they led. (21) So Theramenes and his fellow-ambassadors brought these terms back to Athens; a large crowd surrounded them as they entered, fearing that they had returned unsuccessful; for it was not possible to delay any longer because of the number of those who were dying from hunger. (22) On the next day the ambassadors announced the terms on which the Spartans would make peace; Theramenes was their spokesman, saying that it was necessary to obey the Spartans and pull down the walls. A few people opposed him, but far more agreed and it was decided to accept the peace. (23) Lysandros then sailed into the Peiraieus and the exiles returned, and they tore down the walls with great enthusiasm to the music of flute-girls, thinking that that day was for Greece the beginning of freedom.[4]

Xenophon, *Hellenika* II.2.10–23*

453

1 Men deprived of civic rights; note this last attempt to achieve *homonoia*, concord, compare **112A**.
2 On the frontier of Lakonia.
3 Notably oligarchic.
4 See Meiggs and Lewis no.95 for the Spartan victory dedication at Delphi.

241. The preservation of 'homonoia'

We have suggested that lack of unity (see **236**) was perhaps the major catastrophe for Athens in the last years of the war; serious efforts were made, however, to avoid at least one thing, alienation of the poor as a result of destitution. Although Aristophanes, *Frogs* 1065–1066 (early 405), suggests that men were pretending to be poor in order to avoid serving as trierarchs, at least two men for whom Lysias later wrote speeches (XIX.42–44; XXI.1–11) were prepared to boast of the amounts they had spent during the Dekeleian War. Despite the fact that there were apparently only two *eisphorai* between 411 and 404, there was clearly some private wealth available and the interesting thing is that some of it was spent on what can only be described as welfare payments; the retention of the loyalty of the poor was clearly regarded as more important than the provision of the maximum number of ships possible. Just as earlier (see **198** n.5), relief for those who had suffered from the invasion of Attika was provided by means of a *klērouchia* on Lesbos, so now pay for jury service was revived by the restored democracy (Aristophanes, *Frogs* 1463–1466); in addition, Kleophon introduced an institution known as the *diōbelia*, probably a simple distribution of two obols (see **216, 237**; the expenditure of the treasurers of Athena under this head was already substantial in 410/9, see Meiggs and Lewis no. 84). Aristotle reflected gloomily on the institution; but he was not in Athens in 410/9.

So one of the things which are expedient (for a *polis*) is for the properties of the *politai* to be equal, so that *stasis* does not occur among them, or at any rate not to any great extent. For people who are wealthy are likely to object, as not deserving the same treatment as everyone else; so it is that we often see them attacking the system and engaged in *stasis*. And furthermore human wickedness is something insatiable; originally a mere *diōbelia* was sufficient; but when this is an established institution, people always want more, until there is no limit.

Aristotle, *Politics* (II) 1267 a 37–b 3

242. The 'polis' and the gods

One of the things on which money was spent in the last years of the Peloponnesian War was the maintenance of cult activity; already in the Funeral Speech Perikles had been made to emphasise the importance of joint participation in religious festivals (Thuc. II.38.1); now money was spent on the building of the

Erechtheion (also channelling some money into the hands of the poor); distributions, the so-called *theōrika*, were made to enable the poor to attend religious festivals, and the dramatic performances at the festivals themselves were kept up; indeed much of the money spent by one of the clients of Lysias (see **241**) was spent on ritual activities. When a *polis* ceased to worship its gods it ceased to be a *polis*. In this context it is not surprising that when Alkibiades returned to Athens he turned his attention to the celebration of the rites at Eleusis, which he had been accused of profaning (see also Xen. *Hell.* 1.4.20).

In general, however, everything had gone as Alkibiades wished and 100 triremes with which he intended to set sail were ready manned; at this point a rather splendid desire came over him in relation to the Mysteries. For from the time when Dekeleia was fortified and the enemy by his presence controlled the routes to Eleusis, the procession went by sea and lost all its magnificence; the sacrifices and dances and many of the rites which are performed on the way when they lead forth the procession were perforce abandoned. It therefore seemed an admirable idea to Alkibiades, both from the point of view of reverence for the gods and from that of respect among men, to restore the original appearance of the rite, sending the procession by land and guarding it against the enemy. For either, having ventured and succeeded, he would belittle and humble Agis or he would fight, in full view of his country, a battle which was sacred and approved by the gods in a great and holy cause and would have all the *politai* as witnesses of his worth.

Plutarch, *Alkibiades* 34.2–4

243. The theory of 'homonoia'

Theoretical accounts of democratic views are rare (see Jones, *Democracy*, ch.3); one striking example, however, falls close in time to the practical activities of the Athenian democracy at the end of the Peloponnesian War. For Democritus see p.9.

The *nomoi* would not have forbidden a man to live according to his own resources if it was not the case that by doing so one man may injure another; for envy creates the beginning of *stasis* . . . (255) When those who are able bring themselves to lend and to serve and to oblige, in this already one sees pity and avoidance of destitution and creation of companionship and helping each other and concord (*homonoia*) among the *politai* and other good things which no one could tell in full.[1]

Democritus, fr.245* and fr.255

---

1 Compare **241** and Aristot. *Pol.* (II) 1263 a 35 and (VII)1320 b 10 for the public use of private wealth at Taras.

25 Post-war Athens (404–399)

Whatever the merits, in the eyes of Thucydides (see **227B**, end) and others, of the *politeia* of the Five Thousand, 'while Athens still depended on her ships and rowers for the maintenance of her empire, a constitution which excluded the *thētes* from the full rights of citizenship could only be tolerated as a temporary expedient' (Hignett, *Constitution*, 279); and by July 410, full radical democracy had been restored – and lasted for the remaining six years of the war (see Hignett, *Constitution*, 280–4). Then in the summer of 404, however, came the end of the war, and with it another oligarchical interlude, the régime of the 'Thirty Tyrants' (**244**). To some extent it is self-evident that these two counter-revolutions, of 411 and 404, are to be viewed as a pair, deriving from internal (or internally-generated) factors: if disenchantment with the democracy's record, especially in conducting the war, had set in after the Sicilian disaster and played its part in 411, it will have been all the stronger now that the war had been finally lost, and the reduction of the once supreme Athenian navy to a mere twelve vessels (**240**) will simply have achieved by force what would in any case have come about – the political impotence, for the time being, of the *dēmos*. The oligarchs, by contrast, were renewed and strengthened by the return, as the armistice required, of a host of exiles, many of whom were doubtless eager for revolution and revenge, and some of whom were undeniably prominent amongst the Thirty. Yet in 404 there was a new element in the picture – Spartan involvement and interference – and it goes a long way towards explaining why this post-war revolution followed an even bloodier and more contentious course than its predecessor; see further **244**, and **247** for its long-term impact. By 401 a spirit of reconciliation had prevailed, with democracy restored and extremism repudiated (**245–246**), but the tail had one last sting in it: the trial and execution, in 399, of Sokrates, as the scapegoat for twenty years of folly and failure (**248**).

On these years as a whole see further C. Mossé, *Athens in Decline* (London, 1973), ch. 1.

244. The 'Thirty Tyrants'

As explained above, the régime of the 'Thirty Tyrants' (July–September 404) was a direct outcome of the Athenians' eventual capitulation in the war (**240**) and of the fact, subsequently and consequently, that the Spartans in general and Lysandros in particular were in a position to compel the Athenians towards political change willy-nilly. This they did by giving free rein and overt backing to right-wing extremists: when the *ekklēsia* met to debate the motion of Drakontides (see A, below), Peloponnesian forces were still occupying Peiraieus, and an appearance and speech by Lysandros himself (Lysias XII.74) ensured its safe passage; and although the Spartans then withdrew from Attika, the Thirty discovered that they could manage without this open military support for only a few months before having to ask for a garrison (see B), so that their acts took place against a virtually seamless backcloth of Spartan military occupation. (See further D. Whitehead, 'Sparta and the Thirty Tyrants', *Ancient Society*, forthcoming.) Essentially then the whole episode should be seen as our best-known example of Spartan – or rather Lysandrian – imperialism in general in these years (see **250**), and to this extent it is right to describe the régime as 'a small oligarchy of the type which [Lysandros] had already been instrumental in bringing to power elsewhere' (de Ste Croix, *Origins*, 144, cf. 157; and Cartledge, *Sparta*, 268). Oligarchy, however, is an even less appropriate political label for it than for the régime of 411 (**227**) – if, that is, one's criterion is the number not of those notionally possessing citizenship but of those actually exercising power; and it was the latter yardstick, self-evidently, which led to 'the Thirty' becoming the accepted form of reference, not only in everyday parlance (e.g. Lys. XIII.20, Demos. XXII.52), but also in official terminology (e.g. Tod no.98). An 'oligarchy' of thirty men, in a *polis* the size of Athens, was a nonsense: this was collective tyranny; hence 'the tyranny of the Thirty' (?Aristot. *Ath. Pol.* 41.2) becomes 'the Thirty Tyrants' (Diod. XIV.2.1 and 3.7, etc.), and the traumatic effect of the whole episode (see **247**) finds much of its explanation.

We give here three viewpoints: (A) the Aristotelian *Ath. Pol.*; (B) Xenophon, the contemporary historian; and (C) another eye-witness account, from the non-Athenian Lysias, whose family was directly involved.

(A) In the year of the *archōn* Alexias (405/4) the Athenians had the misfortune to lose the sea-battle at Aigospotamoi, as a result of which Lysandros became master of the *polis* and established the Thirty in the following way. Once the peace had been concluded on condition that the Athenians be governed by their 'ancestral *politeia*',[1] the democrats attempted to preserve the *dēmos*; the upper classes who belonged to the political clubs, together with those exiles who had returned after the peace had been made, were eager for oligarchy; and those (from the upper classes) who did not belong to any club but were otherwise considered to be the best sort of *politai* were aiming for the 'ancestral *politeia*'. This last group included Archinos,[2] Anytos,[3] Kleitophon,[4] Phormisios[5] and many others, but its chief spokesman was Theramenes.

However, once Lysandros had sided with the oligarchs, the *dēmos* was inevitably intimidated into voting the oligarchy into power, on a *psēphisma* drafted by Drakontides of (the deme) Aphidna. (35) So this was how the Thirty were established, in the year of the *archōn* Pythodoros (404/3). And once they had become masters of the *polis* they disregarded every regulation concerning the *politeia* except for the appointment of a *boulē* of 500 and the other officials from a group previously selected by the *phylai*,[6] and the choice of ten colleagues to rule Peiraieus, eleven prison overseers and 300 whip-bearers as their own attendants; in this way they kept the *polis* under their control. At first they behaved moderately towards their fellow-*politai*, and pretended to be administering the 'ancestral *politeia*': they took down from the Areiopagos the *nomoi* of Ephialtes and Archestratos about the Areiopagites;[7] they also abolished those statutes of Solon which were controversial;[8] and they did away with the power of the *dikastai*.[9] In all this they claimed only to be correcting ambiguities in the *politeia* . . . These were their initial measures, which included getting rid of the informers (*sykophantai*) and those mischievous and wicked men who flattered the *dēmos* against its best interests. The *polis* was delighted with all this, thinking that they were doing it for the best of reasons. However, once the Thirty had acquired a firmer hold on the *polis*, none of the *politai* was safe from them: they killed anyone who stood out in terms of property, family and reputation, out of fear of what they might do and with a view to appropriating their property, and within a short space of time they had done away with no fewer than 1,500 men. (36) Theramenes was angry to see the *polis* being ruined in this way, and he urged them to stop their shameful behaviour and to hand over the control of affairs to 'the best men'. At first they opposed this; but when news of Theramenes' proposals reached the people at large and he began to attract mass support, they were afraid that he might become champion of the *dēmos* and overthrow the junta, so they drew up a list of 3,000 of the *politai* who were to be given a share in the *politeia*. But Theramenes attacked this too, on two grounds: because in their desire to give a share to the appropriate people they were giving it only to 3,000 men – as if all merit were confined within that number – and also because they were doing two totally incompatible things, in basing their rule upon force and yet making it weaker than its subjects. The Thirty, however, derided these claims, apart from postponing for a long time the publication of the list of the 3,000 and (until then) keeping to themselves the names of those who had been included . . .

(37) Winter (404/3) had already begun when Thrasyboulos[10] and the (other Athenian) exiles occupied Phyle.[11] The Thirty led out an army against them but were defeated, and decided to disarm the citizen-body

in general and to kill Theramenes. This is how they did it: they put two *nomoi* before the *boulē* and ordered it to vote them through; the first of them gave the Thirty full powers to kill any *politai* who were not included in the list of the 3,000, while the other one forbade participation in their present *politeia* to anyone who had helped to demolish the wall at Ectioneia or had acted in any way in opposition to the Four Hundred who had set up the earlier oligarchy.[12] Theramenes had done both of these things, which meant that once the *nomoi* had been ratified he found himself outside the *politeia* and the Thirty acquired the power to have him killed. And after the removal of Theramenes they disarmed everybody except the 3,000, and stepped up the cruelty and wickedness of their policies in general . . . (38) Subsequently, however, the men from Phyle occupied Mounychia[13] and defeated in battle the Thirty and their forces when they tried to save it; and when the danger was over the men from the *astu* returned, assembled in the *agora* on the following day and deposed the Thirty. They chose instead ten *politai* with full powers to bring the war to an end; but once in office these men did nothing to achieve the object for which they had been elected, sending instead to Sparta for help and a loan of money . . . However, when the men in possession of Peiraieus and Mounychia began to gain the upper hand in the war, as the entire *dēmos* went over to their side, the board of ten originally elected was dissolved and another ten chosen – those deemed to be 'the best men'; and it was under them and thanks to their zealous efforts that a reconciliation was effected and democracy restored.[14]

?Aristotle, *Athenaion Politeia* 34.2–38.3*

(B) This oligarchy came into being as follows. It was resolved by the *dēmos* that thirty men be elected to draft the ancestral *nomoi* as the future basis for the *politeia*. The men chosen were Polychares, Kritias, Melobios, Hippolochos, Eukleides, Hieron, Mnesilochos, Chremon, Theramenes, Aresias, Diokles, Phaidrias, Chaireleos, Anaitios, Peison, Sophokles, Eratosthenes, Charikles, Onomakles, Theognis, Aischines, Theogenes, Kleomedes, Erasistratos, Pheidon, Drakontides, Eumathes, Aristoteles, Hippomachos and Mnesitheides. (11) The thirty were elected immediately after the demolition of the Long Walls and the Peiraieus walls, and they were elected for the purpose of drafting *nomoi* to form the future basis of the *politeia*; in fact, though, they were always 'about to begin' drafting and publication, and they (meanwhile) appointed a *boulē* and the other officials just as they saw fit. (12) Their first act was to arrest and put on trial for their lives those who were generally known to have made their living under the democracy by acting as informers and attacking the *kaloi k'agathoi*;[15] and the *boulē* was glad enough to condemn them, and everyone else to raise no objection –

459

everyone, that is, who could say that he did not belong in that category himself. (13) Next, however, they began to consider how they might be able to treat the *polis* as they liked, and the main outcome of this was that they sent Aischines and Aristoteles to Sparta and persuaded Lysandros to have a garrison sent to help them, just until – as they put it, no doubt – they had got rid of the 'criminals' and established their *politeia*. This garrison they undertook to pay for themselves. (14) Lysandros agreed, and helped them to secure the despatch of garrison-troops, with Kallibios as *harmostēs* . . .[16]

(15) For a time at first Kritias and Theramenes thought alike and were friends; however, once Kritias had acquired a taste for killing large numbers of people – the result of the fact that the *dēmos* had once exiled him – Theramenes tried to restrain him . . . (17) But still the mass murders continued, until it became clear that many people were getting together in opposition and wondering what the *politeia* was coming to. At this juncture Theramenes spoke out again, saying that it would be impossible for the oligarchy to survive unless 'a reasonable number of others' were brought in to share the control of affairs. (18) By this time Kritias and the rest of the Thirty were afraid, particularly of the possibility that the *politai* might rally round Theramenes, so they now proceeded to publish a list of 3,000 men whom they claimed were to have a share in things . . . (20) A review under arms was then held, with the 3,000 in the *agora* and those not on the list in various other places; the order was given to lay down arms, and thereupon, while everyone was off duty, the Thirty sent round the garrison-troops and their Athenian sympathisers to seize the arms of everybody except the 3,000 and carry them up for storage in the temple on the Akropolis. (21) Once this was done they considered themselves free to do whatever they liked and began to kill large numbers of people, some out of personal hatred and others for the sake of their money. The money was needed, amongst other things, to pay the garrison-troops, so they decided that they themselves, each member of the Thirty, should arrest a *metoikos*, kill him and confiscate his property . . .[17] (23) As to Theramenes, they now considered him to be an obstacle in the way of their doing what they wanted, so they began to intrigue against him: in private conversations with the members of the *boulē* they endeavoured to slander him by suggesting that he was undermining the *politeia*, and then they called together the *boulē* as a whole – having instructed some youths, the most audacious they could find, to stand by with daggers under their arms. (Speeches by Kritias and Theramenes follow; Theramenes' name is struck from the list of the 3,000, and he is led away to execution.)

(4.1) After Theramenes had died in this way the Thirty began to behave on the basis that they now had nothing to fear and could rule as tyrants: they issued a proclamation forbidding entry to the *astu* to anyone not on the list and evicted the people involved from their estates, so as to take over the lands for themselves and their friends. Many of those who had sought refuge in Peiraieus were driven from there as well, and both Megara and Thebes were filled with the refugees. (2) But now it was that Thrasyboulos, with 70 men, set out from Thebes and seized the strong fortress of Phyle . . .[18]

Xenophon, Hellenika II.3.2; 3.11–23;* 4.1–2

(c) 'It was Perikles who persuaded my father Kephalos to come to this country, where he lived for thirty years,[19] and neither he nor, until now, we (his sons) have been a party to any law-suit either as plaintiff or defendant; on the contrary, our life under the democracy was such as to avoid all offence, whether giving it or taking it. (5) Then, however, those scoundrels and informers the Thirty established their rule, declaring that the *polis* ought to be purged of unjust men and that the rest of the *politai* should devote themselves to goodness and justice – professions which they preached but did not, in their effrontery, practise. I shall endeavour to remind you of this by speaking first of my own concerns and then of yours.

(6) Theognis and Peison it was[20] who initiated discussions amongst the Thirty about the *metoikoi*, claiming that some of them were hostile to the *politeia*, and that the Thirty therefore had a splendid pretext for making money under the guise of exacting punishment; in any case, they said, the *polis* was impoverished and the régime needed cash. (7) And their colleagues were easily persuaded to agree to this, as they were men who set little store by murder but a great deal by acquiring money. They resolved accordingly to arrest ten (*metoikoi*), two of whom were to be poor men; this was in order that they could explain to the others that the policy was designed not to make money but to benefit the *politeia*, just like any other perfectly justifiable act. (8) So they divided the chosen households out between them and began their visitations. Me they found entertaining foreign guests, whom they sent packing before handing me over to Peison; the others went to the workshop and made a list of the slaves.[21] (9) I asked Peison whether he would be willing to spare me, for a price. He replied that he would – if the price was a high one. I therefore said that I was prepared to give him a talent of silver, and he agreed to this arrangement. Now I was well aware that he had regard for neither gods nor men, but all the same it seemed imperative in the circumstances to make him give his word. (10) When he had sworn – calling down utter destruction upon himself and his children if he should not spare me once he had taken the silver – I went into my bedroom and opened my money-chest. Peison noticed this and came in; and when he saw what it

461

contained he called in two of his minions and told them to seize what was in the chest. (11) Well, men of the jury, since he now had not the sum that we had agreed on but *three* talents of silver, together with 400 staters of Kyzikos, 100 darics and four silver cups, I begged him to give me journey-money. (12) His reply was that I should think myself lucky to escape with my life. As we were leaving, Peison and I, we were met by Melobios and Mnesitheides, who were leaving the workshop; they encountered us just by the door and asked where we were going. Peison told them that we were on our way to my brother's, to examine what was in that household as well; so they told him to carry on his way, but me to accompany them to (the house of) Damnippos. (13) Peison came up to me and urged me to keep quiet and not to worry, for he would be coming there himself. When we got there we found Theognis, guarding some others, and they handed me over to him and went off again. Under the circumstances I made up my mind to take a risk, as death was already staring me in the face: (14) I called Damnippos over and said to him, 'You are a friend of mine, and now I have come into your house. I have done nothing wrong; they want to kill me for my money. This is my plight, so please do whatever is in your power to save me.' He said that he would, and decided that he had better mention the matter to Theognis, whom he believed would do anything at all for money. (15) However, while he was in conversation with Theognis, I made up my mind, as I happened to be familiar with the house and knew that it had doors at both front and back, to try to save myself thereby: my reasoning was that if nobody saw me I should be saved, while if I were caught I expected that if Damnippos had persuaded Theognis to take the money I would be released all the same, and if he had not I should be killed all the same. (16) Having thought the matter through in this way I made my escape while they were keeping guard on the front door. I had to pass through three doors myself, but as it happened they were all open. I went to (the house of) the *nauklēros* Archeneos and sent him into the *astu* for news of my brother (Polemarchos); and he returned with the news that Eratosthenes had arrested Polemarchos in the street and hauled him off to prison. (17) And once I knew what had happened I sailed across, on the following night, to Megara; Polemarchos, however, received from the Thirty their usual order to drink hemlock, without their even telling him why he had to die – much less letting him defend himself in a court of law. (18) And when he was being brought out of prison, dead, they did not allow his funeral to be conducted from any of our three houses but hired a shed and laid him out in that. We had plenty of cloaks, yet they refused our request to use one for the funeral; it was our friends giving whatever they could – a cloak here, a pillow there – who saw to his interment. (19) The Thirty had 700 shields of ours, as well as all that silver and gold, with bronze and jewellery and furniture and women's clothes in quantities beyond any of their expectations; also 120 slaves,[22] of which they took the best for themselves and put the rest into public service. Their desire for profit was enormous, insatiable, and it showed them up in their true colours: for Polemarchos' wife happened to have some twisted gold earrings, and Melobios had no sooner entered the house than he removed them from her ears! (20) Not even the smallest fraction of our property did they spare: we were rich, so they treated us just as badly as other men would have done in anger at great crimes. This was not what we deserved from the *polis*, we who had undertaken all the *chorēgiai*,[23] contributed to many *eisphorai*,[24] shown ourselves well behaved and done whatever was required of us; when we had not made a single personal enemy but had ransomed many Athenians from the enemies of the state. Such was our reward from them for living as *metoikoi* very differently from their own conduct as *politai*.'

Lysias XII (Against Eratosthenes) 4–20

1 This is improbable: see Hignett, *Constitution*, 285; a private undertaking, by Theramenes, that the democracy would be curtailed is much more likely.
2 See further **245**.
3 See further **248**.
4 See **80D**.
5 See further **246**.
6 'From the *phylai*' is Hude's emendation of 'from the 1,000 (*chilioi*)': such a body is not otherwise attested, and it seems in any case too small a pool from which to draw more than 500.
7 See **123**.
8 See ?Aristot. *Ath. Pol.* 9.2.
9 This probably does not mean the suspension of the *dikastēria* but an insistence that they simply administer the law rather than interpret it.
10 On his part on the democratic side in 411 see Thuc. VIII.73–77.
11 A mountain village in northern Attika.
12 See **227B**.
13 A hill inside Peiraieus, commanding the two lesser harbours.
14 See further **245**.
15 *Kaloi k'agathoi*: see **143**.
16 On the *harmostēs* see **250**.
17 Compare c, below; and see in brief Whitehead, *Ideology*, 154–5.
18 With the results described above, A; for Xenophon's version, too long to excerpt here, see *Hell.* II.4.2–33.
19 See Davies, *Families*, 587–90.
20 Two member of the Thirty: see the list which begins B, above. Three further members appear later in the story: Melobios and Mnesitheides, and the defendant himself, Eratosthenes.
21 The family workshop (*ergastērion*) made shields; see further below.

22 Many of these will have been workers in the shield-workshop (n.20) – but not all.
23 See **142** with n.8.
24 See **312**.

245. Democracy restored

Our principal sources on the regime of the Thirty (**244**A and B) go on to describe how through the agency of the Spartan king Pausanias the warring factions in Attika were reconciled and, ultimately, democracy was restored. Here is the account from the Aristotelian *Ath. Pol.* Compare with it Xen. *Hell.* II.4.24–43, and see further Hignett, *Constitution*, 293–8.

It was the Spartan king Pausanias, together with the ten mediators who later came from Sparta at his request, who brought about the peace and the reconciliation. Rhinon and his associates[1] were commended for their goodwill towards the *dēmos*, and although they had been entrusted with their duties under an oligarchy they submitted their *euthynai*[2] under a democracy. And nobody, either of those who had remained in the *astu* or those who had returned from Peiraieus, brought any complaint against them; on the contrary it was on the strength of what he had done that Rhinon was immediately elected *stratēgos*.

(39) The reconciliation took place, in the year of the *archōn* Eukleides (403/2), on the following terms:

(i)[3] Those Athenians who had remained in the *astu* but now wished to leave should have Eleusis to live in, retaining full (Athenian citizen-) rights and the income from their properties (elsewhere in Attika), but with complete self-government of their own.

(ii) The temple (of Demeter and Persephone at Eleusis) should be common to both parties, and administered in the traditional manner by the Kerykes and the Eumolpidai.[4]

(iii) The men from Eleusis should not be allowed into the *astu*, and the men from the *astu* should not go to Eleusis – except, in either case, for the Mysteries.

(iv) (The men from Eleusis) should contribute from their revenues to the allied fund, just like the other Athenians.[5]

(v) If any of those leaving (the *astu*) wished to acquire a house in Eleusis they should secure the agreement of the owner (to sell); if mutual agreement could not be reached, each party should choose three assessors and the owner should accept whatever price these men fixed. If, however, the settlers wished to live with Eleusinians of their choice, they should do so.

(vi) Those wishing to emigrate (to Eleusis) should register, in the case of

464

those in Athens, within ten days of the swearing of the oaths of reconciliation, and should leave within twenty; and the same should apply to those abroad, with the period counted from when they returned to Athens.

(vii) No settler in Eleusis should be permitted to hold any office in the *astu* without re-registration as a resident in the *astu*.

(viii) Homicide trials, in cases where someone had killed or wounded a person with his own hands, should be conducted in accordance with traditional practice.

(ix) There should be a complete amnesty as regards past events, excluding (only) the Thirty and the Ten and the Eleven and those who had governed Peiraieus[6] – and not even them, if they were prepared to submit *euthynai*. The men who had governed Peiraieus should submit *euthynai* to the people of Peiraieus, and those who had held office in the *astu* to those with taxable property there, after which those who wished to do so might leave.

(x) Each party should make its own repayment of the money which it had borrowed for the war.[7]

(40) When the reconciliation had been effected on these lines, however, those who had fought the war together with the Thirty were afraid: many of them had a mind to emigrate (to Eleusis) but they postponed their registration, as one always tends to do, until the last moment. And when Archinos saw how many were involved he wished to hold them back, and did so by cancelling the days remaining for registration; this had the result of compelling large numbers of them to remain, against their will, until they had recovered their confidence. This was clearly a fine and statesmanlike act by Archinos; and so too was his subsequent prosecution, with a *graphe paranomōn*,[8] of Thrasyboulos, for his *psēphisma* proposing to give citizenship to all who had taken part in the return from Peiraieus, some of whom were obviously slaves. And the same goes for a third occasion, too, when one of those who had returned sought to contravene the amnesty: Archinos hauled him before the *boulē* and persuaded it to have him executed without trial; his argument was that now was the time when they would show whether or not they wanted to preserve the democracy and abide by their oaths, for letting the man go would encourage others (to do the same) whereas executing him would serve as an example to all. And this is precisely what happened: after this man's death nobody ever again violated the amnesty.[9] Instead it is clear that the Athenians' attitude, both private and public, to the misfortunes which had taken place was the most fine and most statesmanlike imaginable: not only did they disregard all charges relating to previous events but they even made public repayment of the money which the Thirty had received from the Spartans for the war[10] – this despite the

465

clause in the agreement stipulating that both parties, those from the *astu* and those from Peiraieus, should make their own separate repayments; they felt that this should be the first step towards concord (*homonoia*).[11] In other *poleis*, those who have established democratic rule do not even think of making such contributions out of their own pockets; their concern is to redistribute the *chōra*!

They also brought about a reconciliation with the settlers in Eleusis, two years after they had gone to live there; this was during the year of the *archōn* Xenainetos (401/0).

?Aristotle, *Athenaion Politeia* 38.4–40.

1 I.e. the second board of Ten (see **244**A, end, with n.6, below). Rhinon has already been mentioned with approval in 38.3.
2 See **52** with n.6.
3 We number these clauses purely for convenience.
4 See **227** with n.18.
5 This 'allied fund' is somewhat mysterious, but we take it to be money required by the Spartans from their allies; these now of course included the Athenians (see **240**, end). Compare Lys. XXX.22.
6 The author's *two* boards of Ten (see **244**A) are not otherwise attested, so possibly the text is faulty here and should read '. . . the Thirty, the Ten who governed Peiraieus, and the Eleven'; see Moore, *Aristotle*, 270–1.
7 But see below.
8 See **310**.
9 Compare Isoc. XVIII, esp.2–4 and 23–24. Less charity is implied in (e.g.) Lys. XXVI.
10 See Xen. *Hell*. II.4.28, Lys. xii.59.
11 See **243**.

246. The proposal of Phormisios

The year of the amnesty (**245**), 403/2, was a year of fresh starts of many kinds in Athens: for example the Ionic Greek alphabet, having been preferred to the native Attic (with fewer letters) by some individual masons throughout the Peloponnesian War period, was at last formally adopted for official use; and more substantively, between 403 and 401 a revision and codification of the *nomoi*, first begun after the democratic restoration of 410, was systematically carried through to form the basis of Athenian law in the fourth century (see **307**). In the strictly political sphere, however, novelty was clearly the last thing that most Athenians wanted. On the contrary they had tired of extremism, of whatever kind, and were content to be led by Archinos and others along a moderate middle course: thus the citizenship decree of Thrasyboulos (see **245**) was abandoned, or at any rate temporarily shelved (see Tod no.100; Whitehead, *Ideology*, 156–8), while at the other end of the political spectrum a proposal to limit the citizen-body to landowners also found no favour. See further: Hignett, *Constitution*, 296–7.

(A) The *dēmos* had returned from Peiraieus and had voted for reconciliation with the men in the *astu* and for an amnesty with regard to what had happened; but there was a fear that the masses, now re-established in their old powers, might turn again to outraging the rich. Many speeches were devoted to this subject, and Phormisios – one of those who had returned with the *dēmos* – brought in a resolution to the effect that as well as the return of those in exile the citizenship should be given not to everybody but (only) to those who had land. The Spartans also wanted to see this happen. If this *psēphisma* had been passed it would have meant the exclusion from the community of about 5,000 Athenians; so, to prevent this, Lysias wrote the following speech for one of the prominent politicians. Whether it was actually delivered on this occasion is uncertain, but its composition is at any rate suitable for a real debate.

Dionysius of Halikarnassos, *Lysias* 32 (Introduction to Lysias XXXIV, *Against the subversion of the ancestral politeia in Athens*)

(B) 'Just when we were beginning to think, Athenians, that the disasters which have befallen the *polis* have made such an impression on the memory that not even our descendants would seek a different *politeia*, these men pick this very time to try to deceive us – after all the evils we have suffered as we tried both political systems – with the very same *psēphismata* with which they tried twice before! (2) Yet it is not they who astonish me but you who give them a hearing: I have never known men with worse memories than you, or else readier to be evilly treated by such people as these, who shared in what happened at Peiraieus quite by accident, while really holding the same views as the men of the *astu*. What, may I ask, was the point of returning from exile if you are now to vote yourselves into slavery? (3) Personally, Athenians, whether the criterion (for citizenship) is property or birth, I myself am not disqualified – indeed on both counts I am better qualified than my opponents – but my opinion is that the only way that the *polis* can survive is for all Athenians to share in the *politeia*. For when we still had our walls and our ships and money and allies there was no thought of excluding any Athenian; on the contrary we allowed the Euboians the right of inter-marriage with us;[1] so are we now to drive away the existing *politai*? (4) No, if you will listen to me; nor, after (losing) our walls, should we deprive ourselves also of all these hoplites and cavalrymen and archers;[2] rather keep them, and you will be securer in your democracy, better able to overcome your enemies and more useful to your allies. For you are well aware that during the (two) oligarchies which we have experienced it was not the landowners who controlled the *polis*: many of them died and many more were driven from the *polis*; (5) and although the *dēmos* brought these (exiles) back and restored your *polis* to you, they were not so bold as to share in it themselves.³ If you will listen to me, then, you will not deprive your benefactors of their motherland – as far as that were possible for you – nor will you put more faith in words than in deeds and in the future rather than the past, especially if you bear in mind that however much those who fight for oligarchy may profess to be making war on the *dēmos*, their real aim is *your* property; and they will get it, if they can catch you bereft of allies. (6) Their argument is that there is no salvation for the *polis*, given our present circumstances, if we do not do what the Spartans want. But for my part I challenge these men to tell us, if we do what the Spartans require, where the advantage for the masses will be; and if we do not, it will be finer by far to die fighting than to vote ourselves a plain death-sentence.'

Lysias XXXIV 1–6 (*Against the subversion of the ancestral politeia in Athens*)

1 The right of inter-marriage (*epigamia*) was of course normally exercised within a particular citizen-body, but as a definable component of citizenship it might perfectly well be granted by one *polis* to another. The date of this concession to the Euboians is unknown, but perhaps belongs in 411/10.
2 Even if Dionysius' figure of *c.*5,000 (see A) is far too low, it is frankly incredible that Phormisios' proposal was to disfranchise men of the economic level of hoplites, let alone cavalrymen; the speaker is simply trying to influence those upon whom the vote would predominantly depend. See also next note.
3 I.e. in both 411 and 404 the full restoration of democracy was preceded by a phase of 'moderate' (i.e. genuine) oligarchy; see **227, 244**. In fact chs.4–5 of this speech do not seem to envisage the *dēmos* taking part in the decision; but since, as Dionysius noted, we cannot be sure that it was actually delivered, it would be unwise to attempt to draw conclusions about the constitutional context, which is in any case chronologically uncertain.

247. Retrospective idealisation of democracy

After the excesses of the Thirty (**244**) it comes as no great surprise to find signs of an idealising view, in retrospect, of the radical democracy which their rule had temporarily displaced. Here two old men, writing in the 350s, recall the episode which they had lived through in their youth: Isocrates (who also points the other side of the moral, with regard to the régime of 411) and Plato, in his autobiographical *Seventh Letter*. (N.B. Letters purporting to survive from antiquity are very often spurious, and some of the thirteen ascribed to Plato may be so, but VII has a strong claim to authenticity.)

(A) 'Did not the *dēmos* itself, because of the depravity of the demagogues, desire the oligarchy which was established under the Four Hundred?¹

And have not we, all of us, because of the madness of the Thirty, become more democratically minded than the men who occupied Phyle?'

Isocrates VIII (*On the Peace*) 108

(B) 'Once, when I was a boy, I naturally believed, just like everyone else, that as soon as I had become my own master I would immediately embark upon public life in the *polis*; but then certain things occurred in the *polis* which affected me in the following way. What happened was that the *politeia* of that time came in for abuse from many quarters and was changed, with 51 men being established, after the change, as rulers: eleven in the *astu*, ten in Peiraieus – both these groups being concerned with the *agora* and the other things involved in urban administration – and thirty as absolute and overall rulers. Now some of these men happened to be relatives and friends of mine,[2] and of course they immediately urged me to do the natural thing and join them. And it was no wonder that I felt as I did, young as I was: I imagined, you see, that under their administration the *polis* would inevitably be led away from a life of injustice to a just way, so I was extremely interested in what they would do. But then, of course, I observed how short a time it took before these men had made the previous *politeia* seem like a Golden Age – especially in their treatment of my elderly friend Sokrates:[3] I would have no hesitation in calling him the most just man of his time, yet they sent him, with some others, to find one of the *politai* and bring him in by force to be executed; (325) the object of this was, of course, to implicate Sokrates in their doings whether he liked it or not, but he disobeyed them, risking everything rather than be party to their unholy crimes.[4] So naturally, seeing this and all their other monstrous acts, I was horrified and cut myself off from the evils of that time; then, not long afterwards, the régime of the Thirty and their whole *politeia* fell.'

Plato, *Seventh Letter* 324B8–325A7

1 See **227**.
2 Notably Kritias, first cousin of Plato's mother.
3 See **237, 248**.
4 See in full Plato, *Apology* 32C–D.

248. The trial and death of Sokrates

The political upheavals of the last twelve years of the Peloponnesian War had one more victim to claim: in the spring of 399 the Athenians tried, condemned and executed the seventy-year-old philosopher Sokrates (**237, 247B**). Formally the charge brought by Meletos and his fellow plaintiffs (see B, below) was a *graphē asebeias*, a public prosecution for 'impiety', but it is unlikely that such a crime was precisely defined in law (see D. M. MacDowell, *The Law in Classical Athens* (London, 1978), 197–202), and in this instance our various versions of the written indictment (see A) seem to embrace at least two disparate elements. But perhaps it is pointless to look for logic in the Athenians' attitude to this extraordinary man, who had irritated them for so many years with his questions, who had amused them with his quietly unconventional life-style, and who had latterly, and more seriously, become indelibly associated with and (allegedly) influential upon at least two men who could be seen as instrumental, in their different ways, in Athens' ruin – Alkibiades and Kritias. So finally the amusement and irritation turned to something blacker; and in a prosecution for which, like others in Athenian law, there was no fixed penalty, the jury endorsed the plaintiffs' call for Sokrates' execution.

See further: W. K. C. Guthrie, *Socrates* (Cambridge, 1971), esp. 58–65; M. I. Finley, *Aspects of Antiquity* (Harmondsworth, 1972), ch. 5.

(A) I have often wondered what the arguments were by which the men who drew up the *graphē* against Sokrates persuaded the Athenians that he deserved to die at the hands of the *polis*. For the *graphē* against him went something like this: 'Sokrates is guilty of not recognising the gods whom the *polis* recognises and of bringing in other, novel deities instead; he is also guilty of corrupting the young'.[1]

Xenophon, Memorabilia I.I.I

(B) 'There are many reasons, Athenians, for me not to be aggrieved by what has happened – the fact, that is, that you have voted to condemn me – and the main one is that what has happened is what I expected would happen.[2] Much more surprising to me than that is the number of votes cast on each side: I never thought, personally, that it would be such a close thing, yet it now appears that if a mere thirty votes had gone the other way I would have been acquitted.[3] And even as it is, it seems to me that I *have* indeed been acquitted as far as the prosecution by Meletos is concerned; and not only that, it is perfectly clear that if Anytos and Lykon had not (also) come forward to accuse me, Meletos would have forfeited his 1,000 drachmas for not having obtained one-fifth of the votes.[4]

The fact is, though, that he is demanding the death-penalty. Very well. But what on earth am *I* to propose to you, Athenians, as the alternative penalty? Obviously it must be a suitable one – but what? What do I deserve to suffer or pay?

My life has not been a quiet one, despite my disregard for the things that most men care about: making money, running a household, holding high military or domestic posts, and all the other things – offices, clubs, intrigues – that go on in our *polis*; I thought that I was really too upright to survive if I went in for all that. So instead of embarking on a course which would have benefited neither you nor myself, I set myself instead the task of benefiting each one of you, privately and individually, in the very best way that I know how: I tried to persuade each one of you not to put personal advantage before personal well-being – that is, becoming as good and as wise a man as possible – and not to put advantage before well-being in the case of the *polis* either, or in anything else. What then do I deserve to suffer for behaving in this way? If I must be truthful about my deserts, Athenians, I would have to claim some reward – and a suitable one at that. So what *is* 'suitable' for a poor man who is your benefactor and who needs leisure for giving you instruction and encouragement? Well, Athenians, nothing could be more suitable for such a man than (free) maintenance at public expense; at any rate he deserves it more than your Olympic victors do, whether they have won with one horse or two or four![5] Such men give you the appearance of good fortune, I the reality; and I need the support, not they. So if I am obliged to propose a penalty which is both appropriate and just, this is it – (free) maintenance at public expense.[6]

Perhaps I seem in this, just as when I was talking about pitiful entreaties,[7] to be deliberately perverse; but that is not so, Athenians. The fact of the matter is that I am myself convinced that I never willingly wrong any man; it is you that I cannot persuade of this, because we have had such a short time to discuss it together. It seems to me that if it was your custom, as it is in other societies, to devote not one single day but many to the hearing of capital trials, I would have convinced you, but as it is, to dispose of grave allegations in so little time is no easy task. Of course, convinced as I am that I do not wrong anyone, I can hardly be expected to wrong *myself* by asserting that I deserve something bad and by proposing some penalty accordingly. Why should I? For fear of suffering the penalty that Meletos proposes for me, when, as I said, I do not know whether it is a good thing or a bad?[8] Am I supposed to suggest instead something which I know very well to be bad? Prison, perhaps? But why should I spend my life in prison, a slave to successive boards of Eleven?[9] A fine, then, with imprisonment until I have paid it? That would be just the same in my case, as I have been trying my best to explain: I could not pay it, because I have no money! I could always suggest exile, of course, and you might very well agree to that. But what a coward I should be, hanging desperately on to life, if I were so stupid as to be unable to see that you, my fellow-*politai*, have run out of patience with my discourses and speeches; you have found them too irksome and irritating, so now you are seeking to be rid of them. Will others find them easy to bear, then? Far from it, Athenians. So a fine life I should have if I left Athens at my age and spent the rest of my days trying one *polis* after another and being thrown out every time! I know perfectly well, you see, that wherever I go the young men will listen to my conversation, just as they have done here: if I send them away they will have me driven out by their elders, and if I do not, their fathers and (other) relatives would do it for their sake.'

Plato, *Apology* 35E–37E

(c) 'Since you executed Sokrates the sophist,[10] Athenians, because it was clear that he had been the teacher of Kritias, one of the Thirty who put down the *dēmos*, is Demosthenes to succeed in snatching his friends from your hands?'

Aeschines 1 (*Against Timarchos*) 173

1 On the wording of the indictment compare the fuller, more formal version of Favorinus *apud* Diog. Laert. II.40; and in general Plato, *Seventh Letter* 325A–C.
2 This is an extract from Plato's *Apology*, a work cast in the form of Sokrates' defence-speeches at his trial. It is twice stated in it that Plato (then aged 28) attended the trial, and we have no good reason to doubt this; nonetheless the *Apology* reads like a work of art rather than of reporting.
3 The jury was one of 500 (or to be exact 501), so it is fair enough to claim that a 280/220 split was a close vote.
4 This was one of the procedural rules for a *graphē* prosecution.
5 Free maintenance (*sitēsis*) in the *prytaneion*: see **73** Intro.
6 With the help of friends, Sokrates later (38B) proposes a fine of 30 minas, and it is this which in the second vote the jury weighs against the death-penalty – choosing the latter by an increased majority.
7 See 34B–35D.
8 See 28B–29B.
9 See **67** with n.5.
10 Sokrates was *not* a sophist; to pick one determinant out of many, he did not give formal teaching for a fee (see W. K. C. Guthrie, *The Sophists* (Cambridge, 1971), 27–54); but the failure of most Athenians to draw, or care about, the distinction dates from at least as early as 423, when Aristophanes made Sokrates his sophist-paradigm in *Clouds* (see **156**).

Part IV

The Fourth Century

26 Spartan imperialism

With the end of the Peloponnesian War and the consequent dissolution of the Athenian empire, the Spartans had a second chance, 75 years after 479, of an unchallenged Aegean *hēgemonia*. Its implementation, however, and above all that 'freedom for the Greeks' which Sparta had claimed to be going to war to restore (Thuc. 1.139.3), lay at first chiefly in the hands of Lysandros, around whom some of the trappings of a personality cult had by now arisen (see **249**) – though there were others in the Spartan leadership, notably king Pausanias, who found themselves at odds with him in the style and substance of policy-making (see Xen. *Hell.* II.4.29). At all events, although the 390s saw an intensification of those internal problems – political, social and (in Greek eyes) moral – which while always endemic in Sparta were now to lead directly to her catastrophic defeat at Leuktra (see Ch.28), the period between 401 and 395 found Spartan aims and preoccupations at their most outward-looking for eighty years. Ultimately, though, the desultory Asian campaigning, even in the hands of the strong new king Agesilaos, brought few concrete results – except for the outbreak of the Corinthian War (**254**).

For a modern study of the period 405 to 386 see C. D. Hamilton, *Sparta's Bitter Victories: politics and diplomacy in the Corinthian War* (Ithaca, N.Y., 1979); his model of Spartan political life is, however, too schematic.

249. The cult of Lysandros

Between 408 and 404 Lysandros turned himself into the single most influential individual not only in Sparta but in the Greek world as a whole, for the simple reason that the immediate future of so much of that world, with Athenian defeat imminent, lay effectively in his hands (see **250**). And to say that in these years he became a cult figure is no loose modern metaphor, for Plutarch here testifies to this in literal fact. Admittedly the only source mentioned is Duris of Samos (*c*.340–*c*.260), a writer who often put sensationalism before veracity; in this instance, however, one of his assertions has been archaeologically confirmed (the festival known as the Lysandreia (see below): an early fourth-century statue-base of a four times winner at it), so, as Davies notes (*Democracy*, 182), Duris may thus also be right in his claim that Lysandros was the very first *living* Greek to be so honoured – a century before such things became at all usual.

Out of the spoils of victory Lysandros set up at Delphi bronze statues of himself and of each of his admirals, as well as golden stars of the Dioskouroi[1] – which disappeared before the events at Leuktra.[2] Also, in the treasury of Brasidas and the Akanthians[3] there was deposited a trireme made of gold and ivory, two cubits long, which Kyros sent to Lysandros to mark his victory; and Anaxandrides the Delphian writes that money of Lysandros' was also deposited there, a silver talent and 52 minas, with 11 staters in addition – a statement which is at odds with the accepted view of Lysandros as a poor man. At any rate Lysandros at this time had acquired more power than any Greek ever before him and was believed to be subject to a self-important pride greater even than his power. After all, as Duris writes, he was the first of the Greeks to whom the *poleis* erected altars and made sacrifices as if to a god, and the first also to whom songs of triumph (paeans) were sung. The beginning of one of them which has been preserved is as follows: 'The *stratēgos* of noble Greece, from wide-spaced Sparta, we shall hymn, crying "O Paian!"' Also, the Samians voted that their festival of Hera be called the Lysandreia.[4]

The poets played their part also: Lysandros kept Choirilos[5] constantly with him, to celebrate his achievements in verse; and when Antilochos composed some verses in his honour Lysandros was so pleased that he filled his cap with silver and gave it to him. And when Antimachos of Kolophon and a certain Nikeratos of Herakleia competed with each other at the Lysandreia with poems about him, he awarded the crown to Nikeratos; Antimachos was angry and suppressed his own poem, but Plato, then a young man and an admirer of Antimachos and his poetry, attempted to cheer and console him in his distress at this defeat, telling him that it is the ignorant who suffer from their ignorance just as the blind from their blindness. However, when Aristonoüs the harpist, a victor six times at the Pythian Games, informed Lysandros disdainfully that if he were to win yet again he would have the victory announced under Lysandros' name, Lysandros replied, 'As my slave, I take it?'

Plutarch, *Lysandros* 18

1 The Dioskouroi: **75** with n.12.
2 The catastrophic Spartan defeat in Boiotia in 371 (see **273**); the disappearance of these offerings was evidently construed as prefiguring it.
3 Brasidas had persuaded Akanthos out of the Athenian alliance in 424 (Thuc. IV.84–88; see in general **192**). On cult for Brasidas as a hero – i.e. *after* his death – in Chalkidike see Thuc. V.11.1.

4 In 405 Samian loyalty *to Athens* had been rewarded by a grant of Athenian citizenship to the whole community (Meiggs and Lewis no.94); by now, though, a Lysandrian dekarchy (see **250**) was in power there (Xen. *Hell.* II.3.6–7).

5 Choirilos of Samos, epic poet.

250. Modes of control in the Spartan empire

Whatever restoration of liberties the Greeks may fondly have expected with Athens' defeat, the actual result was that the Athenian empire became the Spartan empire – thanks principally, it is clear, to Lysandros, who even before 404 (see Plut. *Lys.* 5.3–4) had been fostering the personnel and mechanisms of oppression: chiefly a conjunction of garrison-commander (*harmostēs*) and ruling junta of ten (dekarchy). (For the 'Thirty Tyrants' of Athens in this context see **244**) The whole nexus was crucial, and activated by cash: as Davies puts it (*Democracy*, 155), 'Sparta was being offered an overseas empire, wherein the Aegean states contributed the money which financed the ships which protected the garrisons which guaranteed the regimes which ran the states.' The case of Athens shows us, as it showed Lysandros' opponents, the sort of problems to which such a policy gave rise, and it was not kept up for long (see **253**); for the time being, though, its dividends were too tempting to refuse, and Lysandros stood supreme as its architect and guarantor.

See further: H. W. Parke, 'The development of the second Spartan Empire', *JHS* 50 (1930), 37–79.

(A) In Greece the Spartans, having now brought the Peloponnesian War to an end, had the acknowledged *hēgemonia* both on land and at sea. Lysandros was their appointed admiral, and they gave him the task of visiting each of the *poleis* where he had set up the men whom the Spartans call harmosts; for they disliked democracies and wished the *poleis* to have oligarchic governments. They also levied tribute from the people whom they had conquered in the war, and although before this time they had not used coined money[1] they now collected from the tribute more than 1,000 talents a year.[2]

Diodorus XIV.10.1–2

(B) Lysandros also suppressed the democracies and the other *politeiai*, leaving in each *polis* a Spartan harmost together with ten rulers chosen from the clubs which he had organised throughout the *poleis*. This he did indiscriminately, in hostile *poleis* and also in those which had become his allies; and he sailed along in a leisurely manner, establishing for himself thus the *hēgemonia* of Greece. He did not, you see, appoint these rulers on the basis of birth or wealth: it was to gratify these foreign supporters and friends that he allotted control of affairs, giving them sovereign charge of

477

rewards and punishments. He also took part personally in many massacres, helping to drive out his friends' enemies. It was thus an intolerable example of Spartan rule that he gave the Greeks: the comic poet Theopompus likened the Spartans to barmaids, in that they allowed the Greeks a sip of sweetest freedom and then poured in the vinegar, but he was thought a fool for saying so; for from the very start the taste was bitter and harsh, because Lysandros not only denied the common people control of affairs but put the *poleis* in the hands of the most bold and contentious of the oligarchs.[3]

Plutarch, *Lysandros* 13.3–5

1 See **53, 265**.
2 No doubt the figure has been rounded up, but it may not be ridiculously high; compare Davies, *Democracy*, 155.
3 Compare also 19.1–4, and *Lykourgos* 30.4–5.

251. Sparta disciplines Elis

The Spartans' peace with Athens in 404 – just as in 421 – had been concluded with little or no reference to the wishes and interests of their allies in the Peloponnesian League; and, just as in 421, their allies were aggrieved. The Spartans must have recalled what the grievances of 421 had led to (**202**), and decided to assert their authority before there could be any repetition; and Xenophon here describes how Elis was singled out for chastisement. He dates this episode, which filled two campaigning years, 'at the same time as the campaigns of Derkylidas in Asia' (see **252**), but this does not necessarily imply complete overlap (which would mean 399–397), and 400–399 is the soundest dating.

At the same time as the campaigns of Derkylidas in Asia the Spartans were taking action against Elis. For a long time they had been angry with the men of Elis, who had first made an alliance with the Athenians and Argives and Mantineians[1] and had then prohibited the Spartans from competing in either the horse races or the athletics contests[2] – the pretext being that a judgment had been given against them; and not content with that, when Lichas[3] had made over his chariot to the Thebans and the Thebans had been announced as victors, the Eleians had beaten him, old man though he was, when he had come forward to crown the charioteer, and had driven him out. (22) And later, when (king) Agis, in accordance with an oracle, had been sent to sacrifice to (Olympian) Zeus, the Eleians had refused to allow him to pray for victory in war, saying that it was a principle going back to earliest times that Greeks should not consult the oracle in connection with a war against other Greeks; so Agis had left without making his sacrifice.

478

(23) With all these grounds for anger, then, the *ephoroi* and the assembly resolved to make the men of Elis see sense: they therefore sent envoys to Elis to say that in the view of the Spartan authorities the Eleians ought, in all justice, to grant independence to their outlying (perioikic) *poleis*.[4] The Eleians replied that they would not do so, as the *poleis* were theirs by right of conquest; so the *ephoroi* ordered the troops to be mobilised, and Agis, at the head of the army, advanced into Eleian territory by way of Achaia, along the (river) Larisos. (24) However, shortly after the army had arrived in the enemy *chōra* and had begun to ravage it, there was an earthquake, which Agis regarded as a sign from the gods, and so marched out of the *chōra* again and disbanded the army The result of this was that the Eleians grew much bolder than before and began to send envoys round all the *poleis* which they knew to be disenchanted with the Spartans. (25) However, later in the year the *ephoroi* again ordered the levying of troops for an invasion of Elis, and, with the exception of the Boiotians and the Corinthians, all Sparta's allies – including the Athenians – joined Agis on the campaign. As soon as Agis had arrived in Eleian territory, by way of Aulon, the men of Lepreon revolted from the Eleians and came over to him; and they were followed in quick succession by the men of Makistos and Epitalion. Then, as he was crossing the river (Alpheios) he was joined by the Letrinians, the Amphidolians and the Marganians as well. (26) This induced him to go on to Olympia and offer sacrifice to Olympian Zeus – and this time nobody made an attempt to stop him! After the sacrifice he marched on the *astu* (of Elis), cutting down trees and firing crops as he passed through the *chōra* and also capturing huge numbers of sheep, cattle and slaves, which had the result, once it became known, of attracting many more of the Arkadians and Achaians as volunteers to join the army and get a share of the plunder; indeed this expedition became a sort of re-provisioning operation for the entire Peloponnesos. (27) When he reached Elis, Agis began to do damage to the suburbs and the fine gymnasia; the *polis* itself was unfortified, and it is thought that Agis was unwilling rather than unable to capture it. But in any case there was a group led by Xenias – the man of whom it was said that he measured out in sackloads the money he got from his father – which was eager to gain the credit for bringing the place over to the Spartans; so, while the *chōra* was being ravaged and Agis' army was in the neighbourhood of Kyllene, these men, with swords in their hands, rushed out of a house and began a massacre. Amongst those they killed was a man who looked like Thrasydaios, the champion of the *dēmos*, which led them to believe that it was indeed Thrasydaios whom they had killed; and the result of this was that, while the *dēmos* completely lost heart and did nothing, (28) the murderers supposed that their task was completed, and

those who sympathised with them came out and assembled under arms in the *agora*. In fact, however, Thrasydaios had got drunk and was still lying on the spot asleep; and when the *dēmos* realised that he was not dead they crowded round his house on all sides like a swarm of bees round its leader. (29) Thrasydaios put himself at their head, and in the ensuing battle the *dēmos* was victorious, with the men who had attempted the violent coup fleeing to the Spartans. Agis then crossed the Alpheios again and withdrew, but he left behind a garrison at Epitalion, near the Alpheios, with Lysippos as harmost and the Eleian exiles; he then disbanded the army and went back home.

(30) For the rest of that summer and the following winter Lysippos and his men ravaged and plundered the *chōra* of the Eleians; and during the next summer Thrasydaios sent to Sparta and offered to pull down the walls of Phea and Kyllene and to relinquish control of the Triphylian *poleis* of Phrixa and Epitalion, as well as of the Letrinians and Amphidolians and Marganians, and of Akroreia and Lasion, to which the Arkadians were laying claim. Epeion, however, the *polis* between Heraia and Makistos, the Eleians felt that they had a right to keep: this was because, as they maintained, they had bought the whole *chōra* from the people who possessed the *polis* at the time; the price had been 30 talents, and they had paid it. (31) But the Spartans decided that there was no more justice in taking property from the weaker party by forced sale than by forced seizure, so they compelled the Eleians to give up Epeion too. They did not, however, strip the Eleians of their guardianship of the temple of Olympian Zeus, even though there was nothing ancient about it: their reasoning was that the rival claimants were peasants and not qualified to hold the position.[5] These terms were agreed, and a peace and alliance concluded between the Eleians and the Lakedaimonians, which of course thus brought the war between them to an end.

Xenophon, *Hellenika* III.2.21–31

1 See **204–205**.
2 At the Olympic Games, which the Eleians managed: see **11**.
3 See the introduction to Ch.28.
4 See below.
5 See **11** (and Xen. *Hell.* VII.4.28).

252. Beginning of Spartan campaigning in Asia Minor

Persian financial backing between 412 and 404 had been decisive in Sparta's victory in the Peloponnesian War, and the Spartans had evidently been ready to forget their role as liberators when agreeing to the King's price – Persian control, once more, of the Greek *poleis* of Asia Minor (**231**). However, after its shaky start in the hands of the satraps Tissaphernes and Pharnabazos, the link between Sparta and Persia had come to depend upon the personal relationship between Lysandros and Kyros (**233**), the younger son of the Great King himself, and Kyros was a man whose ambitions outstripped his prospects. When his elder brother, on their father Dareios' death in 405, succeeded to the throne (as Artaxerxes II), Kyros began to canvass support for a rebellion; and, as we see here, chief amongst those whose blessing was sought – and given – were the Spartans. Forrest (*Sparta*, 123) expresses surprise at this, but needlessly: Lysandros will surely have advocated it, and even his opponents will have realised how much Sparta stood to gain from the possible defeat of the legitimate Persian régime and in consequence the implicit repudiation of the treaties of 412. (We are not sure whether to accept the 407 'Treaty of Boiotios' proposed by Lewis, *Sparta and Persia*, 123ff.; a purely informal understanding between Lysandros and Kyros remains a possibility.)

After the *stasis* in Athens had ended, as described,[1] Kyros sent messengers to Sparta to appeal to the Spartans to do the same for him as he had done for them in their war against the Athenians. The *ephoroi* considered this a just request, and sent orders to Samios, their admiral at that time, to assist Kyros in any way required. And for his own part Samios was ready and willing to do what Kyros asked: he took his own fleet and sailed with Kyros' fleet round the coast to Kilikia, where he prevented the governor of Kilikia, Syennesis, from opposing Kyros on land while he was marching against the King. (2) The story of that campaign – of how Kyros collected together an army and led it up-country against his brother, of how the battle took place in which he was killed, and of how afterwards the Greeks made their way safely back to the sea – has been recorded by Themistogenes the Syracusan.[2]

(3) At all events, Tissaphernes was considered to have been extremely valuable to the King in the war against his brother, and he was sent down to the coast as satrap not only of the areas which he himself had formerly governed but also of those which had been under Kyros; and no sooner had he arrived than he demanded that all the (Greek) *poleis* of Ionia be his subjects. Now these *poleis* not only wanted to be free but at the same time were afraid of Tissaphernes, because instead of following him they had chosen to support Kyros, while he was alive; they therefore refused to admit him and instead sent envoys to Sparta to appeal to the Spartans, as the champions of all Greece, to take them also, the Greeks of Asia, under their protection, and so prevent the devastation of their territory and the loss of their liberty. (4) Accordingly the Spartans sent Thibron to be their harmost, with an army of 1,000 emancipated helots (*neodamōdeis*) and 4,000 men from the rest of the Peloponnesos. Thibron also requested 300 cavalrymen from the Athenians, offering to pay their wages himself, and the Athenians sent him some of those who had served in the cavalry

under the Thirty (Tyrants), with the idea that for them to go abroad and die there would be to the advantage of the *dēmos*. (5) When they had arrived in Asia Thibron also raised some troops from the Greek *poleis* on the mainland – for at that time all the *poleis* would obey any order given them by a Spartan. Realising how strong the Persians were in cavalry Thibron did not venture down into the plains with this army but was content to prevent them from ravaging whatever part of the country he happened to be in. (6) However, once he had been joined by the troops who had made their escape after marching up-country with Kyros, he did then face Tissaphernes in pitched battles on level ground. He also gained possession of several *poleis*: Pergamon came over to him voluntarily, and so did Teuthrania and Halisarna, which were ruled by Eurysthenes and Prokles, descendants of Damaratos the Spartan (king) – who had been presented with the territory as a royal gift, for taking part in the invasion of Greece;³ and Thibron was also joined by the brothers Gorgion, ruler of Gambrion and Palaigambrion, and Gongylos, ruler of Myrina and Gryneion – these *poleis* too having been gifts from a Persian King, to that Gongylos who, alone of all the Eretrians, had supported the Persian cause and been exiled for it.⁴ (7) There were also some weak *poleis* which Thibron took by storm. The place known as 'Egyptian' Larisa, however, would not yield to him, so he surrounded it with his army and laid siege to it: he tried, unsuccessfully, all sorts of ways of capturing it, including sinking a well and digging a conduit from it, to channel off their water-supply, but the enemy kept dashing out from behind their walls to throw wood and stones into the shaft, and when Thibron then built a wooden shed to cover and protect the well, the Larisaians countered even this, by rushing out at night and setting fire to it; so to all appearances he was achieving nothing at all, and the *ephoroi* sent him orders to leave Larisa and march on to attack Karia.⁵ (8) However, when he was already in Ephesos and about to start the march on Karia, Derkylidas arrived to take command of the army. Derkylidas was a man with the reputation of being a great schemer, and was indeed nicknamed Sisyphos.⁶ Thibron therefore went back home – where the allies accused him of allowing his army to plunder their friends; and he was condemned and exiled.

Xenophon, Hellenika III. I. 1–8

1 See **245**.
2 This is almost certainly a coy pseudonym for Xenophon himself, whose *Anabasis* covers precisely this subject-matter. For Kyros' campaign and its aftermath, therefore, see that eye-witness account.
3 See **55**.
4 For these Greek dynasts under Persian patronage see in brief de Ste Croix, *Origins*, 38–9.

5 Note this: the strategy was being directed at long distance, by the *ephoroi*.

6 Sisyphos, 'most crafty of men' (Homer, *Iliad* VI.153), and proverbial on that account.

253. Agesilaos takes command in Asia

Xenophon narrates the campaigns of Derkylidas, somewhat anecdotally, directly following those of Thibron (*Hell.* III.1.9–2.20), and contrives to make it clear that even with more time at his disposal (399–397) the 'great schemer' achieved little more than his predecessor. The Spartans were simply not taking the Asian war seriously enough. But in the winter of 397/6 they began to. By now there was a new Eurypontid king in Sparta – Agesilaos, half-brother of Agis, and preferred to Agis' son on the basis of rumours of adultery involving Alkibiades (Xen. *Hell.* III 3 1–4; Plut. *Lys.* 22 and *Ages.* 3); Lysandros had seen to this, hoping to recover his own influence thereby; and in the spring of 396 the two of them set out to put the war in Asia to rights.

It was after this[1] that news arrived in Sparta from a Syracusan named Herodas. While in Phoinikia with a *nauklēros* he had seen Phoinikian triremes, some of them sailing in from other places, others there already with a full complement of men, and others still being made ready; and upon hearing that there were to be 300 of them in all, he had sailed on the first boat leaving for Greece and reported to the Spartans that the King and Tissaphernes were preparing this fleet – though he did not know, he said, where they planned to use it. (2) This news put the Spartans on their mettle and they began to summon contingents from their allies and discuss what ought to be done. Lysandros felt that the Greeks' fleet would give them clear superiority at sea, and he also took into account the fact that the land force which had gone up-country with Kyros had come to no harm, so he persuaded Agesilaos to undertake an expedition into Asia, provided he were given 30 Spartiates, 2,000 emancipated helots (*neodamōdeis*) and total allied levies of 6,000. And Lysandros was also making calculations of another kind: he was eager himself to accompany Agesilaos on the expedition because the dekarchies which he had established in the *poleis* had been thrown out by order of the *ephoroi*, who had proclaimed (a return to) the 'ancestral *politeia*',[2] and he wanted Agesilaos to help him set them up again. (3) Agesilaos declared that he was willing to undertake the campaign, and the Spartans gave him all the forces he had asked for, with provisions for six months; and then after making all the proper sacrifices, including the ones necessary when crossing the (Lakonian) border,[3] he set out. Messengers were sent round the *poleis* with orders as to the number of men required from each place and where[4] they were to report. Agesilaos himself, however, had made up his mind to go and offer sacrifice at Aulis, at the very spot where Agamemnon had sacrificed when he sailed to Troy.5 (4) However, when he arrived there the *boiōtarchoi*6 got to hear of his plan to offer sacrifice and sent out some cavalry to order him to stop; they also took the victims which had already been offered and threw them down from the altar. Infuriated, Agesilaos called upon the gods to witness what had happened, and then boarded his trireme and sailed away. At Gerastos7 he collected together as much of his army as he could and made his way with his forces to Ephesos.

Xenophon, Hellenika III.4.1–4

1 The conspiracy of Kinadon (**264**).
2 See **250**. In this context 'ancestral *politeiai*' mostly meant genuine oligarchies, as opposed to the collective tyranny of the dekarchies. Note also that when this happened is a matter of dispute: R. E. Smith, 'Lysander and the Spartan Empire', *CPh* 43 (1948), 145–56, argued that the Lysandrian arrangements survived until 397, but it is more likely that they had been repudiated as early as 403/2 (H. W. Parke, *JHS* 50 (1930), 53–4; A. Andrewes, *Phoenix* 25 (1971), 206–16; de Ste Croix, *Origins*, 157). If true, this means that the former members of the Athenian empire recovered some measure of their freedom at more or less the same time as did Athens herself (**245**), and also that Lysandros' opponents had scored an early success against the war-victor; but he was far from finished yet (see **266**).
3 See **50B**.
4 Or possibly 'when' (as elsewhere in Xenophon, e.g. *Hell.* III.3.6).
5 On the Boiotian coast, opposite Euboia. For Agamemnon there see above all Euripides, *Iphigeneia in Aulis*.
6 The chief officials of the Boiotian League.
7 The south-eastern tip of Euboia; more commonly Geraistos.

254. Preliminaries to the Corinthian War

While the Spartans were busy with the war in Asia, their allies, old (Thebans, Corinthians) and new (Athenians), had been busy preparing to stab them in the back at home. None of these three had provided any troops for Agesilaos to take to Asia; and all three were now prominent – to the delight of the Persians – in bringing about the so-called Corinthian War (395–387). See S. Perlman, 'The causes and the outbreak of the Corinthian War', *CQ* n.s.14 (1964), 64–81; A. Andrewes, 'Two notes on Lysander', *Phoenix* 25 (1971), 217–26. We are fortunate enough to have *two* contemporary witnesses of these events, Xenophon (A) and the 'Hellenica Oxyrhyncia' (B), on which see p.13; also I. A. F. Bruce, *An Historical Commentary on the 'Hellenica Oxyrhyncia'* (Cambridge, 1967), 1–27 and 50–61.

(A) Tithraustes[1] now appeared to believe that Agesilaos was contemptuous of the King and his doings, and, so far from leaving Asia, had every hope of taking on the King and capturing him; and he had no idea what to do about this. He therefore sent Timokrates the Rhodian to Greece, with gold to the value of 50 silver talents and orders to give it to the leading men in the *poleis*, in return, if possible, for firm guarantees that they would start a war with the Spartans. Timokrates arrived in Greece and handed over the gold to Androkleidas, Ismenias and Galaxidoros in Thebes, to Timolaos and Polyanthes in Corinth, and to Kylon and his supporters in Argos. (2) The Athenians did not take their share of it,[2] but they were eager for the war nonetheless, in the belief that they would recover their empire. And those who had received the money naturally began now to create ill-feeling against the Spartans in their own *poleis*; and once they had established this anti-Spartan hatred they brought the most important *poleis* into coalition with each other.

Xenophon, Hellenika III.5.1–2

(B) At about the same time,[3] a trireme sailed out from Athens – without the knowledge of the *dēmos*: Demainetos, its [master?], had, it is said, secretly shared his plan with the *boulē*, and once some of the (other) *politai* had joined in with him he went down with them to Peiraieus, launched a ship from the dockyards and set sail to join Konon.[4] (2) This led to an uproar in which those Athenians with reputation and judgment were indignant, declaring that to begin a war against the Spartans would give the *polis* a bad name. As for the *bouleutai*, they were alarmed at the uproar, and called the *dēmos* together and pretended to have had no part in the episode; and once the masses had come together, those of the Athenians who supported Thrasyboulos and Aisimos and Anytos[5] got up and pointed out that the Athenians were putting themselves at great risk unless they absolved the *polis* from responsibility. (3) The moderate, property-owning Athenians[6] were content with the situation as it stood;[7] and on this occasion the masses and democrats were frightened enough to listen to their advisers and send word to Milon, the (Spartan) harmost of Aigina, telling him that he could punish Demainetos for having acted without the consent of the *polis*. Before this, however, their attitude had been aggressive and anti-Spartan virtually all the time.[8] (II.2) This opposition was being whipped up by Epikrates and Kephalos and their supporters, for it was they who were most eager to involve the *polis* in a war – and this had been their aim not merely after they had had dealings with Timokrates and had taken his gold, but long before that. It is nonetheless stated, by some, that Timokrates' money was responsible for the creation of this faction, as well as of the similar ones in Boiotia and the other *poleis* mentioned, but this is simply ignorance of the fact

485

that they had all begun to hate the Spartans long before this and had been on the lookout for a chance to involve the *poleis* in a war; for the plain fact was that the Spartans were detested – by the Argive and Boiotian factions, for favouring their political opponents, and by the group in Athens, because it wanted to rob the Athenians of their peace and quiet and lead them on to war and meddlesome interference,[9] thus giving *them* the opportunity to make money out of public funds.

'Hellenica Oxyrhyncia' I.1–3 and II.2

1 Tissaphernes' successor (see Xen. *Hell.* III.4.25–26).
2 But see B, below; and compare **327** with n.4.
3 Spring 396.
4 The Athenian *stratēgos* of 407–405, now in command of the *Persian* fleet: see Ch.27.
5 I.e. what we might term the moderate democrats, less extreme than Epikrates and Kephalos (below). On this and the other groups involved see I. A. F. Bruce, 'Athenian foreign policy in 396–395 B.C.', *Classical Journal* 58 (1963), 289–95.
6 Probably the same as 'those Athenians of reputation and judgment' (above).
7 I.e. peaceful relations with Sparta.
8 For the short section omitted here (II.1) see **258**.
9 I.e. *polypragmosynē* (**175**).

255. Abandonment of the war in Asia

In 396 and 395 Agesilaos achieved more in the war in Asia than either of his predecessors (see Xen. *Hell.* III.4.5–29, IV.1.1–40), and more was planned for 394 (IV.1.41). Before it could be accomplished, however, events back in Greece had supervened: the opening campaign of the Corinthian War (summer 395) was a multiple disaster for the Spartans, with a defeat in Boiotia, the death of Lysandros there, and the disgrace and exile of king Pausanias shortly afterwards (III.5.3–25); so it was only to be expected that the other king, Agesilaos, was sent instructions to hurry home.

Once the Spartans knew for certain that Timokrates' money had come into Greece and that the most important *poleis* had formed a war coalition against them, they realised that their own *polis* was in danger and considered it essential to mobilise their army; (2) they therefore made preparations to do this, as well as immediately despatching Epikydidas to recall Agesilaos. When Epikydidas arrived in Asia he explained the whole state of affairs to Agesilaos and made it clear that Sparta was asking him to come as quickly as possible to the aid of his country. (3) Agesilaos was dismayed to hear this, and to reflect upon the honours and the hopes of which he would thus be robbed; nevertheless he called together the allies, told them what the orders from the *polis* were, and declared that it was essential to go to the aid of his country. 'But if things go well over there', he added, 'you allies may be sure that I shall not forget you, but shall come back again to do whatever you ask of me.' (4) Many wept to hear this, yet they all voted to go with Agesilaos to help Sparta, and then, if things went well there, to take him back with them again to Asia.

(5) So the troops made ready to follow him; and Agesilaos left Euxenos as harmost in Asia, together with a garrison of at least 4,000 men to enable him to protect the *poleis*. Agesilaos could see for himself that most of the soldiers preferred to stay in Asia rather than go on a campaign against (other) Greeks, yet at the same time he wanted to take with him the best troops available and as many of them as possible; so what he did was to offer prizes for whichever of the *poleis* furnished the best contingent, and whichever mercenary commander joined him with the best-equipped company of hoplites, of archers, and of peltasts.[1] He also told the cavalry commanders that he would also present a prize of victory to whichever one of them, too, produced the best-mounted and best-equipped squadron; (6) and he declared that he would award all these prizes at the Chersonesos, once they had crossed from Asia into Europe – the object of this being to make it clear to them that they needed to keep their contingents in good order. (7) Most of the prizes turned out to be finely-wrought arms and armour, for hoplites and cavalry alike; there were also golden crowns, and all in all the prizes cost at least four talents; however, the result of this great outlay of money was that the army was equipped with expensive arms and armour. (8) After the crossing of the Hellespontos, Menaskos, Herippidas and Orsippos were appointed as the Spartans' judges, together with one judge from each of the allied *poleis*; and when they had reached their decisions Agesilaos marched on with his army – following exactly the same route as Xerxes had taken in his invasion of Greece.[2]

Xenophon, Hellenika IV.2.1–8

---

1 On peltasts (infantry more lightly armed than hoplites) see **257**.
2 No doubt there were solid practical reasons for this; nonetheless Agesilaos clearly enjoyed following grandiose precedents (as in the initial sacrifice at Aulis: **253**), and the whole episode described in this passage reverberates with them (e.g. Xerxes' review in Hdt. VII).

27 The resurgence of Athens

The early years of the fourth century saw a quite remarkable revival of Athenian fortunes. The revival was to a certain extent artificial, occurring with the help of Persian money, and it apparently came to nothing; for despite the fact that from 395 Sparta faced the hostility of Persia and of much of Greece, in 387/6 Sparta became once more, with Persian backing, the *hēgemōn* of Greece. But Persian money not only, following the provocation of the outbreak of the Corinthian War (see **254**), helped the revival of Athens, it made possible the use in Greece of mercenaries on a greater scale than ever before (see Ch.32 Intro. for the link between Persian money and the use of mercenaries in the 360s); it was a group of these mercenaries which first dented the legend of Spartan invincibility (**257**), a legend finally shattered at Leuktra in 371 (see **273**).

256. The intervention of Persia in Greece

By early 393, the initial impetus of the war against Sparta had died away and Persian support for the war-effort was vital. Fresh from the naval victory at Knidos, Pharnabazos and the Athenian Konon, serving with Persia, arrived just in time.

And when those who held the *polis* of the Kytherians,[1] in fear lest they be captured by assault, abandoned the walls, (Pharnabazos) let them depart for Lakedaimon under truce and himself repaired the wall of the Kytherians and left a garrison and Nikophemos as harmost[2] on Kythera. Having done this and sailed to the isthmus of Corinth, and exhorted the allies to fight with a will and show themselves faithful men in the cause of the King, he left them the money he had and sailed off home. (9) But Konon said that if he let him have the fleet he would provide its keep from the islanders and would sail to his own country and use it to rebuild the Long Walls and the wall round Peiraieus for the Athenians; he said that he knew that nothing would be a more serious blow to the Lakedaimonians and 'So,' he said, 'you will gratify the Athenians in this way and punish the Lakedaimonians; for you will undo for them the

488

achievement for which they laboured most.' And when Pharnabazos heard this he gladly sent him to Athens and in addition gave him money for the work of fortification.

Xenophon, *Hellenika* IV.8.8–9

1 The island of Kythera, off the coast of Lakonia.
2 See **250**.

257. Mercenary tactics

Light-armed troops and cavalry had of course long been used as adjuncts to the heavily-armed infantry formation characteristic of Greek warfare, the hoplite phalanx; light-armed troops in particular had often been foreign mercenaries, notably the peltasts who were so important to the success of Brasidas at Amphipolis (see **192**). But the most spectacular achievement of light-armed troops occurred under the command of the Athenian Iphikrates in 390, in the course of the Corinthian War, following earlier small-scale successes (Xen. *Hell.* IV.4.14–17); the achievement was due in no small part to Iphikrates' solution of the problem of how to discipline mercenaries.

Thereafter mercenaries, barbarian as well as Greek, and their commanders are central features of Greek warfare. The reasons are various, not just the fact that Thrakians were already skilled at the sort of fighting which was needed against hoplites, but also the fact that it was not possible to take a hoplite and make him a different kind of soldier (the Theban reaction was to reinforce the essential nature of the hoplite, see **271**). Once the demand arose and the monetary resources needed became available, usually from Persia, there was a ready supply of mercenaries from the poorer areas of the Greek world, already used to piracy (see **82**); and the evident success of the mercenary in warfare led to the recruitment of hoplite mercenaries by Persia and by Persian satraps, whether acting for the King or in revolt. A romantic halo came to surround their chiefs, perhaps in part because they represented centres of power which rivalled that of the *polis* (the Athenian Chabrias actually had to be recalled by Athens from fighting Athens' ally Persia, Diod. XV.29.3). See in general H. W. Parke, *Greek Mercenary Soldiers* (Oxford, 1933), chs.4–14; Davies, *Democracy*, 198–201.

But those in the *astu* of the Corinthians, namely Kallias the son of Hipponikos, the *stratēgos* of the Athenian hoplites, and Iphikrates, commanding the peltasts, seeing that the Spartans were few in number and not accompanied by peltasts or cavalry, thought that it was safe to attack them with the peltast force. For if they proceeded on the road,[1] they would be fired at on their unprotected side and destroyed; but if they tried to attack, they themselves would easily escape the hoplites with their very lightly-armed peltasts. With this decision they led their troops out. (14) And Kallias drew up his hoplites not far from the *polis*, while Iphikrates took the peltasts and attacked the unit. And when the

Lakedaimonians had been fired at and some wounded and some killed, they ordered the shield-bearers to pick them up and convey them to Lechaion. And in truth these were the only men in the unit who were saved. The *polemarchos* then ordered the men of the first ten years from maturity to attack the peltasts. (15) But when they attacked they caught no one, since they were hoplites at a javelin's throw from peltasts. For Iphikrates had ordered these to retreat, before the hoplites came up with them; and when the Spartans retreated in a scatter since they had attacked as fast as each man was able, the men with Iphikrates turned round, and some of them again fired straight at them and others fired, by running along on the side, at their unprotected flank. And at once in the first attack they shot down nine or ten of them. And when this happened they now pressed home their attack much more boldly. (16) And since the Spartans were having a bad time, the *polemarchos* again ordered an attack, by the men of the first fifteen years from maturity. And as they retreated, even more of them fell than the first time. The best men were already dead when the (Spartan) cavalry came up to them, and they mounted another attack together. But when the peltasts retreated, at this point the cavalry made a mistake in their attack; for they did not press home their attack on the peltasts until they killed some of them, but attacked and retreated along with the (hoplite) sallies. And by attacking and being killed off in the same way again, the Spartans became ever fewer and more demoralised, while their enemies became bolder and their attackers ever more numerous. (A few eventually escaped, but about 250 were killed.)

Xenophon, *Hellenika* iv.5.13–16

1 The Spartan hoplites were returning to their base at Lechaion, after going part of the way towards Sikyon, along with the cavalry (who continued for a while) and the men they were both escorting.

258. Athenian ambitions

The disastrous defeat of Athens in the Peloponnesian War did not lead to despair and the acceptance of subordination; long before there was any hope of concerted opposition to Sparta in Greece, the Athenians were active, as this passage shows; they also made pre-emptive alliances with Boiotia, Lokris and Eretria in 395–394 (Tod nos. 101–3) and they had begun to rebuild their walls even before the battle of Knidos in 394 (see **259**), a battle which ended Spartan naval supremacy and therefore the threat to Athenian food supplies in the event of Athenian misbehaviour in the eyes of Sparta. See R. Seager, 'Thrasybulus, Conon and Athenian imperialism', *JHS* 87 (1967), 95–115.

For (already in 397) they sent equipment and men to the ships with

Konon, and ambassadors were sent [again] to the King of Persia, under
the leadership of [?] krates and Hagnias and Telesegoros; all of these were
arrested by Pharax, who was the Spartan naval commander at the time,
and sent back to Sparta, where they were executed.

'Hellenica Oxyrhyncia' II. 1

259. The walls of Athens

Without her walls, pulled down at the end of the Peloponnesian War (see 240),
Athens was defenceless; and the shift at Athens to an aggressive stance made their
rebuilding imperative.

(A) In the month of Skirophorion in the archonship of Diophantos (the
last month of 395/4) the following sums were disbursed for the work day
by day – for the teams bringing the blocks, 160 drachmas, for iron tools,
53 drachmas. In the archonship of Euboulides (394/3), for the section
beginning from the *sēmeion*[1] as far as the pillar between the gates by the
shrine of Aphrodite on the right as one goes out, 790 drachmas;
contractor, Demosthenes the Boiotian, including the transport of the
blocks.

Tod no. 107

(B) And when he arrived, (Konon) built much of the wall, providing his
crews for the purpose and giving money for carpenters and masons and
spending whatever else was necessary. There were, however, parts of the
wall which the Athenians fortified along with the Boiotians and other
poleis which volunteered.

Xenophon, *Hellenika* IV.8.10

1 Perhaps milestone.

260. The Athenian version

The Athenian belief that they would recover their empire may seem odd to
modern eyes; but the capacity for self-delusion of at least one Athenian at the
time emerges well from Isocrates' account of Konon as a general – in fact in the
service of Persia.

But who does not know of Konon, who was first among the Greeks
because of his numerous virtues, how when he fell on hard times[1] he
chose to go to Euagoras[2] rather than anyone else, thinking that refuge
with him was the safest for his own person and that he himself would the

491

soonest be able to come to the help of his *polis*. And despite having many earlier successes he was regarded as having made in this case the best decision he ever made . . . (54) For when the two of them saw that Athens was subject to the Spartans and had suffered a terrible reverse, they were grieved and angered; for one of them was a native Athenian, the other had been made a *politēs* by law because of his many great services.³ And as they were considering how they might relieve Athens of its sufferings, the Spartans soon provided an opportunity. For, ruling the Greeks both by land and by sea, they became so arrogant that they even tried to ravage Asia.⁴ (55) So Konon and Euagoras seized this opportunity and, since the generals of the King did not know how to manage affairs, they pointed out to them that they must not make war against the Spartans by land, but by sea, considering that if they put together an army by land and won with it only affairs in Asia would benefit, but that if they won by sea the whole of Greece would share in the victory. (56) Which is what occurred; for the generals were persuaded to act in this way and a fleet was collected; the Spartans were defeated at sea⁵ and deprived of their empire, the Greeks were freed and our *polis* recovered some of its old glory and became *hēgemōn* of the allies.

Isocrates IX (*Euagoras*) 52–56*

1 After the battle of Aigospotamoi, see **239**.
2 See **239** and Ch.32 Intro.
3 In fact *after* the battle of Knidos.
4 Ceded to Persia in 412, see **252**.
5 At the battle of Knidos, see **256**.

261. The financial recovery of Athens

During the last years of the Peloponnesian War, financial stringency had forced Athens to create a token coinage in bronze instead of silver. The supersession of this coinage apparently falls, not surprisingly, just after Persian money began to arrive (see **254**); the subject was clearly topical when the *Ekklesiazousai* was performed in 392.

Bystander: Don't you remember when we voted for those coppers?
Chremes: That was an issue which turned out badly for me! For after selling some grapes I went away with my mouth full of coppers, and then went to the *agora* to buy some barley. Then just as I was holding out my bag, the herald shouted, 'No one is to use copper at all in the future; for we're using silver.'

Aristophanes, *Ekklesiazousai* 815–822

262. The thirst for empire

Despite an attempted rapprochement between Sparta and Persia in 392, in neither of whose interests it was to see Athens recover, Athenian enterprise recovered a substantial amount of the ground lost in 404. Apart from the narrative of Xenophon, an inscription of 387 (Tod no.114, just before the peace of Antalkidas, see **263**) shows Athens *de facto* in control of Klazomenai and imposing the *eikostē*, or 5 per cent harbour tax, which had been briefly tried as an alternative to the tribute towards the end of the Peloponnesian War. Another inscription (B, below), for all the evidence it provides of Athenian *polypragmosynē*, also shows the very real role of defender of the Greek *poleis* of Asia against Persia that Athens had come to play.

(A) But the Athenians, thinking that the Spartans were again preparing a naval force, sent out Thrasyboulos of (the deme) Steiria against them with 40 ships. When he had sailed he did not mount an expedition to Rhodes, thinking that he would not easily be able to defeat the friends of the Spartans, since they held a fort and Teleutias was there with a fleet to help them; also that those on his side would not fall under the control of the enemy since they held the *poleis*, were much more numerous and had won one battle. (26) So he sailed to the Hellespontos and, since no one was there to oppose him, he thought that he would be able to achieve something for the *polis*. And so first, learning that Amedokos the king of the Odrysai and Seuthes the king by the sea were at war, he reconciled them to each other and made them friends and allies of the Athenians, thinking that if they were friends the Greek *poleis* situated in Thrake would be more likely to pay attention to the Athenians. (27) These *poleis* and, because the King was a friend of the Athenians, the *poleis* in Asia being well disposed, he sailed to Byzantion and farmed out the tithes on the ships sailing out of the Black Sea.[1] And he converted Byzantion from an oligarchy to a democracy, so that the *dēmos* of the Byzantians was not distressed at seeing as many Athenians as possible present in the *polis*. (28) Having achieved this, he also made friends of the Kalchedonians and sailed away out of the Hellespontos. And finding on Lesbos that all the *poleis* except Mytilene were on the side of the Spartans, he attacked none of them before he had assembled in Mytilene the 400 hoplites from his own ships and those exiles from the *poleis* who had fled to Mytilene, and recruited in addition the strongest of the Mytilenians; he then instilled hope in the Mytilenians that if they captured the *poleis* they would be rulers of all Lesbos, in the exiles that if they stood together and went against one *polis* at a time they would all succeed in being restored to their countries, in his troops that if they won Lesbos over to the *polis* they would have achieved an abundant supply of money. After offering these encouragements he gathered the men together and led them against

493

Methymna. (29) But Therimachos, who happened to be the Spartan harmost, when he heard that Thrasyboulos was approaching, took the troops from his own ships and the Methymnians themselves and any Mytilenian exiles who happened to be there and went to meet him on the boundaries. A battle followed and Therimachos was killed there, many of the others were killed as they fled. (30) Thereupon Thrasyboulos brought over some of the *poleis* and plundered money for his soldiers from those which did not come over.

Xenophon, *Hellenika* IV.8.25–30

(B) . . .] in Erythrai; (it was to be reported that) it had been agreed by the *dēmos*: that none of the *stratēgoi* could come to terms with those in the (*akro*)*polis* without the permission of the *dēmos* of the Athenians; that none of them could restore to Erythrai any of the exiles whom the Erythraians might expel without the permission of the *dēmos* of the Erythraians;[2] and as for saving the Erythraians from the *barbaroi*, reply was to be made to the Erythraians that the *dēmos* of the Athenians had agreed [. . .

SEG XXVI.1282

1 Thereby usurping the position of Byzantion.
2 Presumably when the (*akro*)*polis* had been captured.

263. 'Koinē eirēnē'

The Athenians finally went too far, allying with the rebel Akoris in Egypt and helping Euagoras on Cyprus, now in open rebellion from Persia. The Persian reaction was to back Sparta in her desire to control Greece in order to achieve her own objectives in the east. The response to a general war was a common peace, *koinē eirēnē*, and it is interesting that this was actually advocated by Andocides III (*On the peace*) 17, in 392/1, on the occasion of the earlier move by Sparta to seek a rapprochement with Persia. But despite its fair-sounding title the common peace of early 386, like its successors, was not peace by agreement; it was peace at the behest of Persia and underwrote the hegemony of Sparta. See G. L. Cawkwell, 'The King's Peace', *CQ* n.s. 31 (1981), 69–83.

And now Antalkidas returned with Tiribazos, having arranged that the King should be an ally (of the Spartans) if the Athenians and their allies were unwilling to accept the peace terms which he had laid down. (Antalkidas now gained control of the Hellespontos.) (28) So he prevented the ships from the Black Sea from sailing to Athens, and brought them in to the harbours of his allies. (29) So the Athenians, seeing that the enemy fleet was large and fearing lest they be subdued as they had been before, now that the King was an ally of the Spartans, and being exposed to the pirates on Aigina, were as a result very anxious to accept the peace terms. The Spartans for their part, with one unit as a garrison at Lechaion and another at Orchomenos, and needing to guard the *poleis*, lest those which they trusted were captured and those which they distrusted rebelled, and being involved in fighting at Corinth, were resentful of the war. And the Argives, knowing that an expedition had been mounted against them and realising that the subterfuge of claiming immunity because of a sacred period would no longer avail them, were themselves also anxious to make peace. (30) So when Tiribazos commanded those willing to attend to the peace terms which the King sent down to assemble, they all came at once. And when they were assembled, Tiribazos showed the royal seals and read out the terms. They were as follows. (31) 'King Artaxerxes thinks it right for the *poleis* in Asia to be his and of the islands Klazomenai[1] and Cyprus, but for the other Greek *poleis* small and large to be autonomous, except for Lemnos and Imbros and Skyros, these to belong to the Athenians as of old. Whoever does not accept these peace terms, I will make war on him by land and sea, providing ships and money, alongside whoever *is* willing to accept them.'[2]

(32) After hearing these terms, the ambassadors of the *poleis* took the news back home. And everyone else swore to observe these terms, but the Thebans claimed to swear on behalf of all the Boiotians. But Agesilaos said that he would not accept the oath, unless they swore that any *polis* whether small or large should be autonomous, as the terms of the King laid down. But the Theban ambassadors said that these were not their instructions. 'Go then and ask', Agesilaos said, 'and tell the Thebans that if they do not swear as they should, they will be excluded from the peace.' So the ambassadors went. (33) But Agesilaos refused to wait, because of his hatred for the Thebans, and after persuading the *ephoroi* he performed the sacrifice for the start of a campaign. And when he had performed the sacrifice for crossing the (Lakonian) border[3] and had reached Tegea, he sent some of the cavalry around the *perioikoi* to rouse them and sent the commanders of the allied contingents round the *poleis*. But before he set off from Tegea, the Thebans arrived saying that they were letting the *poleis* (in Boiotia) be autonomous. And so the Lakedaimonians went off home and the Thebans were forced to accept the peace terms, letting the *poleis* of Boiotia be autonomous. (34) But the Corinthians for their part did not dismiss the Argive garrison. So Agesilaos told these two that he would make war on them, on the first if they did not dismiss the Argives, on the second if they did not leave Corinth. So they both took fright and the Argives left and the *polis* of the Corinthians became independent;[4] and the murderers and those who

shared the responsibility of their own accord left Corinth; and the other *politai* gladly accepted back the earlier exiles.

Xenophon, *Hellenika* v.1.25–34*

1 Klazomenai was hardly an island, see Map 1.
2 This means in practice Sparta.
3 See **50B**.
4 Corinth and Argos had in 392 united into a single (democratic) *polis*, see G. T. Griffith, 'The union of Corinth and Argos', *Historia* 1 (1950), 236–56; this process had involved the murder or exile of opponents of the scheme in Corinth.

28 Sparta, Athens and Thebes

As agents for the enforcement of the King's Peace (263), Agesilaos and the Spartans dominated the 380s; and Xenophon describes (Hell. V.2–3) how eagerly they grasped this opportunity for action against Mantineia (see 295), Phleious (291), Olynthos and Thebes (see 268 Intro.), as well as issuing threats against Corinth, Argos and others. Yet already there were signs that the Spartans were as likely to fall victim to their own weaknesses as to anyone else's strengths, with revolution and conspiracy in the 390s (264, 266), and with unprecedented opportunities for wealth and power undermining the chaste austerity of the 'Lykourgan' ethos (265). More fundamental still was (267) Spartan *oliganthrōpia*, literally 'fewness of men', an increasingly acute crisis in the always precarious Lakonian-Messenian demographic structure which to some Greek observers had clear moral roots and which was certainly now to have clear military consequences. The 370s saw the rise of two formidable rivals to Sparta in the pursuit of *hēgemonia*: Athens, with a new (anti-Spartan) Aegean *hēgemonia* (269), and Thebes, at the centre of a reconstituted Boiotian League (270–272); and for the Spartans and their admirers two centuries of invincibility, in fable and reality, came to an abrupt and shattering end on the battlefield at Leuktra (273–274).

See further: R. J. Seager, 'The King's Peace and the balance of power in Greece, 386–362 B.C.', *Athenaeum* 52 (1974), 36–63.

264. The conspiracy of Kinadon

The Spartans lived in constant fear of a helot revolt, a repetition of the 460s (169), but it was not only the helots whom they had to watch: in their elaborately hierarchical socio-political system there were others inferior to and resentful of the full Spartiate 'Equals', and with a better chance than the helots of doing something about it; and Xenophon tells of an unsuccessful attempt, in the first year of the reign of Agesilaos (399 or 398), to mobilise them in revolution.

See further: Forrest, *Sparta*, 124–5; de Ste Croix, *Origins*, 93; Cartledge, *Sparta*, 273–5 and 312–14; E. David, 'The conspiracy of Kinadon', *Athenaeum* 57 (1979), 239–59.

Before the first year of the reign of Agesilaos had elapsed, and as he was making one of the prescribed sacrifices on behalf of the *polis*, the prophet declared that the gods were revealing a conspiracy of the most terrible kind. Agesilaos sacrificed again, but the prophet said that the signs were worse still; and after the sacrifice had been offered for a third time, the prophet declared, 'Agesilaos, I see signs here just as if we were in the midst of our enemies.' This led them to offer sacrifices to the powers that turn evil aside and keep men from harm, but it took a lot of time and trouble before finally they obtained good omens and could stop. And within five days of this sacrifice someone informed the *ephoroi* of a conspiracy and named its ringleader as Kinadon. (5) This Kinadon was a robust and courageous young man – but not one of the Equals. The *ephoroi* asked how the plan was to be executed, and the informer told them that Kinadon had taken him to the edge of the *agora* and told him to count how many Spartiates were present. 'So,' said the man, 'I counted king, *ephoroi*, *gerontes* and about forty others, after which I asked Kinadon why on earth he had had me count them; and his reply was that I should consider these men my enemies and all the others in the *agora*, more than 4,000 of them, as my allies. He also commented on the people that we met here and there in the streets, pointing out "enemies" in their ones and twos and calling everyone else "allies"; and in the countryside, of course, any Spartiate that we came across was an "enemy", being the owner of the estate, but in each case there were plenty of "allies" too.' (6) The *ephoroi* then asked how many men, according to Kinadon, were party to the plan, and the informer told them that on that point Kinadon had said that the actual conspirators, with himself and the other leaders, were only a few, albeit a trusty few; but the leaders preferred to say that it was they who were conspiring with everyone else – helots, emancipated helots (*neodamōdeis*), the Inferiors[1] and the *perioikoi*[2] – for all these groups made no secret of the fact, whenever mention was made of the Spartiates, that they would gladly eat them raw. (7) The *ephoroi* then continued their questioning by asking how the revolutionaries planned to get their hands on arms and armour, and the informer replied that Kinadon had said: 'Obviously those of us who are in the army have arms and armour of our own. As to the mob' – and he had then led the man into the ironmonger's and shown him all the knives, all the swords, all the skewers, all the axes and hatchets and all the sickles – 'all tools which men use for work on the land or in wood and stone are also weapons, and most of the other crafts too use implements which make perfectly good weapons, especially against men who have no weapons at all.' Finally the man said that he had asked Kinadon when all this was to happen, and that Kinadon's answer had been that his orders were to stay in town.

(8) After hearing all this the *ephoroi* realised what a well-planned plot the man had described, and they were most alarmed: they did not even convene the so-called small assembly³ but simply called together and consulted one or two individual members of the *gerousia*. The plan they devised was to send Kinadon and some other young men to Aulon,⁴ with orders to bring back from there some of the Aulonites and helots whose names had been written on his *skytalē*;⁵ and they also instructed him to bring back the woman, said to be the most beautiful in Aulon, who was believed to be corrupting all the Lakedaimonians, young and old alike, who went there. (9) Kinadon had undertaken work of this kind for the *ephoroi* before,⁶ so of course on this occasion they simply handed him the *skytalē* which named those who were to be arrested; and when he asked which of the (other) youths he should take with him, he was told to go to the senior of the (three) guard-commanders⁷ and ask for six or seven of the men he happened to have available. In fact, though, the *ephoroi* had seen to it that the guard-commander knew whom to send, and that the men to be sent knew that it was Kinadon whom they were to arrest. They also told Kinadon that they would be sending three waggons with him, so that he would not have to bring the prisoners back on foot; this concealed as best they could the fact that there was going to be only *one* prisoner – Kinadon himself. (10) Why they did not have him arrested inside the *polis* was partly because they were ignorant of how large the conspiracy was, and partly because they wanted to hear from Kinadon the names of his fellow-activists before they could learn that they had been betrayed and make their escape. So their intention was that Kinadon should be arrested and detained, and when he had told his captors the names of the other conspirators they were to write them down and send them back to the *ephoroi* without delay. So gravely indeed did the *ephoroi* view the whole affair that they sent out a squadron of cavalry with the men going to Aulon. (11) And once Kinadon was in custody, a cavalryman rode back to Sparta with the list of names that he had given them; and the prophet Tisamenos and the other principal ringleaders were immediately arrested. Kinadon was then brought back and interrogated; he admitted everything and (again) named his accomplices. Finally he was asked what his aim had been in acting as he did, and he replied: 'To be second to none in Lakedaimon.' For this he was instantly bound in a collar, hands and neck, and dragged through the *polis* with his companions, lashed and goaded as he went. So much then for these men and their punishment.⁸

Xenophon, *Hellenika* III.3.4–11

1 Possibly men who had failed to keep up their contributions to the messes (**54**) – but this is the only occurrence of the term, and it remains obscure; see most

recently Cartledge, *Sparta*, 313–15. Kinadon himself was evidently one of them.

2 See **44** n.4.

3 We have no idea what this body was; see de Ste Croix, *Origins*, 347.

4 A town in Messenia.

5 A staff or baton used (exclusively in Sparta, it would appear) as a cypher for dispatches, which were written lengthwise on a strip of papyrus wound round it and therefore decipherable only by an official with another *skytalē* of the same size (Plut. *Lys.* 19.5–7; see also Thuc. 1.131.1).

6 Probably, as Jones suggests (*Sparta*, 99), as a member of the *krypteia*, or Secret (Youth) Police (see Plut. *Lyk.* 28).

7 *Hippagretai*; see Xen. *Lak. Pol.* IV.3–4.

8 It culminated, we may be sure, in their execution.

265. The root of all evil

Already in the fifth century the cherished ethos of 'Lykourgan' Sparta (Ch. 5), chaste and – within its own special terms – egalitarian, had been diverging ever further from the facts of life; in a group of Equals there should not, for example, have been individuals wealthy enough to enter four-horse chariots at the great Games (e.g. Lichas (**251**, and Thuc. v.50.4); see in general Isoc. VI.55 and esp. Paus. VI.2.1–3, with de Ste Croix, *Origins*, 354–5); but the ethos was now, in the fourth century and at the height of its idealisation by conservative philosophers, to come under stress as never before and ultimately to be weakened beyond hope of repair. (Within this period, at any rate; for Sparta's second revolution, in the second half of the third century, see Forrest, *Sparta*, 143–50.) Amongst other contentious matters (**267**), the sources have a lot to say about wealth and corruption, and this may not altogether miss the mark: we may naturally be sceptical of the moralist Plutarch (A, below) and his insistence that these problems arose out of nowhere in the reign of Agis (427–399), but it is a plain fact that from 412 and particularly 404 onwards the Spartans were exposed to them, collectively and individually, as never before; and equally plain is the disappointment of Xenophon (B), a lifelong admirer of things Spartan (*philolakōn*), when fourth-century Sparta failed to live up to the old ideals.

(A) And the calculations of Lykourgos did not prove false, so long did his *polis* stand first in Greece for good government (*eunomia*)[1] and reputation: for a period of 500 years it used the *nomoi* of Lykourgos, and none of the fourteen kings after him, down to Agis son of Archidamos, made any change in them. For the institution of the *ephoroi* was not a slackening but a tightening of the *politeia*, and although it was thought to have been done in the interests of the *dēmos* it actually consolidated the position of the aristocracy.[2] (30) However, during the reign of Agis coined money flowed into Sparta for the first time, and with the coinage came greed and a desire for wealth. Lysandros was responsible for this: he was

himself impervious to corruption by money but he filled his country
with the love of riches and with luxury, by bringing home gold and
silver from the war and thus subverting the *nomoi* of Lykourgos.³

Plutarch, *Lykourgos* 29.6–30.1

(B) If I were to be asked whether I think that the *nomoi* of Lykourgos still
remain unchanged to this day, I certainly would not be rash enough to
say so. I know, you see, that in former times the Lakedaimonians
preferred to live together at home with modest possessions rather than be
harmosts in the *poleis* and become corrupted there by flattery.⁴ I know,
too, that there was once a time when they were afraid to be found in
possession of gold, whereas nowadays there are some who even boast of
what they have acquired. Then again there used once to be expulsions of
aliens (from Sparta)⁵ and a prohibition upon (Spartans) travelling abroad,
and I am aware that the reason for this was to prevent the *politai* from
being filled with lazy self-indulgence through contact with *xenoi*; but I
am also aware, now, that their supposed leaders have made it their
ambition to spend their whole lives as harmosts in foreign parts. There
was a time when they tried to be worthy of leadership, but now they put
far more effort into exercising rule than being worthy of it. In earlier
days the Greeks naturally turned to Sparta and begged her to lead them
against those who were thought to be doing wrong; today, however,
many are calling upon one another to prevent a revival of Spartan rule.⁶
And should we be surprised that these reproaches are levelled against
them? Certainly not: for it is clear that they obey neither god nor the
nomoi of Lykourgos.

Xenophon, *Lakedaimonion Politeia* 14

1 See **45, 47**.
2 See **52**.
3 Compare *Lysandros* 2.4–5 and esp. 16–17.
4 Harmosts: see **250**.
5 *Xenēlasiai*: see **56**.
6 This may well refer to the early stages of the Athenian-inspired alliance of 377
   (see **269**).

266. King Lysandros

Among its other deficiencies (**265**), the 'Lykourgan' ethos had never found a way
to accommodate successful and charismatic individuals, particularly if they came
from outside the two royal houses. Two such men had made major contributions
to Sparta's success in the Peloponnesian War: the first of them, Brasidas, had died
before the jealousies which he had aroused (see **192**, end) became a serious

problem, but Lysandros had ended the war with unprecedented power and prestige (**249–250**), and the fact that he then suffered a serious policy defeat surprisingly soon afterwards (**253**) will only have encouraged him to regain the ascendancy. He sought to do this first as kingmaker and *éminence grise*, but Agesilaos did not care, in the event, to be a puppet (see below). So what then? Plutarch, apparently using Ephorus, tells here of a plot which, if true, reveals that Lysandros had had enough of the pursuit of merely *de facto* supremacy and was now out for it *de iure*. It may of course be too good to be true (so for instance Davies, *Democracy*, 160), but not necessarily; and either way it is significant for what the Spartans were prepared to believe of him.

Agesilaos made no further use of Lysandros in the (Asian) war, and once his term of office had expired Lysandros sailed back to Sparta in dishonour, not only angry with Agesilaos but hating the whole *politeia* even more than before; so he decided to waste no time now in putting into effect the plans for revolutionary change which, so it is thought, he had devised and concocted long before. They were as follows. Of the Herakleidai who had joined forces with the Dorians and returned to the Peloponnesos[1] there was a large and distinguished stock flourishing in Sparta, but not every family belonging to it had a share in the succession to the throne: the kings came from two *oikoi* only, and were called Eurypontidai and Agiadai; the rest had no special privileges in the *politeia* by right of birth, and the honours which recognise individual excellence lay open to anyone with the ability to acquire them. Now Lysandros belonged to one of these (Heraklid but not royal families); and when his achievements had brought him a great reputation, many friends and a position of power, it vexed him to see the *polis* growing through his efforts and yet ruled by kings who were no better born than he was. He therefore made up his mind to put an end to the rule of the two *oikoi* and to restore it to all the Herakleidai in common – or as some maintain, not to the Herakleidai (only) but to (all) the Spartiates[2] – in order that it should be the prerogative not of those *descended from* Herakles but of those who *like* Herakles were picked out on the basis of personal excellence, the criterion which had raised Herakles to divine honours; and his hope was that if the kingship was awarded on such a principle as that, no Spartiate would be chosen in preference to himself. (25) So his first task was to win over his fellow-*politai* by his own efforts, and to that end he memorised a speech written for the purpose by Kleon of Halikarnassos. Next, realising that the novelty and the magnitude of his innovatory scheme called for decidedly audacious support, he brought, so to speak, the machinery of the tragic stage to bear upon the *politai*, by collecting and preparing oracles and oracular responses; this was because he believed that Kleon's clever rhetoric would do him no good unless he brought the *politai* under the influence of his argument by first terrifying and subduing them with some sort of religious fear and superstition. At all events Ephorus says that after unsuccessfully attempting to corrupt the priestess at Delphi and, through Pherekles, to win over the ones at Dodona[3] as well, Lysandros went (to Libya) to the temple of Ammon and talked to the god's interpreters there; however, when he offered them a large sum in gold they were affronted and sent men to Sparta to denounce him; and when he had been acquitted of their charges these Libyans declared, as they left, *'We* shall pass better judgments than yours, Spartiates, when you have come to Libya to live with us' – for it was prophesied in a certain ancient oracle that the Lakedaimonians would settle in Libya.

(Plut. goes on to recount Lysandros' death in battle in Boiotia in 395, chs.27–29; see also Xen. *Hell.* III.5.6–25.) (30.3) Some time later, according to Ephorus, a dispute of some kind arose in Sparta in connection with the allies, and it became necessary to examine Lysandros' private papers; and when Agesilaos went to his house to do this he found there the book containing the speech about the *politeia*, which argued that the kingship ought to be taken away from the Eurypontidai and Agiadai and put up for competitive selection from the best men. Agesilaos was eager to display the speech to the *politai* and show them what sort of a man their fellow-citizen had been, but the chief of the *ephoroi* at that time, Lakratidas, held him back; his view, as a prudent man, was that they should not dig Lysandros up again but bury the speech along with him, as it was a wickedly persuasive piece of work.

Plutarch, Lysandros 24.2–25.3; 30.3–4

1 See **3, 44**.
2 So Plut. himself in *Ages.* 8.3 (and Diod. XIV.13.2).
3 The oracle of Zeus, in Epeiros: see H. W. Parke, *Greek Oracles* (London, 1967), *passim.*

267. Spartan 'oliganthrōpia'

We noted earlier Sparta's extreme reaction to the capture of 120 Spartiatai at Pylos (**190 191**), and although it is impossibly difficult to fix exact figures (for the problems see Forrest, *Sparta*, 131–7; de Ste Croix, *Origins*, 331–2; Cartledge, *Sparta*, 307–18), it seems safe to say that the number of 'Equals' was in chronic, possibly accelerating, decline throughout the classical period: there were 5,000 of them at Plataiai in 479 (Hdt. IX.10.1, etc. – out of *c*.8,000 in all, VII.234.2) but only 700 at Leuktra in 371 (see **273**), 400 of whom were killed there (Xen. *Hell.* VI.4.15). Aristotle, in the passage below, calls this *oliganthrōpia* ('fewness of men'), and attributes Sparta's 'ruin' to it. Why? The reasons that he puts forward (or implies) seem sound and coherent enough: property – especially land – was increasingly unequally distributed, thanks to inheritance laws which produced *nouveaux pauvres* economically disqualified from citizenship (compare *Pol.* (II) 1271 a 26–37, 1272 a 12–16); and meanwhile incentives needed to be offered to attempt to arrest a declining birth-rate, as the 'obvious' solution (that of enfranchising outsiders) was even more unthinkable in Sparta than in other *poleis*. Even before Leuktra, the Spartans had been forced to reject an appeal for help from Polydamas of Pharsalos for lack of manpower; see Xen. *Hell.* VI.I.2–19.

Spartan institutions are also open to criticism as regards inequality of property, for what has come about is that some men own too much and others very little indeed, and this has meant the concentration of the *chōra* in a few hands. And it is the *nomoi* which are partly responsible for the evils of this situation: for (Lykourgos) made it dishonourable, and rightly so, to buy or sell existing estates, yet he did allow freedom to alienate land by gift or bequest – despite the fact that the result is inevitable and identical! Also, nearly two fifths of the entire *chōra* is owned by women, partly because so many women inherit it as heiresses (*epiklēroi*) and partly because of the practice of giving large dowries. It would be better if dowries were prohibited, or else limited to a small or modest size (and also the marriage of heiresses more tightly controlled);[1] but as things stand the guardian of the heiress can give her in marriage to whomever he likes, and in the event of his death before this has been arranged his heir can give her to whomever *he* likes. So here are the very reasons why, in a *chōra* capable of supporting 1,500 cavalrymen and 30,000 hoplites, there are actually fewer than 1,000 in all. And events themselves have shown up the deficiencies in this system of theirs: a single blow was too much for the *polis*,[2] ruined by its *oliganthrōpia*. It is said that under the earlier kings they used to share their citizenship with others, which meant that in those days there was no *oliganthrōpia*, despite the lengthy wars; and once, it is claimed, the Spartiatai numbered as many as 10,000. Nonetheless, whether this is true or not, it is better to keep a *polis* full of men by first equalising the property. Even the *nomos* about parentage stands somewhat in the way of correcting this: the lawgiver, you see, wanted there to be as many Spartiatai as possible and offers inducements to the *politai* to have as many children as possible – hence the *nomos* which exempts the fathers of three sons from military service, and fathers of four from tax; yet it is clear that if many sons are born and the *chōra* correspondingly divided the result will inevitably be many poor men.

Aristotle, *Politics* (II) 1270 a 15–1270 b 6

1 Some such clause as this has clearly dropped out of the text.
2 The defeat at Leuktra (**273**).

268. The Sphodrias affair

We have already seen (263) Agesilaos in 386 indulging his hatred of the Thebans by dissolving the Boiotian League, in the name of the King's Peace. The Athenians worried him less; but in the course of the next eight years he was prepared nonetheless to lend his support, *post eventum*, to opportunist Spartan initiatives against them both. Spartan self-confidence had led to an attempt to check the growing power of Olynthos and the Chalkidian League; and in 382 a Spartan commander, Phoibidas, on his way to Olynthos, accepted an invitation from the pro-Spartan Theban leader Leontiades to occupy the Theban *akropolis*, which led to the withdrawal of *c*.300 of his opponents to Athens and the execution of their leader Ismenias (Xen. *Hell.* v.2.24–36). So there was a Spartan garrison on the citadel, the Kadmeia, until the winter of 379/8, when – with the blessing of the gods, according to the pious Xenophon – the exiles regained control (*Hell.* v.4.1–18); and then occurred the episode described here. Consult also the versions in Diodorus (xv. 29.5–8) and Plutarch (*Ages.* 24.3–26.1, *Pelop.* 14); and on Sphodrias' trial see de Ste Croix, *Origins*, 133–7.

The Thebans, for their part, were also alarmed[1] at the thought of standing entirely alone in a war against the Spartans, so they came up with the following stratagem: by bribery – or so it was suspected – they induced Sphodrias, the (Spartan) harmost at Thespiai,[2] to invade Attika, and so force the Athenians into war against the Spartans. Sphodrias agreed to this, and made out that his intention was to seize Peiraieus, which still had no gates. After giving his soldiers an early dinner he led them out of Thespiai (by night), claiming that they would reach their destination, Peiraieus, before daybreak; (21) however, when the sun rose he was still at Thria,[3] and from then on he made no effort to keep his presence a secret but seized flocks and looted houses before turning back. Meanwhile some of the people whom he had encountered during the night had fled to Athens and told the Athenians that a huge army was coming against them; and of course the Athenians, cavalry and hoplites, had immediately armed themselves and were standing guard over their *polis*. (22) Also, there happened to be some Spartan envoys, Etymokles, Aristolochos and Okyllos, in Athens at the time, staying with their *proxenos* Kallias; and when the Athenians heard the news of what was happening they arrested these men and kept them under guard, on the assumption that they too were part of the plot. They, however, were dumbstruck by the whole affair and protested in their defence that if they had known of the plan to capture Peiraieus they would never have been so stupid as to put themselves in the Athenians' hands in the *astu* – indeed actually to stay with their *proxenos*, where they would be most speedily found. (23) They added that the Athenians too would conclude that even the Spartan *polis* had known nothing of the affair, and they were convinced, they insisted, that it would be found that the Spartan authorities had put Sphodrias to death. The Athenians therefore judged that the envoys were ignorant of the plot and set them free. (24) And in fact the *ephoroi* did recall Sphodrias, to stand trial for his life. He, however, was afraid and disobeyed their summons; yet in spite of his disobedience, when it came to the verdict he was acquitted. To many people this seemed without doubt the most unjust verdict ever known in Sparta. (The reason was the influence of Agesilaos, because of the love-relationship between his son Archidamos and Sphodrias' son Kleonymos.) (34) And now the pro-Boiotian group in Athens pointed out to the *dēmos* that so far from punishing Sphodrias the Spartans had actually praised him for his intrigue against Athens; and as a result the Athenians equipped Peiraieus with gates, began building ships, and threw their whole-hearted support behind the Boiotians.[4]

Xenophon, *Hellenika* v.4.20–24; 34

1 I.e. as well as the Athenians (*Hell.* v.4.19).
2 Sphodrias had been left at Thespiai (a few miles west of Thebes) by the young Spartan king Kleombrotos, once he had realised that the coup in Thebes was a *fait accompli*.
3 In the plain between Athens and Eleusis.
4 Indeed before the spring of 377 they were in alliance with them (see **269**B; Diod. xv.29.7–8).

269. The second Athenian empire

The events of 404 had freed the Greek world from half a century and more of Athenian imperialism – but was Spartan imperialism any better? By 380 one Athenian, at any rate, was prepared to say openly that it was worse (Isoc. IV (*Panegyrikos*) 100–118); more important, even before then some at least of Athens' former allies and subjects had been coming to similar conclusions, notably the Chians, who in summer 384 entered into an alliance with the Athenians 'for all time' (Tod no.118). The Athenians were at pains in the document to stress that the alliance did not infringe the King's Peace (**263**), which was a nice irony, as they well knew that it was precisely the Peace, or rather the Spartans' exploitation of it, which was likely to drive more and more cities to accept Athenian *hēgemonia*. By 378 this had begun to happen, and early in 377 the Athenians were in the happy position of being able to 'advertise' an anti-Spartan alliance open to all-comers.

See further: G. L. Cawkwell, 'The foundation of the second Athenian Confederacy', *CQ* n.s.23 (1973), 47–60. Astonishingly, our main source for this period, Xenophon's *Hellenika*, makes no mention of all this, so our best literary source is Diodorus (A, below); but fortunately we also have the foundation-charter on stone (B), 'the most interesting epigraphical legacy of fourth-century Athens' (Tod).

(A) The Athenians sent out their most distinguished men as envoys to the *poleis* that were subject to the Spartans, urging them to cling on to their common liberty. This was because the Spartans, relying on the great size of the forces at their disposal, were ruling these subjects contemptuously and harshly, and so many of them were beginning to turn to the Athenians. The first people to give way and revolt were the men of Chios and Byzantion, followed by the Rhodians and Mytilenians and some of the other islanders;[1] and with the movement growing ever stronger throughout Greece, many *poleis* attached themselves to the Athenians. The (Athenian) *dēmos*, elated by the goodwill of the *poleis*, established a common synod of all the allies and appointed representatives to it from each *polis*; and it was agreed by common consent that, although the synod should meet in Athens, every *polis* great and small should cast only one vote, on an equal basis. It was also agreed that all *poleis* should be autonomous, under Athenian *hēgemonia*.[2]

The Spartans realised that they were powerless to check the momentum of the *poleis* towards revolt, but they strove eagerly nonetheless for reconciliation with the people they had wronged by promising, through envoys and in friendly statements of their own, to become their benefactors. But they were equally assiduous in their planning and preparations for war, for they expected that the Boiotian war would be a major and time-consuming one for them, with the Thebans in alliance with both the Athenians and the other Greeks who were members of the synod.

Diodorus XV.28.2–5

(B) In the archonship of Nausinikos (378/7); Kallibios son of Kephisophon, of (the deme) Paiania, was secretary; in the seventh prytany,[3] (that of the *phylē*) Hippothontis. It was resolved by the *boulē* and the *dēmos*, with Charinos of (the deme) Athmonon as secretary; Aristoteles proposed:

May fortune favour the Athenians and the allies of the Athenians. In order that the Lakedaimonians shall allow the Greeks to be free and autonomous, living at peace in secure possession of their [entire *chōra*], and in order that [the common peace which was sworn by the Greeks] and the King may be valid and [last for ever],[4] in accordance with the terms agreed, the *demos* shall resolve:

If any of the Greeks or the *barbaroi* who live on [the mainland][5] or the islanders wishes to be an ally of the Athenians and their allies – provided they are not (subjects) of the King – let him be one, free and autonomous, living under whatever *politeia* he chooses, admitting no garrison, submitting to no governor and paying no tribute, (which is to say) on the same terms as the Chians and Thebans and the other allies. For those who do make an alliance with the Athenians and their allies the *dēmos* shall renounce all Athenian possessions, whether private or public, that there may be in the [*chōra*] of those making the alliance, and shall give them a guarantee of this. And if in Athens there should chance to be *stēlai* disadvantageous to any of the *poleis* [making] the alliance with the Athenians, the *boulē* currently in office shall be empowered to destroy them.

From the archonship of Nausinikos it shall not be permissible for any Athenian to acquire either privately or publicly any house or estate in allied territories, whether by purchase or mortgage or any other means whatever.[6] If any (Athenian) does buy or acquire or take out a mortgage on (such property) in any way at all, it shall be open to any of the allies to report him to the synod of the allies, whose members shall sell the property and give half to the denouncer; the other half shall be the common property of the allies.

If anyone should make war upon those who have entered the alliance, whether by land or by sea, the Athenians and their allies shall support them both by land and by sea with all their strength and to the best of their ability.[7]

If anyone, whether official or private citizen, proposes or puts to the vote a proposal which conflicts with this *psēphisma* and seeks to cancel any of the provisions in it, he shall be stripped of his citizen-rights and his property confiscated, with a tithe of one-tenth going to the goddess (Athena); he shall then stand trial before the Athenians and their allies on a charge of destroying the alliance, and (if found guilty!) shall be sentenced either to death or else exile from (the territory) which the Athenians and their allies rule; and if he is condemned to death he shall not be buried in Attic or allied soil.

The secretary of the *boulē* shall inscribe this *psēphisma* on a stone *stēlē* and set it up beside (the statue of) Zeus the Liberator; the money for the inscription of the *stēlē*, 60 drachmas, shall be provided from the Ten Talent Fund[8] by the treasurers of the goddess. On this *stēlē* shall be inscribed the names of those *poleis* both which are in the alliance at present and which may become allies later. And as well as inscribing these matters, let the *dēmos* choose three envoys to go at once to Thebes and persuade the Thebans of whatever advantages they can. The following men were chosen: Aristoteles of (the deme) Marathon,[9] Pyrrandros of (the deme) Anaphlystos, Thrasyboulos of (the deme) Kollytos.[10]

The following *poleis* (are) allies of the Athenians:[11]

Chios, Tenedos	Thebes
Mytilene	Chalkis
Methymna	Eretria

Rhodes, Poiessa	Arethousa
Byzantion	Karystos
Perinthos	Ikos
Peparethos	Pall--
Skiathos	----
Maroneia	----
Dion (Euboia)	----
Paros, O --	----
Athenai Diades, P --	----

(*side*)

The *dēmos* of [The]ra;[12] [Abde]ra; [Thas]os; [Chalki]dians from [Thrake]; Ainos; Samothrake; Dikaiopolis; Akarnania; Kephallenia; Pronnoi; Alketas (and) Neoptolemos;[13] (*erasure*);[14] Andros; Tenos; Histiaia; Mykonos; Antissa; Eresos; Astraios; from Keos – Ioulis, Karthaia, Koresia; Elaios; Amorgos; Selymbria; Siphnos; Sikinos; Dion from Thrake; Neapolis; the *dēmos* of Zakynthos in Nellos.[15]

Tod no.123

1 Chios, Mytilene, Methymna (another *polis* of Lesbos), Rhodes and Byzantion are the first names on the list appended to the charter-inscription (B, below). Separate documents survive for Chios (Tod no.118) and Byzantion (121), preceding the general charter, and for Methymna (122) and others following it.

2 For these arrangements see more fully B, below.

3 This establishes the date as February–March 377. (Diodorus' account, A above, is wrongly set in 377/6.)

4 This is a deliberate erasure, or an attempt at one, from a time when the Athenians were evidently less concerned to appease the Persians. See also n.14, below.

5 Or possibly 'in [Europe]'.

6 Compare Isoc. XIV. 44, Diod. XV. 29.8.

7 'The alliance is thus in form, if not in fact, strictly defensive' (Tod).

8 See Rhodes, *Boule*, 103 with n.7.

9 I.e. the proposer of the decree (and indeed of a second one also, inscribed on this same stone (lines 91–6) but only fragmentarily preserved; we omit it here).

10 *Not* Thrasyboulos the hero of Phyle (**244, 245, 262**), who had died in 388.

11 Almost 60 names follow, in 2 columns at the foot of the stone's main face (before the second decree moved by Aristoteles; see n.9, above) and continuing on to its left side. We follow this layout here, at least for the face, but draw attention to the fact that the names represent groups of allies won during a 5-year period and in an order determinable by the several epigraphic 'hands'; see Tod's commentary (esp. pp.66–9), and P. J. Rhodes, *Greek Historical Inscriptions 359–323 B.C.* (LACTOR no.9), 2–3. A few individual problems are mentioned in the following notes.

509

12 So J. E. Coleman and D. W. Bradeen, *Hesperia* 36 (1967), 102–4, in preference to [Kcrky]ra.
13 Alketas was king of the Molossians (of Epeiros), and Neoptolemos his son.
14 Another deliberate erasure. Early editors read a final 'n' and restored [Iaso]n, tyrant of Pherai (see Ch.32), but a longer name seems necessary; see A. G. Woodhead, *American Journal of Archaeology* 61 (1957), 367–73, and Rhodes (n.11, above), 3.
15 See Xen. *Hell.* VI.2.2.

270. The Boiotian War

From 377 onwards the new Athenian alliance (**269**) grew steadily, but within Greece itself these years were chiefly remarkable for the growth of the power of Thebes and the fear which this caused in Sparta. If this sounds like a repetition of the Pentekontaëtia – reading now Thebes for Athens – then the campaigns of 378–376 continue the parallel, showing Spartan strategy in Boiotia just as ineffectual as it had been in the Archidamian War in Attika. For the narrative of this 'Boiotian War', which fulfilled the Spartans' gloomy expectations of it (**269**A), see Xen. *Hell.* V.4.35–63; we give here an anecdotal passage from Plutarch which illustrates the period more obliquely.

After Sphodrias had been acquitted and the Athenians had got to hear of it, they were inclined to war.[1] Then Agesilaos came in for some very severe criticism (within Sparta): it was felt that he had opposed the course of justice in a trial so as to gratify an absurd and childish desire and had made the Spartan *polis* accessory to great breaches of morality against the Greeks. Kleombrotos[2], moreover, had no enthusiasm for a war against the Thebans, but when Agesilaos saw this he simply brushed aside his own legal exemption – which he had previously invoked – from campaigning[3] and personally led an army into Boiotia. There he inflicted some damage on the Thebans but suffered some himself in turn, and this led Antalkidas[4] to remark, when Agesilaos was wounded on one occasion, 'Yes, it's a fine tuition-fee you are taking from the Thebans, for teaching them to fight when they neither wanted to nor knew how!' For the Thebans are said to have become more genuinely warlike at this time than ever before, thanks to their schooling, as it were, by the many Spartan campaigns against them. Indeed this is why long ago Lykourgos, in one of his three so-called *rhētrai*, forbade frequent campaigns against the same enemy, to prevent them from learning how to fight a war.[5]

The Spartans' allies too were angry with Agesilaos, on the grounds that he was seeking to destroy the Thebans not because of any public grievance but out of some quarrelsome fury of his own, and they therefore said that they had no wish, year after year, to be dragged hither and thither to destruction when they were so many and the Lakedaimonians whom they followed so few. And this was the occasion, so it is said, when Agesilaos, wishing to refute their argument from numbers, devised the following scheme: he ordered all the allies to sit down intermingled with one another, and the Lakedaimonians to sit separately by themselves; then his herald called upon the potters to stand up first, which they did, and then the smiths, and then the carpenters and builders, and so on through all the other crafts. In this way virtually all the allies rose to their feet – but not a single Spartan; for they were forbidden to learn and practise a banausic craft [6] And then of course Agesilaos laughed, and said: 'You observe, men, how many more *soldiers* we are sending out than you!'

Plutarch, Agesilaos 26

1 See **268**.
2 His fellow-king.
3 He had completed 40 years of military service, and had cited this fact when refusing to go and coerce the Thebans in 379/8 (Xen. *Hell.* v.4.13; Plut. *Ages.* 24.2).
4 The negotiator of the King's Peace (**263**), which is therefore sometimes known by his name.
5 Compare *Lykourgos* 13.5–6.
6 *Banausia*: see **13**. The Spartans and crafts: **53** with n.9.

271. The Sacred Band

Many things lie behind the Spartans' defeat by the Thebans at Leuktra in 371 (**273**), and we have already looked briefly at some of them which arise on the Spartan side. The Theban perspective is much less well documented; Xenophon, above all, is woefully inadequate here; but it is clear enough that the purely military aspect is as significant as any. The Spartans' supremacy had always rested upon their 'professional' (**270**) hoplite army, and anyone seeking to challenge that supremacy had to face and beat that army, either by enlisting the services of genuine professionals, i.e. mercenaries, with all the risks attendant thereon, or else by upgrading their own domestic forces to the required level. The Thebans, to an extent greater than any of their contemporaries, eschewed the first course of action and put their faith in the second – chiefly by the creation of the Sacred Band (*hieros lochos*), 'an élite force of 300 men who combined full-time training with homosexual pair-bonding and with the idealistic emotional cohesion of a secret society' (Davies, *Democracy*, 200). It seems to have been established in 378, after the expulsion of the Spartan garrison (**268** Intro.), for its creator Gorgidas (see below) was *boiōtarchos* in that year (Plut. *Pelop.* 14.1) and is no longer heard of after 377; but after its first success, at Tegyra in 375, the crucial reorganisation by Pelopidas paved the way for its consummate triumph – Leuktra itself.

See further: H. W. Parke, *Greek Mercenary Soldiers* (Oxford, 1933 [1970]), 90–2. (On the *Carthaginian* Sacred Band, possibly formed in imitation of the Theban one – though at 2,500 much larger – see Diod. XVI.80.4, XX.10.6.)

It was Gorgidas, so they say, who first formed the Sacred Band, out of 300 picked men, for whom the *polis* provided exercise and maintenance and who had their encampment on the citadel. This in fact is why they were (also) called the *polis* Band, for at one time the proper name for an *akropolis* was a *polis*.[1] But some say that this unit was made up of lovers and their beloved; and a jocular remark of Pammenes[2] is recorded, to the effect that Homer's Nestor was no tactician when he told the Greeks to form in companies by *phylai* and clans, 'so that clan might give support to clan, and *phylai* to *phylai*',[3] for he ought to have stationed lover by beloved. This is because in times of danger men of the same *phylē* and clan care little for one another, whereas a body of men that is held together by the friendship between lovers is indissoluble and unbreakable, since both the lover and his beloved are ashamed to show cowardice before each other and so both stand firm in danger for their mutual protection[4] . . . It is also said that until the battle at Chaironeia (in 338) the Band was never beaten; and when, after that battle, Philippos was inspecting the corpses and stopped at the spot where the 300 were lying mingled with one another, where they had all faced and fought his spearmen, he was amazed, and on learning that this was the Band of lovers and beloved he wept and said, 'A miserable death to those who suspect these men of doing or suffering anything shameful!'[5] . . .

(19) . . . So Gorgidas, by distributing this Sacred Band among the entire front ranks of the hoplite phalanx, did not make the excellence of these men stand out; nor did he use their strength against a common object, for it was obviously dissipated when intermixed with a larger and inferior body. Pelopidas, however, saw how their excellence shone out at Tegyra, where they fought around him in a single unit,[6] so he never again divided or dispersed them but treated them as a single body and as such made them bear the brunt of the danger in the greatest conflicts . . .

Plutarch, *Pelopidas* 18–19*

1 This is true enough, though hardly for the 370s.
2 A prominent Theban general of the 360s and 350s: see for instance Diod. XV.94.2–3, XVI.34.1–2.
3 Homer, *Iliad* II.363.
4 See on this Parke, *op. cit.* 91.
5 On this battle see **349**.
6 See *Pelopidas* 16–17; Diod. XV.37.1–2.

272. Epameinondas

The problem of 'Periklean Athens' (148) highlighted the hazards in ascribing complex events and developments to the influence of single individuals, however dominant; but it will at least be conceded that the great years of Thebes, in the 370s and 360s, coincided with the inspired leadership and fruitful partnership of two great Thebans – Pelopidas (c.410–364) and Epameinondas (d.362). Plutarch wrote Lives of them both, of which only the *Pelopidas* survives (though the *Epameinondas* was excerpted by Pausanias, IX.13–15) – and unfortunately so, as, whatever the contribution of Pelopidas (e.g. 271), most scholars see that of Epameinondas as the greater. Here Plutarch describes an encounter between him and the Thebans' arch-enemy Agesilaos.

See further: G. L. Cawkwell, 'Epameinondas and Thebes', *CQ* n.s.22 (1972), 254–78.

During this time (the 370s) the Spartans met with many reverses, both on land and at sea; and the greatest of them was at Tegyra, where for the first time they were overcome and defeated by the Thebans in a pitched battle.[1] All parties were thus resolved to conclude a general peace, and envoys from all Greece met together at Sparta to fix its terms.[2] One of them was Epameinondas, a man of repute for culture and philosophy but not yet tried and tested as a *stratēgos*. Seeing all the others cowering before Agesilaos, he alone had the spirit to speak out and deliver an address, not only on behalf of the Thebans but on that of Greece as a whole, demonstrating how war made Sparta great at the expense of the sufferings of everyone else and urging that peace be made on just and equal terms, for it would last only if everybody involved were made equal. (28) Watching as the Greeks listened to Epameinondas with the utmost admiration and attention, Agesilaos asked him whether he thought it 'just and equal' for Boiotia to be independent (of Thebes). Epameinondas' reply, immediate and bold, was to ask whether Agesilaos for his part considered it 'just' for Lakonia to be independent (of Sparta). Agesilaos sprang from his seat at this and angrily insisted that Epameinondas say plainly whether he would grant Boiotia independence, but Epameinondas only answered again in the same way, by asking whether Agesilaos would grant Lakonia independence. This threw Agesilaos into a violent temper, and he was glad of the excuse for immediately erasing the name of the Thebans from the peace-treaty and declaring war upon them. As for the rest of the Greeks, he told them to go home, now that they were reconciled with each other – healing their curable breaches in peace and their incurable ones in war; for to settle and remove all their disputes was a hard task.

Plutarch, *Agesilaos* 27.3–28.2

1 In 375: see **271**.
2 In 371 (but before Leuktra): see Xen. *Hell.* VI.3; T. T. B. Ryder, *Koine Eirene* (Hull, 1965), 64–70 and 127–30.

273. Leuktra

In the summer of 371 the Thebans crushed the Spartans at Leuktra in Boiotia: Xen. *Hell.* VI.4.1–14. This chapter has pursued various lines of development which can be seen as leading up to this, but the perspective of hindsight should not deceive us: *at the time* the Thebans' victory seemed like, and indeed was, a stupefying reversal of certainties; the unthinkable not merely thought but accomplished. Here are three immediate reactions: in Sparta (A) a stiff upper lip; in Athens (A) grudging recognition; and in Thebes (B), naturally enough, one of (surely) many songs of triumph.

(A) The (Spartan) war-commanders could see that, of the whole Lakedaimonian army, almost 1,000 were dead; they saw too that about 400 of the 700 Spartiates who had been there had fallen; and they realised that none of their allies had any heart left for the fight – some of them indeed not even being sorry at what had happened. They therefore called the most important men together and discussed what to do. Everyone agreed that they should recover their dead under a truce, and so they naturally sent a herald to ask for one. The Thebans, for their part, then erected a trophy[1] and gave back the enemy dead under truce. (16) Subsequently a messenger was sent off to Sparta with the news of the disaster; and he arrived there on the last day of the Gymnopaidiai festival, with the men's chorus in (the theatre). When the *ephoroi* were told of the disaster they were deeply grieved – inevitably so, it seems to me; yet instead of ordering the chorus out they allowed the contest to finish; and although they gave the names of all the dead to the relatives concerned, they instructed the women to bear their suffering in silence, without any cries of lamentation. And on the following day the relatives of the men who had died were to be seen openly going about bright and cheerful, whereas those whose menfolk had been reported to be still alive were not much in evidence, and the few that did come out of doors looked sad and humiliated. (17) The *ephoroi* then called up the two remaining regiments (*morai*), up to and including the men with 40 years' service,[2] and they also sent out the men up to the same age who belonged to the (four) *morai* which had gone on the original expedition into Phokis, in a call-up which had extended only to those of 35 years' service. In addition they ordered out those who had been left behind on the previous occasion because of official duties. (18) Agesilaos had not yet recovered from his illness,[3] so the *polis* ordered his son Archidamos to take command. The men of Tegea marched with him enthusiastically, since at that time Stasippos and his faction, who were pro-Spartan and very influential in the *polis*, were still alive. The Mantineians too flocked in from their villages and joined the expedition, being then under an aristocratic government.4 The Corinthians, Sikyonians, Phleiasians and Achaians also came along with alacrity, and other *poleis* sent out troops as well. In addition both the Spartans themselves and the Corinthians began to man triremes, and asked the Sikyonians to join them in this, their intention being to ferry the army across (the Corinthian Gulf) in these ships. (19) And Archidamos then performed the necessary sacrifices for crossing the border.5

Immediately after the battle the Thebans had sent a messenger, crowned with garlands, to Athens, where they had not only made it clear what a great victory had been won but urged the Athenians to come and help them: it was now possible, they said, to make the Spartans pay for everything that they had done to them. (20) At the time the Athenian *boule* happened to be in session, on the *akropolis*, and when its members had heard what had happened it was clear to all that they were extremely vexed; they did not offer the herald any hospitality,6 and made no reply to his request for help; so he left Athens and went away.

Xenophon, *Hellenika* VI.4.15–20

(B)

Xenokrates7
Theopompos8
Mnasilaos

When the spear of Sparta was (still) strong, Xeinokrates (*sic*) won by lot the task of bearing trophies to Zeus, having not been afraid of the army from Eurotas or the Lakonian shield. 'The Thebans are greater in war' proclaim trophies of victory won by the spear at Leuktra – nor did we run in second to Epameinondas.9

Tod no.130

1 On this practice see Pritchett, *War* II, 246–75.
2 I.e. the full levy: see **270** with n.3.
3 See *Hell.* V.4.58.
4 See **291**.
5 See **50B**.
6 This was perhaps not obligatory, but certainly customary: see for instance **172B**; also Meiggs and Lewis nos.87 and 92, Tod nos.97, 98, 116, 118, 121, 122, 129, etc.
7 One of the seven *boiōtarchoi* at Leuktra: Paus. IX.13.6–7 (Diod. XV.53.3); see also Paus. IV.32.5–6.

8 Mentioned in Plut. *Pelop.* 8.2.

9 This 'might be interpreted as a veiled protest against the undue glorification of that general, but the poem does not enable us to determine precisely the nature of the services rendered by Xenokrates and his two fellow-officers' (Tod).

274. Lakonia invaded

'The significance of the battle of Leuktra is perhaps most clearly revealed in the fact that, during the wars between Sparta and Thebes which followed it, the parts hitherto played by the two states are reversed. Thebes now becomes the invader of the Peloponnesos, as Sparta before had been the invader of Boiotia. Thebes is now the aggressor; it is as much as Sparta can do to defend her own land' (Bury and Meiggs, *Greece*, 369). During the next twenty years the Thebans invaded the Peloponnesos on seven occasions: 'they acted out a role, as guarantor of freedom from Spartan domination, which the Athenians declined and the Thebans therefore made their own' (Davies, *Democracy*, 215). Ultimately the most important consequence of all this was the re-establishment of an independent Messenia (**301**); but the very first of the invasions, led jointly in winter 370/69 by Epameinondas and Pelopidas and undertaken at the request of the newly-formed and militant Arkadian League (see **300**), was chiefly noteworthy for its penetration into the heart of Lakonia itself. See in general, on the consequences of Leuktra, J. Buckler, *The Theban Hegemony, 371–362* B.C. (Cambridge, Mass., 1979).

When Agesilaos had left Arkadia and the Arkadians had got word that his army had been disbanded, they themselves, still in full force, made an expedition against Heraia, because it had not only refused to join the Arkadian League but had taken part with the Spartans in their invasion of Arkadia; so they entered Heraian territory and began to burn the houses and cut down the trees. However, news then came that the Thebans who had set out to help them had reached Mantineia, so they left Heraia and went to join forces with the Thebans. (23) And once the two armies had united, the Thebans were very pleased with the situation from their point of view: they had brought help to Arkadia, but now saw nobody still there to fight; so they made preparations to leave. However, the Arkadians and Argives and Eleians urged them to lead the way immediately into Lakonia, pointing out how many men the Thebans had and lavishing praise on their army. And indeed the Boiotians, exulting in their victory at Leuktra, were now all in training as soldiers; and they were followed by the Phokians, whom they had made their subjects,[1] by all the *poleis* of Euboia, the east and west Lokrians, the Akarnanians, and the men of Herakleia[2] and Malis, as well as cavalry and peltasts from Thessaly. Seeing this, and maintaining that Lakedaimon was deserted, they begged the Thebans not on any account to turn back before invading the Spartans' *chōra*. (24) The Thebans listened to what they had to say, but also took into account, against it, that Lakonia was said to be extremely difficult to invade, with garrisons, they believed, posted at the most accessible points of entry – as indeed they *had* been: Ischolaos was at Oion, in Skiritis, with a force of emancipated helots and about 400 of the youngest exiles from Tegea,[3] and there was another force on guard at Leuktron, above Maleatis. The Thebans also calculated that the Spartans would speedily concentrate their strength, and would fight nowhere better than in their own territory; and consideration of all this made them naturally reluctant to agree to invade Lakedaimon. (25) At this juncture, however, some men arrived from Karyai with a report that there were no Spartan forces there; moreover they undertook to act as guides themselves, and told the Thebans to put them to death if they were found to be deceiving them in any way. Some of the *perioikoi*, too, came to call upon the Thebans to intervene, promising to revolt if only the Thebans would make an appearance in the *chōra*, and declaring also that even now the *perioikoi* were being called up by the Spartiates but were refusing to help them. And accordingly, after hearing these same arguments from all sides, the Thebans were convinced: they themselves went in by way of Karyai, leaving the Arkadians to take the route through Oion in Skiritis (where they overcame Ischolaos and his men, joining the Thebans at Karyai; the combined force then continued south, burning and pillaging Sellasia, and so came within sight of Sparta itself). (27) . . . The invaders did not even attempt to cross the bridge and attack the *polis*, for they could see the Spartan hoplites ready to face them at the temple of (Athena) Alea; instead, keeping the Eurotas on their right they passed by, burning and plundering houses full of many valuables. (28) As for the people in the *polis*, the women could not even bear to see the smoke, for they had never set eyes on an enemy before, but the Spartiates, posted in small detachments here and there, stood guard over their unwalled *polis*.[4] There were not many of them, however, and the fact was obvious. The authorities also decided to issue a proclamation to the helots, guaranteeing freedom to all armed volunteers who joined the ranks and helped in the war; (29) and it was said that at first more than 6,000 of them enlisted, with the result that when they had been added to the ranks the Spartans were alarmed for a second time, as there seemed to be far too many of them; however, once the mercenaries from Orchomenos had remained loyal, and support had also come from Phleious, Corinth, Epidauros, Pellene and some other *poleis*, the Spartans began to feel less nervous about the men they had enlisted. (30) Meanwhile the invading army had continued on as far as Amyklai and crossed the Eurotas there. Wherever the Thebans made camp they immediately began cutting down trees and stacking as many of them as possible in front of their lines, for protection; the Arkadians, by contrast, did none of this, preferring to leave camp and go looting amongst the houses. Anyway, on the third or fourth day of this, the cavalry advanced in battle order into the racecourse in (the sanctuary of Poseidon) the Earthshaker – the Thebans, in full force, with the Eleians and all the Phokians, Thessalians and Lokrians who were serving. (31) Drawn up to face them was the Spartan cavalry, and an extremely small body it looked; however, the Spartans had set an ambush of about 300 of their younger hoplites in the house of the Tyndaridai,[5] and they came running out at the same moment as their cavalry charged. The enemy failed to stand up to this and gave way, and the sight put many of their infantry to flight as well, but eventually the Spartans gave up their pursuit and the Theban army stood its ground and settled down in camp again. (32) The Spartans now saw more grounds for confidence that the invaders would make no further move against the *polis*; and indeed the army did abandon its position and march off on the road to Helos and Gytheion, burning all the unfortified *poleis* on the way and mounting an assault on Gytheion, where the Spartans' dockyards are, for three days. Some of the *perioikoi* too not only took part in this attack but joined forces with the troops who were serving with the Thebans.

Xenophon, *Hellenika* VI.5.22–25; 27–32

1 See **336**.
2 See **189**.
3 See **273**A.
4 See **164**.
5 The Dioskouroi; see **75** with n.12.

275. The Athenians under pressure

Despite the openly anti–Spartan stance of their 377 alliance (**269**), we have already seen that the Athenians were less than jubilant when Sparta had finally succumbed to the new power, Thebes (**273**); and before the second Theban invasion of the Peloponnesos the Athenians had been persuaded into an actual alliance with Sparta (see A, below). This apparent *volte-face* is in fact less startling than it might seem: the highly successful early years of the new Athenian *hēgemonia* owed at least part of their explanation to the fact that potential Spartan opposition had been diverted by Thebes, yet even before Leuktra it had become clear that the Athenians had more to fear from their (unnatural) ally than from their ostensible enemy; and now the Thebans were entering the 360s as buoyant as the Spartans had entered the 370s. Buoyancy would *not* be an appropriate word in the Athenians' case, at least not financially speaking. The archonship of Nausinikos had seen not only the establishment of the new Aegean alliance but also new financial and administrative institutions commensurate with its needs (see for instance **312**), yet even so Athenian financial embarrassment on various levels is a recurrent theme from then on. We find many telling examples of this, such as the glimpse in Xenophon (*Hell.* VI.2.37) of the *stratēgos* Iphikrates having to hire out his rowers as farm labourers in Kerkyra, but the best illustration is provided by another *stratēgos*, Timotheos son of Konon, whose financial difficulties of the 370s and 360s became almost proverbial; as well as the passage given here (B), from Book II of the *Economics* ascribed to Aristotle (see below), see Austin and Vidal-Naquet, *Economy* no. 124.

(A) When the Athenians heard about this[1] they were perplexed as to what ought to be done with regard to the Spartans, and in accordance with a resolution of the *boulē* they held a meeting of the *ekklēsia*. As it happened, in Athens at the time were some envoys both from the Spartans themselves and from such allies as they still had, so naturally these Spartans – Arakos, Okyllos, Pharax, Etymokles and Olontheus – had their say, and their message was virtually the same in all cases: they reminded the Athenians that always in times of great crisis they and the Spartans had stood by one another in defence of right; the Spartans, for example, could lay claim to having expelled the tyrants from Athens,[2] and the Athenians to having hurried to the Spartans' aid when they were hard pressed by the Messenians.[3] (34) What a fine thing it had been, they went on, when the two states had been acting together, in concert, such as in their memorable joint resistance to the *barbaroi*. It would be recollected that when the Athenians had been chosen by the Greeks to have the naval *hēgemonia* and be guardians of the common funds, this had been with the willing agreement of the Spartans;[4] and equally when all the Greeks had had no hesitation in picking out the Spartans to have the *hēgemonia* by land, this had been with the willing agreement of the Athenians. (35) In fact one of the envoys said something like this: 'Gentlemen, if you can agree with us and we with you, there may be hope of bringing to pass the old saying about "tithing the Thebans".'[5] The Athenians, however, were not in a particularly receptive mood, and a murmur arose to the effect that 'this is what they may say *now*, but when they were doing well they turned against us'. But of everything that the Spartans said, the key point appeared to be that when they had beaten the Athenians in the (Peloponnesian) war and the Thebans were pressing for Athens to be laid waste, they, the Spartans, had opposed this.[6] (Further speeches follow, and a pro-Spartan consensus is established.) (49) After this the Athenians were not prepared, in their deliberations, to listen to people speaking against (the proposed alliance), and they voted to go to the Spartans' aid in full force, choosing Iphikrates as *stratēgos*. (And the following year, 369, the alliance is formally concluded: VII.1.1–14.)

Xenophon, *Hellenika* VI.5.33–35; 49

(B) Timotheos of Athens, while fighting a war against the Olynthians[7] and at a loss for silver, struck a bronze (coinage) and gave it to his soldiers.[8] When they protested he told them that the traders and retailers would all sell (to them) just as before. He told the traders that when any of them were given bronze coins they should use them to buy goods sent for sale from the *chōra* or brought in as booty, and he said that if they brought him any bronze that was left over he would give them silver for it.

When he was waging war near Kerkyra[9] and was in (financial) difficulties, with the soldiers demanding their pay and threatening to go over to the enemy, he called them together in assembly and announced that the bad weather was preventing the silver from reaching him (from Athens); however, since he had no shortage of provisions he said that they could have the three months' rations which they had already received as a free gift;[10] and they, supposing that Timotheos would never have made them such an offer unless he really was expecting the money, held their peace about the wages, which enabled him to proceed with his plans.

And while besieging Samos[11] he actually sold to the Samians the fruits and produce of their fields, and so had plenty of money for the wages of his soldiers.

[Aristotle], *Economics* II.2.23[12]

1 The Thebans' invasion of Lakonia (**274**).
2 See **74**.
3 See **169**.
4 So also Thuc. 1.95.7; *contra*, Isoc. XII.52 and ?Aristot. *Ath. Pol.* 23.2. See also **167**.
5 Compare *Hell.* VI.3.20. On the tithe of one tenth see **109**C, and Pritchett, *War* I, ch.5.
6 See **240**.
7 In 364, in the course of Athenian attempts to recover control of the northern Aegean; see further **337**.
8 For the coins see E. S. G. Robinson and M. J. Price, 'An emergency coinage of Timotheos', *Numismatic Chronicle* (1967), 1–6.
9 In 375.
10 See in general Pritchett, *War* I, ch.2, esp.34–41.
11 In 366; compare Isoc. XV.111.
12 As stated above, the *Economics* has come down to us as a work of Aristotle, but it is in fact the product of at least two writers of a later period. Book II is effectively a catalogue of dozens of stratagems, many undatable, employed by individuals and communities in financial crises; for another example see **287**.

29 The polis and its economy

The difficulties in the way of characterising changes in the economy of Greece between the fifth century and the fourth are almost insuperable. We possess a great deal of evidence for economic activity in the fourth century; but almost all of it is from Athens and there is no way of telling whether Athens was qualitatively different from other fourth-century *poleis* or merely larger and better documented. Similarly, we do not know the extent to which practices amply attested in the fourth century were already characteristic of the fifth. In some cases we can see continuity: the position of Peiraieus in the fifth century is already clear (see **159**) and is perpetuated in the fourth (**276**); the mines are already a major factor in individual and collective wealth in the fifth century (see **161**) and it is largely accidental that it is the fourth century which provides evidence for their organisation (**277**). We happen to know of the composition of the substantial estate of the father of the orator Demosthenes, but such estates probably already existed in the fifth century (**278**). With our knowledge of the chariots maintained by Alkibiades (see **219**), it is no surprise to find in the fourth century wealth used for ostentatious display and land mortgaged to raise money not for productive investment but for further display (**279–280**). Both in the fifth century and in the fourth, Athens was dependent on imported grain; the regulation of the grain trade and the system of financing it are likely to be characteristic of both centuries (**281** and **309**). Athens had founded Amphipolis (**132**) in part to control access to strategic materials and the same concern is apparent in the fourth century (**282**).

Is there then no change, and is our expectation of one simply the result of our knowledge that Athens was in the end defeated by Philippos of Makedon (Ch. 34), having failed in the fourth century to gain and hold an empire which could make available the resources provided by the empire lost in 404?

It is perhaps possible to suggest that the relative lack of imperial revenue, compared with the fifth century, did have an effect on the internal finances of Athens, burdened with the payments demanded by the democracy; the result was perhaps a greater dependence on the wealth of rich *metoikoi* and other foreigners; and the contrast which their emergence highlighted with the traditional respect for citizen status perhaps provoked reflection. At the same time the restoration of the Athenian democracy in 403 and the apparent impossibility of introducing any other system provoked utopian longings for the exclusion of *banausoi* from the *polis* (**283–285**).

The evident disparity between resources and demand also provoked reflection, however primitive, on economic matters: at Athens, Xenophon composed the *Poroi*; elsewhere, a literature grew up on financial stratagems. The shift from citizen armies to mercenaries (around whom there also grew up a literature, see **299**) involved great expense without the productive capacity of the citizen body being increased, and it is not surprising that many of the recorded financial stratagems involve mercenaries (**286–287**).

276. Athens and Peiraieus

Perikles had told the Athenians that their imperial position gave them access to goods from all over the world (see **154**) and it is remarkable that in 380, six years after the King's Peace had put an end to the first Athenian attempt to recover the empire, Isocrates could make the same claim.

Moreover, Athens has made the rest of her arrangements with such *philoxenia*[1] and friendliness to everyone that they are suitable both for those who wish to make money and for those who wish to enjoy the wealth they have and are of service both to those who are prosperous and to those who have suffered disaster in their own *poleis*; both find something here, the former somewhere very pleasant to stay, the latter an extremely safe refuge. (42) And since no one has a *chōra* that is self-sufficient, but one that is lacking in some respects and produces more than is needed in others, and since there was no obvious answer to the problem of where to dispose of surpluses and whence to import what was still needed, Athens came to the rescue here also; for she created an *emporion*, Peiraieus, in the middle of Greece with such an abundant stock that it is easy to get there all the things which it is hard to get individually elsewhere.

Isocrates IV (Panegyrikos) 41–42

1 See **158**.

277. The organisation of the mines at Laureion

The earliest epigraphical evidence for the leasing out of the right to work a mine belongs to 367/6, but refers back at least to 374/3, and it looks as if the creation of the second Athenian empire provoked not only the reorganisation of the *eisphora* system in 378/7 (see **312**), but also that of the mines at Laureion. Nonetheless, there must have been a broadly similar system in the fifth century (see **161**) and it is remarkable how casual the identification of a mine still seems. The example below, of 367/6, follows a standard form, in which the *pōlētai* (sellers of leases), having received an account of what was available from another board of officials, describe the leases sold (see Isager and Hansen, *Aspects*, 99–106)

(A) But why should I speak of the past? For at this very moment there are many who are involved in the mines in this way. (17) Indeed, if my proposals were adopted, the only novelty would be that just as individuals with slaves have acquired a permanent source of revenue, so the *polis* also would acquire public slaves, until there were three for every Athenian. (18) Anyone who wishes may consider each proposal individually and see if they are possible. Now it is clear that the community would be in a much better position to find the cost of the slaves than individuals; and it is easy for the *boulē* to issue a proclamation that anyone who wishes is to bring slaves and then buy those who are brought. (19) And when they have been bought, why should anyone be less ready to hire from the community than from an individual, since the conditions will be the same? People certainly rent sacred land and property as well as houses and rights to collect certain taxes from the *polis*.[1] (20) And in order to secure the slaves who have been bought, the community can demand guarantors from those who hire them, as in the case of those who rent rights to collect certain taxes. And indeed it is easier for someone who rents a right to collect a tax to commit a crime than for someone who hires slaves. (21) For how could one detect publicly-owned money which is being embezzled, since privately-owned money is identical; but with a fine laid down for someone who sold or embezzled slaves branded with the public seal, how could anyone steal them? So far, then, it seems possible for the *polis* to acquire and secure slaves. (22) But now someone will perhaps wonder whether, given that there are numerous workmen, numerous hirers will also appear; he can take courage from the reflection that many of those who have slaves will hire public ones in addition, for the resources available for exploitation are considerable; and there is a large number of slaves who are growing old in the mines; and there are many others, Athenians and *xenoi*, who would not wish or be able to work themselves, but would gladly procure livelihoods by the exercise of thought. (23) And if in the first instance 1,200 slaves were got together, it is likely that in five or six years they would be no less than 6,000 as a result of the revenue accruing. And if every one of these produced an obol a day clear, the revenue would be 60 talents a year; (24) and if one put aside 20 of these to purchase other slaves, it would already be possible for the *polis* to use the remaining 40 for whatever other purpose was necessary. And when the number is up to 10,000, the revenue will be 100 talents. (25) And if there are any who still remember how much revenue came in from the slaves before the occupation of Dekeleia,[2] they can support my contention that much more than this is possible. And also relevant is the fact that although countless men have always laboured in the silver mines, they are no different now from their state as described by our ancestors. (26) And the present state of affairs makes it clear that there would never be more slaves there than the works actually need; for the miners find that there is no end to the shafts and galleries. (27) And it is no less possible now than earlier to open new workings, but no one would have the knowledge to say whether there is more silver ore in the open workings or in the untouched parts. (28) Why then, someone will ask, are there not many people engaged in opening new workings, as there used to be? The reason is that those involved in mining are now poorer; for recently they have set to work again, but the risk for someone opening a new working is considerable; for someone who finds a rich seam becomes wealthy, (29) but anyone who does not loses all that he spends. So people nowadays are somewhat reluctant to run this risk. I think, however, that I have some advice to offer also on how the least risk might attach to opening new workings. (30) There are ten *phylai* in Athens; if then the *polis* gave each of them the same number of slaves and they explored new workings at their collective risk, if one found silver, it would be profitable for all, (31) whereas it is clear that if two or three or four or five found it the workings would be even more profitable. Of course, it is quite unlikely on the basis of past experience for them all to find silver. (32) Similarly, it is possible for individuals to get together and share the risk, with its diminution as the result. Nor is there any reason to fear that if public enterprise is involved in this way it will harm individuals or *vice versa*; rather, just as allies make each other stronger the more there are, so also with silver mines, the more there are working there, the more riches will be found and extracted. (33) This then is my explanation of how I think the *polis* may be organised so as to provide from public funds an adequate livelihood for all Athenians.[3]

(34) If, however, anyone reckons that one would need a large capital outlay for all these profits and does not think that enough money would come in to the treasury, he should not be disheartened as a result. (35) For it is not the case that it is necessary for everything to be done at once for any benefit to accrue; rather, any building or ship or slave, once available, will at once produce some benefit. (36) Indeed it is actually preferable to do things bit by bit rather than all at once. For by building houses or ships *en masse* rather than gradually we should produce something inferior at greater expense; and if we attempted to acquire an

enormous number of slaves, we should be forced to acquire poor quality ones at a high price. (37) But if we do things as we can, we could carry on with those which are recognised as effective and if any mistake was made we could avoid repeating it. (38) Furthermore, if everything was done at once, we should have to provide all the resources; but if some projects were carried out and some left pending, existing revenue would cover what was necessary. (39) Perhaps, however, what seems most alarming to everyone is the possibility that if the *polis* acquired too many slaves, the workings would be overloaded; but we should be relieved of this fear if we did not deploy more men each year than the workings actually needed. (40) So I think that the easiest course of action is also the best. But if it is argued that it would not be possible to pay anything to the treasury because of the (direct) taxes levied during the recent war,[4] the answer is to manage the *polis* for the coming year on the money produced by the indirect taxes during the war; any additional product deriving from the conclusion of peace and from the encouraging of *metoikoi* and traders, and from the fact that more is imported and exported when there are more people here, and from the increase in harbour and market revenues – *this* can be taken and used to increase our revenues as far as possible. (41) And if anyone fears lest this effort should be in vain if war broke out, he should reflect that if these projects were carried out war would be much more dangerous for an attacker than for the *polis*. (42) For what is more serviceable in war than men? For we should be able as a community to man many ships; and there would be many infantry who would be able to oppress the enemy, if they were encouraged to come. (Xenophon goes on to consider in detail the garrisoning of the mining area.) (49) So not only would the revenue from the slaves increase the means of support of the *polis*, but with a greater concentration of men around the mines there would be substantial revenue from the *agora* there and from the public buildings in the mining area and from the furnaces and all the other installations. (50) And a very populous *polis* would certainly develop there, if my plan were carried out; and property there would be just as valuable to its owner as that near the town (*astu*). (51) And I must add that if what I suggest were done, not only would the *polis* be better off materially, it would also be more amenable and more law-abiding and better at fighting. (52) For those who were assigned to training would undertake it much more assiduously if they got more keep in the gymnasia than by taking part in torch races; and those who are assigned to guard duty, to serve as peltasts[5] or to patrol the *chōra* would do all those things more readily if keep were provided in every case.

Xenophon, *Poroi* iv.16–52*

(B) In the first prytany, of the *phylē* Hippothontis, (the following) mines were leased: Dexiakon in Nape at Skopia, of which by land the boundaries are on all sides (the property of) Nikias of (the deme) Kydantidai,[6] lessee Kallias of (the deme) Sphettos: 20 drachmas. Diakon at Laureion, of which by land the boundaries are to the east the lands of Exopios, to the west the mountain, lessee Epiteles of (the deme) Kerameis: 20 drachmas. At Sounion in the (lands) of the sons of Charmylos, of which by land the boundaries are, to the north (the property of) Kleokritos of (the deme) Aigilia, to the south (the property of) Leukios of (the deme) Sounion, lessee Pheidippos of (the deme) Pithos: 20 drachmas. Poseidoniakon in Nape, one of those inscribed on the *stēlē*[7] in the (lands) of Alypetos, of which by land the boundaries are the (property) of Kallias of (the deme) Sphettos and Diokles of (the deme) Pithos, lessee Thrasylochos of (the deme) Anagyrous: 1,550 drachmas. Hagnosiakon, one of those inscribed on the *stēlē*, lessee Telesarchos of (the deme) Aixone: 1,550 drachmas. Artemisiakon, one of those inscribed on the *stēlē*, lessee Thrasylochos of (the deme) Anagyrous: 150 drachmas.

M. Crosby, Hesperia 10 (1941) 14, no.1, lines 40–52

1 The resulting income was one of the normal forms of *polis* revenue.
2 See **229**.
3 This is clearly a long-term aim; the more modest aim of meeting the expenses of the democracy occurs in the summing-up at VI.1.
4 The War against the Allies (see **339**), defeat in which effectively ended the second Athenian empire.
5 See **257**.
6 Grandson of the fifth-century general Nikias, see **161B**.
7 That is, in the records of previous years.

278. The estate of the father of Demosthenes

The long legal battle in 363–361, fought by Demosthenes (later a leading politician, see Ch.34) to recover his patrimony from his guardians, has fortunately left us with an account of its remarkably diverse contents.

'So the size of the estate is clear from these depositions in particular. For three talents is the assessment on fifteen talents and that is the *eisphora* which they were prepared to pay. But you will see even more clearly if you listen to an account of the estate itself. For my father, men of the jury, left two workshops, both with very skilled workmen; there were 32 or 33 sword-makers, worth up to five or six minas and in no case less than three,[1] from whom he drew a yearly revenue of 30 minas clear; and there were 20 furniture-workers, held as surety for a debt of 40 minas, who produced twelve minas clear for him. And then there was up to a talent in money out on loan at a drachma (per mina per month), on which the interest each year came to more than seven minas. (10) And this was the amount of productive capital which he left, as these men themselves will admit; the sum of the principal is four talents and 5,000 drachmas and the income for one year is 50 minas. Apart from all this, he left ivory and iron, which the workers used, and wood for furniture worth up to 80 minas, dye and copper bought for 70 minas, a house worth 3,000 drachmas, furniture, plate, gold ornaments and clothing, my mother's apparel, all this worth up to 10,000 drachmas, and in the house 80 minas in money. (11) This then is what he left in hand; in addition there was a maritime loan[2] to Xouthos of 70 minas, 2,400 drachmas with the bank of Pasion,[3] 600 with that of Pylades, 1,600 in the hands of Demomeles the son of Demon, a talent or so out on loan also in two hundreds or three hundreds. And the sum again of these moneys is more than 8 talents and 50 minas. You will find if you look that it all comes to up to fourteen talents.'

Demosthenes XXVII (*Against Aphobos* A) 9–11

1 The jury will have assumed that the men are slaves.
2 See **281**B.
3 See Isager and Hansen, *Aspects,* 175 and 225.

279. Private wealth

Despite the fact that Athens was a democracy, the attitude of the *dēmos* to great wealth was ambiguous, expecting money to be spent on communal purposes (see **142** and **144**), but worshipping an Alkibiades (see **219**). Demosthenes, prosecuting Meidias for insulting behaviour, appealed to the ideology which lay behind the expectation – but Meidias was acquitted.

'This then is how I have conducted myself towards you, but how has Meidias conducted himself? He has never been the head of a *symmoria*,[1] despite the fact that no one has deprived him of any of his inheritance, that from his father being substantial. (158) So in what way is he outstanding, what are his services and his great outlays? I do not see, unless this is what one considers – he has built such a large house at Eleusis that it overshadows everyone else in the area, he takes his wife to the Mysteries or anywhere else she wants to go with the white pair from Sikyon, and himself struts around the *agora* with three or four hangers-on, talking about beakers and drinking-horns and cups so that passers-by can hear. (159) I do not know how the things which Meidias owns in luxury and excess benefit the mass of Athenians; but I do see that the insults he perpetrates, in his pride in his possessions, affect many of us at random. You ought not indeed ever to respect or admire such behaviour or to judge a man's desire for respect by such criteria – whether a man builds a splendid house or owns many maid-servants or much furniture; you should rather consider the man whose splendour and desire for respect appears in the fields in which the whole mass of you have a share; and you will find that none of these fields concerns him.'

Demosthenes XXI (*Against Meidias*) 157–159

1 See **312**.

280. Land and debt

The picture drawn by Demosthenes of a wealthy élite at Athens concerned with ostentatious display is borne out by the evidence of *horoi* from Attika, markers to indicate that a piece of land is mortgaged; it is clear since the work of M. I. Finley, *Studies in Land and Credit in Ancient Athens* (New Brunswick, 1952); 'Land, debt and the man of property', *Political Science Quarterly* 68 (1953), 249–68, that land was mortgaged not to raise capital for productive enterprises, but to provide money for conspicuous expenditure.

Horos on land (put up as security) for the dowry of Hippokleia daughter of Demochares of (the deme) Leukonoion: one talent; by whatever it is worth in excess it is hypothecated to the members of (the *phylē*) Kekropis, to the members of the family (*genos*) of the Lykomidai, to the members of (the deme) Phlya.

M. I. Finley, *Land and Credit*, 160 no. 146

281. The grain trade

The vital importance of imported grain to Athens is clear from the fact that it was a fixed item on the agenda of one meeting of the *ekklēsia* each month (see ?Aristotle, *Ath. Pol.* 43.4); not surprisingly, the litigation arising out of the system for financing the process provides a large part of the subject matter for the speeches on private law matters in the Demosthenic corpus; on the system, see G. E. M. de Ste Croix, 'Ancient Greek and Roman maritime loans', in H. Edey and B. S. Yamey (eds.), *Debits, Credits, Finances and Profits* (London, 1974), 41, making it clear that the maritime loan was a standard institution by the late fifth century.

(A) 'Indeed all your other benefactors have been useful to us for a period, but if you look you will see that Leukon helps us continually, and by supplying a commodity of which our *polis* most stands in need. (31) For you are clearly aware that we use more imported grain than anyone else. Now the grain which comes in from the Black Sea is equal in amount to the whole of what arrives from the other *emporia*. This is not surprising; for this is the result not only of the fact that this area has the largest supply of grain, but also of the fact that Leukon is its ruler and has granted exemption from taxes to those who convey grain to Athens and proclaims that those sailing to you load first. For, possessing exemption for himself and his children, Leukon has granted it to all of you. Now consider what this amounts to. (32) For he exacts a thirtieth from those who export grain from his kingdom; now around 400,000 *medimnoi* of grain come here from his kingdom – one can see this from the return in the hands of the *sitophylakes*;[1] so he gives us 10,000 *medimnoi* in 300,000 and about 3,000 in the remaining 100,000. (33) Now, so far is he from depriving the *polis* of this gift that, having created an additional *emporion*, Theudosia, which those who sail thither say is in no way inferior to the Bosporos,[2] he has granted the exemption to you there also. Although there is much I could say, I ignore all the other ways in which Leukon and his ancestors have helped you; but when there was a shortage of grain the year before last, not only did he send you enough grain, he sent you so much that there was a surplus of fifteen talents in money, of which Kallisthenes had the administration.'[3]

Demosthenes xx (*Against Leptines*) 30–33

(B)   Contract
Androkles of (the deme) Sphettos and Nausikrates of Karystos lent Artemon and Apollodoros of Phaselis 3,000 drachmas of silver to go from Athens to Mende or Skione and thence to the (Crimean) Bosporos, but, if they wish, (only) as far as Borysthenes (Olbia) on the left-hand side of the Black Sea, and back to Athens, at a rate of 225 drachmas per thousand, but if they set sail from the Black Sea for the Hieron after the heliacal rising of Arcturus[4] at a rate of 300, on a security of 3,000 Mendaian amphoras[5] of wine, which will sail from Mende or Skione on the twenty-oared ship of which Hyblesios is *naukleros*. (11) And they put this down as security, not owing any money to anyone else on its security, nor will they make any further borrowing on its security. And they will convey all the goods acquired by way of trade in the Black Sea back to Athens on the same ship. And if the goods come safe to Athens the borrowers will repay the lenders the money due under the contract within twenty days after their return to Athens, in total except insofar as all those on board jointly agree to jettison something or if they have to hand over anything to an enemy; otherwise they will pay in total. And they will provide the security to the lenders to hold unencumbered, until

they repay the money due under the contract. (12) And if they do not make repayment within the agreed time, it will be legal for the lenders to pledge or sell the security for their current value. And if some of the money due to the lenders under the contract is still not recovered, the lenders will be able to claim from Artemon and Apollodoros, from their entire landed property and from their entire maritime assets, wherever they may be, as if they were people who had lost a suit and were overdue for payment; and it will be possible for one or both of the lenders to claim. (13) And if they do not get into the Black Sea, having remained in the Hellespontos for ten days after the heliacal rising of Sirius,[6] if they have discharged their cargo anywhere where the Athenians do not have an agreement over *sylai*[7] and have returned from there to Athens, they are to pay the interest due under the contract the year before. And if the ship on which the goods are travelling suffers some disaster, but the security is saved, what survives is to belong jointly to the lenders. And on these matters nothing is to have greater authority than the contract. Witnesses: Phormion of (the deme) Peiraieus, Kephisodotos of Boiotia, Heliodoros of (the deme) Pithos.

?Demosthenes xxxv (*Against Lakritos*) 10–13

1 Supervisors of the grain supply, attested at a number of Greek *poleis*, apart from Athens.
2 That is, the Crimean Bosporos, Leukon's kingdom.
3 The money presumably accrued from sale of the surplus.
4 After mid-September, when the weather began to worsen; the Hieron lay at the entrance to the Bosporos.
5 The size of the container known as an amphora varied from community to community.
6 In July.
7 See **83** with n.1; absence of an agreement over *sylai* signified that the lenders could not distrain on the security once it had been discharged.

282. The supply of 'miltos'

The Athenians not only took steps to make sure that the grain they needed arrived, they also saw to the availability of *miltos* (red ochre, a waterproof paint for shipbuilding and therefore a strategic necessity). We possess copies of a sequence of decrees (of between 400 and 350), passed by the tiny communities of Karthaia, Koresos and Ioulis on the island of Keos, all of them very much under the thumb of Athens. None of the decrees is identical with any other, though there is much overlap; we give the one passed by Koresos; the one passed by Karthaia is very fragmentary, the one passed by Ioulis requires in addition that all *miltos* made be sold to Athens (Koresos may have made such a provision earlier) and provides for an exemption from taxation, the details of which are unfortunately missing.

Theogenes proposed: that the *boulē* [and the *dēmos* of Koresos agree, concerning the request put by the Athenian] envoys, that the export of *miltos* [to Athens should take place] as in the past. And so that the *psēphismata* [formerly passed by the Athenians] and the Koresians about the *miltos* should be enforced, let it be exported on the ship [designated by the Athenians and on] no [other] ship; and let the producers pay [to the *nauklēroi*] a *naullos* (transport charge) of one obol per [talent]. And if anyone exports on another ship [let him be liable to . . .?]. And let this *psēphisma* be inscribed on a stone *stēlē* and [placed in the sanctuary of] Apollo and let the *nomos* be (enforced) as previously. [Let information] be lodged with the *astynomoi*,[1] and let the *astynomoi* submit the matter to a law court [for adjudication within 30] days; let whoever makes a denunciation or gives information [receive half? . . .]; and if the informer is a slave, if he belongs to the exporters, [let him be free and receive three-] quarters, and if he belongs to someone else, let him be free [and receive . . .?]. Let there be transfer of law-suits to Athens for whoever makes a denunciation or gives information.[2] If the Athenians [pass any other *psephismata*] on the safeguard of the *miltos*, let [the *psēphismata*] come into force from the moment of their arrival. Let the [producers] pay the tax of one-fiftieth to the collectors of the tax. Let the Athenians [be invited] to receive hospitality (*xenia*) at the *prytaneion* till tomorrow.

Tod no.162

1 Local officials.
2 A practice reminiscent of the fifth-century empire, see **134** n.7.

283. Isolation from foreigners

Precisely in the period when Athens was becoming more cosmopolitan than ever and perhaps more dependent on the wealth of foreigners, Plato longed to restrict the activities of the most common visitor to Athens, who came to make money and in so doing enriched Athens.

Now the first type of visitor and one who in all periods makes his visits for the most part in summer, like birds of passage – the majority of this type comes by sea just like a bird, trading in order to make money and visiting other *poleis* in the summer season; the officials established for the purpose must receive such men in *agorai* and harbours and public buildings outside the *polis*, taking care that none of these *xenoi* introduces any innovation[1] and administering justice to them uprightly, dealing with them as need arises, but as little as possible. (Plato goes on to deal

531

with those whom we should call tourists, ambassadors and a category of visitors peculiar to his ideal *polis*.)

Plato, *Laws* (xii) 952D–953E[2]

1 Compare **56**.
2 Compare 915C.

284. The 'polis' and trade

In a long and important passage, worth reading in its entirety (*Politics* (vii) 1326 a 16–1328 b 23), Aristotle lays down in outline the characteristics of an ideal *polis*. In contrast to Plato's authoritarian dream, Aristotle's is an attainable ideal and he provides a lucid and sensible discussion of size of population, size of territory, position in relation to the sea, possession of a navy, character of population and basic requirements. Although in the passage we quote Plato's concerns (see **283**) return, there is also a greater, albeit uneasy, awareness of the role of foreigners and trade in the life of a *polis*; Aristotle also assumes at the outset that a *polis* will contain a large number of slaves, *metoikoi* and *xenoi*, and accepts that, in a large *polis*, *metoikoi* and *xenoi* may usurp citizenship; for this and other reasons he wishes to limit the size of a *polis*, though he recognises that a trading community will be a large one.

And among necessary concerns (for a *polis*) is the acquisition of whatever happens not to be available there and the export of whatever is produced in surplus; for the *polis* must engage in trade for its own sake and not for that of others;[1] but those who do provide their service as an *agora* for everyone do so in order to raise revenue. But a *polis* which does not need to engage in this kind of grasping activity does not need to have an appropriate *emporion*. But since as it is we observe that many areas and *poleis* possess ports and harbours conveniently situated for the *polis*, so as not to occupy the same *astu* nor to be too far off and to be defended by walls and other defences of this kind, it is clear that if there is any benefit to be derived from the possession of ports and harbours, this benefit will accrue to the *polis*, while it is easy to exclude any harmful influence by proclaiming and laying down by *nomos* who may and who may not have dealings with each other.

Aristotle, *Politics* (vii) 1327 a 25–40

1 By serving as an entrepôt; contrast the pride of Isocrates in this role played by Athens (**276**).

285. Class and status

The distance travelled by Athens in the course of her development can be seen most clearly in the fact that in seeking examples of the exclusion of *banausoi* (see 13) from the political heart of the *polis*, Aristotle has to go to Thessaly (a similar regulation obtained at Thebes, see *Politics* (III) 1278 a 25).

And it is proper that below this place (the *akropolis*) there should be created an *agora* of the kind which is customary in Thessaly, which they call the free *agora*; this is the one which must be kept clear of all merchandise and no worker or farmer or anyone else like that approach it unless summoned by the *archontes*. The place would acquire a certain cachet if the gymnasium of the older men was also situated there; for it is proper for this institution also to be divided according to age, and for some of the *archontes* to spend some time with the younger men and for the older men to pass their time near the (seat of the) *archontes*. For being under the eyes of the *archontes* best creates true respect and the reverence appropriate to free men. But it is necessary for the *agora* for merchandise to be quite distinct from this one and separate, with a position convenient for the things brought in by sea and for those from the *chōra*.

Aristotle, Politics (VII) 1331 a 30–1331 b 4

286. The revenues of the 'dēmos'

Another measure of the development of Athens may be found not so much in the simple fact that the *Poroi* of Xenophon, composed in Athens in the 350s, is the only treatise on public finance to have come down to us from antiquity – for in truth it is very naive – but in the fact that the treatise is designed to enable every Athenian to live without working (see 277A), the classic aristocratic ideal. Xenophon, however, clearly believed in the practicability of his proposals and ended his tract with a passionate advocacy of a policy designed to secure peace, arguing no doubt rightly that more visitors would come to Athens in time of peace and that war was expensive, less plausibly that merely by eschewing war, behaving well towards others and deploying moral suasion, Athens would secure her interests.

(1) I myself have always thought that a *politeia* reflects the character of the leading men (of the *polis*). But some of the leading men at Athens have said that they recognise justice no less than other men, but that owing to the poverty of the masses they are forced to be somewhat unjust as far as the *poleis*[1] are concerned. This made me think whether by any means the *politai* might be maintained entirely from their own land, which would certainly be the justest way. I felt that, if this were so, they would be relieved of their poverty, and at the same time cleared of the suspicion with which they are regarded by the Greeks.

(2) Now as I consider my ideas, one thing seemed clear at once, that the *chōra* is by its nature able to provide ample revenues. So that the truth

of what I say may be recognised, I shall first describe the nature of Attika.

(3) The extreme mildness of the seasons here is shown by the actual products. At any rate, plants that would not even grow in many places bear fruit here. Not less productive than the land is the sea around the land. And the good things which the gods send in their seasons all begin earlier here and finish later than elsewhere. (4) And the land is not only outstanding in the things that bloom and wither annually, but has good things that last for ever. For there is an abundance of stone, from which beautiful temples and altars are made, and magnificent statues of the gods. Many Greeks and *barbaroi* have need of it. (5) Again, there is land that bears no fruit if sown, and yet, when quarried, provides keep for many times the number it would support if it grew grain. And there is silver below ground, certainly the gift of divine providence: at any rate, although there are many nearby *poleis* by land and sea, into none of them does even a thin vein of silver ore extend.[2]

(6) One might reasonably suppose that the *polis* lies at the centre of Greece and even of the whole inhabited world. For the further we are from her, the more unbearable is the cold or heat we meet with; and everyone who wishes to cross from one end to the other of Greece passes Athens as the centre of a circle, whether he goes by water or by land. (7) Then too, though Athens is not wholly sea-girt, all the winds bring her the goods she needs and she exports whatever she wishes as if she were an island; for she lies between two seas. And she receives a great deal by way of overland trade as well; for she is part of the mainland. Further, on the borders of most *poleis* live *barbaroi* who trouble them; (8) but even the *poleis* which are neighbours of Athens are remote from the *barbaroi*.

(II) All these advantages, as I have said, are, I believe, due to the *chōra* itself. But consider what would happen if in addition to enjoying the blessings that are indigenous, we first of all looked after the interests of the *metoikoi*.[3] For in them we have one of the very best sources of revenue, in my opinion, since they are self-supporting and, so far from receiving payment for the many services they render to *poleis*, they pay a special tax. (2) I think that we should look after their interests sufficiently if we abolished on the one hand those disabilities which do not profit the *polis* and seem to be a mark of dishonour for the *metoikoi*, and on the other hand the service of *metoikoi* as hoplites along with the citizens (*astoi*). For the danger to someone on service is considerable; and it is a big thing to be away from their children and homes. (3) And the *polis* too would be better off if the *politai* served with each other rather than, as happens at the moment, have Lydians and Phrygians and Syrians and other *barbaroi* of all sorts drawn up with them; for there are many such among the *metoikoi*. (4) In addition to the advantage of these men being removed from the levy, it would also enhance the reputation of the *polis* if the Athenians were seen to trust themselves rather than foreigners for their fighting. (5) And I think that if we gave the *metoikoi* a share in the other things in which it is an honour to share and in particular in service in the cavalry, we should make them better disposed towards us and at the same time make the *polis* stronger and greater. (6) Then, since there are many vacant houses and plots within the walls, if the *polis* gave the right of *enktēsis* to those who intended to build, who applied and seemed suitable,[4] as a result I think that more and more worthy people would wish to live at Athens. (7) And if we established an office of *metoikophylakes* like that of *orphanophylakes*[5] and there was some additional honour for those who displayed the largest number of *metoikoi* in their care, this also would make the *metoikoi* better disposed and, it seems likely, all those without a *polis* would wish for the status of *metoikos* at Athens and increase her revenues.

(III) I shall now explain how the *polis* is also the pleasantest and most profitable as a place of trade. For in the first place, then, it has the best and safest anchorages for ships, where it is possible for people to run into port and remain without fear in bad weather. (2) But on the other hand also, in the majority of *poleis* it is necessary for traders to convey goods of some kind away, since they have coins which are useless elsewhere; but in Athens more useful things are to be found to export than anywhere else and if they do not wish to convey any goods away, even if they export coins, they will be exporting a marvellous object of trade. For wherever they dispose of it they will everywhere get much more than their outlay. (3) And so if someone offered prizes to the supervisors of the port for whoever dealt with disputes most equitably and most swiftly, so that someone who wished to sail off was not prevented, as a result many more would come here and more eagerly too.[6] (4) It is also an excellent and fine thing to honour traders and *nauklēroi* with front seats in the theatre and sometimes offer public *xenia* to those who seem to benefit the *polis* by means of their substantial ships and cargoes. For being honoured in this way they would hasten to us as to friends, not only for the sake of gain but also for the honour. (5) And the more people who settled or came here, the greater, clearly, would be the amount imported and exported or re-exported, sold or rented out, raised in dues.

(6) Now for such increases in our revenues as these there is no need to incur any additional expenditure or do anything except pass favourable *psēphismata* and look after their interests. But in the case of the other sources of revenue which I think could exist, I recognise that some outlay will be necessary in order to acquire them. (7) But I am not without hope

that the *politai* would pay taxes readily for such purposes, thinking how much the *polis* paid when it sent help to the Arkadians under the command of Lysistratos, how much when it served under Hegesileos.[7] (8) I know that triremes are often sent out at great expense and that this expense is incurred when it is on the one hand quite unclear whether it will be for better or for worse, on the other hand quite clear that people will never get back what they pay and will never share in any success. (9) But they would never make so good a purchase as with the money they advanced for the outlay I envisage. For someone who paid an *eisphora* of ten minas, drawing three obols a day, would get almost 20 per cent, as on a maritime loan;[8] someone who paid five minas, over $33\frac{1}{3}$ per cent. (10) But most Athenians would get more in a year than they would contribute; for those who advance a mina will get nearly two minas in revenue, and this on an investment at home, which is regarded as the safest and most enduring of human institutions. (11) In fact, I think that many *xenoi* also would contribute if they were going to be recorded as benefactors for all time and that there would even be some *poleis* anxious for inclusion. And I hope that some kings and tyrants and satraps would wish to share in such a reward. (12) Now when the money was available for the outlay it would be a fine and excellent thing to build lodgings for *naukléroi* around the harbours in addition to the existing ones, and places suitable for traders for buying and selling and also public lodging houses for visitors. (13) And if houses and premises for tradespeople were built in Peiraieus and in the *astu*, they would be at the same time an ornament to the *polis* and a source of substantial revenues. (14) And I think it would be a good idea to see whether, just as the *polis* has triremes which it owns, it would be possible for it to acquire also merchant vessels for itself and rent them out with guarantors like other public property. For if this also should seem feasible, a substantial income would accrue therefrom. (Xenophon turns to the mines, see **161** and **277**.)

Xenophon, Poroi i–iii

1 Of the second Athenian empire; Kos, Chios, Rhodes and Byzantion had just rebelled, see **339**.
2 The island of Siphnos had silver mines, but they were not worked after the archaic period; the only other major source of silver in the Greek world was in Thrake (see **132** and **327**).
3 See **160**.
4 For the link between citizenship and land-holding and for the rare grants of the right to own land, *enktēsis*, made by Athens and other *poleis*, see Austin and Vidal-Naquet, *Economy*, 96.
5 Guardians for *metoikoi*, like guardians for orphans.
6 It looks as if this proposal of Xenophon was actually implemented, with the

creation in about 350 of special commercial courts, deciding cases within a
month. (These courts also existed on Thasos.)
7 In 366 (or 364) and 362/1.
8 See **281**B. Xenophon here alludes to his long-term plan of providing three
obols a day for all *politai*, see **277** n.3.

287. A financial stratagem

No other schemes as elaborate as those of Xenophon are attested; but fiscal
problems were common in Greek *poleis* and we give one example of a means of
overcoming such problems, in effect a forced loan at a nominal rate of interest.
The silver raised was used to strike the only issue of large silver ever produced by
Klazomenai; and it is interesting that the need for the expedient was caused by the
use of mercenaries (see Diod. xv.18.2–4 for the probable occasion), paid in the
first instance by their commanders. It is also worth remarking that the *Poroi* of
Xenophon and the *Economics* (of the period of Alexander the Great) handed down
with the Aristotelian corpus are examples of a genre of literature that flourished
in the fourth century, that of technical handbooks; the little work of Aeneas
Tacticus (see **299**) also belongs in this class.

The Klazomenians, owing mercenaries twenty talents in pay and being
unable to find it, were giving the commanders four talents in interest
each year. And since they failed to reduce the principal, and went on
spending in vain, they struck an iron coinage of twenty talents, with the
face-value of the silver. This they distributed proportionately among the
wealthiest in the *polis*, and received from them silver to the same
amount. Through this expedient, private individuals possessed a currency which was good for their daily needs, and the *polis* was relieved
of its debts. Next, they paid interest out of revenue to those who had
advanced the silver[1] and little by little distributed repayment among
them proportionately and got back the iron coins.

[Aristotle] *Economics* II.2.16b

1 Presumably less than the 20 per cent per annum paid to the mercenary
commanders.

30 War and revolution

The wholesale devastation of Attika after the fortification of Dekeleia by the Spartans (see **229**) had been something new in Greek warfare; but the years from 394 to 386 saw the devastation of much of the north-east Peloponnesos (even the sanctuary of Perachora in the territory of Corinth was fortified, at some point before 371, see R. A. Tomlinson, *Annual of the British School at Athens* 64 (1969), 155) and Boiotia was ravaged by the Spartans in the 370s. It is not surprising that such sufferings were accompanied by an exacerbation of existing conflicts between democrats and oligarchs or that the fourth century saw a resurgence of tyranny as a general phenomenon (see **317** Intro.), quite apart from the spectacular tyranny of Dionysios of Syracuse and its aftermath (**294–297**). Even Athens was now haunted by a fear of tyranny (see **25B**).

At the same time, the use of mercenaries (see **257** and **287**, also **298**) came to be taken for granted, not least in internal strife. A casual notice in Polyaenus (a writer of the second century A.D. on stratagems), relating to the Corinthian War, is revealing: 'Iphikrates was in Corinth; learning that the opposite side intended to bring in some mercenaries by night from Sparta . . .' (III.9.45). These are probably the remains of Xenophon's Ten Thousand (see **252**); but with Persian money available, the practice was often repeated.

One reaction to the troubles of the fourth century and the ambitions of the great powers was the resuscitation or creation of leagues of small communities, usually ethnically related; the development looks forward to the Hellenistic period. At the same time the gloomy succession of Common Peaces (**263**), even if they were primarily instruments of domination by one great power or another, because of their provision in principle for autonomy, created a presumption that a *polis* should be free, a presumption not without influence when the Greek world was faced with Philippos II and his successors (Chs. 33–4).

288. Disruption of harvests in Boiotia

After the Spartan attempt to hold the *akropolis* of Thebes had ended in failure, Agesilaos set out to ravage the territory of Thebes in an attempt to reduce her to submission (compare **270**). Exploiting the separatist tendencies of the *poleis* of Boiotia, he based himself on Thespiai in 378 (Xen. *Hell.* v.4.38 and 41) and invoked the support of Tanagra in 377 (*ibid.* 49).

The Thebans were now suffering greatly from lack of grain, since they had not harvested their crops for two years; so they sent some men and two triremes to Pagasai for grain, allowing them ten talents. But while they were buying the grain, Alketas the Spartan, who was holding Oreos, manned three triremes, taking care that no news should get out. And when the grain was being brought across, he captured it and the ships and took alive no less than 300 men.

Xenophon, Hellenika v.4.56

289. Indestructible Plataiai

The will to survive of the *polis*, even in the face of terrible odds, appears clearly from the case of Plataiai, twice dissolved and twice re-established (see **62**).

Twice it happened that they were driven from their homes and then taken back to Boiotia. For in the war between the Peloponnesians and the Athenians, the Lakedaimonians reduced Plataiai by siege;[1] but it was restored during the peace which the Spartan Antalkidas established between the King of the Persians and the Greeks,[2] and the Plataians returned from Athens. But a second disaster was destined to befall them. There was no open war with the Thebans; in fact the Plataians claimed that the peace held as far as they were concerned, because when the Lakedaimonians seized the Kadmeia they had no part either in the plan or in its execution.[3] But the Thebans maintained that as the Lakedaimonians had themselves made the peace and then broken it all alike were freed from its terms. The Plataians, therefore, looked upon the attitude of the Thebans with suspicion, and maintained strict watch over their *polis*. Those whose fields were at a distance from the town did not go even to these for the whole day but, knowing that the Thebans were accustomed to conduct their assemblies with everyone present and at the same time to prolong their discussions, they waited for their assemblies and then even those whose farms lay farthest away looked after their lands at their leisure. But Neokles, who was at the time *boiōtarchos* at Thebes, being aware of the Plataian trick, proclaimed that every Theban should attend the assembly armed, and at once led them, not by the direct way from Thebes across the plain, but along the road to Hysiai by

Eleutherai and Attika, where not even a lookout had been placed by the Plataians; the plan was to reach the walls about noon. The Plataians, thinking that the Thebans were holding an assembly, were in the fields and cut off from the gates. With those caught within the *polis* the Thebans came to terms, allowing them to depart before sunset, the men with one garment each, the women with two. What happened to the Plataians on this occasion was the opposite of what happened to them formerly when they were captured by the Lakedaimonians and Archidamos. For the Lakedaimonians reduced them by preventing them from getting out of the town, building a double wall; the Thebans on this occasion by preventing them from getting within the wall. The second capture of Plataiai occurred two years before the battle of Leuktra, when Asteios was *archōn* at Athens (373/2). The Thebans destroyed all of the *polis* except the sanctuaries, but the method of its capture saved the lives of all the Plataians alike, and on their expulsion they were again received by the Athenians. When Philippos after his victory at Chaironeia[4] introduced a garrison into Thebes, one of the means he employed to humble the Thebans was to restore the Plataians to their homes.

Pausanias IX.1.3–8

1 See **184** and **186**.
2 See **263**.
3 See **268** Intro.
4 See **349**.

290. 'Stasis' at Corinth

The outbreak of the Corinthian War had been marked by a democratic revolution at Corinth (Diod. XIV.86.1; see **254**); as the war developed into one of attrition, a group in Corinth began to advocate peace.

But the Argives and Athenians and Boiotians and those of the Corinthians who had had a share in the money from the King[1] and had been chiefly responsible for the outbreak of the war realised that if they did not get rid of those who had begun to incline towards peace, the *polis* would be in danger of once more going over to Sparta; so they undertook to organise a massacre. And first of all they planned the most impious thing imaginable; for other people, even if someone is legally condemned to death, do not execute him during a festival. But they chose in advance the last day of the (festival of Artemis) Eukleia for the slaughter, when they thought that they would catch most people in the *agora*. (3) When the signal was given to those who had been told whom it was necessary to kill, they took their swords and struck them down, some as they stood in groups, others as they sat, others in the theatre, others even while they were serving as judges. When the plot was realised, the best men fled, some to the statues of the gods in the *agora*, others to the altars; at that point the conspirators, without any trace of piety and without any respect at all for legality, some giving orders and others obeying, killed their enemies even on holy ground, so that even some of those who were not being attacked, but were law-abiding men, were horrified at the impiety. (4) In this way many of the older men were killed; for they happened rather to be in the *agora*; but the younger men, since Pasimelos had suspected what was going to happen, were undisturbed in the Kraneion. And when they heard the uproar and some of those who had escaped from the plot reached them, they thereupon rushed up onto Acrocorinth and beat off the Argives and others who attacked them. (5) While they were considering what to do, the capital fell from a column although there was no earthquake or wind. And when they sacrificed, the omens were such that the priests said that it was better to go down; and at first they left the territory of Corinth with the intention of going into exile; but when their friends and mothers and brothers came and put pressure on them and some of those who were in power swore an oath, undertaking that they would suffer no harm, some of them then returned home.

Xenophon, Hellenika IV.4.2–5

1 See **254**; also **263** n.4.

291. The 'dioikismos' of Mantineia

Sparta not only used the King's Peace (**263**) to detach the *poleis* of Boiotia from Thebes, she also used her power in the Peloponnesos to break up the *polis* of Mantineia into its constituent villages.

When affairs there[1] had been settled as they wished, the Spartans decided to punish those of their allies who had attacked them during the war or been better disposed towards the enemy than towards Sparta and arrange things so that they could not be disloyal. So first of all they sent to the Mantincians and ordered them to pull down their wall, saying that they would not otherwise trust them not to join the enemy. (2) For they said that they had observed that they had sent corn to the Argives when they were fighting against them and that sometimes they would not join them on a campaign, alleging a truce as an excuse, and that when they did follow, they were useless allies. They also said that they realised that the Mantineians were resentful if the Spartans had some success and delighted if they suffered any misfortune. They also said that their treaty with the Mantineians which had been made for thirty years after the battle of Mantincia[2] had run out this year. (The Spartans attacked and Mantineia capitulated after a siege.) (5) But the Spartans said that they would not make peace unless the Mantineians split up into villages (*kōmai*). The Mantineians, thinking that they had no choice, agreed to do this also. (6) And when those who favoured Argos and the leaders of the *dēmos* thought that they would be killed, Agesipolis' father[3] persuaded him to grant them safe conduct if they left the *polis*; there were sixty of them. And the Spartans stood on either side of the road, beginning at the gates, holding their spears, watching those who came out. And despite the fact that they hated them they kept their hands off them with less difficulty than the oligarchs among the Mantineians. I cite this as a remarkable example of discipline. (7) The wall was then destroyed and Mantineia split up into four parts, which had been the original settlements. And at first they were angry, since they had to destroy their existing houses and build others; but when those who had estates were living nearer to them, since these estates were around the villages (*kōmai*), and they were under an aristocracy and were rid of the obnoxious demagogues, they were pleased with what had happened. And the Spartans sent them not one single commander (*xenagos*),[4] but one for each village; and they joined up much more readily from the villages than when they were under a democracy.[5]

Xenophon, Hellenika v.2.1–7*

1 In Corinth, see **263**.
2 In 418, see **205**.
3 Pausanias (see **245**), exiled in 395.
4 See **50B**.
5 Not surprisingly, the Mantineians provided help to Sparta after the battle of Leuktra (Xen. *Hell.* VII.4.18 = **273**); but they opposed Theban ambitions in the Peloponnesos despite the fact that they had re-synoikised meanwhile (VI.5.3; VII.5.1), see S. and H. Hodkinson, *Ann. Br. Sch. Athens* 76 (1981), 239.

292. Sparta and the 'stasis' in Phleious

After the King's Peace, the Spartans were induced by exiles from Phleious to procure their return; this was eventually achieved by force of arms and a temporary garrison (Xen. *Hell.* v.3.25); the early stages of the process are very revealing on the impact of a great power on the politics of a small one.

(A) When the exiles from Phleious realised that the Spartans were investigating how each of their allies had behaved towards them in the war, they thought that their opportunity had come, went to Sparta and explained that as long as they were at Phleious the *polis* had received the

Spartans within the walls and had followed wherever they led; but since they had been exiled, the Phleiasians would not follow them anywhere and refused to receive the Spartans within their gates, while accepting everyone else. (9) So when the *ephoroi* heard this they thought that the matter demanded attention. And sending to the *polis* of the Phleiasians they said that the exiles were friends of the *polis* of the Lakedaimonians and were in exile without having committed any crime. But they said they wished to arrange their return not by force but by agreement. When the Phleiasians heard this they were afraid that if the Spartans marched against them some of those within would let them into the town. For there were many relatives of the exiles within and people otherwise well disposed towards them and, as is true in the majority of *poleis*, people who wanted revolution and the restoration of the exiles. (10) So because of such fears the Phleiasians voted to receive back the exiles and restore them the property over which there was no dispute and to pay its value from public funds to any who had bought their property; and they agreed that if there was any dispute between the two groups it should be decided in court. And this then is what was done concerning the Phleiasian exiles at that stage.

Xenophon, Hellenika v.2.8–10

(B) But the *polis* of the Phleiasians insolently refused any of their rights to the returned exiles. It behaved in this way because it had been praised by (the Spartan king) Agesipolis for quickly providing a great deal of money for him for his campaign and because it thought that with Agesipolis away Agesilaos would not march out against it, it seemed impossible that both the kings would be away from Sparta at the same time. For the exiles asked that disputes should be judged in an unbiased court; but the Phleiaisians forced the cases to be settled in the *polis*. And when those who had returned asked what sort of a case it was when those who were guilty were also the judges, they paid no attention. (11) Thereupon, those who had returned went to Sparta to complain about the conduct of the *polis*, along with some of those who had not been exiled, but who were prepared to say that many of the *politai* did not think that they were getting their deserts. Angered by this, the *polis* of the Phleiasians fined everyone who had gone to Sparta without the *polis* sending them. (12) Those who had been fined were reluctant to return home, but stayed in Sparta and explained that those who had forced this through were those who had exiled them and had excluded the Spartans, those who had bought their property and were using force to retain it; they had now arranged for them to be fined as well, so that in the future no one would dare to go and expose what was happening in the *polis*. (13) And since the Phleiasians really did seem to be behaving in an insolent way, the *ephoroi* proclaimed an expedition against them. This was not displeasing to Agesilaos; for the friends of Podanemos, who were among those who had returned from exile, were the *xenoi* of his father Archidamos, the friends of Prokles the son of Hipponikos his own *xenoi*.

Xenophon, *Hellenika* v.3.10–13

293. More 'stasis' in the Peloponnesos

The Common Peace of 375/4 (Xen. *Hell.* vi.2.1), which left Thebes bloody but unbowed, meant as a result a weakening of Spartan authority in the Peloponnesos; Diodorus' picture of the consequences, although no doubt somewhat lurid, is likely to be on the whole true to the pattern of what occurred.

Now after autonomy had been granted to every *dēmos*, the *poleis* entered a period of great disturbance and *stasis*, especially those in the Peloponnesos. For having had oligarchic institutions and now making foolish use of the possibilities of democracy, they exiled many of the best men and condemned them by bringing trumped-up charges against them. And so falling into *stasis*, they were guilty of expulsions and confiscations of property, particularly against those who had been leaders of their countries during the *hēgemonia* of the Lakedaimonians. For at that time they had exercised authoritative control over the *politai* and later when the mass of the *dēmos* acquired its freedom it gave no quarter. And first of all the exiles of the Phigaleians[1] got together and seized the place called Heraia, a stronghold. Starting from there, they attacked Phigaleia and since as it happened they did so when the Dionysia festival was being celebrated they fell unexpectedly on those who were seated in the theatre; they killed many and persuaded some to join in their folly and then retreated to Sparta. And the exiles from Corinth, many of whom were living among the Argives,[2] attempted to return; they were received into the *polis* by some associates and friends, but were denounced and surrounded; because they were about to be seized and feared the maltreatment which would follow their capture, they killed each other. The Corinthians, blaming many of the *politai* for having participated in the attempt with the exiles, killed some and exiled others. And in the *polis* of the Megarians, certain individuals attempted to change the *politeia* and were overcome by the *dēmos*; many were killed, some were exiled. Likewise also among the Sikyonians certain individuals attempted a revolution and having failed were killed. And among the Phleiasians many who had been exiled seized a stronghold in the *chōra* and collected a band of mercenaries; there was a battle with those in the *polis* and in the victory of the exiles over 300 of the Phleiasians were killed. But later, when their sentries betrayed the exiles, the Phleiasians won and killed over 600 of them; the rest they compelled to leave the *chōra* and flee to Argos.[3]

Diodorus xv.40

1 The context makes it clear that anti-Spartan democrats have taken control of this small *polis* in the Peloponnesos.
2 See **263** and **290**.
3 Presumably as being democrats; for Phleious see **292**.

294. Dionysios establishes his tyranny in Syracuse

However brilliant the Syracusan success against the Athenians in 415–413 (**220–226**), neither Athens nor any other Greek state represented as much of a constant and serious danger to Sicily as did Carthage. It was principally the Carthaginian threat which lay behind the establishment and the success of Sicily's first wave of 'military monarchs' (**118**; Andrewes, *Tyrants*, 131–6), in the late sixth and early fifth centuries. And at the end of the fifth century with its democratic interludes much the same happened again; fear of Carthage and the chronically unstable socio-political situation combined to throw up, in Syracuse, a man with the ambition and ability to seize supreme power and hold on to it for almost 40 years.

On Dionysios see Andrewes, *Tyrants*, 137–42; A. G. Woodhead, *The Greeks in the West* (London, 1962), 87–94; Davies, *Democracy*, 201–11; and **295**, below.

. . . When the misfortune which had befallen Akragas became generally known,[1] such a panic seized Sicily that some of the Sicilian Greeks decamped to Syracuse and others removed their children, their wives and their entire possessions to Italy. Some of the people of Akragas had evaded capture, and when they reached Syracuse they attempted to lodge accusations against their *stratēgoi*, maintaining that the ruin of Akragas was on account of their treachery. And it so happened that the Syracusans too came in for criticism from the rest of the Sicilian Greeks, on the grounds that they were choosing the sort of leaders who might very well be responsible for the destruction of the whole of Sicily. Nevertheless, when a meeting of the assembly was convened in Syracuse, nobody, despite the great fears hanging over them, had the nerve to offer any advice about the war. However, while everyone was at a loss what to do, Dionysios the son of Hermokrates[2] came forward and accused the *stratēgoi* of betraying their cause to the Carthaginians; and he attempted to stir up the masses to exact their punishment, urging them not to wait upon the futile procedure which the *nomoi* prescribed but to pass judgment then and there. The *archontes* then fined Dionysios, as the *nomoi* required, for creating an uproar; but Philistos – the man who later wrote the *History*[3] – paid the fine, and encouraged Dionysios to speak out

545

with whatever he had to say. Indeed Philistos, who was a very wealthy
man, added that if they wanted to go on all day fining Dionysios he
would put up the money on his behalf. So from then on, full of
confidence, Dionysios kept stirring up the masses and, throwing the
assembly into confusion, he accused the *stratēgoi* of having taken bribes to
jeopardise the safety of Akragas. His accusations extended also to the rest
of the most distinguished Syracusans, whom he represented as friends of
oligarchy, and so he advised them to elect as *stratēgoi* not the most able
men but rather those most favourably disposed towards the *dēmos*[4] . . .
(92) By tailoring every word of this demagogic harangue to suit the
prejudices of his audience – as well as his own purposes – Dionysios
whipped up the assembly into a frenzy of anger: the *dēmos* had long hated
the *stratēgoi* for what it considered to be their bad conduct of the war and
now, stung into action by the words of Dionysios, immediately dismissed some of them from office and chose other *stratēgoi* – including
Dionysios, who had acquired a reputation for exceptional courage in the
battles against the Carthaginians and was therefore greatly admired by
the Syracusans.

So, with his hopes thus raised, Dionysios devoted all his ingenuity to
becoming tyrant of Syracuse. For example, after taking up his office (as
general) he neither participated in the meetings of the *stratēgoi* nor
associated himself with them in any way, and while acting in this fashion
began to spread reports that they were negotiating with the enemy; he
did so because he hoped in this way to strip them of their power
completely and establish himself as sole general. The most respectable of
the *politai* began to suspect why he was acting in this manner, and spoke
disparagingly of him whenever there was a public gathering; but the
common mob, ignorant of his intentions, applauded him, declaring that
at long last the *polis* had found a reliable champion . . . (93) And when
letters were brought from Gela requesting the dispatch of more troops,
Dionysios seized this opportune means of achieving his own purpose, for
he it was who was dispatched with 2,000 infantry and 400 cavalry, and he
lost no time in reaching Gela. The *polis* of Gela was temporarily in the
charge of Dexippos the Spartan, a Syracusan appointee. Dionysios
arrived there to find the wealthiest men in a state of *stasis* with the *dēmos*;
so he accused them in an assembly, secured their condemnation, put
them to death, and confiscated their property. And with the money thus
raised he proceeded to pay the city's garrison-troops, under Dexippos'
command, the wages which were owing to them, while to his own men,
who had come with him from Syracuse, he promised to pay double the
wage that the *polis* had determined. By this means he won the loyalties
both of the troops in Gela and of his own forces. He also won the support
of the Gelan *dēmos*, who considered him responsible for their liberation;

for in their envy of their most able fellow-citizens they stigmatised the superiority of such men as, from their point of view, despotism. Consequently they sent off envoys to sing his praises in Syracuse and announce decrees in which they had honoured him with rich gifts . . .

(Dionysios himself then returned to Syracuse, reiterated his claim that his fellow-*stratēgoi* were traitors, and made known his intention to resign from office.) (94) . . . The Syracusans were agitated at what Dionysios had said, and word of it spread through the whole army; but for the moment each man, full of anxiety, departed to his own home. However, the assembly met again the following day, and Dionysios won strong support when he lodged all sorts of accusations against the *archontes*, as well as stirring up the *dēmos* against the *stratēgoi*. Finally some of his audience cried out that he should be appointed general with full powers (*stratēgos autokratōr*), without waiting until the enemy were storming the walls: the magnitude of the war, it was argued, made necessary such a *stratēgos*, through whom their cause could prosper; as to the accusations of treachery, they were irrelevant to the present situation and would be discussed at another assembly. It was also pointed out that when the 300,000 Carthaginians had been conquered at Himera, Gelon had been *stratēgos autokratōr*.[5] (95) And soon the masses, as they invariably do, swung towards the worse choice, and Dionysios was appointed *stratēgos autokratōr*. Thereupon, with everything having gone according to plan, he proposed a decree to double the troops' pay: if this were done, he maintained, they would all be more eager for the fight ahead; and there was no need for anxiety about the money, for it would be easy to raise.

After the assembly had been adjourned, quite a few of the Syracusans began to condemn what had been done – as if it had not been their own sovereign decision;[6] for as their thoughts turned to their own prospects they began to imagine the sort of régime which was to come. In their desire to ensure their liberty, these men had unwittingly set up a despot in Syracuse. But Dionysios, for his part, was concerned to forestall any change of heart by the mob, and so began to look for some means of asking for a bodyguard; for if this were granted it would be easy to set himself up as tyrant. He therefore issued immediate orders that all men of military age up to forty should bring rations for thirty days and report to him under arms at Leontinoi – which at this time was a Syracusan garrison-post, and full of exiles and foreigners: these men were eager for revolution, and Dionysios hoped to enlist their support; he also expected that the majority of the Syracusans would not even come to Leontinoi. Then, while he was encamped at night in the countryside he made out that there was a conspiracy against him and had his servants raise an outcry and uproar; he then took refuge on the *akropolis* (at Leontinoi) and passed the night there, keeping fires burning and summoning the most trustworthy of his soldiers. At daybreak, when the Syracusans had arrived *en masse* at Leontinoi, he proceeded to implement his plan by delivering a long and plausible speech, and thus persuaded the mob to grant him 600 soldiers of his choice to be his guard. He did this, it is said, in imitation of Peisistratos the Athenian[7] . . . and thus put his tyranny into effect. (96) He immediately selected more than 1,000 Syracusans, men with no property but no shortage of boldness and spirit, equipped them with costly armour and raised their hopes with lavish promises. The mercenaries he won over by summoning them and talking to them in a friendly manner. He also made changes in the military posts, entrusting them to his most faithful supporters . . . and lost no time, either, in marrying the daughter of Hermokrates, the man who had conquered the Athenians;[8] he also gave his own sister in marriage to Polyxenos, Hermokrates' brother-in-law. This he did because he wanted to establish a relationship with such a distinguished family – and so strengthen his tyranny. Afterwards he summoned the assembly and got rid of his most influential opponents, Daphnaios and Demarchos.

And so Dionysios, once a clerk and an ordinary private citizen, had become tyrant of the largest *polis* in the Greek world; and he maintained himself in power until his death, by which time he had been tyrant for 38 years.[9]

Diodorus XIII.91–96.4*

1 Its capture by the Carthaginians, in their invasion of 406 (Diod. XIII.85–91.1).
2 *Not* Hermokrates 'who had conquered the Athenians', who is mentioned later: see below with n.8.
3 Philistos of Syracuse (*c*.430–356), contemporary and friend of Dionysios, wrote a *History of Sicily*.
4 See 303A.
5 See 118.
6 See the remarks of Diodotos in 210C.
7 See 69.
8 See 218, 221, etc.
9 I.e. 405–367.

295. Further measures of Dionysios

The activities of Dionysios are chronicled by Diodorus, in the interstices of events in mainland Greece, in Books XIII–XV; and we pick out two passages which illustrate his methods of consolidating and extending his power.

(A) In Sicily, Dionysios, the tyrant of the Sicilian Greeks,[1] having now concluded peace with the Carthaginians,[2] planned to devote himself more to strengthening his tyranny – on the assumption that now that the

Syracusans had been relieved of the war they would have plenty of time in which to attempt to recover their liberty. Dionysios realised that the Island³ was the strongest part of the *polis* and could be easily defended, so he spent a lot of money on a wall to divide it from the rest of the *polis*; high towers were built into the wall at frequent intervals, while in front of it were places of business and colonnades capable of accommodating the populace. He also constructed on the Island, at great expense, a fortified *akropolis*, to serve as a place of refuge in an emergency; and within its wall he enclosed the dockyards which are connected with the small harbour called Lakkion. These dockyards, with space for 60 triremes, had a blocked-off entrance through which only one vessel at a time could come in. As to the territory of Syracuse, he picked out the best of it and presented it as gifts to his friends and his officers; the rest he distributed in equal portions to *xenoi* and *politai* alike – including in the designation '*politai*' the manumitted slaves, whom he named New Citizens (*neopolitai*). He also distributed the houses amongst the mob, except for the houses on the Island, which he gave to his friends and his mercenaries.

And when it seemed to him that he had organised his tyranny satisfactorily he led out his forces against the Sikels: he was eager to bring all the independent peoples under his control, but the Sikels especially, because of their previous alliance with the Carthaginians.⁴

Diodorus XIV.7.1–5

(B) Dionysios realised that it was his mercenaries who were most hostile to him;⁵ he was afraid, indeed, that they might cause his downfall, so first of all he arrested Aristoteles, their commander. Then, after the rest of them had approached him *en masse* and under arms to demand their wages, he declared that he was sending Aristoteles back to Sparta, to be tried by his fellow-citizens;⁶ and in lieu of wages he offered the mercenaries, who numbered about 10,000, the *polis* and territory of Leontinoi. They gladly agreed to this, because the land was so good, and after dividing it out amongst themselves in allotments they made their home in Leontinoi. As for Dionysios, he recruited other mercenaries, and relied on them and on his freedmen for the maintenance of his rule.

After the disaster suffered by the Carthaginians, the survivors from those Sicilian *poleis* which had been enslaved gathered together, recovered their native lands and revived in strength. In Messana Dionysios settled 1,000 men from Lokroi and 4,000 from Medma,⁷ together with 600 Messenians from the Peloponnesos who were exiles from Zakynthos and Naupaktos.⁸ However, when he realised that the Spartans were offended that the Messenians whom they had driven out were being settled in a *polis* with such a significant name, he moved them from

Messana and gave them a place by the sea, chopping off some of the territory of Abakaine and annexing it to theirs. The Messenians named their *polis* Tyndaris, and by living in mutual concord and enfranchising many new *politai* their numbers soon exceeded 5,000.

Diodorus XIV.78.1–6

1 Diodorus actually wrote 'tyrant of the (native) Sikels', which is nonsense; but given Syracusan dominance (note, e.g., XIII.112.1), hindsight could certainly represent Dionysios as tyrant of the Sikeliotai (Sicilian Greeks).
2 See Diod. XIII.114.1.
3 Ortygia.
4 See further XIV.7.6–9 (end).
5 The occasion is 396, after another (unsuccessful) Carthaginian invasion.
6 Sparta had been supporting Dionysios since 404 (XIV.10.2–3 and *passim*).
7 Both Lokroi and Medma are in southern Italy, in fact.
8 They had been settled in Naupaktos by the Athenians, see **169**.

296. The condition of Sicily before the arrival of Timoleon

At his death in 367/6 Dionysios was succeeded by his son of the same name, who ruled comfortably and competently enough for a decade. From 357/6 onwards, however, Dionysios II had too many persistent problems for comfort – first the philosopher zealot Dion (on whom see Westlake, *Essays*, ch.15) and then the emergence of more tyrants and renewed Carthaginian offensives; and by the 340s the general situation in Sicily, described here by Plutarch, cried out for the intervention of Timoleon (**297**).

The state of affairs in Syracuse before Timoleon's journey to Sicily was as follows. No sooner had Dion driven out Dionysios the tyrant than he was himself killed, by treachery, and those who had helped him to liberate Syracuse were divided amongst themselves. The *polis* was thus continually exchanging one tyrant for another; it was in fact virtually deserted, thanks to the multitude of its problems; and as for the rest of Sicily, part of it, because of the wars, was ruined and already entirely without *poleis*, while such *poleis* as there were had been taken over by *barbaroi* of mixed races and unemployed soldiers, who readily fell in with the successive dynastic changes. In the tenth year (of his exile)[1] Dionysios collected together some mercenaries, drove out Nysaios, who was at that time master of Syracuse, recovered control of affairs and established himself afresh as tyrant. That he had been robbed, by a small force, of the greatest tyranny of all time was inexplicable; but more inexplicable still was his return from humble exile to become master of the men who had thrown him out. Accordingly, those of the Syracusans who remained in the *polis* were the slaves of a tyrant who was unreasonable at the best of times but who now, after all his many misfortunes, had become a savage. The best and most distinguished Syracusans, however, turned to Hiketas the ruler of Leontinoi, put themselves in his hands, and chose him as their general for the war – not because he was actually preferable to any of the acknowledged tyrants but because he was their only resort, and they could have some faith in a man who was a Syracusan by birth and possessed forces to match those of Dionysios.

(2) Meanwhile the Carthaginians had invaded Sicily with a large army and were casting their shadow over these developments. This alarmed the Sicilian Greeks, who wanted to send envoys to Greece to seek help from the Corinthians – not only because they trusted them on account of their kinship[2] and the benefits which they had often received from them in the past, but also, more generally, because the Corinthians were reckoned to be lovers of liberty and haters of tyrants, having waged most of their wars, and the greatest ones, not for their own imperialist aggrandisement but for the liberty of the Greeks.

Plutarch, *Timoleon* 1–2.2

1 I.e. 346.
2 Syracuse was a Corinthian *apoikia*: see **20**.

297. Timoleon's solutions

The response of the Corinthians, when asked for help by Syracuse in 345 (**296**), was to send them a modest force of mercenary troops under the command of 'an elderly nonentity' (Davies, *Democracy*, 240): Timoleon son of Timodemos. Timoleon's anti-tyrannical credentials, in point of fact, were fairly spectacular, as in the 360s he had arranged the assassination of his elder brother, at that time tyrant in Corinth itself (see Plut. *Tim.* 3.4–7.1); nonetheless, neither the Corinthians nor anybody else could reasonably have predicted the transformation which he was to bring about in Sicily over the following decade – ridding it, however temporarily, of predators both internal (the tyrants) and external (the Carthaginians), and making valiant efforts to reshape and revive its whole political, social and demographic structure. His prestige and his power were enormous – in fact, he was a tyrant himself in all but name.

With Plutarch's account, below, compare Diodorus XVI.82–83. And see further H. D. Westlake, *Timoleon and his Relations with Tyrants* (Manchester, 1952); *id.*, *Essays*, chs.16 and 17; R. J. A. Talbert, *Timoleon and the Revival of Greek Sicily 344–317 B.C.* (Cambridge, 1974); Davies, *Democracy*, 240–2.

When he had become master of the citadel (of Syracuse),[1] Timoleon neither repeated the experience of Dion[2] nor spared the place on account of its beauty and expensive buildings; instead, to guard against the suspicion which had brought first slander and then ruin upon Dion, he issued a proclamation that any Syracusans who wished should appear with iron tools and help in the demolition of the tyrants' fortifications. And once they had reflected that that day with its proclamation marked the securest possible beginning of liberty, the Syracusans all turned up to overthrow and demolish not only the citadel but the houses and tombs of the tyrants as well. As soon as he had levelled off the site Timoleon housed the jury-courts there – thus pleasing the *politai* by making democracy triumph over tyranny.

However, in the *polis* which he had taken there were not *politai* enough: some had died in the wars and the civil disturbances, while others had fled from the tyrants into exile . . . Timoleon and the Syracusans therefore decided to write to the Corinthians and urge them to send settlers to Syracuse from Greece . . . (23) When these letters from Timoleon had been delivered in Corinth, at the same time as the arrival of Syracusan envoys who begged them to be solicitous for Syracuse and to become its founders (*oikistai*) again, the Corinthians did not seize the opportunity for aggrandisement or appropriate Syracuse for themselves. Instead, in the first instance, they visited the sacred Games in Greece and the greatest of the festivals, and proclaimed by heralds that they, the Corinthians, had overthrown the tyranny in Syracuse and driven out the tyrant, and now called upon Syracusans and any other Sicilian Greeks who wished to settle in Syracuse as free and autonomous *politai*, allotting its land between themselves on just and equal terms. Secondly they sent messengers to Asia (Minor) and the islands – where they had been told most of the scattered exiles were living – and invited them all to come to Corinth, assuring them that the Corinthians, at their own expense, would provide them with *stratēgoi* and ships and ensure them safe passage . . . However, when these men had assembled in Corinth there proved to be too few of them, and so they begged to be allowed to take fellow-settlers both from Corinth itself and the rest of Greece. This increased their numbers to as many as 10,000, whereupon they sailed to Syracuse. But by this time large numbers of people from Italy and Sicily, too, had flocked to Timoleon; and when their numbers had risen to 60,000, according to Athanis,[3] Timoleon divided out the land between them, and sold the houses, for 1,000 talents – thereby, at one and the same time, making it possible for the original Syracusans to purchase their own houses and supplying the community, by this device, with ample funds . . .

(24) And seeing Syracuse starting to revive and fill up with people in this way, with its *politai* streaming into it from all sides, Timoleon was eager to liberate the other *poleis* as well, and to root out tyrannies from Sicily altogether. He therefore marched into their territories and compelled Hiketas to sever his links with the Carthaginians and agree to

demolish his citadels and live in Leontinoi as a private individual. As for Leptines, who was tyrant of Apollonia and numerous other strongholds, he surrendered himself when in danger of being taken by force; Timoleon spared his life and sent him off to Corinth, thinking it a fine idea to have the tyrants of Sicily on show to the Greeks in the mother-city, living the lives of humble exiles[4] . . .

(35) So this was how Timoleon rooted out the tyrants and put an end to their wars. He had found the whole of the island reduced to savagery by its troubles and hated by its inhabitants; yet his measures made it so civilised and so universally desirable that others sailed to Sicily to live in the very places from which, previously, their own *politai* used to flee. Akragas and Gela, for example, great *poleis* which had been devastated by the Carthaginians after the Attic (i.e. Peloponnesian) War, were now resettled – Akragas by Megellos and Pheristos and their associates, from Elea,[5] and Gela by Gorgos and others, who sailed from Keos with a party which included (some) original Gelan *politai*. To such men as these Timoleon not only offered safety after the great wars and a peaceful place in which to settle, but he was so zealous in supplying everything else for them that he was revered as a founder (*oikistēs*). Everyone else felt the same about him, too; and no conclusion of a war, no legislation, no settlement of territory and no constitutional arrangements seemed complete without Timoleon on hand to apply the finishing touches, just like a master craftsman finishing off some piece of work with a touch of divinely-inspired and fitting grace.

Plutarch, Timoleon 22–24* and 35

1 For what led up to this see Plut. *Tim.* 9–21.
2 Dion had been criticised for not demolishing it (Plut. *Dion* 53.1–2).
3 A fourth-century historian.
4 See further, on the tyrants, *Tim.* 30–34.
5 Elea (the Roman Velia), a Phokaian *apoikia* in southern Italy (Hdt. 1.167.3–4).

298. The use of mercenaries

Two vignettes may be presented to show the casual use of mercenaries by Greek *poleis* in the fourth century, relating (A) to the tiny *polis* of Kleitor in Arkadia in the period just before the foundation of the second Athenian empire and (B) to a destitute Corinth in the 360s.

(A) (Sphodrias),[1] hearing that the Kleitorians were fighting the Orchomenians and using a force of mercenaries, came to an agreement with them that the force should join him if he needed it.

Xenophon, Hellenika v.4.36

(B) Now the Corinthians, thinking that it would be difficult to survive, having been defeated earlier by land and now having the Athenians as enemies in addition, decided to collect mercenaries, both infantry and cavalry.

Xenophon, Hellenika VII.4.6

1 See **268**.

299. The security of the 'polis'

One of the most remarkable texts of the fourth century to survive is the *Poliorketika*, or 'Siegecraft' of an Aeneas who is probably the Stymphalian mentioned by Xen. *Hell.* VII.3.1; it is mainly devoted to preventing the capture of a *polis*, and its unconscious assumptions throw the prevalence of political struggle and *stasis* into sharp relief.

(A) One must deal with those in the *polis* who wish to reverse the established order in the way already mentioned. But it is very important to achieve *homonoia*[1] among the mass of the *politai* for the time being, winning them over by a variety of means and relieving debtors by a reduction or abolition of interest, in particularly dangerous situations even remitting part of the capital – all of it, even, if necessary – since men of this kind who are waiting their opportunity are very dangerous; those who lack the necessities of life are to be well provided for.

Aeneas Tacticus XIV.1

(B) In a *polis* which is not of one mind and where people are suspicious of each other, it is necessary to possess foresight and take care over mass excursions to watch a torch-race or a horse-race or other contests, and over any festival or procession which takes place outside the *polis*, with public participation and under arms, and over public and ceremonial hauling-up of ships, and over obsequies of the dead. For it is possible on an occasion like this for one side to be overcome.

Aeneas Tacticus XVII.1

(C) If there are any exiles, one must proclaim what penalties attach to any citizen (*astos*), *xenos* or slave who absconds. (6) And if anyone associates with any of the exiles or with anyone sent by them, or sends or receives letters, there must be a penalty or fine. And there must be inspection of outgoing and incoming letters, before men who are designated beforehand. (7) One must make a list of those who have more than one set of arms and armour, and no one may export any, or receive them as a pledge. No one may hire soldiers or hire himself out without permission of the *archontes*. (8) No *astos* or *metoikos* may sail off without a passport and announcement must be made in advance that ships are to anchor by those gates which are designated in an attached list.

Aeneas Tacticus x.5–8

1 Compare 241.

300. The foundation of Megalopolis

Given Spartan hostility to combinations between *poleis*, evinced in the insistence on the detachment of the *poleis* of Boiotia from Thebes and of Corinth from Argos, and in the attempted dismemberment of the Chalkidian confederacy in the 380s, it is not surprising that one reaction to the Spartan defeat at Leuktra was the creation of combinations between *poleis* – now against Sparta; the first step was taken by the Arkadians, and it is a measure of Xenophon's sympathy for Sparta that he manages to ignore the Arkadian initiative in founding Megalopolis in his account of the aftermath of Leuktra (*Hell.* vi.5.1–14). The reality of Arkadian unity emerges interestingly from the decree reproduced below, B, which in form perhaps betrays Athenian influence.

(A) It was with this sort of end in mind[1] that the Arkadians synoikised and Epameinondas of Thebes might fairly be called the *oikistēs* of their *polis*; for it was he who encouraged the Arkadians to synoikise, and sent 1,000 picked Thebans and Pammenes to defend them, in case the Spartans attempted to prevent the foundation (of Megalopolis). (The list of *oikistai* and *poleis* involved in the foundation follows.)

Pausanias VIII.27.2[2]

(B) God. Good fortune. It was resolved by the *boulē* of the Arkadians and the Ten Thousand[3] that Phylarchos son of Lysikrates of Athens should be *proxenos* and benefactor of all the Arkadians, himself and his descendants. These were the *dāmiorgoi*[4] . . . (a list of 50 *dāmiorgoi* is added, of whom ten come from Megalopolis, five each from Tegea, Mantineia, the Kynourioi, Orchomenos, Kleitor, Heraia and Thelphousa, three from the Maenalioi and two from Lepreon).

Tod no.132

1 Self-defence.
2 The account in Diodorus xv.72.4 differs over date (368/7, but 371/0 according to Pausanias viii.27.8) and number of communities involved.
3 The name of the Arkadian *ekklēsia*, probably derived from a notional figure for the number of hoplites.
4 The chief federal officials.

301. Independence for Messenia

The most dramatic consequence of Leuktra was the recovery of independence by Messenia, after some 400 years (see **45**), which changed for ever the balance of power within the Peloponnesos. It also encouraged historians to write histories of the early history of Messenia, which are entirely fictional.

(A) But Epameinondas, who was ambitious by nature and anxious for everlasting glory, advised the Arkadians and the other allies to refound Messene, which had been destroyed many years before by the Lake-daimonians and was in a suitable position for a base against Sparta. When everyone agreed, he sought out those of the Messenians who remained and included anyone else who wished in the foundation and re-founded Messene with a large population. So, dividing up the land among them and building the town, he restored a great Greek *polis* and gained a great reputation among all men.

Diodorus xv.66.1

(B) And then after their victory at Leuktra the Thebans sent messengers to Italy, Sicily and Euesperides[1] and summoned all Messenians every-where back from their wanderings to the Peloponnesos. And they came quicker than one might have expected, from love for their land and country and because of the hatred of the Spartans which had remained with them . . . (27.9) And the Messenians returned to the Peloponnesos and were restored to their own land 287 years after the capture of Eira, when Dyskinetos was *archōn* at Athens, in the third year of the hundred and second Olympiad, when Damon of Thourioi won for the second time.[2] The time during which the Plataians were in exile from their own land was not a long one,[3] nor that during which the Delians lived at Adramyttion after they had been ejected from their country by the Athenians.[4] And the Minyan Orchomenians, driven from Orchomenos by the Thebans after the battle of Leuktra, were restored to Boiotia by Philippos the son of Amyntas, along with the Plataians. And when Alexander deprived the Thebans themselves of their *polis*, Kassandros the son of Antipatros founded Thebes again not many years later. The Plataian exile seems to have been the longest of those mentioned, but even it did not last for more than two generations. But the Messenians were wanderers outside the Peloponnesos for some 300 years,[5] in the course of which they clearly lost none of their original customs, nor did they forget the Doric dialect; rather they have preserved its purity down to our own time more than the other Peloponnesians.

Pausanias IV.26.5; 27.9–11

1 Some Messenians had taken refuge at Messana (see **295**) and in Euesperides near Kyrene.

2 In 370/69, the solemnity of the dating echoes that in **184**.

3 See **289**.

4 See Thuc. III. 104.

5 Apart, of course, from those who remained as helots, see **45**. Pausanias looks back to the Second, not the First Messenian War.

302. Protection of democracy

The King's Peace of 387/6 had enshrined the principle of *polis* autonomy, initially to the advantage of Sparta; but when the second Athenian empire was founded in 378/7 (see **269**), it accepted this principle and built on it, describing specific elements of autonomy; an alliance between Athens and Kerkyra of 375 goes one step further, guaranteeing help in the preservation of the existing constitution, in this case democracy. It is another attempt to secure protection in the insecure world of the fourth century

Alliance of Kerkyrans and Athenians for all time. If anyone goes with warlike intent against the land of the Kerkyrans or against the *dēmos* of the Kerkyrans, the Athenians are to help with all their strength, as the Kerkyrans request, as far as possible. And if anyone goes against the *dēmos* of the Athenians or against the land of the Athenians with warlike intent by land or by sea, the Kerkyrans are to help with all their strength, as far as possible, as the Athenians request. And it is not to be possible for the Kerkyrans to make war or peace without the agreement of the Athenians and the majority of the allies; and they are to behave in other respects according to the *psēphismata* of the allies (the oaths to be sworn by the two sides follow).

Tod no. 127

31 Athenian politics and society

Athenian politics and society in the fourth century, when set beside those of the fifth, show many obvious similarities and continuities but also some interesting and important differences. The restored democracy of 403 survived unchallenged until its enforced removal in 322 by Makedonian *diktat*, but by then it had long been viewed without enthusiasm by the conservative theorists (**303**) and increasingly changed in ethos and practice from the Periklean ideal: the gulf between advice and accountability (**212**) widened (**314**); the methods of practical politics grew less edifying (**305, 310**); and ordinary men needed financial inducement to join in actively shaping their own lives (**304**). Yet the inducement appears to have done its work, for in a diminishing citizen-body proportionately more Athenians came to attend the *ekklēsia* in the fourth century than they had done in the fifth (see M. H. Hansen, 'How many Athenians attended the ekklesia?', *GRBS* 17 (1976), 115–34); and in a less generally aggressive radical democracy we find more willingness now to give scope to professionalism and expertise, especially in the crucial sphere of finance (**307, 309, 311, 313, 315**).

See further: P. J. Rhodes, 'Athenian democracy after 403 B.C.', *Classical Journal* 75 (1980), 305–23.

303. Attitudes to democracy in fourth-century political thought

While enthusiasm for democratic institutions was *rising* amongst ordinary Athenians (see introduction, and **304**), the reverse was true at the more rarified level of political thought. In these extracts Plato, Isocrates and Aristotle discuss in their characteristically different ways – satire (A), sentimental conservatism (B) and logical analysis (C) – some of the theoretical and practical problems, as they conceived them, of democracy, liberty and egalitarianism. With the passage of Isocrates compare the idealisation of monarchy in IX (Euagoras) 49–50 and, in general, the attitude of Xenophon.

(A) (Conversation between Sokrates and Adeimantos)
'Of course democracy, or so I suppose, comes about when the poor

defeat their opponents, killing some and banishing others, and then give the rest equal rights in the *politeia* and the holding of offices – which as a rule, under this system, are filled by lot.'

'That is indeed,' he agreed, 'how a democracy is established, whether achieved by force of arms or by frightening the opposition into retreat.'

'Well then,' said I, 'what sort of society will this be? And for that matter what sort of *politeia* will it have? I ask this because the answer, clearly, will reveal to us the character of the Democratic Man.'

'Clearly.'

'First things first, then: it is of course true, is it not, that (in a democracy) one is free – that the (democratic) *polis* is full of liberty and free speech and that everyone there is free to do what they like?'

'That is what we are told, certainly.'

'And given such freedom it is obvious that each man would arrange whatever mode of private life-style pleased him best.'

'Obviously.'

'So under a democratic *politeia* one would find every sort of human being imaginable.'

'Inevitably, yes.'

'In all probability, then,' said I, 'democracy is the most attractive of all the *politeiai*; just like a dress embroidered with all the different-coloured flowers, all the different characters woven into a democracy would give it a most attractive appearance. Indeed,' I added, 'perhaps for this reason most people would judge it to be the finest *politeia*, just like children and women looking at fine embroidery.'

'Very likely.'

'Well then, my friend,' said I, 'here in a democratic society we have a splendid opportunity to go *politeia*-hunting.'

'Why should that be?'

'Because it will contain all possible types of *politeia*, thanks to the freedom there; and anyone wishing to found a *polis*, as we are doing now, should perhaps be made to visit a democratic *polis* and treat it as a *politeia*-supermarket, picking out for his own foundation whichever model was most appealing.'

'A good idea,' he said. 'There would at any rate be no shortage of examples.'

'In such a *polis*,' I continued, 'there is no compulsion to exercise authority, not even upon those who are capable of so doing; nor for that matter to submit to the authority of others against one's will. One need not fight in wartime, or stop fighting in peacetime, if one has no enthusiasm for a peace which everyone else is observing; and if there is any *nomos* debarring you from holding office or sitting on a jury, you will nonetheless do both if the opportunity arises! (558) It is a marvellously pleasant way of behaving, in the short run, is it not?'

'Perhaps so – in the short run.'
'And then think of the mild and gentlemanly attitude of some of those who have been sentenced in court. Or have you not noticed that in a democracy men condemned to death or exile continue nonetheless to stay where they are, walking about in public, and attracting about as much attention as wandering spirits?'
'Yes,' he said, 'I have often seen this.'
'And as for the solemn principles that we laid down when founding our *polis*, the democratic state is very easy-going here; no splitting hairs, but simply disparagement of the whole business. We said that nobody without exceptional natural gifts would ever become a good man unless he had been educated from earliest childhood in goodness and schooled in all its aspects. But the democratic state grandly tramples all this sort of thing underfoot, setting no store at all by the background and habits of those who seek a public career; provided they declare themselves friends of the masses, that is the only criterion which counts.'
'All very splendid, I'm sure.'
'These then are the characteristics of democracy,' said I, 'and others closely related to them. And it would seem to be a most agreeable form of *politeia*, anarchic and varied, treating all men alike as equal – whether they *are* equal or not.'
'Yes,' he said, 'you paint a familiar picture.'

Plato, Republic 557A–558C

(B) 'Those who directed the *polis* in those days (of Solon and Kleisthenes) did not establish a *politeia* which, while hailed in name as the acme of impartiality and mildness, showed itself to be no such thing in practice, to those living under it; nor was it one which trained the *politai* in such a way that they regarded unruliness as democracy, lawlessness as liberty, outspokenness as equality, and the freedom to do everything that they wanted as happiness. On the contrary it detested and punished such men, and by doing so made every one of the *politai* better and wiser. (21) But what contributed most to the excellence of their government of the *polis* was the fact that of the two recognised kinds of equality – the one which gives the same to everybody and the one which gives each man his due[1] – they did not fail to appreciate which was the more useful: the one which holds that the good and the bad deserve the same treatment they examined and rejected as unjust, (22) preferring the one which rewards and punishes each individual according to his deserts; this was the principle on which they governed the *polis*, not filling official positions by drawing lots amongst everybody but picking out those judged to be best suited for each particular task. They did this because they believed that it would lead to everyone else's emulating the character of those, whoever they were, who were in charge of affairs. (23) Moreover they considered this method of appointment to be more democratic even than the casting of lots: with sortition, it was felt, the issue would be determined by chance, and the offices would often fall to the supporters of oligarchy, whereas by pre-selecting the worthiest men the *dēmos* would have the power to choose those who were most attached to the existing *politeia*.

(26) To put it in a nutshell, the men of that time had resolved that the *dēmos* ought to act like a tyrant – appointing officials, punishing offenders and settling disputes – and that those men who could afford the time and possessed sufficient means should devote themselves to the common good as if public servants, (27) entitled, if they acted justly, to public commendation – no further honours than that – and liable to the severest punishments, mercilessly applied, if they governed badly. And how could there be a more secure or a more just democracy than this, appointing the most able men to public office and giving the *dēmos* sovereignty over them?'

Isocrates VII (*Areopagitikos*) 20–23; 26–27

(c) A fundamental principle of the democratic *politeia* is liberty; this is what one is always told, as if only under a democracy do men have a share in liberty; and every democracy is said to have liberty as its objective. However, one aspect of liberty is to govern and be governed in turn. The popular conception of justice, you see, operates in terms of numbers and not in terms of worth, and by *that* idea of justice the masses must necessarily be sovereign and the decision of the majority final – and indeed in itself an embodiment of justice; for the argument holds that each of the *politai* must have an equal share. And the result of this is that in democracies those without property are more powerful than those with it, because there are more of them, and majority decisions are sovereign. This then is one sign of liberty which all democrats set up as a cornerstone of the *politeia*. Another is the idea that each man should live as he pleases: this, they maintain, is what liberty is for, if *not* living as one pleases means the life of a slave. So here is the second cornerstone of democracy – and from it has come the idea that it is best to be governed by nobody at all, or else, failing that, by everyone in turn; and this is how the principle makes its contribution to equality of liberty.[2]

(1318 a 3) And it is the admittedly democratic concept of justice – the idea of equality for all, numerically – which gives rise to what is thought to be the extreme form of democracy and (rule of) the *dēmos*. It is equality, you see, for the propertyless to have no larger share of government than the propertied; the propertyless alone must not be sovereign, but all equally; in this way the *politeia* would be felt to offer

561

equality and liberty. However, it is the next step in the argument which presents the problem: how is the equality to be achieved? Are the property-assessments of 500 (rich) men to be defined as equal to those of 1,000 (poor) men, so that the 1,000 and the 500 have equal power? Or is democratic equality not to be set up in this manner but instead by a division into classes on a property basis, and then the control of elections and the *dikastēria* by a group drawn equally from the 500 and the 1,000? Will this be the justest *politeia*, in terms of the popular conception of justice, or should it rather operate by counting heads? The democrats maintain, you see, that what the majority decides *is* justice, whereas for the oligarchs justice is whatever those with more property want, for in their view the criterion ought to be the amount of property one owns. Yet both these standpoints involve *in*equality and *in*justice: for the will of the few means tyranny, given the principle – of oligarchic justice – that if one individual owns more than the other men of property he has the right to sole rule; if on the other hand the will of the numerical majority prevails, they will act unjustly, as was said earlier, by confiscating the property of the rich minority! So the sort of equality on which both parties would agree has to be determined by examining their respective definitions of justice. We are told (by the democrats) that the decisions of the majority of the *politai* ought to be sovereign. Let us accept this, then, but with a qualification: since chance has created two component parts of the *polis*, the rich and the poor, let any decision reached by both, or by a majority (of each), be sovereign; but if the two classes carry opposing resolutions let it be the decision of the majority in the sense of the larger property-assessment. If, for example, there are ten rich men and twenty poor ones, and opposing votes have been cast by six of the rich men and fifteen of the poorer men, this means that four rich men have sided with the poor and five poor men with the rich; so then the side with the larger property-assessment, when the assessments of both classes on either side are added together, wins the day.[3] If however the totals fall out equal, this has to be deemed an *impasse* common to both sides, just as it is today if the *ekklēsia* or a *dikastērion* is split and the decision made by casting lots or some such device.

It is extremely difficult, then, to discover the truth about equality and justice. Nonetheless to do so is easier than to dissuade those who are in a position to manipulate it to their own advantage; for it is always the deprived who seek equality and justice, while those in power do not give it a thought.

Aristotle, *Politics* (VI) 1317 a 40–b 17; 1318 a 3–b 5

1 See more fully, C.
2 For what now follows see **126**.
3 On the schematic assumption that rich men will be twice as rich as poor men

(see above) this vote may be expressed as 17 property-units (i.e. (6 × 2) + 5) versus 23 (i.e. (4 × 2) + 15); the latter group thus prevails, satisfying both timocratic and numerical justice. See in general F. D. Harvey, 'Two kinds of equality', *Classica et Mediaevalia* 26 (1965), 101–46, esp. 110–23.

304. Payment for attending the 'ekklēsia'

During the Peloponnesian War period the Athenian authorities had attempted to solve the problem of declining attendance at the *ekklēsia* by use of the 'red rope' (**211**). The latest reference to this, however, dates from 392 (Aristoph. *Ekkles.* 376–379), and we may assume that the punitive approach was abandoned soon afterwards in favour of a positive incentive, pay, which had already been introduced and was presumably already having some effect; certainly in the long term the carrot turned out to be more effective than the stick (see p. 558).

See further: Hignett, *Constitution*, 396–7; M. H. Hansen, *GRBS* 17 (1976), 132–3.

At first the Athenians rejected the idea of payment for attendance at the *ekklēsia*. However, with poor attendances, and the *prytaneis* trying many devices to make the masses attend and ratify proposals by their vote,[1] Agyrrios took the first step by instituting (a payment of) one obol. Subsequently Herakleides of Klazomenai, the so-called 'king',[2] (raised it to) two obols, and then Agyrrios again to three obols.[3]

(62.2) The *dēmos* receives the following payments:[4] a drachma for the ordinary meetings of the *ekklēsia*, and one and a half for the *kuria ekklēsia*.[5]

?Aristotle, Athenaion Politeia 41.3; 62.2

1 More devices, evidently, than the 'red rope'; but we know no details.
2 A native of Klazomenai (in Asia Minor), Herakleides' services to Athens (see for instance Meiggs and Lewis no. 70) secured him Athenian citizenship, and even (according to Plato, *Ion* 541D) election as *stratēgos*.
3 'The increase to 3 obols was recent when Aristophanes produced his *Ekklesiazousai* in the spring of 392, and the whole evolution described in *Ath. Pol.* 41.3 must have occurred within three years, for in view of the financial difficulties of Athens in and after 403 it is unlikely that pay for attendance at the assembly could have been introduced even at the rate of 1 obol until 395' (Hignett, *Constitution*, 396–7).
4 I.e. at the time of writing, the 320s.
5 The *kuria ekklēsia*: see **308**.

305. The demes

Since Kleisthenes, the Attic demes (**76**) had functioned as the 'grass roots' of

Athenian political life; see in brief R. J. Hopper, *The Basis of the Athenian Democracy* (Sheffield Inaugural Lecture, 1957), 13–15. It was here, after all, that Athenian citizenship was grounded in a tangible definition: following Perikles' *nomos* of 451/0 (**128**), which after lapsing during the Peloponnesian War had been re-enacted in 403/2, a *politēs* was, precisely, a man born of two Athenian parents and enrolled amongst his fellow-demesmen at the age of eighteen (?Aristot. *Ath. Pol.* 42.1). Yet as the prerogatives of citizenship had grown ever more desirable in the fifth century, at least one episode, the Egyptian grain affair (**128**), had shown how easily the demes and their registers could serve as a flashpoint for jealousy and victimisation; and in the fourth century it seems to be the clear indication of our sources that this sort of thing increased still further. (In addition to the case illustrated here, B, note the notorious Agasikles: Hypereides IV.3; Whitehead, *Ideology*, 50 and 53.) Evidently further scope for it was provided in 346/5, with the procedure referred to by Aeschines (A, below), created by the *psēphisma* of Demophilos; see most recently on this J. K. Davies, 'Athenian citizenship: the descent-group and the alternatives', *Classical Journal* 73 (1977), 105–21, at p.112.

(A) 'There have been revisions of the registers in the demes, and each of us has submitted to a vote about himself, to determine who is a genuine Athenian and who is not. And for my part, whenever I go to the *dikastērion* and listen to the cases being contested, I see that the same argument always prevails with you: (78) whenever the prosecutor says "Men of the jury, this fellow has been excluded under oath by the men of his deme, relying not on any accusation or testimony against him but on their own personal knowledge", you immediately raise a cheer, believing that the man on trial has no right to be a member of the *polis*. This, I imagine, is because you believe that when anyone has clear personal knowledge of something he does not need argument or testimony as well.'

Aeschines I (Against Timarchos) 77–78

(B) 'As many of you know, Athenians, when this man Euboulides[1] indicted the sister of Lakedaimonios for impiety he failed to secure a fifth of the votes;[2] and it was of course because I gave evidence in that trial – justly, but against him – that he hates me and is therefore attacking me now. Again, gentlemen of the jury, when he was serving on the *boulē*, and (within the deme) was in charge both of the oath and of the lists of the demesmen, what did he do? (9) Well first of all, when the demesmen had gathered together he took up the whole day in making speeches and recording *psēphismata*. This was no coincidence, but deliberately directed against me, so as to delay the vote on my case until as late as possible; and so it did. Those of us demesmen who swore the oath numbered 73, but we did not begin the voting until very late in the evening, with the result that when *my* name was called night had already fallen. (10) There were 60 or so cases at issue, and I was the very last of all those called on that day, by which time the more elderly of the demesmen had gone back to the country; the deme, you see, gentlemen of the jury, lies four and a half miles out of the *astu*, and since the majority live there,[3] most people had left. Those remaining numbered no more than 30; and in that number were all the men that my opponent had set up against me. (11) When my name was called he took the floor and started slandering me, speaking quickly, at length, and in a loud voice – just as now – though without producing a witness in support of his accusations, either from the demesmen or the other *politai*. He called upon the demesmen to strike my name from the register. (12) I insisted that the case be resumed next day, because of the lateness of the hour and because, taken by surprise, I had nobody there to give me assistance: this would give *him* the opportunity to present his case at leisure, bringing forward any witnesses he might have, while I for my part could defend myself in front of all my fellow-demesmen and summon my relatives as witnesses; and I was ready to abide by whatever decision was reached. (13) But he ignored my proposition, beginning at once to hand out votes to those of the demesmen who were (still) present and allowing me no opportunity either to make any defence or to establish any proof of my own. His henchmen came forward and voted. By now it was dark, and Euboulides was handing out two or three votes for each of them to place in the urn! The proof of this is that although no more than 30 men voted, over 60 votes were counted – to universal amazement.

(14) To prove that what I say is true – that the vote did not take place in a quorate assembly and that there were more votes than voters – I shall bring you witnesses. To be sure, I am not in a position to call as witnesses any of my friends, or any other (trustworthy) Athenians, for it was late and I had not asked anyone to be there; but I can resort instead to the testimony of the very men who have wronged me.'

Demosthenes LVII (Against Euboulides) 8–14

1 See also **163D**.
2 Compare **248B** with n.4.
3 The deme in question is Halimous – a 'city' deme in Kleisthenic terms but nonetheless several miles, as we see, from the *astu* (where we gather the deme held its assemblies). Note also that most Halimousioi, or so the speaker claims, still lived in the deme in which their sixth-century ancestors had been first registered. It is hard to assess how far this was generally true.

306. The ephebic oath

Greek warfare in the fourth century, as we have seen (**257, 298**, etc.), underwent several major developments, notably the increased use of light-armed troops and, especially, of mercenaries. Apart from the special case of Sparta, only the Thebans appear to have dug in their heels against this with any real success (270–271), but the Athenians, while compelled to follow the trends as much as anyone else, did at the same time see a need to keep alive for as long as possible the traditional mode of citizen hoplite fighting and a belief in its central place in the life of the *polis*. We may take it that there had always been military training *of some sort* for young Athenian males, whether or not they were actually required at that stage for active service (as in Thuc. I.105.4) or defence duties (Thuc. II.13.7), but in fact it is not until the fourth century, and indeed not until the 330s, that we hear of the *ephēbeia*, a compulsory and standardised two-year programme of military training for citizen youths between the ages of 18 and 20 (see ?Aristot. *Ath. Pol.* 42); this formalisation, very probably the work of the *nomos* of Epikrates in 336/5, will have been one of the consequences of the Greeks' defeat at Chaironeia in 338 (see 349). From then on, therefore, the institution blended the contemporary (as in the non-hoplite elements in the training itself; see *Ath. Pol.* 42.3) with the traditional, as in the solemn oath sworn by all the raw *ephēboi*. We have several versions of it in the literary sources, notably Lyk. *Leok.* 76, but we give here the one which survives on an inscription from the deme Acharnai – cut on the same stone as a copy of the oath allegedly sworn by the Athenians before the battle of Plataiai in 479.

Gods. The priest of Ares and Athena Areia, Dion son of Dion of (the deme) Acharnai, dedicated (this *stēlē*).

The ancestral oath of *ephēboi*, which the *ephēboi* must swear: 'I will not disgrace the sacred arms, nor will I abandon the man beside me wherever I may be stationed. I will fight in defence of what is sacred and holy, and I will not hand on the motherland (to posterity) diminished but greater and better, both as far as I myself am able and with all the others; and I will gladly obey those who govern well, and the established statutes, and those which may be well established in the future; and if anyone sets out to destroy (them) I will not permit it, both as far as I myself am able and with all the others; and I will honour the ancestral rites. Witnesses (to this) are the gods Agraulos, Hestia, Enyo, Enyalios, Ares and Athena Areia, Zeus, Thallo, Auxo, Hegemone, Herakles, boundaries of the motherland, wheat, barley, vines, olive-trees, fig-trees.'

Tod no. 204

307. 'Nomothesia'

The fifth-century Athenian democracy, through the *ekklēsia*, passed both laws (*nomoi*) and decrees (*psēphismata*), apparently indiscriminately; but it would seem that in the fourth century – from the 403/2 restoration, to be exact – a reasonably consistent attempt was made to distinguish between laws and decrees as being enactments on quite different levels, and therefore calling for different procedures both of creation and, when necessary, revision. Building on work on the law-code begun between 410 and 404 (Thuc. VIII.97.2 (see **227B**, end); Lysias XXX), the restored democracy, as we learn here from Andocides, attempted to produce by *nomothesia* a body of legislation permanent, stable and rationalised; and *nomothesia* (the procedure) and *nomothetai* (the officials), operating under progressively refined procedural guidelines, then became a regular feature of the fourth-century *politeia*.

See further: A. R. W. Harrison, 'Law-making at Athens at the end of the fifth century B.C.', *JHS* 75 (1955), 26–35; Rhodes, *Boule*, 49–52; D. M. MacDowell, 'Law-making at Athens in the fourth century B.C.', *JHS* 95 (1975), 62–74 (and *The Law in Classical Athens* (London, 1978), 48–9); M. H. Hansen, '*Nomos* and *psephisma* in fourth-century Athens', *GRBS* 19 (1978), 315–30, and 'Did the Athenian *ekklēsia* legislate after 403/2 B.C.?', *ib.* 20 (1979), 27–53.

'After your return from Peiraieus you decided to forgo revenge and let bygones be bygones; you set more store by the safety of the *polis* than by the righting of private wrongs, so you resolved that both sides should observe an amnesty in respect of what had happened.[1] And in accordance with this resolve you elected twenty men to take charge of the *polis* until the *nomoi* had been laid down – the *nomoi* of Solon and the statutes of Drakon to be in force meanwhile. (82) However, after you had appointed a *boulē* by lot and elected *nomothetai* you began to discover that there were many of the *nomoi*, both those of Solon and those of Drakon, under which, because of earlier events, large numbers of the *politai* were liable to prosecution. You therefore called a meeting of the *ekklēsia* to discuss these matters, and voted that all the *nomoi* should be scrutinised, and the ones which passed this scrutiny then inscribed in the *stoa* (*basileios*). Read out the *psephisma* for me: (83) "It was resolved by the *dēmos*, on the proposal of Teisamenos, that the Athenians be governed in accordance with ancestral practice, using the *nomoi* and weights and measures of Solon and the statutes of Drakon – the ones we used before. Whatever extra (*nomoi*) are necessary shall be inscribed upon tablets by the following *nomothetai* elected by the *boulē*,[2] displayed for all to see before the (statues of the) *epōnymoi*,[3] and handed over to the officials during this present month. (84) However, the *nomoi* thus handed over shall be scrutinised beforehand by the *boulē* and the 500 *nomothetai* elected by the demesmen, when they have sworn their oath; and it shall be open to any private individual who wishes to do so to come before the *boulē* and give his advice on how the *nomoi* might be improved. And when the *nomoi* have been laid down they shall be in the charge of the Council of the Areiopagos, to the end that the officials shall apply only such *nomoi* as are in force. Those *nomoi* which are approved shall be inscribed on the wall, just where they were inscribed previously, for all to see."

567

(85) And so, gentlemen, the *nomoi* were scrutinised, in accordance with this *psēphisma*, and the ones which were approved were inscribed in the stoa.'

Andocides 1 (*On the Mysteries*) 81–85

1 See **245**.
2 Evidently their names were appended, but Andoc. does not give them.
3 The ten heroes after whom the Kleisthenic *phylai* had been named (see **76**, end).

308. Formalisation of 'ekklēsia' agendas

From ch. 43 of the Aristotelian *Ath. Pol.* we learn that in the second half of the fourth century there existed permanent standing orders prescribing the matters to be discussed at different meetings of the *ekklēsia*. (Compare ch. 61.1 on the duties of the *stratēgoi*.) As usual with such information we are left in ignorance on the (to us) central question of when the practice first began; the best and most recent investigation (M. H. Hansen, 'How often did the *ekklēsia* meet?,' *GRBS* 18 (1977), 43-70, esp. 68–70) puts it in the period 362–354. See also Rhodes, *Boule*, 55–7.

The *prytaneis* also give written notice of meetings of the *ekklēsia*. One meeting (in each prytany) is plenary (*kuria*), at which there must be a vote on whether the officials appear to be doing their duties well, and discussions about (the supply of) grain and about the defence of the *chōra*. This is the day also when those who wish to do so initiate impeachments (*eisangeliai*)[1] and when public announcement is made of the inventories of confiscated property and also of claims to inherit properties and (to marry) heiresses[2] – this so that nobody may be in ignorance of any vacant estates. Also, in the sixth prytany (only), in addition to the matters mentioned they take a vote on the question of whether or not to hold an *ostrakismos*;[3] and they hear complaints (*probolai*) against informers – whether Athenians or *metoikoi*,[4] and up to three of each – and against anyone who has failed to fulfil a promise made to the *dēmos*. The second meeting (in each prytany) is the one for petitions, when anyone who wishes to do so may appear as a suppliant and address the *dēmos* on any subject he likes, private or public. The two other meetings (in each prytany) deal with other matters, though the *nomoi* prescribe that these must include three discussions of sacred matters, three connected with heralds and embassies, and three concerning secular matters.

?Aristotle, *Athenaion Politeia* 43.4–6

1 See M. H. Hansen, *Eisangelia* (Odense, 1975).

2 Heiresses (*epiklēroi*): see Lacey, *Family*, 139–47 and *passim*; D. M. MacDowell, *The Law in Classical Athens* (London, 1978), 95–108.

3 See **79**

4 *Metoikoi*: see **160**.

309. The prescripts of 'psēphismata'

The movement towards a more precise and bureaucratic tone in Athenian democratic procedures in the fourth century is reflected in changes and developments not only of substance (e.g. *nomothesia*, **307**) but also of form, as is clear from a simple comparison of the prescripts of fourth-century decrees with those of the fifth century. We juxtapose here a typical example of each, though it should be recognised that there was some scope for variation, especially (and significantly) in the fifth century. One might fairly say that in the fifth century items of relevant information were frequently omitted – for instance in A, below, the secretary's name is not recorded (compare e.g. Meiggs and Lewis nos. 31 and 46), nor, more importantly, the *archōn*-date (compare e.g. **172B**) – whereas in the fourth century an already fulsome preamble was sometimes amplified by still further information in the form of an eye-catching heading (see for instance Tod nos. 167, 173, 198). See further: A. S. Henry, *The Prescripts of Athenian Decrees* (*Mnemosyne* Suppl. no. 49, 1977).

(A) *The fifth century*

It was resolved by the *boulē* and the *dēmos*; (the *phylē*) Antiochis held the prytany; Drakontides was chairman, Diognetos proposed (the motion).

Meiggs and Lewis no. 52, lines 1–2

(B) *The fourth century*

In the year of the *archōn* Chairondas (338/7), in the tenth prytany, (that of the *phylē*) Pandionis; Philippos son of Antiphemos of (the deme) Eiresidai was secretary; on 27 Thargelion, the third of the prytany; the question was put by [- - - - -] of (the deme) Erchia, (chairman) of the *proedroi*.[1] It was resolved by the *dēmos*; Hegesippos son of Hegesias of (the deme) Sounion proposed (the motion).

Tod no. 178, lines 1–5

1 In the fourth century nine *proedroi* took over from the *prytaneis* the job of presiding in the *boulē* and the *ekklēsia*; see Rhodes, *Boule*, 25–8.

310. The 'graphē paranomōn'

The *graphē paranomōn* was a public prosecution – which is to say that any Athenian who felt so inclined could initiate it – of someone who had allegedly framed an illegal or unconstitutional proposal, whether in a law or a decree; a defendant found guilty paid a fine, in addition to seeing his measure annulled, and three such convictions meant disfranchisement (*atimia*). The procedure is first attested for 415 (Andoc. 1.17 and 22; see also **227**) but it became especially characteristic of the fourth century, where as Aeschines says here it was little more than a routine hazard of public life.

See further: M. H. Hansen, *The Sovereignty of the People's Court in Athens in the Fourth Century* B.C. *and the public action against unconstitutional proposals* (Odense, 1974), 28–65; D. M. MacDowell, *The Law in Classical Athens* (London, 1978), 50–2.

'I myself have heard from my own father – a man who died at the age of 95, having shared with the *polis* in every one of its toils, which often in his leisure hours he used to recount to me – that in the early days of the restored democracy[1] one only had to mention '*graphē paranomōn*' to a *dikastērion* for a conviction to be as good as secured. What, after all, is more wicked than a man whose words and actions are unlawful? (192) And the hearings too, so he used to say, were not of the same kind as nowadays: the jurors were far more severe even than the prosecutor himself upon the proposers of illegal measures, and they often used to call the clerk back and have him read out the (relevant) *nomoi* and the (offending) *psēphisma* a second time. Also the proposers of illegal measures used to be convicted if they contravened so much as a single syllable of the *nomoi*; they did not need to transgress the entire statute-book! But the procedure as it is conducted these days is utterly ridiculous: the clerk reads out a statement of the illegality as charged and the jurors' minds wander on to some other matter, just as if they were listening to an incantation, or something in which they had no involvement. (193) And already, thanks to the tricks of Demosthenes, you have accepted a shameful custom in the *dikastēria*. I refer to your allowing the legal procedures of the *polis* to become perverted: the accuser is on the defensive, the defendant fills the role of accuser, and as for the jurors, they sometimes forget what they are there to judge and are obliged to vote on matters which were never theirs to decide. And if by any chance the question at issue is actually broached, by the defendant, his plea is not that the motion was lawful but that once upon a time some other man made an equally unlawful motion yet was acquitted. This, I gather, is the plea in which Ktesiphon has so much faith now.[2] (194) And once the famous Aristophon of (the deme) Azenia had the nerve to boast in court that he had been acquitted in a *graphē paranomōn* 75 times![3] Not so the venerable Kephalos, the man with the reputation of being the staunchest of democrats: he by contrast took pride in the exact opposite, saying that although he had been the sponsor of more *psēphismata* than anyone else he had never once been prosecuted in a *graphē paranomōn*.[4] And this, it seems to me, is the right thing to be proud of, for (in those days) it was not purely the rival politicians who used to prosecute each other in a *graphē paranomōn*, but friends against friends, if any harm to the *polis* was involved. (195) To prove the point, witness the fact that Archinos of (the deme) Koile brought a *graphē paranomōn* against one of his comrades in the return from Phyle, Thrasyboulos of (the deme) Steiria, who had put down some motion which contravened the *nomoi*;⁵ and Thrasyboulos was convicted, for although his services to the state were so recent the jury did not take them into account; their opinion was, you see, that just as on that occasion Thrasyboulos had brought them back from exile, so now, by making an illegal motion, he was driving them out again. (196) But this is not what happens today, far from it: today men prosecuted in a *graphē paranomōn* find themselves championed by eminent *stratēgoi* and by some of those who have been granted free maintenance at public expense.⁶ And if you interpreted this as ingratitude you would have every justification; for if anyone who has been honoured in a democracy – a *politeia* kept safe by the gods and by the *nomoi* – dares to assist those who make illegal proposals he is destroying the *politeia* which did him honour.'

Aeschines III (Against Ktesiphon) 191–196

1 I.e. from 403/2.
2 The defendant Ktesiphon is being prosecuted (in 330) for his proposal that Demosthenes be given a golden crown at the forthcoming Dionysia festival.
3 Aristophon (c.435–c.335) was a leading figure in Athens between 403 and the late 340s; even so it is hard to credit that he was prosecuted in a *graphē paranomōn* more, on average, than once a year! See Hansen, *op. cit.* 31; S. I. Oost, 'Two notes on Aristophon of Azenia', *CPh* 72 (1977), 238–40.
4 Compare Demos. XVIII.251. Kephalos (not to be confused with the father of the orator Lysias: see **244**C) was a democratic politician prominent in the 390s; see **254**B.
5 See **245**.
6 See **73** Intro.; **248**B with n.5.

311. The Forty and the Arbitrators

Ch.53 of the Aristotelian *Ath. Pol.* outlines what might be termed the procedure of first resort in the fourth-century Athenian legal system. Any dispute not settled by *private* arbitration (on which see A. R. W. Harrison, *The Law of Athens* II (Oxford, 1971), 64–6; D. M. MacDowell, *The Law in Classical Athens* (London, 1978), 203–6) could be taken to the 40 tribe judges – an enlarged, latterday version of the circuit-judges of Peisistratos (see below) – who by a financial criterion either decided it on their own authority or passed it to a *public* arbitrator. The system of public arbitration, instituted in 399, was one of a year's compulsory service by all 'veteran' *politai* (i.e. men in their sixtieth year, see below) and evidently derived from the view that men of that age, however ordinary, had perforce acquired the requisite general experience and sagacity. See further Harrison, *op. cit.* 66–8; MacDowell, *op. cit.* 207–11.

The Forty also are appointed by lot, four from each *phylē*, and to them go the other law-suits.[1] Previously there were thirty of them, who used to try cases on a circuit through the demes,[2] but after the oligarchy of the Thirty (Tyrants) they became forty. Up to the sum of 10 drachmas they have the authority to settle cases themselves, but beyond that figure they hand them over to the Arbitrators (*diaitētai*), who then take it up and, if they cannot reconcile the parties, give a decision. If what they have decided is acceptable to both sides and they abide by it, the case is at an end. But if either party appeals to the *dikastērion*, the Arbitrators place the depositions, the challenges and the (relevant) *nomoi* in jars, separate ones for the plaintiff and for the defendant; they then seal the jars, add the Arbitrator's decision written on a tablet, and hand everything over to the four men (of the Forty) who handle the cases of the *phylē* of the defendant.[3] These men then take up the case and bring it before the *dikastērion* – a court of 201 jurors when the sum involved is less than 1,000 (drachmas) and of 401 when it is more than 1,000; and it is not permitted to use *nomoi* or challenges or depositions other than those used in front of the Arbitrator, which have been sealed in the jars. The Arbitrators are men in their sixtieth year.[4]

?Aristotle, *Athenaion Politeia* 53.1–4

1 I.e. other than the suits previously mentioned (ch. 52.2–3) which had to be settled within one month.
2 See **70** and **125**; MacDowell, *op. cit.* 206–7.
3 This of course assumes that the defendant is a *politēs*; for foreigners, who were outside the tribal system, see ch. 58.2 (with Whitehead, *Ideology*, 92).
4 This was 'the year that marked the end of their liability for military service. To be more exact, it was the forty-second year from a man's registration in a deme as an adult citizen' (MacDowell, *op. cit.* 207).

312. The 'eisphora'

Eisphorai were extraordinary capital levies upon the property of the residents, citizen and (free) non-citizen, of Athens and Attika – as well as of several other *poleis* – based on the individual's own declared assessment (*timēma*) of his taxable capital, and spent 'on war and national security' (Demos. xx.18). The history of the institution in Athens is full of problems and controversies, especially as regards the fifth century (see **197** with n.7). But it is clear enough that 378/7, the archonship of Nausinikos, saw a substantive reform of the system – coinciding (uncoincidentally) with the creation of the second Athenian empire (**269**): not only does Polybius, in the passage below, imply that something new happened then, but Demosthenes in 355 could still speak of 'the *eisphora* from (the year of) Nausinikos' (XXII. 44). The taxpayers were divided into 100 groups, called *symmoriai*, each of which represented the same fraction of the total taxable capital and so distributed the burden equitably. The threshold of liability was set lower than that for liturgies (**144**); nonetheless the whole institution took on a quasi-liturgical character from 362 onwards with the *proeisphora*, payment of the whole levy in advance by the 300 richest individuals who then reimbursed themselves from the rest.

See further: C. Mossé, *Athens in Decline 404–86* B.C. (London, 1973), 28.

Who does not know that when the Athenians, together with the Thebans, entered into the war against the Spartans,[1] sending out 10,000 soldiers and manning 100 triremes, they decided to meet the expenses of the war by levying *eisphorai*, and so made a valuation of the whole of Attika, including the houses and the other property? Nonetheless the overall valuation fell short of 6,000 talents by 250.[2]

Polybius II.62.6–7

1 The date is 378/7, when the war which P. mentions began (see Diod. XV.25); the archonship of Nausinikos (*ib.* 25.1, Demos. XXII.44, etc.).
2 I.e. it was 5,750. This figure seems to have served for the rest of the fourth century. Demos. XIV.19, Philochorus *FGrH* 328 F46.

313. General financial organisation and management

Finance is another department of Athenian public life where it is probable that procedural changes were adopted in or soon after 403/2 and quite certain that more followed in the course of the fourth century. During the fifth century all authorised public expenditure had been made from a single central treasury, but under the system described in the Aristotelian *Ath. Pol.* (which was very probably introduced in 403/2) the board of ten Receivers (*apodektai*) conducted a *merismos*, an annual distribution of monies to all the various boards and officials entitled to spend them (?Aristot. *Ath. Pol.* 48.2; Tod no.116, lines 18–23). More significant than that, though, is the fact that we now meet important state treasurers, *elected* to office and holding it for a *four-year* term (see A, below), and two new treasuries or funds in their charge: the stratiotic, or military, and the theoric (B). The inauguration-date and the precise character and function of these funds, particularly the theoric, are obscure matters, but it is plain enough that they were basically identifiable with, respectively, war and peace, so that the question of which of them should siphon off the state's surplus annual revenues became one of the prime political issues of the period (C, D). See further Rhodes, *Boule*, 88–113; Austin and Vidal-Naquet, *Economy* nos.111 and 115.

(A) The officials in charge of the routine administration are all appointed by lot except for the treasurer of the military fund, the commissioners of the theoric fund and the superintendent of the water supply; these are elected by show of hands, and those elected hold office from one (Great) Panathenaia festival to the next.[1] All the military officials too are elected.[2]

?Aristotle, *Athenaion Politeia* 43.1

(B) 'Previously, Athenians, the *polis* used to elect a copy-clerk (*antigrapheus*)[3] who reported once every prytany to the *dēmos* about the revenues. However, because of the trust which you came to place in Euboulos,[4] those who had been elected commissioners of the theoric fund held also – until the *nomos* of Hegemon came into being[5] – the offices of the *antigrapheus* and of the Receivers. In addition they controlled the dockyards, built a naval arsenal, and were surveyors of roads; in fact virtually the whole administration of the *polis* was in their hands.'

Aeschines III (*Against Ktesiphon*) 25

(C) 'You were at that time (349/8) on the point of sending your entire forces to Euboia and Olynthos; and Apollodoros, who was a member of the *boulē*, had a *psēphisma* included in the agenda of that body, which was passed and so came before the *dēmos* as a *probouleuma*. And what it proposed was that the *dēmos* should decide whether the money left over from public administration should be stratiotic or theoric. The *nomoi* prescribed, you see, that (only) in time of war should the money left over from public administration be stratiotic, whereas Apollodoros believed that the *dēmos* should have the power to do whatever it liked with its own property; and as all of you bore witness, he had sworn an oath to do his best for the Athenian *dēmos* in that crisis. (5) And when the issue came to a vote, nobody was prepared to vote against the use of this money as stratiotic; and even now, whenever the matter is spoken of at all, everyone concedes that Apollodoros made the best proposal and yet suffered unjustly for it. So the proper object of your anger is the man whose arguments deceived the jurors, not those whom he took in: I refer to the fact that a *graphē paranomōn* was lodged by this fellow Stephanos,[6] who came before the *dikastērion* with false witnesses to claim that Apollodoros had been a debtor to the state for 25 years; and by making all sorts of accusations that were irrelevant to the charge he won his case against the *psēphisma*.'

[Demosthenes] LIX (*Against Neaira*) 4–5

(D) In the archonship of Lysimachides (339/8) they postponed work on the ship-sheds and the arsenal because of the war against Philippos, and decreed, on the motion of Demosthenes, that all the monies be stratiotic.

Philochorus *FGrH* 328 F 56a

1 I.e. for 4 years. See, however, Rhodes, *Boule*, 235–7.
2 See further ch.61; compare also **126**, and [Xen.] *Ath. Pol.* 1.3.
3 See Rhodes, *Boule*, 238–9.
4 Euboulos (*c*.405–*c*.335), the leading Athenian statesman of the years 355–346: see G. L. Cawkwell, 'Eubulus', *JHS* 83 (1963), 47–69; C. Mossé, *Athens in Decline 404–86 B.C.* (London, 1973), 53–7. His power-base was the theoric fund (**141** with n.4; **216** n.5), which was either created or at least substantially reorganised in the second half of the 350s; Rhodes, *Boule*, 105 with n.6. If the latter, the reorganisation was indeed substantial, for if *theōrika* existed at all in the fifth century they were simply distributions of money to the poor to enable them to attend religious festivals (**242** Intro.), and modern scholars have found it very difficult to trace the process whereby this expanded into a much more comprehensive poor-relief institution ('the cement of the democracy', one contemporary politician called it: Plut. *Moralia* 1011B) and the officials in charge of it correspondingly increased in stature (See J. J. Buchanan, *Theorika* (Locust Valley, N.Y., 1962), with the review by G. E. M. de Ste Croix, *CR* n.s.14 (1964), 190–2; Cawkwell, *op. cit.*; A. R. Hands, *Charities and Social Aid in Greece and Rome* (London, 1968), 98–9; Rhodes, *Boule*, 105–7 and 235–40.) At any rate we may plausibly see the hand of Euboulos behind the policy, during his period of predominance, of declaring surplus revenues as theoric rather than stratiotic, which was not reversed until 339/8 (C, D).
5 The exact provisions of the *nomos*, of *c*.335, are obscure (see Rhodes, *Boule*, 235–40 *passim*) but apparently its general concern was with limiting the cumulative tenure of major financial offices.
6 See **310**; and on this particular case M. H. Hansen, 'The theoric fund and the *graphē paranomōn* against Apollodorus', *GRBS* 17 (1976), 235–46.

314. Orators versus generals

In the middle of the fourth century Demosthenes declared that 'as things are, our affairs have reached such a shameful state that each of the *stratēgoi* is put on trial for his life two or three times in the courts, yet none of them dares to fight for his life even once with the enemy' (Demos. IV.47). The claim gives every appearance of rhetorical exaggeration – yet it has recently been investigated and verified (by M. H. Hansen, *Eisangelia* (Odense, 1975), 58–65; see also Pritchett, *War* II, ch.1). Demosthenes also makes the point that the situation would be different if the jurors sitting in judgment upon the *stratēgoi* (at their *euthynai*) had been, as soldiers, eye-witnesses of the campaigns in question. Obviously what he had chiefly in mind here was the excessive reliance on mercenary troops in this period; but his comments and the problems to which they pertain focus also upon a rift between orators and generals – the men who made policy and the men who attempted to put it into effect – of which we see signs in the fifth century (**212**), but which in the fourth grew ever wider and more problematical.
  See further: S. Perlman, 'Political leadership in Athens in the fourth century B.C.', *La Parola del Passato* 22 (1967), 161–76; M. H. Hansen, *The Sovereignty of the*

People's Court in Athens in the Fourth Century B.C. *and the public action against unconstitutional proposals* (Odense, 1974), 22–7.

(A) 'So far are we different from our ancestors that whereas *they* chose the same men as both spokesmen of the *polis* and *stratēgoi* – in the belief that the man best able to give good advice on the speakers' rostrum would be the man best able to counsel himself, when left to his own devices – what *we* do is the opposite of this: (55) those whose advice we follow on matters of the greatest importance we do not think worthy of election as *stratēgoi*, as if we consider them lacking in intelligence, while those to whom nobody would go for advice on matters either private or public we send out (as *stratēgoi*) with plenipotentiary powers, as if we consider them likely to be wiser in that situation, and better able to give counsel on the affairs of the Greeks as a whole than on those which are at issue here at home.'

Isocrates VIII (On the Peace) 54–55

(B) Phokion[1] saw that the public figures of his day had distributed amongst themselves as if by lot the work of the *stratēgos* and of the public speaker: some of them, including Euboulos, Aristophon, Demosthenes, Lykourgos and Hypereides, were simply speaking and making proposals to the *dēmos*, while (such others as) Diopeithes and Menestheus and Leosthenes and Chares advanced themselves by being *stratēgoi* and waging wars. Phokion, however, wished to recover and restore the *politeia* of Perikles and Aristeides and Solon which had, as it were, a perfect disposition of effort in both spheres: for each of those men showed himself to be, as Archilochus puts it,[2] 'both a squire of the warlike god (Ares) and with knowledge too of what the lovely Muses give'.[3] He also saw that the goddess (Athena) was a goddess of war as well as of statecraft, and was addressed as such. (8) Having taken this stand, therefore, his domestic policies were always directed towards peace and quiet, and yet he was *stratēgos* more often than anyone else, whether in his day or earlier times. He neither sought this nor canvassed for it, but when the *polis* called upon him he did not flee or run away. It is agreed in fact that he was a *stratēgos* 45 times – without ever once being at the elections himself; he was always absent when summoned and voted into office.[4] (9.5) Once, during a heatwave, he saw Polyeuktos of (the deme) Sphettos advising the Athenians to go to war with Philippos (of Makedonia) and then panting and sweating so much, being of course an excessively fat man, that he needed frequent gulps of water. At this Phokion declared, 'A most suitable man, this, to persuade you to vote for the war! But what do you suppose he will do when he faces the enemy with breastplate and shield if he is in danger of choking to death when making you a prepared speech?'

Plutarch, *Phokion* 7.3–8.1; 9.5

1 An Athenian general and politician prominent between the 340s and his death in 318; see Plut. *Phokion*.
2 Archilochus of Paros, seventh-century poet.
3 There is in fact no good evidence for Solon as a military man.
4 If this figure can be accepted it exceeds even the tenure of Perikles in the fifth century (**148**).

315. Qualifications for public office: the need for experience

Fifth-century Athenian democracy operated on the principle that anyone and everyone was not merely entitled but also competent to play a part, however modest, in running the *polis*. In the fourth century the doctrine still held good, but greater store came to be set by expertise and experience. And this is true not only of Athens (on which see Rhodes, *Boule*, 218–21) but to some extent of Greek cities in general, as we see in the passage below. It is a fragment, first published in 1943, of the *Laws* (*Nomoi*) of Theophrastus of Eresos on Lesbos (*c*.370–288/5), a pupil of Aristotle's, and in 322 Aristotle's successor as head of the Lykeion philosophical institute in Athens. And indeed Theophrastus here takes up a problem which had already been adumbrated by Aristotle (in *Politics* (v) 1309 a 32 ff.) – the qualifications appropriate to those seeking high office.

For textual problems, and commentary, see J. J. Keaney and A. Szegedy-Maszak, *Transactions of the American Philological Association* 106 (1976), 227–40, and J. H. Oliver, *GRBS* 18 (1977), 321–39 (though parts of Oliver's translation (330–2) seem to us faulty).

What is best is that a man should win trust by virtue of his life-style and upbringing, not his property; and this is exactly what will happen as the result of education and good practices in the *politeia*. At any rate the *nomos* basing office-holding upon census-classes seems in general to be too old-fashioned, because it would often thwart the true leaders: neither Epameinondas nor Pelopidas[1] nor, from Athens, Iphikrates and Chabrias[2] (would) have been *stratēgoi*, nor those earlier – and better – men Aristeides and Themistokles.[3]

So all in all the question of which offices ought to be filled on the basis of wealth and excellence (together, or excellence) only, or wealth (only), seems to call for some investigation. In appointing treasurers, for example, as has been said, wealth is the consideration,[4] whereas for the guardianship of the *nomoi* or some other similar position one looks for justice; and for a *stratēgos*, whether he controls affairs outside or inside the *polis*, adequate financial resources are needed as well as personal excellence – together with the third attribute of which we spoke, experience. And these are indeed the three requirements – taking loyalty as read – for office: personal excellence, sufficient wealth, and practical wisdom. The first and second of these are necessary for all offices, while practical wisdom is rather appropriate to some offices but absolutely essential for the highest ones. And in a way it is sufficient if an honest assessment is made of both (the first and second criteria), for they are generally good for observing situations and splendid, of course, at recognising critical moments; so as a result a choice is made on the basis of a candidate's good fortune and ability. However, while some people do consider one or the other of these, because they pick out the best citizens, most people, whose judgment is very poor, look (only) at the man's property. It is true, as was said before, that some offices in particular call for trust-worthiness, others for practical wisdom and cleverness, and others again for someone who takes pains and, distasteful though this may be, does his job boldly and aggressively. But it is not easy by *nomos* to assign the right person to each, so it is those who scrutinise the candidates who need to choose the most suitable.

Since some offices, as was said, also call for experience, it is a good idea in these cases always to bring in some of the younger men, so that without detriment to the administration of the *polis* they may be trained by those with the knowledge. This is exactly what Hagnon once advised the Athenians to do in the case of their *stratēgoi*, using hunting with hounds as an illustration; there, he maintained, lovers of hunting always bring in puppies.[5] And this approach is actually employed, even now, by some of the well-organised lesser *poleis*, such as Karystos and Kythnos: they appoint three men from amongst those who have served as *stratēgoi*, in conjunction with two younger men. In this office above all the most serious situations are bound to arise; nevertheless some sort of mixture on these lines, bringing together the so-called generations, will produce both good order and the combined abilities of the two ages. Witness the gymnasiarchy:[6] those who elect *two* men for this, an elder and a younger, have the right idea; the older man brings discipline when he participates, while the younger becomes the leader of the hard exercises by stripping down and joining in himself. The point is that it is not right that both should have the same physical burden; what they share is the organisa-tional responsibility, and the requirement there is a high level of perceptiveness. However, anyone who plans to hold high office ought first to hold other posts, as was said in the case of the *stratēgoi*: it is absurd if someone who has not been a tribal commander (*taxiarchos*) or even a tribal cavalry-commander (*phylarchos*) becomes a *stratēgos* immediately. As was decided before, some offices are suitable for preliminary experi-ence, others best left until last – for two reasons: under this system the man expecting (to hold office) is made both very eager and also ambitious to be put to the test, because of the placing of the higher posts, or else, as used to be the case in Epeiros, the delay (in reaching them). In some places it is actually a legal requirement that the candidate for high office be chosen from the lower ones, or from those reckoned to lead on to the higher ones; this is so in Phokis, for example, where they appoint the *stratēgoi* from ex-*phylarchoi* and ex-treasurers. And in general nobody should hold (high) office without having served at least on the *boulē*, as in Amprakia; for it always pays to choose someone to join the younger man who is already gaining experience of public affairs.

Theophrastus, *Fragmentum Vaticanum de eligendis magistratibus* B, lines 8–22[1]

1 The two great fourth-century Theban leaders: see 271–274.
2 Athenian *stratēgoi* active in the first half of the fourth century.
3 In neither of these cases does the implication of poverty stand up to scrutiny – see Davies, *Families*, 48–53 (Aristeides) and 212–17 (Themistokles) – which casts doubt on the others too; the rags-to-riches *stratēgos* has all the appearance of a cliché.
4 Note the survival in Athens of the restriction (however disregarded in practice) of the office of treasurer of Athena to members of the very highest Solonian census-class, the *pentakosiomedimnoi* (see 67). ?Aristot. *Ath. Pol.* 47.1.
5 Hagnon, father of Theramenes, was a prominent Athenian in the second half of the fifth century (Davies, *Families*, 227–8). It may have been as one of the *probouloi* of 413 (226–227; Lys. xii.65) that he gave this advice.
6 An office, in Athens and many other *poleis*, involving management of the public sports grounds and the athletic activities there.

32 Thessaly and Persia

Behind the decision of Philippos II to attack Persia (see **350**), implemented by his son Alexander the Great, there lie both a growing awareness in Greece that it could and should be done and the type of hegemony briefly exercised by Iason of Pherai.

Persian money often seemed in the fourth century to control the Greek *poleis* like so many puppets (Diod. xv.70.2; Xen. *Hell.* vii.1.27); there were nonetheless real weaknesses in the Persian position. The post of satrap itself was often in effect hereditary (see Xen. *Hell.* iv.1.32) and large areas of the Persian empire were actually ruled by local dynasts owing nominal allegiance to Persia. The Hekatomnids, for example, were able to create a virtually independent kingdom in Karia (see **339**), and Euagoras ruled Cypriot Salamis from 411 to 374/3, years which included a period of open rebellion from Persia.

The Persian royal house was also sometimes a prey to internecine strife, as in the sequence of events which led up to the attempt of Kyros on the throne (see **252**). The subsequent escape of his mercenaries, the Ten Thousand, the invasion of Asia by Agesilaos and the successes of Athens all helped to create an impression of Persian weakness. It may be that this picture is overdrawn (so C. G. Starr, 'Greeks and Persians in the fourth century B.C.', *Iranica Antiqua* 11 (1975), 39–99; (1977), 49–115), but the important thing is that it existed, and existed alongside Greek resentment of Persian influence. The Persian monarchy succeeded during the reign of Philippos II of Makedonia in restoring central authority throughout the empire; but the notion of a Greek crusade against Persia had already come into being.

Meanwhile, a single individual in one of the *poleis* of Thessaly managed briefly to unite under his control one of the most backward areas of Greece and use the manpower so acquired to dominate central Greece. His heirs were finally suppressed by Philippos, who took over both much of his approach and his ambition to conquer Persia. The dream of Isocrates had almost come true.

316. Thessaly and Pherai

It is difficult to provide a coherent account of Thessaly in the archaic and classical periods before Iason, since it emerges into the light only when involved in the affairs of more important communities. We know that Thessaly as a whole had some form of common political organisation, with – intermittently – an elected head or *tagos* (Thuc. IV.78); but although we happen to know from an inscription that there was a *tagos* in office in 424 (*SIG* 274), he played no part when Brasidas made his great march north (see **192**).

Real power in the *poleis*, characterised by the denial of full rights to much of the population (see **285**), was held by narrow oligarchies. The oligarchs were great landowners, their estates worked by dependent peasants known as *penestai* and of similar status to the helots of Sparta (Aristotle, *Pol.* (II) 1269 a 36). There was also below the very greatest landowners a numerous class of men with large *klēroi* (Aristotle, fr. 498), also probably worked by *penestai*; these men formed the large force of cavalry which was unique to Thessaly and for which the region was famous.

At the turn of the fifth and fourth centuries, two casual references reveal to us a split within the oligarchy in one of the *poleis* of Thessaly, Larisa; this split initially let in Archelaos, the king of Makedonia between about 413 and 399, then provided an opportunity for Lykophron of Pherai, father of Iason.

See in general H. D. Westlake, *Thessaly in the Fourth Century* B.C. (London, 1935).

(A) It was near this date, and at about the time of an eclipse of the sun (September 404), that Lykophron of Pherai, who wanted to make himself ruler of all Thessaly, defeated in battle those among the Thessalians who opposed him, the Larisaians and others, and killed many of them.

Xenophon, *Hellenika* II.3.4

(B) (There are various ways in which an oligarchy may lose power, for instance) when the members of the oligarchy curry popularity with the mob, as the *politophylakes*[1] at Larisa courted popularity with the mob because it elected them . . .

Aristotle, *Politics* (V) 1305 b 28–30

1 An office at Larisa.

317. The rise of Iason

One can see in the early fourth century some traces of Spartan interest in Thessaly; but nothing is clear until Polydamas of Pharsalos (see **267** Intro.) came to Sparta to warn of the power of Iason. The survival of an independent

Pharsalos up to this point finds its explanation in Aristotle's remark (at *Politics* (v) 1306 a 10), on the preservation of a united front by the Pharsalian oligarchy, in contrast to what had happened at Larisa. With the career of Iason it is worth comparing and contrasting that of Euphron of Sikyon (Xen. *Hell.* VII.1.44–6; 2.11–15; 3.2–12).

'So I know well that you are familiar with the name of Iason; for he possesses great power and is very famous. It is he who, after concluding a truce, met me and spoke these words: (5) "Polydamas, that I could bring over your *polis* even against your will you may conclude from the following facts. For I have the greatest number and the largest of the *poleis* of Thessaly as my allies and it was while you were fighting with them against me that I subdued them. And you also know that I have up to 6,000 mercenary troops, with whom, I think, no *polis* could easily contend. For just as many men could no doubt come from somewhere else; but the armies of *poleis* include men who are already past their best and those who are not yet mature; and very few men in each *polis* are in training. But no one receives pay from me who cannot do what I can do . . . (8) So it is clear to us that if Pharsalos and your dependent *poleis* came over I should easily be appointed *tagos* of all the Thessalians; and that, when Thessaly has a *tagos*, her cavalry amounts to 6,000 and her hoplites to more than 10,000. (9) And when I consider their strength and their spirit I think that if one looked after them there would be no people to which the Thessalians would need to be subject. For Thessaly itself is a flat land; but all the people round about are subject when a *tagos* is appointed here and nearly all of them there are javelin-throwers; so it is likely that our strength in peltasts would be overwhelming. (10) And the Boiotians and all the others who are fighting the Spartans are my allies and they are ready to follow me if only I free them from the Spartans. And I know well that the Athenians would do anything in order to become my allies; but I do not think that I will make friends with them.[1] For I think that it would be even easier to win an empire by sea than by land. (11) To see if my calculations are reasonable, consider this also: by holding Makedonia, whence the Athenians get their wood, we shall be in a position to construct far more ships than they. And are we or the Athenians more likely to be able to man these ships with crews, given that we have so many and such robust *penestai*? And are we more likely to be able to feed our sailors, we who because of its abundance here actually export grain elsewhere, or the Athenians, who do not even have enough for themselves unless they import it? (12) And it is also indeed likely that we should have a more abundant supply of money, since we do not look to miserable little islands, but tax peoples who live on the mainland. For all those round about pay tribute when Thessaly has a *tagos*.[2] And you know that the King of the Persians has become the richest of men by taxing the mainland, not islands. *Him* I think it would be even easier to reduce to subjection than Greece. For I know that everyone there except one is trained rather to be a slave than to display any vigour, and I know how large a force it was that went up-country with Kyros and with Agesilaos and reduced the King to desperation."'

Xenophon, *Hellenika* VI.1.4–12*3

1 Iason *may* have been bluffing, see **269** n.14.
2 See **316** Intro.
3 Polydamas went on to demand a force of Spartiatai, and the Spartan inability to accede to the request is the first explicit recognition of Spartan *oliganthrōpia* (see **267**).

318. The end of Iason

After Leuktra, the Thebans sent to Athens, whence they received no reply (see **273**), and to Iason, who came south at once; he persuaded both the Thebans and the Spartans to agree to a truce, 'perhaps acting in order that the two sides being at enmity with each other should both need him' (Xen. *Hell.* VI.4.25). He then returned north as quickly as he had come.

And on arriving at Herakleia, he destroyed the wall of the Herakleots, clearly not afraid in case anyone should march against his kingdom if this route was opened up, but rather worried in case anyone should seize Herakleia, situated as it was in the pass,[1] and block him if he wished to march anywhere in Greece. (28) And when he had returned to Thessaly, he was at the height of his power, both because he had legally been appointed *tagos* of the Thessalians and because he kept a large number of mercenaries with him, infantry and cavalry, all of them trained so as to be of the highest quality. And his power was even greater because he already had many allies and many others wished to become his allies. He was the greatest of the men of his time because no one could look down on him. (29) And as the Pythian Games approached, he instructed the *poleis* to prepare oxen and sheep and goats and pigs for the festival for sacrifice. And it was said that although he made quite moderate demands on each *polis* no less than 1,000 oxen were provided along with more than 10,000 of the other animals. And he announced that there would be a prize of a golden wreath for the *polis* which produced the finest ox as the first sacrifice for the god (Apollo). (30) And he ordered the Thessalians to prepare as if for an expedition at the time of the Pythia; for he had the intention, it was said, himself to preside over the festival of the god and the games.[2] Even now, however, it is not clear what his intention was over the sacred treasure; and it is said that, when the

Delphians asked what they should do if he took any of the treasure of the god, the god replied that he would take care of it. (31) So great a man, then, and with such great plans, was struck down and killed by seven young men who approached as if they had a quarrel with each other, after he had conducted a review and inspection of the Pheraian cavalry and when he was already seated (in judgment) and replying if anyone approached him with a request. (32) And when the bodyguards standing beside him came rushing to his aid, one of the assassins was struck with a spear and killed while still actually striking Iason; another was caught as he mounted his horse and died of the many wounds he received; but the rest leapt on the horses which were waiting ready and escaped. And wherever they went among the Greek *poleis*, they were mostly honoured; from which it is clear that the Greeks were very afraid lest Iason become their master.

Xenophon, Hellenika VI.4.27–32

1 Of Thermopylai, see Map 3; and **189**.
2 Note that control of Delphi was also a major step in the advance of Philippos (Ch.34).

319. Isocrates on Persia

As early as 380, Isocrates urged reconciliation between Sparta and Athens, Spartan recognition of Athenian *hēgemonia*, and war against a Persia explicitly described in the passage quoted below as militarily weak. Given, however, the number of Greeks who fought as mercenaries for Persia, we may doubt whether a feeling that it was a Greek duty not to fight each other but to fight Persia was yet very widespread. (Compare the views of another intellectual, Plato, on war between Greek and Greek, Austin and Vidal-Naquet, *Economy* no.131.) Later evidence, however, suggests that the notion of a crusade against Persia became more general and Isocrates had the satisfaction in 346 of composing his *Philippos* (V), preaching the notion to someone already converted.

'But it is not reasonable to form an estimate of the power of the King from those achievements where he has fought with one or other of us,[1] but from those where he has fought alone and for himself. First, then, in the case of the revolt of Egypt, what has he achieved against those who hold the country? Did he not send the best-known of the Persians to conduct this war, Abrokomas and Tithraustes and Pharnabazos? And did they not remain for three years, suffering more damage than they inflicted, and finally withdraw in such disgrace that the rebels are no longer content with their freedom, but are seeking to rule over their neighbours? (141) After this he mounted an expedition against Euagoras, who is the ruler of a single *polis* and was abandoned by the terms of the treaty;[2] he inhabits an island, has been defeated by sea and has only 3,000 peltasts for the defence of the *chōra*; and yet the King cannot overcome in war so slight a power, but has already wasted six years and, if one can predict the future on the basis of what has happened, it is much more likely that someone else will revolt before Euagoras is subdued – so slow is the King in accomplishing anything . . . (145) And indeed there are no grounds for fearing either the army which accompanies the King or the bravery of the Persians; for they were clearly exposed by the men who marched up-country with Kyros to be no better than those stationed by the sea.'

Isocrates IV (*Panegyrikos*) 140–145*[3]

1 Athens or Sparta.
2 The King's Peace of 387/6, see **263**.
3 See Austin and Vidal-Naquet, *Economy*, no.108, for Isocrates' obsession with an invasion of Persia as a way of ridding Greece of footloose mercenaries, a menace which Isocrates almost certainly exaggerated (see **297** for the lack of enthusiasm for Timoleon's invitation to settle in Sicily); also the important article of N. H. Baynes, 'Isocrates', *Byzantine Studies and other Essays* (London, 1955), 144–67.

320. The decline of Persia

The last section of Xenophon's *Education of Kyros* (possibly an addition by another hand) contains a long account of Persian degeneration after the death of Kyros the Great, a decline in religion and morality, deteriorating physical prowess, the abandonment of education, and the growth of luxury. The polemic concludes with an account of military decline (A, below), also the theme of an amusing vignette from Xenophon (B). The embassy to Sousa which he describes, in connection with the so-called Peace of Pelopidas in 367, clearly stimulated contempt for Persia at a less rarefied level than that of philosophy or rhetoric.

(A) How then can one do other than expect them to be in every respect worse in war than before? It was their custom in earlier times for landowners to provide cavalry who served wherever they were needed and for those who served as guards on the frontiers to be paid; but now the leading men have made into cavalrymen all their porters, bakers, cooks, wine-pourers, bath-attendants, those who serve and remove food, those who put them to bed and wake them up, and those who anoint them and rub them with cosmetics and otherwise condition them; the result is that *these* men serve for pay. (21) A large force is made up from them, but they are of no use for war. What is happening itself

585

makes this clear; for their enemies move about their *chōra* more easily than their friends . . . (26) And so since they themselves realise how ill-prepared they are for war, they abandon the attempt, and none of them any longer prepares for war without hiring Greeks,[1] whether they are fighting each other or whether the Greeks are attacking them; they have even decided to make war on Greeks by means of Greeks.

?Xenophon, *Education of Kyros* VIII.8.20–26*

(B) When all the ambassadors had returned home, the Athenians put Timagoras to death, since Leon accused him of not having shared accommodation with him and of having consulted with Pelopidas on everything. Of the other ambassadors, Archidamos of Elis praised the proposals of the King, because he had honoured Elis above the Arkadians; while Antiochos, because Arkadia was humbled, did not accept the gifts which were offered and reported back to the Ten Thousand[2] that the King had plenty of bakers and cooks and wine-pourers and porters, but that he had searched everywhere for men who could fight the Greeks without being able to find any. And in addition he said that he thought that the supposed great wealth of the King was a pretence, since the much vaunted golden plane-tree would not even provide enough shade for a grass-hopper.

Xenophon, *Hellenika* VII.1.38

1 Compare Austin and Vidal-Naquet, *Economy* no. 132, for the Aristotelian view of the superiority of Greeks over *barbaroi*.
2 Here the Arkadian assembly, see **300B**.

33 The rise of Makedonia

The kingdom of Makedonia lay on the northern fringe of the Aegean, set against a hinterland of non-Greek peoples – Illyrians, Paionians and Thrakians. Were the Makedonians themselves Greeks? By the yardsticks which the Greeks themselves recognised (encapsulated in Hdt. VIII.144.2) the answer is, and was, ambiguous; and so was the role of Makedonia in the Greek world before the second quarter of the fourth century, with kings such as Alexandros I (c.498–c.454) playing a part in the Persian War (**114**) and Perdikkas II (c.454–c.413) in the Peloponnesian (**177, 192**) but with no consistent impact upon Greek affairs. A sketchy picture of developments can be pieced together (**321**), but they were slow. In 359, however, came the accession to the throne of king Philippos II, father of Alexander (III) the Great, and his reign (359–336) marks a watershed, not simply in Makedonian history but in Greek history as a whole. (For the spectacular archaeological finds at Vergina in 1977, including a royal tomb which may well be that of Philippos II, see N. G. L. Hammond, '"Philip's tomb" in historical context', *GRBS* 19 (1978), 331–50.) His dealings with the Greeks, whom by 338 he had conquered, form the subject of Ch.34; here, first, the texts and documents have been chosen to illustrate the Makedonian domestic background and the influence of Philippos upon it.

See further: G. T. Griffith, 'The Macedonian background', *Greece and Rome* 12 (1965), 125–39; Ellis, *Philip II*, ch.1; Hammond and Griffith, *Macedonia*, chs.1–4.

321. Makedonia before Philippos

The sum total of our information about Makedonia before the accession of Philippos II is paltry even by the standards to which historians of the ancient Greek world are generally accustomed; and it is often pure chance that we have even what does survive. Here are two examples. In the course of chronicling the campaigning of the Archidamian War, Thucydides (A) has occasion to digress, briefly, upon the early history of Makedonia and its people. (Compare Justin VII.1–5; and see Ellis, *Philip II*, 34–42.) And it is thanks only to a Latin inscription found in 1911 in Perrhaibia in northern Thessaly (B) that we can add to our meagre knowledge of king Amyntas III, the father of Philippos, and the only fourth-century Makedonian king before Philippos to enjoy a reign of any length (393–370/69; see on it Hammond and Griffith, *Macedonia*, 172–80). The stone, dating from the year A.D. 101, is the record of an appeal to the Roman emperor Trajan to settle a border dispute between Elimiotis, a district of upper Makedonia, and Doliche, one of the three members of the north Perrhaibian *tripolis*; and it makes reference back to a judgment on the same issue by Amyntas. As the original editors pointed out, this does not necessarily prove that the area was under the direct rule of Amyntas, who may simply have been called in as a convenient third-party arbitrator (so too Hammond and Griffith, *Macedonia*, 178); we see no way of telling, and present the text chiefly as an illustration of the often curious transmission of historical information.

(A) So they assembled at Doberos[1] and made preparations to cross straight over the mountains and invade lower Makedonia, the domain of Perdikkas. Up-country, the Lynkestians and Elimiots and other peoples are also part of Makedonia: they have their own kings but are nonetheless allies and subjects of the coastal Makedonians. This country by the sea – which we now know as Makedonia – was first acquired by Alexandros the father of Perdikkas and his ancestors, who were originally descendants of Temenos from Argos;[2] they became kings of Makedonia by defeating and driving out from Pieria the Pierians – who later settled in Phagres and other places under Mount Pangaios, beyond the (river) Strymon, so that even today the country between the foot of Pangaios and the sea is still called the Pierian Valley – and from Bottia, so called, the Bottiaians, who now live as neighbours of the Chalkidians. They also acquired a narrow strip of Paionia, extending along the river Axios from the interior to Pella and the sea; and by driving out the Edonians they gained possession of the country called Mygdonia, beyond the Axios as far as the Strymon. They also expelled, from the country now called Eordia, the Eordians – most of whom were killed, though a few still live near Physka – and from Almopia the Almopians. And these Makedonians also conquered, and still hold, certain places that belonged to other peoples: Anthemous, Grestonia, Bisaltia, and much of (upper) Makedonia. In its entirety, however, Makedonia is its name; and at the time of Sitalkes' invasion Perdikkas son of Alexandros was its king. (100) Faced with so large an invading army, Perdikkas' Makedonians were unable to put up any resistance, and so retreated to the country's various strongholds and fortresses.[3] These were few, however: the ones which now exist in Makedonia were built by a later king, Perdikkas' son Archelaos,[4] who also built straight roads and in general organised his country for war by providing more cavalry, arms[5] and other equipment than all his eight royal predecessors put together.

Thucydides II.99–100.2

(B) Since I am satisfied that on the stone *stēlē* which is set up in the forum at Doliche the borders between Doliche and Elimiotis are inscribed in accordance with the royal prescription made by Amyntas, father of Philippos, my decision is that the border begins from the boundary-stone which is on the road above Geranae between Azoros and Onoreae and Petreac in Doliche . . .

A. J. B. Wace and M. S. Thompson, *Annual of the British School at Athens* 17 (1910–11), 193–204, lines 11–23

1 The army of Sitalkes, the Odrysian king of Thrake, preparing in 429/8 to attack Makedonia.
2 Temenos was one of the Herakleidai (3, 44). Compare Hdt. VIII.137–9.
3 It is important to observe that Makedonia is a land without *poleis*.
4 *c*.413–399.
5 This would seem to mean infantry, but see 323.

322. The Companions

The king of the Makedonians was no absolute monarch but from various standpoints *primus inter pares*: around and next to him stood his Companions (*hetairoi*), the aristocratic landowners who fought alongside him as cavalrymen. The origins of such a group, analogous to the Homeric nobility (6), are no longer determinable; but we may infer from the passage below – from a patently hostile witness, the Greek historian Theopompus – that during the reign of Philippos their numbers were increased (by grants of land from conquered territories) and their designation extended to take in non-Makedonians.

See further: Ellis, *Philip II*, 21–7, esp.26–7; Hammond and Griffith, *Macedonia*, 152–60, 395–404, 408–10.

In the forty-ninth book of his (*Philippic*) *Histories* Theopompus writes as follows of the profligate way of life of Philippos and his *hetairoi*. 'When Philippos had become master of a large fortune,[1] did he spend it quickly? Quickly would not be the word: he threw it out and tossed it away, for he was the world's worst manager. And those around him were no better: to be blunt about it, not one of them knew how to live an upright life or manage a household sensibly. And it was Philippos himself who was to blame for this: insatiable and extravagant, he did everything in a hurry, whether getting or giving; and as a soldier, you see, he could never spare the time for reckoning up his income and expenditure. His *hetairoi*, moreover, were men who had flocked to him from here, there and everywhere – some from Makedonia itself, others from Thessaly and the rest of Greece. And they had not been picked on merit! On the contrary, virtually all men of a lewd, disgusting or arrogant way of life, whether Greeks or *barbaroi*, had gathered in Makedonia under the name of "Companions of Philippos"; and any who were not of such a character when they went there very soon became like all the rest, under the influence of Makedonian life and habits. The fact was that they were impelled to abandon an orderly life and behave like prodigals and bandits, partly by the wars and campaigns and partly by the extravagant way of living.' (225) . . .[2] 'Neglectful of what they had, they coveted what they did not have – despite the fact that they possessed quite a large part of Europe: for I believe that, although the *hetairoi* at this time[3] numbered no more than 800, they enjoyed the revenues of as much land as the 10,000 Greeks who had the best and largest estates.'

Theopompus, FGrH 115 F224–225

1 See **327**.
2 The beginning and the bulk of this fragment (which is preserved by two writers, Polybius and Athenaeus) enlarges upon the sexual antics of the *hetairoi* of Philippos.
3 'Probably about 340' (Hammond and Griffith, *Macedonia*, 408).

323. The 'Foot-Companions'

The *hetairoi* will always have served as the Makedonian cavalry (**322**) – but what of the infantry? We are told that at the beginning of his reign Philippos could already muster 10,000 'foot-men' (*pezoi*) to fight the Paionians and the Illyrians (see **326**), and Demosthenes spoke in 349 of his 'foot-companions' (II. 17); but it is not at all clear when and how such a force first took shape. An ostensibly attractive clue comes in a fragment, translated here, of the fourth-century Greek historian Anaximenes of Lampsakos, who appears to ascribe the institution of the *pezetairoi* to (king) 'Alexandros', but in fact this datum is notorious for creating more difficulties than it solves, both as regards what Anaximenes meant and as to how far, if at all, we should believe him. If 'Alexandros' was really meant (rather than 'Archelaos': see **321A**), there are problems with both of the pre-Philippos kings of that name – with Alexandros II because his reign was so very short (370/69–369/8), and with Alexandros I because of indications in Thucydides that in his day there was no effective, organised Makedonian infantry. (This latter solution thus requires the assumption that the innovation was ahead of its time, in Makedonian terms, and had little or no lasting effect: so for instance Ellis, *Philip II*, 53.) Nor is it easy to accept Griffith's reasoning (in Hammond and Griffith, *Macedonia*, 705–9) in favour of Alexander (III) the Great. However, in view of the Greeks' well-known habit of attributing virtually any development, military, political or whatever, to a single individual whenever possible, we agree with the conclusions about this passage reached by P. A. Brunt, 'Anaximenes and king Alexander I of Macedon', *JHS* 96 (1976), 151–3: 'all that it permits us to infer is that the institutions he mentions are earlier than the time of Philip II . . . and perhaps somewhat remote'.

In the first book of his *Philippics* Anaximenes, when talking of Alexandros, says: 'Then, after making the most renowned men accustomed to serving as cavalry he gave them the name of *hetairoi*; but the majority, that is the foot-men (*pezoi*), he divided into companies (*lochoi*) and decads and other commands, and designated them *pezetairoi*. He did this in order that both groups might have a share in the royal companionship and so continue in their steadfast loyalty to him.'

Anaximenes, FGrH 72 F4

324. Philippos in Thebes

Born in either 383 or 382, the young Philippos spent three of his early teenage years (at some time between 369 and 365) as a diplomatic hostage in Thebes. In the view of Ellis (*Philip II*, 43–4), 'we can scarcely credit the stories circulated by some ancient and modern authors that he learnt and developed at this time many of the military ideas with which he was to inculcate the Macedonian army a decade and more later'. This seems to us unnecessarily sceptical: see rather the remarks of Hammond and Griffith, *Macedonia*, 205–6 and 424 5. With Plutarch's version, given here, compare Diod. xv.67.3–4 and xvi.2.2–4.

Having arrived in Makedonia, settled the disputes there and brought back the exiles, Pelopidas took as a hostage the king's brother Philippos, together with 30 other sons of the most distinguished men, bringing them to live in Thebes; thus he showed the Greeks what progress the Theban state had made in the respect paid to its power and the trust placed in its justice. This was the Philippos who subsequently went to war to deny the Greeks their liberty, but who at this time was a boy. In Thebes he lived with Pammenes,[1] and because of this was believed to have become an enthusiastic follower of Epameinondas[2] – perhaps because he grasped how effectively Epameinondas conducted wars and the role of a *stratēgos*. Yet that was only a small part of what made Epameinondas outstanding: it was his self-control, his justice, his greatness of heart and his gentleness which made him a truly great man, and these were qualities in which Philippos had no share, by either nature or imitation.

Plutarch, Pelopidas 26.4–5

1 See **271** with n.2.
2 See **272**, etc.

325. The condition of Makedonia in 359. The measures of Philippos surveyed

In 359, at the death of his brother Perdikkas (III), Philippos succeeded to the Makedonian throne. (Justin asserts that in the first instance he was regent for his infant nephew Amyntas, but the most recent modern studies doubt this: see J. R. Ellis, *JHS* 91 (1971), 15–24, and *Philip II*, 250 n.10; Hammond and Griffith, *Macedonia*, 208–9 and 702–3.) And his accession was seen – with hindsight – as heralding the end of 40 chaotic years, occupied by the reigns of eight ineffectual kings in Makedonia. Here Diodorus sets the scene for the transformation to come.

See further: Ellis, *Philip II*, 44–7 (accession) and 52–6 (army); Hammond and Griffith, *Macedonia*, chs. 5 (accession) and 12 (army).

When Perdikkas was defeated in a great battle by the Illyrians[1] and fell in the action, his brother Philippos, who had escaped from detention as a hostage, succeeded to the throne. But his kingdom was in a sorry state: more than 4,000 Makedonians had fallen in the battle, and the remainder, panic-stricken, had become terrified of the Illyrian forces and had lost heart for continuing the war. Also at about this same time the Paionians, who are neighbours of the Makedonians, began, in contempt of them, to ravage Makedonian territory; the Illyrians began to assemble large forces and make preparations for an invasion of Makedonia; and a certain Pausanias, who was related to the Makedonian royal house, began to make plans with the help of the king of the Thrakians to stake his claim to the Makedonian throne. Likewise the Athenians also, who were hostile to Philippos, were seeking to restore Argaios to the throne,[2] and they had already sent off a *stratēgos*, Mantias, with 3,000 hoplites and a considerable naval force. (3) So because of the disastrous battle and the magnitude of the dangers pressing in upon them the Makedonians were utterly at a loss. Nevertheless, despite the fears and dangers which threatened them, Philippos was not dismayed by the magnitude of the perils that lay in store: instead, bringing the Makedonians together in a series of assemblies[3] and using the persuasive power of his oratory to exhort them to courage, he filled them with heart; and once he had satisfactorily organised the deployment of his forces for the better and equipped his men suitably with weapons of war, he held constant musters of the men under arms and competitive drill-manoeuvres. He also devised the close-packed order and the equipment of the phalanx – imitating the heroes at Troy, with their shields held closely together;[4] he was indeed the originator of the Makedonian phalanx.[5] He was also gentle in his dealings with men, and sought by his gifts and promises to become supreme in popular favour, as well as making skilful moves to counteract the multitude of impending dangers.

Diodorus XVI.2.4–3.3

1 The Dardanians, to be precise (both here and in **326**).
2 Argaios had ruled, briefly, in the 390s or 380s, as a rival to Amyntas III.
3 On the relationship between the assembly and the army see Hammond and Griffith, *Macedonia*, 383–92, esp. 389ff.

4 See Homer, *Iliad* XIII.131–133.

5 On this sort of claim compare **323** Intro.

326. Defeat of the Paionians and Illyrians

Philippos' first task was to secure his northern frontier, against the Paionians and, especially, the Illyrians (Dardanians). See further: Ellis, *Philip II*, 47–8 and 56–8; Hammond and Griffith, *Macedonia*, 210–14.

Once relieved of the war with the Athenians[1] Philippos decided that he had a good opportunity to attack the Paionians, having heard that their king, Agis, had died. He therefore led an expedition into Paionia, defeated the *barbaroi* in battle and compelled the Paionian people to acknowledge allegiance to the Makedonians. However, he still had enemies left – the Illyrians – and he was eager for the glory of fighting and defeating them also; so, having at once called an assembly and suitably urged on his soldiers to war, he led into Illyrian territory an expeditionary force consisting of no fewer than 10,000 foot-men (*pezoi*) and 600 cavalrymen. When Bardylis the Illyrian king learned that his enemies had come, his first move was to send off envoys to negotiate an armistice on the basis of both sides' retaining control of the *poleis* that they currently possessed. Philippos, however, declared that although he was eager for peace he would not agree to it unless the Illyrians withdrew from all the Makedonian *poleis*;[2] so the envoys came away unsuccessful, and Bardylis, relying upon his previous victories and the courage of his Illyrians, came out with his forces to meet the enemy; he had 10,000 picked foot-men and about 500 cavalrymen. When the two armies approached each other and, with loud shouts, engaged in battle, Philippos – in command of the right wing and the flower of the Makedonian fighters – ordered his cavalry to ride past the ranks of the *barbaroi* and attack them in the flank, while he himself engaged them in a frontal assault and began a hard-fought battle. The Illyrians, however, formed themselves into a square and courageously entered the fray; and at first for a long time the battle was evenly poised because of the courage shown by both sides. As many were killed and still more wounded, the risk of defeat swung first one way and then the other, being constantly counterbalanced by the bravery of the combatants; but subsequently, with the (Makedonian) cavalry pressing from the flanks and the rear, and Philippos and his champions contending heroically, the mass of the Illyrians was put to flight. When the pursuit had been kept up for a considerable distance and large numbers of Illyrians had been killed as they fled, Philippos gave his trumpeter an order to recall the Makedonians, erected a trophy of victory and buried his own dead. As for the Illyrians, they sent envoys, withdrew from all the Makedonian *poleis*,[2] and secured their peace. More than 7,000 of them, though, had been killed in this battle.

Diodorus XVI.4.2–7

1 Over Amphipolis (see **337**).
2 A misnomer: see **321** n.3.

327. Mines and coinage

In addition to other natural resources (such as timber, see **317**), Makedonia was well placed as regards possession – or else acquisition of possession – of precious metals. According to Herodotus the silver mines of Mount Dysoron, near Lake Prasias, yielded Alexandros I a talent of silver a day (Hdt.v.17.2), and we know of others still further up-country at Damastion. But the richest deposits lay further east, beyond the Strymon (Hdt. VI.46–47, VII.112; Thuc. I.100–101; Plut. *Kim.* 4.1–2; etc.); and Philippos did not wait long before laying hands on them.

See further: Ellis, *Philip II*, 33–4 (mines) and 235–9 (coinage); Hammond and Griffith, *Macedonia*, 662–7.

After this[1] Philippos went to the *polis* of Krenides,[2] and after increasing its size with a mass of settlers re-named it after himself: Philippoi. Then, turning to the gold mines in its *chōra*, which were altogether paltry and unimportant, he contrived to increase their output to such an extent that they were able to yield him revenues of more than 1,000 talents. So very soon he amassed a fortune from these mines, and thus with the abundance of money elevated the Makedonian kingdom to ever greater and greater superiority: for with the gold coinage which he struck – which came to be known, after him, as Philippeioi – he organised a considerable force of mercenaries,[3] as well as bribing many Greeks to betray their native cities.[4]

Diodorus XVI.8.6–7

1 In Diodorus' dating 358/7, but actually 356. On the episode as a whole see Ellis, *Philip II*, 68–70; Hammond and Griffith, *Macedonia*, 246–50.
2 In Thrake, north east of Mt Pangaios. According to Diod. XVI.3.7 Krenides (the name means 'Springs') had been founded by the Thasians in 360. See further Hammond and Griffith, *Macedonia*, 358–61.
3 See Demos. IX (*Third Philippic*) 47–50. Philippos adopted the Attic weight-standard for his gold coinage, not for commercial reasons but as a way of asserting his Greekness.
4 Compare **254** with n.2; also **348**, and the remarks of Hyperides, *Against Demosthenes* cols.24–26.

328. Land and settlement

The Makedonian army, like all others in the Greek world, rested upon a socio-economic basis of landownership, great and small; so the king's distribution of land, especially that of newly-conquered territories (A, below), could serve as either tangible reward for military service already rendered or for the creation of more men eligible for such service in future. See further. Ellis, *Philip II*, 55; Hammond and Griffith, *Macedonia*, ch.20.

(A) When Philippos saw that the men of Methone[1] were permitting their *polis* to be used as a base of operations for his enemies, he laid siege to it;[2] and although the Methonaians held out for a time they were subsequently overpowered and forced to hand over their *polis* to the king, who stipulated that its *politai* should all leave Methone with one article of clothing apiece. Philippos then razed the *polis* and distributed its *chōra* amongst the Makedonians. It was during this siege that he was unfortunate enough to be struck in the eye by an arrow and lost the sight in it.[3]

Diodorus XVI.34.4–5

(B) As to the number of his forces,[4] the lowest figures put forward are 30,000 infantry and 4,000 cavalry, and the highest 40,000 infantry and 5,000 cavalry. To provision these forces he had no more than 70 talents, according to Aristoboulos;[5] Duris[6] writes of maintenance for only 30 days; and Onesikritos[7] claims that he had debts of 200 talents besides. However, even though he was setting out with such small and meagre resources he did not board ship before enquiring into the circumstances of his *hetairoi*,[8] and allotting a farm to one, a village to another, and to another the revenue from some settlement or harbour. And when at last virtually all the crown property had been expended and written off, Perdikkas[9] asked him what he was leaving for himself. 'My hopes,' declared Alexander. 'In that case,' said Perdikkas, 'we will share them with you, as we are serving with you,' and with that he declined the property which had been recorded as his gift; and some of the other friends of the king did the same. Nonetheless, upon those who wanted and would accept his favours Alexander eagerly bestowed them, and used up in these distributions most of what he possessed in Makedonia.

Plutarch, *Alexander* 15.1–6

1 A Greek *apoikia* on the Thermaic Gulf.
2 In the winter of 355/4. It fell the following spring. See Hammond and Griffith, *Macedonia*, 254–8.
3 The right eye, according to other sources.
4 Alexander the Great's, for his Asian invasion of 334.
5 Aristoboulos of Kassandreia, one of the early (indeed contemporary) 'Alexander-historians', and an important source for Arrian's *Anabasis*.

6 See **249**.
7 Onesikritos of Astypalaia, a less important (albeit contemporary) 'Alexander-historian'.
8 See **322**.
9 A Makedonian noble, briefly prominent in the power-struggle after Alexander's premature death in 323.

329. Discipline in the Makedonian army

An inscription from Amphipolis, dating from the late third or early second century, preserves a list of regulations governing the behaviour of the Makedonian army in camp. It is likely, though not certain, that its provisions are substantially those of the time of Philippos II and Alexander.

(A¹) (Rubric missing): [---] making no reply to the patrols, but in silence demonstrating that they are present and on their feet.
Patrols: In each *stratēgia*¹ the tetrarchs are to take turns on patrol, without a light, and they are to punish any guard (found) sitting or [sleeping] by (a fine of) a drachma for each offence; the secretaries shall see to (its) collection [--].
(B¹) (Rubric missing): [---] shall punish, according to the regulations, those (found) not bearing any of the arms appropriate to them: two obols for the *kotthybos*,² the same for the *kōnos*,³ three obols for the *sarissa*,⁴ the same for the dagger, two obols for the greaves, a drachma for the shield. In the case of officers, double for the arms mentioned, two drachmas for the corslet, a drachma for the half-corslet. The secretaries and the chief attendants (*archypēretai*) shall exact the penalty, after indicating the defaulters to the king. Discipline relating to booty: [If] any men bring booty into the camp, the *stratēgoi* shall go out to meet (them, at a point) three stades in front of the encampment, taking the speirarchs and tetrarchs [and] the other officers, and with them sufficient (numbers of) [attendants]; and they shall not permit those who have taken the booty to keep it. If any disorderliness [of this kind] should occur, the [officers] and the speirarchs and tetrarchs and the chief attendants shall repay the value [of what each of the men] owes.
(A²) (Rubric missing): [-- if they do not indicate to the] king those who are in breach of discipline, they are to be punished by (a fine of) three-twelfths (of a drachma) and handed over to the *hypaspistai*,⁵ if the latter have already sent in the written denunciation of the offenders.
On making camp: When they have finished the enclosure for the king and pitched the rest of the tents, and an intervening space has been created, they shall at once make a bivouac for the *hypaspistai* [---].
(B²) On [foraging]: If anyone [goes foraging in enemy (territory), a

reward for the information] is to be announced, and there shall be given [---. And if anyone] sets fire to crops or [cuts down] vines [or] commits [any other] disorderly act, [the *stratēgoi* shall announce] a reward for the information [--].

(A³) Passwords: Let them also receive the [password . . . when] they close the passages of the [king's enclosure ---].

L. Moretti, *Iscrizioni Storiche Ellenistiche*
no. 114, A¹; B¹ lines 1–18; A²; B² lines 14–18; A³ lines 5–7

1 The largest unit (perhaps 1,000 men) of the Makedonian army. Its subdivisions (q.v. below) are, in descending order of size, the *speira*, the *tetrarchia* and the *lochos*.
2 A term not otherwise attested; it would seem to mean a protective garment for the abdomen, for those without corslets.
3 The conical helmet.
4 The long stabbing-spear or pike.
5 An élite corps of guards.

330. The royal squires

One of Philippos' most urgent tasks was to improve the internal cohesion of his kingdom, which might otherwise – especially in the cantons of Upper Makedonia display and follow tendencies which were naturally centrifugal (see 321A). Loyalty was crucial at all levels (compare 322, 323); and Arrian here describes one method which Philippos employed to ensure it. (See also Q. Curtius Rufus VIII.6.3–6.) Here again, despite what the sources themselves say, it is likely that he developed rather than created the institution: see Hammond and Griffith, *Macedonia*, 168 n.1 and 400–1.

It was a practice dating back to the time of Philippos that when the sons of powerful Makedonians reached adolescence they should be enlisted in the king's service, their duties being general attendance upon his person and the particular task of guarding him while he slept. Also whenever the king rode out it was these youths who received the horses from the grooms and led them up, mounted the king in the Persian manner and shared with him in the rivalry of the chase.

Arrian, *Anabasis* IV.13.1

331. The marriages of Philippos

It is likely that the Makedonian nobility in general and the royal family in particular was never completely monogamous; but it is equally likely that its polygamous tendencies were welcomed, and extended, by Philippos – and for reasons essentially, as the third-century biographer Satyrus observes in the extract here, of 'war'; today we should probably call it power-politics. The women concerned are not all mentioned in the correct chronological order, but the basic point is clear enough; for the problems of the passage consult Ellis, *Philip II*, 211–17.

Philippos always married with war in mind. At any rate, in the 22 years of his reign, as Satyrus says in his *Life of Philippos*, he married Audata the Illyrian and had by her a daughter, Kynna;[1] and he also married Phila, a sister of Derdas and Machatas.[2] And in his desire to conciliate the nation of the Thessalians he had children by two Thessalian women: one of them was Nikesipolis of Pherai, who bore him a daughter, Thessalonike;[3] the other was Philinna of Larisa, by whom he fathered Arridaios.[4] He also acquired the kingdom of the Molossians by his marriage to Olympias, by whom he had Alexander (the Great) and Kleopatra.[5] And when he took control of Thrake, Kothelas the king of the Thrakians came to him bringing his daughter Meda and many gifts; Philippos married her, adding her to Olympias.[6]

Athenaeus (XIII) 557B–D

1 Or Kynnane. Audata was probably the daughter or niece of Bardylis (see **326**), but we do not know whether the marriage preceded Philippos' defeat of the Illyrians, in which case it was effectively forced upon him in the early months of his reign (so Ellis, *Philip II*, 47–8), or followed it, as part of the peace (so Hammond and Griffith, *Macedonia*, 214–15).

2 I.e. a princess of Elimiotis (see **321B**), by now one of the cantons of Upper Makedonia. The marriage possibly preceded the one to Audata: Ellis, *Philip II*, 46.

3 In 352. A late source asserts that Nikesipolis was a niece of Iason (see Ch. 32); we do not agree with Ellis, *Philip II*, 261 n.108, that this is 'hardly credible' (cf. Hammond and Griffith, *Macedonia*, 278–9).

4 In 358 or early 357. The son, (Philippos) Arridaios, was feeble-minded, which further assisted Alexander's already strong claim to the succession in 336 (see next note); even so Arridaios became a puppet king for six years (323–317) after the early death of his half-brother.

5 The marriage took place in 357, and Alexander was born in July 356. Even leaving aside (as of course one must) Alexander's later status and success, it is clear that this marriage was the most important of all Philippos' seven (see next note): whatever the exact status of his various *wives*, Olympias was his only *queen*.

6 In *c*.339. The probable order of these marriages is thus: Phila, Audata, Philinna, Olympias, Nikesipolis, Meda (and finally, in 337, Kleopatra, niece of his general Attalos).

332. The achievements of Philippos in the eyes of his son

When Alexander's troops mutinied at Opis in Babylonia in 324, Arrian tells us that the king saw fit to remind them, amongst other things, of how his father Philippos had taken them almost literally from rags to riches. Here is an extract from the speech, which 'is Arrian's own composition, but the substance may go back, if not to Alexander, at least to Ptolemy. Rhetorical it undoubtedly is, but a solid basis of fact underlies it' (J. R. Hamilton, *Alexander the Great* (London, 1973), 26); see also Hammond and Griffith, *Macedonia*, 657–62.

'I shall begin my speech in the first place with my father Philippos. This is only right and proper: for Philippos took you over as helpless vagabonds, most of you wearing skins, pasturing a few sheep up in the mountains, and fighting – badly – to keep them from Illyrians and Triballians and the neighbouring Thrakians. He gave you cloaks to wear instead of skins; and he brought you down from the mountains into the plains, having made you men fit to battle with the *barbaroi* on your borders – men whose hope of survival lay no longer in mountain strongholds but in innate courage. He made you *polis*-dwellers[1] and organised you with good *nomoi* and habits; and as for those very *barbaroi* who until then had been harrying and plundering you and your possessions, he made you their masters instead of their slaves and subjects. He also added most of Thrake to Makedonia, and by seizing the most convenient coastal towns opened up the country to commerce,[2] and enabled you to work the mines in safety.[3] He made you rulers of the Thessalians, who for years had been frightening you to death, and by humbling the Phokian people made your highway into Greece broad and easy instead of narrow and difficult.'[4]

Arrian, Anabasis VII.9.2–4

1 Not really: see **321** n.3.
2 I.e. importing.
3 See **327**.
4 See Ch.34.

34 Philippos and Greece

The death of Iason of Pherai (**318**) naturally led to anarchy in Thessaly; this anarchy then encouraged Theban intervention (the Thebans even went on to intervene in Makedonia, see **324**); the final result was a Thessaly divided between Alexandros of Pherai (and his supporters) and the rest, a division which provided an easy opening for Makedonia when she began to expand under Philippos II. Theban expansionism in the north had meanwhile also provoked the Phokians in self-defence to seize the treasure of Delphi in order to pay for mercenaries with whom to defend themselves; for a time they dominated central Greece, even becoming involved in Thessaly in competition with Makedonia; but it was the Sacred War between the Phokians and their opponents which Philippos eventually ended in 346, making his entry into Greece thereby.

See in general J. R. Ellis, *Philip II* (London, 1976), chs. 4–8; Hammond and Griffith, *Macedonia*, chs. 5–21.

333. Anarchy in Thessaly

After his death, the family of Iason attempted in the first instance to retain power, but failed to hold much more than Pherai. See further: Westlake, *Thessaly* (op. cit. p.581), ch.6.

During this year (369/8) Polydoros of Pherai, the ruler of Thessaly, was poisoned by his nephew Alexandros after being invited to a party;[1] and this nephew Alexandros succeeded him and ruled for eleven years. But having acquired his power illegally and by force he managed the affairs of his empire by adopting the same approach. For those in power before him had treated the masses with moderation and had been loved as a result, while he was hated for his harsh and violent rule. (3) So some men from Larisa, known as the Aleuadai because of their noble birth,[2] fearing his lawlessness, conspired together to overthrow him. And going from Larisa to Makedonia, they persuaded Alexandros its king[3] to join with them in getting rid of the tyrant. (4) But while they were occupied in this way, Alexandros of Pherai learnt of their attempt against him and gathered together those who were available for a campaign, intending to join battle in Makedonia. But the king of the Makedonians, accompanied by the exiles from Larisa, stole a march on his enemy and reached Larisa with his army; he was let into the walled circuit by the Larisaians and got control of the *polis* apart from its *akropolis*. (5) He then took this by siege and got control of the *polis* of Krannon; at first he agreed with the Thessalians to give the *poleis* back, but then, in contempt of public opinion, introduced substantial garrisons and held the *poleis* himself. Meanwhile, Alexandros of Pherai, under pursuit and much alarmed, returned to Pherai.

Diodorus xv.61.2–5

1 Xenophon reports, more accurately, that Iason was initially succeeded by his brothers Polyphron and Polydoros; the former killed the latter and was then killed by Alexandros, the son of Polydoros (*Hell.* vi.4.33–4).
2 Descended from Aleuas, who himself claimed descent from Herakles.
3 Oldest brother of Philippos II and, briefly, successor to their father, Amyntas III.

334. Athens and Thessaly

The divisions within Thessaly (see **333**) emerge very clearly from the alliance with the Athenians made by the enemies of Alexandros – in the name of all the Thessalians – in 361/60.

> Gods
> In the archonship of Nikophemos
> Alliance of Athenians and
> Thessalians for all time

It was resolved by the *boulē* and *dēmos*; (the *phylē*) Leontis held the prytany, Chairion son of Charinautos of (the deme) Phaleron was secretary, Archippos of (the deme) Amphitrope was president, on the twelfth day of the prytany, Exekestides proposed: concerning the matters raised by the Thessalian ambassadors, the *dēmos* voted to accept the alliance – and may good fortune follow – on the terms proposed by the Thessalians and that there should be an alliance between them and the Athenians for all time. And all the allies of the Athenians should be allies of the Thessalians and *vice versa*. And the *stratēgoi* and *boulē* and cavalry-commanders and cavalry of the Athenians should swear this oath: 'I will help with all my strength as far as I am able, if anyone goes against the community (*koinon*) of the Thessalians with warlike intent or overthrows the *archōn* whom the Thessalians have elected or sets up a tyrant in Thessaly.' And they should swear also the usual oath. And in order that the Thessalians may swear in turn, the *dēmos* should choose five men from among all the Athenians, who will go to Thessaly and administer this oath to Agelaos who is the *archōn* and the *polemarchoi* and the cavalry-commanders and the cavalry and the *hieromnēmones*[1] and the other *archontes*, such as hold office on behalf of the *koinon* of the Thessalians, 'I will help with all my strength as far as I am able, if anyone goes against the city of the Athenians with warlike intent or overthrows the *dēmos* of the Athenians.'[2] And the Thessalian ambassadors who are in Athens should swear the same oath in the presence of the *boulē*. And it is not to be possible for the Thessalians to end the war against Alexandros without Athenian agreement or for the Athenians to do so without the agreement of the *archōn* and *koinon* of the Thessalians. And the *dēmos* is to praise Agelaos who is the *archōn* and the *koinon* of the Thessalians, since they have efficiently and eagerly carried out everything which the *polis* requested of them, and is to praise the Thessalian ambassadors who have come here and invite them to hospitality in the *prytaneion* till tomorrow.[3] And the treasurers of Athena are to remove the *stēlē* concerning the alliance with Alexandros.[4] (Procedural details follow.)

Tod no. 147, lines 1–40

1 Priests in Thessaly.
2 Compare **302**.
3 Compare **172B**.
4 The alliance belongs early in his reign, soon after 369; he had engaged in numerous acts of war against Athens and it is surprising that the *stēlē* had not already been removed.

335. The Thebans in Thessaly

The most energetic exploiters in the first instance of the division of Thessaly between Alexandros of Pherai and his enemies were not the Makedonians or the Athenians, but the Thebans; the first expedition of Pelopidas after the accession of Alexandros of Pherai in 369 evidently restrained him for the time being and Pelopidas was able to go on to remove a competing Makedonian force (see **333**) and even intervene in the affairs of Makedonia (see **324**). A second expedition a year later was also mainly occupied with Makedonia, where the rebel Ptolemaios had succeeded in murdering the king Alexandros, and culminated in the capture of Pelopidas and his companion Ismenias by Alexandros of Pherai.

So when the Thebans heard of this, they were angry and at once despatched an army, though they appointed other men as its commanders, disapproving of Epameinondas for some reason . . . (29) But when the *stratēgoi* of the Thebans accomplished nothing by their invasion of

Thessaly, but were forced by inexperience or ill-fortune to retire in disgrace, the *polis* fined each of them 10,000 drachmas and sent Epameinondas off with an army . . . (Alexandros), however, terrified by the very reputation and name and the distinction of the generalship of Epameinondas, 'although a fighting cock, crouched down with folded wings, like a slave',[1] and at once sent men to him to offer an apology. Epameinondas could not bear to let the Thebans make peace with and become friends of such a man, but made a truce for thirty days, recovered Pelopidas[2] and Ismenias and retreated.

Plutarch, *Pelopidas* 28–29★

1 From a poem of unknown authorship.
2 Despite Pelopidas' death in 364, Thebes remained a dominant force in Thessaly; Alexandros' position was much weakened and he was murdered by his wife and her three brothers in 358.

336. The Sacred War

It is not surprising that after Leuktra the Thebans, as we see here, should have attempted to invoke the authority of the shrine of Delphi against the Spartans; their attempt, however, to apply the same technique to the Phokians rebounded, and when the latter reconciled themselves to outright use of the treasure of Apollo they were able to raise a force of mercenaries which dominated central Greece from the mid-350s down to 346.

(In 355/4) the so-called Sacred War[1] broke out and lasted for nine years. For Philomelos the Phokian, a man of extraordinary audacity and lawlessness, seized the shrine at Delphi and kindled the Sacred War, for some such reasons as these. When the Lakedaimonians had fought the war of Leuktra against the Boiotians and been defeated, the Thebans brought a suit against the Lakedaimonians in the presence of the Amphiktyones[2] on the grounds of their seizure of the citadel of Thebes, the Kadmeia, and had them condemned to pay a large fine; and the Phokians, who had cultivated a large part of the sacred land known as Kirrhaian, were prosecuted in the presence of the Amphiktyones and condemned to pay a fine of many talents. And when they did not pay what they owed, the *hieromnemones*[3] accused the Phokians in the presence of the Amphiktyones and asked the council, if the Phokians did not pay the money to the god, to consecrate the land of those who were defrauding the god. Likewise they said that the others who had been condemned should pay what they owed, among whom were the Lakedaimonians; and if they did not obey they should be branded together as villains. But when the Greeks joined in ratifying the decisions

603

of the Amphiktyones and the *chōra* of the Phokians was about to be consecrated, Philomelos, who was the most notable of the Phokians, spoke to his compatriots and said that they could not pay the money because of the size of the fine and that to stand by and watch their *chōra* being consecrated was not only cowardly, but was also dangerous since it involved the destruction of the livelihood of them all. And he tried to show, as far as possible, that the judgments of the Amphiktyones were unjust; for very large fines had been inflicted when only an extremely small piece of land had been cultivated. So he advised them to treat the fines as invalid and showed that the Phokians had strong grounds for their complaint against the Amphiktyones; for of old they had held the control and guardianship of the oracle; and he cited Homer, the oldest and greatest of the poets as a witness, quoting 'Now Schedios and Epistrophos ruled over Phokians . . . Who held Kyparissos and rocky Pytho.'[4] So he said that they should claim the guardianship of the oracle as being an ancestral right of the Phokians; and he promised that the attempt would succeed if they made him *stratēgos* with full and complete powers for the whole attempt.

Diodorus XVI.23

1 See **84**.
2 See **84**.
3 Officials of the Amphiktyones.
4 The ancient name of Delphi (Homer, *Iliad* II.517 and 519).

337. Athens and Amphipolis

One of the prime objectives of Athenian foreign policy in the middle of the fourth century was the recovery of Amphipolis, lost in 424 (see **192**); Aeschines here, in the course of narrating how he presented the Athenian claim to Amphipolis to Philippos II, documents the early stages of the Athenian attempt.

'Just after the deaths of Amyntas and of Alexandros,[1] the eldest of his sons, Perdikkas and Philippos being children and their mother Eurydike being abandoned by those who had seemed to be her friends, (27) Pausanias was making an attempt on the throne; he was an exile, but was dominant at that particular moment, with many supporters and a Greek army at his back; he had taken Anthemous and Therma and Strepsa and a number of other places;[2] the Makedonians were disunited, but the majority were in favour of Pausanias: at that moment the Athenians elected Iphikrates *stratēgos* to fight against Amphipolis,[3] the Amphipolitans at the time possessing the *polis* and enjoying the *chōra*.'

Aeschines II (*On the mismanaged embassy*) 26–27

1 See **333** n.3.
2 Moving in from the east.
3 Amyntas had in 371 recognised the Athenian claim to Amphipolis.

338. Problems in the Athenian confederacy

The life of the Athenian confederacy founded in 377 (**269**) was abruptly terminated, in fact if not in name, by the war of 357–355 (**339**) – thereby lasting considerably less well than its fifth-century counterpart. Why? All went well enough for a decade (see in brief T. T. B. Ryder, *Koine Eirene* (Oxford, 1965), 77–8), but thereafter we begin to see signs of allied disaffection and of Athenian highhandedness (*ib.* 88–9). It may be wrong to exaggerate this into a repetition of the fifth century (see on this G. T. Griffith in P. D. A. Garnsey and C. R. Whittaker (eds.), *Imperialism in the Ancient World* (Cambridge, 1978), 127 44; J. Cargill, *The Second Athenian League* (Berkeley, 1981); a different view in G. L. Cawkwell, 'Notes on the failure of the second Athenian Confederacy', *JHS* 101 (1981), 40–55), but it seems undeniable that in the 360s and 350s the Athenians were prepared, where necessary, to infringe both the letter and the spirit of the 377 Charter – with, for example, judicial interference on Keos (Tod no.142) and a cleruchy at Poteidaia (Tod no.146; Poteidaia was not actually a member of the confederacy). In the inscription below, the city of Arkesine (on the island of Amorgos) thanks and rewards the Athenian who, in the 350s, has been their governor for a period of at least two years. Clearly Androtion has been a model and humane *archōn* – but he (and his garrison – see below) ought perhaps not to have been in Arkesine at all. (For an allegedly less scrupulous governor see Aeschines 1.107.)

Resolved by the *boule* and the *dēmos* of Arkesine: since Androtion[1] has been a good man with regard to the *dēmos* of Arkesine, and in governing the *polis* caused no distress to any of the *politai* or any of the foreigners visiting the *polis*; and (since) he lent money to the *polis* at a critical time without wishing to charge any interest; and (since), with the *polis* in difficulties, he paid the wages of the garrison troops himself, and on recovering the money at the end of the year exacted no interest; and (since this) saved the *polis* twelve minas in expenditure every year; and (since) he ransomed any men[2] he came across who had been captured by the enemy: let Androtion son of Andron, of Athens, be crowned with a golden crown worth 500 drachmas, in recognition of his excellence and justice and goodwill towards the *dēmos* of Arkesine; and let him be recorded as a *proxenos* and benefactor of the *polis* of Arkesine,[3] both himself and his descendants; and let him be exempt from all taxes.[4]

Tod no.152

1 Androtion (*c.*410–340) was a local historial of Attika (Atthidographer) as well as a public figure; for his political career see Phillip Harding, *Historia* 25 (1976),

186–200. It is likely that his governorship of Arkesine (or the whole of Amorgos?) fell in the first half of the 350s.

2 Citizens of Arkesine, presumably.

3 This means he will look after the interests of Arkesine, and its citizens, in Athens (see **43**), though appointments as *proxenos* were by now, increasingly, purely honorific.

4 After a small gap, the inscription resumes with a record, seemingly, of a resolution of 'the allies', but only three mutilated lines of it survive.

339. The Revolt of the Allies

Trouble for Athens in 357 began in Euboia, which had developed sympathies with Thebes after the battle of Leuktra (see **273**).

While these things were going on, the inhabitants of Euboia fell into *stasis* among themselves, and when one side summoned the Boiotians to its assistance and the other the Athenians, war broke out in Euboia. Several battles and skirmishes took place, in which sometimes the Thebans were superior and sometimes the Athenians carried off the victory. No important pitched battle occurred, yet, even when the island had been devastated by internecine warfare and many men had been killed on both sides, the two sides barely came to an agreement as a result of this lesson taught by the disasters and made peace with each other.[1]

Now the Boiotians returned home and remained quiet, but the Athenians suffered the revolt of Chios, Rhodes, Kos and, moreover, Byzantion, and became involved in the war called the War with the Allies which lasted three years.[2] The Athenians chose Chares and Chabrias as *stratēgoi* and dispatched them with an army. The two *stratēgoi*, on sailing against Chios, found that allies had arrived to assist the Chians from Byzantion, Rhodes and Kos, and also from Mausolos, the ruler of Karia.[3] They then drew up their forces and began to besiege the city by land and sea. Now Chares, who commanded the infantry, advanced against the walls by land and began to fight the enemy who poured out on him from the *polis*; but Chabrias, sailing up to the harbour, fought a severe naval engagement and was worsted when his ship was shattered by a ramming attack. While the men on the other ships withdrew in time and saved their lives, he, choosing death with glory instead of defeat, fought on for his ship and died of his wounds.[4]

Diodorus XVI.7.2–4

1 The entire war in fact lasted a month and fell in 357/6; see Tod nos. 153–4 for a new alliance with Karystos and measures to prevent a recurrence of the troubles which had threatened Eretria.

2 In fact only parts of 357/6 and 356/5.

3 In fact nominally a Persian satrap, but in practice largely independent (see S. Hornblower, *Mausolus* (Oxford, 1982), esp. ch.7).

4 The war came to an end when Chares, short of money (compare **287**), helped the satrap Artabazos in rebellion against Persia and Persia threatened war on Athens. Although Athens had lost the most important of her allies, it is interesting to note that those who were left were prepared to vote for a garrison in Andros (Tod no.156).

340. Athens and Persia

Although the early years of the reign of Philippos (see **325–327**) had seen not only the safeguarding of his kingdom from attack, but also its expansion (partly at the expense of Athens, with the capture of Amphipolis in 357), the chief enemy of Athens in 354/3 is clearly still Persia. In urging the Athenians not to seek war with Persia, Demosthenes shows a healthy respect for the power of Persia (contrast **319–320**).

'I agree that the King is the common enemy of all Greeks, yet I would not on that account advise you to undertake a war against him by yourselves apart from the rest; for I observe that the Greeks themselves are by no means common friends of each other, but that some of them place more confidence in the King than in some of themselves. From this state of things I conclude that it is in your interest to be careful that your grounds for beginning a war are fair and just, but to prepare everything which is necessary and settle on that.'

Demosthenes xiv (*On the symmories*[1])3

1 See **312** Intro. for their role in the collection of Athenian revenue; their relevance to preparations for war is obvious.

341. Philippos in Thessaly

When, after 355/4, the power of the Phokians grew at the expense of that of Thebes (see **336**), they followed the Theban practice of intervention in Thessaly. In moving in 353 to increase the role of Makedon in Thessaly, Philippos had the justification of being the avenger of the shrine of Delphi.

Afterwards Philippos, summoned by the Thessalians, entered Thessaly with his army and at first fought against Lykophron the tyrant of Pherai on behalf of the Thessalians;[1] but afterwards, when Lykophron had summoned help from the Phokians, Phayllos the brother of Onomarchos[2] was sent with 7,000 troops. Philippos, however, defeated the Phokians and ejected them from Thessaly. Onomarchos then raised his entire force and, in the expectation of mastering the whole of Thessaly, came in haste to the help of those on the side of Lykophron. Philippos with the Thessalians joined battle with the Phokians, but Onomarchos with his superior numbers won two battles and killed many of the Makedonians. Philippos was in the greatest danger and his soldiers deserted him in despair; but he spoke encouragingly to the greater number of them and just managed to restore discipline.

Diodorus XVI.35.1–2

1 Lykophron had succeeded to the position of Alexandros of Pherai (see **333**). Diodorus XVI.14.1–2 records an earlier move against Pherai in 358/7 and 31.6 the seizure of its harbour Pagasai in 354/3. Perhaps because of their uncertainty over Philippos' intentions, the Thessalians, despite their opposition to Phokis (29.1), were easily bribed by the Phokians into inactivity.
2 Successors of Philomelos (see **336**) in command.

342. Philippos blocked at Thermopylai

The next stage of the war provides a rare example of the Athenian war machine functioning efficiently; Philippos returned to Thessaly and defeated Onomarchos, at a battle witnessed by Chares and an Athenian fleet, 'by chance', according to Diodorus XVI.35.3–6. Hardly: Chares no doubt had a precise function to perform and it was his presence with a fleet which made it possible to get news of the disaster back to Athens. It was the absence of naval patrols and the information they provided (in contrast to the fifth century) which made it hard for the Athenians to react to the moves of Philippos; but now they could and did.

It is incredible how much glory Philippos won in the eyes of everyone by this victory; they regarded him as the avenger of sacrilege and the defender of religion; he had emerged as the only person who could exact vengeance for something which should have been expiated with the whole strength of the entire world; as a result he was fit to be regarded as closest to the gods, since the majority of the gods had been re-established by him. But the Athenians, when they heard the outcome of the war, seized the pass of Thermopylai in order to prevent Philippos crossing into Greece,[1] just as they had seized it before on the approach of the Persians;[2] but neither the reason nor the action were similar; for then they had acted in defence of the freedom of Greece, now of public sacrilege, then in defence of temples against the ravaging of the enemy, now in defence of the ravagers of temples and in opposition to their avengers.

Justin VIII.2.5–9

1 In 352.
2 See **III**.

343. Philippos in Thrake

Philippos had won some successes in Thrake in the period down to early 353, but these had been largely undone by Athenian activity while Philippos was engaged in Thessaly (see **342**). In 352/1, he returned to Thrake, operating with impunity on the shores of the Propontis. It is at this point that Demosthenes emerges as the consistent advocate of Athenian opposition to Philippos, recognising in 346 (see **346**) the tactical necessity of peace, but only to welcome its breakdown a few years later.

'I think it is necessary first of all to remind you of a few of the things which have happened. You remember, men of Athens, that news came to you two or three years ago that Philippos was besieging Heraion Teichos[1] in Thrake. At the time it was (the month of) Maimakterion;[2] there were many speeches and you made a great deal of noise and voted to launch 40 ships and to embark on them the men under 45 and to collect an *eisphora*[3] of 60 talents. (5) Thereafter the year passed, Hekatombaion, Metageitnion, Boedromion;[4] in that month, after the celebration of the Mysteries,[5] you just managed to send off Charidemos with ten ships and no soldiers and five talents of silver. For when it was announced that Philippos was ill or dead – both pieces of news came – you thought that an expedition was no longer appropriate and abandoned its despatch. But that *was* the opportunity; for if we had then promptly sent an expedition there, as we voted, Philippos would not have been preserved to trouble us now '

Demosthenes III ((Third Speech) on Olynthos) 4–5

1 On the north shore of the Propontis.
2 Roughly November 352.
3 See **312**.
4 Roughly July to September 351.
5 See **242**.

344. Philippos and Olynthos

Philippos had in 357/6 made an alliance with Olynthos, head of the Chalkidian cities, an alliance which had served both parties well, since both gained at the expense of Athens; about 350/49, however, Olynthos offered refuge to two pretenders to the Makedonian throne; in doing so, it seriously miscalculated the power and will of Philippos, who moved to deal with Olynthos in the autumn of 349.

In Europe, Philippos the king of the Makedonians marched against the Chalkidian *poleis*; he besieged and destroyed the fortress of Geira[1] and having terrified some of the other small towns he forced them to submit.

Diodorus XVI.52.9

1 Or Zeira, in other manuscripts; we do not know where this place was or whether either name is correct (the attested site of Zereia has been suggested; it is quite impossible that Stageira, the *polis* where Aristotle was born, could be referred to as a fortress, *contra* Ellis, *Philip II*, 94–5).

345. The reaction of Demosthenes

The Olynthians appealed to Athens for help. The strategic arguments over whether it was in the Athenian interest to help or whether Athens was able to help effectively can probably not be resolved; in the event, the Athenians were involved at more or less the same time in an attempt to assert their control over Euboia which ended in the loss of everywhere except Karystos; little help was sent and Olynthos fell (see Ellis, *Philip II*, 98–9). The attack of Philippos on Olynthos is remarkable, however, for Demosthenes' argument that Philippos must be opposed at all costs (and earlier Olynthian hostility to Athens forgotten). Speech IV, the so-called *First Speech against Philippos*, was probably delivered in the winter of 351/0, after a hostile move against Olynthos by Philippos on his way back from Thrake; I–III, the *Speeches on Olynthos*, were made after the full-scale assault had begun.

See further: G. L. Cawkwell, 'The defence of Olynthus', *CQ* n.s. 12 (1962), 122–40.

'The things which happened then[1] cannot be undone; but now an opportunity has come with another war, which is why I dealt with those events, so that you do not do the same thing over again. How then, men of Athens, shall we make use of this opportunity? For if you do not send help with all the strength at your disposal, consider how you will turn out to have run all your campaigns in the interest of Philippos . . . (8) So what else is there to do, but to send help vigorously and promptly? I have no idea. For apart from the shame which would cover us if we abandoned any of our undertakings, there seems to me to be much to fear from the consequences, with the Thebans disposed as they are towards us, the Phokians financially exhausted and no one to prevent Philippos having won his present objectives from turning to affairs here.'

Demosthenes III ((*Third Speech*) *on Olynthos*) 6–8★

1 See 343.

346. The Peace of Philokrates

Philippos began to indicate his desire for an accommodation with Athens already in 349/8, before the fall of Olynthos; he needed to consolidate his position in Thrake and also (his alliance with Thessaly depended thereon) to settle the

Phokian issue once and for all; Athens now had no choice but to agree and to watch Phokis dismembered. Those responsible for the Peace of Philokrates (named after the head of the Athenian envoys) in 346, including Demosthenes, naturally competed to disown it. But its necessity at the time could not be gainsaid.

See further: G. L. Cawkwell, 'Aeschines and the Peace of Philocrates', *REG* 73 (1960), 416–38; 'Demosthenes' policy after the Peace of Philocrates', *CQ* n.s.13 (1963), 120–38; 200–13.

(A) The members of the *synedrion*[1] then passed a decree to admit Philippos and his descendants to the Amphiktyony and to give him two votes which had previously been held by the now defeated Phokians. They also decreed that the three *poleis*[2] in the possession of the Phokians should lose their walls and that the Phokians should have no access to the shrine or the council of the Amphiktyony; that they should not be permitted to acquire horses or arms until they had repaid to the god the money they had plundered; that those of the Phokians who had fled and any others who had had a share in robbing the shrine were to be under a curse and subject to arrest wherever they might be; that all the *poleis* of the Phokians were to be razed and the inhabitants moved to villages, none of which should have more than 50 houses;[3] the villages were to be at least a stade away from each other; that the Phokians were to possess their territory and pay each year to the god a tribute of 60 talents until they had paid back the money in the accounts at the time of the robbing of the sanctuary. Philippos, furthermore, was to hold the Pythian games together with the Boiotians and Thessalians, since the Corinthians had shared with the Phokians in the sacrilege committed against the god. The Amphiktyones and Philippos were to hurl the arms of the Phokians and their mercenaries down the crags and burn what remained of them and sell the horses. The Amphiktyones, consequent upon all this, laid down regulations for the custody of the oracle and other matters relating to piety towards the gods and the general peace and concord of the Greeks. Thereafter, when Philippos had helped the Amphiktyones give effect to their decrees and had dealt courteously with all, he returned to Makedonia, having not merely won for himself a reputation for piety and excellent generalship, but having also made considerable preparation for the aggrandisement that was destined to be his. For he was ambitious to be appointed *stratēgos* of Hellas in supreme command and to prosecute the war against the Persians. And this was what actually happened.

Diodorus xvi.60

(B) '"Is it then necessary for us to do what we are told[4] because of our fears in this respect? Do *you* recommend this?" Far from it. What I do recommend is that we should do nothing unworthy of ourselves *and* avoid war, while appearing to everyone to be reasonable and make just proposals. With respect to those who think we should remain entirely obdurate and do not foresee the war that will follow, I wish to offer this consideration. We are allowing the Thebans to keep Oropos;[5] and if someone asked us why, insisting on an honest reply, we should say that it was in order not to go to war. (25) And we have now in the treaty abandoned Amphipolis to Philippos[6] and are allowing the Kardians to be separated from the other Chersonesitans and the Karian[7] to hold the islands of Chios, Kos and Rhodes and the Byzantians to detain our ships, clearly thinking that the respite afforded by peace is the source of greater benefits than resistance or controversy over these matters. Is it not foolish and entirely perverse, if this is our attitude to everyone individually on matters of vital concern, now to fight all of them over the phantom issue at Delphi?'

Demosthenes v (*On the Peace*) 24–25

1 Council of the Amphiktyony.
2 Of the Boiotians.
3 Compare **291**.
4 To endorse the reconstruction of the Amphiktyony with Philippos holding the position once held by the Phokians, see A.
5 Some politicians had held out the hope that the Peace of Philokrates would provide for its return; for Oropos, see **186** n.4.
6 Athens had again had hopes of getting Euboia in exchange.
7 Mausolos, see **339**.

347. The drift back to war

After 346 Philippos was not idle, expanding his control of Thrake, intervening in Euboia; a Thucydides might have said that the Athenians were compelled to go to war. The war was actually provoked when Philippos attacked Perinthos and Byzantion in 340; he had had Artabazos and Memnon, exiled subjects of the King of Persia, at his court from 353/2 and no doubt saw the final subjugation of the Hellespontine area as the last step before the invasion of Asia. Both *poleis* resisted, with Athenian help.

And Chares[1] set off for the meeting of the generals of the King leaving his ships at Hieron,[2] in order that they could escort the merchant fleet from the Black Sea. But when Philippos realised that Chares was not there he at first tried to send his ships to seize the merchant fleet; when he failed in the attack, he sent his soldiers across to Hieron and got control of the ships; there were no less than 230 in total. And separating out the enemy ones,[3] he broke them up and used the wood for his siege engines and got control also of a great deal of corn and leather and money.

Philochorus, *FGrH* 328 F 162

1 The Athenian commander, see **339**.
2 See **281** n.4.
3 The Athenian ships principally, no doubt.

348. Athens or Greece?

Apart from the purely Athenian aspect of the opposition to Philippos, there was a Panhellenic one. But despite the disclaimer of VIII.42, Demosthenes could not really distinguish the power of Athens from the freedom of Greece; all who opposed Athens were traitors to Greece. The reality was not so simple – not only did Philippos appear as a defender against the barbarians to the Greeks of Thrake (Diodorus XVI.71.2), he appeared also as a defender to the small *poleis* of Greece which had suffered at the hands of the great. The most eloquent account of their position is that of the second-century historian of the rise of Rome, Polybius of Megalopolis.

So while we may praise Demosthenes for many things, we may blame him for one, for having recklessly and uncritically cast bitter reproaches at the most distinguished men in Greece by saying that the associates of Kerkidas, Hieronymos, and Eukampidas in Arkadia were betrayers of Greece because they joined Philippos, and for saying the same of Neon and Thrasylochos, the sons of Philiadas, in Messene, the associates of Myrtis, Teledamos and Mnaseas in Argos, those of Daochos and Kineas in Thessaly, those of Theogeiton and Timolas in Boiotia, and several others in different *poleis*. But in fact all these men were perfectly and clearly justified in thus defending their own rights, especially those from Arkadia and Messene. For they, by inducing Philippos to enter the Peloponnesos and humbling the Lakedaimonians, in the first place allowed all the inhabitants of the Peloponnesos to breathe freely and to gain some impression of liberty; and next by recovering the territory and *poleis* of which the Lakedaimonians in their days of power had deprived the Messenians, Megalopolitans, Tegeans and Argives, they unquestionably increased the power of their native communities. With such an object in view, it was not their duty to fight against Philippos and the Makedonians, but to take every possible step for their own honour and glory. Had they in acting thus either allowed their communities to be garrisoned by Philippos, or abolished their laws and deprived the citizens of freedom of action and speech to serve their own ambition and place themselves in power, they would have deserved the name of traitor. But if, preserving the rights of their respective communities, they simply differed in their judgment of the facts, thinking that the interests of Athens were not identical with those of their *poleis*, they should not have been called traitors for this reason by Demosthenes. Measuring everything by the interests of his own community, thinking that the whole of

Greece should have its eyes turned on Athens, and if people did not do so, calling them traitors, Demosthenes seems to me to have been mistaken and very far from the truth.

Polybius xviii.14.1–11

349. The battle of Chaironeia

Raising the sieges of Perinthos and Byzantion, Philippos dealt initially with problems in the interior of Thrake; meanwhile, the Amphiktyony manufactured an excuse for his intervention and in the autumn of 339 he marched swiftly to Elateia, *south* of Thermopylai.

(A) 'It was evening when someone arrived with the news for the *prytaneis* that Elateia had fallen. Upon this, they at once got up in the middle of supper; some of them expelled the people from the booths in the *agora* and burnt the coverings, others sent for the *stratēgoi* and called the trumpeter; the *polis* was in a state of uproar. The next day at dawn the *prytaneis* summoned the *boulē* to the *bouleutērion*, while you went to the *ekklēsia*; before the *boulē* had begun to deliberate and prepare for the *ekklēsia*, the whole *dēmos* was seated ready. (170) And then when the *boulē* came and the *prytaneis* announced the news which had been brought to them and introduced the messenger and he spoke also, the herald asked, "Who wishes to speak?," but no one came forward . . . (174) I said then, "I think that those who are completely shattered on the grounds that the Thebans are on the side of Philippos do not realise how things actually are; for I am sure that if this had been so, we should not now be hearing that he is at Elateia, but that he is on our borders. I know well that he has come in order to organise affairs in Thebes . . ."' (Demosthenes went on to recommend and then to bring about an alliance between the Athenians and the Thebans, who now perceived Philippos as a threat.)

Demosthenes xviii (*On the Crown*) 169–174*

(B) So Philippos, having failed to get the alliance of the Boiotians, nevertheless decided to fight both of them[1] together. So he waited for the last of his allies to arrive and then marched into Boiotia, with more than 30,000 infantry and no less than 2,000 cavalry. Both sides were eager for the battle and were well matched in intention, zeal and courage, but the king had the advantage in numbers and in generalship. For he had fought many battles of different sorts and had been victorious in most cases, so that he had wide experience of military operations. On the Athenian side, the best of their *stratēgoi* were dead, Iphikrates, Chabrias and Timotheos too; and the best of those who were left, Chares, was no better than any ordinary soldier in the activity and counsel required of a *stratēgos*.

(86) The armies deployed at dawn (i.e. at Chaironeia), and the king stationed his son Alexander, young in age but outstanding for his bravery and swiftness of action, on one wing, placing with him his best commanders, while he himself at the head of an élite corps exercised the command over the other; and he deployed individual units where the occasion required. On the other side, the Athenians, dividing the line according to nationality, assigned one wing to the Boiotians and commanded the other themselves. The battle was hotly contested for a long time and many fell on both sides, so that for a while the struggle permitted hopes of victory to both.

Then Alexander, eager to show his father his prowess and second to none in excess of zeal, and also with many good men at his side, first succeeded in breaking the solid front of the enemy line and, striking down many, he fought those opposite him into the ground. As the same success was won by his companions, gaps in the solid front were opened. Corpses piled up, until finally those with Alexander forced their way through and put their opponents to flight. Then the king also in person hazarded an advance, not conceding credit for the victory even to Alexander; he first forced back the troops stationed opposite him and then by compelling them to flee became the man responsible for the victory. More than 1,000 Athenians fell in the battle and no less than 2,000 were captured. Likewise, many of the Boiotians were killed and not a few taken prisoner. After the battle Philippos raised a trophy, gave up the dead for burial, gave sacrifices to the gods for victory, and rewarded according to their deserts those of his men who had distinguished themselves for bravery.

Diodorus XVI.85.5–86

1 The Athenians and the Boiotians.

350. The settlement of Greece

Philippos' appetite grew with eating, and after the battle of Chaironeia he became the man who would fulfil earlier, inchoate Greek ambitions (see **319–320**) and lead an invasion of Persia. The settlement of Greece in general was generous, particularly generous to the Athenians; it could, indeed, hardly have been otherwise; for it would not have seemed very plausible for someone who had actually attacked Athens to claim to be invading Persia in order to avenge the destruction of the temples of Athens in 480. The murder of Philippos in 336 did not prevent the invasion of Asia; the enterprise was only delayed, to be carried out by Alexander the Great – but that is the theme of M. Austin, *The Hellenistic World* (Cambridge, 1981).

Meanwhile, the role of leader of Greece was congenial to a man who had earlier set out to provide Makedonia with a Greek capital at Pella and, as patron, paid for the erection of public buildings in other Greek *poleis*. The constitutional arrangement which Philippos created is known to modern scholars as the 'League' of Corinth; but it was almost certainly yet another Common Peace (see **263**) now with an unchallenged *hēgemōn*.

(A) After he had settled matters in Greece, Philippos ordered that envoys should be summoned to Corinth from all the states with a view to consolidating his settlement. He there propounded a covenant of peace for the whole of Greece, giving each state the share that it deserved, and he created a council of representatives to serve as a sort of common senate. Only the Spartans refused to have anything to do with the king or with the covenant; they considered that a settlement imposed by the victor instead of being agreed on by the states concerned meant enslavement, not peace. Next, the military contributions were fixed that the individual states were to make, whether to assist the king against attack or for making war under his command. But everyone realised that these arrangements were directed against the Persian empire.

Justin IX.5

(B) In this year (337/6) king Philippos, proudly conscious of his victory at Chaeroneia and seeing that he had dashed the confidence of the leading Greek *poleis*, conceived of the ambition to become the *hēgemōn* of all Greece. He spread the word that he wanted to make war on the Persians on the Greeks' behalf and to punish them for the profanation of the temples, and this won for him the loyal support of the Greeks . . . A general congress was accordingly held at Corinth. He spoke about the war against Persia, and by raising great expectations won the representatives over to war. The Greeks elected him *stratēgos autokratōr* of Greece, and he began great preparations for the Persian campaign. He prescribed the number of soldiers that each *polis* should send for the joint effort, and then returned home to Makedon.

Diodorus XVI.89★

(C) [Oath. I swear by Zeus, Earth, Sun, Pose]idon, A[thena, Ares and all the gods and goddesses.] I will abide [by the peace and I will not break the] treaty [with Philippos the Makedonian, nor] will I bear arms [with malicious intent against any of those] who abide by [their oaths, either by land] or by sea, [nor] will I seize with warlike intent [a *polis* or] fort [or harbour] of any of those [who participate in the peace] by any device [or trick, nor] will I overthrow the monarchy of Philippos [or his heirs or the *politeiai* existing] in each state when they swore [the oaths concerning] the peace, [nor will I myself do anything] against this [treaty nor] will I allow anyone else to do so, as far as [I am able; and if anyone does anything] which breaks [the treaty, I will help those who are wronged] as they request and I will make war against the transgressor [of the common peace] as is [decided by] the common council and as the *hēgemōn* [requests and I will not] desert . . . (a list of those swearing follows).[1]

Tod no. 177[2]

1 The list makes it clear that the number of representatives was related to the size of the contingent furnished by each community.
2 A speech preserved as XVII in the Demosthenic corpus and attacking the misconduct of Alexander the Great makes it clear that in 336 he largely renewed the treaty to which this oath relates: the preservation of existing *politeiai*, their defence against exiles, the role of the common council and *hēgemōn* and collective action against a transgressor all appear, as well as more general concepts such as freedom, non-aggression and the security of the seas. The speech also asserts that Philippos and Alexander both used the guarantee for existing *politeiai* to preserve their own supporters in power in a number of Greek communities.

Chronological table

Before 490 B.C., most Greek dates are more or less approximate; in particular, an internally coherent set of synchronisations in Herodotus offers a rather different view of archaic chronology from that found in later writers. The synchronisations, linked by the presence of Alyattes in both, may be represented diagrammatically (see below).

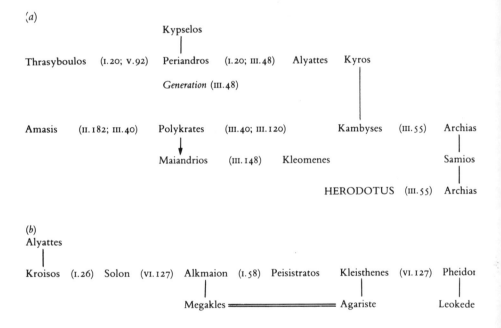

(a)

		Kypselos			
Thrasyboulos	(1.20; v.92)	Periandros	(1.20; III.48)	Alyattes	Kyros
		Generation (III.48)			
Amasis	(II.182; III.40)	Polykrates	(III.40; III.120)	Kambyses (III.55)	Archias
		Maiandrios	(III.148)	Kleomenes	Samios
				HERODOTUS (III.55)	Archias

(b)
Alyattes

Kroisos	(1.26)	Solon	(VI.127)	Alkmaion	(1.58)	Peisistratos	Kleisthenes	(VI.127)	Pheidon
				Megakles ======= Agariste					Leokede

Undue precision is not to be expected from Herodotus; generations vary in length and people of different ages, such as Herodotus and Archias (almost certainly his senior), are obviously synchronised because their *careers* overlapped. *Very roughly*, one can calculate that the Corinthian tyranny (conventional dates 650–585) and the tyranny of Pheidon were essentially sixth-century affairs. This calculation (rather more than four generations from Herodotus to Kypselos) is perfectly compatible with a calculation based on Fig. 13, p.216 (five generations from Thoukydides, son of Melesias, to Kypselos), unless one makes the wholly unwarranted decision to accept 597/6 as the date when the Athenian grandson of

Kypselos was *archōn*. Such conventional dates depend on the calculations of scholars of the late fifth century and later, who drew up lists of kings and magistrates. Such lists are only of value if they depend on archival material and we can see no reason to suppose that such archival material existed; Thucydides clearly did not know of any and the fact that the high chronology was at Athens enshrined in inscribed lists of *archontes* in the late fifth century (see Meiggs and Lewis no.6, accepting their reliability) tells us nothing about the material on which it was based.

We prefer Herodotus.

The Dark Ages

1200 onwards	Destruction of Mycenean centres in Greece
1050	Renewal of Greek contacts with Cyprus
1050–950	Ionian colonisation of Asia Minor coast
1000	Dorian invasion
Before 800	Foundation of *emporion* at Al Mina
776	Conventional date for first Olympic Games
Before 775	Foundation of *emporion* at Pithekoussai
750–700	Invention and diffusion of Greek alphabet
About 735	Foundation of first Sicilian colony: Naxos
About 730–710	Spartan conquest of Messenia
Before 700	Homer

The Archaic period

687	Kingdom of Lydia founded by Gyges (687–52)
664	Foundation of Saïte dynasty in Egypt under Psammetichos I (664–610)
632	Attempted tyranny of Kylon at Athens
About 630	Foundation of Kyrene
621	Drakon lawgiver at Athens
About 600	Foundation of Naukratis
595–586	First Sacred War for control of Delphi
594/3	Solon *archōn* at Athens
572	Marriage contest organised by Kleisthenes of Sikyon
569–525	Amasis king of Egypt
561	Peisistratos' first tyranny at Athens
560–546	Kroisos king of Lydia
559–556	Miltiades the elder becomes tyrant in Thrakian Chersonesos
559	Kyros becomes ruler of Persia
550	Kyros conquers Media
546	Peisistratos' final tyranny at Athens (546–528) Kyros conquers Lydia
530	Death of Kyros; accession of Kambyses
528/7	Death of Peisistratos; rule of Hippias at Athens
525	Death of Amasis of Egypt; Persian conquest

525–520	Fall of Polykrates tyrant of Samos
521	Dareios seizes power in Persia
520–490	Kleomenes king of Sparta
514	Harmodios and Aristogeiton murder Hipparchos at Athens
512	Dareios conquers Thrake
510	Expulsion of Peisistratids from Athens
508/7	Isagoras *archōn* at Athens; reforms of Kleisthenes
505	Beginning of tyranny at Gela
501/500	Institution of ten generals at Athens
499	Ionian revolt from Persia
498	Sardis burned by rebels
494	Battle of Lade followed by sack of Miletos
493/2	Themistokles *archōn* at Athens; Phrynichos prosecuted for staging *Milesians*
491	Gelon tyrant of Gela
490	Death of Kleomenes of Sparta
	First Persian expedition; battle of Marathon
487/6	Athenian *archontes* chosen by lot
486	Death of Dareios; accession of Xerxes
485	Gelon becomes tyrant of Syracuse
483	Discovery of new vein of silver at Laureion
480	Persian and Carthaginian invasions of Greece and Sicily. Battles of Artemision, Thermopylai, Salamis and Himera
479	Battles of Plataiai and Mykale

The Classical period

478/7	Delian League against Persia founded under leadership of Athens
	Between 469 and 466 Greeks defeat Persians at Eurymedon River
466	Collapse of tyranny at Syracuse
464	Earthquake in Sparta; helot revolt in Messenia
461	Reforms of Ephialtes at Athens
	War between Athens and Sparta (First Peloponnesian War 461–446)
459	Athenian expedition to Egypt
458	Battles of Tanagra and Oinophyta: Athenian conquest of Boiotia
447	Parthenon begun in Athens
446	Thirty Years' Peace between Sparta and Athens and their allies
441–439	Revolt of Samos
435–433	War between Corinth and Kerkyra
431	Second Peloponnesian War begins, see pp.334–6
429	Death of Perikles
428	Revolt of Lesbos
425	Athenian success at Pylos

421	Peace of Nikias between Athens and Sparta and their allies
418	Battle of Mantineia
415–413	Athenian expedition to Sicily
412	War renewed: Spartan treaties with Persia
411	Coup of Four Hundred at Athens
409	Carthaginians invade Sicily
405	Dionysios I becomes tyrant of Syracuse
	Spartans destroy Athenian fleet at Aigospotamoi
404	Siege and capitulation of Athens
404–403	Régime of Thirty Tyrants at Athens
401–399	Expedition of Kyros and the Ten Thousand against Persian King
399	Death of Sokrates
396–394	Agesilaos' campaigns in Asia Minor
395	Corinthian War breaks out
394	Persians defeat Spartan fleet at Knidos
387/6	Peace of Antalkidas ('King's Peace') between Persia and Greek states
379/8	Liberation of Thebes
378/7	Second Athenian League founded
375	Iason *tagos* of Thessaly
371	Battle of Leuktra
370	Death of Iason
367	Death of Dionysios I
362	Battle of Mantincia
359	Philippos II becomes king of Makedon
356	Sacred War breaks out
348	Philippos captures Olynthos
346	Peace between Philippos and Athens (Peace of Philokrates)
344	Timoleon reaches Sicily
338	Philippos defeats Thebans and Athenians at Chaironeia
337	'League of Corinth' founded; declares war on Persia
336	Death of Philippos

TABLES OF RULERS

Kings of Sparta

(within the period covered by this book)
(For the problems in computing such a list see Forrest, *Sparta*, 19–22, and Cartledge, *Sparta*, 341–6)

Agiads		Eurypontids	
Archelaos	*c.*790–*c.*760	Charillos	*c.*780–*c.*750
Teleklos	*c.*760–*c.*740	Nikandros	*c.*750–*c.*720
Alkamenes	*c.*740–*c.*700	Theopompos	*c.*720–*c.*675
Polydoros	*c.*700–*c.*665	Anaxandridas I	*c.*675–*c.*660

Chronological table

Eurykrates	c.665–c.640	Archidamos I	c.660–c.645
Anaxandros	c.640–c.615	Anaxilas	c.645–c.625
Eurykratidas	c.615–c.590	Leotychidas I	c.625–c.600
Leon	c.590–c.560	Hippokratidas	c.600–c.575
Anaxandridas II	c.560–c.520	Agasikles	c.575–c.550
Kleomenes I	c.520–490	Ariston	c.550–c.515
Leonidas	490–480	Demaratos	c.515–491
Pleistarchos	480–459	Leotychidas II	491–469
Pleistoanax	459–409	Archidamos II	469–427
Pausanias	409–395	Agis	427–399
Agesipolis I	395–380	Agesilaos	399–360
Kleombrotos	380–371	Archidamos III	360–338
Agesipolis II	371–370		
Kleomenes II	370–309		

Kings of Persia

(within the period covered by this book)
(Note that these are Hellenised approximations to Persian names, e.g. Kyros for Kurash)

Kyros 559–530
Kambyses 530–522
(Pretenders to the throne, 522–521; see Hdt. III.61–79)
Dareios I 521–486
Xerxes 486–465/4
Artaxerxes I 465/4–425/4
(Pretenders to the throne, 425/4–424/3; on this 'Year of the Four Emperors' see Lewis, *Sparta and Persia*, 69ff.)
Dareios II 424/3–405/4
Artaxerxes II 405/4–359/8
Artaxerxes III 359/8–338/7

Kings of Egypt (26th Dynasty)

(Note that these are Hellenised approximations to Egyptian names, e.g. Psammetichos for Psamtik)

Psammetichos I 664–610
Nekos 610–595
Psammetichos II (Psammis in Hdt.) 595–589
Apries 589–569
Amasis 569–525
Psammetichos III (Psammenitos in Hdt.) 525, whereafter the Persians rule in Egypt (see **93**)

Indexes

Index of ancient sources

N.B. (i) Numbers refer to passages, not to pages
(ii) An asterisk (*) indicates abridgement

A: LITERARY SOURCES

Aelian, *Varia Historia* XIII.24.3: **79D**

Aeneas Tacticus, *Poliorketika* X.5–8: **299**C;
XIV.1: **299**A; XVII.1: **299**B; *see also* **287**

Aeschines (Aeschin.) I (*Against Timarchos*)
77–78: **305**A; 173: **248**C; II (*On the
mismanaged embassy*) 26–27: **337**; III
(*Against Ktesiphon*) 25: **313**B; 191–196:
310; *see also* **157**

Alcaeus, fr. D12 (Page), lines 6–13: **24**; *see
also* **17, 23**

Anaximenes, *FGrH* 72 F4: **323**

Andocides (Andoc.) I (*On the Mysteries*)
81–85: **307**; *see also* **214, 230, 233, 263**

Androtion, *FGrH* 324 F6: **79**E; *see also* **84,
338**

Aristophanes (Aristoph.), *Acharnians* 17–22:
211 (with scholiast on l.22);
61–90: **147** (with scholiast
on l.67); 502–508: **160**C;
509–539: **180**A
Clouds 90–104: **156**
Ekklesiazousai 815–822: **261**
Frogs 549–578: **163**C
Knights 923–926: **201**
Peace 605–610: **180**B
see also **73, 159, 200, 207,
241, 248** n.10

Aristotle (Aristot.) *Politics* (I) 1252 a 24–
1253 a 7: **7**; (II) 1265 b 33–42: **48**;
1267 a 37–b 3: **241**; 1270 a 15–b
6: **267**; 1274 b 5–8: **40**A; 1274 b
15–18: **65**A; (III) 1275 b 32–39:
78; 1285 a 1–10: **50**C; 1285 a
29–b 4: **23**; (IV) 1297 b 16–28:
22; (V) 1305 b 28 30: **316**B; 1313
b 19–25: **32**B; (VI) 1317 a 40 b
17: **303**C; 1317 b 18–1318 a 3*:
126; 1318 a 3–b 5: **303**C; (VII)
1327 a 25–40: **284**; 1331 a 30–b
4: **285**
Nicomachean Ethics (II) 1122 b 19–
23: **153**; fr. 549 Rose: **19**B
see also **8, 13, 47**B, **49, 51, 59** n.5,
67 n.9, **141**A, **315**

Aristotle (?Aristot.), *Athenaion Politeia* 2:
66; 3: **63**; 4: **65**B; 5: **66**; 6–12*: **67**; 13; **68**;
16.2–9: **70**; 17.1: **70**; 17.3–19.1: **72**; 21.1–
2: **76**; 21.3: **77**; 21.4–6: **76**; 22.1–6*: **79**A;
see also 22.2: **119**; 22.5: **120**; 23.1–2: **122**;
23.4–5: **129**; 24: **137**; 25*: **123**; 26.2: **124**;
26.3: **125**; 28.3–4: **216**; 29.1–2: **227**A; 29.3:
80D; 29.4–5: **227**A; 31–33: **227**A; 34.1: **238**;
34.2–38.3*: **244**A; 38.4–40: **245**, 41.3: **304**;
43.1: **313**A; 43.4–6: **308**; 53.1–4: **311**; 62.2:
304

[Aristotle], *Oikonomika* II.2.16 b: **287**;
II.2.23: **257**B

Arrian, *Anabasis* IV.13.1: **330**; VII.9.2–4: **332**

Athenaeus, *Deipnosophistai* (VI) 263C–D:
19A; (XIII) 557B–D: **331**; 576A–B: **19**B; (XV)
695A–B: **73** (= D. L. Page, *Poetae Melici
Graeci* nos.893–6)

Democritus fr.245: **243**; fr.255: **243**

Demosthenes (Demos.) III ((*Third Speech*)
on Olynthos) 4–5: **343**; 6–8*: **345**; V (*On
the Peace*) 24–25: **346**B; XIV (*On the
symmories*) 3: **340**; XVIII (*On the Crown*)
169–174*: **349**A; XX (*Against Leptines*) 30–
33: **281**A; XXI (*Against Meidias*) 157–159:
279; XXVII (*Against Aphobos A*) 9–11: **278**;
XXXV (*Against Lakritos*) 10–13: **281**B; LVII
(*Against Euboulides*) 8–14: **305**B; 30–36*:
163D; LIX (*Against Neaira*) 4–5: **313**C; *see
also* **158**D, **248**C, **280, 310, 312, 313**D, **314,
348**

Diodorus (Diod.) XI.43.3: **160**A; XI.50: **167**;
XI.76: **172**A; XII.9–11*: **174**; XII.20: **40**B;
XIII.91–96.4*: **294**; XIII.106: **239**; XIV.7.1–
5: **295**A, XIV.10.1–2: **250**A; XIV.78.1–6:
295B; XV.28.2–5: **269**A, XV.40: **293**;
XV.61.2–5: **333**; XV.66.1: **301**A; XVI.2.4–
3.3: **325**; XVI.4.2–7: **326**; XVI.7.2–4: **339**;
XVI.8.6–7: **327**; XVI.23: **336**; XVI.34.4–5:
328A; XVI.35.1–2: **341**; XVI.52.9: **344**;
XVI.60: **346**A; XVI.85.5–86: **349**B; XVI.89*:
350B; *see also* **118, 159**; p.301; **180**

Dionysius of Halikarnassos, *Lysias* 32: **246**A
(= intro. to Lysias XXXIV, *Against the
subversion of the ancestral politeia in Athens*)

Index of ancient sources

Euripides, *Suppliant Women* 888–900: **160B**
'Hellenica Oxyrhyncia' I.1–3: **254B**; II.1: **258**; II.2: **254B**; *see also* **162** n.5
Herodotus (Hdt.) I.1–2.1: **2B**; I.6: **90**; I.23–24*: **29A**; I.26–28: **90**; I.46.1: **90**; I.59–62.1: **69**; I.64: **69**; I.65–66.1: **47A**; I.66–68: **58**; **1.69–77***: **91**; I.82: **59** I.131–132: **97**; I.134.1–2: **98**; I.141–171*: **92**, *see also* I.168: **18B**; II.1.2: **93**; II.154: **94A**; II.164–167: **13**; II.178–180: **94B**; III.39: **31**; III.44–47: **31**; III.48–53: **28**; III.60: **32A**; III.80–83: **89**; III.88–97: **96**; III.142–143: **34**; IV.137 and 142: **101**; IV.150–159: **16A**; V.28–37*: **102**; V.39–42.2: **61**; V.49–51*: **103**; V.57–58.2: **4**; V.62–65.3: **74**; V.66: **75**; V.67–68: **30**; V.69–70: **75**; V.71: **64A**; V.72.1–2: **75**; V.73–75: **75**; V.77.1–2: **75**; V.78: **75**; V.92β–η.1: **27**; V.96–97: **104**; V.99–126*: **105A**; VI.1–32*: **105B**; VI.34–41*: **106**; VI.43–49.1*: **107**; VI.56–57: **50A**; VI.94–117*: **108**; VI.108: **62**; VI.125: **100**; VI.126–131: **26**; VI.131.1: **80A**; VII.1: **109A**; VII.32: **109B**; VII.104: **55**; VII.132–133.1: **109C**; VII.138–139: **110A**; VII.144.1–2: **161A**; VII.145: **110B**; VII.153–156: **35**; VII.165–166: **118**; VII.205.2–207: **111A**; VIII.15–18*: **111B**; VIII.30: **117**; VIII.41: **112B**; VIII.61: **112C**; VIII.105–106: **99**; VIII.132: **113**; VIII.142.4–5: **25A**; IX.63–64: **114**; IX.80–81.1: **115A**; IX.90.1–2: **116A**; IX.106: **116B**; *see also* **1**, **3**, pp.66 and 128; **71** n.3; pp.183 and 205; **128, 139, 143** n.3, **327**
Hesiod, *Works and Days* 213–273: **10**; *see also* **7**
Homer, *Iliad* II.188–277*: **6**; VI.212–236: **5B**; XII.307–330*: **5A**; XVIII.490–508: **9** *Odyssey* I.178–188: **14**; VI.4–10: **17A**; XIV.285–297: **2A**; *see also* **1, 7, 11, 36, 47B, 88, 271, 336**
Ibycus fr.263 (Page), lines 10–22 and 46–48: **33**
Isocrates (Isoc.) IV (*Panegyrikos*) 41–42: **276**; 140–145*: **319**; VII (*Areopagitikos*) 20–23: **303B**; 26–27: **303B**; VIII (*On the Peace*) 54–55: **314A**; 108: **247A**; IX (*Euagoras*) 52–56*: **260**; XVI (*On the team of horses*) 26–27: **80B**; *see also* **269**
Justin VIII.2.5–9: **342**; IX.5: **350A**
Livy VIII.22.5–6: **15A**
Lysias (Lys.) XII (*Against Eratosthenes*) 4–20: **244C**; XXV (*Defence against a charge of subverting the democracy*) 12–13: **144**; XXXIV (*Against the subversion of the ancestral politeia in Athens*) 1–6: **246B**; *see also* **241, 242**
Old Oligarch: *see* [Xenophon]
Pausanias (Paus.) II.24.7: **57**; IV.26.5: **301B**;

IV.27.9–11: **301B**; V.7.6–8.8*: **11**; VIII.27.2: **300A**; IX.1.3–8: **289**; X.8.1–2: **84**; *see also* **272**
Philochorus, *FGrH* 328 F30: **79C**; F56a: **313D**; F162: **347**; *see also* **45, 128** n.2
Pindar, *Olympian* XIII.1–46b: **12B**; *see also* **29**; p.277; **175**
Plato, *Apology* 35E–37E: **248B**
　　Gorgias 515E: **141B**
　　Laws (V) 745B–E: **17B**; (XII) 952D–953E: **283**
　　Republic (VIII) 557A–558C: **303A**
　　Seventh Letter 324 b 8–325 a 7: **247B**
　　see also **48, 51, 52A, 139A, 155, 158D, 249, 284**
Pliny, *Natural History* XXXV.151–152*: **29B**
Plutarch, *Agesilaos* 26: **270**; 27.3–28.2: **272**
　　Alexander 15.1–6: **328B**
　　Alkibiades 34.2–4: **242**
　　Aristeides 7*: **121**
　　Kimon 8.7–9: **150**; 12.6–13.5: **131**; 13.6–8: **142A**; 15.2: **80C**
　　Lykourgos 1.1–3: **47B**; 5.6–8: **51**; 6: **49**; 7.1–2: **52A**; 8–9: **53**; 26.1–3*: **51**; 27.3–4: **56**; 29.6–30.1: **265A**
　　Lysandros 13.3–5: **250B**; 18: **249**; 24.2–25.3: **266**; 30.3–4: **266**
　　Nikias 3*: **142C**; 11.1–6: **213**
　　Pelopidas 18–19*: **271**; 26.4–5: **324**; 28–29*: **335**
　　Perikles 6.2–3: **146**; 7.8: **139A**; 8.3–4: **146**; 9.1–2*: **148**; 9.2–3: **141A**; 11.1–3: **145**; 11.5–6: **139B**; 12.1–2: **138**; 13.6–14*: **151**; 14: **146**; 15–16.3*: **148**; 16.3–5: **142B**; 20–21.1: **175A**; 32: **157**; 37.2–end: **128**
　　Phokion 7.3–8.1: **314B**; 9.5: **314B**
　　Themistokles 19.2–4: **159**
　　Theseus 25.1: **158B**; 36: **18A**
　　Timoleon 1–2.2: **296**; 22–24*: **297**; 35: **297**
　　see also **54, 159**
Polybius II.62.6–7: **312**; XVIII.14.1–11: **348**
Posidonius fr.60 Edelstein/Kidd: **19A**
Sophocles, *Oidipous at Kolonos* 258–262: **158C**; *see also* **150**
Strabo, *Geography* VI.2.2: **15B**; VI.3.2–3*: **46**; VIII.1.2: **3**; VIII.4.10: **45**; VIII.5.4: **44**; VIII.6.22: **20**; X.3.18: **158D**; X.4.17–19: **88**; XIV.2.28*: **1B**
Theognis 39–52: **21**; 145–148: **36**; 183–192: **21**
?Theophrastus, *Fragmentum Vaticanum de eligendis magistratibus* B, lines 8–221: **315**
Theopompus, *FGrH* 115 F224–225: **322**; *see also* **162**

Thucydides (Thuc.) I.2.5–6: **158A**; I.3: **1A**;
I.5–8: **82**; I.10.1–2: **164**; I.12.4–15: **81**;
I.17–18.1: **60**; I.23.4–6: **165A**; I.31–55*:
176; I.56–57.5: **177**; I.66–67: **178**; I.69.4–
5: **182**, I.70.2–71.3: **87**; I.72–77.4*: **179**;
I.80–81: **183A**; I.83: **183A**; I.86.3–87.3:
183B; I.89–99*: **130**, *see also* I.89.3–90.3:
166; I.93.1–2: **166**; I.100.2–101: **132A**;
I.102–103.3: **169**; I.103.4: **170**, I.104:
132B; I.107–108.3: **171**; I.109–110*: **132B**;
I.113–115.1: **173**; I.118.2: **165B**; I.121.2–3:
183C; I.122.1: **183C**; I.126.1–2: **181**;
I.126.3–11: **64B**; I.127: **181**; I.135.2–
138.2*: **168**; I.139–146: **194A**; II.1–2.3:
184; II.7–9.3*: **185**; II.10.1–2: **186**; II.13.2–
end: **194B**; II.14: **207**; II.15:8; II.16–17.3:
207; II.18–23*: **186**; II.24: **195**; II.37: **149**;
II.38: **154**; II.40–41*: **149**; II.45.2: **163B**;
II.47.3–4: **196**; II.51.4–54: **196**; II.59–60.1:
208; II.61.2–63.2: **208**; II.65: **209**; II.67.1:
230A, II.68.5–8. **175B**; II.93–94: **187**; II.99–
100.2: **321A**; III.2–3: **197A**; III.10.2–6: **136**;
III.19: **197B**; III.36: **210A**; III.37–38: **210B**;
III.39: **198A**; III.42–43: **210C**; III.47 and 50:
198B; III.82.1: **135A**; III.86.: **217**; III.92–93:
189; IV.8: **190**; IV.15: **190**; IV.26: **190**;
IV.27.3–28: **212**; IV.38.5–41: **190**; IV.50:
230B; IV.51: **199**; IV.55: **191**; IV.59.4–61.3:
217; IV.65: **217**; IV.78*: **192**; IV.79–81:
192; IV.108*: **192**; V.4–5.1: **218**; V.14–
20.1: **193**; V.21–25*: **202**; V.43: **203**; V.48:
204; V.74–75.3: **205**; V.89–97: **206**; VI.1.1:
219; VI.6: **219**; VI.8: **219**; VI.11.6–12: **219**;
VI.15–16.5: **219**; VI.24–26: **219**; VI.27–29:
214; VI.32.3: **220**; VI.35: **220**; VI.41: **220**;
VI.45: **220**; VI.53: **214**; VI.60–61.1: **214**;
VI.63: **221**; VI.72–73: **221**; VI.88.3–8: **222**;
VI.91–92.1: **228**; VII.8: **223**; VII.16–17.1:
223; VII.18–19.2: **229A**; VII.27–28.2: **229B**;
VII.27.5: **162C**; VII.47–49: **224**; VII.50.3–4:
224; VII.85–87: **225**; VIII.1–2: **226**; VIII.4:
226; VIII.24.4–6: **232**; VIII.29: **231**;
VIII.43.2–4: **233A**; VIII.45.1–2: **233B**;
VIII.48.1–4: **227B**; VIII.48.5–7: **235**; VIII.49:
227B; VIII.53–54: **227B**; VIII.58: **233C**;
VIII.65–68: **227B**; VIII.86.4–7: **215**;
VIII.89.2–90.3: **227B**; VIII.96.1–3: **227B**;
VIII.97–98.1: **227B**; *see also* **1B**, **3**, **56**, **62**
n.2, **71**, **72**, **127**; p.246; **148**, **156**, **159**;
p.301; **167**; p.322; pp.333–4; **188**; p.406
Vaticanus graecus 1144, fol.222ʳᵛ: **79B**
Xenophon (Xen.) *Hellenika* I.1.14–15: **236**;
I.5.1–9: **234**; I.7.1–15*:
237; I.7.34–35: **237**;
II.2.10–23*: **240**; II.3.2:
244B; II.3.4: **316A**;
II.3.11–23*: **244B**;

II.4.1–2: **244B**, III.1.1–
8: **252**; III.2.21–31: **251**;
III.3.4–11: **264**; III.4.1–
4: **253**; III.5.1–2: **254A**;
IV.2.1–8: **255**; IV.4.2–5:
290; IV.5.13–16: **257**;
IV.8.8–9: **256**; IV.8.10:
259B; IV.8.25–30: **262A**;
V.1.25–34*: **263**;
V.2.1–7*: **291**; V.2.8–
10: **292A**; V.3.10–13:
292B; V.4.20–24: **268**;
V.4.34: **268**; V.4.36:
298A; V.4.56: **288**;
VI.1.4–12*: **317**;
VI.4.15–20: **273A**;
VI.4.27–32: **318**;
VI.5.22–25: **274**;
VI.5.27–32: **274**;
VI.5.33–35: **275A**;
VI.5.49: **275A**; VII.1.38:
320B; VII.4.6: **298B**
Education of Kyros
VIII.8.20–26*: **320A**
Lakedaimonion Politeia
(*Lak. Pol.*) V.2–6: **54**;
VIII.1–4: **52B**; XIII.1–5:
50B; XIV: **265B**; XV.1–8:
50B
Memorabilia (*Mem*). I.1.1:
248A; II.3.3: **162A**;
III.6* **155**
Poroi I–III: **286**; IV.2–12:
161C, IV.14–16: **161B**;
IV.16–52: **277A**
see also **47B**, **98**, **239**, **269**,
271, **287**, **300**, **303**
[Xenophon] (the 'Old Oligarch'), *Athenaion
Politeia* I.1–2: **143**; I.4–8: **143**; I.10–12:
160D; I.14–15: **135B**; II.11–12: **140**; *see also*
144, **147**, **194**, **227**

B: INSCRIPTIONS

D. W. Bradeen and M. F. McGregor,
Studies in Fifth-Century Attic Epigraphy
(1973), 71–2: **172B**
M. Crosby, *Hesperia* 10 (1941), 14 (no.1):
277B
M. I. Finley, *Studies in Land and Credit*
no.146: **280**
L. H. Jeffery and A. Morpurgo Davies,
Kadmos (1970), 118: **39**
R. G. Kent, *Old Persian*, 136: **95A**
Meiggs and Lewis no.2: **37**; no.4: **43**; no.5:
16B; no.6c: **71**; no.8: **38**; no.9:**12A**; no.12:
95B; no.13: **86**; no.17: **85**; no.23: **112A**;

Meiggs and Lewis (*contd*)
    no.27: **115**B; no.33: **127**; no.34: **133**;
    no.44: **163**A; no.52: **134**, **309**A; no.67:**188**;
    no.69: **200**; no.79A: **162**B; no.86: **65**C
L. Moretti, *Iscrizioni Storiche Ellenistiche*
    no.114: **329**
Supplementum Epigraphicum Graecum (*SEG*)
    X.47: **152**; XII.87: **25**B; XII.391: **42**B;
    XXVI.1282: **262**B

Sylloge Inscriptionum Graecarum (*SIG*)[4] no.2:
    41; no.4: **42**A
Tod no.34: **83**; no.107: **259**A; no.123: **269**B;
    no.127: **302**; no.130: **273**B; no.132: **300**B;
    no.147: **334**; no.152: **338**; no.162: **282**;
    no.177: **350**C; no.178: **309**B; no.204: **306**
A. J. B. Wace and M. S. Thompson, *ABSA*
    17 (1910–11), 193ff.: **321**B

Index of Greek words

N.B. Unless otherwise indicated, numbers refer to passages (and their introductions), not
to pages. (G) indicates an entry in the Glossary

agōgē, **54**
agōn, **11**, **12**, **51**, **55**, **57**, **114**, **142**C, **146**
agora (G), p.21, **9**, **30**, **46**, **69**, **79**C, **92**, **142**,
    163D, **178**, **180**A, **194**A, **211**, **244**, **247**,
    251, **261**, **264**, **277**A, **279**, **283–285**, **290**,
    349A
aisymnētēs, **23**
akropolis, p.21, **17**B, **34**, **64**, **67**, **69**, **72**, **75**,
    92, **105**A, **112**B, **131**, **134**, **142**A and C,
    151, **157**, **190**, **193**, **194**B, **195**, **207**, **244**B,
    262B, **268**, **271**, **273**A, **285**, **288**, **294**,
    295A, **333**
apoikia/apoikos (G), p.1, **7**, Ch.2 *passim*,
    28, **45**, **46**, **81**, **88**, **105**A, **116**B, **135**, **136**,
    139, **154**, **158**A, **168**, **174**, **176–178**, **186**,
    189, **200**, **206**, **219**, **296**, **297**, **328**A
archōn (G), **18**A, **31**, **50**, **57**, **63**, **64**B, **65–68**,
    71, **79**C, **119**, **120**, **122**, **124**, **135**, **147**,
    150, **172**B, **184**, **193**, **200**, **202**, **227**, **232**,
    244A, **245**, **285**, **289**, **294**, **299**C, **301**B,
    309, **334**
aretē, **5**, **33**, **53**, **56**, **142**C, **143**, **163**B, **167**,
    192, **225**
astos, **21**, **34**, **83**, **89**, **92**, **128**, **286**, **299**C
astu (G), p.1, **9**, **53**, **69**, **70**, **74**, **76**, **108**,
    142A, **142**, **166**, **174**, **187**, **196**; p.385;
    207, **244**, **245**, **246**, **247**, **251**, **257**, **268**,
    277A, **284**, **286**, **305**B
atimia/atimos, **240**, **310**

banausia/banausos, **13**, **270**, p.522, **285**
barbaros (G), **1**, **3**, **7**, **13**, **25**A, **69**, **80**B, **81**,
    82, **99**, **103**, **104**, **108**, **109**C, **110**A, **111**B,
    112A, **113**, **116**, **130**, **131**, **138**, **140**, **147**,
    148, **162**, **165**B, **166**, **175**, **179**, p.333,
    182, **185**, **194**A, **219**, **262**B, **269**B,
    275A, **286**, **296**, **322**, **326**, **332**
basileus (G, under *archōn*), **38**, **63**
boiōtarchos, **184**, **253**, **271**, **273** n.7, **289**
boulē/bouleutērion/bouleutēs (G), **25**B, **38**, **41**,
    65, **67**, p.152, **75**, **77**, **79**, **92**, **112**A, p.235,
    119, **126**, **134**, **137**, **141**, **143**, **152**, **172**B,
    186, **200**, **215**, **227**, **237**, **244**, **245**, **254**B,
    269B, **273**A, **275**A, **277**A, **282**, **300**B,
    305B, **307**, **309**, **313**C, **315**, **334**, **338**,
    349A

chōra (G), p.1, **8**, **17**, **44**, **47**A, **50**, **53**, **65**B,
    70, **76**, **81**, **105**B, **112**A, **130**, p.287, **159**,
    160B, **162**C, **166**, **171**, **172**A, **174**,
    175A, **183**C, **190**, **191**, **193**, **200**, **207**, **209**,
    220, **224**, **228**, **229**, **245**, **251**, **267**, **269**B,
    274, **275**B, **276**, **277**A, **285**, **286**, **293**, **308**,
    319, **320**A, **327**, **328**A, **336**, **337**
chorēgia/chorēgos, **142**C, **144**, (**153**), **244**C

dēmokratia, **80**, **89** n.2, **143** n.3
dēmos (G), p.19, **16**B, **21**, **24**, **25**B, **35**, **38**,
    42, **43**, **48**, **49**, **51**, **52**A, **65**C, **66–70**, **75**, **76**,
    79, **80**, **85**, **86**, **89**, **102**, **104**, **108**, **112**A,
    pp.235–6, **121**, **123**, **126–128**, p.246, **131**,
    134, **135**, **138**, **139**, **142–149**, p.277, **152**,
    154, **155**, **157**, **159**, **160**, **167**, **171**, **172**B,
    176, **180**, **181**, **198**, **200**, **209**, **210**, **213**,
    214, **216**, **218**, **220**, **226**, **227**, **234–236**,
    239, p.456, **244–246**, **248**C, **251**, **254**B,
    262, **268**, **269**, **282**, **286**, **291**, **293**, **294**,
    302–304, **308**, **309**, **313**, **314**B, **334**, **338**,
    349A
dikastērion/dikastai (G), **67**, (**70**), **121**, **123**,
    125, **126**, **134**, **141**A, **159**, **200**, **227**, **237**,
    244A, **303**C, **305**A, **310**, **311**, **313**C
diōbelia, **141** n.4, **216**, **237**, **241**

eisphora, p.236, **144**, **197**B, **201**, **241**, **244**C,
    277, **278**, **286**, **312**, **343**
ekklēsia (G), p.22, **16**B, **25**B, **34**, **41**, **65**B, **67**,
    p.152, **77**, p.235, **119**, **123**, **126**, p.246,
    138, **143**, **145–147**, **152**, **159**, **176**, **181**,
    186, **194**A, p.385, **207**, **208**, **210**, **211**, **219**,
    226, **227**B, **237**, **238**, **240**, **244**, **275**A, **281**,
    300B, **303**C, **304**, **307–309**, **349**A
emporion (G), p.52, **15**, **81**, **92**, **94**, **116**B,
    132A, **276**, **281**A, **284**

enktesis, **286**

ephoros, **47**A, **48**, **49**, **50**B, **52**, **58**, **61**, **69**, **183**, **184**, **193**, **202**, **233**C, **240**, **251–253**, **263–266**, **268**, **273**A, **292**

epiklēros, **267**, **308**

epimachia, **176**, **181**, **204**

eunomia, **12**B, **45**, **47**A, **56**, **58**, **60**, **143**, **265**A

euthynai, **65**B, **126**, **210** n.7, **227**A, **245**, **314**

genos, **76**, **280**

gerousia/gerontes (G), **47**A, **48**, **49**, **50**A, **51**, **52**, **61**, **167**, **264**

graphē paranomōn, p.236, **210** n.7, **227**, **245**, **310**, **313**C

hēgemonia/hēgemōn (G), **105**B, **122**, p.246, **130**, **136**, **137**, **148**, **154**, **164**, **167**, **173**, **175**A, **179**, p.333, p.337, **226**, p.475, **250**, p.488, **260**, p.497, **269**, **275**, **293**, **319**, **350**

hektēmoroi, **66**

hippeis, **65**B, **67**, **124**, **201**

homonoia, p.447, **240**, **241**, **243**, **245**, **299**A

horos, **67**, **280**

isēgoria, **75**, **143** n.3, (**160**D)

isonomia, **34**, **73**, **89**, **102**, **192**

kaloi k'agathoi, **143**, **145**, **146**, **156**, **190**, **235**, **244**B

klēros/klērouchia/klērouchoi, **53**, **75** n.14, **135**, **139**B, **198**B, **241**, **316**

klērōsis ek prokritōn, **120**, **122**, **124**

koinon, **134**, **334**

kōmē, **7**, **8**, **164**, **291**

metoikos (G), **83**, **134**, **160**, **162**B, **194**, **214**, **244**, p.521, **277**A, **284**, **286**, **299**C, **308**

misthos, **126**, **137**, **141**, **142**, **148**, (**304**)

nauklēros (G), **168**, **244**C, **253**, **281**B, **282**, **286**

naukraroi, **64**A, **76**

neodamōdeis, **252**, **253**, **264**, (**274**)

nomos (G), **25**B, **47**B, **50**, **52**B, **55**, **59**, **63**, **65**, **67**, **70**, **71**, p.152, **75**, **79**, **80**D, **88**, **89**, **97**, **124**, **149**, **163**D, **174**, **210**B, **227**, **237**, **243**, **244**, **246**, **265**, **267**, **282**, **284**, **294**, **303**, **306–308**, **310**, **311**, **313**, **315**, **332**

nomothetēs, **25**B, **40**, **47**B, **65**, **88**, **174**, **227**B, **307**

oikistēs, p.53, **16**, **18**, **106**, **176**, **189**, **297**, **300**A

oikos/oikia (G), **5**, **7**, **10**, **12**B, **16**B, **52**B, **54**, **55**, **60**, **100**, **102**, **167**, **168**, **266**

ostrakismos, **79**, **120**, **121**, **146**, **148**, **168**, **169** n.9, **213**, **308**

pentakosiomedimnoi, **65**B, **67**, **124**, **315** n.4

perioikoi, **44**, **45**, (**50**B), **53**, **58**, **169**, **189**, **190**, **194** n.9, **263**, **264**, **274**

philoxenia, **5**, **158**, **160**, **276**

phoros, **130**, **134**, **152**, **154**, **177**, **200**, **201**

phratria, **16**B, **128**

phylē (G), (3), **16**B, **17**B, **18**, **30**, **38**, **39**, **49**, **67**, **75**, **78**, **79**C, **80**A, **119**, **120**, **127**, **133**, **134**, **150**, **163**A, **174**, **186**, **227**, **244**A, **269**B, **271**, **277**, **280**, **307**, **309**, **311**, **334**

poinikastēs, **39**

polemarchos (G), **50**B, **63**, **69**, **73**, **108**, **112**A, **119**, **257**, **334**

pōlētai, **65**C, **67**, **162** n.2, **163**A, **172**B, **277**

polis (G), pp.1–4, pp.7–8, p.14, p.18, p.22, pp.27–9, **1**, **5**, **7–10**, **13**, pp.52–4, **14**, **16–18**, **20**, pp.66–7, **21–24**, **26**, **27**, **31**, **32**, **35**, p.87, **36**, **37**, **39–46**, **49**, **50**B, **52**B, **53–57**, **60**, p.128, **64**, **65**, **67**, **69**, **70**, **75**, **76**, **79**, p.168, **81–88**, **90–92**, **94**B, **96**, **101**, **102**, **104–108**, **110**A, **111**A, **112**, **122**, **126–128**, pp.246–7, **129**, **130**, **132**B, **134–140**, **142**C, **143–149**, p.277, **150**, **151**, **153–155**, p.287, **158–164**, **166**, **167**, **170–172**, **174–176**, **178–181**, **183–186**, **189**, **192–198**, **200**, **202**, **203**, **205–210**, **213–215**, **217–220**, **222**, **224**, **226–229**, **232**, **235**, **238**, **240–242**, **244–257**, **259**, **260**, **262–271**, **273**, **274**, pp.521–2, **276**, **277**A, **281**A, **283–287**, p.538, **288–303**, **305–307**, **310**, **313**B, **314–319**, **321** n.3, **326**, **327**, **328**A, **332–335**, **337–339**, **344**, **346**, **348**, **249**A, **350**

politeia (G, under *polis*), **16**B, **22**, **44**, **47**B, **48–51**, **53**, **56**, **60**, **63**, **65–68**, **76**, **78**, **79**, **80**D, **88**, **119**, **123**, **126**, **137**, **143**, **145**, **148**, **149**, **172**, **174**, **202**, **227**, **244**, **246**, **247**, **250**, **253**, **265**A, **266**, **269**B, **286**, **293**, **303**, **307**, **310**, **314**B, **315**, **350**C

politēs (G, under *polis*), pp.1–4, **4**, **13**, **27**, **31**, **35**, **40**, **46**, **50**B, **52**B, **76**, **78**, **80**B, p.168, **89**, **128**, p.246, **139**A, **144**, **145**, **158**A, **159**, **167**, **172**A, **174**, **175**A, **184**, **193**, **194**A, **210**, **214**, **218**, **227**B, **241–244**, **246**B, **247**, **248**, **254**B, **260**, **265**B, **266**, **267**, **286**, **292**B, **293–295**, **297**, **299**A, **303**, **305**, **307**, **311**, **328**A, **338**

polypragmosynē, **175**, **254**B, **262**

probolai, **237**, **308**

probouloi, **226**, **227**, **315** n.5

proedroi, **25**B, **227**B, **309**B

prostatēs, **66** n.4, **94**B, **135**A, **155**

proxenos/proxenia (G), **5**, **43**, **50**A, **83**, **135**, **197**A, **203**, **268**, **300**B, **338**

prytaneia/prytaneis (G), **25**B, **41**, **65**, p.235, **126**, **134**, **152**, **157**, **200**, **227**, **237**, **304**, **308**, **309**, **334**, **349**A

prytaneion (G, under *prytaneia*), 30, 41, 42, 63, 137, 172B, 282, 334
psēphisma (G), 25, 131, 134, 157, 163D, 172B, 175A, 180, 194A, 224, 227, 244A, 245, 246, 269B, 282, 286, 302, 305, 307, 309, 310, 313C

rhētra, 38, 49, 51–53, 85, 270

skytalē, 264
stasis (G), 21, 60, 66–69, 86, 89, 102, 113, 135A, 158A, 172A, 174, 209, 217, 227B, 241, 243, 252, 293, 294, 299, 339
stēlē (G), p.21, 16B, 25B, 41, 65C, 127, 134, 142C, 166, 172B, 193, 269B, 277B, 282, 306, 321B, 334
stratēgos/stratēgia (G), 50C, 65B, 92,105A, 107, 108, 112A, p. 236, 119, 122,126–128, 134, 148, 150, 168, 171, 172B, 173, 175B, 181, 190, 192, 193, 197, 198B, 205, 208, 209, 212, 217, 219–221, 223–225, 227, 228, 230B, 236, 237, 239, 245, 249, 257, 262B, 272, 275, 294, 297, 304, 308,

310, 314, 315, 324, 325, 329, 334–337, 339, 346, 349, 350B
sylē, 83, 281B
symmachia, 176, 219 n.3
symmoria, 279, 312, (340)
synoikismos, 8, 18, 63, 88, 164, 197A, 207

technai, 13, 53
temenos, 5A, 30, 34
theōrika, 141, 216 n.5, 242, 313 n.4
thesmothetai (G, under *archōn*), 63, 134
thētes, 67, (p.456)
triērarchia/triērarchoi, 112A, 144, 195
tyrannos, 23, 64, 68, 70–72, 113, 116A, 118, 138

xenēlasia, 56, 194, 265B
xenia/xenos (G), 5, 14, 19B, p.67, 33, 43, 44, 74, 75, 83, 90, 91, 102, 103, 106, 112A, 118, 134, 154, 158, 160, 163D, 172B, 194A, 265B, 277A, 282–284, 286, 292B, 295A, 299C

zeugitai, 65B, 67, 124

Index of names

N.B. Unless otherwise indicated, numbers refer to passages (and their introductions), not to pages

A PERSONS

Achilles, Homeric hero, 1A, 6, 9, 73
Agamemnon, Homeric hero, 6, 24, 33, 58, 253
Agasikles, Spartan king (C6), 47A, 58
Agesilaos, Spartan king (C4), 253–255, 263, 264, 266, 268, 270, 272–274, 288, 292B, 317
Agesipolis, Spartan king (C4), 291, 292B
Agis, Spartan king (C5), 193, 229, 233B, 242, 251, 253, 265
Ahura(mazda), Persian god, 95A, 105A
Alexander the Great, pp.13 and 16, 301B, pp.580 and 587, 323, 328B, 329, 331, 332, 349B, 350
Alexandros I, king of Makedon (C5), 25A, 111, 114, 168, 321A, 323, 327
Alexandros II, king of Makedon (C4), 323, 333, 335, 337
Alexandros, tyrant of Pherai (C4), 333–335
Alkibiades, Athenian politician and general (C5), 156, 175A, 203–205, p.385, 213–215, 219, 221, 223, 227B, p.437, 228,

229, 233–236, 239, 242, 248, 253, p.521, 279
Alyattes, king of Lydia (C6); 28, 90
Amasis, king of Egypt (C6), 31, 91, 94
Amyntas (III), king of Makedon (C4), 321, 337
Anakreon of Teos, poet (C6), 72
Anaxagoras of Klazomenai, philosopher (C5), 146, 157
Anaxandridas, Spartan king (C6), 58, 61, 62
Anaxila(o)s, tyrant of Rhegion (C5), 118, 172A
Antalkidas, Spartan diplomat (C4), 263, 270, 289
Antiphon, Athenian oligarch (C5), 227
Anytos, Athenian politician (C5/4), 244A, 248, 254B
Aphrodite, 97, 259A
Apollo, 8, 11, 12, 16, 28, 46, 47A, 49, 50A, 81, 84, 86, 88, 91, 92, 94B, 95B, 109C, 115A, 142C, 167, 174, 189, 193, 197A, 282, 318, 336
Apries, king of Egypt (C6), 16A
Archelaos, king of Makedon (C5), 316, 321A

Archidamos, Spartan king (C5), **5, 146, 182,** **183A, 186**

Archidamos, son of Agesilaos, **268, 273A,** **289**

Archilochus of Paros, poet (C7), **18, 314B**

Archinos, Athenian politician (C5/4), **244A,** **245, 246, 310**

Ares, **11, 12, 24, 133, 306, 314B, 350C**

Aristagoras, tyrant of Miletos (C6/5), **102–** **105**

Aristeides, Athenian politician and general (C5), **121, 129, 137, 168, 193, 213, 314B,** **315**

Aristogeiton, Athenian tyrannicide (C6), **72, 73**

Ariston, Spartan king (C6), **58**

Aristophon, Athenian politician (C4), **310,** **314B**

Aristoteles, Athenian oligarch (C5), **240,** **244B**

Artaphrenes, Persian satrap (C6/5), **75, 102,** **104, 105**

Artaxerxes I, King of Persia (C5), **108,** **132B, 168, 230B**

Artaxerxes II, King of Persia (C4), **252, 263**

Artemis, **28, 90, 289**

Aspasia, Milesian mistress of Perikles (C5), **128, 157, 180**

Astyages, king of the Medes (C6), **90, 91**

Astyochos, Spartan admiral (C5), **227B,** **231, 232, 233B**

Athena, **8, 12, 14, 17B, 25B, 49, 50B, 58,** **64B, 69, 73, 92, 112A, 142C, 151, 152,** **159, 163A, 194B, 274, 306, 314B, 350C**

Bias of Priene (C6), **90, 92**

Brasidas, Spartan general (C5), **187, 192,** **193, 249, 257, 266, 316**

Chabrias, Athenian general (C4), **257, 315,** **339, 349B**

Chares, Athenian general (C4), **314B, 339,** **342, 347, 349B**

Charondas of (?) Katana, lawgiver (?C5), **7,** **40A, 174**

Chilon, Spartan *ephoros* (C6), **58, 69**

Damaratos (Demaratos), Spartan king (C6/5), **55, 75, 252**

Dareios I, King of Persia (C6/5), **55, 75, 81,** **89, p.183, 95, 96, 101, 102, 104–109**

Dareios II, King of Persia (C5), **233C, 252**

Demosthenes, Athenian general (C5), **190,** **193, 223–225, 229B**

Demosthenes, Athenian politican (C4), **340,** **343, 345–346, 348–349**

Derkylidas, Spartan general (C4), **251–253**

Diomedes, Homeric hero, **5B, 73**

Dion, Syracusan philosopher-politician (C4), **296, 297**

Dionysios I, tyrant of Syracuse (C5/4), p.66, **32**, p.538, **294–296**

Dionysios II, tyrant of Syracuse (C4), **296**

Dionysos, **8, 12, 30, 63, 96, 142C, 150, 156**

Douketios, Sikel leader (C5), **172A**

Drakon, Athenian lawgiver (C7), **63, 65,** **67, 307**

Duris of Samos, historian (C4/3), **249, 328B**

Epameinondas, Theban leader (C4), **272–** **274, 300A, 301A, 315, 324, 335**

Ephialtes, Athenian politician and general (C5), **123, 124, 131, 139, 148, 244A**

Euagoras, ruler of Cyprus (C5/4), **239, 260,** **263, p.580, 319**

Euboulos, Athenian politician (C4), **313B,** **314B**

Eurymedon, Athenian general (C5), **190,** **217, 219, 223–225**

Gelon, tyrant of Syracuse (C6/5), **35, 110B,** **118, 294**

Gorgidas, Theban leader (C4), **271**

Gylippos, Spartan general (C5), **223, 225,** **229**

Hagnon, Athenian politician and general (C5), **157, 216, 315**

Harmodios, Athenian tyrannicide (C6), **72,** **73, 214**

Hera, **42B, 45, 94B**

Herakles, **11, 12, 44, 47B, 62, 74, 108, 113,** **266, 306**

Hermes, **11, 214**

Hermokrates, Syracusan politician and general (C5), **217, 220–222, 231, 294**

Hestia, **17B, 38, 306**

Hieron, tyrant of Gela (C6/5), **35, 172A**

Hiketas, tyrant of Leontinoi (C4), **296, 297**

Hipparchos, son of Peisistratos (C6), **4,** **72–74**

Hipparchos, ostracised 488/7, **79A and E,** **213**

Hippias, son of Peisistratos (C6/5), **71, 72,** **74, 104, 108**

Histiaios, tyrant of Miletos (C6/5), **101,** **102, 105**

Hyperbolos, Athenian politician (C5), **79C,** **121, 163C, 213**

Hypereides, Athenian politician (C4), **314B**

Iason, tyrant of Pherai (C4), **269 n.14,** p.580, **316–318,** p.600, **333**

Iphikrates, Athenian general (C4), **257, 275,** p.538, **315, 337, 349B**

Ismenias, Theban leader (C4), **254A, 268**

Kallikrates, Athenian architect (C5), **151, 163A**

Kambyses, King of Persia (C6), **31, 81, 89, 93, 96, 109A**

Kephalos, father of Lysias (C5), **244C**

Kephalos, Athenian politician (C4), **254B, 310**

Kimon, Athenian general (C5), **18A, 80C, 128, 130, 131, 141A, 142A, 145, 148, 150, 168, 169, 173**

Kinadon, Spartan revolutionary (C4), **264**

Kleisthenes, tyrant of Sikyon (C6), **26, 30, 75, 80A**

Kleisthenes, Athenian lawgiver (C6), **71,** p.152, **75–80,** p.235, **119, 120, 128,** p.262, **141, 216, 303B, 305**

Kleombrotos, Spartan king (C4), **268** n.2, **270**

Kleomenes, Spartan king (C6/5), **55** n.1, **61, 62, 74, 75, 103, 104**

Kleon, Athenian politician (C5), **142C, 160C, 163C, 190, 193,** p.362, **198, 200, 201, 210, 212, 216, 220** n.2

Kleophon, Athenian politician (C5), **216, 237, 238, 241**

Konon, Athenian general (C5/4), **230, 236, 237, 239, 254B, 256, 258, 259B, 260**

Kritias, Athenian revolutionary (C5), **53, 244B, 248**

Kroisos, king of Lydia (C6), **31, 47A, 58, 69, 90–92, 100**

Kybebe (Cybele), **105A**

Kylon, failed Athenian tyrant (C7), **64, 69**

Kypselos, tyrant of Corinth (C7 or 6), **27**

Kyros, first King of Persia (C6), **81, 89–93, 96, 98, 320**

Kyros, Persian pretender (C5/4), **209, 234, 249, 252, 253, 317, 319**

Laches, Athenian general (C5), **193, 203, 217, 219**

Lamachos, Athenian general (C5), **175A, 193, 219, 223**

Lampon, Athenian seer (C5), **146, 174, 193**

Leon, Spartan king (C6), **47A, 58, 61**

Leonidas, Spartan king (C5), **61, 111, 114**

Leotychidas (II), Spartan king (C5), **116A, 130**

Lichas, Spartan (C5), **202, 233A, 251, 265**

Lygdamis, tyrant of Naxos (C6), **69**

Lykophron, tyrant of Pherai (C5/4), **316, 341**

Lykourgos, legendary (?) Spartan lawgiver, p.95, **47, 49–54, 56, 61, 65, 88, 265–267, 270**

Lykourgos, Athenian aristocrat (C6), **68, 69**

Lysandros, Spartan general (C5/4), **234, 239, 240, 244,** p.475, **249, 250, 252, 253, 265A, 266**

Mardonios, Persian general (C5), **25A, 107, 108, 109** n.2, **113, 114**

Mausolos, ruler of Karia (C4), **339, 346B**

Megakles, Athenian aristocrat (C6), **26, 68, 69, 100**

Miltiades (1), Athenian aristocrat (C6), **18, 106**

Miltiades (2, nephew of 1), Athenian aristocrat (C6/5), **71, 101, 106, 108**

Myronides, Athenian general (C5), **148, 171**

Nikias, Athenian general and politician (C5), **142C, 161B, 193, 203, 212, 213, 216, 219, 223–225**

Olympias, mother of Alexander the Great (C4), **331**

Onomarchos, Phokian general (C4), **341, 342**

Paches, Athenian general (C5), **198B, 210A**

Pammenes, Theban general (C4), **271, 300A, 324**

Pasion, Athenian banker (C4), **278**

Pausanias, Spartan general and regent (C5), **114, 115A, 129, 130, 168, 230**

Pausanias, Spartan king (C5/4), **240, 245,** p.475, **255, 291**

Peisandros, Athenian oligarch (C5), **227**

Peisistratos (1), tyrant of Athens (C6), **28,** p.128, **64A, 68–72, 79E, 106, 108, 125,** p.287, **161, 214, 216, 294**

Peisistratos (2, grandson of 1), **71**

Pelopidas, Theban leader (C4), **271, 272, 274, 315, 320, 324, 335**

Perdikkas, king of Makedon (C5), **177, 192, 321A**

Periandros, tyrant of Corinth (C6), **27–29**

Perikles (1), Athenian general and politician (C5), **5, 25, 128, 131, 138, 139,** p.262, **141, 142, 145, 146, 148, 149, 151, 152, 154, 156, 157, 163, 173, 175, 180–182, 186,** p.362, **194, 200, 207–209, 216, 220** n.2, **242, 244C, 276, 305, 314B**

Perikles (2, son of 1), **128, 237**

Pharnabazos, Persian satrap (C5/4), **233C** with n.3, **236, 252, 256, 319**

Phayllos, Phokian general (C4), **341**

Pheidias, Athenian architect and sculptor (C5), **151, 180B**

Pheidon, king or tyrant of Argos (C7 or 6), 26, 42, 57
Philippos (II), king of Makedon (C4), 25, 117, 271, p.538, 289, 301B, 313D, 314B, p.580, 321–332, p.600, 337, 340–350
Philomelos, Phokian general (C4), 336
Phokion, Athenian general and politician (C4), 314B
Phormion, Athenian general (C5), 175B
Phormisios, Athenian oligarch (C5), 244A, 246
Phrynichus, Athenian tragedian (C5), 105B
Phrynichos, Athenian general (C5), 227B, 235
Pittakos, tyrant of Mytilene (C6), 23, 24, 90
Pleistoanax, Spartan king (C5), 171, 173, 193, 205
Polydamas, tyrant of Pharsalos (C4), 267, 317
Polydoros, Spartan king (C7), 49, 53
Polyeuktos, Athenian politician (C4), 314B
Polykrates, tyrant of Samos (C6), 31–34, 60, 81
Poseidon, 12, 92, 112A, 115A, 159, 180, 227B, 274, 350C
Protagoras of Abdera, philosopher (C5), 155
Psammetichos (I), king of Egypt (C7), 94A

Simonides of Keos, poet (C6/5), 72, 105A
Sokrates, Athenian philosopher (C5), 141B, 151, 155, 156, 237, 247B, 248, 303A
Solon, Athenian lawgiver and poet (C6), p.7, 23, p.128, 63, 65–68, 77, 79A, 80D, 120, 128, p.287, 162, 216, 244A, 303B, 307, 314B
Sphodrias, Spartan (C4), 268, 270, 298

Thales of Miletos, philosopher (C6), 91, 92
Theagenes, tyrant of Megara (C7), 21, 64B
Themistokles, Athenian politician and general (C5), 81, 112, 113, 121, 123 n.5, 159, 160A, 161A, 166, 168, 172, 230, 315
Theopompos, Spartan king (C8/7), 49, 52
Theramenes, Athenian politician (C5), 216, 227, 236, 237, 240, 244
Theseus, legendary Attic king, 8, 18, 112A, 158B
Thibron, Spartan general (C4), 252, 253
Thoukydides, Athenian politician (C5), 145, 146, 148, 213
Thrasyboulos, Athenian politician and general (C5/4), 244–246, 254B, 262A, 269 with n.10, 310
Timoleon, Corinthian lawgiver in Sicily (C4), 296, 297

Timotheus, Athenian general (C4), 275, 349B
Tissaphernes, Persian satrap (C5/4), 227B, 231, 233, 234, 252, 253
Tolmides, Athenian general (C5), 148, 173

Xerxes, King of Persia (C5), 55, 81, 99, 108–113, 118, 165B, 168, 255

Zaleukos of Lokroi, lawgiver (?C6), 40B
Zeus, 5B, 6, 7, 8, 10, 11, 12, 17B, 34, 45, 47A, 49, 50, 64B, 75, 85, 94B, 97, 105A, 112A, 115A, 134, 147, 169, 193, 251, 269B, 273B, 306, 350C

B PLACES

Abdera, 18
Aigina, 81, 107, 110
Aigospotamoi, 239
Amorgos, 338
Amphipolis, 192, 202, 337
Arginousai, 237
Argos, 26, 30, 57, 59, 202–205
Athens, Attika, 8, 18, 25, 26, 62–80, 87, 100, 104–106, 108–110, 119–187, 189–232, 235–248, 254–263, 268–269, 275–286, 302–315, 317, 320, 325, 334, 337–340, 342, 345–350

Boiotia, 75, 171, 173, 193, 240, 254, 288
Byzantion, 130, 339

Carthage, 118
Chaleion, 83
Chalkis (Euboia), 15, 75, 108, 134
Chersonesos, 106
Chios, 38, 92, 99, 136, 199, 339
Corinth, p.28, 12, 20, 27–29, 75, 81, 176–178, 183, 193, 202, 204, 240, 254, 290, 293, 296–297
Crete, 37, 39, 47, 88
Cyprus, 105, 130, 132

Dekeleia, 229
Delos, 69, 130, 142
Delphi, 12, 16, 18, 46, 49, 64, 74, 84, 94, 115, 266, 336

Egesta, *see* Segesta
Egypt, 2, 13, 16, 31, 93–94, 109, 132–133
Eion, 130
Eleusis, 8, 151, 245
Elis, 85, 251
Ennea Hodoi, 132; *see also* Amphipolis
Ephesos, 90

Index of names

Epidauros, 28
Eretria, p.28, 4, 105, 108
Euboia, 165, 173, 189, 226
Eurymedon, 131

Gela, 35

Heraia, 85
Herakleia (Black Sea), 19
Herakleia (Greece), 189, 318

Illyria, 325–326
Ionia, 92, 101–102, 105, 107, 129
Ischia, see Pithekoussai

Karia, 1, 105
Keos, 282
Kerkyra, 28, 43, 81, 135, 176, 302
Klazomenai, 287
Kos, 339
Kyme (Asia), 92
Kyme (Italy), 15
Kyrene, 16
Kyzikos, 42, 236

Lakedaimon, Lakonia, see Sparta
Larisa, 333
Laureion, 277
Libya, 16
Lokris (West), 43, 82, 86; see also Chaleion, Oiantheia
Lydia, 90, 100
Lykia, 5

Makedonia, 7, 25, 192, 321–350
Mantineia, 291
Marathon, 108
Massalia, 19
Megalopolis, 300
Megara, 21, 64, 140, 170
Megara (Sicily), 15, 17, 35
Melos, 206
Messenia, 45–46, 132, 169, 301
Miletos, 27, 92, 101–105
Mykenai, p.28, 164
Mytilene, 23–24, 90, 136, 197–198, 210

Naukratis, 94
Naxos (Aegean), 102, 130
Naxos (Sicily), 15

Oiantheia, 83
Olympia, 11–12, 47, 69, 136

Olynthos, 344

Paionia, 325–326
Parnassos, 3
Peiraieus, 159, 187, 268, 275
Persia, 81, 89–99, 101–117, 129–133, 147, 168, 208, 227, 230–231, 233–234, 252–256, 258, 260, 263, 269, 319–320, 340, 350
Pherai, 316–318
Phigaleia, 293
Philippoi, 327
Phleious, 292–293
Phoinikia, 2, 4, p.52, 132–133
Phokaia, 92
Phokis, 336
Phthiotis, 1
Pithekoussai, 15
Plataiai, 62, 113–114, 184, 289
Poteidaia, 177
Pylos, 190, 212

Rhodes, 339

Salamis, 112
Samos, 16, 28, 31–34, 42, 81, 133, 136, 227
Sardis, 91, 100, 105
Segesta, 172, 219
Sicily, 172, 214, 217–225, 296
Sigeion, 41
Sikyon, 26, 29–30, 75, 293
Sparta, p.28, 31, 44–62, 74, 87–88, 91, 103, 109, 130, 132, 160, 164–171, 173–174, 178, 180–198, 202–205, 212, 219, 223, 225–226, 228–236, 238–240, 244–245, 249–258, 260, 262–275, 289–301
Sphakteria, 190
Syracuse, 20, p.66, 35, 118, 172, 220–225, 294–297

Taras, 46
Tegea, 47, 58
Teos, 18, 92
Thasos, 132
Thebes, 62, 184, 268–275, 289, 301, 324, 335, 349
Thera, 16
Thermopylai, 111, 342
Thessaly, 74, 171, 192, 316–318, 333–335, 341
Thourioi, 174
Thrake, 192, 343

Index of subjects

N.B. Unless otherwise indicated, numbers refer to passages (and their introductions), not to pages

agriculture, p.2, pp.52–3, **15**, p.95, p.128, **70, 95B**, p.287, **159, 229B, 286**; *see also* land

alphabet, p.20, **2, 4**, p.53, **246**; *see also* dialects

altars, p.2, **34, 62, 64B, 94B, 97, 131, 157, 249, 253**; *see also* cult, festivals, gods, priests, sacrifices, temples

archaeological evidence, p.19, p.28, pp.52–3, **16, 29, 44, 82**, pp.183–5, **151, 249**, p.538

Areiopagos, **25B, 63, 65B, 67, 70, 75, 80C, 120, 122, 123, 307**

aristocracy, p.28, **5, 6, 10, 11**, p.53, **14**, p.66, **21, 22, 24, 26, 48, 50, 51, 70, 80C**, p.168, **82, 98, 128**, p.247, p.262, **163n.2, 265A, 273A, 291, 322**

bribery, **10, 74, 75, 102, 103, 141, 142, 157, 168, 173n.3, 193, 210, 217, 225, 244C, 254, 265, 266, 268, 294, 327**

castration, **28, 96, 99**

cavalry, **22, 35, 58, 74, 137, 185, 186, 191, 194B, 225, 227n.23, 229B, 236, 246B, 252, 255, 257, 264, 267, 268, 274, 286, 294, 298B, 316–318, 320A, 321A, 323, 326, 328B, 334, 349B**

coinage, p.22, p.53, **16, 35, 42, 53, 136, 161, 231, 250A, 261, 265, 275B, 286, 327**

commerce, *see* trade

crafts, **13, 29B, 32A, 53, 81, 160, 162C, 229B, 264, 270, 278**; *see also* pottery

cults, p.1, p.28, **8**, p.53, **16n.5, 17B, 18, 30, 34, 50, 70, 73, 84, 92, 94B, 95, 97, 142C, 153, 158D, 163A, 200, 214, 242, 249**

debt-bondage, p.3, p.128, **65–68, 162**

democracy, p.66, **22, 25D**, p.87, **38, 48, 49, 51, 72**, Ch.7 *passim*, p.168, **89, 101, 107**, Ch.11 *passim*, p.246, **135, 139, 143, 146, 148, 149, 155**, p.287, **159, 172n.1, 174, 198**, p.385, **209, 210B, 216, 227, 235, 241, 243**, p.456, **244–247, 250, 262**, p.521, p.538, **290, 291, 293, 297, 302**, p.558, **303, 310, 313n.4**

dialects, p.21, p.28, **3**, p.53, **39, 41, 301B**; *see also* alphabet

election(s), **51, 63, 119, 120, 124, 126, 143, 219, 221, 227, 237, 244, 294, 303, 313**

epigraphical evidence, pp.19–23, **16**, p.87, **37, 38, 39, 41, 82, 132, 151, 172n.6, 269n.11, 277, 306, 316, 321**

epitaphs, p.20, **41, 43, 127, 133, 163n.2**

exile(s), p.1, **23, 31, 35, 75, 79, 102, 104, 134, 158, 168, 173, 181, 214, 218, 227B, 228, 239, 240**, p.456; **244, 246, 248B, 262, 263, 274, 289, 292–294, 296, 297, 299C, 301, 303A, 310, 324, 333, 337**

festivals, p.28, **8, 12, 28, 30, 38, 43, 46, 64B, 70, 72, 73, 92, 96, 111A, 114, 136, 151, 154, 160C, 193, 194B, 197A, 200, 205, 237, 242, 249, 273A, 290, 293, 297, 299B, 313A, 318**

food, **5A, 39, 50, 54, 112B, 141A, 163C, 190, 225, 240**

gods/goddesses, p.1, **5–8, 10–12, 14, 16, 17B, 24, 25B, 27, 28, 34, 35, 37–39, 40B, 42B, 45, 46, 47A, 49, 50, 58, 62, 64B, 69, 75, 81, 84–86, 88, 90–92, 94B, 95–97, 99, 105A, 106, 108, 109C, 112, 115, 116, 120, 134, 142C, 150–153, 158D, 163A, 167, 169, 174, 181, 183B, 189, 193, 196, 198B, 214, 227B, 242, 248, 249, 251, 253, 264, 266, 268, 269B, 273B, 286, 290, 306, 310, 314B, 318, 336, 342, 346A, 349B**

grain imports, p.2, p.53, **155, 197A, 217, 226**, p.521, **281, 288, 308, 317**

helots, **44, 46, 58, 115A, 132A, 162, 169, 170, 190, 192, 264, 274**

heralds, **9, 46, 69, 92, 107, 109, 147, 172B, 174, 184, 194A, 200, 261, 273A, 297, 308, 349A**

homosexuality, **72, 268, 271**

hoplites, p.53, p.66, **22, 137, 169, 173, 190–194, 219, 224, 227B, 228, 246B, 255, 257, 262, 267, 268, 271, 274, 286, 300n.3, 306, 317**

land/landownership, p.1, p.52, **15B, 16, 17, 44–46, 50B, 53, 66, 86, 139**, p.287, **159, 172A, 173, 174, 175A, 183, 186, 194A, 198B, 207–209, 218, 228, 245, 246, 267, 269B**, p.521, **277B, 278–280, 286, 291, 294, 295, 297, 301A, 312, 316, 322, 328, 335, 346A**; *see also* agriculture

law, 9, 10, 23, 25B, p.87, 37–40, 47, 49, 50,
    52B, 55, 56, 59, 63, 65, 67, 70, 71,
    p.152, 75, 79, 80D, 83, 86, 88, 124–126,
    128, 134, 149, 174, 179, 210B, 237, 244,
    246, 267, 282, 303, 307, 310, 311, 313,
    315, 332
literacy, p.21, p.28, 4, 121
liturgies, 142C, 144, 153, 244C, 312

mercenaries, p.1, p.52, 31, 69, p.185,
    91–94, 161C, 172A, 183C, 192, 194A,
    224, 229B, 252, 255, p.488, 257, 274,
    p.522, p.538, 293–296, 298, 299C,
    306, p.580, 317–320, 327, p.600, 336,
    346A; *see also* peltasts
metals, p.3, 5B, 6, 14, 22, 53, 91, 92, 96,
    100, 115, 140, 161, 194B, 229A, 234,
    244C, 249, 275B, 277A, 286, 327
mines, 132A, 155, p.287, 161, 169, 228,
    p.521, 277, 286, 327
monarchy, p.27, 6–8, 16, 22, 23, 33, Ch. 5
    passim (esp.50), 63, 75, p.168, 81, 89,
    95, 96, 159, 168, 175A, 193, 266, 267,
    p.538, Chs. 33–34 *passim*

oaths, 16B, 38, 39, 42A, 46, 50B, 63, 67, 83,
    91, 92, 116B, 119, 129, 134, 148, 150,
    169, 172B, 193, 221, 227, 237, 244C,
    245, 263, 290, 302, 305A, 306, 313C,
    334, 350C
oligarchy, 22, p.87, 48, 49, 52A, 66, 68,
    p.168, 89, 135B, 143, 146, 159, p.385,
    214, 219, 227, 235, 236, 238, p.456,
    244–247, 250, 262, p.538, 291, 293,
    294, 303C, 316, 317
Olympic games, 11, 12, 26, 47B, 57, 64, 69,
    82, 100, 106, 111A, 219, 248B, 251, 265
oracles, p.52, 16, 18A, 20, 27, 30, 45, 47A,
    49, 50, 58, 64B, 69, 74, 91, 92, 100,
    106, 110, 112B, 114, 156, 167, 169, 174,
    193, 196, 207, 226, 251, 266, 335, 346A

peltasts, 212, 229B, 255, 257, 274, 277A,
    317, 319
piracy, 2, 14, 15B, 31, 81, 82, 83, 92,
    257
population (size and growth), p.28, p.52,
    20, p.497, 267, 284, 297
pottery, p.28, 14, 29B, p.128; *see also* crafts
priests/priestesses, p.2, 16A, 18A, 27, 34,
    35, 39, 47A, 50, 58, 74, 75, 76, 112,
    163A, 184, 193, 227B, 266, 306

sacrifices, p.2, 16, 18A, 26, 30, 39, 40B,
    46, 50, 62, 64B, 69, 75, 97, 134, 142C,
    152, 153, 163A, 172B, 174, 193, 227,
    242, 249, 251, 253, 263, 264, 273A,
    290, 318, 349B

sea/sea-power, 1A, 2, 10, 29A, 31, 44, 81,
    82, 90, 103, 110–113, 116, 122,
    129–132, 140, 143, 159, 160, 161A, 167,
    175A, 176, 183, 185, 187, 190, 192,
    194, 195, 197, 198, 206, 208, 209, 224,
    226, 228, 229, 231–234, 236, 239, p.
    456, 252, 253, 256, 260, 262, 282, 286,
    288, 317, Ch. 34 *passim*
slaves, p.3, 7, 13, p.53, 18A, 35, 78,
    93, 101, 108, 128, 130, p.287, 160D,
    161–163, 169, 173, 175B, 194A, 210A,
    214, 225, 228, 229B, 232n.1, 244C, 245,
    251, 277A, 282, 299C, 335; *see also*
    debt-bondage, helots
sophists, p.9, 155, 156, 157, 210B,
    248n.10
sortition, 16, 51, 65B, 67, 76, 89, 108, 112A,
    120, 122, 124, 126, 137, 143, 150,
    163A, 202, 227B, 303, 307, 311

taxes, 39, 42, 70, 96, 134, 144, 160A, 161,
    163D, 193, 201, 262, 267, 277A, 281A,
    282, 286, 312, 317, 338
temples, p.2, 8, 12B, p.53, 16B, 17A,
    28, 30, 32, 46, 47A, 49, 50, 58, 62, 64B,
    69, 74, 84, 90, 92, 94, 97, 102, 105A,
    108, 134, 138, 142C, 151, 164, 192,
    193, 196, 201, 207, 214, 219, 245, 266,
    342, 350
trade, p. 27, 2, pp. 53, 14, 15, 53, 81,
    p.183, 94, 140, 154, p.287, 275B, 276,
    281, 284–286, 332
tyranny, 8, Ch. 3 *passim*, 41, 48, 50B, 51,
    52B, 60, 64, 68–76, 78, 79, 80B, p. 168,
    81, 89, 101, 106, 108, 113, 118, 120,
    121, 128, 138, 148, p.277, 172A, 175A,
    208, 210B, 214, 227, 244, 275A, 286, p.
    538, 294–297, 303B, 316–318, 333–335,
    341

walls, 17B, 82, 110n.2, 129, 131, 132A,
    142A, 151, 166, 167, 169, 170, 171,
    177, 197A, 198, 199, 207, 227B, 240,
    244, 246B, 256, 259, 291, 318, 346A
water/water supply, 8, 16A, 32A, 50B, 53,
    142A, 152, 174, 252, 313A
wealth, p.53, 14, 21, 36, 53, p.128, 67, 81,
    82, 100, 141, 142, 144, 149, p.277,
    p.287, 161, 174, 183, 213, 233B, 241,
    243, 251, 265, p.521, 276, 278, 279,
    303C, 315, 320B
women, p.3, 2B, 6, 7, 9, 10, 16B, 19, 21,
    26, 31, 46, 52A, 59, 61, 63, 69, 72, 78,
    157, p.287, 162B, 163, 174, 180A, 264,
    267, 273A, 274, 279, 280, 289, 331

xenophobia, 56, 265B, 283, 285